The Schlieffen Plan

Foreign Military Studies

History is replete with examples of notable military campaigns and exceptional military leaders and theorists. Military professionals and students of the art and science of war cannot afford to ignore these sources of knowledge or limit their studies to the history of the U.S. armed forces. This series features original works, translations, and reprints of classics outside the American canon that promote a deeper understanding of international military theory and practice.

Series editor: Roger Cirillo

An AUSA Book

The Schlieffen Plan

INTERNATIONAL PERSPECTIVES ON THE GERMAN STRATEGY FOR WORLD WAR I

Edited by
Hans Ehlert, Michael Epkenhans,
and Gerhard P. Gross

English translation edited by
Major General David T. Zabecki, USA (Ret.)

UNIVERSITY PRESS OF KENTUCKY

Copyright © 2014 by Zentrum für Militärgeschichte und Sozialwissenschaften der Bundeswehr (ZMS)

Published by special arrangement with Zentrum für Militärgeschichte und Sozialwissenschaften der Bundeswehr (ZMS). The original edition was published under the title *Der Schlieffenplan: Analysen und Dokumente*, edited by Hans Ehlert, Michael Epkenhans, and Gerhard P. Gross (Munich: Odenberg, 2006).

English-language edition published by the University Press of Kentucky

Scholarly publisher for the Commonwealth,
serving Bellarmine University, Berea College, Centre College of Kentucky, Eastern Kentucky University, The Filson Historical Society, Georgetown College, Kentucky Historical Society, Kentucky State University, Morehead State University, Murray State University, Northern Kentucky University, Transylvania University, University of Kentucky, University of Louisville, and Western Kentucky University.
All rights reserved.

Editorial and Sales Offices: The University Press of Kentucky
663 South Limestone Street, Lexington, Kentucky 40508–4008
www.kentuckypress.com

Cataloging-in-Publication data is available from the Library of Congress.

978-0-8131-4746-8 (hardcover : alk. paper)
978-0-8131-4747-5 (pdf)

This book is printed on acid-free paper meeting the requirements of the American National Standard for Permanence in Paper for Printed Library Materials.

Manufactured in the United States of America.

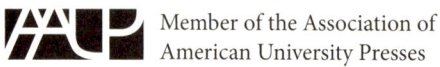 Member of the Association of
American University Presses

Contents

Map Key   vii

Introduction: The Historiography of Schlieffen and the
Schlieffen Plan   1
  Hans Ehlert, Michael Epkenhans, and Gerhard P. Gross

The Sword and the Scepter: The Powers and the European System
before 1914   17
  Klaus Hildebrand

The Moltke Plan: A Modified Schlieffen Plan with Identical Aims?   43
  Annika Mombauer

The Schlieffen Plan—A War Plan   67
  Robert T. Foley

There Was a Schlieffen Plan: New Sources on the History of German
Military Planning   85
  Gerhard P. Gross

"This Trench and Fortress Warfare Is Horrible!" The Battles in Lorraine
and the Vosges in the Summer of 1914   137
  Dieter Storz

The Military Planning of the Austro-Hungarian Imperial and Royal
Army and the Schlieffen Plan   189
  Günther Kronenbitter

French Plan XVII: The Interdependence between Foreign Policy and
Military Planning during the Final Years before the Outbreak of the
Great War   209
  Stefan Schmidt

Russian Forces and the German Buildup at the Outbreak of
World War I   247
  Jan Kusber

The Southern Envelopment: Switzerland's Role in the Schlieffen and
Moltke Plans   261
  Hans Rudolf Fuhrer and Michael Olsansky

The British Army, Its General Staff, and the Continental Commitment,
1904–1914   293
  Hew Strachan

Belgium: Operational Plans and Tactics of a Neutral Country   319
  Luc de Vos

Appendix: Deployment Plans, 1893–1914   339

Glossary of German Military Terms and Acronyms   527

List of Contributors   533

Index   539

Photographs follow page 188

General Map Key

General Terms and Notes:

Lagenskizzen	Situation Sketches
Aufmarsch	Deployment
Alpenjäger	Mountain Light Infantry
Grenzschutz	Border Security
Ersatz	Replacement
Landwehr	Territorial Reserve
Bahnfahrt	Rail Movement
Stellungen am 10.9.	Positions on 10 September
Rückmärsche am:	Retrograde March on:
10 Armee Korps	Ten Army Corps
6 Ersatz Korps	Six Replacement Corps
22.	22nd Mobilization Day
Die mit diesem Pfeil bezeichneten Verbände wurden in den nächsten Tagen weggezogen.	The red arrows indicate the French units that were withdrawn in the following days.

Cavalry

☆   Fortress

┿┿┿┿┿   Fortified Position

Examples of Military Unit Designations:

Armee d'Alsace	Army of Alsace
6. Armee	Sixth Army
G.	Guards Corps
G.R.	Guards Reserve Corps
XV.	XV Army Corps
XIV.R.	XIV Reserve Corps
III.b	III Bavarian Corps, or…..
III.B.	III Bavarian Corps
I.b R.	I Bavarian Reserve Corps
2.G.R.	2nd Guards Reserve Division
G.E.	Guards Ersatz Division
28.	28th Division
30.R.	30th Reserve Division
6.E.	6th Ersatz Division
2.B.L.	2nd Bavarian Landwehr Division

 7.   7th Cavalry Division

60.I.Br.	60th Infantry Brigade
55.E.Br.	55th Ersatz Brigade
60.L.Br.	60th Landwehr Brigade
1.b L.Br.	1st Bavarian Landwehr Brigade

© ZMSBw
07028-02

Introduction

The Historiography of Schlieffen and the Schlieffen Plan

Hans Ehlert, Michael Epkenhans, and Gerhard P. Gross

Anniversaries generally provide a good opportunity to commemorate historical personalities or important events of the past. Such a personality is Field Marshal Count Alfred von Schlieffen. Despite the fact that he, contrary to his famous predecessor Field Marshal Count Helmuth von Moltke the Elder, did not fight a battle or directly conduct or win or lose a war, there is no escaping him when considering Prussian-German military history in general and the prehistory of the First World War in particular. Schlieffen and his *Denkschrift für einen Krieg gegen Frankreich* (Memorandum for a War against France), which he wrote more than one hundred years ago during the winter of 1905–1906, are important elements of the cultural memory that explain the outbreak of the First World War in the summer of 1914. According to the 1998 twentieth edition of the German *Brockhaus Encyclopedia,* Schlieffen tried "to meet the requirements of the modern war by establishing the technical troop requirements. For him the highest form of the operational art was the double envelopment and the subsequent annihilation of the enemy." *Brockhaus* further reads: "The basic idea of the Schlieffen Plan of 1905 was the concentration of the mass of the German field army in the west and a simultaneous strategic defense in the east." The operational objective was the annihilation of the French Army within a few weeks without having a force ratio superiority. "In the case of a war against Russia as well, the intent was to shift the center of gravity immediately to the east."[1]

For decades that interpretation has shaped our knowledge of the prehistory of the First World War. All assessments, starting from key academic publications, through newspaper articles on the occasion of anniversaries, up to pertinent sections in federal German schoolbooks describe the Schlieffen Plan in a similar way. Only a few years ago, an American historian and, significantly for the further course of the debate he started, former U.S. Army major, Terence Zuber, questioned in an increasingly aggressive approach that traditional and generally acknowledged interpretation. The following chapters of this book will address the debate Zuber initiated.[2]

However, in order to understand why the debate launched by Zuber created quite a stir and (like the earlier Fischer controversy of the early 1960s)[3] eventually resulted in various degrees of rancor, it is necessary to start with a closer look at Schlieffen, the Schlieffen Plan, and its historiography.

In the history of the Prussian-German Great General Staff (*Grosse Generalstab*) it was Schlieffen who, after his legendary predecessor, the victor of the Battles of Königgrätz and Sedan, Moltke the Elder, left the most important imprint. Schlieffen's immediate predecessor, Colonel General Count Alfred von Waldersee, served as chief of the Great General Staff for only a short period. Owing to Waldersee's political ambitions, he got caught up in the wheels of politics and was summarily replaced in 1891. Schlieffen, who had already served on the General Staff during the wars of 1866 and 1870–1871, had been a department (*Abteilung*) head since 1884. When he finally succeeded Waldersee in office in February 1891 his objective was "to administer his office in the spirit of Moltke."[4] According to his first biographer, Major General Hugo Freiherr von Freytag-Loringhoven, Schlieffen in 1913, like Moltke before him, declared with an astonishing frankness that he intended "never to be active in politics . . . but when occasionally asked for his opinion, he was emphatic on decisively belligerent actions."[5]

Today, it is no longer possible to establish with certainty what Schlieffen specifically proposed at any certain time, either officially or in background talks with members of the German Foreign Office. It is particularly difficult to evaluate his influence on the Wilhelmine-era *eminence grise* of German foreign policy, Privy Councillor (*Geheimrat*) Friedrich von Holstein. The exact records of when and on what occasions Schlieffen deemed it necessary to become active behind the scenes and how he proceeded were lost when the German Army Archive at Potsdam was destroyed during an Allied bombing raid in the closing days of World War II.

Since 1871, the long-serving chancellor of the German Reich, Otto von Bismarck, had worried increasingly about the dangers of a two-front war. He devised a sophisticated alliance system to protect Germany from such a threat. But when in 1890 the kaiser declined to renew the 1887 Russian-German Reinsurance Treaty and the Franco-Russian alliance followed, Bismarck's nightmare became a reality by 1892, only two years after his resignation from office. As far as we know today, there is no doubt that all his life Schlieffen as the chief of the *Grosser Generalstab* was very preoccupied with the impact the changed situation on the European continent would have for Germany. Various political crises, especially the First Morocco Crisis, prompted him to offer advice to the responsible political leaders.[6]

In contrast to the strategic situation before 1890, Germany's self-imposed loss of its Russian ally, which then turned to the "archenemy" France, forced the German military leadership to search for solutions to what seemed to be the now inevitable scenario of a two-front war. This was all the more necessary as Schlieffen soon realized that the Reich's leadership did not even think about forming new alliances. Instead, the political leaders were convinced that they would be able to pursue with relatively low risk a policy of a "free hand" both on the continent and globally.

These shifts in the old political-strategic structure of the Bismarck era forced the chief of the General Staff to find solutions to the strategic problems compounded by the changes in the alliance systems and the central geographic position of the Reich in Europe. The impact of growing industrialization and mechanization would also greatly influence any future war. Thanks to the development of the railroads, the mobilization times and thus the requirements for the deployment of military forces to the borders of the enemy countries had been further and further compressed during the second half of the nineteenth century. Moreover, other technical developments revolutionized warfare: artillery projectiles could be fired over greater distances and with more accuracy than ever before, and at the same time their destructiveness continually increased at a breathtaking pace. The same was true for rifles and machine guns. On the other hand, some of the traditional military branches lost their importance, especially the cavalry, which had often in the past decided battles through its mobility. The command of million-man armies in the age of national war was vastly different from the relatively small armies of the traditional "cabinet wars" during the period when the Reich was established.[7]

Schlieffen understood these changes very clearly. After he left office he published in 1909 and 1911 his ideas on the changing character of warfare in the age of mass armies in the journal *Deutsche Revue*.[8] According to Schlieffen, these changes made it no longer feasible to "pursue a strategy of attrition if maintaining millions requires billions." Nonetheless, the achievement of a "decisive and terminal success" would require "attack on two or three sides, that is, against the front and one or two of the flanks."⁹

During his tenure of active service Schlieffen had tried to take into consideration this realization of the problems of warfare under the conditions of the modern industrial age. In his opinion, the changing character of war and the geographical situation of the Reich made it imperative to plan a short, rapid war. Considering that situation, combined with the newly established Franco-Russian alliance, his plan focused on dividing if possible the war of two fronts into two wars of one front each. In particular, it was essential in the first war to achieve quickly an annihilating victory, using the ancient Battle of Cannae as a model. That in turn would make war on the other front easier or even unnecessary. The plan and its basic operational idea was developed by Schlieffen during the course of many *Generalstabsreisen* (staff rides) and *Kriegsspiele* (war games) and repeatedly reevaluated. The result "promised" the responsible political leaders of the Wilhemine era who wanted to wage a war, and the military who wanted to win it, a quick and convincing victory—provided they adhered strictly to the plan.

Reality in 1914, however, was totally different. The German offensive became bogged down near Paris, and the outcome of the subsequent grueling, years-long trench warfare offered no victory, but instead disgraceful military defeat.

Neither the defeat itself nor even the causes for the war were subjected to an objective analysis afterward. Political and military leaders alike looked for scapegoats to blame for the final disaster of November 1918. "Well, in a sense it was a preemptive war," confessed former German chancellor Theobald von Bethmann Hollweg in February 1918 speaking to Conrad Haussmann, a Reichstag deputy from the *Fortschrittliche Volkspartei* (Progressive People's Party). "But war was hanging threateningly over our heads. It would have come two years later even more dangerously and inescapably. And as the military said, it was still possible then to fight without being defeated, which would not be true two years hence! Oh, those military people!" The comments of the former chancellor referred to the responsibility of the General Staff, while of course not fully accepting his own.¹⁰ After all, it had been Bethmann Hollweg who in late June and early July 1914 had decided to use the crisis between Serbia and the Dual Monarchy caused by the death of the heir to the Austro-Hungarian throne, Archduke Franz Ferdinand, to take the deliberate risk of a great European war. With the exception of a "short winter of criticism," as noted by historian Markus Pöhlmann, the military on its part soon focused exclusively on the question of why Schlieffen's "recipe for victory" did not work. Around Christmas 1920 the *eminence grise* of World War I historiography, General Hermann von Kuhl, stated incontrovertibly, "A decision in France in 1914 could have been achieved and Count Schlieffen's campaign plan inevitably would have led to victory if we had adhered to and consequently executed it."[11] Similar positions were advanced by others, including the former chief of the *Feldeisenbahnwesen* (Field Railway Service) and last *Erste Generalquartiermeister* (first quartermaster general) of the Imperial Army, General Wilhelm Groener, and retired lieutenant colonel and later director of the German Army Archive Wolfgang Foerster—both members of what would soon be called the "Schlieffen School." Their critics, including the long-term chief of the Operational Division of the *Oberste Heeresleitung* (OHL—Supreme Army Command), Major General Georg Wetzell, tried to point out the weaknesses of the Schlieffen Plan and even declared openly that Moltke did not "water down, but improve" the plan. It was difficult, however, for the opponents of the Schlieffen School to make themselves heard. The *Reichsarchiv,* having interpretational authority over First World War historiography, tried to restrict if not to prevent completely any access to the relevant files.[12]

The publications issued on the occasion of the centennial of Schlieffen's birthday in 1931 had the strong support of Groener and especially the president of Germany, former field marshal Paul von Hindenburg. Those publications continued to demonstrate the high esteem in which Schlieffen was held within both the internal and the public debates on war and strategy.[13] The fact that all those publications did not include the actual transcriptions of Schlieffen's original *Denkschrift* of 1905–1906, "Krieg gegen Frankreich," or of his last *Denkschrift* of 28 December 1912 on a war against France and Russia, is a strong indicator that dealing with Schlieffen even two decades after his death was a highly charged issue—one that was not really about approaching historical truth. When retired lieutenant general Wilhelm Marx in 1934 requested the publication of Schlieffen's December 1912 *Denkschrift,* the director of the *Reichsarchiv* refused with the typical justification: "The *Denkschrift* contains statements, the publication of which would damage the German position on the issue of the war guilt issue. Count Schlieffen wanted to lead the right wing of the German Army through the territory of the Netherlands. To the extent the military elements of the *Denkschrift* can be released for military historical considerations, this has already been done in the publication *Graf Schlieffen und der Weltkrieg,* published by myself."[14]

Thus, Foerster as the director of the *Reichsarchiv* made it clear that it was more than his concern about the explosive political nature of Schlieffen's *Denkschriften* that prevented him from publishing the documents. He also wanted to keep previously unknown details secret for military reasons, because the General Staff continued to think and plan "in the spirit of Schlieffen." The chief of the German Army General Staff at the time, General Ludwig Beck, made that quite clear. When he had Schlieffen's *Generalstabsreisen Ost* (General Staff Ride East) documents—significantly not the "*West*" version—issued, he expressly declared them a model and even "an important teaching aid for contemporary war. The independent use of military historical processes and the increasingly deep immersion in the issue of a possible war gave birth to [Schlieffen's] idea of the annihilation of the enemy, his Cannae lesson."[15]

It took less than two years for the practical implementation of those lessons envisaged by Beck. As noted by historian Karl-Heinz Frieser, the Wehrmacht leadership during the winter of 1939–1940 planned a "three-dimensional Cannae" against France in the spirit of Schlieffen, albeit with important modifications that modern war technology had made possible and which were to ensure success.[16] During the fighting in the spring of 1940 these plans proved so successful that Hitler and the responsible generals essentially succumbed to the "delusion of the worldwide blitzkrieg," and the attempt to implement that delusional idea eventually ended in the total disaster of 1945.[17]

Following the catastrophe of World War II, during the early years of the German Federal Republic, Schlieffen and his "plan" were of interest only for historians at best. During the 1950s historical scholarship initially proceeded from totally different assumptions, but nonetheless did start to take a closer look into the underlying causes of what historian Friedrich Meinecke called the "German Disaster." Soon, however, the scholarship started to analyze thoroughly the outbreak of the First World War, "the great seminal catastrophe of this century," as George F. Kennan called it. Consequently, the study of Schlieffen and the interpretations of his "lessons" were inevitable. In the early 1950s, historian Gerhard Ritter, one of the doyens of military historiography in the young Federal Republic of Germany, started the basic trend for the study of Schlieffen that continued throughout the subsequent decades. It was a trend that was seldom challenged.

As much as Ritter saw Schlieffen in the tradition of Moltke the Elder, and as much as he was convinced that the chief of the General Staff was a "pure military technician, not at all a political figure nor a war-fighter," it was difficult to avoid the judgment "that the sum of his dealings, the great campaign plan of 1905, had been even more cataclysmic for German politics than the excessive arming of the German High Seas Fleet during the era of Tirpitz."[18] Ritter continued, "The responsibility for that lies only to a smaller degree with the chief of the General Staff. Its full weight must be borne by the political leadership of the German Reich for having accepted such a plan without contradiction, even without thorough consideration and discussion of its political consequences."

This was both an unambiguous and strong judgment. In contrast to the analyses of the interwar period, abundant in publications about Schlieffen and his "plan," Ritter now cast the debate about Schlieffen and the Schlieffen Plan in a totally different dimension. Unlike his predecessors, Ritter was not primarily interested in who failed when and in which position in the General Staff. Instead, his interest focused on the failure of *Staatskunst* (statecraft), which surrendered itself in an almost grossly negligent way to *Kriegshandwerk* (military tradecraft) and made itself dependent on a plan based on a singular case. Ritter also dissected the plan with great sharpness. In the subsequent debate he had a crucial advantage. In 1956, Ritter not only had been able to publish the alleged original of Schlieffen's notorious *Denkschrift*, "*Krieg gegen Frankreich*," including all the maps, but he also had access to the notes in the German Army Archive on the original documents, which had been lost during World War II.[19]

Although Ritter endeavored to point out the shortcomings in Schlieffen's planning—including the insufficient arming of the army, the "distorted" assessment of the position of Belgium and the Netherlands, and the questionable idea of a *Totalsieg* (total victory) in a two-front war—he nevertheless clearly emphasized the plan's basic ideas. According to Ritter's analysis, Schlieffen's sole objective was to attempt to "seek the decision with outflanking maneuvers and flank attacks."[20] While Schlieffen as chief of the General Staff generally followed Moltke the Elder, he also went beyond the latter's ideas. Schlieffen did not content himself with "devising the initial deployment of the German armies and leaving further action as required by the respective situation and conduct of the enemy to the genius of the commander-in-chief, to his imagination and willpower." Instead, Schlieffen wanted to determine in advance the whole campaign down to the details, as a strictly closed, centrally controlled general action of a million-man army, based on a single operational principle.[21]

Ritter's interpretation of the Schlieffen Plan and especially his analysis of the political explosiveness and the military shortcomings of the supposed "recipe for victory" soon became widely accepted. The consensus in the "guild" of military historians did not necessarily exclude critical examination of the modifications Moltke the Younger had made to the Schlieffen Plan. That approach received more emphasis during the 1990s,[22] but the conviction that Schlieffen's successor relied on the basic principles of the plan, in particular the wide envelopment (*Umfassung*), was never questioned.

Historians were not the only ones interested in Schlieffen and his plan. The founding fathers of the *Bundeswehr* also tried to learn from Schlieffen. As opposed to their predecessors in the World War I–era *kaiserliche Armee* or the World War II–era *Wehrmacht,* it was not their intent to use Schlieffen's ideas as the basis for the deployment plans of NATO during the Cold War period. For the responsible generals of the *Bundeswehr* the establishment of a reasonable relationship between "statecraft" and "military tradecraft" and the primacy of politics were indispensable because of the painful experiences of the previous decades. Such was even more critical, considering the responsibility the *Bundeswehr* leaders had to bear in the age of nuclear war. General Adolf Heusinger, the first *Bundeswehr* chief of staff, was particularly involved in this process.[23]

The far-reaching and basically undisputed consensus over Schlieffen, his "plan," and its implications for historical scholarship, military leadership, and the public has been questioned in principle by Terence Zuber. According to Dr. Zuber, the Schlieffen Plan is nothing more than a "myth" that was concocted by the German General Staff in hindsight to acquit themselves of their failures during the Great War. Without anticipating the respective arguments of those who participated in the debate about the "Schlieffen Myth," Zuber's thesis was a surprise in two respects. On the one hand, it seemed astonishing because so many high-ranking German generals had made it clear as early as the beginning of the First World War that the German operations in August–September 1914 had been based on Schlieffen. As Prussian war minister Lieutenant General Erich von Falkenhayn noted in his diary on 10 September 1914, after he received the report about the shifting of the German forces on the left wing; "One is left speechless hearing those instructions. They only prove one thing with certainty, that our General Staff has completely lost its head. Schlieffen's notes have come to an end, and so have the wits of Moltke."[24] The Bavarian military representative to OHL, Lieutenant General Karl Ritter von Wenninger, reacted in a similar manner. On 7 September he reported to Munich that "Schlieffen's operational plan of 1909 has been implemented—as I heard—without significant changes, and even after the initial confrontation with the enemy." It was only "what was written on the last page of Schlieffen's draft—the closing in of the northern and southern army wings toward the center to accomplish the greatest Cannae of world history, on the Catalaunian Fields," that unfortunately had to be abandoned.[25] On 16 February, after the Battle of the Marne, Wenninger wrote in his diary: "Falkenhayn without doubt has his own thoughts, while Moltke and his subordinates were completely sterile. They could only turn the handle and run Schlieffen's film and were clueless and beside themselves when the roll got stuck."[26]

Two primary questions immediately rose concerning Zuber's thesis: (1) Did he correctly interpret the existing sources? and (2) Was his source basis sufficient to support such far-reaching conclusions? Since Zuber's provocative thesis caused such a stir, it seemed reasonable to bring together all sides in the debate to the Military History Research Institute in Potsdam in the autumn of 2004. The objective of such a meeting was to discuss Zuber's pertinent theses and perhaps convince him to modify them if necessary, in order to establish a basis for debate. The inclusion of an analysis of the strategy and planning of the other European states that figured prominently in the prehistory of the First World War would also provide an opportunity for an international comparative forum, one which frequently had been suggested but had not yet been convened. That, of course, meant that the conference would include discussion and analysis of the operational planning of the other states involved in the world war, including Austria-Hungary, Great Britain, France, Russia, and Belgium, the principal victim of the German steamroller. Switzerland was also included, although it did not play a significant role in the developments prior to the war. Those conference papers represent the main body of this volume.

In his chapter, Klaus Hildebrand discusses the relationship between "statecraft" and "military tradecraft" from a comprehensive and comparative European perspective. Hildebrand explains how the specific interrelationship of both elements affected the "increasingly strategic thinking and action on the part of the statesmen" and "caused a system of alliances and ententes to emerge which, interacting with other important factors, had a determining influence on the course and outcome of the July [1914] Crisis." As he emphasizes, however, the way into that crisis had not at all been predetermined. On the contrary, recent research has correctly indicated the attempts at the time to avoid the allegedly imminent Great War. The various political blocs were not at all as unchangeable as general opinion has come to believe them to be. It was the dilemma of the pre–World War period that those elements which were supposed to promote peace actually encouraged war, "because in the end they made an already unstable system unpredictable." As much influence as the military may have had over the details, Hildebrand argues that "there is no doubt that it was politicians, not military men, who in the imperialist system of the European concert of nations before 1914 made the final decisions." That system, however, was sure to fail "when one of its protagonists dared to venture all or nothing." As such, the system was unable to offer any prescription, "either by revelation, by knowledge, by prophesying, or by doctrine." Instead, its solutions were "oracular, ambiguous and impenetrable."

The other conference papers focused on the exact actions of the principal actors, first and foremost on the military level, but also on the political. Terence Zuber, who initiated the debate on Schlieffen and his plan, advanced his original thesis that the Schlieffen Plan was a mere myth, a blatant invention of former General Staff officers who had wanted to justify their own failures after the war. Zuber debated with his critics, Annika Mombauer, Robert T. Foley, and Gerhard P. Gross, on that issue in detail. Zuber not only stated that Schlieffen did not have the forces to carry out the plan he allegedly had developed, but he also stuck to his thesis that a detailed war plan providing for a wide envelopment of Paris would have been a contradiction of existing Prussian military doctrine.

Zuber further argued that one should not overestimate the importance of Schlieffen's notorious *Denkschrift*. The very fact that it had been kept in a generally accessible drawer by Schlieffen's daughters and not in a safe at the General Staff is an argument against its importance. He also concluded that an analysis of Schlieffen's *Aufmarschplanung* (deployment plan) East or West proves that the chief of the *Grosser Generalstab* was an advocate of defensive counterattacks rather than offensive envelopment operations. This conclusion supports Zuber's notion that the German Reich was by no means a power tightly focused on waging a war.

In her chapter, Annika Mombauer describes at great length the commonalities and differences between Moltke the Younger and his predecessor. Her analysis of the continuing effects of Schlieffen's thinking is very important for the evaluation of the Schlieffen Plan, despite the changes Moltke had to make in order to deal with the changed political-strategic framework just prior to 1914. Mombauer stresses the offensive character of the German *Aufmarschplanung* before 1914, a characteristic that had been obvious to all involved immediately before the start of the war. She also notes the close connection between the political world and the military. Zuber, who seemed to be thinking purely in military terms, overlooked that connection, which incorrectly distorted the realities in the German Reich. As Mombauer concludes, any attempt to represent a war prepared and "almost fanatically evoked" by

Schlieffen and his successor "in retrospect as German defensive war" would mean being taken in "by the post-war apologists of the General Staff members, including those who argued uncritically that Schlieffen had developed an infallible recipe for victory."

Robert T. Foley also thoroughly analyzes Zuber's thesis. He points to the fundamental change in the strategic situation of the German Reich that took place after 1905, which completely forced the responsible planners to prepare for a new war scenario—a rapid war on one front. Under the circumstances, the only option was a campaign against France, where the weak French left flank would be enveloped and destroyed. The proof of that plan lies in Schlieffen's *Generalstabsreisen* (staff rides). In Foley's opinion, the importance of those staff rides was completely underestimated by Zuber.

Gerhard P. Gross also discusses Zuber's theses at length, based on hitherto completely unknown sources. Gross argues that Zuber's source basis was not sufficient to support his conclusion. Zuber overlooked important material, including the published excerpts from the pre-1914 *Aufmarschanweisungen* (deployment directives), and the extremely rich collection of papers bequeathed by General of Artillery Friedrich von Boetticher containing important copies of originals of the Schlieffen papers, as well as insightful correspondence with former colleagues and friends of Schlieffen. The insights of these documents as well as other sources previously overlooked or not researched thoroughly indicate that Schlieffen's actual operational thinking fundamentally contradicts Zuber's thesis. What cannot be overlooked is the fact that Schlieffen repeatedly considered the issue of how German forces would be able to defeat the French Army in a rapid battle of annihilation on French territory through a large-scale envelopment. Schlieffen's operations plans, however, were far less dogmatic than previously thought. This is well illustrated in the *Kriegsspiele* (war games) and *Generalstabsreisen,* and especially in the copies of the maps of Schlieffen's last *Generalstabsreise,* where both the western and eastern envelopment of the Fortress Paris were war-gamed through in detail. Schlieffen's *Denkschrift* of 1905, Gross continued, was neither an operational plan for a war against France nor a two-front war elaborated in detail. Rather, it served as a further operational directive for his successor. Zuber is correct on that point.

Dieter Storz in his chapter studies the battles in Lorraine and in the Vosges Mountains. During the postwar debates the plans for the operations of the Sixth and Seventh Armies and the bloody battles on the German left flank were much too important to be neglected. Storz convincingly points out the difference between planning and reality. There can be no doubt, he notes, about Schlieffen's basic idea of enveloping the French Army with the German right wing, as the surviving Bavarian sources suggest.

A key assumption of Zuber's thesis is that since the German Reich only defended itself, a further examination of the German deployment, or of Schlieffen's and Moltke's deliberations, would add little to further debate. In his chapter, however, Günther Kronenbitter examines in detail the deployment plans of Germany's most important ally prior to 1914, the Austro-Hungarian Dual Monarchy and its Imperial and Royal Army. Kronenbitter correctly points out the rather astonishing phenomenon that despite the political alliance and the relatively close contacts between the respective chiefs of the General Staffs, Moltke the Younger and Franz Conrad von Hötzendorf, the two armies did not have a common operational plan. According to Kronenbitter, the agreements between the two armies remained rather vague until the very end of the war.

Whether or not the planning of the allies was more specific is dealt with in Stefan Schmidt's chapter, which focuses on the development of the French Army's Plan XVII. Based on new sources from French archives, Schmidt makes the case that although the French leadership was aware that the power shift on the Continent had maneuvered the German Reich into a more and more precarious position, the French still supported Czarist Russia with "all available means" to deprive Germany of its "capability for attack" in the east. Although the French plan did not provide any details of deployment, it relinquished the necessary political space to France's ally in the east for the sake of maintaining peace. Such an approach fit with the French conviction that only an *offensive à outrance* would guarantee a victory, which under the existing circumstances could only be achieved with the help of Russia. According to Schmidt, "Thus, a plan initially conceived to guarantee the military triumph of France led to greater insecurity and exacerbated the security dilemma, which during the July 1914 crisis led the Great Powers to seek their salvation no longer in peace, but in war."

Jan Kusber focuses on France's most important ally, Russia. He offers a detailed account of the structural deficiencies of the Czarist Empire, which were strikingly exposed by the defeat in the Russo-Japanese War and the revolutionary unrest of 1905–1906. That unrest could only be quelled to a limited degree. Russia's responsible political and military leadership saw themselves more as the driven than as the driving force in the July 1914 crisis. From the Russian perspective, the notorious Russian general mobilization did not necessarily mean a shift to an offensive posture. Instead, mobilization had been necessary to "compensate at least to some degree for the assumed faster pace of the German mobilization."

As Hew Strachan argues in his chapter, Britain at the outbreak of the First World War was always a "special case." Strachan follows Britain's lengthy and complicated path toward its "Continental commitment" of August 1914. What was significant in his discussion is the insight that the process had been an object of consideration at a much earlier stage than previously assumed. Against this background, the influence of the Anglo-French staff talks during the Second Morocco Crisis should not be overrated, especially since the responsible political leaders would have kept open their final decision about the support of France. Indeed, the final decision was to join a Continental war not on behalf of Belgium, but rather on behalf of Britain's Entente partner France.

The development of the Belgian state in the first half of the nineteenth century and the corresponding dilemma of all Belgian governments in planning the defense of their own neutral territory is discussed by Luc de Vos. He also notes the Belgian sense of uncertainty about exactly who their possible wartime enemy might be—an uncertainty that lasted nearly to the last moment. The Belgian defense plans, which he was the first to describe since they had been returned from archives in Moscow, indicate that while the Belgian General Staff understood correctly the direction of the German deployment, they nevertheless failed to deploy their forces in time because of the concerns over their neutrality.

Switzerland was in a similar position to a certain degree. In their chapter Hans Rudolf Fuhrer and Michael Olsansky focus on Switzerland's plans for a European war. As they indicate, the mutual sympathies between Switzerland and Germany, irrespective of the problems in planning and conducting military operations given the geography of Switzerland, would have rendered a military conflict unthinkable. "In general, both sides were well disposed toward each other."

A summary of the papers and the course of the discussions during the conference show that without a doubt Zuber launched an important debate. To refer to the Schlieffen Plan as a myth, however, falls short of historical reality. Nonetheless, these collected conference papers demonstrate clearly how important a thesis's rubbing against the grain of previous research can be for the further progress of the scholarly debate over the long and short routes to the First World War, from both national and international comparative perspectives. The discussion prompted new questions and offered new answers, not least through the new sources that recently have been discovered. In this respect, Zuber's provocative thesis, although it may not have been convincing in the end, contributed significantly to advancing the research. This is both important and encouraging.

This volume publishes in the appendix for the first time the German deployment plans, which previously had been thought lost. These documents demonstrate that Schlieffen's basic operational considerations, in particular the envelopment concept, provided the basis for his successor's deployment plans, despite some modifications. The documents place the discussion about the development of operational thinking within the Great General Staff prior to 1914 on a solid footing, and thus greatly advance the research.

This book is a translation of the German original that was published by the Military History Research Institute in 2006 under the title *Der Schlieffenplan: Analysen und Dokumente*. Zuber's paper was the second chapter of that original edition. Regrettably, Dr. Zuber declined permission for his chapter to be included in this English edition. Additional information on his thesis can be found in his book *Inventing the Schlieffen Plan: German War Planning, 1871–1914* (Oxford, 2003) or on his Web site, www.terencezuber.com.

Notes

1. "Schlieffenplan," in Brockhaus, *Die Enzyklopädie* (Mannheim: Leipzig, 1998), 19:364.

2. Terence Zuber, *Inventing the Schlieffen Plan: German War Planning, 1871–1914* (New York: Oxford, 2003).

3. In his 1961 book *Griff nach der Weltmacht: Die Kriegzielpolitik des kaiserlichen Deutschland 1914–1918* (published in English as *Germany's Aims in the First World War*), German historian Professor Fritz Fischer argued that Germany had deliberately started the First World War in an attempt to become a world power. http://en.wikipedia.org/wiki/Fritz_Fischer-cite_note-Moses_pages_386-387-0#cite_note-Moses_pages_386-387-0

4. Quoted in Hugo Freiherr von Freytag-Loringhoven, "Generalfeldmarschall Graf von Schlieffen: Lebensgang und Lebenswerk," in *Alfred Graf von Schlieffen, Gesammelte Schriften*, ed. Grossen Generalstab (Berlin, 1913), 1:xivf.

5. Ibid., 1:xviii.

6. Cf., for example, Ivo N. Lambi, *The Navy and German Power Politics, 1862–1914* (Boston, 1984), 242f., as well as Heiner Raulff, *Zwischen Machtpolitik und Imperialismus: Die deutsche Frankreichpolitik 1904/06* (Düsseldorf, 1976), 126–134, each on the state of the discussion at that time. A new assessment including all files has yet to be made. Gerd Fesser, *Reichskanzler Fürst von Bülow: Architekt*

der deutschen Weltpolitik (Leipzig, 2003), 111, assumes that neither Schlieffen nor Holstein and Bülow intended a preemptive war in 1904–1905.

7. Cf. the articles in the collective volume *Das Militär und der Aufbruch in die Moderne 1860 bis 1890: Armeen, Marinen und der Wandel von Politik, Gesellschaft und Wirtschaft in Europa, den USA sowie Japan,* ed. Michael Epkenhans and Gerhard P. Gross (Munich, 2003).

8. "Der Krieg in der Gegenwart," in *Schlieffen, Gesammelte Schriften,* 11–22; also, "Über Millionenheere," in *Schlieffen, Gesammelte Schriften,* 23f.

9. "Der Krieg in der Gegenwart," in *Schlieffen, Gesammelte Schriften,* 17.

10. Notes by Conrad Haussmann on a talk with Bethmann Hollweg on 24 February 1918, cited in Fritz Fischer, *Griff nach der Weltmacht: Die Kriegszielpolitik des kaiserlichen Deutschland 1914/18,* 2nd ed. (Königstein, 1978), 85.

11. Quoted in Markus Pöhlmann, *Kriegsgeschichte und Geschichtspolitik: Der Erste Weltkrieg. Die amtliche deutsche Militärgeschichtsschreibung, 1914–1956* (Paderborn, 2002), 316.

12. Cf. Pöhlmann, *Kriegsgeschichte und Geschichtspolitik,* 314–320.

13. Cf. in this context the chapter by Gerhard P. Gross in this volume. However, a comprehensive study has yet to be prepared that, going beyond the work of Pöhlmann, will thoroughly examine the assessment of Schlieffen after his death and include even the most obscure journals and the relevant bequeathed papers and those that seem not so relevant at first glance. The papers of General Friedrich von Boettcher, which have so far not been considered, are a good example.

14. Foerster to the Reichswehrministerium, 12 September 1934, cited in Pöhlmann, *Kriegsgeschichte und Geschichtspolitik,* 317.

15. Alfred von Schlieffen, *Dienstschriften des Chefs des Generalstabes der Armee Generalfeldmarschall Graf von Schlieffen,* ed. Generalstab des Heeres, vol. 2, *Die Grossen Generalstabsreisen—Ost—aus den Jahren, 1891–1905* (Berlin: Einleitung, 1938).

16. Karl-Heinz Frieser, *Blitzkrieg-Legende: Der Westfeldzug 1940* (München, 1995), 418. In this context the connection between the concept of a breakthrough (which Schlieffen had rejected) and the concept of the envelopment (*Umfassung*) (which he advocated) are to be particularly emphasized. Cf. in detail page 418f.

17. Cf. ibid., 437–441.

18. Gerhard Ritter, *Staatskunst und Kriegshandwerk: Das Problem des "Militarismus" in Deutschland,* vol. 2, *Die Hauptmächte Europas und das Wilhelminische Reich (1890–1914)* (Munich, Vienna, Zurich, 1960), 240f.

19. Gerhard Ritter, *Der Schlieffen-Plan: Kritik eines Mythos* (Munich, 1956).

20. Ritter, *Staatskunst und Kriegshandwerk,* 2:248.

21. Ibid.

22. Cf. in particular the work by Annika Mombauer, *Helmuth von Moltke and the Origins of the First World War* (Cambridge, 2001).

23. Cf. Georg Meyer, *Adolf Heusinger: Dienst eines deutschen Soldaten 1915 bis 1964* (Hamburg, 2001), 628, 807f.; Heusinger especially endeavors to preserve the

given scope of action of politics versus the military, despite the continuously narrowing scopes of action in the nuclear age: Bruno Thoss, *NATO-Strategie und nationale Verteidigungsplanung: Planung und Aufbau der Bundeswehr unter den Bedingungen einer massiven atomaren Vergeltungsstrategie 1952 bis 1960* (Munich, 2006).

24. Diary entry by Falkenhayn of 10 September 1914, cited by Holger Afflerbach, *Falkenhayn: Politisches Denken und Handeln im Kaiserreich* (Munich, 1994), 185.

25. Bericht des Bayerischen Militärbevollmächtigten im Grossen Hauptquartier Generalleutnant von Wenninger an den bayerischen Kriegsminister Kress von Kressenstein vom 7 September 1914, cited in Bernd F. Schulte, *Europäische Krise und Erster Weltkrieg: Beiträge zur Militärpolitik des Kaiserreichs, 1871–1914* (Frankfurt a.M., 1983), 262.

26. Ibid., 279.

The Sword and the Scepter
The Powers and the European System before 1914

Klaus Hildebrand

I

When turning to the study of the relationship between the "scepter" (statecraft) and the "sword" (military tradecraft) during the run-up to the First World War, one encounters a dramatic event in connection with the July Crisis that took place on 31 July 1914 at the Ballhausplatz in Vienna. Even while German chancellor Theobald von Bethmann Hollweg was reversing the policy he had been pursuing in the crisis thus far, that of encouraging Austria-Hungary to move militarily against Serbia, he was trying on 29 and 30 July to move the Dual Monarchy toward accepting the British offer of mediation. Simultaneously, the chief of the German Great General Staff, Helmuth von Moltke the Younger, was urging the very opposite. From Moltke's Viennese counterpart, Colonel General Franz Conrad von Hötzendorf, he demanded immediate mobilization "against Russia," and implored the Austrian chief of the General Staff to "Reject latest English initiative to preserve the peace. For the preservation of Austria-Hungary, perseverance in the European war is the ultimate measure. Germany will go along with this absolutely."[1] The more-than-surprised reaction of the Austro-Hungarian foreign minister, Leopold Berchtold von und zu Ungarschitz when commenting on Moltke's telegram, has often been quoted: "A fine piece of work! Who rules in Berlin? Moltke or Bethmann?"[2]

This rhetorical question transforms the scene almost into a tribunal, before which the "almost grotesque perversity"[3] of the Schlieffen Plan is glaringly exposed. Gerhard Ritter's outraged condemnation of a fateful victory of "military tradecraft" over "statecraft," of the "helpless dependency of Germany's political leadership on the military's planning,"⁴ and of a disastrous triumph of militarism as the "exaltation and overestimation of the soldier"⁵ would seem to be unmistakably confirmed. Without wanting to call into question whether over the course of the July Crisis the military establishment in Germany, as in other European states, was gaining in influence, and without overlooking at least in Germany's case the crucial fact that her mobilization and the onset of war could hardly any longer be differentiated, significant advances in research have made it necessary to supplement Ritter's hypothesis in several aspects—and finally to revise it.

There is no need here to go farther into British historian Niall Ferguson's extravagant position that militarism on the eve of the First World War was "politically in decline."⁶ Rather, the emphasis on the military and an increase in its importance to all of the actors on the political stage was undeniable.⁷ This trend toward the emergence of an "armaments culture"⁸ can be observed not only in the three nonparliamentarian empires, but also in France and Great Britain. Often quoted in this context is the famous remark made by French chief of staff Joseph Joffre during the early months of 1912, indicating the degree to which his mind was totally preoccupied with thoughts of war. When he was asked, "Don't you think we will have a war?" he answered: "Certainly I think so. I have always thought so. It will come. I shall fight it and I shall win."

Joffre's confident prognosis on the prospects of war corresponds with a similar statement made in January 1914 by French president Raymond Poincaré. Beyond any political experiment aiming at preserving peace through deterrence, he had long before begun to concentrate on preparations for the coming war. "In two years we will have war. All of my thoughts are directed at forearming ourselves for it."⁹

British naval officers, subjected to the novel concept of professionalization under the modernization program of First Sea Lord Admiral Sir John A. Fisher, were thinking along entirely similar lines. Lieutenant Commander J. M. Kenworthy, later Lord Strabolgi, characterized the representative attitudes of his comrades on the eve of the Great War: "We prepared for war . . . , we talked about war, we thought about war, and we hoped for war. For war would be our chance, was for what we had been trained."¹⁰

And Winston S. Churchill, then minister of trade and siding with the "economists," when reporting on the debate on the naval estimates for 1909, which the spiraling arms race was propelling into ever more expensive dimensions, quipped: "The Admiralty had demanded six ships, the budgeteers offered four, and we compromised finally on eight."¹¹

Across the whole of Europe a "cult of the offensive"[12] reigned triumphant. Although this mind-set was more prevalent on the Continent, Britain nonetheless did not remain unaffected by the militarization of society,[13] and during the last decade prior to 1914 its military professionals were reckoning firmly with war against Germany.[14] The cult of the offensive subjected the military planning of one country after another to its pull. There was a sort of "offensive mysticism"[15] challenging politics. We should not, however, allow such generalizations to mislead us into ignoring important differences in detail. True, the military professionals in France, for example, were certainly convinced in the spring of 1913, "that it would be better for France if the conflict were not put off for too long,"[16] as Chief of Staff Joffre put it to General Henry Wilson, the British director of military operations. Likewise, the French ambassador in St. Petersburg, Maurice Paléologue, repeatedly reassured the Russians of his country's absolute loyalty to its obligations under the treaty of alliance.[17] For the political motive of winning over Great Britain's entry into the war, and despite its orientation toward preserving its alliances and dedication to *l'offensive à outrance*,[18] France nevertheless planned to have its covering forces halt ten kilometers from the German borders,[19] despite the fact that the French cabinet expected the imminent outbreak of war by 20 July. Also out of consideration for its British Entente partner, France also vowed on 31 July to respect unequivocally Belgian neutrality, quite unlike the dissembling Germans.[20]

Militarism was widespread among the populations of Europe, owing in large part to the popularization of this phenomenon in all five countries by the emerging mass-market press.[21] The defects of policy were drowned under the din of war cries, limiting the options available to statecraft. But quite aside from this, another mighty influence was coming into effect, one that had been emerging since the final third of the nineteenth century. As early as 17 February 1872, Austro-Hungarian foreign minister Julius Andrássy, impressed by Prussia's three victorious wars of unification, described it thus: "The consequence of the recent wars is that 'might makes right.' . . . any foreign policy is the right one when it is strategically correct."[22] German chancellor Leo von Caprivi expressed the same conviction two decades later, according to which, "every political issue . . . can be reduced in the end to a military factor."[23] In other words, Germany's Schlieffen Plan,[24] France's Plan XVII,[25] and the British agreements with France concerning military cooperation in the event of war[26] all had a growing, albeit variously pronounced, influence on political decision-making, especially following the Second Morocco Crisis of 1911.

The opposite, however, applies as well when one considers the strategic consequences of the French alliance for the Czarist Empire in light of one of the specific variants of Russia's Plan 19 for an offensive against Germany.[27] And in Austria-Hungary, the members of the "fronde of the diplomatic cadets,"[28] as the group including Alexander von Musulin, Alexander Graf Hoyos und János Forgách, Friedrich Szápáry, Otto Graf Czernin und Leopold von Andrian-Werburg, Georg von Franckenstein, and Emanuel von Urbas has been called, were more ready to go to war than many representatives of the military, with the notable exception of General Conrad von Hötzendorf.[29]

In "the subconsciousness of the soul,"[30] to use a contemporary phrase coined by publicist Theodor Wolff, European statesmen probably were adopting more of a strategic thinking orientation than even they were aware. Thus, any notion of a fundamental separation between statecraft and military tradecraft does not hold up under close scrutiny. Military thinking had a growing influence on political action. The statesmen themselves, who in the final event were responsible for the course and outcome of the July Crisis, were thinking in military terms. Some, though not all, were doing so by preference, and not all with the same degree of intensity. The basic pattern, however, was the same.[31] They all acted under the spell of alliances and ententes, which became ever more powerful until they finally became sacrosanct.

But these alliances also served to reinforce the no longer sufficient powers of the individual states, a fact that contributes to an explanation of the change in British foreign policy.[32] The alliances also produced autonomous effects, from which no actor could remain aloof, either by choice or from lack of option. When war finally threatened, there was no turning back without running the risks of lost allies and the threat of isolation. Avoiding just those risks seemed in every case more important than preserving the peace.

To be specific here, the point is not to obscure responsibility for the outbreak of the First World War, to plunge it into a darkness where all cats are gray. Austria's willingness to go to war with Serbia following the 28 June 1914 assassination of Archduke Franz Ferdinand caused Germany consciously to accept extreme risk in order to achieve a diplomatic victory. In no way different was the reaction of Russia, which showed itself more willing to accept military conflict than political defeat. This left France with no other choice but to place loyalty to its Russian ally over the preservation of the European peace. And with that, Britain's decision to embark upon a passage of arms became practically inevitable, for fear of isolation and the loss of credibility as an ally.[33] Nevertheless, the timeless and pivotal question still remains: Why did diplomatic interaction between the actors, that concert of European nations that we will have opportunity to examine more closely, break down as soon as one of its members, for whatever reason, challenged the status quo, even at the cost of a major war?

II

The specific interrelationship between statecraft and military tradecraft that was characteristic of European political history between the turn of the century and 1914, the increasingly strategic thinking and action on the part of statesmen, caused a system of alliances and ententes to emerge. Interacting with other important factors, that system had a determinant influence on the course and outcome of the July Crisis. Its establishment and framework replaced the European System of Otto von Bismarck, which, without generally rejecting war as a political tool or option, served according to the intention of its leading proponent one central purpose—the preservation of the general peace.[34]

After the kaiser dismissed Bismarck in 1890, all that started to change, slowly at first and then rapidly after the turn of the century. In 1892, proponents in Russia and France, who had been pressing even before the lapse of the Reinsurance Treaty, finally succeeded in concluding a military convention that by 1894 assumed the character of a formal defensive alliance. Directed against Britain at first, the alliance from 1899 on was aimed against Germany, which it threatened on two fronts. Independently at first, but then as a direct reaction to this change in the concert of nations, Bismarck's successors in Germany began to transform the double alliance with Austria-Hungary.[35] No longer was it considered an alliance for the purpose of preserving the peace. Rather, it was seen by those responsible in Wilhelmine Germany as an instrument for victory in a passage at arms. For Germany, the result of a progressive process of self-isolation and foreign encirclement was that the Double Alliance finally became an alliance "through thick and thin."

In the years immediately before and after the turn of the century, the conformation of the European political world widened following the appearance on the global stage of the United States and Japan.[36] The focus of the imperialist movement began to shift from the dispersed colonial world back to its European center. The developing trend toward the establishment of antagonistic camps and blocs—Germany and Austria-Hungary here, France and Russia there—intensified significantly. Its pace accelerated considerably and finally transformed qualitatively. This fundamental transformation of the political scene had its origins in Germany and the British reaction.

There can be no doubt that it was the construction of a German battle fleet that played a key role in revolutionizing the political scene. Actually, it did not have much to do as such with the fact that Germany, like other nations, wanted a big navy. The crucial element was the fact that the Tirpitz Plan[37] was not based on a cruiser fleet operating on the high seas, but rather on a German battle fleet operating on the British doorstep. Britain, therefore, felt fundamentally challenged. This characterized the singularity of German imperialism at the turn of the century.[38]

The British recognized the threat much earlier than the Germans would have assumed.[39] The trend toward abandoning the long-standing British policy of "splendid isolation," which became apparent under the last government formed by Robert A. Salisbury in 1895, was exacerbated by the German challenge. The result culminated in the "strategic revolution"[40] of Great Britain's foreign policy, and the abandonment of Lord Salisbury's classic maxim: "Isolation is less dangerous than to be drawn into a war that is none of our affair."[41]

Comforted by the security offered by their insular position, maritime powers generally tend to react to political and military challenges with more equanimity than do geographically less favored continental powers. But when they feel their invulnerability is in danger, the reaction can be exceptionally determined, as illustrated by Great Britain's stance during the Napoleonic era, or America's war-fighting efforts in the Second World War. It was in this spirit, one profoundly influenced by the disappointing experience in the Boer War, that a new generation of British politicians led by Joseph Chamberlain and Arthur Balfour cast about for allies. Britain felt its own military power to be inadequate, because, among other factors, the introduction of conscription was completely out of the question. The solution, then, was to seek reinforcement in the form of alliances, ententes, and conventions.

In 1902 Britain concluded a defensive alliance with Japan and reached a compromise with France over colonial interests, leading to the Entente Cordiale of 1904 and to the Asia Convention with Russia in 1907. The issues at the heart of these agreements, Morocco and Egypt in the case of the former, and Persia, Afghanistan, and Tibet in the latter, were not without repercussions in Europe. The result was that although still considering itself as the arbiter of international politics, and although claiming complete freedom of action for itself, Britain over the course of time was becoming a member of one of the two camps dividing Europe. The British position was not unambiguous, but rather half-and-half in its own understanding, and incalculable for others.

The *opérations contre Allemagne*,[42] which had been ongoing since 1905, resulted in the agreement to commit a British expeditionary corps on the Continent in the event of war. And while Great Britain thus grew into its role as a member of the Triple Entente, that nation nevertheless remained an incalculable factor. The process apparently had nothing whatsoever to do with Foreign Secretary Edward Grey's illusionary hope of enjoying the advantages of an alliance without having to bear the disadvantages arising from its obligations. Against all evidence to the contrary, he remained convinced that military agreements and political decisions could be kept separate in principle. "Well, the military experts held conversations," he said in 1911 to Prime Minister Herbert Asquith, referring to the pertinent staff talks of 1906. "What they agreed on I never found out. In fact, the situation was that the governments had full freedom of action while the military knew what they had to do, should the word come."[43]

Willingly or not, Britain made its arrangements with Russia, which seemed invincible and capable of doing a colossal amount of damage to the British in India,[44] as well as with France, which because of its Russian alliance could not be allowed to become an enemy.[45] Conversely, fear of Germany was driving both France and Russia "right into England's arms," as noted in the assessment by Paul von Hintze, German military plenipotentiary at the czarist court in 1909.[46] It was, therefore, the problematic logic of the constellation of powers on the one hand, and the challenge at sea on the other, that turned Wilhelmine Germany initially into Britain's rival. And once the power struggle escalated into an ideological one—equally true for both sides—Germany finally became Britain's enemy.[47] The objectively weaker but nonetheless more dangerous of the two nations had drawn Britain's enmity upon itself.[48]

The power of the alliances to ensnare and bind all of the actors, including Britain, grew stronger from crisis to crisis between 1905 and 1914. Thus, when Britain by 1911 at the latest had decided the naval arms race in its own favor,[49] it ceased to seek compromise with Germany in even general terms. Britain's foreign policy persisted under the spell of strategic considerations. Focusing by preference on its sheer survival in case of war, it still seemed rigid. In the central elements of its thought processes and courses of action, it was indistinguishable from those of the other actors. Belonging to a bloc, even an alliance, albeit in a British way, was now more important than a return to the "old diplomacy" and its freedom of action.[50]

Despite Britain's self-image as being the most advanced of civilizations, it was nonetheless haunted by the fear of decline and decay,[51] as it fell more and more into a "security dilemma."[52] Indeed, all of the state actors of the period, each in his own way, were "hoist on their own alliances,"[53] as observed by Jules Cambon, the French ambassador in Berlin, who repeatedly warned about the affinity between the system of alliances and the threat of war.[54] For all their power, the members of the two blocs lacked the necessary flexibility and thus lost their diplomatic freedom of action as the price of strategic power projection because they erroneously believed that a military balance was the same as political equilibrium.

Desiring finally to get a grip on the German threat, French foreign minister Théophile Delcassé as early as 1904 proposed an *alliance politique* with Great Britain, over and above the Entente Cordiale and in addition to the Franco-Russian alliance. "If we could lean on Russia and England both, how strong we then would be against Germany!"[55] Although not wanting for the present to turn this idea into action, two years later even Britain's Foreign Secretary Grey was prepared to take up this dangerous thought: "An *entente* between Russia, France and us would offer absolute safety. If it should ever become necessary to put Germany in check, it could be done."[56] And it was Russian foreign minister Sergey D. Sazonov who, in the spring of 1914, just prior to the outbreak of the Great War, floated the idea to transform the so-called "Triple Entente" into a new "Triple Alliance" to guard against the perceived aggressiveness of Germany "for all time to come."[57]

Whether such a hermetically tight system of deterrence would have had a pacifying effect is a fundamental question that must remain unanswered. That the quest for absolute security for one side implies absolute insecurity for the other can be regarded as a commonplace of historical experience. But apart from this we can simply say that because of Britain's refusal to enter into a firm or even a publicly proclaimed alliance, the Great Powers were denied the one advantage of a true bloc system—the chance of predictability. Problematically, Great Britain stood aloof from the idea of a perfect *alliance à trois*.[58] This was primarily because of domestic political considerations rooted in its parliamentary constitution, but also because of the desire to avoid encouraging any war tendency on the part of Russia, which since 1912 had been growing excessively in strength.[59] Put another way, although Britain's parliamentary structure would allow only the conclusion of secret military agreements, the obligations those agreements entailed proved nonetheless to be determinant.

Charles Hardinge, permanent undersecretary in the Foreign Office, remarked in January 1909: "We cannot afford to sacrifice our entente with Russia in any way."[60] This was just as true during the July Crisis as at the time of Grey's admission a few days prior to the war: "We cannot allow ourselves to stand aside and watch France's position being weakened."[61] Significantly, it was not the military and political agreements as such that Britain had entered into over the years, notably the important exchange of notes between Grey and Cambon of 22 and 23 November 1912,[62] that were the determining factors for both Britain and the European System in the summer of 1914.[63] Rather, it was the motives underlying those military agreements and political ententes, along with other international trends, that induced Britain to enter the war like all the others, to bow to the overwhelming imperatives of alliances, claiming Germany's violation of Belgian neutrality as its justification. It was the fear of losing or even duping Russia and France, leaving Britain standing alone, isolated, and abandoned.

The consideration of each of the powers for its allies and entente partners had an overpowering effect and forced them to make concessions, especially Germany to Austria-Hungary and Great Britain to Russia. Unlike in the Balkan Wars of 1912–1913, the Czarist Empire in the summer of 1914 was no longer willing to back down. Russia did not want any future conflict with Austria-Hungary and Germany to end in another "diplomatic Tsushima," as Russia had suffered in the Bosnian Annexation Crisis in 1908.[64] The same holds true for Austria-Hungary, whose aggressiveness in July 1914 was not likely to be deterred as easily by a "bucket of cold water"[65] from Berlin as it had been during the Adriatic Crisis of 1912. On the contrary, Germany in sheer terror of losing the last of its allies not only gave Austrian aggression free rein, but it even encouraged it. Berlin sought to break the chains of an encirclement that was as much self-made as foreign-caused through a diplomatic forward strategy, and in doing so it accepted the risk of a major war.

All of the actors on the European stage were gripped by the "Hobbesian Fear"[66] of losing all credibility as an ally and in the end standing isolated. With their influence, power, honor, and prestige at stake, and without consideration of a future war, they all deliberately decided to put the preservation of their alliances, ententes, and agreements ahead of preserving the peace. No one wanted the big war, but neither did anyone want to avoid it at the cost of a diplomatic defeat.

Aside from the existence of the almighty alliances, aside from the conviction that the coming struggle was inevitable, aside from the immanent fatalism of war expectations, and aside from the directionless activity arising from it, there was during the final years prior to the First World War a completely different tendency within the European concert of nations. That in turn gave rise to the hopes that the unbroken series of crises, conflicts, and military disputes might yet turn out well in the end. All of that took place in the middle of what Eduard Berstein early in the 1890s had already called "cold war,"[67] the policy of détente.

III

The fact can neither be ignored nor underestimated that the years and decades of the pre–World War era was also what Emil Daniels, political editor of the *Preussischen Jahrbücher,* diagnosed in the spring of 1914 as the predominating trend of his time—an "era of reduced tensions."[68] Historians subsequently have discovered this long-neglected line of inquiry, leading to the emergence of what H. M. Scott called a "history of détente" for the decade prior to 1914.[69] This approach questions the teleology of a development that regards the crises between 1905 and 1914 as leading virtually without alternative directly to the First World War. In fact, it marks a return to the historical perspective of individuals acting in their contemporary environment of uncertainty, which helps to explain better their actions. Holger Afflerbach, along with Friedrich Kiessling[70] and Klaus Wilsberg,[71] are the principal advocates of this new direction of inquiry. Afflerbach sees the Triple Alliance less as a "community of gains" than as an "insurance society." He even goes so far as to advance the idea that the perpetuation of the peace seems to have been the guiding principle of European statesmanship of that time. The warmongering of the General Staffs, according to his argument, had no real limiting effect on the responsible politicians. That establishes a true counterpoint to Ritter's theory of militarism as the rule of the military over the political. Accordingly, Afflerbach reaches the conclusion: "The First World War was a possible outcome, but it was neither an inevitable one, nor even very probable."[72]

What could justify such an exaggerated thesis? It is indeed a fact that statesmen on all sides tried to escape the ties and bonds of their alliances in order to reclaim freedom of action. This they did more timidly than boldly, and without threatening their existing obligations, however fragile they might have been. Certainly, ideas did arise in public debate that took into account that highly civilized modern societies would only stand to lose from war, whereas they would benefit from peace, and that an armed struggle might lead, as Moltke the Elder pessimistically predicted, to "thirty years of war"[73] and in no way short or glorious. Or as French ambassador Paléologue in St. Petersburg wrote presciently on 20 August 1914, a modern war "could not be ended by a political treaty after a battle like Solferino or Sadowa," but rather would be "to the death," and a question of "national existence."[74] Paléologue did not fail to overlook that war was not, as some contemporaries believed, a cure for social ills, but rather, as some predicted, it would end in upheaval and revolution.[75] Regardless, such insights, as Ernest Bloch noted, brought little light "to the darkness of the lived moment," no matter how true they now may seem in hindsight.

What is rather obvious is that it was just those existing alliances and ententes that seemed to have a restraining influence on their members in critical situations. This is true for the Austrian attitude toward Germany during the Algeciras Conference in 1906, and it can be seen in the French reservations toward Russia's activities during the Bosnian Annexation Crisis of 1908–1909. It is also characteristic for the course of the Balkan Wars of 1912 and 1913, with Britain restraining Russia, and Germany restraining Austria.[76]

The determining factor for the policy of détente was, however, the efforts to reduce tensions and find compromise between the members of opposing blocs. These efforts were as numerous as they were closely spaced. They seem, however, less spectacular or memorable than that series[77] of crises, conflicts, and military disputes that, notwithstanding, did not automatically have to end in the First World War. There was another side to the story. The so-called bloc system during the years and decades prior to 1914 was not so solid as commonly thought. On the contrary, it proved to be rather "unstable,"[78] to use the term coined by Friedrich Kiessling.

That is why the negotiating under the détente process was never directly from bloc to bloc.[79] Typically there were no such constituted organs as the Delian League of Athens or Sparta's Peloponnesian League, or in the second half of the twentieth century America's NATO or Russia's Warsaw Pact. The pre–World War I blocs did multiply considerably the existing tensions between their members; however, reducing those tensions remained in the realm of bilateral efforts. The individual actors were quite aware that success or failure of their attempts to reduce tensions would have immediate effects on the status of the blocs and their relations with one another. Détente and power politics were inseparably interconnected. But that means in consequence that by the Morocco Crisis of 1911 at the latest there was a European consciousness that the emergence of the blocs involved obvious dangers, and that a reduction of tensions was required. As Austro-Hungarian foreign minister Leopold Graf Berchtold noted on 15 December 1912, "But Europe, divided and disunited, should keep in mind that its fate here is directly at stake, that a categorical imperative demands that in this most serious question it appear not as two divided camps, but as a united front, reasonable and purposeful."[80]

Aside from the oft-repeated "topos of the inevitability of war,"[81] there was also the one of "the avoided war."[82] That was based on the notion that all of the crises, conflicts, and even the small wars of the age had up to the present turned out all right without turning into the big war. But the idea also had to do with the fact that the policy of détente seemed to be successful in the eyes of the German cabinet, although jeopardized by the mass emotions whipped up by the press.[83] Moreover, it should not be overlooked that the blocs themselves were not free of internal tensions. The uneasy cohabitation of Great Britain and Russia, for example, had to manage the antagonisms resulting from the concept of an endgame[84] between the two empires. Those tensions had never entirely been put to rest, and their effects rippled from the frontiers of India to the heart of Europe.

The Anglo-French relationship also produced sufficient room for doubts, such as those of the Russians in 1914 about whether in the final event Great Britain would really go to war at France's side.[85] During his tenure in office from 1906 to 1911, Russian foreign minister Aleksandr P. Izvol'skiy made an obvious effort to win more freedom of action for his country. With Russia tipping the scales, the balance would be altered between France and Britain on the one side, and Germany and Austria-Hungary on the other.[86] Austria-Hungary's Foreign Minister Berchtold, who came into office in 1912, tried to qualify Germany's preeminence in the Triple Alliance, albeit more subtly than did his predecessor, Alois Lexa von Aehrenthal.[87] The state secretary of the German Foreign Office, Alfred von Kiderlen-Wächter, firmly rejected the Double Monarchy's effrontery in attempting to make Germany the tool of its Southeast European policy, preferring, for at least one historic moment in true Bismarckian style, Great Power autonomy and European peace over the cultivation and perfecting of the alliance.[88] Even Britain's foreign secretary, Lord Grey, saw the reason for his actions as the reconciliation of bloc and détente policies—that is, finding new partners without losing the old.[89]

Finally, a number of bilateral efforts at compromise and détente remain that cannot be discussed in detail here, but which regardless of their specific and overall failure nevertheless fed the anxieties of the respective alliance or entente partners, casting doubt upon the continued existence of the blocs.[90]

Repeatedly such efforts to find a settlement were undertaken by Russia and Austria-Hungary, conservative and plagued by the fear of revolution as they were. Both powers were especially concerned about their mutual southern and eastern European zones of contention. The efforts extended from the Mürzsteg Program, resulting from the meeting for foreign ministers in Buchlau in 1908, to the options for the negotiation of disputed Polish-

Ukrainian issues in 1914. Russia and Germany also pursued settlements, as typified by the meeting of the monarchs in Björkoe in 1905 and the "*entrevues*" in Potsdam in 1910 and Baltischport in 1912. Bethmann Hollweg speculated during the July Crisis of 1914 whether it might be possible, once the "Serbian business" was decided in Germany's favor, "to reach an arrangement with Russia, disappointed by the Western Powers, with regard to a then-satisfied Austria-Hungary."[91]

Such initiatives played a role between Austria and France and extended from financial cooperation to political relations. Austria's objective, more so under Foreign Minister Alois von Aehrenthal than under his successor, Leopold Berchtold, was to secure more independence for Austria from its German ally. And as France noted, "belonging to different political associations could not have any disruptive influence on our relations with one another."[92] There were some initiatives even between France and Germany, whose reciprocal policies of détente advanced so favorably that their relationship, as defined by Klaus Wilsberg, "was less of a threat to peace in Europe in 1914 than in 1911."[93]

There were also opportunities between Austria and Britain, since the British, despite their disinterest in an active policy of détente with the Dual Monarchy, still had a fundamental interest in preserving the Habsburg Empire as part of the "general détente between Vienna and the Western Powers."[94] This corresponded with Austrian intentions to make the formation of the blocs more tolerable through a rapprochement with Great Britain, since Austria felt that British intermediation was often more useful than the political maneuverings of its German ally.[95] Finally, and not least significantly, Germany and Britain sought mutual rapprochement as evidenced by early colonial agreements at the turn of the century, reciprocal soundings in search of an alliance, the Haldane Mission of 1912, and in Bethmann Hollweg's 1914 successful strategy of peripheral détente in dealing with the Baghdad Railway and the Portuguese colonies.[96] Those tentative initiatives, however, became abruptly obsolete with the announcement of Anglo-Russian negotiations over a naval convention.[97]

To be sure, these efforts at rapprochement, détente, and the loosening of the blocs, all of which failed, reveal what was characteristic for the policy of détente as a whole—in the long run it was unsuccessful. The general state of the tottering European System was such that whenever anything about any attempts to alter the existing state of affairs became known, it caused major and often existential anxieties on the part of those directly or indirectly affected. Each feared standing alone in the outcome of any such experiment. In the event of an apparent Russo-German rapprochement, such as the "Specter of Potsdam"[98] that produced such disquiet in Austria following the "*entrevue*" of 1910, France feared for its Russian alliance, which seemed to be the cornerstone and even the very essence of its state policy. Such a rapprochement between Berlin and St. Petersburg, noted Ambassador Paléologue in his diary for 23 June 1914 and quoting French prime minister René Viviani, would almost be the end of France: "That would be terrible! It would mean the loss of our national independence! . . . It would not just be the end of the Republic, it would be the end of France!"[99]

Contrary to commonly held belief, recent research has shown that in the years and decades prior to 1914 the blocs were anything other than monolithic. Therein lay the chance, and it was indeed a clear one to contemporary observers, that war would once again be avoided as it had been in past crises. This contributes to explaining the confidence on all sides going into the July Crisis. Looking back at all the questions, this optimistic assumption alone propelled even more urgently the fateful course of events. For as Friedrich Kiessling remarked, "Détente and tension are mutually dependent." He concluded, "Détente, which was initially conceived among other things to manage the risks inherent in the confrontation of blocs, merely had the result of exacerbating the security dilemma."[100] In other words, what was supposed to have served peace actually encouraged war, because in the end it made an already unstable system unpredictable.

IV

It was just this incalculability of the European political system during the Age of Imperialism between 1900 and 1914—let us call it the Imperialist System for short—that distinguishes it so characteristically and problematically from other forms of organizing the relations between nations. It was a system in sharp contrast to the open balance of power of the age of Bismarck in the nineteenth century, or the closed bloc system during the Cold War period of the second half of the twentieth century. What does this mean, then?

The concert of nations, so skillfully cultivated by Bismarck, provided a freedom of action to the five participants that almost amounted to a nonsystem. It had such flexibility that all existing relationships between the Great Powers could be regarded as valid for a limited time only. In principle, each power could combine with any other against any other. "*Renversement des alliances*" was a constitutive characteristic of the system's existence. It resisted every tendency toward solidification, permanence, and bloc-building, which primarily were demanded by the militaries of the continental European states. Such initiatives were also the subject of strident calls from the various national public opinions, but the system remained basically viable until its breakdown in 1890. It was just this inconsistency of the confused patchwork of alliances that promoted the understanding that lay at the system's heart. That which was supposed to be prevented, the outbreak of a revolutionizing struggle, the Bit War, might happen at any time.

The never-ending, institutionalized, and even inflamed rivalries that were characteristic of the Balance of Power System moved the actors to caution, which successfully prevented them from crossing the threshold of military conflict between the Great Powers. There indeed were some conflicts that resorted to military means, even localized and limited wars, but these could be prosecuted without endangering the system. Bismarck's system, consisting of too much tension and not enough détente, was all in all so fragile that it seemed calculable, at least with regard to the cardinal question of war and peace. Undoing the balance of terror meant endangering the peace. Preserving the balance of terror prevented the outbreak of war.[101]

The problem of war and peace was quite different under the recent nuclear age international system. That system was a monolithic bloc system, underpinned by the singular experience of the military use of the atomic bomb in 1945. That made the responsible heads of the blocs constantly aware of the risk of radical annihilation. Détente could indeed exist within the framework of this bloc system, but without casting any doubt on the existence of the system or the persistence of the blocs themselves. Moreover, wars were actually waged on the periphery of this bipolar world, but they were not permitted to alter the status quo in any fundamental way. Overall, the nuclear system was extremely predictable—each actor knew what he could do and what he had to avoid if he did not want to run the risk of war. Hence, peace was preserved.[102]

The Imperialist System of the early years of the twentieth century had quite different features. Its structure was a mixture, an indefinite alloy. It was a bloc system with tendencies toward détente that called its own existence into question. Its actors blended planning for war with systematic peace policies. They built their alliances to win the coming war, while at the same time trusting in just those alliances to ensure diplomatic victory below the military threshold. They built up their militaries far too greatly to avoid falling victim to the military in the areas of domestic and international policy, but they built them up far too little to give each actor enough power of its own to make the alliances obsolete. Of course, politics reigned supreme, but it became increasingly intermixed with strategy. Considered as a whole, the situation was, if we are to believe with Immanuel Kant in the congruence of democracy and peace, far from democratic enough. And yet it was already much too democratic, if we are to agree with Rudolf Virchow's resigned observation at the end of the nineteenth century: "It used to be governments who were for war, now the peoples want war."[103]

Largely through diplomatic détente, the political balance of terror increasingly came to be reduced to merely the military balance, with its terrors even more diminished. In other words, the aim of the Bismarckian system was to preserve the balance of power and the peace, largely detached from the influences of ideology, social organization, or the internal affairs of its actors. During the Cold War, on the other hand, the nuclear system aimed at the balance between blocs and the avoidance of war, shifting the conflict between the Great Powers to the realms of ideology, social organization, and internal affairs of the actors. The Imperialist System sought to achieve supremacy and victory in war, while including some elements of ideology, social organization, and the internal affairs of its members. All in all, it was a system of half measures and thus a mirror of its times. It was torn between tradition and modernity, between autocracy and democracy, between conservatism and socialism, and between classical art and the avant-garde. From the specific perspectives of statecraft and military tradecraft, it was torn between the cabinet and the mass age.

This state of indecision, which articulated itself as a confusing noise lacking any clear signal, encouraged the tendency to regard grand policy as a grand game. This tendency was already widespread among the rulers and governed alike.[104] The result was a situation that had long since grown serious, was not taken seriously enough soon enough, and seemed at times to vanish into some "land of the absurd."[105] Like Marie Antoinette at the end of her era playing at living the peasant's life without ever experiencing its toils, the representatives of the dying epoch of the "long nineteenth century" played at peace and war, some in earnest and desperation, others flippantly and frivolously. They generally did so without realizing in the slightest the consequences of the stakes that were in play. It was certainly not apparent to them that the coming struggle would be the First World War, at least not with regard to the destructive dimensions of this European catastrophe.

Their cognitive miscomprehension, from which arose their political failure, resulted from the fact that they had lost all sense of the notion that societies and nations could die. If one disregarded the Napoleonic interlude, in which revolution and war had appeared as twin brothers challenging fundamentally the Old World, then war, "the most aggressive form"[106] of international relations, no longer seemed necessarily so destructive that it might actually bring about the end of an age.

Since the eighteenth century, and even since the end of the Thirty Years War, the predominate experience—regardless of the evidence to the contrary—had been that wars between nations were relatively "harmless."[107] Responsible leaders, to whom the burden of their responsibility often seemed lighter than it actually was, risked conflict after conflict like a jousting match, as though they lay under the spell of some collective compulsion to repeat themselves. Their thinking bore the stamps of "reprisal ethics" and "response morality."[108] High politics seemed like a swashbuckling duel, in which honor was dearer than survival. Blinded by the fullness of their own powers, which extended worldwide, they eventually lost sight of reality. Almost superhuman, godlike even, able to rule the world, they proved their own downfall and destroyed each other.

In terms of our own study there is no doubt that it was the politicians, not the military men, who in the Imperialist System of the European concert of nations before 1914 made the final decisions. Their actions, however, were in large part less an expression of statecraft than of military tradecraft—and even of that not entirely but only halfway. On the one hand they were the executors of the military alliances, and on the other hand they were the bearers of the hopes for political détente. As the July Crisis of 1914 unfolded and the alliances functioned so imperatively and so perfectly, seamless and flawless as in no other crisis before, it gave rise to a specific and singular situation.[109] The hope for détente, which hitherto had always prevailed, worked in the absolute contrary sense by promoting conflict. Driven, aside from other contemporary factors, by "honor, fear, and self-interest,"[110] it even helped to confirm the illusionary assumption of the statesmen. This can be seen in the constant references to the end of the Bosnian Annexation Crisis of 1908–1909 and that it would once again be possible to avoid war. Thus, all of the actors saw themselves encouraged, albeit in differing degrees of decisiveness, not to divert from their course of conflict. But at the end of that course lay the First World War.

Undoubtedly, it was not the European Imperialist System in itself that was solely or even principally responsible. That responsibility lies squarely with the actors, the nations, and their representatives. But those were the conditions predisposed by this system, as it was established and practiced by just those statesmen. They developed a dynamic of their own, demanding and even predicating a set of actions, a pattern of behavior, that was accepted as given in every nation and that favored war more strongly than it discouraged it.

Such as it was, the Imperialist System could offer no prescription for their actions—to paraphrase the Apostle Paul—"either by revelation, by knowledge, by prophesying, or by doctrine."[111] No, the answers were oracular, ambiguous, and impenetrable. And finally, when one of its protagonists dared to venture all or nothing, they failed in their entirety. Because even major war still counted as a part of European normality, none of the actors, no matter how grave their individual responsibility for the onset of the military catastrophe, wanted or was even ready or able to believe that the playing at games of power politics had long since turned into an epochal struggle for existence itself.

Notes

This chapter was first published in volume 24 of the *Friedrichsruher Beiträge der Otto-von-Bismark-Stiftung* (Friedrichsruh, 2005).

1. Franz Conrad von Hötzendorf, *Aus meiner Dienstzeit: 1906–1918*, vol. 4, *24. Juni 1914 bis 30. September 1914* (Wien, Leipzig, Munich, 1923), 152.

2. Ibid., 153.

3. Gerhard Ritter, "Der Anteil der Militärs an der Kriegskatastrophe von 1914," *Historische Zeitschrift* 193 (1961): 72–91, esp. 88.

4. Gerhard Ritter, *Staatskunst und Kriegshandwerk: Das Problem des "Militarismus" in Deutschland*, vol. 3, *Die Tragödie der Staatskunst: Bethmann Hollweg als Kriegskanzler (1914–1917)* (Munich, Vienna, Zurich, 1964), 19.

5. Ritter, *Staatskunst und Kriegshandwerk: Das Problem des "Militarismus" in Deutschland*, vol. 1, *Die altpreussische Tradition (1740–1890)*, 3rd ed. (Munich, Vienna, Zurich, 1965), 13.

6. Niall Ferguson, *Der falsche Krieg: Der Erste Weltkrieg und das 20. Jahrhundert* (Stuttgart, 1999), 64.

7. Cf. David G. Herrmann, *The Arming of Europe and the Making of the First World War* (Princeton, N.J., 1996), 219; David Stevenson, *Armaments and the Coming of War: Europe, 1904–1914* (Oxford, 1996), 416f.; and Manfried Rauchensteiner, *Der Tod des Doppeladlers: Österreich-Ungarn und der Erste Weltkrieg* (Graz, Wien, Köln, 1993), 58f.

8. Cf. Michael Epkenhans, "Verlust des Primats der Politik? 'Staatskunst' und 'Kriegshandwerk' 1890–1914," in *Otto von Bismarck und Wilhelm II: Repräsentanten eines Epochenwechsels?*, 2nd rev. ed., ed. Lothar Gall (Paderborn, 2001), 61–83, esp. 67.

9. Quoted in Stephen Schröder, "Das Deutsche Reich und die Verhandlungen über eine anglo-russische Marinekonvention am Vorabend des Ersten Weltkrieges" (Ph.D. diss., University of Bonn, 2003), 220; see page 77.

10. Quoted in Zara S. Steiner, *Britain and the Origins of the First World War* (London, 1977), 193.

11. Winston S. Churchill, *The World Crisis, 1911–1918,* vol. 1 (London, 1938), 24.

12. Stephan van Evera, "The Cult of Offensive and the Origins of the First World War," *International Security* 9 (1984): 58–107; Jack Snyder, *The Ideology of the Offensive: Military Decision Making and the Disasters of 1914* (London, Ithaca, 1984).

13. Cf. James Joll, *Die Ursprünge des Ersten Weltkriegs* (München, 1984), 109ff., 299ff.; Dieter Storz, *Kriegsbild und Rüstung vor 1914: Europäische Landstreitkräfte vor dem Ersten Weltkrieg* (Herford, Berlin, Bonn, 1992), 84ff.

14. Cf. Storz, *Kriegsbild und Rüstung vor 1914,* 55.

15. Cf. ibid., 226.

16. G. P. Gooch and Harold Temperley, eds., *British Documents on the Origins of the War, 1898–1914,* vol. 9, part 2 (London, 1933), 532.

17. Cf. Gerd Krumeich, *Aufrüstung und Innenpolitik in Frankreich vor dem Ersten Weltkrieg: Die Einführung der dreijährigen Dienstpflicht 1913–1914* (Wiesbaden, 1980), 265; see also Gooch and Harold Temperley, eds., *British Documents on the Origins of the War, 1898–1914,* vol. 11 (London, 1938), 125.

18. Cf. Stefan Schmidt, "Frankreichs Aussenpolitik in der Julikrise 1914" (Master's thesis, University of Bonn, 2001), 122f.

19. Cf. John F. V. Keiger, *France and the Origins of the First World War* (London, 1983), 161.

20. Cf. Joll, *Die Ursprünge des Ersten Weltkriegs,* 46.

21. Cf. Klaus Hildebrand, "Europäisches Zentrum, überseeische Peripherie und Neue Welt: Über den Wandel des Staatensystems zwischen dem Berliner Kongress (1878) und dem Pariser Frieden (1919/20)," *Historische Zeitschrift* 249 (1989): 53–94, 63f.

22. Heinrich Lutz, "Politik und militärische Planung in Österreich-Ungarn zu Beginn der Ära Andrássy: Das Protokoll der Wiener Geheimkonferenzen vom 17. bis 19. Februar 1872," in *Geschichte und Gesellschaft: Festschrift für Karl R. Stadler zum 60. Geburtstag,* ed. Gerhard Botz, Hans Hautmann, and Helmut Konrad (Wien, 1974), 23–44, cf. page 29.

23. Caprivi, speaking before the Reichstag on 11 November 1892, in Michael Behnen, ed., *Quellen zur deutschen Aussenpolitik im Zeitalter des Imperialismus 1890–1911* (Darmstadt, 1977), 71.

24. On the debate over the existence and relevance of—and problems surrounding—the Schlieffen Plan, cf. Terence Zuber, "The Schlieffen Plan Reconsidered," *War in History* 6 (1999): 262–305; Terence Holmes, "The Reluctant March on Paris: A Reply to Terence Zuber's 'The Schlieffen Plan Reconsidered,'" *War in History* 8 (2001): 208–232. See also the debate in *War in History* from 2001 to 2003, and also Annika Mombauer, *Helmuth von Moltke and the Origins of the First World War* (Cambridge, 2001), esp. 72ff., and Gerhard Ritter, *Der Schlieffenplan: Kritik eines Mythos* (München, 1956), cf. page 160ff.

25. Cf. Krumeich, *Aufrüstung und Innenpolitik in Frankreich vor dem Ersten Weltkrieg,* 139ff.

26. Cf. Samuel R. Williamson Jr., *The Politics of Grand Strategy: Britain and France Prepare for War, 1904–1914* (Cambridge, 1969), passim, cf. page 367; Steiner, *Britain and the Origins of the First World War,* 194ff.; Hildebrand, "Europäisches Zentrum," 79.

27. Cf. Bruce W. Menning, "Pieces of the Puzzle: The Role of Iu.N. Danilov and M.V. Alekseev in Russian War Planning before 1914," *International History Review* 25 (2003): 775ff.; William C. Fuller Jr., *Strategy and Power in Russia, 1600–1914* (New York, 1992), 430ff.; David Alan Rich, *The Tsar's Colonels: Professionalism, Strategy and Subversion in Late Imperial Russia* (Cambridge, Mass., London, 1998), 217.

28. Expression used by Emanuel von Urbas, former member of this "friendly circle of decision-makers" led by Berchthold, as cited by John Leslie, "Österreich-Ungarn vor dem Kriegsausbruch: Der Ballhausplatz in Wien im Juli 1914 aus der Sicht eines österreichisch-ungarischen Diplomaten," in *Deutschland und Europa in der Neuzeit: Festschrift für Karl Otmar Freiherr von Aretin zum 65. Geburtstag,* ed. Ralph Melville, Klaus Scharf, Martin Vogt, and Ulrich Wengenroth (Stuttgart: Halbbd., 1988), 661–684, cf. page 663.

29. Cf. Günther Kronenbitter, *"Krieg im Frieden": Die Führung der k.u.k. Armee und die Grossmachtpolitik Österreich-Ungarns, 1906–1914* (Munich, 2003), 10f.

30. Theodor Wolff, *Tagebücher 1914–1919: Der Erste Weltkrieg und die Entstehung der Weimarer Republik in Tagebüchern, Leitartikeln und Briefen des Chefredakteurs am "Berliner Tageblatt" und Mitbegründers der "Deutschen Demokratischen Partei,"* ed. T. L. Eingel (Boppard a.Rh.: Bernd Sösemann, 1984), 233.

31. Cf. Herrmann, *The Arming of Europe and the Making of the First World War,* 218ff. See also Gustav Schmidt, "Die Julikrise: Unvereinbare Ausgangslagen und innerstaatliche Zielkonflikte," in *Flucht in den Krieg? Die Aussenpolitik des kaiserlichen Deutschland,* ed. Gregor Schöllgen (Darmstadt, 1991), 187–229, cf. pages 188 and 217f.; Pertti Luntinen, *French Information on the Russian War Plans, 1880–1914,* Studia Historica, 17 (Helsinki, 1984), 205. For the case of Germany, Jost Dülffer, "Zur Einführung: Vermiedene Kriege im internationalen Mächtesystem," in Jost Dülffer, Martin Kröger, and Rolf-Harald Wippich, *Vermiedene Kriege: Deeskalation von Konflikten der Grossmächte zwischen Krimkrieg und Erstem Weltkrieg (1856–1914)* (Munich, 1997), 1–29, cf. page 29, and Jost Dülffer, "Die zivile Reichsleitung und der Krieg: Erwartungen und Bilder 1890–1914," in *Gestaltungskraft des Politischen: Festschrift für Eberhard Kolb,* ed. Wolfram Pyta and Ludwig Richter (Berlin, 1998), 11–28, cf. page 11f.

32. Cf. Joll, *Die Ursprünge des Ersten Weltkriegs,* 107.

33. For an overview of historical research on the July Crisis of 1914 and the outbreak of the First World War, see Annika Mombauer, *The Origins of the First World War: Controversies and Consensus* (London, 2002); Antoine Prost and Jay Winter, *Penser la Grande Guerre: Un essai d'historiographie* (Paris, 2004); for this topic see also the still paramount study by Joll, *Die Ursprünge des Ersten Weltkriegs,* and Hew Strachan, *The First World War,* vol. 1, *To Arms* (Oxford, 2001), 64ff.

34. Cf. Klaus Hildebrand, "'System der Aushilfen?' Chancen und Grenzen deutscher Aussenpolitik im Zeitalter Bismarcks (1871–1890)," in *Flucht in den Krieg? Die Aussenpolitik des kaiserlichen Deutschland*, ed. Gregor Schöllgen (Darmstadt, 1991), 108–131.

35. Cf. Rainer Lahme, "Die Entwicklung des Zweibundes von Caprivi bis Bethmann Hollweg," in *Der "Zweibund" 1879: Das deutsch-österreichisch-ungarische Bündnis und die europäische Diplomatie*, ed. Helmut Rumpler and Jan Paul Niederkorn (Wien, 1996), 195–220; Jürgen Angelow, *Kalkül und Prestige: Der Zweibund am Vorabend des Ersten Weltkrieges* (Köln, Wien, 2000), passim, cf. page 117ff.

36. Cf. Klaus Hildebrand, "'Eine neue Ära der Weltgeschichte': Der historische Ort des Russisch-Japanischen Krieges 1904/05," in *Der Russisch-Japanische Krieg (1904/05)*, ed. Josef Kreiner (Göttingen, 2005), 27–51.

37. Cf. Volker Berghahn, *Der Tirpitz-Plan: Genesis und Verfall einer innerpolitischen Krisenstrategie unter Wilhelm II* (Düsseldorf, 1971).

38. Cf. Ludwig Dehio, "Deutschland und die Epoche der Weltkriege," in *Deutschland und die Weltpolitik im 20. Jahrhundert* (Munich, 1955), 15.

39. Cf. Klaus Hildebrand, *Das vergangene Reich: Deutsche Aussenpolitik von Bismarck bis Hitler*, 2nd ed. (Stuttgart, 1996), 200ff.

40. Steiner, *Britain and the Origins of the First World War*, 207; cf. Williamson, *The Politics of Grand Strategy*, 367.

41. *The Letters of Queen Victoria*, 3rd series, vol. 3, ed. George Earl Buckle (London, 1932), 21: Salisbury to Queen Victoria, dated 12 January 1896.

42. Quoted in Theodor Schieder, "Europa im Zeitalter der Nationalstaaten und europäische Weltpolitik bis zum I. Weltkrieg (1870–1918)," in *Handbuch der europäischen Geschichte*, vol. 6, ed. Theodor Schieder (Stuttgart, 1968), 1–196, cf. page 117.

43. Lord Edward Grey, *Fünfundzwanzig Jahre Politik 1892–1916*, vol. 1 (Munich, 1926), 96. For a discussion of the restrictions on Britain's diplomatic options imposed by the policy decisions of British military officers (in other words, the "new dimension" in the nation's foreign policy), see Steiner, *Britain and the Origins of the First World War*, 189.

44. See also Schröder, "Das Deutsche Reich und die Verhandlungen über eine anglo-russische Marinekonvention am Vorabend des Ersten Weltkrieges," 68.

45. Cf. Erwin Hölzle, *Die Selbstentmachtung Europas: Das Experiment des Friedens vor und im Ersten Weltkrieg* (Frankfurt a.M., Zurich, 1975), 143.

46. Ibid., 141.

47. For the problem of power politics and ideology in Anglo-German relations during the prewar period, see Klaus Hildebrand, "Zwischen Allianz und Antagonismus: Das Problem bilateraler Normalität in den britisch-deutschen Beziehungen des 19. Jahrhunderts (1870–1914)," in *Weltpolitik. Europagedanke. Regionalismus. Festschrift für Heinz Gollwitzer zum 65. Geburtstag am 30. Januar 1982*, ed. Heinz Dollinger, Horst Gründer, and Alwin Hanschmidt (Münster, 1982), 305–331, cf. page 322.

48. Without sharing Keith Wilson's exaggerated thesis that Great Britain practically "invented" the rivalry with Germany in order to distract from its own weaknesses and justify the entente with France and Russia (Keith M. Wilson, *The Policy of the Entente: Essays on the Determinants of British Foreign Policy, 1904–1914* [Cambridge, 1985], especially page 101ff.), for the specific development of Anglo-German relations against the backdrop of the contemporary constellation of power, see Mombauer, *The Origins of the First World War*, 197, and Schröder, "Das Deutsche Reich und die Verhandlungen über eine anglo-russische Marinekonvention am Vorabend des Ersten Weltkrieges," passim.

49. Cf. Klaus Hildebrand, "Julikrise 1914: Das europäische Sicherheitsdilemma. Betrachtungen über den Ausbruch des Ersten Weltkrieges," *Geschichte in Wissenschaft und Unterricht* 36 (1985): 469–500, cf. page 481; Paul G. Halpern, *A Naval History of World War I* (London, 1994), 7ff.

50. Cf. Christel Gade, *Gleichgewichtspolitik oder Bündnispflege? Maximen britischer Aussenpolitik (1909–1914)* Veröffentlichungen des Deutschen Historischen Instituts London, 40 (Göttingen, Zurich, 1997), 192; Schröder, "Das Deutsche Reich und die Verhandlungen über eine anglo-russische Marinekonvention am Vorabend des Ersten Weltkrieges," 128.

51. Cf. the paradigmatic observations of Herfried Münkler, *Über den Krieg: Stationen der Kriegsgeschichte im Spiegel ihrer theoretischen Reflexion* (Weilerswist, 2002), 23.

52. For the fundamental problem of the "vicious circle of security needs and the search for power," which John H. Herz called the "security dilemma," see John H. Herz, "Idealistischer Internationalismus und das Sicherheitsdilemma (1950)," in *Staatenwelt und Weltpolitik* (Hamburg, 1974), 39–56, cf. 39.

53. Quote from Jean Stengers, "July 1914: Some Reflections," *Annuaire de l'Institut de Philologie et d'Histoire Orientales et Slaves* 17 (1963–1965): 120.

54. Cf. Hildebrand, "Julikrise 1914," 485, 491.

55. Maurice Paléologue, *Un grand tournant de la politique mondiale (1901–1906)* (Paris, 1934), 12.

56. G. P. Gooch and Harold Temperley, eds., *British Documents on the Origins of the War, 1898–1914*, vol. 3 (London, 1928), 267.

57. Sazonov to [Aleksandr P.] Izvol'skiy, 4 April 1914, in *Die Internationalen Beziehungen im Zeitalter des Imperialismus: Dokumente aus den Archiven der Zarischen und Provisorischen Regierung*, series 1, vol. 2 (Berlin, 1931), 136f.

58. Cf. Schröder, "Das Deutsche Reich und die Verhandlungen über eine anglo-russische Marinekonvention am Vorabend des Ersten Weltkrieges," passim.

59. For a general discussion, cf. William C. Wohlforth, "The Perception of Power: Russia in the Pre-1914 Balance," *World Politics. A Quarterly Journal of International Relations* 39 (1986/1987): 353ff.; Risto Ropponen, *Die russische Gefahr: Das Verhalten der öffentlichen Meinung Deutschlands und Österreich-Ungarns gegenüber der Aussenpolitik Russlands in der Zeit zwischen dem Frieden von Portsmouth und dem Ausbruch des Ersten Weltkriegs* (Helsinki, 1976).

60. G. P. Gooch and Harold Temperley, eds., *British Documents on the Origins of the War, 1898–1914*, vol. 5 (London, 1928), 550.

61. Quote from Wilson, *The Policy of the Entente*, 7.

62. Johannes Lepsius, Albrecht Mendelssohn Bartholdy, and Friedrich Thimme, eds., *Die Grosse Politik der Europäischen Kabinette 1871–1914: Sammlung der Diplomatischen Akten des Auswärtigen Amtes*, vol. 31 (Berlin, 1927), 544f. The problems surrounding this secret correspondence, which endorsed the consultations between British and French naval and military specialists, were "un caractère officiel" but did not impair the governments' freedom of action. See the interpretation of Schröder, "Das Deutsche Reich und die Verhandlungen über eine anglo-russische Marinekonvention am Vorabend des Ersten Weltkrieges," 72.

63. Cf. Williamson, *The Politics of Grand Strategy*, 361.

64. *Novoye Vremya* of 16 March, quoted in Caspar Ferenczi, *Aussenpolitik und Öffentlichkeit in Russland 1906–1912* (Husum, 1982), 219; cf. Luntinen, *French Information on the Russian War Plans*, 119.

65. Johannes Lepsius, Albrecht Mendelssohn Bartholdy, and Friedrich Thimme, eds., *Die Grosse Politik der Europäischen Kabinette 1871–1914*, vol. 33 (Berlin, 1927), 425.

66. Herbert Butterfield, *History and Human Relations* (London, 1951), 21.

67. Eduard Bernstein, "Die internationale Bedeutung des Wahlkampfes in Deutschland," *Die Neue Zeit* 11, no. 2 (1892/1893): 294.

68. Quoted in Friedrich Kiessling, *Gegen den grossen Krieg? Entspannung in den internationalen Beziehungen 1911–1914* (München, 2002), 7.

69. Cf. Holger Afflerbach, *Der Dreibund: Europäische Grossmacht- und Allianzpolitik vor dem Ersten Weltkrieg* (Wien, 2002), 19.

70. Kiessling, *Gegen den grossen Krieg?*

71. Klaus Wilsberg, *"Terrible ami—aimable ennemi": Kooperation und Konflikt in den deutsch-französischen Beziehungen 1911–1914* (Bonn, 1998).

72. Afflerbach, *Der Dreibund*, 826.

73. *Moltkes Militärische Werke*, ed. Grossen Generalstab, Kriegsgeschichtliche Abteilung I, vol. 4, *Kriegslehren* (Berlin, 1911), 7.

74. Maurice Paléologue, *Am Zarenhof während des Weltkrieges: Tagebücher und Betrachtungen*, 5th ed. (München, 1939), 88.

75. Cf. Hildebrand, *Europäisches Zentrum*, 58f.

76. Cf. Thomas Lindemann, *Die Macht der Perzeptionen und Perzeptionen von Macht* (Berlin, 2000), 296.

77. Kiessling, *Gegen den grossen Krieg?*, 3.

78. Ibid., 322.

79. See the proposal of the British foreign secretary on 21–22 August 1909, that a political agreement should "be one not between two powers alone but between the two great groups of Powers," in order not to frighten the individual powers through bilateral détente. G. P. Gooch and Harold Temperley, eds., *British Documents on the Origins of the War, 1898–1914*, vol. 6 (London, 1930), 284.

80. Quoted in Kiessling, *Gegen den grossen Krieg?*, 190.

81. Wolfgang J. Mommsen, "Der Topos vom unvermeidlichen Krieg: Aussenpolitik und öffentliche Meinung im Deutschen Reich im letzten Jahrzehnt vor 1914," in *Der autoritäre Nationalstaat: Verfassung, Gesellschaft und Kultur im deutschen Kaiserreich* (Frankfurt a.M., 1990), 380.

82. Kiessling, *Gegen den grossen Krieg?*, 306.

83. Cf. Hildebrand, *Europäisches Zentrum*, 63f.

84. Jennifer Siegel, *Endgame: Britain, Russia and the Final Struggle for Central Asia* (London, 2002).

85. Cf. Schröder, "Das Deutsche Reich und die Verhandlungen über eine anglo-russische Marinekonvention am Vorabend des Ersten Weltkrieges," 63.

86. Cf. Dominic B. Lieven, *Russia and the Origins of the First World War* (London, 1983), 32f.

87. Cf. Kiessling, *Gegen den grossen Krieg?*, 215, 217.

88. Cf. Hildebrand, *Das vergangene Reich*, 287.

89. Cf. Gade, *Gleichgewichtspolitik oder Bündnispflege?*, 218, and Kiessling, *Gegen den grossen Krieg?*, 71.

90. The following discussion is based principally on Hildebrand, *Europäisches Zentrum*, 86f.; Kiessling, *Gegen den grossen Krieg?*, passim; and Leslie, "Österreich-Ungarn vor dem Kriegsausbruch," 67ff.

91. Kurt Riezler, *Tagebücher, Aufsätze, Dokumente*, ed. Karl Dietrich Erdmann (Göttingen, 1972), 189 (entry for 23 July 1914).

92. *Österreich-Ungarns Aussenpolitik von der Bosnischen Krise 1908 bis zum Kriegsausbruch 1914: Diplomatische Aktenstücke des österreichisch-ungarischen Ministeriums des Äussern* (Wien, Leipzig, 1930), 7:642.

93. Wilsberg, "Terrible ami—aimable ennemi," 356.

94. Kiessling, *Gegen den grossen Krieg?*, 123.

95. Cf. ibid., 217.

96. Cf. Gregor Schöllgen, *Imperialismus und Gleichgewicht: Deutschland, England und die orientalische Frage 1871–1914* (Munich, 1984), 329ff., 374ff.

97. Cf. Schröder, "Das Deutsche Reich und die Verhandlungen über eine anglo-russische Marinekonvention am Vorabend des Ersten Weltkrieges," 574.

98. Kiessling, *Gegen den grossen Krieg?*

99. Maurice Paléologue, "Au Quai d'Orsay à la veille de la tourmente," *Journal 1913–1914*, 1 January 1913–28 June 1914 (Paris, 1947), 318; cf. also Luntinen, *French Information on the Russian War Plans*, 71, 74.

100. Kiessling, *Gegen den grossen Krieg?*, 321.

101. Cf. Klaus Hildebrand, "System der Aushilfen."

102. Cf. Werner Link, *Der Ost-West-Konflikt: Die Organisation der internationalen Beziehungen im 20. Jahrhundert*, 2nd rev. ed. (Stuttgart, 1988).

103. Quote in Andreas Osiander, "Interdependenz der Staaten und Theorie der

zwischenstaatlichen Beziehungen: Eine theoriegeschichtliche Untersuchung," *Politische Vierteljahrsschrift* 36 (1995): 261.

104. Cf. Michael Salewski, *Der Erste Weltkrieg* (Paderborn, 2003), 65ff.

105. Stig Förster, "Im Reich des Absurden: Die Ursachen des Ersten Weltkrieges," in *Wie Kriege entstehen. Zum historischen Hintergrund von Staatenkonflikten*, ed. Bernd Wegner (Paderborn, 2000), 213.

106. Osiander, "Interdependenz der Staaten und Theorie der zwischenstaatlichen Beziehungen," 256.

107. Ibid.

108. Cf. Klaus Hildebrand, "Die viktorianische Illusion: Zivilisationsniveau und Kriegsprophylaxe im 19. Jahrhundert," in *Macht und Zeitkritik: Festschrift für Hans-Peter Schwarz zum 65. Geburtstag*, ed. Peter R. Weilemann, Hanns Jürgen Küsters, and Günter Buchstab (Paderborn, 1999), 17–28, esp. page 25.

109. For a more detailed discussion, cf. Hildebrand, "Julikrise 1914," 491ff.

110. On the Thucydidian Triad, cf. Donald Kagan, *On the Origins of War and the Preservation of Peace* (New York, 1996), 8.

111. 1 Corinthians 14:6.

The Moltke Plan
A Modified Schlieffen Plan with Identical Aims?

Annika Mombauer

In 1914, Germany went to war with the war plan of the younger Helmuth von Moltke, not with the Schlieffen Plan. An investigation into the nature of the "Moltke Plan" can be based on sources in which Moltke referred to the plan of his predecessor and outlined how his own plan differed from Schlieffen's, thus enabling us to comment on both plans simultaneously. Such statements by Moltke provide evidence for the fact that he and his contemporaries believed that Alfred von Schlieffen had developed a plan that he had intended to be used in a future war. We can thus base our analysis on the conclusion that there was a Schlieffen Plan, and that Moltke's plan was derived from it and contained elements of it.

We have even more precise knowledge of Moltke's war planning, given that we know which plan the chief of the General Staff used in 1914 when war broke out, whereas we are to some extent reliant on speculation regarding Schlieffen's actual intentions in case of war. We simply do not know what he would have done if his demands for preemptive war, for example in 1905, had led to a European war.[1] Moltke, on the other hand, was able to see through Schlieffen's demands for war and to implement his own plans—although of course things did not quite go as planned in 1914, given that the anticipated quick victory in the west was not achieved.

Some of what follows in the discussion below is actually well known and could almost be taken for granted, were it not for the fact that much of what we have come to think of as fact has recently been questioned by Terence Zuber. He has not only queried our understanding of the Schlieffen Plan, but also important aspects of German military planning of the years before 1914, as well as the outbreak of war and the war-guilt question. With this in mind and in view of the controversy that Zuber's thesis has caused, it has become necessary to revisit even what might seem like general knowledge.[2]

According to Zuber, the Schlieffen Plan was merely a postwar invention; it had not really ever existed. And yet, Moltke referred in his war planning directly to Schlieffen's ideas, and there is evidence of many parallels and similarities between the war plans of the two chiefs of the General Staff. The following chapter is based on sources dating from before and after the outbreak of war, and not just on accounts of the postwar years in which disappointed former General Staff officers advanced their own interpretations of why the war began, and—more importantly—why it was lost. It goes without saying that Zuber is right to point out that an allegedly foolproof version of the Schlieffen Plan was invented after the war for the benefit of posterity. However, how can we explain the fact that before and during the war the Schlieffen Plan was a much-debated topic and that the plan was being compared to Moltke's own if not by concluding that such a plan did exist after all?

Zuber's thesis goes far beyond his provocative statement that the Schlieffen Plan was a postwar invention. He also claims that neither Moltke nor Schlieffen ever intended to attack France in case of war, or that, in order to do so and to avoid the fortifications along the Franco-German border, they planned to march through neutral Belgium. If we are to believe Zuber, it was seemingly Belgium, rather than France, that the German troops were aiming for, and Germany merely reacted to a French attack, rather than being the attacker in the west. According to this interpretation, for Germany the First World War did not begin with a German offensive against France. And yet, that this thesis is untenable can be demonstrated clearly with the help of contemporary sources, not least Moltke's own account of Germany's intentions in case of war. As he recorded on 1 August 1914: "Already in the early years the *Auswärtiges Amt* [Foreign Office] told me that France could possibly remain neutral in a war between Germany and Russia. I had such little faith in this possibility that I explained even then that if Russia declared war on us we would have to declare war on [France] immediately if [its] attitude was in doubt."[3]

Such a declaration of war would lead to the implementation of the German war plan, and that plan stipulated that German troops would march in the direction of Luxembourg, Belgium, and France. The plan did not entail stopping short of the borders and waiting for France to beat Germany to it and begin its own offensive.

This investigation of German war planning in the immediate prewar years aims to address Zuber's contentious claims and refute his tendentious conclusions that "the French did not respond to German 'aggression' but rather solely to meet their treaty obligation to the Russians";[4] that "the Russo-French Alliance had the offensive war plan, not the Germans," and that the German *coup de main* on Liège had only been planned because it was assumed that Britain would not remain neutral in a future war and that Belgium would allegedly be found on the side of the Entente.[5] Furthermore, it will be shown that the Schlieffen Plan was not a postwar invention; rather, the Schlieffen Plan was already in evidence before 1914 and was discussed by contemporaries both before and during the war.

This chapter will not address the postwar debate on whether Moltke's plan was inferior to that of his predecessor. Although this was a hotly debated topic after the war, it is of secondary importance to the controversy around Zuber's thesis. Likewise, the moral aspects of Moltke's and Germany's war plan (for example, the violation of Belgian neutrality) will not be analyzed in detail here. However, this investigation will comment on the changes Moltke made to the German deployment plan in the years 1906–1914, and on how his plan differed from the strategic plan of his predecessor. In addition, this chapter will seek to highlight the aims behind Moltke's war plan, and the consequences of his war planning for Germany's military campaign. The question of war guilt also requires further investigation in the context of Zuber's apologetic claims, and it will be asked to what extent Moltke's plan was responsible for the outbreak of war in 1914.

Moltke Plan, Schlieffen Plan: Parallels and Differences

The fact that vociferous and well-known Schlieffen followers attempted in the postwar years to make Moltke the scapegoat for the lost Battle of the Marne and thus for the "squandered victory" should not divert our attention from the fact that it had been Moltke's task as chief of the General Staff to adapt Germany's military plan in line with changing external military and political circumstances. For Wilhelm Groener and other authors of the "Schlieffen School," it went without saying that Moltke had changed and thus adulterated the Schlieffen Plan and that he had squandered Germany's certain recipe for victory.[6] This interpretation became generally widely accepted. What this school of thought liked to overlook, however, was the fact that Moltke and Schlieffen actually developed very similar plans, not least because they faced identical problems and identical external threats in their war planning.

Both chiefs of staff considered Germany to be encircled by potential enemies, but both also knew that the German armies were not strong enough to wage a war against France and Russia simultaneously. Both wanted to find a way to make the future war on two fronts winnable (and as short as possible) by concentrating initially on one of the two enemies: France in the west.[7] Both shared an overly optimistic assessment of the weakness of Germany's future opponents and thought that Germany's numerical inferiority could be made good with the superior quality of German soldiers.[8] Furthermore, both feared that the enemies would in the near future become so strong that their war plan would no longer be able to lead Germany to victory, which is why both men advocated preemptive wars in times of international crises—in 1905, 1909, 1911, 1912, and in 1914.[9]

There were parallels, too, in the restrictions and adversities that both men were subject to. Often, the army increases that they demanded were not granted by the Ministry of War, and despite their important position in the Wilhelmine state, they were ultimately dependent on external actors, such as the Ministry of War, the Reichstag, and of course, the kaiser. It was because of such constraints that their plans always involved demands for army increases, and Schlieffen's famous memorandum of 1905 must be read in this context. It was only following the Agadir Crisis of 1911 that it was possible for Moltke to have some say over army increases, and even then he was never able to achieve the level of increases he repeatedly demanded.[10]

The mobilization orders of the prewar years clearly show that, contrary to what his critics would later claim, Moltke largely adopted Schlieffen's views on how Germany could best escape from its encirclement. Even Moltke's ardent critic Groener wrote after the war, looking back at the years following Schlieffen's dismissal: "In the area of war preparations everything initially stayed the same."[11] In December 1911, for example, Moltke outlined the basis of his operational plan:

> However, the decision of the war is in the fight against France. The [French] Republic is our most dangerous enemy, but we can hope to achieve an early decision here. Once France has been defeated in the first great battles, then the country, which does not have large reserves of people, will hardly be able to continue with a long war, while Russia could divert [the war] after a lost battle into the interior of its vast territory and drag it out for an inestimable time. Germany's entire striving must, however, be aimed at ending the war at least on one side as quickly as possible by way of a few great strikes.[12]

Consequently Moltke's plan demonstrated a number of characteristics that largely correspond to what is usually referred to as the Schlieffen Plan. First, instead of fighting a war on two fronts, Germany was to fight two wars on two fronts in quick succession. Germany needed a speedy victory against France in order to be able to turn against its second enemy, Russia. Moltke explained this necessity, for example, as early as 1909 to the Austro-Hungarian chief of the General Staff Franz Conrad von Hötzendorf:

> In order to be successful against one of the two opponents we have to restrict ourselves with the minimum amount of defense against the other. Our foremost intention must be to achieve a speedy decision. This will hardly be possible against Russia. The defense against France would absorb such great strength that the remaining troops for an offensive against Russia would not suffice to force a decision onto it. . . . In a war on two fronts I will only be able to suggest to H.M. [His Majesty, the Kaiser] to employ the main bulk of the German Army initially against France, leaving only such forces as are necessary to protect our eastern provinces.[13]

Moltke's colleagues were equally aware of Germany's difficult strategic position. General Bruno von Mudra wrote to Moltke in November 1911:

> If in a double[-sided] war it is essential initially to hold the situation on one side with as few forces as possible (numerically and qualitatively speaking) so as to be able to defeat decisively the other side with much more devastating force, then the most pressing task of the country's fortifications is to support this intention with whatever means necessary.[14] As things stand at the moment and for the foreseeable future, there can be no doubt that we must hit France with our main thrust. Once France is beaten in the first battles and has been made conscious by us again of its inferiority, then the most important task has, in my opinion, been achieved. The army leadership then has free rein to use the army also against the eastern opponent.[15]

The second shared characteristic of their plan was that Moltke and his colleagues, like Schlieffen before them, saw Germany's best chance for a quick victory, at least against one enemy, in the west against France, rather than in the east. The mobilization orders of the prewar years demonstrate this clearly, as does Mudra's letter from November 1911: "Here in the east it is imperative to halt the advance of the presumably numerically far superior Russians with tough resistance and to win time for the execution of the initially decisive operations in the western theater of war. France must be defeated by us in decisive battles before the Russians cross the middle or upper Oder River with stronger forces."[16]

There can be absolutely no doubt that the plan was to proceed offensively against France if a war were to result from a conflict between Austria and Russia. Even the kaiser was aware of the direction in which "his" troops would have to march in case of war. During the Bosnian Annexation Crisis of 1908–1909, for example, he was concerned that Austria-Hungary's attitude toward Russia might conjure up a war that would result in the *casus foederis* for Germany. "This [*casus foederis*] necessitates mobilization and a war on two fronts for Germany, that is to say in order to march against Moscow Paris must first be taken."[17]

Both Moltke and Schlieffen agreed also on a third matter. In order to be able to defeat France, they planned to avoid the fortifications along the Franco-German border. That Moltke did not consider this step to be necessitated by a French attack on Belgium, but that this was rather a planned attack on France, is clear from the contemporary evidence. Thus, he wrote to the chancellor in December 1912:

> If the political situation of Europe does not change, we will, owing to Germany's central position, always be forced to fight on several fronts, and therefore will have to be on the defensive on one side with weaker troops in order to be on the offensive on the other. That side can only ever be France. Here a speedy decision can be hoped for, while an offensive war into Russia would be without a foreseeable end. However, in order to be on the offensive against France it will be necessary to violate Belgian neutrality. Only by advancing through Belgian territory can we hope to attack the French army in the open [*im freien Felde*] and defeat them. This way we will face the English Expeditionary Corps [*sic*] and—if we do not manage to come to an agreement with Belgium—also Belgian troops. However, this operation is more promising than a frontal attack against the fortified French eastern front.[18]

It is certainly significant that even vis-à-vis the civilian chancellor Moltke did not attempt to dress up this move as defensive by arguing that he feared a

French offensive into Belgium and wanted to preempt such a move. Rather, he deemed it essential—and this is a fourth parallel between his and Schlieffen's plan—to march Germany's troops through neutral Belgium toward France, regardless of French or Belgian plans. Schlieffen had also intended to march through neutral Holland, but this move had been rejected by Moltke (as we will see). Instead, Moltke aimed to come to an agreement with Belgium, hoping to be able to secure free passage through the neutral's territory. In November 1913, during a meeting with Belgium's King Albert in Potsdam, Moltke was very open ("*déboutonné*")[19] in requesting that Belgium let Germany's troops march through it and into France. He did not shy away from trying to intimidate the Belgian king and his military attaché, though he clearly miscalculated and only made Albert all the more determined to safeguard Belgian neutrality from any violation. The Belgian king was not willing to allow either Germany or France to march through his territory unopposed.

There is plenty of evidence to show that Moltke's unsuccessful blackmail attempt of the Belgian king did not put an end to his plan for an invasion in the west. For example, the Bavarian military plenipotentiary, Hugo Graf von und zu Lerchenfeld, wrote on 4 August 1914 to the Bavarian *Ministerpräsident* Georg Freiherr von Hertling: "Germany cannot respect Belgium's neutrality. The General Staff has explained that even for the sake of English neutrality respecting Belgium would be too much of a price to pay, because an offensive war [*Angriffskrieg*] against France would only be possible along the lines of Belgium. . . . I have to assume that our attitude toward Belgium will result in us falling out with England."[20]

Clearly, the unsuccessful attempt at forcing the Belgians to surrender their neutrality had not led to a change of the German deployment plan. As Lerchenfeld realized, the war in 1914 was an offensive war and not a defense against a French attack through Belgium. The next day, Moltke himself summed up the situation, as Lerchenfeld reported:

> England's joining on our enemies' side no doubt worsened our position. . . . Nonetheless he [Moltke] had absolutely counseled against buying English neutrality at the cost of protecting Belgian territory, if this had even been possible, which he decidedly did not believe. The attack [on France] from German territory would have cost the German Army three months and would have assured Russia such a head start that it would then no longer be possible to count on success on both fronts. We must attack France with all [our] might

immediately via Belgium, in order to achieve a quick reckoning with France. This was the only way to victory.[21]

Here, too, no mention is made of defensive action from German territory.[22] Rather, the statement shows without doubt that Germany launched an attack on France via the territory of neutral Belgium. It was emphatically not a reaction on Germany's part to a French provocation, as Terence Zuber would have us think.

So much for the parallels between Moltke's and Schlieffen's war planning. But what were the differences between the two chiefs of staff's plans? From 1909 onward, Moltke began to make changes to his predecessor's strategy, informed in part by new intelligence about Germany's potential enemies, so that the plan of 1914 differed in important points from that which Schlieffen had put to paper for a preemptive war against France shortly before his retirement. Therefore, it is indeed appropriate not to refer to Germany's war plan of 1914 as the Schlieffen Plan—after all, Moltke had been in office for nine years when war broke out.

The most important difference resulted from Moltke's fear of the effects of an allied blockade on Germany. For that reason he wanted the Netherlands to act as a "windpipe" in case of war. He changed the deployment plan so that Dutch neutrality could be maintained. Luxembourg and Belgium, on the other hand, were in the way of the advancing troops en route to France and their neutrality could not be respected. While this decision had an obviously positive effect on relations between Germany and the Netherlands, it necessitated the *coup de main* on the Belgian fortified town of Liège, and this in turn forced the German troops to launch a surprise attack in the west as soon as possible, and preferably before an official declaration of war had even been made. In contrast, Schlieffen had wanted to march around Liège via Dutch territory, and had therefore not based his planning on a risky *coup de main*.

A further difference between the two plans was that Moltke was no longer able to ignore the enemy in the east to the extent that Schlieffen had, given that Russia's military situation had improved significantly after 1905–1906. It was for this reason that Moltke wanted to deploy more troops there than Schlieffen had stipulated in his memorandum of 1905—and even in his memorandum of 1912.[23] This was in large part because of changed international relations, particularly the improved alliance between Russia and France. In contrast to the situation of 1905, Moltke could no longer assume that Russia would be too weak in a future war to support its alliance partner France. In contrast, Schlieffen had felt as late as 1912: "All of Germany has to throw itself onto one opponent, the one that is the strongest, most powerful and most dangerous, and that can only be France-England. Austria can rest assured: Russia's army intended to go against Germany will not march to Galicia before the dice have been cast in the west. And Austria's fate will not be decided on the Bug, but on the Seine!"[24]

As Moltke's marginal comments on this document show, he did not share Schlieffen's confidence. While he agreed with Schlieffen regarding his views "in case of a war between France and Germany," he foresaw a different scenario "if the Triple Alliance War is started by a war between Russia and Austria-Hungary." He noted: "In that case, Russia must mobilize her entire army and also will immediately face Germany as an opponent." Moltke was convinced that neither France nor Russia would in future be "disengaged spectators," but rather that "both would mobilize simultaneously and will be Germany's enemies. There can be no talk under the current political . . . circumstances that Russia would hesitate to deploy into Prussia."[25]

This realization led to the scrapping of the Eastern Deployment Plan (*der grosse Ostaufmarsch*), which had been developed for some years in parallel to the Western Deployment Plan. It was discontinued in April 1913.[26] From this date onward, Germany only had a single strategic plan which, regardless of the casus belli, had to be implemented in case of war, as was indeed to happen in 1914. This plan concentrated on the west and only stipulated for the east that the Eighth Army should dedicate itself to the "difficult task" of "securing our eastern provinces against a Russian invasion, [and] to support the planned Austrian offensive." However, it was also noted that it should be "considered where in the west the Eighth Army should be deployed if its commitment against Russia were not necessary."[27]

At the same time, Moltke needed to develop a more flexible approach to the enemy in the west. Intelligence revealed that France appeared to have abandoned her defensive strategy and intended to take the offensive in case of war. This was something that Moltke had anticipated earlier when he had remarked on Schlieffen's 1905 memorandum that he "did not consider it a certainty that France would under all circumstances remain on the defensive."[28] For this reason Moltke adapted Schlieffen's plan over the years, wanting to be able to react more flexibly to a possible French offensive than Schlieffen had considered necessary. It was because of these changes and the alleged weakening of the right wing of the German armies on the western front that Moltke was so severely criticized after the Battle of the Marne and following Germany's defeat in 1918. We will look at each of these changes in a little more detail.

Holland and Liège

One of the most important decisions that Moltke made, together with Erich Ludendorff and Gerhard Tappen, was to exclude the Netherlands from the German deployment plan.[29] Tappen remembered after the war that "Moltke had wanted to avoid under any circumstances the infringement of Dutch territory, even the tip around Maastricht."[30] In a marginal note on Schlieffen's memorandum of 1905, Moltke had already commented that it might be possible for the diplomats to come to an arrangement with the Netherlands. This would have been "a great advantage," because the German deployment could make good use of the Dutch railways and because the Netherlands would be "of inestimable value" as an ally.[31] In a 1915 letter Moltke compared his plan directly with Schlieffen's: "in contrast I predicted that with hostile Holland the German [right] army wing would lose such a lot of force that it would lose the necessary power [*Stosskraft*] in the west."[32]

In November 1914, Moltke also compared his plan directly with that of his predecessor and highlighted the differences between them: "Count Schlieffen even wanted to march with the right wing of the German Army through southern Holland. I changed this in order not to force the Netherlands onto the side of our enemies, and preferred to take upon myself the great technical difficulties that were caused by the fact that the right wing of our army had to squeeze through the narrow space between Aachen and the southern border of the province of Limburg."[33]

As early as 1911 Moltke had explained why it would be of great advantage to Germany not to force the Netherlands onto the side of Germany's enemies. He stressed that if Britain were to intervene in a war because of Germany's violation of Belgian neutrality, it would then have to respect Dutch neutrality and would not be able to land its troops on the Dutch coast. Moreover, as we have already seen, Holland was to serve as "a windpipe so that we can breathe," so that, if necessary, a longer war could be survived. The Netherlands would be a way for Germany to access the sea.[34]

However, this change to Schlieffen's original plan brought with it some "technical problems," as Moltke put it. The deployment of the right army wing was slowed down, and troops had to march into Belgium through a relatively narrow corridor. In order for the advance to be possible at all, Liège "would have to be in our hands.... This realization led me to the decision to take Liège by *coup de main*," Moltke explained in a letter in July 1915.[35]

This statement also clearly shows that the German violation of Belgian neutrality was not a response to an expected French or even a British deployment into Belgium, but rather that the march through Belgium was an integral part of the German deployment plan, regardless of the actions of the enemies. Therefore, Zuber's thesis that Germany acted defensively and only tried to preempt a French offensive through Belgium is wrong. Even if, as Zuber repeatedly points out, France and Russia had agreed to march into Germany on the fifteenth mobilization day, this was irrelevant in early August 1914 when Germany's actions forced war on the French with its own attack on its western neighbors. Moltke never denied the necessity of the march through Belgium, not even vis-à-vis the political leadership. In a memorandum of December 1912 he informed the chancellor in no uncertain terms: "In order to go on the offensive against France it will be necessary to violate Belgian neutrality."[36]

The *coup de main* on Liège was a decisive difference between Moltke's plan and Schlieffen's.[37] As we have seen, Moltke expected significant advantages if the Netherlands remained neutral. However, the planned *coup de main* also led to massive logistical problems: some six hundred thousand soldiers of the First and Second Armies, plus horses, equipment, and supplies, had to march into Belgium through a relatively narrow area, just a few kilometers wide.[38] Moreover, the early march of German troops into Luxembourg and Liège meant that it became impossible at the last minute for the political leadership to come to a peaceful agreement at the conference table—although this was not necessarily a disadvantage as far as the military leadership was concerned.[39] What is more, Germany's action united the previously divided British cabinet and established for Britain the perfect pretext for entering the war.

The Strategy in the East

While Schlieffen had been willing to expose East Prussia to a short-term Russian invasion if necessary, Moltke did not want to take the same risk. Hence, he focused his attention more on the east and favored the deployment of larger numbers of troops and the building of better fortifications there. In his memorandum of December 1912 he explained: "We have doubtless to reckon with an invasion in the east, perhaps also in the west, immediately following the declaration of mobilization. . . . We need to increase our troops in this area and put our fortifications on higher alert."[40] Contrary to Schlieffen, Moltke even envisioned possible limited offensives in the east.[41] Georg von Waldersee also advised in May 1914 that Germany should attempt offensives on two sides: "We would immediately relinquish *any* chance of victory if we settled for an offensive on one side only. If the politicians allow themselves to be forced onto the defensive, the German Army may never do so."[42] Thus, Moltke's order for Waldersee, who—much to his displeasure—was sent east in August 1914, cannot have surprised him: "If the Russians come, no defensive, but offensive, offensive, offensive."[43] Despite the fact that only relatively small numbers of troops were being deployed in the east, they were to attempt limited offensives in coordination with the Austro-Hungarian troops.[44] In contrast with Moltke and his colleagues, Schlieffen had not needed to focus on the problem of the eastern front in 1905, given that the Russian troops were hardly in a position at that time to come to the aid of the French or to advance into Germany. It was only the changed international circumstances and the fact that Russia had regained its military strength that necessitated taking the Russian steamroller seriously.

Changing International Circumstances

When Schlieffen's tenure as chief of the General Staff came to an end, Moltke, the allegedly "reluctant military leader," inherited not only Schlieffen's famous 1905 memorandum, but also the same strategic problem of Germany's "encirclement" that had already worried his predecessor. However, even if Schlieffen and his followers felt that he had developed the perfect strategy for a war against France in 1905, this did not of course mean that the same strategy would work years later under different international circumstances. Indeed, Moltke annotated his predecessor's memorandum with notes that clearly show that right from the start he had his own views when it came to military planning, and that he needed to take account of the changing international situation. Moltke's critics, eager to blame him for the loss of the war, criticized him rather unfairly for the fact that under his leadership the German deployment plan had been altered and adapted to those changing international circumstances.

Since 1905–1906, Germany's encirclement by hostile neighbors had begun to be felt even more acutely, and until 1914 the General Staff was increasingly worried about the numerical strength of Germany's future enemies. While the military convention between Russia and Britain was still in the future, and even the strengthening of ties between Britain and France still uncertain when Schlieffen handed over his office, for Moltke they would soon be a fact that he had to acknowledge in his planning. Russia in particular became an increasingly stronger threat, and with this in mind it was his duty to change Germany's strategic plan and adapt it to these external circumstances. Sticking rigidly to Schlieffen's plan was clearly not an option.

News of Russian Army increases did not bode well for the future. Soon, the plan to concentrate nearly all available German troops in the west would no longer be realistic, particularly because starting in 1916–1917 Russia would no longer be slow to mobilize. Moltke's marginal notes on Schlieffen's 1912 memorandum show that he felt Schlieffen had underestimated the strength of the Franco-Russian alliance. In his opinion it was impossible that either Russia or France would remain passive observers in a future war, but rather that "both would mobilize simultaneously and be Germany's enemies. There can, under the current political treaties and circumstances, be no talk of Russia hesitating to march into Prussia if no defensive forces are left there."[45] For this reason there was, in his opinion, little point in continuing to prepare the *grosser Ostaufmarsch*, given that this was based on the premise of France being a passive observer, at least initially. From 1913 on, that plan was no longer updated, leaving Germany with just one strategic plan—the Moltke Plan.

In September 1914, Waldersee, who claimed to have been actively involved in "the creation of the deployment plan," outlined the reasons why he, too, had favored working on only a single deployment, "based on the premise that our main forces would be employed against France under all circumstances by way of entering Belgium, while initially operating defensively against Russia. . . . When war became unavoidable in the last days of July, the political situation was not yet completely certain. There was certainty within the Supreme Army Command, however, that the strike would have to be conducted with all force against France through Belgium."[46]

Waldersee explained that this had been a way to avoid "half measures." "We can only be strong and superior in one place; the most important [objective] is to defeat France and its Western allies."[47] But even this objective was becoming increasingly more difficult than it had been during Schlieffen's time in office.

Flexibility vis-à-vis France

Intelligence regarding the French war plan had led Moltke to suspect that the French were not planning an exclusively defensive strategy for the future. If this were the case, Germany would not be able to make do with the small number of troops in the south that Schlieffen had allocated there, envisaging a French defensive in 1905.[48] Moltke, therefore, aimed at a more flexible strategy in a future war. "If the French come out of their fortification, then they move into the open field. There is no point to continuing to march through Belgium with strong forces if the main French army advances in Lorraine. Then only one thought can be decisive: to attack the French army with all available forces and to defeat it where it can be found. The march through Belgium is therefore not an aim in itself [*Selbstzweck*], but only a means to an end."[49]

That Moltke doubted the French would be on the defensive can be demonstrated by a number of sources, including his marginal note on Schlieffen's memorandum: "If the war is wanted and initiated by France, then it will in all likelihood lead it offensively. If France wants to reconquer the lost provinces, it must march into them, that is, act offensively. I do not consider it settled that France will be defensive in all circumstances. The border fortifications, built soon after the war of [18]70–71 do, however, express a defensive attitude. Yet, this does not correspond with the offensive spirit that has always been inherent in the nation, nor with the currently predominant teachings and views in the French Army."[50]

In 1906 the General Staff exercise was already based on the scenario of a French offensive in the south. As Moltke explained in his maneuver critique, in such a case the German right wing on its way through Belgium would not be able to achieve the decisive quick victory, given that the majority of French troops would be deployed elsewhere.[51] In the following years, Moltke expected that the French decision for the offensive or the defensive would depend on the casus belli.[52] Hence, the deployment plan of 1908–1909 included for the first time the deployment of an army corps to defend the upper Alsace. "Seventh Army will initially be assembled in Lorraine between Metz and Saarburg. This assembly is intended to provide the opportunity to be ready for a French advance south of Metz, as well as to deceive and engage the enemy through our own action against Nancy."[53]

From this year onward the plan was to deploy the Seventh Army (three army corps and one reserve corps) on the Rhine to defend Alsace, as well as the Sixth Army (four corps) in southern Lorraine. From 1910–1911 on, the plan no longer included committing the troops of the Seventh Army elsewhere.[54] The final deployment plan before the outbreak of war envisioned the deployment of both armies in Lorraine. In other words, a total of eight army corps were to deploy on the left wing. Their task was "to stop the French forces deployed here and to prevent their transport to the French army wing."[55]

This is not the place to consider in detail the claims of Moltke's critics that these changes to Schlieffen's plan watered down his recipe for victory and ultimately cost Germany the war. They accused him, for example, of basing his own planning too much on the enemies' plans, rather than forcing his will onto them. However, Moltke was surely obliged to adapt his plan to different external and internal conditions, and Germany clearly needed to have a different war plan in 1914 than the one Schlieffen had devised for a war against France (and Britain[56]) in 1905.[57] But whether his changes were legitimate or not, the fact remains that neither Moltke nor Schlieffen ever had a certain recipe for victory.

The Debate about the Schlieffen Plan

Given that so much contemporary evidence points to similarities and differences between the Schlieffen Plan and the Moltke Plan, Terence Zuber's claims that the Schlieffen Plan did not exist and that Germany's deployment plan of 1914 was defensive does not stand up to scrutiny. Regarding the outbreak of war, Zuber claims: "Far from having an aggressive plan in 1914, the German armies initially stood on the defensive in East Prussia as well as in Lorraine."[58] While it is true that the Germans were on the defensive in these areas, it is somewhat disingenuous to portray this as a defensive strategy overall, given that the defensive position in some areas was adopted in order to enable the German Army to attempt a massive offensive elsewhere—in Luxembourg and Belgium. Many of the documents quoted above prove that in 1914 Germany did not intend to be on the defensive. As we have seen, Germany's first acts of war had been long in the planning and were not, as Zuber would argue, a mere reaction to the actions of the French and British. In addition to the many contemporary sources, Germany's actual deployment in 1914 shows without doubt that Zuber's apologetic interpretation is untenable.

In his effort to prove his point Zuber argues that while there was a "Schlieffen doctrine," there was no Schlieffen Plan. This is a rather fine distinction. It is perhaps more helpful to understand both Schlieffen's and Moltke's plans as an attempt to turn an unwinnable war on two fronts into two separate and potentially winnable wars on one front each. To achieve this aim the intention was initially to go to war in the west and to achieve the necessary quick victory against one enemy, namely France, by attempting to outflank its forces, rather than through a head-on engagement. In this sense the aims of Moltke and Schlieffen were identical "doctrines." Of course, it goes almost without saying that the German deployment plan of 1914 was based on Moltke's and not Schlieffen's ideas, and in that sense Germany did not go to war with a Schlieffen Plan. However, this is an obvious point, rather than a radical revision of all that we have previously assumed, as Zuber maintains.

It is certainly wrong to see Schlieffen's memorandum of 1905 as a precise plan that was to be implemented unchanged at any given point in the future. Even Schlieffen's follower and defender Wolfgang Foerster admits this, and acknowledges at the same time that Schlieffen's memorandum had been intended to shape future war plans, but that it had also been a war plan (*Operationsplan*) itself, designed for the specific situation in 1905. As Foerster outlined in 1955: "[Schlieffen] intended with his operations plan of December 1905 nothing other than to express the operational thinking of an offensive aimed against our western enemies.... This was the operational achievement [*Höchstleistung*] which was to be aimed for. The purpose of his memorandum was to provide the proof for the possibility of its implementation."[59]

Whatever name we attach to the German deployment plan, the fact remains that in 1914 Germany proceeded through Belgium in the direction of France in order to attack the western neighbor, and that this is how its offensive war plan was being put into practice. Of course, France also had an offensive war plan, as Zuber repeatedly stresses. There was, however, a crucial difference in that France did not attack Germany in 1914, and that General Joseph Joffre held the French troops back until he was certain of how Germany would proceed.[60] While the French military leadership considered it important not to be seen as the aggressor, both by France's allies and its own population, the German commanders had no such concerns. The military necessity to fight a war against France quickly outweighed any political qualms regarding the violation of the neutrality of Germany's neighboring countries.

To be clear then, contrary to Zuber's thesis, Germany's troops did not have their sights set on Brussels when they marched into Belgium. Rather, their aim was to defeat the French and British forces from that vantage point. Belgium was not an objective in itself. Nor was Germany attacked by France in 1914—whatever their alliance agreement with Russia might have held in store. Therefore, Zuber's conclusion that he has proven there was no Schlieffen Plan and that he has thus discredited "one of the principal pieces of evidence for German war guilt" is untenable. While he maintains that "without the Schlieffen Plan the political-military situation in 1914 looks very different," he ignores what actually occurred in 1914, and he does not distinguish adequately between the Moltke Plan and the Schlieffen Plan.[61] However, we must consider the outbreak of war with the Moltke Plan in mind. It was Germany's only deployment plan when war loomed in July 1914. Moltke knew that the chances of his plan succeeding were slim, but he was nonetheless willing to take the risk of a war against the Entente.[62] The German military leadership wanted a war, the sooner the better, and they were not willing to wait until their enemies would perhaps one day beat them to it, for this only would have further reduced Germany's chances of victory.

The accusation that Moltke had not known how to solve Germany's strategic dilemma did not develop after 1918, but was already being advanced during the war. Following the loss at the Battle of the Marne, Karl Ritter von Wenninger wrote dismissively in his diary: "Falkenhayn without doubt has his own thoughts, while Moltke and his subordinates were completely sterile. They could only turn the handle and run Schlieffen's film and were clueless and beside themselves when the roll got stuck."[63]

Such sources prove that the Schlieffen Plan was by no means a postwar invention. As Wilhelm Groener noted in his diary during the Battle of the Marne: "The 'plan' of the late Schlieffen has temporarily been mislaid. Perhaps it will be found again."[64] In Groener's opinion one of the main reasons for the failure on the Marne was the fact that the Supreme Army Command had not been "in the picture of Schlieffen's operational thought."[65] For Groener, Schlieffen's plan was more than a concept (*Grundidee*), but rather he already in 1914 considered it "an 'operational plan' that was worked out in all important points. The memorandum of December 1905 actually contains this plan, following several years in which the deployment was worked on in the General Staff according to the plan's principles."[66]

The argument of the invented Schlieffen Plan would no doubt have been completely unfathomable for Groener and other contemporaries of Schlieffen and Moltke. Even if Terence Zuber today doubts its existence, contemporaries were in no doubt that a Schlieffen Plan, a strategic concept for fighting a war on two fronts, did exist, and that Moltke attempted in 1914 with his own version of that plan to achieve the seemingly impossible—to fight a successful war against a numerically superior enemy on several fronts.[67] In the eyes of the General Staff that war was a preemptive war, for in the future Germany's chances of winning against France and Russia would only further decrease, while 1914 appeared to be an opportune moment.

Even the "Supreme War Lord," Kaiser Wilhelm II, had known for some time before 1914 what Germany's strategy would be in case of war. He did not expect his troops to be on the defensive, as Zuber claims the military leadership intended. In a March 1909 meeting with the Saxon minister of war, Max von Hausen, the kaiser declared:

I believe that there will be a conflict of Russia, be it with Austria, be it with the Balkan States within five years. If that conflict between Russia and the Balkan States is restricted to those powers, then we probably have no reason to involve ourselves in this matter. As soon as France indicates, however, to help the Russians to the detriment of the Austrians . . . I will order the mobilization of the entire German Army against France. In that case the friendship with Turkey would also be useful. It would give our allies—the Austrians—an immediate increase of power and would be of advantage for us in as much as we would need fewer forces with which to make war on Russia, and could therefore unfold more power against France.[68]

All the important decision makers in the *Kaiserreich* knew that the future war would begin with Germany's deployment against France—regardless of French actions. To claim today that this war, which had been willed by Moltke and his colleagues at different political junctures, was a defensive war is a misrepresentation of the evidence and a falsification of history.

Notes

1. It is possible that Schlieffen's demand for a preemptive war was one reason why Kaiser Wilhelm II and Chancellor Bernhard von Bülow wanted to replace him in 1905. See Annika Mombauer, *Helmuth von Moltke and the Origins of the First World War* (Cambridge, 2001), 43–44 (and also for further evidence that contemporaries thought that Schlieffen wanted a preventive war in 1905). More (if indirect) evidence that this might have led to his downfall is contained in Wilhelm Dieckmann's manuscript on the Schlieffen Plan, where his chapter headings are "The big chance" (referring to 1905) and "Bülow's victory over Schlieffen" (the relevant sections are unfortunately not contained in the file). It is possible that Dieckmann referred here to demands Schlieffen might have made for preventive war in 1905 that might have led to his dismissal (i.e., Bülow's victory). Dieckmann's manuscript in Bundesarchiv/Militärarchiv, Freiburg (BA/MA), W10/50220. However, as Gerhard Gross shows elsewhere, he was certain that Schlieffen would never have interfered with political decisions and that Schlieffen thus never demanded preventive war. See also below, note 9, and also note 181 in Gerhard Gross's contribution to this volume.

2. Zuber's thesis of the invented Schlieffen Plan has been debated over several years in, among other places, *War in History* and the *Journal for Military History*. For a detailed discussion of the debate, see Annika Mombauer, "Of War Plans and War Guilt: The Debate surrounding the Schlieffen Plan," *Journal of Strategic Studies* 28, no. 5 (2006): 857–885.

3. Helmuth von Moltke, *Erinnerungen, Briefe, Dokumente 1877–1916: Ein Bild vom Kriegsausbruch, erster Kriegführung und Persönlichkeit des ersten militärischen Führers des Krieges,* ed. Eliza von Moltke (Stuttgart, 1922), 21.

4. Terence Zuber, *Inventing the Schlieffen Plan: German War Planning, 1871–1914* (Oxford, 2003), 264.

5. Ibid., 265. "In 1912 Haldane told the Germans that British intervention was a practical certainty. The Germans had to assume that Belgium would then side with the Entente regardless. This led to a series of German measures, among which, in 1911 or 1912, were preparations for a *coup de main* on Liège. . . . The decision to attack Liège therefore arose out of the German appreciation of the political-military situation in 1911–1912 and had nothing to do with the Schlieffen plan." Zuber fails to acknowledge that the plan for a *coup de main* on Liège already existed in 1910 and cannot, therefore, have been arrived at in response to Haldane's mission of 1912. See BA/MA, Nachlass Tappen, N56-5, page 222. For a detailed analysis of the plan for a *coup de main* on Liège, see also Mombauer, *Moltke,* 86–105. Moreover, the argument is disingenuous, given that it goes without saying that decisions dating from 1911–1912 (or 1910, for that matter) had nothing to do with the Schlieffen Plan, given that Schlieffen had retired at the end of 1905. Rather, these are details of the Moltke Plan, and that plan was based on a *coup de main* on Liège as the only way of guaranteeing that German troops could utilize the Belgian railways. Schlieffen had been able to ignore Liège altogether, given that in his plan the fortified town would simply have been avoided with a march through Holland.

6. Groener maintained that Moltke, Stein, and Ludendorff had lacked the courage to implement the Schlieffen Plan in its unadulterated form. Rather than replacing it with something different, Groener bemoaned, they had adulterated it (Groener to Kuhl, 22 September 1935, in Nachlass Hahnke, BA/MA, N36/10). However, Groener overlooked the fact that he had collaborated with Moltke in the years before 1914 and had been involved in making the changes he later criticized. Moreover, it is surely unfair to criticize Moltke for adapting the German deployment plan to changing international circumstances, as any other chief of staff would also have had to do. See also Gotthard Jäschke, "'Schlieffenplan' und 'Marneschlacht,'" in *Militärgeschichte, Militärwissenschaft und Konfliktforschung,* ed. Dermot Bradley and Ulrich Marwedel (Osnabrück, 1977), 185–199.

7. Moltke revealed this intention, for example, in a letter to the Austro-Hungarian chief of the General Staff, Franz Conrad von Hötzendorf, on 21 January 1909: "In order to be successful against one of the two opponents we have to make do with being on the defensive against the other. Our foremost intention must be to achieve a quick decision. To achieve this will hardly be possible against Russia. Defense against France would absorb so much strength that the military force that would remain against Russia would not suffice to force a decision onto it." BA/MA, W10/50315, Forschungsarbeit gemeinsame Kriegsvorbereitung Deutschland und Österreich-Ungarn, f. 15.

8. It was no secret before the war that Germany was numerically inferior to its enemies. See, for example, *Archivrat* Greiner: "Welche Nachrichten besass der deutsche Generalstab über Mobilmachung und Aufmarsch des französischen Heeres in den Jahren 1885–1914?" BA/MA, W10/50267 (RH61/398).

9. Wilhelm von Hahnke commented on Schlieffen's demands for a preventive strike after the war: "During the Moroccan Crisis of 1905 there was a meeting of the *Staatsrat*, chaired by Bülow, with Tirpitz and Schlieffen, among others, in attendance. There was much idle chat. Finally, Bülow asked Schlieffen's opinion. He said: 'Russia is tied up in the East, England still weakened from the Boer War, France behind with its armaments. Before long Germany will have to prove itself with a war. Now is the most convenient time. Therefore my solution is: war with France.' Tirpitz got angry, his fleet was not yet ready, and Bülow lost heart, as with *this* Kaiser a war is impossible." BA/MA, N46/38, Schriftwechsel betr. Schlieffen-Plan, 1919–1932, Wilhelm von Hahnke to Wilhelm Groener, 16 April 1926, f. 49f.

10. See, for example, Schäfer's manuscript "Der Kriegsplan für den Zweifrontenkrieg," 1924, BA/MA, W10/50223; Stig Förster, *Der Doppelte Militarismus: Die deutsche Heeresrüstungspolitik zwischen Status-Quo-Sicherung und Aggression* (Stuttgart/Wiesbaden, 1985); Mombauer, *Moltke*, 174–181.

11. Wilhelm Groener, *Das Testament des Grafen Schlieffen: Operative Studien über den Weltkrieg* (Berlin, 1927), 79.

12. Memorandum, 2 December 1911: "Die militär-politische Lage Deutschlands," BA/MA, W10/50279, f. 19. The memorandum was sent to the chancellor and the minister of war. Moltke's adjutant Friedrich von Mantey later confirmed that Moltke's views of operational matters did not differ from Schlieffen's. Friedrich von Mantey, "Graf Schlieffen und der jüngere Moltke," *Militär-Wochenblatt* 10 (1935): 395–398, 396.

13. Moltke to Conrad, 21 January 1909, in BA/MA, W10/50315, "Forschungsarbeit gemeinsame Kriegsvorbereitung Deutschland und Österreich-Ungarn," f. 15.

14. Marginal note by *Oberquartiermeister* Major General von Stein: "Conforms to our views."

15. Bruno von Mudra to Moltke, 9 November 1911, in *Der Weltkrieg, Kriegsrüstung und Kriegswirtschaft*, vol. 1 (Berlin, 1930), Annex to vol. 1, appendix 40, page 125. Mudra repeated his views in December 1912: Bruno von Mudra to Moltke, 4 December 1912, in ibid., no. 52, page 153.

16. Mudra to Moltke, 9 November 1911, in ibid., no. 40, page 127.

17. Johannes Lepsius, Albrecht Mendelsohn-Bertholdy, and Friedrich Thimme, eds., *Die Grosse Politik der Europäischen Kabinette 1871–1914: Sammlung der Diplomatischen Akten des Auswärtigen Amtes*, vol. 33 (Berlin, 1922–1927), file no. 12349, pages 302–304.

18. Memorandum on the military and political situation, 21 December 1912, *Der Weltkrieg, Kriegsrüstung und Kriegswirtschaft*, vol. 1, Annex to vol. 1, appendix no. 54, pages 163–164 (emphasis A.M.).

19. For details of the visit, see Jean Stengers, "Guillaume II et le Roi Albert à Potsdam en novembre 1913," *Bulletin de la Classe des Lettres et des Sciences Morales et Politiques* (1993): 7–12, passim. See also Mombauer, *Moltke*, 153–167.

20. Ernst Deuerlein, ed., *Briefwechsel Hertling-Lerchenfeld 1912–1917* (Boppard/Rhein, 1973), letter no. 117, page 327 (emphasis A.M.).

21. Ibid., letter no. 119, page 330 (emphasis A.M.).

22. In a study entitled "Deployment and Operational Intentions of the French in a Future German-French War," the General Staff concluded in 1912 that the French would now "deploy along the Belgian border." "Their right flank would then be too vulnerable from [the direction of] Lorraine." This is further evidence against the thesis that Germany had wanted to preempt a French offensive through Belgium. See BA/MA, W10/50267 (RH61/398), page 124.

23. Both memoranda are published in Gerhard Ritter, *Der Schlieffenplan: Kritik eines Mythos* (München, 1956), 141f. A copy of the memorandum dated 28 December 1912 can also be found in BA/MA, N121/35.

24. Schlieffen's memorandum of 28 December 1912 in Ritter, *Der Schlieffenplan*, 181–196, 186; BA/MA, N121/35, f. 5.

25. BA/MA, N121/35, marginal note f. 5.

26. The deployment orders dating from before 1909 had contained a deployment for West and East. For 1909–1910 they contained "Deployment II 'Grosser Ostaufmarsch' against Russia"; for the deployment for 1913–1914 it was noted: "Germany's preparations for war have to be directed primarily against France." And, "In view of the French mood we *cannot* reckon with a war between Germany and England or Russia *alone*." The "Grosser Ostaufmarsch" of the previous four years had thus been abandoned. BA/MA, RH61/v.96.

27. BA/MA, RH61/v.96, deployment orders for 1913/14.

28. Reichsarchiv, *Der Weltkrieg*, 1:62–63. See also Ritter, *Der Schlieffenplan*, 145.

29. See Major von Harbou's letter to the *Reichsarchiv*, 4 April 1925, in which he blamed Ludendorff and Tappen for the changes to Germany's deployment plan. BA/MA, W10/51062. Gerhard Tappen was chief of the General Staff's Operations Department from 1914 until August 1916.

30. Tappen, "Kriegserinnerungen," BA/MA, W10/50661, page 6. "He did not want to march through Limburg because he did not consider it militarily necessary." BA/MA, W10/50276, "Die Militärpolitische Lage Deutschlands," 71–72. However, as the documents contained in this volume show, it remained part of the German deployment plan to march through Holland in case the quick advance through Belgium failed. The deployment instructions for 1913–1914 read: "If Liège has not succumbed by the 12th mobilization day the First Army has to touch Dutch territory during its advance." BA/MA, RH61/v.96.

31. Ritter, *Der Schlieffenplan*, 148.

32. Moltke to Freytag-Loringhoven, 26 July 1915, BA/MA, W10/51063.

33. Moltke, *Erinnerungen*, 17.

34. BA/MA, W10/50276, "Die Militärpolitische Lage Deutschlands," 72–73, partially cited in Ritter, *Der Schlieffenplan*, 178–180. See also Stig Förster, "Der deutsche Generalstab und die Illusion des kurzen Krieges, 1871–1914: Metakritik eines Mythos," *Militärgeschichtliche Mitteilungen* 54, no. 1 (1995): 61–98.

35. BA/MA, W10/51063, Moltke to Freytag-Loringhoven, 26 July 1915.

36. Reichsarchiv, *Der Weltkrieg*, Anlagen, appendix no. 54, 21 December 1912, 1:164.

37. Helmuth von Moltke's son Adam already used the term "Moltkeplan" when referring to his father's war planning. See BA/MA, N78/37. Adam von Moltke, "Eine Antwort an Herrn Walter Görlitz."

38. Leonard C. F. Turner, "The Significance of the Schlieffen Plan," in Kennedy, ed., *The War Plans of the Great Powers, 1880–1914*, ed. Paul M. Kennedy (London, 1979), 61; Arden Bucholz, *Moltke, Schlieffen and Prussian War Planning* (New York, 1991), 266.

39. Waldersee, for example, explained that one reason for discontinuing the Eastern Deployment Plan was the hope that this would prevent the politicians from interfering at the last minute and thus ruining the chance of having the desired war in the west. Georg von Waldersee, "Meine Erlebnisse zu Beginn des Krieges 1914," Ivennack, September 1914, BA/MA, W10/51032, pages 3–4.

40. Memorandum of 21 December 1912, Reichsarchiv, *Der Weltkrieg*, Anlagen, appendix no. 54, page 1:167.

41. Reichsarchiv, *Der Weltkrieg*, vol. 2, *Befreiung Ostpreussens* (Berlin, 1930), 45.

42. Waldersee's memorandum of 18 May 1914, BA/MA, W10/50279, Document 94.

43. Dommes to Waldersee, 14 August 1914, BA/MA, W10/51032.

44. See Gerhard Tappen, "Kriegserinnerungen," BA/MA, W10/50661, page 5.

45. Moltke's marginal notes on Schlieffen's 1912 memorandum in Ritter, *Der Schlieffenplan*, 185.

46. Waldersee, "Meine Erlebnisse," BA/MA, W10/51032, pages 1, 3.

47. Ibid., 4.

48. S. R. Williamson Jr., "Joffre Reshapes French Strategy," in *The War Plans of the Great Powers, 1880–1914*, ed. Paul M. Kennedy (London, 1979), 135; Robert A. Doughty, "French Strategy in 1914: Joffre's Own," *Journal of Military History* 67 (April 2003): 427–454.

49. Cited in Ritter, *Der Schlieffenplan*, 56.

50. Ibid., 145–146; Reichsarchiv, *Der Weltkrieg*, 1:62–63.

51. "Aus der Schlussbesprechung der grossen Generalstabsreise 1906," BA/MA, W10/50897, "Äusserungen des Generals von Moltke über die Möglichkeit einer schnellen Feldzugsentscheidung im Westen," page 138.

52. Moltke's marginal notes on Schlieffen's memorandum in Ritter, *Der Schlieffenplan*, 145.

53. Deployment orders in BA/MA, RH61/V.96. See also Reichsarchiv, *Der Weltkrieg*, 1:61.

54. BA/MA, W10/50730, page 56.

55. BA/MA, RH61/v.96, deployment orders for 1913/14. See also BA/MA, W10/50730, page 62.

56. In an additional memorandum dated February 1906 Schlieffen discussed the scenario of a British involvement in a war between Germany and France, in which case an additional one hundred thousand troops would be found on the enemies' side. Ritter, *Der Schlieffenplan,* 174–178.

57. For a more detailed discussion of this argument, see Mombauer, *Moltke,* 86–105.

58. Zuber, *Inventing the Schlieffen Plan,* 303.

59. Wolfgang Foerster, "Hat es eine Schlieffenplan-Legende gegeben?" *Wehrwissenschaftliche Rundschau* (1952).

60. Doughty, "French Strategy in 1914," 428.

61. Zuber, *Inventing the Schlieffen Plan,* 302.

62. See, for example, Stig Förster on Moltke's doubts regarding Germany's chances to achieve victory: "Der deutsche Generalstab und die Illusion des kurzen Krieges," passim. See also Mombauer, *Moltke,* 287–288.

63. Bayerisches Hauptstaatsarchiv—Kriegsarchiv München, HS 2543, Wenninger diaries, 16 September 1914. For Moltke's role in the Battle of the Marne and the criticism of his leadership, see Annika Mombauer, "The Battle of the Marne: Myths and Reality of Germany's 'Fateful Battle,'" *Historian* 68, no. 4 (winter 2006): 747–769.

64. BA/MA, Nachlass Groener, N46/22, Persönliches Kriegstagebuch 1914–1916, 13 September 1914, f. 28.

65. Ibid., f. 29.

66. BA/MA, Nachlass Groener, N46/40, "Bemerkungen zu der Arbeit von Herrn Universitätsprofessor Dr. Bredt," f. 1.

67. Holger Herwig comes to a similar inescapable conclusion: "Not only Schlieffen's contemporaries, but also the men who implemented his plan in August 1914, had no doubt about the existence and authenticity of a Schlieffen plan." See "Germany and the 'Short War' Illusion: Toward a New Interpretation," *Journal of Military History* 66 (July 2002): 681–693, 683.

68. Sächsisches Hauptstaatsarchiv Dresden, Nachlass M. L. v. Hausen, no. 36.

The Schlieffen Plan— A War Plan

Robert T. Foley

In an article published in *War in History* in 1999, Major Terence Zuber set out to challenge one of the longest-held interpretations about origins of the First World War.[1] Zuber set himself the task of reexamining German war planning during the tenures of Alfred Graf von Schlieffen and Helmuth von Moltke the Younger. Using previously unknown documents, he painted a much more detailed picture of this war planning than had hitherto been available. He showed the minutiae of Schlieffen's deployment plans from 1892 to 1904 and demonstrated how German commentators in the interwar period and later historians, most notably Gerhard Ritter, had simplified and even altered the details of these plans in their writings.

However, Zuber went much farther in his analysis than merely adding much-needed detail to our understanding of German war plans before the First World War. He challenged the traditional interpretation of Schlieffen's memorandum of 1905, the infamous Schlieffen Plan.[2] Indeed, Zuber went so far as to argue that there had never been a Schlieffen Plan. Instead, he contended that Schlieffen's memorandum of 1905 was not a blueprint for a future German deployment, but rather was an elaborate attempt to get more troops out of a reluctant Ministry of War.[3] Going farther, Zuber argued that far from planning to fight an offensive war, Schlieffen had always intended to remain on the strategic defensive and await his enemies' attacks. In Zuber's analysis, neither Schlieffen nor his successor, Moltke the Younger, ever intended to launch an invasion of France with a powerful right wing enveloping the French fortress line. In short, in a challenge to the long-accepted interpretation, Zuber argued that Schlieffen, and later his successor Moltke, never intended Germany to be the aggressor in a future war.[4]

One aspect of Zuber's far-reaching analysis has been critiqued by Terence Holmes. Holmes has subjected Schlieffen's 1905 memorandum to a close textual analysis, and has shown this document to be much more complex than previously understood. He has demonstrated that this memorandum was not the disastrous operations plan with a simplistic drive on Paris assumed by Zuber, but rather a sophisticated document that provided for a variety of scenarios.[5] While Holmes's perceptive analysis of Schlieffen's memorandum is perhaps one of the most important points to come out of the debate, it does not deal directly with some of Zuber's wider claims, and that is the aim of this chapter. It will leave aside the operational detail of the Zuber-Holmes debate and concentrate on an examination of Zuber's wider argument.[6] This chapter will look at some weaknesses in Zuber's sources and at areas ignored in Zuber's analysis to show the problems with his argument, and in doing so it will argue for a more traditional interpretation of Schlieffen and his plan.

Problems with Zuber's Sources

Zuber's radical reinterpretation of German war planning is based largely on two sources, both unavailable to historians until the 1990s. First, he makes extensive use of an unpublished manuscript entitled "Der Schlieffenplan" written by Dr. Wilhelm Dieckmann, a historian based in the *Reichsarchiv* during the interwar period.[7] This manuscript was part of the papers of the Kriegsgeschichtliche Forschungsanstalt des Heeres, the organization responsible for writing the German official history of the First World War. These extensive papers survived the Allied bombing raid on Potsdam that destroyed the German Army Archive only to be confiscated by the Soviets in 1945. They remained in the Soviet Union, unavailable to historians, until they were returned to then-East Germany in December 1988 and the Berlin Wall fell in 1989.[8] As Zuber notes, Dieckmann's manuscript is a crucial source for historians seeking insight into German war planning during Schlieffen's tenure as chief of the General Staff. As a *Reichsarchiv* researcher, Dieckmann had access to planning documents that were destroyed in 1945 and was able to communicate with officers who had themselves taken part in constructing German war plans during the Schlieffen period.

Indeed, Zuber has made good use of Dieckmann's manuscript to show that our traditional interpretation of how Schlieffen intended to fight a two-front war is flawed. Via the Dieckmann manuscript, Zuber has shown that Schlieffen did not commit fully to an early western offensive in 1894, as has been accepted by historians, but rather maintained as the second of his annual plans a viable *Ostaufmarsch* (Eastern Deployment), which split German forces to fight fully in cooperation with the Austrians in the east.[9] In fact, unbeknownst to Zuber, his interpretation is supported by materials in the Austrian archives that show Schlieffen's willingness to work with the Austrian Army.[10]

However, Dieckmann's important manuscript is not without its problems. First, the section Dieckmann had intended to write on the formulation of Schlieffen's war plan for 1905 is missing, seemingly unwritten but perhaps lost in the intervening years. Thus, we have considerable information for Schlieffen's planning from 1892 until 1903, but not the crucial period during which the so-called Schlieffen Plan was committed to paper. Zuber does not seem to think this a problem, believing that there is sufficient evidence within the unfinished manuscript to draw wide conclusions about how Schlieffen intended to fight a future war.[11]

Another significant problem with the Dieckmann manuscript is its sources. While this manuscript is an invaluable source for historians of this period, it is not a substitute for the original records. Dieckmann did not have access to all of the German war planning documents from Schlieffen's time as chief of the General Staff, but instead had to construct his analysis on a relatively limited number. Crucially, Dieckmann did not have access to sources that would have given him firm evidence for how Schlieffen intended to fight a future war. While Zuber sees a conspiracy to deny Dieckmann access to these top-secret planning documents,[12] the fact of the matter is that the *Reichsarchiv* did not have many of the sources necessary to fully reconstruct German war planning before 1914. There were several reasons for this. First, the German Army Archives were in considerable disarray following the 1918 revolution, much material was lost or destroyed in the upheaval, and the *Reichsarchiv* did not possess a complete record of prewar planning.[13] However, perhaps a better reason for the fact that Dieckmann did not have access to planning documents is that these had been destroyed long before the outbreak of the First World War. Given the threat posed by foreign intelligence agencies, the General Staff took the secrecy of its war plans very seriously. Annika Mombauer has shown that prior to the issuing of new deployment orders each year, those of the previous year were burned to prevent their falling into the hands of enemy intelligence.[14] Thus, the very documents that would have given Dieckmann a full understanding of Schlieffen's intentions were more than likely destroyed long before he began writing his manuscript.

This lack of official records forced the *Reichsarchiv* to search for documents wherever they could be found, including those in private possession, and this accounts for the *Reichsarchiv*'s use of the obvious drafts of Schlieffen's 1905 memorandum held by Schlieffen's daughter Elizabeth and son-in-law and former adjutant Wilhelm von Hahnke.[15] It also explains why Dieckmann's manuscript is based on a relatively narrow base of sources. Given the lack of documentation, any reconstruction of German prewar planning was going to be problematic, even for a *Reichsarchiv* researcher, and Dieckmann was forced to rely on the relatively few sources that survived.

Perhaps a bigger problem is Zuber's peculiar interpretation of the manuscript. Zuber states that "there is practically nothing in his manuscript to support the contention that the Schlieffen Plan was the culmination of Schlieffen's strategic thought."[16] However, this is precisely how Dieckmann saw things. Dieckmann divided his work into three sections. The first covers Schlieffen's planning in the first half of the 1890s. The second section examines his planning from the middle of the 1890s till 1903, and the third, unwritten, section was intended to examine the years 1904 and 1905. How Dieckmann titled his sections tells us something about where he was going with his analysis. Section Two is entitled "Der Umgehungsplan," ("The Out-Flanking Plan"). Dieckmann entitled his missing section dealing with the Schlieffen Plan "Der Umfassungsplan" ("The Envelopment Plan").[17]

Indeed, contrary to Zuber's interpretation of the manuscript, Dieckmann's narrative in his first two sections was intended as a buildup to this final section. He shows how Schlieffen first introduced the idea of outflanking the French fortifications in July 1894, but lacked sufficient manpower to launch a holding attack or to defend in Lorraine at the same time as carrying out a powerful offensive around the French fortresses. Dieckmann demonstrated how Schlieffen continually returned to the idea of outflanking the French fortresses throughout his time as chief of the General Staff, but was continually put off from this course of action by a lack of manpower. As Dieckmann put it, in response to the challenge of a two-front war, "there was always only one solution, which Schlieffen had already described as most promising in his memorandum of July 1894—a flank offensive around the left wing of the French fortified front north of Verdun, which had to be simultaneously supported by a frontal attack against this front."[18] Dieckmann's entire manuscript is about showing how Schlieffen continued to attempt to build up the German Army—increase its manpower, develop its heavy artillery, and develop its western fortresses—to permit Germany to take the offensive against France in a future war. Moreover, Dieckmann demonstrated how Schlieffen's ideas about this offensive developed from a relatively shallow outflanking maneuver toward the final grand envelopment of the 1905 memorandum.

Zuber maintains that Dieckmann was incorrect in his interpretation of the evidence and that the examples Dieckmann gives refute his conclusion that the memorandum of 1905 was the culmination of Schlieffen's war planning. However, in my opinion, Zuber does not have enough evidence to refute Dieckmann's interpretation. Dieckmann was intimately familiar with sources we do not have today, including records and individuals associated with Schlieffen's planning, and basing ourselves on his narrative and how he titled the sections of his manuscript, we can infer that he saw a clear progression toward "Umfassung" in Schlieffen's war planning. Simply stating that Dieckmann was misled by the Schlieffen school is not enough to dismiss his conclusions.[19]

Zuber does attempt to make up for the Dieckmann manuscript's missing section and the lack of war planning documentation by examining a number of Great General Staff rides led by Schlieffen and Moltke between 1904 and 1908. These were not published in the interwar period and most were not readily available to researchers until after German reunification.[20] The fact that Schlieffen's staff rides of 1904 (both conducted in the west) and his last *Kriegsspiel* (war game) of 1905 did not follow the pattern of his memorandum of 1905 is further evidence to Zuber that this memorandum was not a true war plan.[21] Zuber then goes on to examine Moltke's staff rides of 1906 and 1908. As these rides did not involve a strong German right wing advancing all the way to Paris, Zuber again concludes that the German war plans under Moltke were not based on Schlieffen's 1905 memorandum.[22]

This, however, amounts to a very narrow definition of what constitutes the Schlieffen Plan. Zuber defines the Schlieffen Plan simply as an operation that has a strong right wing advancing on Paris regardless of enemy action elsewhere. Terence Holmes has already convincingly argued that Schlieffen's memorandum of 1905 was flexible enough to incorporate a variety of scenarios based on French actions and was not simply a drive on Paris, as has traditionally been assumed. Instead, Schlieffen's goal was not Paris, but rather the destruction of the French Army, wherever it might be found.[23] Zuber refuses to acknowledge the validity of this interpretation, because if he did he would be forced to admit that Schlieffen planned to fight an offensive war. Zuber, on the other hand, is convinced by the course of Schlieffen's western staff rides that he would fight any future war defensively.[24]

However, Zuber's use of staff rides as sources of support for his argument is also extremely problematic. One of the key assumptions upon which Zuber's argument is based is that staff rides provide a direct window into war planning.²⁵ He believes that Schlieffen and Moltke used their annual staff rides to test their war plans directly. Thus, based on the course of the staff rides of 1904, 1906, and 1908, Zuber concludes that the real German war plans of this period bore no resemblance to Schlieffen's memorandum of 1905.²⁶ However, with the exception of one year (1905), we have absolutely no evidence that Schlieffen or Moltke used their staff rides to test their war plans directly.²⁷ Indeed, most evidence suggests that these were primarily designed to provide training for staff officers and as a means of assessing staff officers for further promotion. While they may also have been used to test certain aspects of a war plan, again with the exception of 1905, we have no evidence of which aspects of which war plans particular rides were testing, if any at all.

If Zuber had examined the conduct of Schlieffen's staff rides, he might have recognized this limitation. Schlieffen's staff rides were by no means the free-flowing affairs necessary to give war plans a serious test. Hermann von Kuhl wrote about how Schlieffen conducted his exercises: "It is no lie that Graf Schlieffen usually altered now and then the course of General Staff rides and war games. For him, it was less about the free play of the two parties against one another than the carrying out of a particular operational idea. He tested how an operation would take place under particular circumstances, which courses of action a commander could find against the actions of an enemy. To this goal, he often deliberately put difficulties before one commander, while he made the situation easier for the other."²⁸ If, as Zuber would have us believe, staff rides and war games were designed to test war plans, this is a strange way to go about it.

Moreover, if staff rides were used to test war plans directly, this would have made the reports from these rides some of the most secret documents within the German Army. Yet, these reports were marked only *Geheim* (Secret) not *Streng Geheim* (Top Secret) and were distributed relatively widely—copies went to each of the Reich's twenty-five army corps, as well as to many other institutions within the army. No special precautions seem to have been taken to prevent these documents from falling into the hands of Germany's enemies. On the other hand, in 1911 the French were attempting to acquire a copy of the *Taschenbuch des Generalstabsoffiziers* (*General Staff Officer's Handbook*). This prompted Moltke to warn the entire army to be extraordinarily careful with this document and to destroy all old copies.²⁹ No such precautions seem to have been taken with copies of staff ride critiques.³⁰ If these were used to test war plans, surely the General Staff would have held them more closely than a staff officer's handbook. This further supports the view that these rides were primarily designed as training tools, rather than directly as war planning devices.

Indeed, from documents recently found in the archives, we can see that Zuber's interpretation of Schlieffen and his plan is seriously flawed. As part of their research for the history of the First World War, the *Reichsarchiv* summarized the surviving deployment directives of Schlieffen and Moltke the Younger. While the documents available to the *Reichsarchiv* provide only the barest details of the actions of the various armies after deployment, they nonetheless shed considerable light on Schlieffen's and Moltke's war plans in the decade before the outbreak of the First World War. From this, we can see that even in the deployment plan for 1905–1906, that is, before the ideas from the 1905 memorandum were to come into effect, Schlieffen made provisions for advancing through Belgium and Holland to fight the French. In both his *Aufmarschpläne* (deployment plans) for this year, Schlieffen intended to operate offensively against France. In his *Aufmarschplan I,* the entire German Army of twenty-six army corps and twenty reserve divisions organized in eight armies was deployed north of Metz poised to advance through the Low Countries. In his *Aufmarschplan II,* the numbers were reduced to twenty-three army corps and sixteen reserve divisions in seven armies, but these too were deployed to advance against France via Belgium and Holland. Schlieffen even provided for the rapid capture of the Belgian and Dutch rail network: five German cavalry divisions had orders to capture the bridges across the Maas and to secure the rail lines running from Germany.[31]

Thus, we see some serious problems with the sources upon which Zuber has constructed his radical reinterpretation of German war planning before 1914. The first source upon which Zuber constructs his argument, Dieckmann's manuscript, lacks the crucial section covering Schlieffen's planning of 1905 and is based on incomplete sources. Further, Zuber seems to believe that he has some type of secret knowledge that allows him to reject Dieckmann's conclusions. Part of this secret knowledge comes from Zuber's flawed use of another source—a few of Schlieffen's and Moltke's staff rides. Zuber assumes that the scenarios and course of these rides were true indicators of German war plans. However, there is no evidence to suggest that these rides were based on any real war plans or played a significant role in the formulation of war plans. Moreover, new evidence shows the extent to which an invasion of France via the neutral Low Countries was an integral part of Schlieffen's war plans even before his 1905 memorandum was to take effect. Given these problems with his sources and his use of these sources, one must seriously question Zuber's conclusions about German war planning. However, there are other serious flaws in Zuber's analysis that further throw into doubt his interpretation.

Zuber's Lack of Context

Another severe failing in Zuber's analysis is that it looks almost exclusively at the operational aspects of German war planning and virtually ignores the bigger picture. Zuber glosses over issues such as Germany's changing strategic situation and intelligence about enemy deployments and intentions. However, these points are central to understanding German war planning, particularly in the period from 1905 to 1914. Without examining them, we cannot have a complete grasp of German war plans. Indeed, an analysis of German war planning that takes into account these factors produces a very different interpretation from Zuber's.

One important aspect of Zuber's argument is his assertion that when writing his war plans for 1905 and 1906 Schlieffen assumed Germany would have to fight a two-front war. Zuber argues that "by February 1906 the Japanese war had been over for six months and Russia's internal situation was rapidly stabilizing."[32] From this, he concludes that Schlieffen believed the Russian Army would take an active part in a future war. Thus, as Schlieffen's 1905 memorandum dealt exclusively with a war against France, Zuber contends that it was never a real German war plan.[33]

However, an examination of Schlieffen's correspondence with the chancellor, Bernhard von Bülow, and an analysis of German intelligence assessments of Russia during this period do not bear out Zuber's assertion. In one of his articles, Holmes has already mentioned Schlieffen's letter to Bülow dated 10 June 1905.[34] However, he did not quote from this important letter in any length. This is unfortunate, as it shows Schlieffen's true assessment of the Russian Army in this period. He wrote:

> "the East Asian war has shown that the Russian Army is less competent than had been previously assumed by informed opinion and that the war has worsened the Russian Army rather than made it more efficient. It has lost all complaisance [*Freudigkeit*], all confidence [*Vertrauen*], and all obedience.
>
> It is very questionable whether or not an improvement will take place. The Russians lack enough self-awareness [*Selbsterkenntnis*] to carry this out. They see the origins of their defeat not in their own imperfections [*Unvollkommenkeiten*], but rather in the enemy's

superiority in numbers and in the ineffectiveness of particular commanders. The Russian Army lacks the men capable of carrying out the required reforms and who possess the necessary moral fortitude.

Therefore, recent history would suggest that the Russian Army will not improve, but instead will grow more ineffective. The current internal conditions of our great neighboring empire will surely not help, but rather add to this development."[35]

While Schlieffen thought that the Russian Army might in the future take part in a European war, he believed it unlikely in the short term and that, if the Russian Army did fight in Europe, it could easily be defeated even by an army as poor as the Austro-Hungarian Army. Another letter to Bülow dated 18 August supported Schlieffen's evaluation of the worth of the Russian Army by noting the significant Russian losses in the Far East and showing how these losses further reduced the combat power of the Russian Army.[36]

Schlieffen's assessments of the Russian Army in this period were based on intelligence gathered by German observers during the Russo-Japanese War. One of the most important of these observers was Otto von Lauenstein, who was a long-time head of the section of the Great General Staff responsible for intelligence assessments of the Russian Army. Lauenstein accompanied the Russian Army into the field in 1904 and was appalled by what he saw. In December 1905 he wrote a final, damning report of the Russian Army based on his observations: "The deepest basis of success and failure in war lies in the moral realm. . . . The character of the Russian people is marked by a pronounced indolence, an avoidance of compulsion and exertion, an aversion of everything that is difficult and unpleasant for the individual, and a shortage of consistency in thought as well as deed."

Lauenstein had believed that, when push came to shove, these character traits would be overcome by the innate good nature of the Russian officer corps. However, this had not been the case, and Russian officers came in for some of the harshest criticism in his report: "By and large, I did not win a good impression of the Russian officers during the campaign. They lacked moral gravity and any feeling of duty or responsibility. Their strength of will was not hardened." He reported that officers, more concerned with their own comforts, often absented themselves from the front lines. In Lauenstein's opinion, the Russian officer corps, from the top down, failed to show any leadership during the conflict. He believed that this lack of leadership infected the entire army and did much to undermine the famous discipline of the Russian soldiers and reduce the effectiveness of the army. Moreover, Lauenstein believed these problems to be endemic and that the Russian Army was unlikely to recover from them anytime soon.[37]

Thus, contrary to Zuber's assertion, Schlieffen and German intelligence did not believe that the Russian Army was capable of effective offensive action at the end of 1905 and beginning of 1906. Even before the outbreak of the Russian Revolution of 1905, they questioned the ability of the Russian Army to recover rapidly from the Japanese War. After their defeats in the Far East and the revolution at home, both Schlieffen and German intelligence concluded that the Russian Army would not be a threat for the foreseeable future.

Moreover, Schlieffen cannot have been unaware of attempts by the German government during 1904 and 1905 to bring Russia back into the German fold. Zuber's Schlieffen is one uninformed and uninterested in foreign affairs. However, we know that during this period Schlieffen was being kept well informed about foreign affairs from his friend in the Foreign Office, Friedrich von Holstein.[38] Although Holstein was initially opposed to any rapprochement between Germany and Russia, he certainly became a convert to the idea, particularly as Kaiser Wilhelm was intent on pursuing this policy.[39] German diplomats hoped to take advantage of Russia's weakness during the war with Japan and her antagonism with Britain to neutralize the Franco-Russian alliance. Although the treaty signed by Kaiser Wilhelm and Tsar Nicholas in July 1905 at Björkö was ultimately repudiated by both governments, it nonetheless showed that this policy had potential, and it certainly demonstrated the growing closeness between the two states.[40]

Thus, when Schlieffen was writing his memorandum in late 1905 and early 1906, he assumed that Germany would face France alone in a future war. A window of opportunity had been opened that would allow him to return to an idea he had nurtured since 1894. With Russia neutralized, Schlieffen could now employ the entire German Army in the west and have enough manpower to carry out an envelopment of the French fortress system.

Indeed, in the charged atmosphere of the Morocco Crisis, many minds in Berlin turned to the idea of launching a preventive war against an isolated France. Zuber, concentrating solely on the operational level, does not even bother to discuss Schlieffen's advocacy of such a war. Although the argument is old,[41] the case has been given new life recently by historians such as Albrecht Moritz, Fritz Fischer, and Heiner Raulff, who have shown that Schlieffen was one of the German government's greatest proponents of a preventive war against France.[42] At this point in time, Germany was in the grip of a war scare with Great Britain. As the Russo-Japanese War and the

Morocco Crisis took their courses, the Germans became increasingly afraid that Britain, who was allied to Japan and recently to France, might launch a preemptive strike against Germany and the German navy.[43] Schlieffen's answer to this problem was to attack France. In late 1905, the Saxon military plenipotentiary in Berlin reported back to Dresden: "A war against the allies France and Britain continues to be regarded as a possibility at the highest levels here. His Majesty the Emperor has therefore ordered the Chief of the General Staff of the Army and the Chief of the Navy Staff to prepare a joint plan of campaign. His Excellency Count Schlieffen is of the opinion that all available forces of the land army should be marshaled against France.... The war will be decided in France, not at sea. For this purpose the army must be as strong as possible."[44]

Despite significant pressure from the normally taciturn Schlieffen, neither Kaiser Wilhelm nor his chancellor was ready to go quite so far in Schlieffen's bid to break what he perceived as a growing encirclement of Germany.[45] However, in the end, it seems to have been the Minister of War, Karl von Einem, who put the final nail in the coffin of the idea of launching a preemptive war against France. The French had rearmed their artillery with modern guns and the German Army did not yet have these weapons. Einem feared this modern French artillery and argued strongly against war.[46] (Schlieffen even took to calling the Ministry of War the Ministry of Peace.[47]) With the minister of war against the idea, it was easy for the unenthusiastic kaiser and chancellor to dismiss Schlieffen's calls for war.[48] Indeed, there is considerable evidence that Schlieffen's belligerent stance during the Morocco Crisis poisoned relations between Schlieffen and Bülow and the kaiser, which led to Schlieffen's replacement.[49]

Schlieffen's 1905 memorandum was also influenced by what he saw the French doing. First, it was clear that the French Army was shocked by the defeats of their Russian ally in the Far East and what they perceived as their own relative weakness compared to the German Army during the Morocco Crisis.[50] To protect themselves, they threw considerable sums of money into their armed forces. Importantly, they poured money into modernizing their fortresses. In a special budget passed in the summer of 1905, the French Chamber authorized 193 million francs for this project.[51] Divining the intentions of one's enemy has never been an easy task. However, given the weakness of the Russian Army and the amount of money the French were spending on defensive works, it was a pretty safe bet for German intelligence that the French did not intend to attack Germany in 1905 or 1906, regardless of provocation. Thus, for Schlieffen, who clearly wanted to launch a war against France, the only way to defeat the French Army would be to go in and get it.

However, Schlieffen again faced the problem of how to get at the French Army. Many historians have recently cited Martin Köpke's memorandum of 1895, in which he writes of the severe difficulties of fighting through the French fortification line.[52] This challenge, along with the deadliness of modern weapons, certainly prompted Schlieffen to push hard for a modernization of German heavy artillery.[53] However, although much had been done to improve German artillery by 1905, it was still not enough to break through the French fortress line.[54] Indeed, six months after he took over from Schlieffen, Moltke wrote that the armor of the French fortresses would easily withstand the fire of even the heaviest German guns and asked that new super-heavy howitzers be developed.[55] Thus, if Schlieffen wanted to fight the French Army in 1905 or 1906, he would have to get at them via their vulnerable left flank. In other words, the German Army would have to advance through the neutral Low Countries.[56]

To be properly understood, Schlieffen's memorandum of 1905 must be seen in this wider context. It represents a reaction to a radically altered strategic situation. Both Schlieffen and German intelligence assumed that Russia was out of the equation, at least for the short term. If German diplomacy were successful, Russia would be unable to aid France for the foreseeable future. Clearly, this offered an opportunity to deal a blow to France that would once and for all end French rivalry with Germany, and Schlieffen did not miss a chance to advocate a preventive war. Indeed, even the "missing" units of Schlieffen's memorandum can be understood if viewed within this context. The revolution in Russia offered a salient lesson for autocratic Germany. The conservative Schlieffen would certainly have recognized that all of German society would have to be behind any war with France to prevent a similar occurrence in Germany. What better way to do this than to replicate the act that provided the foundation myth for the Second German Empire—a total mobilization of German manpower to face the age-old enemy France?

As Holmes has pointed out, the Germans fielded barely trained *Ersatz* (replacement) troops in the Austro-German War in 1866 and the Franco-German War of 1870–1871.[57] There is no doubt that raising new units after the outbreak of war would be challenging. However, as Holmes has noted, the German Army of 1905–1906 was not the regularized force of 1914. Given differences in recruiting pools, among other things, some German corps districts possessed active units (battalions, squadrons, and batteries) that did not fit into the order of battle of existing units.⁵⁸ These "spare units" could easily provide a core around which to build new formations. Indeed, during the First World War many *Ersatz* units were raised in this way,⁵⁹ and the Ministry of War even managed to raise four new army corps from scratch within six weeks.⁶⁰ Although the quality of these units would not be high, they could be used to free better units for more difficult tasks, as was done in the Wars of Unification.

Conclusion

In the interwar period, German soldiers and historians, stung by their defeat in the First World War and by the war-guilt clause of the Treaty of Versailles, twisted facts and the historical record in an attempt to prove that Germany had fought essentially a defensive war in 1914.⁶¹ Zuber stands in this long line of apologists. Again by the selective use and peculiar interpretation of documents, he hopes to knock away a key element of the case against German war guilt. He has attempted to prove that the Schlieffen Plan, a plan for an offensive war, was never a real German war plan. Instead, he has argued that this was merely a means by which Schlieffen could obtain more troops from an unwilling Ministry of War. Zuber maintains that Schlieffen, and later Moltke, planned to fight a defensive war in German territory as a reaction to a Dual Alliance attack. Any violation of the neutrality of any neighboring states would be in reaction to Entente offensives. In other words, he contends that neither Schlieffen nor Moltke planned a war of aggression. Given the recent research on the outbreak of the First World War, all unexamined by Zuber, this stance is untenable.

If Zuber had lifted his gaze beyond the operational level, he would have recognized that 1905 represented a fundamental shift in the strategic situation, and was perceived as such by Schlieffen and later Moltke. In the aftermath of the Russo-Japanese War and the 1905 Russian Revolution, Schlieffen believed that the Russian Army was a negligible force and would remain such for the foreseeable future. Thus, he could concentrate on a one-front war, which would give him the forces necessary to take the offensive and, hence, maintain the initiative in a war with France. Indeed, he believed the situation to be so favorable that he advocated a first strike against France during the Morocco Crisis of 1905. Given the relative balance of forces in 1905, it is clear that the German Army would have had to have launched their attack against the weakest point in the formidable French defensive system—their unprotected left flank. The only way to do this would have been an advance through Holland and Belgium. In other words, to follow what later became known as the Schlieffen Plan.

Notes

1. I would like to thank Dr. Annika Mombauer for her helpful comments on earlier drafts of this chapter. The analysis, opinions, and conclusions expressed or implied in this chapter are those of the author and do not necessarily represent the view of the Joint Services Command and Staff College, the UK Ministry of Defence, or any other government agency.

2. While Zuber is correct to state that Schlieffen did not complete his memorandum until 1906, I have used the date 1905, as this is the date given on the document.

3. Indeed, Zuber is not the first to argue this. However, he is the first to suggest that this was the prime reason for Schlieffen's memorandum. See Reichsarchiv, *Der Weltkrieg*, vol. 1, *Die Grenzschlachten im Westen* (Berlin: E. S. Mittler, 1925), 55; and Stig Förster, *Der doppelte Militärismus: Die deutsche Heeresrüstungspolitik zwischen Status-Quo-Sicherung und Aggression, 1890–1913* (Stuttgart: Franz Steiner, 1985), 165.

4. Terence Zuber, "The Schlieffen Plan Reconsidered," *War in History* 6, no. 3 (1999): 262–305. While his argument is implied in the above article, it comes out more clearly in his *Inventing the Schlieffen Plan: German War Planning, 1871–1914* (Oxford: Oxford Univ. Press, 2003).

5. Terence Holmes, "The Reluctant March on Paris: A Reply to Terence Zuber's 'The Schlieffen Plan Reconsidered,'" *War in History* 8, no. 2 (2001): 208–232.

6. See Terence Zuber, "Terence Holmes Reinvents the Schlieffen Plan," *War in History* 8, no. 4 (2001): 468–476; Terence Holmes, "The Real Thing: A Reply to Terence Zuber's 'Terence Holmes Reinvents the Schlieffen Plan,'" *War in History* 9, no. 1 (2002): 111–120; Terence Zuber, "Terence Holmes Reinvents the Schlieffen Plan—Again," *War in History* 10, no. 1 (2003): 92–101; Robert T. Foley, "The Origins of the Schlieffen Plan," *War in History* 10, no. 2 (2003): 222–232; Terence Holmes, "Asking Schlieffen: A Further Reply to Terence Zuber," *War in History* 10, no. 4 (2003): 464–479; and Terence Zuber, "The Schlieffen Plan Was an Orphan," *War in History* 11, no. 2 (2004): 220–225.

7. Wilhelm Dieckmann, "Der Schlieffenplan," unpublished manuscript in Bundesarchiv/Militärarchiv, Freiburg (hereafter, BA/MA), W10/50220.

8. If Zuber had looked at the relevant secondary literature on the KGFA files, he would have known their provenance. See Uwe Löbel, "Neue Forschungsmöglichkeiten zur preussisch-deutschen Heeresgeschichte: Zur Rückgabe von Akten des Potsdamer Heeresarchivs durch die Sowjetunion," *Militärgeschichtliche Mitteilungen* 51 (1992): 143–149.

9. Zuber, "The Schlieffen Plan Reconsidered," 274ff; Zuber, *Inventing the Schlieffen Plan*, 141ff.

10. See Kurt von Regenauer, "Materialsammlung zur Darstellung der operativen Verhandlungen des Grafen Schlieffen mit Österreich-Ungarn," BA/MA, W10/50222. These documents were collected by Regenauer from the Austrian archives in January 1939. The collection contains copies of the diary of the Austrian chief of the General Staff, Friedrich Graf von Beck-Rzikowsky, as well as copies of the letters of the Austrian military plenipotentiary in Berlin from 1894 to 1904. Cf. Lothar Höbelt, "Schlieffen, Beck, Potiorek und das Ende der gemeinsamen deutsch-österreichisch-ungarischen Aufmarschpläne im Osten," *Militärgeschichtliche Mitteilungen* 2 (1984): 7–30.

11. Zuber, "The Schlieffen Plan Reconsidered," 270f.; Zuber, *Inventing the Schlieffen Plan*, 136ff.

12. Zuber, "The Schlieffen Plan Reconsidered," 274; Zuber, "The Schlieffen Plan Was an Orphan," 222.

13. Wolfgang Foerster admitted as much in his "Ist der deutsche Aufmarsch 1904 an die Franzosen verraten worden?" *Berliner Monatshefte* (1932), 1060.

14. Annika Mombauer, *Helmuth von Moltke and the Origins of the First World War* (Cambridge, 2001), 39.

15. Cf. Zuber, "The Schlieffen Plan Reconsidered," 267.

16. Ibid., 285. See also Zuber, "The Schlieffen Plan Was an Orphan," 222.

17. Dieckmann, "Der Schlieffenplan," 1–2.

18. Ibid., 57.

19. Zuber, "The Schlieffen Plan Was an Orphan," 222.

20. The *Reichsarchiv* planned to publish Moltke the Younger's staff rides and staff problems, but the outbreak of the Second World War prevented their publication. See Friedrich von Rabenau (chief of the Army Archive) to all army archives, 22 May 1937, U.S. National Archives (USNA), Alfred von Schlieffen Papers, RG 242, M-961/Roll 1.

21. Zuber, "The Schlieffen Plan Reconsidered," 288–289, 291, 296.

22. Ibid., 301–304. Also see Zuber, *Inventing the Schlieffen Plan*, 224–238.

23. Holmes, "Reluctant March," 211–214.

24. Zuber, "The Schlieffen Plan Reconsidered," 288–304.

25. This assumption seems to have originated with Arden Bucholz, *Moltke, Schlieffen and Prussian War Planning* (Oxford, 1991).

26. Indeed, Zuber even uses Moltke's staff problems from 1906 to 1913 to bolster his case. Zuber, *Inventing the Schlieffen Plan*, 232–238.

27. A number of General Staff officers claimed that Schlieffen's staff rides of 1905 were designed to test his new war plan. See Erich Ludendorff, *Mein militärische Werdegang* (Munich: Ludendorffs Verlag, 1933), 96ff.; Hugo Freiherr von Freytag-Loringhoven, *Menschen und Dinge, wie ich in meinem Leben sah* (Berlin: E. S. Mittler, 1923), 102–103.

28. Hermann von Kuhl, *Der deutsche Generalstab in Vorbereitung und Durchführung des Weltkrieges* (Berlin: E. S. Mittler, 1920), 129. Cf. Zuber, *Inventing the Schlieffen Plan*, 147.

29. Chef des Generalstabes der Armee, No. 12209, 28 September 1911, Bayerisches Hauptstaatsarchiv—Kriegsarchiv, München (BayHStA-KA), MKr. 983.

30. Indeed, around 1906 the details of a staff ride seem to have fallen into French hands. Robert A. Doughty, "French Strategy in 1914: Joffre's Own," *Journal of Military History* 67 (April 2003): 437.

31. "Aufmarsch 1905/06," in "Aufmarschanweisungen für die Jahre 1893/94 bis 1914/15," BA/MA, RH61/v.96. My thanks to Dr. Gerhard Gross for a copy of this important document.

32. Zuber, "Terence Holmes Reinvents the Schlieffen Plan—Again," 97.

33. Zuber, "The Schlieffen Plan Reconsidered," 305.

34. Holmes, "The Real Thing," 116.

35. Schlieffen to Bülow, 10 June 1905, reprinted in Robert T. Foley, *Alfred von Schlieffen's Military Writings* (London: Franck Cass, 2002), 159–161.

36. Schlieffen to Bülow, 18 August 1805, in ibid., 161–162. See also 1. Abteilung, Grosser Generalstab, "Zusammenstellung der wichtigsten Veränderungen im Heerwesen Russlands im Jahre 1905," and "Zusammenstellung der wichtigsten Veränderungen im Heerwesen Russlands im Jahre 1906," BayHStA-KA, GSt. 207.

37. Otto von Lauenstein, report of 10 December 1905, BA/MA, PH3/653. Most of the other German observers were similarly dismissive of the Russian Army. See "Berichte über den russisch-japanische Krieg," BA/MA, PH3/653, and "Russisch-japanische Krieg: Korrespondenzen und Berichte 1904–5," BayHStA-KA, GSt. 234.

38. Peter Rassow, "Schlieffen und Holstein," *Historische Zeitschrift* 173 (1952): 297–313.

39. Norman Rich, *Friedrich von Holstein: Politics and Diplomacy in the Era of Bismarck and Wilhelm II*, 2 vols. (Cambridge: Cambridge Univ. Press, 1965), 2:678ff.

40. Roderick R. McLean, "Dreams of a German Europe: Wilhelm II and the Treaty of Björkö of 1905," in *The Kaiser: New Research on Wilhelm II's Role in Imperial Germany*, ed. Annika Mombauer and Wilhelm Deist (Cambridge: Cambridge Univ. Press, 2003), 119–142.

41. See Hugo Rochs, *Schlieffen: Ein Lebens- und Charakterbild* (Berlin: Richard Schröder, 1940), 84ff.; Walter Kloster, *Der deutsche Generalstab und der Präventivkriegs-Gedanke* (Stuttgart: W. Kohlhammer, 1932), 34–44.

42. See Albrecht Moritz, *Das Problem des Präventivkrieges in der deutschen Politik während der ersten Marokkokrise* (Frankfurt: Peter Lang, 1974); Fritz Fischer, *War of Illusions: German Policies from 1911 to 1914*, trans. Marian Jackson (London: Chatto and Windus, 1975); Heiner Raulff, *Zwischen Machtpolitik und Imperialismus: Die deutsche Frankreichpolitik 1904–05* (Düsseldorf: Droste Verlag, 1976), 126–193.

43. Paul M. Kennedy, *The Rise and Fall of Anglo-German Antagonism, 1860–1914* (London: Allen and Unwin, 1980), 267ff.; Jonathan Steinberg, "The Copenhagen Complex," *Journal of Contemporary History* 1, no. 3 (1966): 23–46.

44. Freiherr von Salza und Lichtenau to the Saxon Minister of War, 6 September 1905, quoted in Fischer, *War of Illusions,* 55.

45. In this period, Schlieffen insisted that the French were making preparations for war. The Foreign Office came to the opposite conclusion. See Raulff, *Machtpolitik und Imperialismus,* 126ff.

46. Cf. Karl von Einem, *Erinnerungen eines Soldaten 1853–1933* (Leipzig: v.Hase and Koehler, 1933), 110f.

47. Rochs, *Schlieffen,* 51.

48. Raulff, *Machtpolitik und Imperialismus,* 131ff.

49. Mombauer, *Moltke,* 42–46. Indeed, Holstein was forced to resign over his role in the Morocco Crisis. If, as has been suggested by Rich and Rassow, Holstein and Schlieffen were working together to push for war with France, it is logical that Schlieffen would also have been pressured to resign over the issue.

50. See the report of the German military attaché in Paris, Mutius, "Militär-Bericht Nr.1: Kriegsbereitschaft," in Public Record Office, Kew, German Foreign Ministry Files 16/29 (*Frankreich 95*, vol. 58 [1 Jan 06–31 Dez 06]); Christopher Andrew, "France and the German Menace," in *Knowing One's Enemies: Intelligence Assessment before the Two World Wars,* ed. Ernest R. May (Princeton: Princeton Univ. Press, 1984), 127–149; and David G. Herrmann, *The Arming of Europe and the Making of the First World War* (Princeton: Princeton Univ. Press, 1996), 37–58.

51. 4. Abteilung, Grosser Generalstab, "Jahresbericht 1906: Veränderungen im Festungswesen der westlichen Staaten," 4 December 1906, in BayHStA-KA, GSt. 489.

52. See Stig Förster, "Der deutsche Generalstab und die Illusion des kurzen Krieges, 1871–1914: Metakritik eines Mythos," *Militärgeschichtliche Mitteilungen* 54 (1995): 75; Holger Herwig, *The First World War: Germany and Austria-Hungary 1914–1918* (London: Arnold, 1997), 48.

53. Dieckmann, "Der Schlieffenplan," 21ff.; Eric Dorn Brose, *The Kaiser's Army: The Politics of Military Technology in Germany during the Machine Age* (Oxford: Oxford Univ. Press, 2001), 73ff.

54. Brose, *The Kaiser's Army,* 78ff.

55. Moltke to Kriegsministerium, 6 June 1906, BayHStA-KA, MKr. 990.

56. For Schlieffen's view of the defensive strength of the Low Countries, see Dieckmann, "Der Schlieffenplan," 59ff.

57. Holmes, "The Real Thing," 114.

58. Holmes, "Asking Schlieffen," 467ff.

59. Bruce I. Gudmundsson, "Ersatz Divisions in 1914" and "Mixed Ersatz Brigades," *Tactical Notebook* (July 1993); Bruce I. Gudmundsson, "German Techniques for Forming Units," *Tactical Notebook* (August 1993).

60. Ernst von Wrisberg, *Heer und Heimat 1914–1918* (Leipzig, 1921), 15ff.

61. Holger Herwig, "Clio Deceived: Patriotic Self-Censorship in Germany after the War," *International Security* 12 (1987): 5–44; Annika Mombauer, *The Origins of the First World War: Controversies and Consensus* (London: Longman, 2002), 45–105.

There Was a Schlieffen Plan
New Sources on the History of German Military Planning

Gerhard P. Gross

"There never was a Schlieffen Plan."[1] Several years ago this pointed thesis advanced by Terence Zuber caused a lively debate about operational and strategic planning in the Prussian Great General Staff (Grosser Generalstab) under the leadership of Field Marshal Alfred Graf von Schlieffen and Colonel General Helmuth von Moltke the Younger.[2] Zuber argued that the generally accepted view that, disregarding all political implications, Schlieffen had planned to circumvent the French fortification systems through the BENELUX states and to envelop and destroy the French Army with a strong right attack wing was wrong. This view has prevailed since 1956, when Gerhard Ritter[3] published Schlieffen's *Denkschrift* (Memorandum) of 1905–1906. Instead, Zuber argued:

1. One of the reasons that Schlieffen's *Denkschrift* of 1905 was not the German war plan is that it had not been secured in the files of the General Staff, but rather was kept among Schlieffen's private papers until he died. Afterward it became the property of his daughters.[4]
2. Schlieffen did not plan a great battle of annihilation. Instead, he only wanted to stave off the expected French attacks with a well-aimed counterattack close to the border.[5]
3. In Schlieffen's exercise plans, German troops never practiced the western envelopment of Paris or battles on French ground. His map exercises always took place only in Lorraine or Belgium.[6]
4. Schlieffen's *Denkschrift* of 1905 was not the final point of his opera-

tional planning. Instead, it only served as a reasonable basis for his intended expansion of the German Army.[7]
5. The divisions necessary to carry out the attack operations described in Schlieffen's *Denkschrift* of 1905 were not available. Therefore, the *Denkschrift* did not serve as a basis for the real planning of the General Staff.[8]
6. The campaign plan laid down in Schlieffen's *Denkschrift* of 1905 does not represent the culmination of his philosophy of the operational art. It is rather an isolated aberration of his operational thinking.[9]
7. The political dimension of warfare did not play a role in Schlieffen's operational planning.

According to Zuber, German military historiography after the First World War invented the Schlieffen Plan—understood as the "War against France" *Denkschrift* written by Schlieffen at the turn of the year 1905–1906[10]—in order to cover over the German operational errors made during the first weeks of the war and during the debacle at the Battle of the Marne.[11]

I

Following the destruction of much of the Reich Archive records near the end of World War II, Gerhard Ritter assumed that there would be only a very limited amount of documentation on the operational planning of the Great General Staff under Schlieffen and his successor during the years prior to the First World War. Zuber, however, bases his revisionist interpretation on newly discovered records. Those primarily are the undated and incomplete study by senior archivist Wilhelm Dieckmann titled "Der Schlieffenplan"[12] and the study of the German intelligence assessments before 1914 by archivist Helmuth Greiner.[13] But in the opinion of Zuber's critics, especially Robert Foley, Terence Holmes, and Annika Mombauer, Zuber offers a one-dimensional operational interpretation.

This chapter, then, will scrutinize those issues. First, I will reexamine the situation of the sources in order to establish whether Zuber's interpretation is based on all currently available records, in particular those of the Great General Staff. Here I shall examine if the hitherto unknown documents provide additional weight to one position or the other.

What was the Great General Staff and what do we know of its modus operandi? The Great General Staff, which had been an independent institution since 1837, was headed by the chief of the Great General Staff, who since 1883 enjoyed the right of direct access (*Immediatrecht*) to the kaiser. The tasks of the General Staff included the survey and mapping of the country, as well as the collection of information about foreign armies and the preparation of the forces for wartime. Most importantly, the General Staff was responsible for all issues regarding mobilization and the actual conduct of war.[14]

In addition to the tactical and strategic training of the General Staff officers, the chief of the Great General Staff was responsible for operational and strategic war planning for the German Army.[15] The General Staff's philosophy of operational art was implemented in specific military planning through *Aufmarschanweisungen* (deployment directives) for the individual field armies, which were issued at the beginning of each new mobilization year on 1 April.[16] As part of that process the General Staff's Railway Division prepared the railway deployment of the German Army on the basis of the top secret "Direktiven für den Aufmarsch" (Directives for Deployment), which had been issued by the chief of the General Staff in November–December of the previous calendar year.[17] This procedure was repeated every year, and the *Aufmarschpläne* (deployment plans) were usually destroyed at the end of the mobilization year, as were other top secret written documents of the General Staff.[18]

Because of failures to follow procedures, however, not all originals and copies were destroyed.[19] Thus, the Reich Archive (*Reichsarchiv*) in Potsdam, which was established on 1 October 1919 as a collection point of military records of the Prussian army, had a set of Great General Staff records that later passed into the collection of the Army Archive (*Heeresarchiv*), established on 1 April 1936.[20] In addition to the *Kriegsspiele* (war games) and *Generalstabsreisen* (General Staff rides), this set—even if not complete—contained the *Schlussaufgaben* (key taskings) of Schlieffen and Moltke from the years 1890 to 1914. Furthermore, according to Ritter, a set of Schlieffen's papers was held in the Reich Archive/Army Archive.[21] Today, Germany no longer has a complete official collection of the deployment files (*Aufmarschakten*) once held by the Reich Archive/Army Archive, nor does it have Schlieffen's papers (*Nachlass*) or the *Kriegsspiele*.[22] Even prior to World War II, however, access to the records then available at the Army Archive were restricted and limited to selected persons only.[23] Foremost among that select group was the staff of the Reich Archive Division of the History of War (*Kriegsgeschichtliche Abteilung*), simply called the Historical Division from 1924 on. Among those most prominent individuals with special access was former General Staff officer and future president of the War Historical Research Institute of the Army (*Kriegsgeschichtliche Forschungsanstalt des Heeres*) Wolfgang Foerster, son-in-law of the first president of the Reich Archive; Hermann Ritter Mertz von Quirnheim; Wilhelm Dieckmann; and the former first quartermaster general of the German Army and future Reich defense minister Wilhelm Groener. Although the Reich Archive had an, albeit incomplete, collection of *Aufmarschakten* (deployment plans) and service regulations from Schlieffen and Moltke, they were not published as a document collection in the 1920s. During the immediate post–World War I controversy about the failure to use Schlieffen's "Siegesrezept Schlieffens" (Recipe for Victory) and Schlieffen's *Denkschrift* of 1905, commonly referred to as the Schlieffen Plan, individual sentences from Schlieffen's *Denkschrift* were cited or paraphrased either by the Reich Archive in the German official World War history, *Der Weltkrieg 1914–1918*,[24] or by other former General Staff officers.[25] Only in 1937 and 1938 did the War Historical Division of the General Staff publish two volumes of Schlieffen's official papers, which included his tactical-strategic taskings and the *Generalstabsreisen im Osten* (General Staff Ride in the East).[26] According to Foerster, further publication of the records, especially Schlieffen's plans for the west, was prevented by the outbreak of World War II.[27]

On 14 April 1945, the Army Archive was almost totally destroyed during a British air raid.[28] As a consequence, all the important documents on the General Staff's operational planning before the First World War were apparently irretrievably lost. Schlieffen's papers, however, had been removed to southern Germany before the air raid. Those files were secured by American forces, transferred to the U.S. National Archives in Washington, and later made available to Ritter, who had already been granted access by the Reich Archive prior to 1945. In 1956, Ritter published his documentation of Schlieffen's *Denkschriften* of 1905 and 1912.

Although the archived military records of the German Reich suffered great losses during the Allied air raid, not all records of the Army Archive were destroyed.[29] Immediately after the end of the war in 1945, individual holdings were recovered, including a large part of the records of the War Historical Research Institute. Later, those records were transferred to the Military Archive of the National People's Army (East German Army) in Potsdam and were maintained under record group W10. After German reunification, those records were transferred to the Bundesarchiv/Militärarchiv in Freiburg between 1996 and 2000 and in part were integrated into the already existing record group RH61 "Military Historical Research Institute of the Army," which consisted of individual preserved record holdings. As Zuber and others correctly note, those archival records contain many documents that extend beyond Ritter's knowledge and allow for a new examination of the operational and strategic planning of the General Staff before the First World War.

But did Zuber really base his theories on all relevant record holdings? Information concerning this and other still unresolved questions about the preservation of the operational and strategic planning files of the General Staff can be found in the personal papers (*Nachlass*) of General of Artillery Friedrich von Boetticher, which surprisingly have not yet been studied by historians in this context.[30] Boetticher had been asked by Reich president Paul von Hindenburg and Reich Defense Minister Wilhelm Groener to prepare an appreciation of Schlieffen with appropriate essays and to deliver a speech at the Reich Ministry of Defense on 28 February 1933, the one hundredth anniversary of Schlieffen's birth. Boetticher agreed, on the condition that he be granted unrestricted access to the Reich Archive records and the materials in the possession of Schlieffen's heirs.[31] Based on those documents, Boetticher wrote several articles,[32] including an article about Schlieffen's lifework[33] as a contribution to the history of the Prussian-German General Staff[34] edited by Major General Friedrich von Cochenhausen on the one hundredth anniversary of Schlieffen's birth.

The Reich Archive initially displayed a dilatory attitude toward Boetticher's request for access to the records.[35] But retired Major General Wilhelm von Hahnke, Schlieffen's son-in-law, immediately granted him access to the documents in the possession of the family. Thanks to the fact that Boetticher was very diligent in handling the records, his own personal papers include not only the return list of the Schlieffen records he had borrowed, but also lists of records of the Central Department of the Great General Staff[36] that were handed over to the Reich Archive, as well as Schlieffen's private documents[37] that had been made available by Hahnke. Although these indexes do not contain a complete list of the holdings of the Reich Archive and the private records of Schlieffen's heirs, they indicate for the first time which records had been available to Foerster, Dieckmann, and others for their scholarly research. It is especially important for our problem that Boetticher had been allowed by Groener[38] to make handwritten excerpts of the records available to him, or to make typed copies of them and keep them among his own personal papers. These records supplement the already existing files on *Kriegsspiele, Grosse Generalstabsreisen,* and *Schlussaufgaben* of the General Staff under Schlieffen and Moltke in the holdings of the Bundesarchiv/Militärarchiv under record group PH3, *Bestand Grosser Generalstab*.

Boetticher's personal papers include, among other things, copies and maps of the *Grosse Generalstabsreisen* of 1899, 1901, and 1903, as well as of the *Schlussaufgaben* of 1903, 1904, and 1905. Of particular importance, however, are the copies of the *Grosse Generalstabsreise West* of 1905, which had been considered lost.[39]

Although the operational studies that had been presented in detail by Zoellner[40] and Boetticher[41] were important cornerstones of Zuber's arguments against the existence of the Schlieffen Plan,[42] Zuber analyzed neither those records nor the handwritten fragments in the *Bestand Grosser Generalstab* under record group number PH3/663.[43, 44] Boetticher's indexes of files, however, do not provide any hints as to where Schlieffen's *Denkschrift* of 1905 might have been kept. Had the Schlieffen Plan indeed been kept among family pictures in the drawing room of Schlieffen's daughters, as stated by Zuber?[45] Or was it among the files of the Great General Staff in the Reich Archive?[46] Is the *Denkschrift* of 1905 published by Ritter on the basis of the drafts available to him from the field marshal's papers really the only still extant version of the famous Schlieffen Plan? To answer these questions, it is necessary to reconstruct the respective places where the original of the *Denkschrift*, which had been handed over to Moltke in February 1906, had been kept, and to clarify the level of classification of the *Denkschrift*.

Moltke treated Schlieffen's *Denkschrift* as strictly confidential and did not even disclose it to his closest staff. His department chiefs, Lieutenant Colonel Gerhard von Tappen, General Erich Ludendorff, General Georg Graf von Waldersee, and General Hermann von Stein, all said after the end of the war in 1918 that they had never seen the *Denkschrift* during their periods of service on the Great General Staff. In 1925, the *Denkschrift* was mentioned and partially cited for the first time by Foerster,[47] and in the World War I official history, *Der Weltkrieg 1914–1918*.[48] Prior to that, the operational plans of Schlieffen and Moltke had been discussed in the relevant military literature. There was a general mention of a Schlieffen Plan.[49] To prove the existence of the *Denkschrift*, extracts of it were published in facsimile by Groener in 1927[50] and by Foerster in 1933.[51] However, a comparison of both prints—which Zuber did not make—reveals that they were taken from two different originals.[52] Accordingly then, two different versions of Schlieffen's *Denkschrift* of 1905 existed in the early 1930s. Neither Groener nor Foerster indicate in their works where the originals of their facsimiles had been found. Thanks to Ritter's edition of the *Denkschrift* of 1905, we know that Groener's facsimile was in part incorrectly compiled from three different partial drafts by Schlieffen, which were then in the possession of Hahnke and are now kept at BA/MA (Nachlass Schlieffen, N43). Thus, the preserved copies from Schlieffen's papers, which Hahnke had identified as copies of the original, are titled "War against France," and not "War against France which is Allied with England."[53]

Schlieffen's papers do not include a copy with handwritten marginal notes by Moltke similar to Foerster's facsimile. It merely contains preliminary drafts and two typed copies in which Hahnke, after viewing the *Denkschrift* original with Moltke's written comments, had added Moltke's marginal notes.[54] Consequently, the original *Denkschrift* was not in the possession of Schlieffen's heirs. In 1932–1933, then, it must have been kept at a place to which Foerster had easy access. There is every reason to believe that this place was the Reich Archive and that Foerster, who had been director of the Historical Division of the Reich Archive since December 1931, used his access to publish the facsimile of the original *Denkschrift* of 1905. Do copies of this original memorandum, which probably was destroyed in April 1945, still exist today, and do we have records documenting its existence in the Reich Archive?

Looking for indicators in the relevant literature we again come to Boetticher. In his essay "Schlieffen" he notes that during his studies in 1932 of Schlieffen's operational thinking he made a copy of the original *Denkschrift*.[55] How did Boetticher gain access to the original of the "Schlieffen Plan" and where did he acquire his detailed knowledge of Schlieffen's legacy? Boetticher's excellent knowledge of the late field marshal's written legacy is mainly the result of his friendly relations with Schlieffen's eldest daughter, Elisabeth von Hahnke. After the 1931 death of her husband, Wilhelm von Hahnke, Boetticher was the only person in her circle who was able to assess the military documents in her possession and whom she trusted. Boetticher, therefore, advised the widow at her request on all issues regarding her father's papers. Following his suggestion, she finally on 14 July 1933 handed the papers over to the Reich Archive to be kept secretly and securely. The stipulation was that her property rights would be protected and the papers kept top secret. The papers included the copies of the *Denkschrift* made by Hahnke in the Reich Archive. Access to the documents was subject to her approval. After her death, the sole right of disposition passed to her daughter, Anna Josefa von Hahnke.[56] Any requests to examine and, if applicable, use Schlieffen's papers were turned down by her and her mother.[57]

Boetticher was the only person outside the family who was given unlimited access to the private documents, and who was allowed to dispose of the estate at any time at the request of the family, thanks to his especially trusted relations with the Hahnkes.[58] After the publication of Ritter's *Schlieffenplan*, Boetticher, on behalf of Schlieffen's granddaughter, initiated legal action against Ritter's use of Schlieffen's documents and factual deficiencies in his study on the basis that neither he nor Anna Josefa von Hahnke had authorized the use of the documents.[59] In a lively correspondence on that matter, which included Professors Eberhard Kessel, Gotthard Jäschke, Werner Frauendienst, a former chief of the Army General Staff, General Franz Halder, Walter Görlitz, and Foerster,[60] Boetticher referred to the only still existing copy of the original *Denkschrift* of 1905. It therefore must have been in his possession and archived in the Boetticher papers, which have since been handed over to the Bundesarchiv/Militärarchiv under record number N323/19 Nachlass Boetticher. A comparison of the document found in that file with the facsimile printed by Foerster clearly indicates that this is indeed a copy of the original.[61] Boetticher also described the history of its origins and reveals where the original of the *Denkschrift* of 1905 had been kept. In February 1958 he told Görlitz that he was the only person "who possesses clean copies of all the works of Schlieffen that had not been printed before 1945, among them an exemplar of the *Denkschrift*—the so-called Schlieffen Plan—that Schlieffen had sent to the younger Moltke and which the second president of the Reich Archive, Hans von Haeften, had carefully kept in his iron cabinet."[62]

Initially, Moltke kept this original at the General Staff. When the Reich Archive was established, that original came into its possession and was later transferred to the Army Archive.[63] There, it was either destroyed on 14 April 1945 or it was taken to the Soviet Union by Russian soldiers—a possibility not excluded by Foerster.[64] Perhaps the "Schlieffen Plan" still lies unrecognized and awaits rediscovery in a Russian archive, like many other records on the history of the First World War. The original *Denkschrift* of 1905 was definitely not stored "with the family photos" in the custody of Schlieffen's daughters—as Zuber states to challenge its significance.

Thanks to Groener's directive, the Reich Archive after initial difficulties favorably supported Boetticher in his studies on Schlieffen. In addition to providing files, several staff members, among them Foerster, Stoeckel, von Bose, and Dieckmann, prepared excerpts and compilations for him and offered their expertise. Expressly acknowledging the support provided by the Reich Archive, Boetticher sent a letter of thanks to Haeften, who had received him personally and granted him access to the *Denkschrift* of 1905. Interestingly, it was Dieckmann's and not Foerster's research that Boetticher expected to "very much contribute to developing a deep insight into the problem of Schlieffen," as he told Haeften.[65] This statement is of importance for the source-critical evaluation of Dieckmann's manuscript, "Der Schlieffenplan," which Zuber uses as the basis for his thesis.

How does Zuber categorize Dieckmann's study? With a strange ambivalence, actually. Although Zuber quotes several passages from Dieckmann in his book *German War Planning, 1891–1914* and refers to it as "the most important of the newly found documents,"[66] he also discounts somewhat its value without an explanation, noting, "Dieckmann's manuscript is not a great piece of historical writing."[67] Although Zuber credits Dieckmann with no more knowledge of the Schlieffen Plan than the interested public,[68] and notwithstanding the critical marginal notes by Foerster, it is Zuber's opinion that Dieckmann's presentation of Schlieffen's operational planning is correct and irreplaceable because of the lost records of the Army Archive.[69] Since Zuber's source criticism asks more questions than it answers, it is necessary to subject Dieckmann's manuscript of "Der Schlieffenplan" to another critical review.

Dieckmann[70] was a well-known expert on the German war economy during the first World War. Before he wrote several studies on Schlieffen's operational thinking, he had attracted interest with a number of articles about German war armament,[71] in cooperation with his brother-in-law, Otto Korfes, and as the editor of the armament volume of the official World War History.[72] Best known is Dieckmann's incomplete, undated, and unpublished study "Der Schlieffenplan,"[73] which had already been analyzed by Stig Förster in 1995[74] and used by Zuber as the central source for his theses. It totals 175 pages and consists of the two chapters "Die Operationspläne des grossen Generalstabes in der ersten Hälfte der 90er Jahre" (The Operational Plans of the Great General Staff during the First Half of the 1890s), and "Der Umgehungsplan" (The Envelopment Plan). The text and footnotes of the manuscript contain comments by an unknown editor, and the first forty-three pages include critical marginal notes by Foerster. As Zuber correctly notes, the third chapter, "Der Umfassungsplan" (The Envelopment Plan), listed in the table of contents, is important for the understanding of the Schlieffen Plan. That chapter, however, is missing, as are the maps and tables noted by Dieckmann in the text.

Although undated, it is possible with the help of individual bibliographical references to establish the year 1935 as the earliest feasible time for the completion of the manuscript. The marginal note, "Such a general opinion should be avoided—in particular today," with reference to Dieckmann's criticism of the political efforts to improve the relationship with Russia,[75] tentatively suggests that Dieckmann presented the first two chapters of his manuscript after the conclusion of the Hitler-Stalin Pact in 1939. This would also explain why Dieckmann was not able to complete his planned third chapter "Der Umfassungsplan" (The Envelopment Plan), since at the beginning of the Second World War all work on the First World War was stopped because of a shortage of personnel.[76]

Two issues that are very important for the assessment of the source and that have been totally neglected by Zuber have not yet been mentioned. Why did Dieckmann, a well-known expert on armament who had never served in the General Staff, write a paper about Schlieffen's operational planning? And which new insights into Schlieffen's operational thinking did Boetticher expect from his own research results?

Other manuscripts by Dieckmann on Schlieffen's military planning and operational plans kept among the current holdings of the Bundesarchiv/ Militärarchiv in Freiburg (RH61/W10 "Kriegsgeschichtliche Forschungsanstalt des Heeres") provide answers to these questions. Of particular significance are the incomplete and unpublished manuscript "Notizen und Material für eine Untersuchung über Graf Schlieffen und die Entwicklung des deutschen Heeres"[77] (Notes and Material for a Study on Count Schlieffen and the Development of the German Army), and the handwritten draft (in *Suetterlinschrift*—old German handwriting) of a paper by Dieckmann, "Einige Bemerkungen über die Entstehungsgeschichte des Schlieffenplans" (Some Remarks on the History of the Origins of the Schlieffen Plan).[78] The latter is stored with the same records as his manuscript, "Der Schlieffenplan." Neither manuscript is noted by Zuber.

This is surprising and somewhat incomprehensible considering that the handwritten study on the history of origins of the Schlieffen Plan, the research on the development of the German Army, and his study on the Schlieffen Plan are all linked to each other through handwritten classification marks on the first pages, probably made by Dieckmann himself.[79] These manuscripts, therefore, are connected to each other internally and must be considered together. The general idea connecting all three manuscripts is Dieckmann's thesis of the at least temporary influence of German foreign policy on Schlieffen's operational planning. The manuscript "Notizen und Material für eine Untersuchung über Graf Schlieffen und die Entwicklung des deutschen Heeres" is of particular interest to us. It is not just an extensive collection of notes and material, but is also an—unfortunately—incomplete work on Schlieffen's army and armaments policy, which, among other things, shows the influence of German foreign policy on Schlieffen's operational planning.[80] Because of the references in the footnotes, it is obvious that the incomplete collection of *Denkschriften* (memorandums) and reports on the development of the German Army, which is marked as an annex and stored together with Dieckmann's "Der Schlieffenplan" in RH61 (W10/50220), is directly connected to the manuscript.

Considering his expertise in the field of defense economics, it is little wonder that the Reich Archive tasked Dieckmann with a study on Schlieffen's defense and army policies. Instead, it is somewhat surprising that he developed during the course of his research new insights on the connection between the foreign policy of the Reich, on the one hand, and defense policy and war planning on the other. These insights were of such great interest to Boetticher that he included a copy of Dieckmann's collection of materials in his own records.[81] Since Boetticher completed his archival research in 1932, the collection of annexes and the manuscript can be dated to the time prior to 1932. As the notation already indicates, this study had been completed before Dieckmann's "Der Schlieffenplan." Boetticher's results can be considered a preliminary study, the new insights of which probably induced the directors of the Reich Archive to assign defense expert Dieckmann to study Schlieffen's operational planning, in addition to his other research on war armament.[82] Such an effort would be the actual domain of General Staff officers, but despite Dieckmann's lack of competence in operational issues, he was granted extensive access to the records—contrary to Zuber's contention.

On its own, Schlieffen's 1905 *Denkschrift für einen Krieg gegen Frankreich* stands only as an operational plan for a given war scenario, a typical function of the General Staff at that time. However, the *Denkschrift* only became an important aspect of relevant research—except for Zuber—when the assumption was made that its basic operational ideas of destroying the French Army with an envelopment by the German right flank while deliberately violating Belgian neutrality had been included in the *Aufmarschpläne* of the Great General Staff after 1906. The prevailing literature on the Schlieffen Plan,[83] including that by Zuber, again and again regrets the loss of Schlieffen's and his successor's *Aufmarschpläne*, especially since the Reich Army Archive had maintained a restrictive access and publication policy, thus keeping researchers and scholars in the dark about the contents and extent of the archived *Aufmarschpläne*.[84]

Did, however, the Reich Archive actually have the *Aufmarschpläne* from the service periods of Schlieffen or Moltke? And if the answer is yes, what did the Great General Staff understand by *Aufmarschplan*? The holdings catalog of the Reich Army Archive was probably destroyed,[85] but several statements by Foerster on the Schlieffen Plan give an indication. In his reply to Maurice Paléologue's[86] 1932 comments on the German invasion of Belgium, Foerster stated that the *Aufmarschplan* of the mobilization year 1904–1905 was not completely preserved in the Reich Archive; however, it would probably be possible to reconstruct it in essence from the still available remaining deployment records.[87] After the Second World War Foerster again confirmed the existence of the deployment records, from which the *Aufmarschpläne* would have resulted. He did not, however, indicate their dates. At that time, he also made it clear that the *Aufmarschplan,* in addition to maps, mobilization schedules, war orders of battle, etc., were only a small part of the much more extensive deployment records.[88]

According to General Erich Ludendorff, each numbered field army received a special deployment folder (*Aufmarschmappe*) containing transport lists for the deployment and the war order of battle of that army, as well as general instructions for the troops, information about enemy forces, and the allocation of the field army headquarters.[89] Although many important documents had been destroyed in accordance with prescribed General Staff procedures of the time, the Reich Archive/Army Archive according to Foerster possessed a large number of copies and deployment records from the period prior to the First World War. Not *all* of them were destroyed in 1945. The compilations of the *Aufmarschpläne* of the period from 1893–1994 to 1914–1915 previously had been kept at the Military Archive of the GDR. Since 1996, and not since 2002 as Zuber indicates,[90] those records have been held in the "Generalstab"[91] record group at the Bundesarchiv/Militärarchiv in Freiburg, where they are freely accessible to all interested users. When Zuber carried out his archival research, the copies of the deployment records as well as the only existing copy of Schlieffen's original 1905 *Denkschrift* and many other copies and originals of Schlieffen's operational planning records were stored among the holdings at Freiburg. Zuber apparently did not avail himself of those resources.

In his books and articles Zuber has been right to refer consistently to the importance of the records of the Kriegsgeschichtliche Forschungsanstalt, which he in part newly introduced into the discussion of the operational plans of the Great General Staff. He even translated several of those sources into English and edited them. Some of his comments, however, especially the one about his most important source, "Der Schlieffenplan" by Dieckmann, raise more questions than answers. Nor is it only Zuber's source criticism that leaves many questions unanswered. As his previous writings indicate, he neglected during his archival studies many documents that were available at the Bundesarchiv/Militärarchiv and that are of great importance and value for our topic.

II

In the following section I will subject Zuber's central thesis to a critical analysis on the basis of the sources as we now know them.

1. Zuber maintains that one of the reasons Schlieffen's *Denkschrift* of 1905 was not the German war plan is that it had not been securely stored at the General Staff, but rather kept among Schlieffen's personal papers until he died, when it became the property of his daughters.

Boetticher's writings refute this argument of Zuber's. According to Boetticher, the original *Denkschrift*, which Hahnke had handed to Moltke in February 1906, had been stored as a top secret document at the Great General Staff until the beginning of the war. After the war it was kept in the office of the president of the Reich Archive. Moltke, therefore, had been in possession of his predecessor's *Denkschrift*, and he even attached marginal notes shortly after he received it. However, he neither made the document known to his closest staff nor the war minister. Moltke had cogent reasons for doing so. The *Denkschrift* was based on the then current deployment plans of the year 1906–1907, and thanks to the intensive training and education by Schlieffen, it had become second nature of the leading members of the General Staff to operate according to the basic idea of the *Denkschrift*—in other words, the destruction of the French Army after an extensive envelopment of the French fortification system. Furthermore, because of the existing differences on operational issues[92] between Moltke and Schlieffen, the former could not be interested in making the *Denkschrift* public and binding himself to its details in the long term, all the more since he had not asked for the memorandum. Although Moltke basically shared Schlieffen's general idea concerning the establishment of a *Schwerpunkt* (main effort) in the west and the rapid destruction of the French Army after the envelopment of the French fortification system, he rejected the approach of a too dogmatic fixation on the envelopment with the involvement of Belgium.

Thus Moltke, now acting in Schlieffen's former position, wrote an order to the commanding generals in the field on 26 October 1905, which was signed by the kaiser. He agreed in general with the concept that the "combination of a frontal attack and envelopment" would be "the most certain way to achieve the objective." But then he went on to qualify that it would be necessary that "the enemy be held firmly at the front and thus fixed with the maximum possible strength. . . . Only then can the envelopment prove to be effective."[93] Significantly, Moltke did not inform Schlieffen about his modification of the concept, but the latter eventually learned of it. According to Hahnke, Schlieffen, who did not think much of Moltke's operational capabilities, was profoundly angry about dilution of the concept by his successor. "Count Schlieffen was beside himself with indignation at the sorry effort by his 'second-rate imitator.' Whereas Schlieffen wanted to inculcate the value of envelopment into the army, Moltke crushed that idea." Hahnke concluded, "This may explain Schlieffen's anger, even outrage at the capabilities of his successor. In all his writings about 1807 and 1813 and Cannae, Moltke's ideas at the time appeared to be in agreement with Schlieffen's." But Moltke's apparent change of mind now caused Schlieffen "anguish of mind for the future."[94] These statements indicate that Schlieffen felt defrauded of his lifework by Moltke, although the statements should be considered with a certain degree of reservation because of Hahnke's private relationship with Schlieffen. It stood to reason that Schlieffen wanted to explain personally to his successor in the form of a *Denkschrift* his basic operational ideas, which promised a victory over France.

2. Zuber argues that Schlieffen did not plan the great battle of annihilation. Instead, he merely wanted to ward off the expected French attack with focused counterattacks close to the border.

The last *Kriegsspiel* of December 1905 that Schlieffen commanded in person is used by Zuber as vital evidence for this argument. Although Schlieffen considered the scenario of a war between Austria-Hungary allied with Germany against a coalition of France, Russia, and Great Britain as highly improbable, that possibility is nonetheless very significant in relationship to the German deployment plans of 1914. Since Schlieffen considered it impossible for Germany alone to conduct simultaneous offensives on both the western and eastern fronts, he planned, according to Zuber, a strategic defensive on both fronts in order to defeat at first one and then the other aggressor with counterattacks within the shortest possible time.[95] Zuber thus considers the 1905 *Kriegsspiel* as the completion of Schlieffen's counterattack doctrine, which he developed initially in a *Denkschrift* of 1898[96] and continuously improved until the *Kriegsspiel* of 1905.[97]

Citing Dieckmann, Zuber argues that in his *Denkschrift* of 1898 Schlieffen had wanted to destroy any possible offensive by the French left wing through Luxembourg and Belgium with a counterattack on the French flank. This counterattack, however, was to be executed only in the event that the French attacked prior to the completion of the German deployment, because of France's more rapid mobilization.[98] Therefore, the German deployment was not to be moved too close to the French border.[99] In case of the expected success of the German counterattack, Schlieffen wanted to push the French Army back with a western envelopment of their fortification system and push them against the Upper Rhine.

What Zuber mentions only in passing is the fact that if the French did not attack, Schlieffen wanted to assume the offensive as soon as possible by enveloping the French fortification system through Luxembourg and Belgium.[100] In Zuber's opinion, however, the envelopment should not be too extensive since the German deployment was to serve a double purpose: 1. A counterattack if the French advanced as soon as their deployment was complete; or 2. An offensive if the French remained standing behind their fortifications.[101] This *Denkschrift* shows that Schlieffen kept open both the option of the counterattack and the offensive through Belgium and Luxembourg. However, it is impossible to understand how Zuber came to conclude upon the basis of this *Denkschrift* and Dieckmann's writing that since the time he wrote that *Denkschrift* Schlieffen preferred the counterattack option, and that the modified German *Aufmarschplan* of October 1899 had been based on a counterattack doctrine. Dieckmann clearly indicates that the two armies with eight army corps intended to make the envelopment attack had the same strength as in the previous year's plan and that "the two armies (Fourth and Fifth) intended for the attack on Nancy and the subsequent advance through the French fortification gap had been reinforced with [even] another army corps for a total of eight army corps and one reserve corps."[102] This can hardly be the foundation on which to base a counterattack doctrine. Rather, it is obvious that the chief of the German General Staff focused his operational planning on the anticipated enemy situation and reserved at least two very different options.

Zuber's other arguments, which he advances to support the development of a counterattack doctrine by Schlieffen, are likewise not convincing. His assertion is that the counterattacks Schlieffen had planned in the east to destroy the attacking Russian armies near the border were evidence that Schlieffen had developed a counterattack doctrine.[103] It does not, however, cover the whole issue. For Schlieffen as well as for the entire General Staff, it was a given that, considering their own numerical inferiority, the enemy attacks could only be countered by an offensive of maneuver on both the eastern and western fronts, relying on the German railway network and taking advantage of the local terrain. Consequently, Schlieffen planned to destroy the Russian attacking forces by attacking them himself. "If we want to wage war against France for months, we can hardly ignore the Russians. We cannot watch them march across the Vistula, Oder, and Elbe Rivers while we continue to wage war in France. This is absolutely impossible. If we cannot withdraw forces after the decision [against France], we must try to drive back the Russians at the beginning of the war."[104]

There are also examples for the western front—for example, the great

Ostaufmarsch of the mobilization year 1901–1902, during which Schlieffen abandoned the concept of an immediate offensive against the French Army in favor of counterattacks in recognition of the numerical inferiority of the German forces on the western front. "For the numerically inferior German Army in the west, it is . . . essential to organize its assembly as favorably as possible, i.e., in a way that it will be able to conduct a surprise attack on a wing or a flank of the enemy's army. For this purpose, it seems appropriate to leave the army corps initially in their garrisons and to start their deployment as soon as the direction of the enemy offensive is known."[105]

The examples mentioned clearly indicate that Schlieffen planned counterattacks only in situations of numerical inferiority when an offensive was not possible, because counterattacks were no guarantee for the quick destruction of the French Army, which was mandatory for his strategic plan. Only in case of an immediate large-scale attack by massive French forces did Schlieffen plan a one-off counteroffensive,[106] probably in the mobilization year of 1904–1905. However, as soon as he saw a chance for an offensive, counterattacks became for him the second-choice option only. This was in conformance with his basic conviction that it would not be advisable for the German armed forces to act defensively against the French Army. He nonetheless planned to be numerically superior at the *Schwerpunkt* (center of main effort). "However, we will have a chance to do so only if *we decide* [emphasis in the original] the operations, and not if we wait in a passive posture for whatever the enemy has decided for us."[107]

Since Zuber in support of his thesis cites only anticipated German counterattacks from a position of numerical inferiority as further evidence of a continuous development of a counterattack doctrine by Schlieffen, it is impossible to accept Zuber's assertion that "Henceforth the counter-offensive remained Schlieffen's preferred strategy: he would play it repeatedly in war games on both the west front and the east, culminating in his last great war game of November and December 1905."[108] The *Kriegsspiel* of 1905 was not the final point of a counterattack doctrine Schlieffen had developed since 1898, but one of many *Kriegsspiele* that Schlieffen used to train General Staff officers—as Foley correctly notes.[109] It is not only Schlieffen's explicit reference to the unrealistic scenario on which the *Kriegsspiel* is based,[110] but also his caveats about the use of *Kriegsspiele* that bring us to this conclusion. At the end of his *Schlussbesprechung* (final discussion) with his officers, the outgoing chief of the General Staff emphasized the importance of the *Kriegsspiele* for the training of future leaders and delivered a passionate plea for *Auftragstaktik* (mission-type command and control). Even if the young first lieutenants on the General Staff did not command field armies just then, they were the commanding generals of the future. They and all other subordinate leaders had to understand the ideas and *Absicht* (intent) of the senior field commanders and be able to execute them in an appropriate manner. It was important, therefore, to demand as many difficult and critical decisions as possible from them. Schlieffen considered the *Kriegsspiele* an important training tool for such a purpose. Even if it was imperfect, it offered the opportunity "to try to understand the situation of a large army and the tasks of an army corps operating in it, and to act in the spirit of the commander in chief and in the interest of the whole."[111] Schlieffen could not have expressed the importance of the *Kriegsspiele* for the operational training of General Staff officers more clearly.

As the chief of the General Staff, Schlieffen was responsible for the training and military education of the principal staff assistants of the General Staff in the same way as the regimental commander was responsible for the training of his officers. To ensure unity in analytical methodology, the obligatory prerequisite for *Auftragstaktik*, Schlieffen trained the General Staff officers in this spirit and according to his operational principles.[112] Although Schlieffen did not have any direct control on the selection and training of leaders outside the General Staff, he did have influence on the operational training of those officers through his control of the *Kriegsspiele* and the training areas used by the army corps.[113] It is not without reason that this aspect of Schlieffen's command activity was consistently emphasized after the First World War.[114]

Zuber, who perceives Schlieffen's *Kriegsspiele, Schlussaufgaben,* and *Generalstabsreisen* only as verification of operational planning, completely misjudges their use as training tools. He fails to understand the central task of the German officer as a trainer and instructor of his soldiers, and thus has not realized the importance of those functions for *Auftragstaktik* even today.

3. Zuber argues that in Schlieffen's exercises, German forces never exercised the western envelopment of Paris or battles on French territory. His map exercises always took place only in Lorraine or Belgium.[115]

This central thesis of Zuber's, which is intended to prove the defensive posture of Schlieffen's operational planning, is not tenable. During the map exercises of the *Generalstabsreise West* of 1905, Schlieffen himself commanded the German troops that advanced in a sweeping wheel of the right wing through Belgium and to the Lille-Maubeuge line, enveloping Verdun in the north, and crossing the Seine west of Paris near Rouen. This is documented in the summaries of Schlieffen's last *Generalstabsreise*, compiled by Boetticher with the support of Hahnke in the early 1930s on the basis of the available records in the Reich Archive. The summaries were included in Boetticher's papers, but Zuber apparently did not consider them.[116] Prior to the *Generalstabsreise*, all the senior quartermasters and division heads of the Great General Staff had been required to prepare for possible French countermeasures against a German attack on the left French wing. Among the four options provided by his staff, Schlieffen selected three possible French reactions that seemed plausible to him, and he had them played through. Those included: first, a French attack with all available forces in Alsace between Metz and Strassburg (Option Steuben); second, a French attack on both sides of Metz (Option Kuhl); and third, a French attack supported by Belgium with a prolonged and reinforced left wing west of the Moselle River (Option Freytag). The fourth suggestion by Colonel Matthiass—to regroup the French upon completion of their deployment and to reinforce the left French wing and expand it to Lille, while weakening the center and the right wing—was not considered for further analysis. The reason cited in the files was that this proposal was "contradictory to the national character of the French,"[117] or as Hahnke put it, Schlieffen did not want to embarrass Matthiass, whom he regarded highly.[118]

Neither explanation is convincing. One cannot help suspecting that Schlieffen deliberately excluded the defense option that was most dangerous to his attack. After Schlieffen had defeated all his opponents in a first run, he replayed the situations after conducting an in-process review. However, only the training sites of Option Kuhl II and Option Freytag II are of interest regarding our problem. Although Freytag and Kuhl drew the conclusions from the first run and moved their left flanks farther to the west—Freytag to the level of Lille—and reinforced them, they could not cope with Schlieffen's attack through Belgium. In both cases he outflanked the French troops with his strong right wing and advanced to French territory when they withdrew. In the case of Option Kuhl II, the French evaded to Langres, the Aube, and with their Third and Fourth Armies to the Seine. Thereupon, Schlieffen enveloped them even farther to the right, marched northwest past Paris, and crossed the Seine near Rouen with his Second and Third Armies. After all French counterattacks had failed, he defeated the remainder of the left French wing south of Paris.[119]

In the case of Option Freytag II, Schlieffen followed the retreating French along the east of Paris,[120] crossed the Marne, and cut the French Army off from Paris. Furthermore, he succeeded in forcing the French units to withdraw from the Seine, and pushed them against the Swiss border with a continuing envelopment by his right wing.[121] Although I do not intend to discuss here in detail Schlieffen's operational command and control, it must be noted that in these exercise tasks Schlieffen obviously played through multiple times the basic idea of his *Denkschrift* of 1905 against his best staff members.[122] Of particular note is the fact that the speed of the German advance was indicated in mobilization days. Thus in the case of Option Kuhl II, the Germans crossed the Seine near Rouen on the thirty-fourth mobilization day; in the case of Option Freytag II, Schlieffen succeeded in pushing the French Army toward the Swiss border by the fifty-sixth mobilization day.[123] Zuber's argument that in none of the exercises of the *Generalstabsreise West* of 1905 did German troops ever enter northern France, but that all decisive battles had been waged in Lorraine or Belgium,[124] is unfounded, the more so as it is based on an insufficient number of sources.

4. According to Zuber, Schlieffen's *Denkschrift* of 1905 was not the final point of his operational planning; instead, it only served as a reasonable basis for his intended expansion of the German Army.

This thesis is not new. Even the official military historiography of the Reich Archive regarded the *Denkschrift* as "a program for the further expansion of the army and its mobilization."[125] In the 1920s Walter Elze established: "The *Denkschrift* of 1905 cannot be regarded only as an operationally, but also an organizationally intended memorandum which pointed to a necessary but until now neglected increase of the army during peacetime required to implement the plan."[126]

Stig Förster, too, had already suggested that, in addition to operational planning, Schlieffen's *Denkschrift* included the request to his successor to try to accomplish an expansion of the army in materiel and personnel and to push the War Ministry to enforce universal conscription.[127] New only is Zuber's thesis that Schlieffen wrote his *Denkschrift exclusively* to justify the full enforcement of universal conscription. Zuber, however, does not provide any relevant conclusive evidence for this argument. Scholars do not dispute that during his entire term of office Schlieffen tried to increase the army's combat power through an increase in materiel and personnel. He actually achieved his goal of increasing the strength of the foot artillery units.[128] In many hagiographic writings of the 1920s and 1930s, this is cited as proof of the fact that Schlieffen had not only been an ingenious operational planner, but also the father of the pre–First World War German Army.[129] However, Dieckmann's manuscript "Der Schlieffenplan," which Zuber cites repeatedly to prove his operational thesis, and even more importantly, Dieckmann's study "Notizen und Material für eine Untersuchung über Graf Schlieffen und die Entwicklung des deutschen Heeres," which Zuber does not cite, indicate how much Schlieffen hesitated in pushing his armament expansion requirements with the War Ministry. While Dieckmann and his coauthors in the volume *Kriegsrüstung und Kriegswirtschaft* only hint at their incomprehension of Schlieffen's reserved manner in dealing with the war minister,[130] Dieckmann is more direct in "Der Schlieffenplan." He unmistakably criticizes Schlieffen's approach to the Defense Bill of 1899: "Schlieffen did indeed settle for the few expansion measures included in the defense bill without protest and even accepted that they, instead of being carried out in one step, ... would be implemented gradually."[131]

Although a considerable expansion of the army had been a prerequisite for his intended envelopment operation, Schlieffen, in contrast to his predecessors, showed a surprising deference toward the War Ministry. For example, he neither persistently demanded an increase in the army's personnel strength, nor tried to carry it out—although such was crucial to his operational plans.[132] Dieckmann even goes as far as accusing Schlieffen, in part, of isolating himself during his first years as chief of the General Staff and states that Schlieffen did not live up to his own principle that a commander in chief should not only lead his army to victory, he also should build and equip it.[133] Although Dieckmann emphasized Schlieffen's commitment from 1896 on to the expansion of the foot artillery and the reorganization and expansion of the army in the field, he often criticized Schlieffen's deferential attitude toward the War Ministry. As he characterized Schlieffen's conduct during the negotiations on the Army Bill: "This time Schlieffen again failed to try to convince the relevant authorities to take steps for the radical expansion of the army that would have met the military requirements obvious to him. Without raising any objections, he unconditionally settled for the measures proposed by the War Ministry."[134]

Shortly before his retirement, while probably already working on his *Denkschrift*, Schlieffen even accepted the statement of War Minister Karl von Einem that the development of the army had been completed.[135] Dieckmann presents the picture of a man who had acknowledged the deficiencies of the German Army in personnel and materiel, but was not ready to seriously discuss a solution with the War Ministry, which was responsible for providing the German ground forces with the necessary personnel and equipment. Nor was Schlieffen disposed to question the established procedures. As Ludendorff commented on this behavior, "Unfortunately [Schlieffen] had given up the fight without using his personal influence."[136] Or as Ritter wrote, "Strictly adhering to the traditional boundaries of his department, he repeatedly presented his wishes and demands—sometimes rather far-reaching—to the War Ministry. Sometimes he protested at being completely cut off from the consultations, however, he never claimed decisive influence on the Army Bills."[137] According to Zuber, however, at the end of his term in office Schlieffen suddenly demanded in his *Denkschrift* the complete enforcement of universal conscription and, thus, as Förster aptly notes, introduced not only a totally different German defense policy, but also a decisive change of systems, replacing the small army, which allegedly could be reliably used within the country, with a large one that was suitable for national defense but was probably less well-suited for domestic use.[138]

But why should Schlieffen have drafted a politically highly risky attack plan against France to justify his long-desired expansion of the army? And why especially at the end of his term in office, given that he had always avoided a conflict with the War Ministry, had pursued a hesitant defense policy, and had never overstepped the boundaries of his department before? Based on his experience with the War Ministry, did he really believe that he would be able to convince War Minister von Einem, whom he had never taken into his operational planning,[139] of an isolated operations plan against France in a military-strategic situation favorable to Germany? If this was the case, why did he give this *Denkschrift* only to his successor—of whose capabilities he was not convinced—and not to the War Minister and the kaiser, who would have been able to enforce an increase in personnel strength? Zuber does not provide us with answers to these questions.

5. The divisions necessary to carry out the offensive operations described in Schlieffen's *Denkschrift* of 1905 were not available. Zuber argues, therefore, the *Denkschrift* did not serve as a basis for the real plans of the General Staff.[140]

This thesis is not new either. In 1920 Kuhl had stated that the formation of eight replacement corps (*Ersatzkorps*) from replacement troops would be required for the offensive through Belgium.[141] Further, in the first volume of the Reich Archive's official history it was stated that the force strengths on which Schlieffen's operations plans had been based were not available.[142] Ludendorff too remarked laconically that the replacement and reserve corps earmarked by Schlieffen did not exist in 1905–1906.[143]

Doubts regarding the feasibility of the Schlieffen Plan were raised at an early stage because of the objective fact that the force strength was insufficient. Foerster tried to prove those doubts wrong, claiming that Schlieffen's operational plans had been based on the last *Aufmarschplan* for which he had personal responsibility, that of the mobilization year 1906–1907. But even Foerster had to concede that several reserve corps in that plan were only reinforced reserve divisions, and that in the event of mobilization it would have been very difficult to expand the necessary replacement corps from the regular, but poorly equipped, replacement units.[144] In his debate with Zuber, Terence Holmes noted Foerster's rationale and explained that after the beginning of the war the raising of the replacement units would have been generally possible until their intended commitment in Belgium or near Paris. Holmes is convinced that Schlieffen in his *Denkschrift* requested an immediate program for the mobilization of all available forces to execute his operational plans as soon as war broke out.[145]

Although Holmes's rationale seems to be conclusive in part, it is impossible to ignore that Schlieffen in his *Kriegsspiele* and exercise rides often used notional forces that existed only on paper. When several of his officers confessed that they did not understand his course of action, Schlieffen explained it thusly during the *Schlussbesprechung* (final discussion) of the first *Grosse Generalstabsreise* of 1904: "You, sirs, are probably wondering where the many German reserve corps come from. If we want to march through Belgium, we will be faced with many tasks: the occupation of Belgium, the screening of the Belgian fortifications, and the screening of the Netherlands. We also must hold back reserve forces to cover the flank when we enter France and then have to envelop the French fortifications. More reserve units, therefore, will have to be formed than previously, not using our imaginations, but in conformance with reality and in accordance with the principle that if you want to win you cannot be too strong."[146] However, these explanations by the chief of the General Staff did not convince the members of his closest staff since it was explicitly written in the initial Situation *Blau* (Blue) of the second *Grosse Generalstabsreise* of 1904: "The deployment of the German Army was conducted under the same conditions as the 1st ride. The reserve units have become weaker after doubts were raised as to whether or not it would be possible to establish them at the same strength as in the 1st ride."[147]

This episode clearly indicates two issues. On the one hand, during the exercises of the first *Grosse Generalstabsreise* of 1904 Schlieffen already had used nonexisting units. On the other hand, several of his General Staff officers criticized this as unrealistic and insisted on a more realistic German force estimate for the second *Generalstabsreise*. In consequence, instead of eighteen reserve corps with thirty-six reserve divisions, the assumption was now based on only twenty-three reserve divisions.[148] Although the number of reserve divisions had thus been much reduced, that level was still not equal to the actual strength of the German Army, since for the *Aufmarsch I* "Kriegszustand nur mit Frankreich" (State of War with France Only) fifteen reserve divisions were earmarked for the western and five for the eastern fronts in the mobilization year of 1904–1905.[149] It is without a doubt rather astonishing that in his *Kriegsspiele* Schlieffen was not very particular about the strength of the German armed forces. According to Dieckmann, however, Schlieffen had based his changed *Aufmarschpläne* from 1892–1893 to 1896, which provided for an attack on Nancy[150] supported by strong mortar and howitzer batteries, on an insufficient number of heavy batteries of foot artillery.[151] Foerster commented on these statements by Dieckmann with the following marginal notes: "But Schlieffen must have known that he did not have this many 21 cm mortars at his disposal."[152] And: "The question is raised then: How did Schlieffen intend to operate with insufficient foot artillery until the mobilization year of [18]96?"[153]

These astonished and almost incredulous marginal notes reveal that Schlieffen, to the surprise of Foerster, did not only play with unrealistic force strengths in his *Kriegsspiele,* but he also made a radical change in the center of gravity from the eastern to the western front, focusing on an attack on Nancy, despite the fact that he did not have the heavy artillery that he had formerly considered essential. In the end, Schlieffen had based his deployment plans of those years not always on the real materiel and personnel strengths but—at least at the beginning of his tenure—on his new operational ideas. He lacked, however, the means to achieve those ideas. Considering this fact, it is not surprising that in his *Denkschrift* of 1905 he used German forces that had not existed at that time.

Zuber's assertion, that the *Denkschrift* of 1905 could not have been a real war plan since the twenty-four divisions required to execute the attack plan projected in the *Denkschrift* were missing, does not then hold up. According to Holmes, it was possible—even if with great difficulty—to raise at least a few units after the beginning of the war. That, however, was not the first time that Schlieffen had planned his operations without a sufficient number of troops. In this context, we must consider an additional argument that has not been introduced into the discussion so far. Like his staff, Schlieffen was convinced that the excellent quality of the German troops and their leadership would make up for their inferiority in numbers. Furthermore, it is a fact that Schlieffen based the *Aufmarschplan* of the mobilization year of 1906–

1907—the last one under his responsibility—on the operational planning of his *Denkschrift*.[154]

6. Zuber claims that the campaign plan laid down in Schlieffen's *Denkschrift* of 1905 does not represent the culmination of his philosophy of operational art, but that it rather was an isolated aberration of his operational thinking.

Zuber's thesis, which is based mainly on his assessment of Dieckmann's "Der Schlieffenplan" manuscript and Schlieffen's selected *Kriegsspiele*, is unfounded. It is precisely this study that states that Schlieffen developed his operational planning on the basis of the estimate of the enemy situation and with regard to the political considerations in the direction of a large-scale, situation-oriented envelopment. Zuber should realize this very well. For very obvious reasons, however, he apparently only accepts those statements in Dieckmann's manuscript that fully support his assertions, while ignoring others that contradict his thesis with the hardly convincing justification that "Dieckmann's interpretation must be treated with caution, since he was looking for opportunities to show that Schlieffen wanted to 'make the right wing strong.'"[155]

As a consequence, Zuber fails to appreciate the fact that Dieckmann presents the picture of a chief of the General Staff who, in his *Denkschrift* of 2 August 1897, abandoned the idea of a breakthrough of the French fortification system and stated unmistakably that a German offensive against France would require a route on which it would have to overcome as few fortifications as possible. Having weighed all the options, the only solution for Schlieffen was a northern envelopment of Verdun. Since the narrowness of the approach between the Vosges and the Belgian-Luxembourg border prevented a broad deployment of the German Army, Schlieffen concluded, "an offensive which is to circumvent Verdun should not hesitate to violate the neutrality not only of Luxembourg, but also of Belgium."[156] The objectives of the German offensive were to attack the French rearward lines, to push the French Army away from Paris, and to destroy it.[157]

That was the first time Schlieffen had put into writing the idea of an envelopment of the French fortification system.[158] In 1897, however, there was as yet no question of a large-scale offensive enveloping Paris. The *Aufmarschpläne, Generalstabsreisen,* and *Kriegsspiele* of the years before 1904–1905 indicate that Schlieffen generally adhered to the envelopment idea, although he recognized its risks. His operational intentions, however, varied depending on the anticipated intentions of the French leadership, and he did not focus solely on large-scale envelopment. Thus, in 1902 when Schlieffen thought that the French knew the German envelopment plan and would prepare countermeasures, he decided to change his operational planning. During the mobilization year of 1902–1903, the German Army was to deploy much of its force—the Second to the Sixth Armies with eighteen army corps—directly to the Franco-Luxembourg border, and the First Army was to be used merely as a distant flank screen.

According to Dieckmann, Schlieffen intended to attack both Nancy and the front between Toul and Verdun. He wanted to destroy the expected French attack against the German northern flank with an envelopment operation by the right German wing armies. After that victory, the right German wing was to cross the Meuse downriver from Verdun and proceed against the rearward lines of the French Army.[159] Thus Schlieffen planned to combine the envelopment operation with a counterattack and a frontal assault.[160] Schlieffen also retained this basic idea for the deployment of the following year. The deployment of the mobilization year of 1904–1905, however, indicates a reinforced left and a weakened right wing that did not deploy too far to the north. That deployment enabled Schlieffen to conduct both a large counterattack in Lorraine and an offensive, supported by a frontal attack in Lorraine,[161] with the objective of a decisive battle in the Verdun region.[162] Both options are feasible and indicate that Schlieffen's operations planning was highly flexible. At that point, however, the chief of the German General Staff was not yet planning a deep offensive through Belgium.

That changed during the mobilization year 1905–1906. In contrast to the deployment of the previous year, it was now not only the First and Second Armies with eight army corps and six reserve divisions, but rather the First through Fifth Armies with seventeen army corps and two and a half reserve corps that deployed north of Diedenhofen to the Dutch border.[163] In his *Aufmarschpläne* Schlieffen had never before so directly focused on the right attack wing, which now conformed with the distribution of forces set forth in the *Denkschrift* of 1905. The chief of the General Staff had now decided against a mere northern envelopment of Verdun in favor of a large-scale envelopment by the German right wing to Lille through Belgium in the direction of Brussels. For the first time Schlieffen was determined to violate Dutch neutrality in the event of war.

Why did Schlieffen in 1904 change his previous operational planning and order an *Aufmarschplan* with such far-reaching political and serious operational risks? Although the answer to this question is of vital importance for the understanding of Schlieffen's *Denkschrift* of 1905, Zuber does not even raise it. At the same time, Greiner's study "Welche Nachrichten besass der deutsche Generalstab über Mobilmachung und Aufmarsch des französischen Heeres in den Jahren 1885–1914," which has been analyzed for the first time by Zuber, also refutes Ritter's formerly generally accepted thesis that Schlieffen had based his decision on military-technical considerations only.[164] According to Greiner, it was both political considerations and recent intelligence about the enemy's situation that led Schlieffen in late 1904 to substantially change the German deployment. Since the midsummer of 1904, the 3rd Department of the Great General Staff had been convinced that the deployment of the left French wing had been shifted to the north, and that a French offensive had become improbable because of the Russo-Japanese War. "A French offensive, which was still conceivable until 1904, seemed no longer probable considering the Russo-Japanese War. Rather, it could be assumed that at the onset of war the French would not immediately attack but would wait for the attack of the Germans in a marshaling area, probably behind their fortresses, obviously based on the assumption that the German right wing would circumvent the French fortress line in the north. A deployment rapidly shifted to the north seemed more favorable for such a marshaling than massing the main forces toward Alsace-Lorraine, as previously assumed."[165]

Based on this estimate of the enemy's situation, Schlieffen had to assume that without Russian support the French would no longer maintain a cautious offensive posture as had been previously expected. Rather, they would act defensively and would reinforce their left wing. Against this background, it is understandable why Schlieffen during the *Schlussbesprechung* of the first *Generalstabsreise* in 1904 questioned his own previously favored northern envelopment of Verdun to Mezières. He realized the danger that the German troops might not be able to force the French to withdraw from their fortified positions. Despite the disadvantages involved, including the violation of Dutch neutrality and the loss of surprise because of the long approach routes, Schlieffen for the first time considered an attack with the majority of the German Army on the less-fortified front of Verdun–Lille. Such a large-scale envelopment would enable the German units to envelop the French fortification system completely.[166] Considering that the French had introduced an extensive modernization program for their fortification system as a reaction to the changed strategic situation,[167] this was the *conditio sine qua non* in Schlieffen's operational planning for the years to come.

As we have seen, during the *Grosse Generalstabsreise West* of 1905, Schlieffen played through his new operational concept against his best General Staff officers. The positive results—according to his perspective—were reflected in the deployment planning for the mobilization year 1906–1907, the last one under his responsibility as chief of the Great General Staff.

Thus, Schlieffen again reinforced the right flank wheel for the *Aufmarsch West I*, the state of war with France only. The first operational objectives, with the First Army covering the right flank against Antwerp and the Second Army advancing toward Brussels, indicate the wide range of the envelopment operation by the German right wing as Schlieffen intended. Clearly, these orders do not allow for a different interpretation: "The entire army, except the Seventh Army, will turn left through Belgium. The left wing (Eighth Army) will operate near Metz to cover the left flank of the army, if necessary, in a reinforced position against Verdun."[168] This is not a deployment for a counterattack operation, but for a large-scale envelopment operation covering the whole of Belgian territory and a part of Dutch territory.

In his *Denkschrift* to his successor, Schlieffen supplemented his deployment and mobilization planning, which was binding on Moltke for the mobilization year 1906–1907, with farther-reaching and extensive recommendations for the conduct of the intended operations. Hence, Schlieffen's *Denkschrift* of 1905 was anything but an isolated aberration in his operational thinking. Instead, it contained guidance for similar current and future *Aufmarschplanungen*.

7. If Zuber is correct, the political dimension of warfare did not play a role in Schlieffen's operational planning.

Foley and Mombauer correctly criticize Zuber's analysis for completely ignoring the political background against which Schlieffen developed his operational planning. Zuber does not even hesitate to brush aside Dieckmann's comments about the interdependency of the military and political conditions on Schlieffen's operational planning, stating "Dieckmann's own opinions are generally uninteresting."[169] Zuber's Schlieffen is an apolitical military technocrat whose operational planning developed in a political vacuum. Interestingly, with this image of Schlieffen Zuber follows Ritter's tradition. In contrast to Zuber, however, Ritter discussed the possible political influence on Schlieffen's operational planning in detail before he concluded that Schlieffen "was a mere military technician, by no means a political head, and no war-fighter."[170]

Dieckmann's image of Schlieffen is in sharp contrast with that of an apolitical military technocrat. He argues that Schlieffen did base his operational planning on the respective political situation and he made general operational decisions based on requirements by the political leadership of the German Reich. Dieckmann, therefore, felt he was able to demonstrate that Schlieffen's change of the center of gravity from the eastern to the western front was based not only on military but also on serious political factors. Hence, the decision "to switch the center of gravity of the two-front war to the west and to open the campaign with a breakthrough attack against the French fortification line was to a lesser extent the result of Schlieffen's own initiative . . . but was rather influenced by Kaiser Wilhelm II himself,"[171] in order to facilitate an improvement of Russo-German relations.[172]

The development of the operational plans for the attack in the west was repeatedly influenced by political events. Considering the ongoing German-British alliance talks on the improvement of the German-British relationship, Wilhelm II decided in 1898 to expand the fortress of Metz into only a large-scale defensive bulwark, and not into a base for offensive operations as Schlieffen had wished. This very costly measure only made sense, according to Dieckmann,[173] if the Reich leadership was determined "to change the course of German foreign policy from Russia to England by responding to the English rapprochement efforts."[174] This thesis is supported by the fact that after the German-British relations had again deteriorated during the spring of 1899 Wilhelm II decided to expand the fortress of Metz as Schlieffen had recommended.

According to Dieckmann, Schlieffen also took into account the political intent of the Reich leadership concerning the issue of Belgian neutrality. Thus, Schlieffen's decision to advance through Belgium with the German right wing had been first and foremost a military one; "however, for such a politically important step, military considerations could not have been the only crucial factors. If that had been the case, the General Staff would not have had to take higher politics into account. Instead, they would have already based their operational plan, as we have seen, on the militarily sensible and promising concept of envelopment. Therefore, there must have been other political considerations which led Schlieffen to avoid no longer the idea of a violation of Belgian neutrality."[175] According to Dieckmann, this was because of the fact that since the late 1890s Schlieffen had fully expected Britain's opposition.[176] This assessment was probably based on his weekly background talks with the actual head of German foreign policy of those times, *Geheimrat* (Privy Councillor) Friedrich von Holstein.[177] Thanks to his talks with Holstein, Schlieffen was very well informed about the intentions of German foreign policy.[178] His operational planning, therefore, was based in part on his own estimate of the enemy situation and to a considerable extent on the assessment of the foreign policy situation of the German Reich as provided by the senior officials of the Foreign Office. According to Dieckmann, Schlieffen therefore responded immediately to the British-German rapprochement efforts of late 1901, and in his *Aufmarschplan* for the mobilization year of 1902–1903 he eliminated the passage through Belgium, only to reinclude it in his *Aufmarschplan* for the mobilization year of 1903–1904 immediately after the negotiations had broken down.[179] Unfortunately, the relevant surviving documents do not include Dieckmann's chapter on the Schlieffen Plan. Merely the outline is available.

Mombauer concludes from the chapter headings "Die grosse Chance" and "Bülows Sieg über Schlieffen" that in 1905 Schlieffen had demanded a preemptive war, which Bülow had opposed. According to Mombauer and Foley, Schlieffen during the First Morocco Crisis had been one of the greatest advocates of a preemptive war against France.[180] However, Dieckmann did not share this interpretation. In his statement of 1932 "Hat Graf Schlieffen während der ersten Marokkokrise 1905 den Präventivkrieg gegen Frankreich gefordert?," written in response to an enquiry by Professor Hermann Oncken, he expressly noted with a certain degree of regret that the chief of the General Staff had at no time advocated a preemptive war.[181] Considering this statement, the interpretation seems to suggest that Dieckmann was convinced Schlieffen did not make use of the great opportunity of the year 1905 to bring about a preemptive war, since he willingly acquiesced to the primacy of policy, to the disadvantage of the Reich.

From today's perspective, it is impossible to establish conclusively whether during his tenure as chief of the Great General Staff Schlieffen had urged the Reich leadership to conduct a preemptive war against France.[182] There is every reason to believe that in general Schlieffen was prepared to conduct a preemptive war. In contrast to his predecessors and his successor, however, he did not openly demand it from the Reich's political leadership. Instead he provided his estimate of the situation, "Russia is bound in the East. England is still weakened as a result of the Boer War. France is behind in its armaments," unambiguously only upon the Reich chancellor's request. This is obvious from Hahnke's description of the meeting of the Council of State of 1905, and subsequently implemented as a resolution: "Sooner or later the German Reich must prove its qualifications [to being a Great Power] through a war. Now is the most favorable time. My solution: War against France."[183] This position was in conformance with Schlieffen's ideas, and Schlieffen characterized himself as the senior official of the Reich.[184] And as the chief of the Great General Staff, he was very particular that the departmental boundaries within the administration were not crossed.

The political dimension of warfare did indeed play a role in Schlieffen's operational planning. Schlieffen was, therefore, not an apolitical general who was exclusively focused on operational warfare—as argued by Ritter, Wallach, and Zuber—but a chief of the General Staff who aligned his operations plans with both the military necessities and the political situation.

III

With his thesis, "There never was a Schlieffen Plan," Zuber courageously advanced a provocative theory and initiated a scholarly debate about the operational plans of the German General Staff prior to the First World War. Although his theories were based on newly found sources, his selection from the wealth of available material was biased and his interpretations were one-sided. Additional records available in German archives do not support his central theories, but instead contradict his views on central points. From the analysis of the *Kriegsspiele* and *Generalstabsreisen* Zuber is well able to prove that the operational planning of the Great General Staff was more flexible than previously assumed. However, by restricting himself to the operational aspects, Zuber does not do justice to the complexity of Schlieffen's strategy, all the more so since he completely disregards the political environment in which the German chiefs of the General Staff operated. To clarify this complexity, it is necessary to examine the general strategic classification of the German operations plans prior to the First World War.

Since the unification of the Reich in 1871, the Great General Staff, proceeding from the central geographic position of the Reich, had studied the issue: Is it possible to win a two-front war? And, if so, how is it to be conducted?

In case of a two-front war, Moltke the Elder and Waldersee planned to divide the German armed forces between the eastern and western fronts, conduct a mobile defense against France based on the German fortifications, and conduct regional offensive actions against Russia in coordination with allied Austria-Hungary. This defensive strategy, combined with limited offensive thrusts, was not aimed at a total victory through a battle of annihilation.[185] During the tenures of Moltke the Elder and Waldersee, the consideration of a two-front war—with the exception of the crisis of 1887–1888, when they specifically urged a war against Russia—was a rather theoretical issue. For Schlieffen and Moltke the Younger, on the other hand, it was a real issue because of the political and military developments. In contrast to Moltke the Elder (who had always been able to plan his wars based on a superiority in personnel and materiel and excellent political support by Bismarck), Schlieffen and Moltke the Younger had to plan a two-front war based on numerical inferiority and completely different political and military situations.

Shortly after he assumed office in 1891, Schlieffen came out of the shadows of his powerful predecessor and developed his own operational-strategic concept for a two-front war. For him, the only possible solution to avoid a lengthy war of attrition, which in his opinion was impossible to win, was an offensive. In this context, it was necessary to consider the political environment, space, time, and the military capacities of his own forces and those of the enemy.

During the after-action analysis of the *Generalstabsreise Ost* in 1901, Schlieffen announced his strategic and operational credo based on those determining factors. "Germany has the advantage of being located in the middle between France and Russia and dividing those allies from each other. Yet it would give up that advantage as soon as it should split up its army, which would leave it outnumbered by each of its enemies. Therefore, Germany must be determined to defeat the one while the other is only tied down. But afterward, when the one opponent is defeated, [Germany] must bring about a superiority in numbers in the other theater using the railway, which will be pernicious to the other enemy as well. . . . The first strike must be carried out with full force, and a truly decisive battle must be conducted."[186] Schlieffen's operational and strategic credo does not leave any space for deviating ideas; instead it proclaims the—in his opinion—inviolable assumptions of the German Army's ability to wage a two-front war. Schlieffen's solution for the strategic dilemma of the Reich was therefore both simple and convincing: To use internal lines to split the two-front war into two successive one-front wars with superiority at the respective locations.

To execute this strategy, one of the two opponents had to be defeated decisively and, above all, very quickly. This could be achieved only through offensive and not defensive actions. In addition to offensive operations, it required that the units received tactical-level offensive training, which is exactly what the German Army did.[187] Because of the rapid speed of French mobilization, combined with a lack of operational depth in their defensive area, Schlieffen decided to attack France first. From the very beginning, the planned operation was under extreme time pressure. If the French were not decisively defeated before the Russian Army began to attack, it would spell disaster. Over the course of time the rapid decisive battle became the focus of Schlieffen's operational thinking. A balance with one of the main opponents, if possible Russia, was his strategic focus. But what would be the course of action if the French remained in their fortifications and played for time? What if the Russians mobilized more rapidly than anticipated?

For Schlieffen, there was only one answer to those questions. He had to force the French into a decisive battle. Since he did not think that it would be possible to achieve a frontal breakthrough of the French fortifications because of their strength and the time pressures, he decided to circumvent the cordon of fortifications, marching through Belgium, the Netherlands, and Luxembourg and to envelop and destroy the French Army with a strong German right attack wing. This complete determination to execute an envelopment in order to execute a destructive battle, was, without doubt, the second cornerstone of Schlieffen's operational thinking.

However, Schlieffen's operational plans were far less dogmatic than previously thought. Political considerations certainly influenced part of his assessment of the situation. At times, such as when the center of gravity shifted from east to west, the considerations and decisions of the Reich leadership concerning a rapprochement with Russia or Great Britain were directly reflected in his operations planning. With his flexible operational planning, which Zuber correctly notes, Schlieffen responded immediately when the enemy situation changed. This can be seen clearly both in the decision made against the background of the Russo-Japanese War and the decisions he made when the intelligence on the enemy situation available to him indicated that the French Army (in contrast to previous assessments) would not attack. Based on that scenario, in the case of a war against France, the German right wing would envelop the French fortification system on a large scale, violating the neutrality of Belgium, the Netherlands, and Luxembourg, and thereby destroy the French Army. Schlieffen's operational objective, therefore, was the rapid destruction of the French Army in a one-front war, since he could not know whether and when Russia or Great Britain would enter the war to support France. Nonetheless, Schlieffen maintained a high degree of flexibility in the course of the intended envelopment. As soon as the French fortification system had been bypassed, he could envision the decisive battle of destruction (*Vernichtungsschlacht*) taking place at various locations in western France.

The western envelopment of Paris, which every schoolbook today notes as a dogmatic cornerstone of the Schlieffen Plan, was the worst-case option for Schlieffen. He surely did not wish for it because of the personnel strength of the German forces. Nonetheless, he played the option through with his best officers in order to be able to execute it if necessary. His last *Aufmarschanweisungen* for the mobilization year of 1906–1907 were based on his operational considerations for the *Aufmarsch I* war against France. He summarized his instructions in his *Denkschrift* of 1905 as a future benchmark for his successor, who did not share his views on many operational issues. In addition to Schlieffen's operational principles, the *Denkschrift* also included the indirect request to Moltke—as something of an appendix—to get approval from the War Ministry for the field expansion of the Metz fortress and an increase in the German Army's overall personnel strength. But since Schlieffen lacked the ability to assert himself in the disputes among the departments of the Reich government, he failed on both counts. Against the political background of 1905, the difficulty of accomplishing those objectives in the immediate future was inevitable.

During his tenure in office Schlieffen wrote only a few *Denkschriften*. Why did he choose this medium and give Moltke a *Denkschrift* summarizing his basic operational ideas after his retirement? Thanks to the writings of the Schlieffen School in the 1920s and 1930s, the Great General Staff under Schlieffen until recently has often been considered a monolithically thinking and planning organization, subjecting itself to the will of its chief without discussion. But is this really true? Could it be that there had been no differing factions and divergent operational-strategic concepts in the General Staff? Answering this question would clarify many open questions about the functioning of the Great General Staff. The *Schlussbesprechung* of the *Grosse Generalstabsreise West* of 1904 indicates that during the last years of Schlieffen's tenure his operational planning had indeed been criticized internally, which in turn affected the further exercises conducted by the chief of the General Staff. This criticism centered on Moltke the Younger, who—at least from Schlieffen's subjective point of view—had been forced on him. It is possible that Moltke was surrounded by a group of ambitious General Staff officers who at least indirectly challenged Schlieffen's claim to leadership, which he did not want to relinquish. This was not an uncommon phenomenon during an imminent change in office. After Schlieffen's successor had been designated, many young General Staff officers considered the seventy-two-year-old outgoing chief of the General Staff to be a lame duck. Schlieffen, like all those affected by relinquishing a powerful office, was fully aware of this fact. What would be more suitable from Schlieffen's point of view than to remind his successor of his own vital basic operational ideas, to present his own position clearly for the record, and to preserve his life's work?

Schlieffen was right. Although in the subsequent years Moltke adhered to the basic principles of Schlieffen's operational planning, his marginal notes on the *Denkschrift* show that two premises of the intended large-scale envelopment did not convince him. Moltke doubted the French would conduct defensive operations as Schlieffen assumed, but did not exclude the probability of a lengthy war.[188] Moltke's reservations about Schlieffen's planning were so strong that as early as the mobilization year of 1908–1909[189] he abandoned the violation of the neutrality of the Netherlands, and thus the passage through Dutch territory. Mombauer has shown clearly with the help of the *Aufmarschplanungen* that Moltke considered the Netherlands the economic lifeline of the Reich in the event of war.[190] Consequently, Moltke since that time focused his operational considerations on a rapid occupation of the fortification and railway junction at Liège. In order to continue to conform to what in his opinion was the correct western offensive, he decided from the mobilization year of 1909–1910 on in favor of the very risky coup de main on Liège.[191]

This, however, put the German operations under even more time pressure and prevented virtually any opportunity for a political solution in case of war. The astonishingly rapid regeneration of the Russian Army following the Russo-Japanese War increased the danger of a two-front war in Moltke's opinion. Nevertheless, he continued to focus on the west. In contrast to Schlieffen, however, he ruled out the possibility that German eastern territory would be given up completely. When the General Staff received increasing intelligence indicators that in case of war the French Army would immediately mount a large-scale offensive[192] in Lorraine, Moltke saw confirmation of his skepticism toward Schlieffen's planning. After consulting his key staff members, he increased the German forces in Alsace-Lorraine beginning in the mobilization year of 1909–1910. It was a region he was not prepared to give up. During the mobilization year 1913–1914, the five armies of the right attack wing with their seventeen army corps and nine reserve corps were opposed to the two French armies with six army corps and two reserve corps of France's left wing.[193] In case of a massive French attack into Lorraine, Moltke was prepared to abandon the envelopment through Belgium, since the rapid destruction of the French Army seemed to be ensured nevertheless.[194] That was an option that Schlieffen had also considered, at least briefly, as a response to an immediate French offensive.

Moltke did not inform his predecessor of these changes. Neither he nor any of his staff members sought advice from Schlieffen after the latter retired—a fact that annoyed him greatly.[195] While Moltke severed all professional ties with his predecessor, he did inform the Reich government of his operations plans.[196] And in contrast to Schlieffen, he notified even the war minister of his war plan in order to ensure the meeting of his personnel requirements across departmental lines.[197] Although Moltke the Younger was not given the personnel increases that in his opinion were urgently needed, he was, like his predecessor, convinced that the higher quality of German troops would make up for most of the numerical deficiency.

Since 1905 the strategic situation had changed to the disadvantage of the German Reich. While in 1906 the only possible option had been a war against France, on the eve of the First World War Moltke assumed that the opponents would be France, Russia, and Great Britain. Schlieffen's successor had continually adapted German operational planning to develop the situation based on his assessment of the enemy. Moltke's operations plan against France differed in essential elements from that of his predecessor, particularly the reinforcement of the German left wing, the abandoning of the march through Holland, and a rapid conquest of Liège. Thus in 1914, the German soldiers did not enter the field with a Schlieffen Plan, but rather with a Moltke Plan.[198]

Despite those operational changes, Moltke adhered to the basic principles on the conduct of a two-front war as developed by Schlieffen:

1. To pursue war not in a defensive and reactive manner, but to take the offensive and wage warfare based on the initiative.
2. To use the interior lines to divide the two-front war into two one-front wars, which are then waged in sequence.
3. To establish a center of gravity through an offensive in the west and delay in the east.
4. To conduct a rapid battle of destruction with the strong right wing after a successful passage through Luxembourg and Belgian territories and the envelopment of the French fortification system. (Exception: French large-scale attack against Alsace-Lorraine)
5. After the victory, to transport the preponderance of the victorious units to the eastern front using the railway and then to defeat the enemy that had been delayed.

However, it was an indispensable prerequisite of this strategic doctrine that the initial enemy had to be rapidly annihilated in a truly decisive battle. Therefore, the time factor hung over all those plans like the sword of Damocles. The operational planning involved a very high risk factor and by no means ensured victory; rather, it was more of an emergency solution. The alternative of informing the Reich government of the hopelessness of a two-front war and thus inducing it to change its foreign policy was inconceivable because of the German General Staff's own image of itself. Doing so would have thrown into question the position of the army in the structure of the Reich. Since neither Schlieffen nor Moltke was ready to admit defeat in military matters, they decided not to untie the Gordian Knot of the two-front war through defensive means, but to cut it with an offensive.

Thus, the basic operational-strategic doctrine developed by Schlieffen—a Schlieffen Plan—did exist. His successor strictly adhered to it despite making some operational changes. That plan was even applied by the Wehrmacht in a modified form during the Second World War. However, it was not a defensive doctrine, as argued by Terence Zuber.

Notes

1. Terence Zuber, *Inventing the Schlieffen Plan: German War Planning 1871–1914* (Oxford, 2003), 5, 219.

2. Cf. Terence Zuber, "The Schlieffen Plan Reconsidered," *War in History* 6, no. 3 (1999): 262–305; Terence Holmes, "The Reluctant March on Paris: A Reply to Terence Zuber's 'The Schlieffen Plan Reconsidered,'" *War in History* 8, no. 2 (2001): 208–232; Terence Zuber, "Terence Holmes Reinvents the Schlieffen Plan," *War in History* 8, no. 4 (2001): 468–476; Antulio J. Echevarria II, "An Infamous Legacy: Schlieffen's Military Theories Revisited," *Army History* 53 (2001): 1–8; Terence Holmes, "The Real Thing: A Reply to Terence Zuber's 'Terence Holmes Reinvents the Schlieffen Plan,'" *War in History* 9, no. 1 (2002): 111–120; Terence Zuber, "Terence Holmes Reinvents the Schlieffen Plan—Again," *War in History* 10, no. 1 (2003): 92–101; Robert T. Foley, "The Origins of the Schlieffen Plan," *War in History* 10, no. 2 (2003): 222–232; Terence Holmes, "Asking Schlieffen: A Further Reply to Terence Zuber," *War in History* 10, no. 4 (2003): 464–479; Terence Zuber, "The Schlieffen Plan Was an Orphan," *War in History* 11, no. 2 (2004): 220–225; Annika Mombauer, "Of War Plans and War Guilt: The Debate Surrounding the Schlieffen Plan," *Journal of Strategic Studies* 28, no. 5 (2005): 857–858; Robert T. Foley, "Debate: The Real Schlieffen Plan," *War in History* 13 (2006): 91–115.

3. Gerhard Ritter, *Der Schlieffenplan: Kritik eines Mythos* (Munich, 1956).

4. Zuber justifies this as follows: "The first sheet in the 'Schlieffen Plan' file N 43/137 at the Bundesarchiv/Militärarchiv proudly announces in a beautiful feminine hand that the plan is *Eigentum von Elisabeth von Hahnke geb. Gräfin Schlieffen und Gräfin Maria Schlieffen. . . .*" Cf. Zuber, *Inventing the Schlieffen Plan*, 45, note 69.

5. ". . . Schlieffen's operational thought was moving in the direction of the use of rail mobility to launch surprise counteroffensives to encircle and destroy the enemy on or near friendly territory, and toward deep penetration into enemy territory." Zuber, *Inventing the Schlieffen Plan*, 219.

6. "The German troops fought only in Belgium or Lorraine: they never entered

France at all" (Zuber, "Terence Holmes Reinvents the Schlieffen Plan," 471) and "The goal was not to sweep around to the west of Paris but to defeat the French army in battles near the frontier and then to break the French fortress line" (Zuber, "The Schlieffen Plan Reconsidered," 280); Terence Zuber, "Der Mythos vom Schlieffenplan," in *Der Schlieffenplan: Analysen und Dokumente*, ed. Hans Ehlert, Michael Epkenhans, and Gerhard P. Gross (Paderborn, 2006), 45-78.

7. "The point was not to develop a radically new scheme of maneuver, but to readdress the issue which Schlieffen had felt throughout his career to be the most serious problem facing the German Army: Germany's failure to utilize exhaustively either trained manpower or her total available manpower" (Zuber, *Inventing the Schlieffen Plan*, 213-214).

8. "Non-existent units can hardly be used in a war plan. For this reason alone, the Schlieffen plan could have been an exercise or a policy paper, but not a war plan" (Zuber, *Inventing the Schlieffen Plan*, 197).

9. "Most important, there is practically nothing in this manuscript to support the contention that the Schlieffen Plan *Denkschrift* was the culmination of Schlieffen's strategic thought. In fact, it demonstrates that this *Denkschrift* was an isolated aberration" (Zuber, "The Schlieffen Plan Reconsidered," 285).

10. Cf. Wolfgang Foerster, "Hat es eine Schlieffenplan-Legende gegeben?," *Wehrwissenschaftliche Rundschau* (1952): 601.

11. Cf. Zuber, *Inventing the Schlieffen Plan*, 5; Zuber, "Der Mythos vom Schlieffenplan," 45-78.

12. Wilhelm Dieckmann, "Der Schlieffenplan," BA/MA, RH 61/347 (W10/50220), f. 48-226.

13. Helmuth Greiner, "Welche Nachrichten besass der deutsche Generalstab über Mobilmachung und Aufmarsch des französischen Heeres in den Jahren 1885-1914: Wie wurden sie ausgewertet, und wie lagen die tatsächlichen Verhältnisse?," BA/MA, RH 61/398 (W10/50267), f. 1-157.

14. Cf. Helmut Otto, *Schlieffen und der Generalstab: Der preussisch-deutsche Generalstab unter der Leitung des Generals von Schlieffen 1891-1905*, Militärhistorische Studien 8, neue Folge (Berlin, 1966), 38-53.

15. In the following, the German Army is understood as the contingent army of the German Empire.

16. Cf. Wilhelm Groener, *Lebenserinnerungen: Jugend, Generalstab, Weltkrieg*, ed. Friedrich Freiherr Hiller von Gaertingen, Deutsche Geschichtsquellen des 19. und 20. Jahrhunderts, 41 (Göttingen, 1957), 72.

17. On the work routine in the General Staff, cf. Groener, *Lebenserinnerungen*, 70-74; Erich Ludendorff, *Mein militärischer Werdegang: Blätter der Erinnerung an unser stolzes Heer* (München, 1924), 73-74, 93-95; Hermann von Staabs, "Aufmarsch nach zwei Fronten: Auf Grund der Operationspläne von 1871-1914," *Militär-Wochenblatt* (Berlin, 1925), 24-25.

18. On this, cf. Annika Mombauer, *Helmuth von Moltke and the Origins of the*

First World War (Cambridge, 2001), 39–40; Ludendorff, *Mein militärischer Werdegang*, 74.

19. Cf. "Mobilmachungsplan für das Deutsche Heer," 9 October 1913 (D.V.E. Nr. 219) (Berlin, 1913), 33, sec. 17.

20. Cf. Foerster, "Hat es eine Schlieffenplan-Legende gegeben?," 601–605, here pages 602–604.

21. Cf. Ritter, *Der Schlieffenplan*, 8.

22. *Nach Angaben in dem Inventar archivalischer Quellen des NS-Staates: Die Überlieferung von Behörden und Einrichtungen des Reichs, der Länder und der NSDAP*, vol. 2, *Regionale Behörden und wissenschaftliche Hochschulen für die fünf ostdeutschen Länder, die ehemaligen preussischen Ostprovinzen und eingegliederte Gebiete in Polen, Österreich und der Tschechischen Republik mit Nachträgen zu Teil 1.* (Munich, 1995) (Texte und Materialien zur Zeitgeschichte, vol. 3, part 2). This is kept at the Special Archive Moscow under Fond 545 Kriegsgeschichtliche Forschungsanstalt des Heeres and under Fond 1256 as well as 1275 on the Chef der Heeresarchive Nachlass- und Aktenverzeichnisse sowie Bestandsübersichten des Reichs/Heeresarchivs, 271–272.

23. After the end of World War II, this resulted in the accusation of secretiveness. See Peter Rassow, "Schlieffen und Holstein," *Historische Zeitschrift* 173 (1952): 297–313, here 301.

24. Cf. *Der Weltkrieg 1914–1918*, vol. 1, *Die Grenzschlachten im Westen*, ed. Reichsarchiv (Berlin, 1925), 9–13.

25. For example, Wolfgang Foerster, *Aus der Gedankenwerkstatt des Deutschen Generalstabes* (Berlin, 1931); Wolfgang Foerster, *Graf Schlieffen und der Weltkrieg* (Berlin, 1921); Wilhelm Groener, *Das Testament des Grafen Schlieffen: Operative Studien über den Weltkrieg*, 2nd ed. (Berlin, 1929); Hermann von Kuhl, *Der deutsche Generalstab in Vorbereitung und Durchführung des Weltkrieges* (Berlin, 1920).

26. Generalstab des Heeres, ed., *Generalfeldmarschall Graf von Schlieffen, Dienstschriften*, vol. 1, *Die taktisch-strategischen Aufgaben aus den Jahren 1891–1905* (Berlin, 1937); Generalstab des Heeres, ed., *Generalfeldmarschall Graf von Schlieffen, Dienstschriften*, vol. 2, *Die Grossen Generalstabsreisen—Ost—aus den Jahren 1891–1905* (Berlin, 1938).

27. Cf. Foerster, "Hat es eine Schlieffenplan-Legende gegeben?," 602.

28. On the history of the Reich Archive/Army Archive and its destruction, see Helmut Otto, "Das ehemalige Reichsarchiv: Streiflichter seiner Geschichte und der wissenschaftlichen Aufarbeitung des Ersten Weltkrieges," in *Potsdam, Staat, Armee, Residenz*, ed. Bernhard R. Kroener (Frankfurt/Main, Berlin, 1993), 421–434.

29. Today, the preserved files of the Great General Staff are kept in record group PH 3 of the Federal Achive/Military Archive (BA/MA).

30. During the First World War, Friedrich von Boetticher (1881–1967) was a General Staff officer assigned to the Railway Department (*Eisenbahnabteilung*). After several assignments in the Reich Ministry of Defense, he was commander of the Artillery School in Jüterbog from 1929 to 1933. From 1933 until the end of the war in

1945 he served as military attaché at the embassy in Washington, and between 1938 and 1945 he simultaneously served at the German Mission in Mexico. From 1942 to 1945 he was general on special duty at the Wehrmacht High Command. Owing to his assignment in the Field Railway Department of the General Staff, he maintained good relations with Groener. His papers are archived under the record group number N 323 at the Federal Archive/Military Archive (Bundesarchiv/Militärarchiv); it is accessible to all. The record group comprises 4.1 linear meters. The information provided by the Federal Archive's Central Database on personal papers refers to the contents as follows: "Denkschriften Wilhelm Groeners; Auszüge aus Dienstschriften und Privatunterlagen des Generalfeldmarschalls Graf Alfred von Schlieffen, Korrespondenz zu militärgeschichtlichen Fragen," www.bundesarchiv.de/zdn (19 August 2005).

31. Cf. "Boetticher an Frauendienst," Bielfeld 30 May 1957, BA/MA, Nachlass Boetticher, N 323/52. Cf. also Anschreiben des Reichswehrministers (Letter of the Reich Defense Minister), 23 January 1931, BA/MA, Nachlass Boetticher, N 323/49.

32. Friedrich von Boetticher, *Der Kampf gegen die Übermacht* (Berlin, 1926); Friedrich von Boetticher, "Graf Schlieffen als Lehrmeister und Wegweiser," *Wissen und Wehr* 14 (1933): 71–83; Friedrich von Boetticher, *Graf Alfred Schlieffen: Sein Werden und Wirken* (Berlin, 1933).

33. Friedrich von Boetticher, "Der Lehrmeister des neuzeitlichen Krieges," in *Von Scharnhorst zu Schlieffen 1806–1906: Hundert Jahre preussisch-deutscher Generalstab*, ed. Friedrich von Cochenhausen (Berlin, 1933), 249–319.

34. Friedrich von Cochenhausen, ed., *Von Scharnhorst zu Schlieffen 1806–1906: Hundert Jahre preussisch-deutscher Generalstab* (Berlin, 1933), was published at the instigation of the Reich Defense Ministry.

35. The Reich Archive tried to put off Boetticher, claiming that the material had not yet been organized and could therefore not be given to him. However, thanks to the support by Groener, Boetticher asserted his request and was granted access to the documents he wanted to inspect. Boetticher to Hahnke, 19 October 1931, BA/MA, Nachlass Boetticher, N 323/53.

36. In accordance with Boetticher's file lists, the Reich Archive kept all *Kriegsspiele* (war games) of Schlieffen and Moltke the Younger except for the *Kriegsspiele* of 1891, 1892, 1894, and 1895, a large number of Schlieffen's operational studies, in particular those of the years 1904 and 1905, as well as the documents on all *Grosse Generalstabsreisen* (Great General Staff rides) of the years 1891 to 1914 (BA/MA, Nachlass Boetticher, N 323, not dated, Index of file pages of the Central Department of the former Great General Staff, which had been transferred to the Reich Archive). Furthermore, another file index (BA/MA, Nachlass Boetticher, N 323, undated) proves that numerous *Denkschriften* and operational studies of Schlieffen were kept in the Reich Archive (for example, Schlieffen's *Denkschrift* of April 1891 about a War of the Triple Alliance against France and Russia). They were used by Foerster and others in relevant works as evidence for their theories.

37. Hahnke provided Boetticher with records about several extensive *Gener-*

alstabsreisen of Schlieffen, the *Schlussaufgabe* and other *Chefaufgaben* of the Great General Staff, and several studies and *Denkschriften* of Schlieffen (for example, about the German and French infantries), as well as private letters of his father-in-law (BA/MA, Nachlass Boetticher, N 323/53, Aktenverzeichnis undated). Boetticher's records also show that in the early 1930s the ownership issues regarding part of Schlieffen's records were not clarified between the Reich Archive and Schlieffen's heirs.

38. See Friedrich von Boetticher, *Schlieffen: Viel leisten, wenig hervortreten—mehr sein als scheinen,* Persönlichkeit und Geschichte, 7 (Göttingen, Berlin, Frankfurt/Main, 1957), 5.

39. Grosse Reise 1905, BA/MA, Nachlass Boetticher, N 323/9. In addition to the postmortem session of 17 July 1905, this file contains several summaries and maps of the exercises carried out during the staff ride. Those records had been compiled at the Reich Archive. A note by Hahnke states that the summaries are based on files 2680, 2681, and 2682 as well as maps 2500, 2501, and 2502 of the Reich Archive. The maps were drawn by order of Boetticher on the basis of photographs and blueprints from the Reich Archive original by the graphics service of Jüterbog Artillery School (BA/MA, Nachlass Boetticher, N 323/9, 1).

40. Zoellner, "Schlieffens Vermächtnis," *Militärwissenschaftliche Rundschau,* Sonderheft 4 (1938): 1–56, here pages 48–52.

41. Boetticher's comments in both Boetticher, "Der Lehrmeister des neuzeitlichen Krieges," 310–313, and Boetticher, *Schlieffen,* 66–68, are not discussed by Zuber.

42. Cf. Zuber, *Inventing the Schlieffen Plan,* 203–206.

43. Grosse Generalstabsreise (Fall Steuben) 1905/1906, BA/MA, Grosser Generalstab, BA/MA, PH/663, f. 1–56.

44. Zuber examined file PH 3/663. In his list of references, however, he wrongly indicates it as "Grosse Generalstabsreise 1906" (Zuber, *Inventing the Schlieffen Plan,* 307). In Zuber, "Terence Holmes Reinvents the Schlieffen Plan," 471, he writes: "This exercise has survived only in Zoellner's article."

45. Cf. Zuber, "Der Mythos vom Schlieffenplan," 45–78.

46. Zuber mentions several times, and also in his documentation for *German War Planning, 1891–1914: Sources and Interpretations,* Warfare in History (Woodbridge, UK, 2004), 51, that "the original Schlieffen plan Denkschrift, which was not in the Reichsarchiv but in the possession of Schlieffen daughters until 1937, and was surely thereafter a closely held secret."

47. Cf. Foerster, *Schlieffen und der Weltkrieg,* 29–35.

48. Cf. *Der Weltkrieg 1914–1918,* vol. 1, *Die Grenzschlachten im Westen,* ed. Reichsarchiv (Berlin, 1925), 1:55–58.

49. Cf. Freiherrr von Freytag-Loringhoven, *Folgerungen aus dem Weltkrieg,* 10th ed. (Berlin, 1917), 46; Kuhl, *Der deutsche Generalstab,* 150–177; Landmann, "Deutscher Ost- oder Westaufmarsch 1914?," *Militär-Wochenblatt* 108, no. 12 (1923): 273–275; Hermann von Kuhl, "Zum Aufsatz Deutscher Ost- oder Westaufmarsch 1914?," *Militär-Wochenblatt* 109, no. 13 (1924): 293–297; Erich Ludendorff, *Krieg-*

führung und Politik (Berlin, 1922), 69–71; Georg Steinhausen, *Die Grundfehler des Krieges und der Generalstab* (Gotha, 1919), 18.

50. Cf. Groener, *Das Testament des Grafen Schlieffen*, 8–9.

51. Cf. Wolfgang Foerster, "Graf Schlieffen und der Weltkrieg," *Wissen und Wehr* 14 (1933): 63–70, here page 65.

52. While Groener's reconstruction is compiled from different passages including the beginning and the end of the *Denkschrift*, Foerster's facsimile is the first page of the *Denkschrift* with handwritten comments added by Moltke in 1911. Furthermore, Groener's *Denkschrift* version is titled "Krieg gegen das mit England verbündete Frankreich" (War against France allied with England) and Foerster's is "Krieg gegen Frankreich" (War against France).

53. Cf. Ritter, *Der Schlieffenplan*, 143–145. Only three preliminary drafts are titled "War against France allied with England." See Ritter, *Der Schlieffenplan*, 141–144; BA/MA, Nachlass Schlieffen, N 43/137 and 138.

54. Cf. Friedrich von Boetticher, "Graf Schlieffen als Urheber des Unglücks Deutschlands und Europas," BA/MA, Nachlass Boetticher, N 323/33, page 3; Ritter, *Der Schlieffenplan*, 144.

55. Cf. Boetticher, *Schlieffen*, 106 note 66.

56. Anna Josefa von Hahnke an das Heeresarchiv Potsdam, 6 October 1943, BA/MA, Nachlass Boetticher, N 323/32.

57. "Ich bedauere es ausserordentlich, dass ich [. . .] die Genehmigung zur Einsichtnahme und gegebenenfalls Benutzung der Briefe aus grundsätzlichen Erwägungen heraus Niemanden erteilen vermag." (I deeply regret that I . . . am not in a position to grant permission to anybody to view and, if applicable, use the letters due to principal considerations.) Anna Josefa von Hahnke to Weniger, 6 October 1943, BA/MA, Nachlass Boetticher, N 323/32.

58. Anna Josefa von Hahnke, 7 October 1943, BA/MA, Nachlass Boetticher, N 323/32.

59. H. J. Klasing, lawyer and notary, an den Verlag Oldenbourg (to Oldenbourg publishing house), Bielfeld 29 January 1957, BA/MA, Nachlass Boetticher, N 323/28; Friedrich von Boetticher an das Bundesministerium der Verteidigung Bonn (to the Federal Ministry of Defense), Bielfeld 9 January 1957, BA/MA, Nachlass Boetticher, N 323/28.

60. The correspondence is kept in BA/MA, Nachlass Boetticher, N 323/31, 33, 52, and 178.

61. As Boetticher correctly indicates, in several passages his copy deviates from the version compiled by Ritter on the basis of Hahnke's materials. However, these differences are marginal and do not change the tenor of the *Denkschrift*.

62. Boetticher to Görlitz, Bielfeld 21 February 1958, BA/MA, Nachlass Boetticher, N 323/52.

63. Cf. Foerster to Boetticher, Irschenhausen 4 September 1957, BA/MA, Nachlass Boetticher, N 323/52.

64. By his own accounts, Foerster lost a copy while fleeing from the Russian

armed forces. Foerster to Boetticher, Irschenhausen 25 November 1957, BA/MA, Nachlass Boetticher, N 323/52.

65. Boetticher to Haeften, 11 December 1931, BA/MA, Nachlass Boetticher, N 323/53.

66. Zuber, *German War Planning, 1891–1914: Sources and Interpretations,* 49.

67. Ibid., 50.

68. Zuber justifies this with the argument that Foerster refused Dieckmann access to the *Denkschrift* handed over to the Reich Archive by Schlieffen's daughter in 1931 because of Dieckmann's critical remarks. Cf. Zuber, *German War Planning, 1891–1914: Sources and Interpretations,* 51.

69. Cf. ibid., 49.

70. After his release as a reserve lieutenant and his study course of national economy and history, Wilhelm Dieckmann (1893–1944), married to the eldest daughter of Reich Archive president Hermann Ritter Mertz von Quirnheim, became an archivist assistant in 1923, an archivist (*Archivrat*) in 1926, and a senior archivist (*Oberarchivrat*) in 1936 in the Reich Archive. As a well-known expert on the German war economy, he wrote a number of articles on German war armament before and during the First World War, and in cooperation with his brother-in-law, Otto Korfes, he wrote the supplementary volume of the official war history *Der Weltkrieg 1914 bis 1918, Kriegsrüstung und Kriegswirtschaft: Die militärische, wirtschaftliche und finanzielle Rüstung Deutschlands von der Reichsgründung bis zum Ausbruch des Weltkrieges.* Since 1935 he had served as a reservist in the 9th Infantry Regiment in Potsdam. From the outbreak of the war, he commanded the 477th Infantry Replacement Battalion. After 30 April 1940, he was released from active military service and resumed his job at the War Historical Research Institute (Kriegsgeschichtlichen Forschungsanstalt). As a member of the Confessing Church and during his service period in the 9th Infantry Regiment, he was in contact with resistance circles and was privy to the preparations for the 20 July 1944 Plot. On the basis of complicity he was arrested by the Gestapo and died in prison under unexplained circumstances on 13 September 1944. Cf. Ines Reich, *Potsdam und der 20. Juli 1944: Auf den Spuren des Widerstandes gegen den Nationalsozialismus* (Freiburg i.Br., 1994), 70–71; Sigrid Wegner-Korfes, "Realpolitische Haltung bei Offizieren der Familien Mertz von Quirnheim, Korfes und Dieckmann," *Zeitschrift für Militärgeschichte* 25, no. 3 (1986): 226–233.

71. Wilhelm Dieckmann, *Die deutsche Holzverkohlungsindustrie in der Kriegswirtschaft* (Berlin, 1923); *Die Behördenorganisation in der deutschen Kriegswirtschaft 1914–1918,* Schriften zur kriegswirtschaftlichen Forschung und Schulung (Hamburg, 1937); "Deutsche Rohstoffwirtschaft im Weltkrieg," *Wirtschaftskrieg: Die Wirtschaft als Kampfträger und Kampfobjekt im totalen Kriege,* Schriftenreihe der Deutschen Wirtschaftszeitung, 6 (Berlin, 1938), 45–57.

72. *Der Weltkrieg 1914 bis 1918, Kriegsrüstung und Kriegswirtschaft,* vol. 1, *Die militärische, wirtschaftliche und finanzielle Rüstung Deutschlands von der Reichsgründung bis zum Ausbruch des Weltkrieges* (Berlin, 1930).

73. Dieckmann, "Der Schlieffenplan," BA/MA, RH61/347 (W10/50220), f. 48–226.

74. Stig Förster, "Der deutsche Generalstab und die Illusion des kurzen Krieges, 1871–1914: Metakritik eines Mythos," *Militärgeschichtliche Mitteilungen* 54 (1995): 61–95, here page 75 n. 46.

75. "Mit solchen Bestrebungen vertrug es sich in der Tat schlecht, militärische Massnahmen zu treffen oder vorzubereiten, die ihre unverkennbare Spitze gegen Russland hatten." (With these intentions it could indeed hardly be tolerated to adopt or prepare military measures that were undoubtedly directed against Russia.) Dieckmann, "Der Schlieffenplan," BA/MA, RH61/347 (W10/50220), f. 92.

76. Cf. Markus Pöhlmann, *Kriegsgeschichte und Geschichtspolitik: Der Erste Weltkrieg. Die amtliche deutsche Militärgeschichtsschreibung, 1914–1956* (Paderborn, 2002), 156.

77. BA/MA, RH61/355 (W10/50228), f. 35–194.

78. Dieckmann, "Der Schlieffenplan," BA/MA, RH61/347 (W10/50220), f. 1–13. A typed version of "Einige Betrachtungen über die Entstehungsgeschichte des Schlieffenplans" with slight changes in the title is stored in BA/MA, RH61/355 (W10/50228), f. 210–232.

79. The manuscript of "Notizen und Material für eine Untersuchung über Graf Schlieffen und die Entwicklung des deutschen Heeres" contains the notation II E.1, the manuscript of "Der Schlieffenplan" the notation II E.2, and the handwritten draft of the paper "Einige Bemerkungen über die Entstehungsgeschichte des Schlieffenplans" the notation II E.3. The incomplete and unpublished manuscript of "Graf Schlieffens Einfluss auf die Entwicklung des deutschen Heeres," BA/MA, RH61/355 (W10/50228), f. 195–247, by Dieckmann which is in part typewritten and in part handwritten does not contain any classification marks.

80. Wilhelm Dieckmann, "Notizen und Material für eine Untersuchung über Graf Schlieffen und die Entwicklung des deutschen Heeres," BA/MA, RH61/355 (W10/50228), f. 40, 131–136.

81. This copy is stored at BA/MA Freiburg, Nachlass Boetticher, N 323/18.

82. For example, Wilhelm Dieckmann, "Die Vorbereitung für die Versorgung des deutschen Heeres mit Munition vor Ausbruch des Weltkrieges" (1939), BA/MA, W10/50777. Regarding further studies by Dieckmann on defense history, cf. Matthias Herrmann, *Das Reichsarchiv (1919–1945): Eine archivische Institution im Spannungsfeld der deutschen Politik*, 2 vols. (Berlin, 1994), Annex 28, pages 533–542.

83. Cf. Boetticher, *Schlieffen: Viel leisten, wenig hervortreten—mehr sein als scheinen*, 2nd. reviewed ed. by Friedrich-Christian Stahl, Persönlichkeit und Geschichte, 7 (Göttingen, Zurich, Frankfurt/Main, 1973), 111 n. 139. Regarding this issue, Ritter writes that the strategic planning can only be deduced from "nur aus den jährlichen 'Aufmarschplänen' und aus den sie vorbereitenden operativen Entwürfen des Generalstabschefs zu erkennen seien" (the annual *Aufmarschpläne* and the operational drafts by the Chief of the General Staff in preparation of them). Ritter, *Der Schlieffenplan*, 31; Otto, *Schlieffen und der Generalstab*, 151.

84. Cf. Rassow, "Schlieffen und Holstein," 301–303.

85. It cannot be excluded that the Special Archive Moscow keeps personal papers and records lists as well as inventory lists of the Reich/Army Archive in Holdings 545, *Kriegsgeschichtliche Forschungsanstalt des Heeres,* and Holdings 1256 and 1275 on the chief of Army Archives.

86. Maurice Paléologue, "Un prélude a l'invasion de la Belgique," *Revue des Deux Mondes* 102, 5 (1932): 481–524.

87. Wolfgang Foerster, "Ist der deutsche Aufmarsch 1904 an die Franzosen verraten worden?," *Berliner Monatshefte: Zeitschrift für Vorgeschichte und Geschichte des Weltkrieges* 10, no. 2 (1932): 1053–1066, here 1060–1061.

88. Cf. Foerster, "Hat es eine Schlieffenplan-Legende gegeben?," 603–605.

89. Cf. Ludendorff, *Mein militärischer Werdegang,* 94–95.

90. In 2002, the file was included in the Holdings RH 61, "Kriegsgeschichtliche Forschungsanstalt des Heeres." According to the entries in the list of users, three users examined this file—in 1985, 1990, and 1995.

91. After the Military Preliminary Archive (the former Military Archive of the GDR) was closed in 1996, the file RH61/96 was sent from Potsdam to the Bundesarchiv/Militärarchiv in Freiburg. In the Military Archive of the GDR it was stored under the shelf mark Pr 3.2.12.1./2, and belonged to the sub-holdings "Chef des Generalstabes des Feldheeres" in the holdings "Generalstab" of the main group "Preussische Armee." It was only at the BA/MA that the documents were placed among the records of the Kriegsgeschichtliche Forschungsanstalt des Heeres, since they contained papers by members of the Kriegsgeschichtliche Forschungsanstalt des Heeres. A preliminary finding aid on the holdings of RH61, which was completed in 2002, lists the former Records Pr 3.2.12.1./2 for the first time under the shelf mark RH61/96.

92. During the *Grosse Generalstabsreise West* of 1904 Schlieffen and his successor disagreed considerably on operational issues: "Graf Schlieffen frägt mich ab und zu um meine Ansicht, und diese deckt sich fast nie mit der seinigen. Man kann sich keine grösseren Gegensätze denken, als unserer beiderseitigen Ansichten." Helmuth von Moltke, *Erinnerungen, Briefe, Dokumente 1877–1916: Ein Bild vom Kriegsausbruch, erster Kriegführung und Persönlichkeit des ersten militärischen Führers des Krieges,* ed. Von Eliza von Moltke (Stuttgart, 1922), Tagebuchnotiz vom 18 June 1904, page 292; cf. also: Ernst Buchfinck, "Der Meinungskampf um den Marnefeldzug," *Historische Zeitschrift* 152 (1935): 286–300, here page 294.

93. Kaiserliche Ordre, Berlin, 26 October 1905, BA/MA, Nachlass Boetticher, N 323/23.

94. Anhang zu Kaiserliche Ordre, Berlin, 26 October 1905, BA/MA, Nachlass Boetticher, N 323/23.

95. Chef des Generalstabes des Armee, Kriegsspiel November/Dezember 1905, Berlin, 23 December 1905, BA/MA, PH 3/646, f. 1–36.

96. Foerster dates this *Denkschrift* by Schlieffen to the year 1899, with reserva-

tion, and reproduces it in excerpts. Foerster, "Ist der deutsche Aufmarsch 1904," 1060–1062.

97. Cf. Zuber, *Inventing the Schlieffen Plan*, 160.

98. At that time, the French Army was able to complete its deployment after about three weeks, while the German armed forces were operational only after four weeks.

99. Cf. Dieckmann, "Der Schlieffenplan," RH61/347 (W10/50220), f. 119–120.

100. "However, if the French did not conduct an offensive and left the initiative to the Germans, the two armies of the right wing (First and Second Armies) were to march off to the right to 'cross the Maas between Donchery and Stenay,' actually to advance around the French fortress front from the north." Dieckmann, "Der Schlieffenplan," RH61/347 (W10/50220), f. 173–174.

101. Dieckmann, "Der Schlieffenplan," RH61/347 (W10/50220), f. 173; cf. also Foerster, "Ist der deutsche Aufmarsch 1904," 1063.

102. Cf. Dieckmann, "Der Schlieffenplan," RH61/347 (W10/50220), f. 180–181.

103. "This exercise clearly illustrates Schlieffen's developing doctrine: a true mass German army conducted mobile counter-offensive operations on German territory in order to fight battles of annihilation against the attacking enemy army." Zuber, *Inventing the Schlieffen Plan*, 183.

104. Kriegsspiel 1905 Ost, BA/MA, Nachlass Boetticher, N 323/10, page 23.

105. Cf. Dieckmann, "Der Schlieffenplan," RH61/347 (W10/50220), f. 206.

106. Cf. Boetticher an Marcks, 18 December 1931, BA/MA, Nachlass Boetticher, N 323/53.

107. Cf. Dieckmann, "Der Schlieffenplan," RH61/347 (W10/50220), f. 64–65.

108. Zuber, *Inventing the Schlieffen Plan*, 162.

109. Cf. Robert T. Foley, "Der Schlieffenplan: Ein Aufmarschplan für den Krieg," in *Der Schlieffenplan: Analysen und Dokumente*, ed. Hans Ehlert, Michael Epkenhans, and Gerhard P. Gross (Paderborn, 2006), 101–116.

110. "However unrealistic or even impossible its realization is, it offers enough interest to deal with it." Chef des Generalstabes der Armee, Kriegsspiel November/Dezember 1905, Berlin, 23 December 1905, BA/MA, PH 3/646, f. 1.

111. Chef des Generalstabes des Armee, Kriegsspiel November/Dezember 1905, Berlin, 23 December 1905, BA/MA, PH 3/646, f. 35–36.

112. "It was in the nature of the position of the chief of the General Staff that his educational work could not extend directly to the practical training of units. Rather, he was responsible for educating and teaching the intellectual elite of the Prussian-German officer corps for the purposes of higher command, for developing a high-quality class of leaders able to meet the requirements of modern army command and control, and for developing a new generation of apt young military leaders. . . . To this end Count Schlieffen relied, in addition to the systematic training of his officers in the technique of general staff duty, which was basically incumbent on the subordinate senior quartermasters, mainly on the annual *grossen Generalstabsreisen* led by himself and the *operativen Kriegsspiele*, also on the *strategisch-taktischen*

Aufgaben which he assigned to junior officers considered for a duty in the general staff at the end of each training year ... and finally the large *Kaisermanöver* [Kaiser Maneuvers] held each autumn under his command." Graf Schlieffen als militärischer Erzieher, unveröffentlichtes und undatiertes Manuskript von Wolfgang Foerster, BA/MA, Kriegsgeschichtliche Forschungsanstalt des Heeres, RH61/355 (W10/50228), f. 1-34, here f. 15-16. See also Zusammenstellung der Bestimmungen und Gesichtspunkte für die Winterarbeiten der Generalstabsoffiziere (Verfügung Graf Schlieffen, dated 21 January 1902, Nr. 9491, BA/MA, Nachlass Boetticher, N 323/22).

113. Cf. Boetticher, "Der Lehrmeister des neuzeitlichen Krieges," 296.

114. Cf. Boetticher, "Graf Schlieffen als Lehrmeister und Wegweiser," *Wissen und Wehr* 14 (1933): 71-83; Walter Elze, *Graf Schlieffen*, Veröffentlichungen der Schleswig-Holsteinschen Universitätsgesellschaft, 20 (Breslau, 1928), 5-9; Freiherr von Freytag-Loringhoven, *Generalfeldmarschall Graf von Schlieffen: Sein Leben und die Verwertung seines geistigen Erbes im Weltkrieg* (Leipzig, 1920), 30-39.

115. Cf. remark no. 6, Zuber, "Terence Holmes Reinvents the Schlieffen Plan," 471, and "The goal was not to sweep around to the west of Paris but to defeat the French army in battles near the frontier and then to break the French fortress line" (Zuber, "The Schlieffen Plan Reconsidered," 280).

116. Boetticher's summaries are based on the detailed after-action analysis session of the *Generalstabsreise* by Schlieffen and the operations drafts of other participating parties. These latter operations drafts were no longer among the Reich Archive records in the early 1930s. However, Boetticher was able to trace the movements of the other parties with the help of the after-action session and the maps available. File N 323/9 contains the blueprint made by Boetticher and the photographs of maps in the Reich Archive records as well as a large map each for Option Steuben, Option Freytag, and Option Kuhl. They were drawn by the graphics service of Jüterbog Artillery School on the basis of Boetticher's map copies.

117. Grosse Reise 1905, Vorbemerkung, BA/MA, Nachlass Boetticher, N 323/9, page 2.

118. Grosse Reise 1905, BA/MA, Nachlass Boetticher, N 323/9, page 6.

119. Cf. Grosse Reise 1905, BA/MA, Nachlass Boetticher, N 323/9, pages 3 and 4.

120. Option Freytag shows that under certain conditions the general staff was quite ready to forgo the western envelopment of Paris and advance east of Paris. The decision of General von Kluck, whose chief of staff, Major General Hermann von Kuhl, had played Option Kuhl against Schlieffen when he was a major in 1905, to lead the First Army in August 1914 along the east of Paris was not a sudden inspiration, but was based on operational considerations made by Schlieffen during the *Generalstabsreise* of 1905.

121. Cf. Grosse Reise 1905, BA/MA, Nachlass Boetticher, N 323/9, pages 5-7.

122. Cf. on this also Boetticher, "Der Lehrmeister des neuzeitlichen Krieges," 310-312; Ritter, *Der Schlieffenplan*, 44-45; and Zoellner, "Schlieffens Vermächtnis," 48-52.

123. Cf. Grosse Reise 1905, BA/MA, Nachlass Boetticher, N 323/9, pages 6-7.

124. "It is therefore not surprising that in none of these three war games did the German right wing even enter northern France. Rather, in this exercise, as in all of Schlieffen's west-front exercises, battles were fought in Lorraine or Belgium." Zuber, *Inventing the Schlieffen Plan*, 204.

125. *Der Weltkrieg 1914–1918*, vol. 1, *Die Grenzschlachten im Westen*, ed. Reichsarchiv (Berlin, 1925), 55.

126. Elze, *Graf Schlieffen*, 14.

127. Cf. Förster, *Der Doppelte Militarismus*, 164–165; Jäschke, "'Schlieffenplan' und 'Marneschlacht,'" 187; Eberhard Kessel, ed., *Generalfeldmarschall Graf Alfred Schlieffen Briefe* (Göttingen, 1958), 10.

128. The German Army of the period had two branches of artillery. The foot artillery was the heavier branch, while the field artillery was the lighter and more mobile branch.

129. On this cf. Boetticher, "Der Lehrmeister des neuzeitlichen Krieges," 300–308.

130. "As much as Graf Schlieffen agreed at that time with the plans of the government and army administration, the chief of the General Staff was little involved in the details of their implementation, contrary to previous practice." *Der Weltkrieg 1914 bis 1918, Kriegsrüstung und Kriegswirtschaft*, vol. 1, *Die militärische, wirtschaftliche und finanzielle Rüstung Deutschlands von der Reichsgründung bis zum Ausbruch des Weltkrieges*, 44.

131. Dieckmann, "Der Schlieffenplan," BA/MA, RH61/347 (W10/50220), f. 161.

132. Two quotes by Dieckmann illustrate his criticism: "All the more it was, as one should think, the duty of a chief of the General Staff conscious of his responsibility for the future fate of the Reich to become the standard bearer of this idea and to use all the authority of his position to convince the relevant agencies of the need for a quick resumption of army expansion, in particular now that its implementation was in danger. But none of this happened. Without any objections Schlieffen resigned himself to the fact that further armament increases would be delayed for years until the expiration of the Seven-Year Military Bill (*Septennat*) in 1894" (Dieckmann, "Notizen," BA/MA, RH61/355 [W10/50228], f. 39–40), and "As mentioned, Schlieffen was not even involved in the drafting of the Army Bill [*Caprivis*], which was extremely important for the further development of the German Army, given alone the resulting introduction of the two-year service period. Not only did he leave it at the fact that the draft of the bill was sent to him, the chief of the General Staff of the Army, 'for his information' only, he also explicitly directed that on the issue to what extent the Army Bill was consistent with any requirements as seen by the General Staff 'a particular comment of the General Staff . . . was not to be expected'" (BA/MA, RH61/355 [W10/50228], f. 43–44).

133. Cf. Dieckmann, "Notizen," BA/MA, RH61/355 (W10/50228), f. 51.

134. Cf. Dieckmann, "Notizen," BA/MA, RH61/355 (W10/50228), f. 186.

135. Cf. *Der Weltkrieg*, "Kriegsrüstung, Anlagenband," Nr. 27, pages 92–93; Gerhard Ritter, *Staatskunst und Kriegshandwerk: Das Problem des "Militarismus" in*

Deutschland, vol. 2, *Die Hauptmächte Europas und das Wilhelminische Reich (1890–1914)* (Munich, Vienna, Zurich, 1960), 267.

136. Ludendorff, *Mein militärischer Werdegang*, 102.

137. Ritter, *Staatskunst und Kriegshandwerk*, 2:259.

138. Cf. Förster, *Der Doppelte Militarismus*, 165.

139. War Minister Karl von Einem did not have any particular ideas on Schlieffen's operations plans. It seems that Moltke the Younger introduced him to the plans of the General Staff only in 1912. Cf. Ritter, *Staatskunst und Kriegshandwerk*, 2:261.

140. Cf. Zuber, *Inventing the Schlieffen Plan*, 214; Zuber, "The Schlieffen Plan Reconsidered," 266.

141. Cf. Kuhl, *Der deutsche Generalstab*, 169.

142. Cf. *Der Weltkrieg 1914–1918*, vol. 1, *Die Grenzschlachten im Westen*, ed. Reichsarchiv (Berlin, 1925), 61.

143. Cf. Ludendorff, *Mein militärischer Werdegang*, 101.

144. Cf. Foerster, *Aus der Gedankenwerkstatt des Deutschen Generalstabes*, 40–41.

145. Cf. Holmes, "The Real Thing," 113–114; Holmes, "Asking Schlieffen," 467–472.

146. "Übersicht über die Operationen der 1. Grossen Generalstabsreise 1904," BA/MA, Nachlass Boetticher, N 323/8, pages 10–11.

147. "2. Grosse Reise 1904," BA/MA, Nachlass Boetticher, N 323/8, page 3.

148. "Übersicht über die Operationen der 1. Grossen Generalstabsreise 1904," BA/MA, Nachlass Boetticher, N 323/8, page 4; "2. Grosse Reise 1904, Kriegsgliederung," BA/MA, Nachlass Boetticher, N 323/8, page 3.

149. Cf. "Mobilmachungsjahr 1904/05," in *Der Schlieffenplan: Analysen und Dokumente*, ed. Hans Ehlert, Michael Epkenhans, and Gerhard P. Gross, Zeitalter der Weltkriege, 2 (Paderborn, 2006), 389–393. The number of nineteen reserve divisions was the peacetime strength of the German Army in the summer of 1904. Cf. Ludwig Rüdt von Collenberg, *Die deutsche Armee von 1871 bis 1914*, Forschungen und Darstellungen aus dem Reichsarchiv, 4 (Berlin, 1922), 66–67.

150. Cf. Ritter, *Der Schlieffenplan*, 36–39; Dieckmann, "Der Schlieffenplan," BA/MA, RH61/347 (W10/50220), f. 68–72.

151. It was only at the beginning of the mobilization year of 1896 that Schlieffen had the available artillery units intended for his attack.

152. Dieckmann, "Der Schlieffenplan," BA/MA, RH61/347 (W10/50220), f. 76.

153. Ibid., f. 77.

154. In *Aufmarsch West I* (War on the Western Front Only) in the mobilization year of 1906–1907, the whole German Army without occupation troops deploys eight armies consisting of twenty-six army corps, twelve reserve corps, three reserve divisions, eleven cavalry divisions, and twenty-six and a half Landwehr brigades to the west. The right army wing, six armies with twenty-two army and seven reserve corps, deploys to the area between Diedenhofen and Düsseldorf and takes a turn to the left through Belgium. The first deployment objectives are Antwerp for the First Army and Brussels for the Second Army. Cf. "Aufmarsch 1906/07," in *Der Schlieffen-*

plan: Analysen und Dokumente, ed. Hans Ehlert, Michael Epkenhans, and Gerhard P. Gross, Zeitalter der Weltkriege, 2 (Paderborn, 2006), 409–417.

155. Zuber, *Inventing the Schlieffen Plan,* 163.

156. Dieckmann, "Der Schlieffenplan," BA/MA, RH 61/347 (W-10/50220), f. 115; see Ritter, *Der Schlieffenplan,* 39.

157. "The conditions north of Verdun are more favorable. Naturally, the Maas, too, will be defended, but not by considerable forces. The right wing at least will be free and we will probably be able to force a crossing of the river in a bypass. Once this is accomplished, the march can be directed against the rear communications of the enemy and, if this succeeds, the French army can be pushed away from Paris." This briefly describes the essence of the offensive: the destruction of the enemy. Dieckmann, "Der Schlieffenplan," BA/MA, RH 61/347 (W-10/50220), f. 114–115.

158. Cf. Ritter, *Der Schlieffenplan,* 37–39.

159. See Dieckmann, "Der Schlieffenplan," BA/MA, RH 61/347 (W-10/50220), f. 207–210.

160. "Here as everywhere neither the frontal attack nor the envelopment or bypass could lead to victory, only a combination of both." Schlieffen remarks of 16 May 1902 cited in Dieckmann, "Der Schlieffenplan," BA/MA, RH 61/347 (W-10/50220), f. 210.

161. Boetticher does not exclude that Schlieffen wanted to use this deployment to react to an expected large-scale attack of forty infantry and four cavalry divisions between Metz and Saarburg and to defeat the French in Lorraine. Cf. Boetticher to Marcks, 18 December 1931, BA/MA, Nachlass Boetticher, N 323/53, pages 3–4. On the side of the 3rd Department of the General Staff, a French attack on Lorraine was expected before 1904. However, the relevant records do not contain any hints to the large-scale attack of the French Army as expected by Boetticher.

162. Cf. Ritter, *Der Schlieffenplan,* 41. Ritter bases his statements on Foerster's sketch in "Ist der deutsche Aufmarsch 1904," page 1061. However, this sketch does not only picture the *Aufmarsch I* against France but also the *Aufmarsch II,* state of war with Russia and France. Cf. Ehlert, *Der Schlieffenplan,* 389–393.

163. Cf. Ehlert, *Der Schlieffenplan,* 394–399.

164. Cf. Ritter, *Der Schlieffenplan,* 42–45.

165. Greiner, "Welche Nachrichten besass der deutsche Generalstab," BA/MA, RH 61/398 (W-10/50267), f. 95.

166. Cf. "Übersicht über die Operationen der 1. Grossen Generalstabsreise 1904, Schlussbesprechung," BA/MA, Nachlass Boetticher, N 323/8, pages 5–8.

167. Cf. Foley, "Der Schlieffenplan," 101–116.

168. Cf. Ehlert, *Der Schlieffenplan,* 409–417.

169. Zuber, *German War Planning, 1891–1914: Sources and Interpretations,* 49.

170. Ritter, *Staatskunst und Kriegshandwerk,* 2:240; similar also, Jehuda L. Wallach, *Das Dogma der Vernichtungsschlacht: Die Lehren von Clausewitz und Schlieffen und ihre Wirkungen in zwei Weltkriegen* (Frankfurt/Main, 1967), 108. "There is no doubt that Schlieffen represents the prototype of a new kind of the apolitical soldier

who only lives for his profession and is not interested in anything beyond his narrow technical horizon."

171. Dieckmann, "Der Schlieffenplan," BA/MA, RH61/347 (W10/50220), f. 96–97.

172. "It will not be a mistake to view them in the context of the, already mentioned, vigorous efforts by the German kaiser himself to establish closer connections with the eastern neighbor. Obviously, the monarch regarded the relief from German pressure which this shifting provided for Russia as another means to facilitate the rapprochement efforts." Dieckmann, "Der Schlieffenplan," BA/MA, RH61/347 (W10/50220), f. 97–98.

173. In this context, Dieckmann states: "What importance the monarch attached to such an increase in the defense potential at the western border is also illustrated by the fact that he was prepared to spend several hundred million Marks to implement his Metz expansion plan . . . , while at the same time he agreed to the costs for the army program of 1899 . . . being restricted to the utmost, as we will see later." Dieckmann, "Der Schlieffenplan," BA/MA, RH61/347 (W10/50220), f. 154.

174. Dieckmann, "Der Schlieffenplan," BA/MA, RH61/347 (W10/50220), f. 153.

175. Ibid., f. 230.

176. "Diesen Zusammenstoss [mit Grossbritannien] hat der Soldat Schlieffen mit dem Weitblick eines überragenden Staatsmannes als unvermeidlich kommen sehen." Ibid., f. 164.

177. Cf. on this: Boetticher, "Briefwechsel mit Frauendienst und Rein," BA/MA, Nachlass Boetticher, N 323/52. During those talks Holstein provided Schlieffen with the opportunity to read important files of the Foreign Office. Neither Moltke nor Waldersee had such an opportunity. In contrast to his predecessors, Schlieffen was therefore well informed about German foreign policy. Cf. Otto, *Schlieffen und der Generalstab*, 57. According to Hahnke, Schlieffen even wrote his *Denkschrift* of 1905 in close agreement with Holstein. Moreover, the political foundations of several operations plans and *Generalstabsreisen* were probably based on joint talks. Cf. Friedrich von Boetticher, *Schlieffen: Viel leisten, wenig hervortreten—mehr sein als scheinen*, 2nd. reviewed ed. by Friedrich-Christian Stahl, Persönlichkeit und Geschichte, 7 (Göttingen, Zurich, Frankfurt/Main, 1973), 62.

178. It cannot be proved whether and to what extent Schlieffen informed the state secretary in the Foreign Office, the Reich chancellor, or the kaiser—apart from Holstein—of his operations planning. According to the secret diary of the chief of the General Staff, there had been no information in writing. Reich chancellor Bernhard Fürst von Bülow stated to the Reich Archive on 9 July 1920 that there had been no exchange of opinions between himself and Schlieffen on this issue. ("Die Verletzung der Neutralität," BA/MA, RH61/96, f. 145.) However, according to Kolster, Bülow had been informed about a possible passage of German troops through Belgium. See Walter Kolster, *Der deutsche Generalstab und der Präventivkriegs-Gedanke*, Beiträge zur Geschichte der nachbismarckischen Zeit und des Weltkriegs, 13 (Stuttgart, 1932), 77. Cf. also Wallach, *Das Dogma der Vernichtungsschlacht*, 62.

179. Cf. Dieckmann, "Der Schlieffenplan," BA/MA, RH61/347 (W10/50220), f. 210.

180. Cf. chapters in this volume.

181. The only explanation for Schlieffen's restraint in my opinion is to be found in Schlieffen's *firm principle, to which he always adhered,* to never get involved in higher politics without being asked. Indeed, during his entire term in office Schlieffen had never approached the leadership of the Reich to stir up a war. Wilhelm Dieckmann, "Hat Graf Schlieffen während der ersten Marokkokrise 1905 den Präventivkrieg gegen Frankreich gefordert?" (Did Graf Schlieffen Demand a Preemptive War against France during the Morocco Crisis of 1905?, BA/MA, RH61/355 [W10/50228], page 258.)

182. On the discussion of Schlieffen's preemptive war plans, see Ivo Nikolai Lambi, *The Navy and German Power Politics, 1862–1914* (Boston, 1984), 241–245; Heiner Raulff, *Zwischen Machtpolitik und Imperialismus: Die deutsche Frankreichpolitik 1904/06* (Düsseldorf, 1976), 126–144; Ritter, *Der Schlieffenplan*, 102–138.

183. Letter by Hahnke to Groener, 16 April 1926, Schriftwechsel betr. Schlieffen-Plan, 1919–1932, Nachlass Groener, BA/MA, N46/38, f. 49–50.

184. Cf. Michael Epkenhans, "Verlust des Primats der Politik? 'Staatskunst' und 'Kriegshandwerk' 1890–1914," in *Otto von Bismarck und Wilhelm II: Repräsentanten eines Epochenwechsels?,* ed. by Lothar Gall, Otto-von-Bismarck-Stiftung wissenschaftliche Reihe, 1 (Paderborn, 2002), 61–83, here page 1.

185. Cf. Arden Buchholz, *Moltke, Schlieffen and Prussian War Planning* (New York, Oxford, 1991), 58–108.

186. Heeres, ed., *Generalfeldmarschall Graf von Schlieffen, Dienstschriften,* 222.

187. Cf. Gerhard P. Gross, "Das Dogma der Beweglichkeit: Überlegungen zur Genese der deutschen Heerestaktik im Zeitalter der Weltkrieg," in *Erster Weltkrieg Zweiter Weltkrieg: Ein Vergleich. Krieg, Kriegserlebnis, Kriegserfahrung in Deutschland,* ed. Bruno Thoss and Hans-Erich (Paderborn: Militärgeschichtliche Forschungsamt, 2002), 143–166.

188. "This war will grow into a world war which Britain will enter as well. Only few people have an idea about the extent, duration and the outcome of such a war. Today nobody can imagine how this all might end." Moltke to Haeften, 31 July 1914, BA/MA, Nachlass Hans von Haeften, N 25/1. On the issue of short or long wars, cf. Förster, "Der deutsche Generalstab und die Illusion des kurzen Krieges," 61–95; Stig Förster, "Der Krieg der Willensmenschen: Die deutsche Offizierselite auf dem Weg in den Weltkrieg 1871–1914," in *Willensmenschen: Über deutsche Offiziere,* ed. Ursula Breymacher, Bernd Ulrich, and Karin Wieland (Frankfurt/Main, 1999), 23–36.

189. Already in the year before, the First Army was to march through the Maastricht area via Brussels to Oudenarde and the Second Army was to approach the northwest of Binche far into Belgium. Cf. *Aufmarschanweisungen 1907–1908,* in the appendix.

190. Cf. Annika Mombauer, "Der Moltkeplan: Modifikation des Schlieffenplans

bei gleichen Zielen," in *Der Schlieffenplan: Analysen und Dokumente*, ed. Hans Ehlert, Michael Epkenhans, and Gerhard P. Gross, Zeitalter der Weltkriege, 2 (Paderborn, 2006), 79–100, Förster, "Der Krieg der Willensmenschen," 29.

191. In case the attack on Liège had not been completed, Moltke also planned the passage through the territory of the Netherlands territory. Cf. *Aufmarschanweisungen 1908–1909* to *1913–1914*, in the appendix.

192. Cf. Wallach, *Das Dogma der Vernichtungsschlacht*, 134.

193. Cf. *Aufmarsch 1913–1914*, in the appendix.

194. Cf. Dieter Storz, "'Dieser Stellungs- und Festungskrieg ist scheusslich!' zu den Kämpfen in Lothringen und in den Vogesen im Sommer 1914," in *Der Schlieffenplan: Analysen und Dokumente*, ed. Hans Ehlert, Michael Epkenhans, and Gerhard P. Gross, Zeitalter der Weltkriege, 2 (Paderborn, 2006), 161–204.

195. According to Groener, a few weeks before his death Schlieffen tried to receive information from General von Stein regarding the current situation of his plan, but Stein avoided the issue. Groener was convinced that after his leave-taking Schlieffen was "completely neutralized" in military issues (Über den Schlieffenplan, Nachlass Groener, BA/MA, N 46/51, f. 79, 85). According to Hahnke, this was the only case in which "ein höherer Generalstabsoffizier und berufener Führer Graf Schlieffen's Rat in operativen Fragen eingeholt hat. Moltke, Stein, Waldersee, Ludendorff haben es niemals für für der Mühe wert gehalten, je des Grafen Schlieffens Ansicht in operativen Fragen einzuholen; Graf Schlieffen versuchte verschiedentlich, diese Herren zu einer operativen Aussprache zu bringen. Zu seinem grössten Schmerze wichen die Genannten einem solchen Gespräche stets aus." Graf Schlieffen's französischer Operations-Entwurf gegen Deutschland, BA/MA, Nachlass Boetticher, N 323/19.

196. Moltke informed Reich chancellor Theobald von Bethmann Hollweg in writing about his operations planning in his *Denkschrift* of December 1912 (printed in Erich Ludendorff, *Urkunden der Obersten Heeresleitung* [Berlin, 1922], 51–60). According to his own statement, Bethmann had already received oral information about the military planning of the General Staff. "Von dem Aufmarschplan für den Zweifrontenkrieg habe ich lange vor dem Kriege Kenntnis gehabt. Einen bestimmten Zeitpunkt vermag ich nicht anzugeben." (Letter by Bethmann Hollwegs to the Reich Archive of 27 May 1920.) According to his own statement, the state secretary of the exterior, Gottlieb von Jagow, too, had been informed of the planning of the General Staff long before the beginning of the war. (Letter by Jagow to the Reich Archive of 28 July 1920.) Both quotes from "Die Verletzung der Neutralität," BA/MA, RH61/96, f. 145. Cf. Wallach, *Das Dogma der Vernichtungsschlacht*, 61–62.

197. Cf. Ritter, *Staatskunst und Kriegshandwerk*, 2:261.

198. Cf. also Jäschke, "'Schlieffenplan' und 'Marneschlacht,'" 186–196.

"This Trench and Fortress Warfare Is Horrible!"

The Battles in Lorraine and the Vosges in the Summer of 1914

Dieter Storz

In 1977 the major German television network ZDF broadcast a feature on the Battle of the Marne titled *Generals*. In the film, commentator Sebastian Haffner uses a large map to introduce the audience to the situation. With his hand pointing to Lorraine, he says: "We may forget about everything that happened here at the southern part of the western front. There was constant bloody and acrimonious fighting, but nothing was decided."[1] This chapter focuses on those events in Lorraine, and it can be safely said even at this point that there will be no objections to Haffner's second statement.

The battles in Lorraine and in the Vosges were separated from the remaining western front by the fortified zones of Metz–Diedenhofen (Thionville) and Toul–Nancy. Those battles were secondary actions within the overall German western offensive. The planning and conduct of the western campaign in 1914 stirred up heated discussions after the war. The events that took place on the left wing of the German Army raised their own controversy about not only the two southern battles, but also their influence on the greater Battle of the Marne. Although there was less at stake in the south and there has been less written about it, the subordinate dispute was no less fierce than the main debate. And yet, there was general agreement that the battles in Lorraine and in the Vosges produced unfavorable results for Germany. Not that the Germans were defeated there. Rather, the results achieved, in terms of the operational impact or the damage inflicted on the enemy's combat capabilities, were at odds with the number of forces committed to the task and the sacrifices they had to make.

Criticism was directed at the senior German military leadership—the Supreme Army Command (*Oberste Heeresleitung*—OHL) and the subordinate field headquarters operating in what was called the "Imperial Territories" (*Reichslande*), which included the "Bavarian" Sixth Army and the Seventh Army to its south. The dispute involved the degree to which the various headquarters and leaders should be held responsible for the undesirable course of events.

The controversy focused on two issues. First, there was the issue of why the Sixth Army did not stop and withdraw well away from the French advancing into Lorraine, in order to assume a more favorable position from which to launch a devastating counterattack. The Sixth Army instead terminated that move on 20 August by launching a hardly promising large-scale frontal attack that resulted in an "ordinary victory" instead of the intended Cannae-like defeat of the French. This limited success was followed by a so-called pursuit that did not really develop but instead changed into fierce frontal clashes stretching over some two weeks. During this phase the French—like the Germans—relied on their fortifications. The principle that attacks against such objectives were better avoided was basic military knowledge. Why the German advance was nevertheless made and why it took so long until it was aborted and the troops were withdrawn from that impasse is the second focus of the discussion. In the center of that feud was the former Sixth Army chief of staff, Major General Konrad Krafft von Dellmensingen.

Krafft's first public statement on the matter[2] was triggered by a book review. In a review of the first volume of the *Reichsarchiv* series on the World War, Lieutenant Colonel Georg Wetzell,[3] who during the last year of the war was the chief of the Operations Division at OHL, put the main blame for the failed Lorraine operation on OHL itself for not being able to carry out the actual operational intent. But Wetzell also criticized the impetuosity of Sixth Army headquarters. "A leadership paying more attention to keeping a cool head, instead of being ruled by a pugnacious hot heart and the mood of the belligerent troops, might have waited for the development along the line of Metz–St. Avold–Sarre Union–Phalsbourg during the following days, and would have broken forward from there or from an even more rearward position. Such was appropriately recommended, but unfortunately not ordered by the Supreme Army Command several days later as a devastating Cannae-strike."[4]

Several years later Krafft was again criticized, this time by Wilhelm

Groener,[5] who in 1914 had been the chief of the *Feldeisenbahnwesen* (Field Railway Service). In two books Groener portrayed himself as the grail keeper of Schlieffen's heritage. The suggestive titles of his chapters on the Lorraine campaign indicate clearly that he questioned the purpose of those battles and their conduct in general. Groener called them "Die Extratour in Lothringen" (The Extra Tour in Lorraine)[6] and "Die Kette der Irrtümer in Lothringen" (The Chain of Errors in Lorraine).[7] Krafft's most critical opponent in the postwar controversy was the last to join the debate—Hermann Ritter Mertz von Quirnheim, long-term president of the *Reichsarchiv*.[8] It was not, however, his position that made Mertz a particular threat. It was the fact that in his capacity as the General Staff officer Ia (chief of operations) of the Sixth Army he had been Krafft's closest professional associate. While Wetzell combined his criticism with a dutiful praise for the high capabilities of Krafft and Sixth Army commander Crown Prince Rupprecht of Bavaria,[9] Mertz attacked his former superiors with an aggressiveness that could not but result in a breach.[10] It remains unclear what made him abandon the solidarity of former Sixth Army officers, to which he previously had adhered.[11] The publicly aired controversy over the battles in the Imperial Territories in the summer of 1914 has only recently been thoroughly described and analyzed.[12] In 2002 a biography of Krafft was published by Thomas Müller, discussing the Lorraine campaign in detail.[13] The attention paid to this little-known and not even symbolic battle of the First World War is largely owing to the rather unusual and favorable availability of German source material. The *Bayerisches Kriegsarchiv* (Bavarian War Archive) in Munich holds not only the extensive personal papers of Krafft, but also the files of the Sixth Army. Hence, unlike for most other events, there are many original source documents to draw on for analyzing the fighting in Lorraine during the first year of the war.

The Objective of the Operations in Lorraine and the Vosges

The starting point of any study of the German leadership in the Imperial Territories must be the *Aufmarschanweisung* (Deployment Directive) sent to the headquarters of the Sixth Army upon mobilization. The crucial elements are included in Section IV: Special Instructions:

> 38. The German deployment against France is based on the following intent [*Absicht*]: The *main forces of the German Army* will advance through Belgium and Luxembourg into France. Their advance, if the intelligence on the French deployment (cf. Annex

19b) is correct, is intended as a turn while the Fifth Army secures the pivot point of Thionville–Metz.

The security of the left flank of the main forces will be ensured by the army forces deployed to the Imperial Territories southeast of Metz (Sixth and Seventh Armies and Higher Cavalry Command 3), in addition to the fortresses of Thionville and Metz.

44. *The army forces deployed to the Imperial Territories southeast of Metz*: The Higher Cavalry Command 3 [Höherer Kavallerie Kommandeur], . . . the Sixth Army (III Bavarian Corps, II Bavarian Corps, XXI Army Corps, I Bavarian Army Corps, I Bavarian Reserve Corps, and the Citadel of Bitche), and the Seventh Army (XV Army Corps, XIV Army Corps, XIV Reserve Corps, and presumably two Italian cavalry divisions as well as the fortresses of Strasbourg, including the Feste Kaiser Wilhelm II, Neubreisach, and Upper Rhine fortifications), *will be subordinate to the joint senior command* of the senior-most of the two army commanders.

The joint senior commander is tasked to advance toward the Moselle downriver of Frouard and the Meurthe, capturing Fort de Manonviller, in order to block the assembled French forces and prevent their redeployment to the left wing of the French army.

This task might be superseded by the French launching an attack with superior forces between Metz and the Vosges. If the army forces in the Imperial Territories are thus forced to withdraw, their movements should be such as to prevent a threat to the left flank of the main forces posed by an envelopment of the Nied position [*Niedstellung*]. If required, the Sixth Army will detach units to reinforce those forces holding the *Nied* position.

If the Sixth and Seventh Armies do *not* encounter superior French forces, elements of the Sixth Army and Higher Cavalry Command 3 might deploy via Metz or in the south to join the battle on the left bank of the Moselle.

45. If a French offensive expands into upper Alsace, it would not be unfavorable for our operation in general so long as the enemy does not advance beyond the line of Feste Kaiser Wilhelm II–Breusch–Strasbourg. Holding this line and preventing its circumvention west of the Feste Kaiser Wilhelm II is the mission of the governor of Strasbourg.

46. *During the deployment movements* the security of upper

Alsace and southern Baden is a responsibility of the commanding general of the Seventh Army....

The task of the commanding general of the Seventh Army in upper Alsace and southern Baden is only *temporary*. The joint commanding general of the forces in the Imperial Territories should seek to *use the strongest possible elements of the Seventh Army in direct coordination with the Sixth Army.*[14]

The composition, deployment areas, and missions of the Sixth and Seventh Armies remained basically unchanged from what they had been in 1909–1910.[15] The measures to be taken by the senior German commander in the Imperial Territories depended on the actions of the French. There were three different logical courses of action. The offensive action against the Moselle and Meurthe is not only emphasized by being noted first, it is also underlined in the written orders.

The *Aufmarschanweisung* later played an important role in the justification or criticism of the performance of the Sixth Army's senior leadership, at least for the first stage of the fighting up to 22 August, when the Moselle–Meurthe line was reached.

Sixth Army headquarters received the *Aufmarschanweisung* on 2 August.[16] The contents of this deployment directive had not previously been known to the commanders or staff officers. The reactions within the staff varied. Krafft breathed a sigh of relief: "Thank God, a complete decision!"[17] Mertz, however, reported that later on that day Krafft and Rupprecht had shown themselves "to be little satisfied with the mission they were given."[18] To Mertz himself it seemed "as if the *Oberste Heeresleitung* would have to spend the next weeks frozen at the North Pole."[19] What he meant was that OHL had somewhat relinquished the actual command and control of the operations by making provisions in advance for the Sixth Army to react automatically to various possible developments. As Mertz summarized his impressions: "If one of my former students at the *Kriegsakademie* had written such a sophisticated and roundabout directive I would have had enough reason to question his qualifications to become a General Staff officer. I do, however, wholeheartedly recognize *one* advantage of that instruction: You can make what you want out of it!"[20]

The de facto senior commander of the German forces in the Imperial Territories was to be the chief of staff of the senior field army commander.[21] As Karl Deuinger described in his work about the campaign in Lorraine and in the Vosges, the assignment of the Bavarian crown prince as the formal commanding general and senior combat leader was obviously a function of his royal position.[22] Rupprecht, however, was neither without talent nor uneducated in military affairs. During his earlier service in peacetime he had taken his duties seriously.[23] The surviving records of that period clearly indicate that he did more than simply sign documents put in front of him. To his subordinates he had been a superior to be respected for his professional competence. In his personal war diary he filled many pages with extensive descriptions of situations[24]—not included in the published edition[25]—which show that he approached his tasks with professionalism. Rupprecht was not one of the amateur strategists of the "small maps, large arrows" school, as Terence Zuber described it.

Krafft undoubtedly had more extensive military training and a far better grasp of his tradecraft. In Rupprecht, however, he had a command partner who was far more capable of arguing with his chief of staff based on well-founded reasons than could Prussian Crown Prince Wilhelm in dealing with his own chief of staff, Lieutenant General Konstantin Schmidt von Knobelsdorff.

In retrospect it seems a matter of course that Krafft, the peacetime chief of the Bavarian General Staff, became the chief of the General Staff of the Bavarian Army Supreme Command (the Sixth Army). That assignment was, in fact due to a coincidence of other personnel decisions. Originally, the Prussians wanted one of their own General Staff officers in that position, which they in fact did have during the war with the Austro-Hungarian Army. But the Prussian chief intended for the Sixth Army, Schmidt von Knobelsdorff, was claimed by the German crown prince when he received the command of the Fifth Army, which originally had Krafft assigned as the chief of staff. Krafft, therefore, became available to assume a position with the Bavarian Army, and that coincided with the wishes of the Bavarian crown prince.[26] Thus, the Great General Staff did the Bavarians a favor, which obliged the Bavarian senior command in the Imperial Territories to show particular loyalty in return.[27] This might well have contributed to the fact that the Sixth Army did not always demonstrate the self-confidence in dealing with OHL that the critics later demanded of it.

Immediately after having received the *Aufmarschanweisung*, Krafft wrote a "First estimate of the situation and tasks . . . for the initial operations of the Sixth and Seventh Armies." Krafft summarized the basic idea of the *Anweisung* (instruction) as follows:

> In any case, it must be ensured that the group in the Imperial Territories tasked with the security of the [German] army's flank secures

the necessary time and flexibility for the thrusts of the decisive [right] wing. In the event that the mass of the French army should turn against the [German] forces in the Imperial Territories, it will secure the time for [the right wing] to turn to southeast and provide support. All considerations must be subject to this purpose. Under no circumstances can the army group allow itself to be defeated. It is the shield with which OHL protects the left flank.[28]

Krafft clearly realized that the *Aufmarschanweisung* assigned a supporting role within the broader operation to the Sixth and Seventh Armies, whereas the German Army's right wing was to affect the decision. He sent the completed text of his instruction to Colonel General Helmuth von Moltke. Mertz, who later claimed to have made a defensive interpretation of the OHL *Aufmarschanweisung*, did not find fault with the written explanations of his chief of staff. "There can be no doubt that the army chief [of staff, Moltke] having read this statement could sleep easy knowing that he would have the senior German commander in the Imperial Territories well in hand."[29]

To be forced to adapt to the actions of the enemy made the task much more difficult. This was so not only because the German Army had been trained always to take the initiative, even and especially when the situation was unclear, but also because there had been practically no intelligence on the intent of the French.[30]

The analysis conducted by the *Reichsarchiv* interpreted the *Aufmarschanweisung* as if the attack against the Moselle and Meurthe had been contingent upon certain preconditions, whereas waiting and luring the French into the Lorraine trap would have been the intended normal course of action.[31] The joint commanding general's control of the operations in the Imperial Territories was thus painted in unfavorable colors from the very beginning. This interpretation, of course, elicited vehement opposition from Krafft, which he voiced both publicly and internally.[32] "*It was not the German attack that was . . . tied to certain preconditions*—except for one but rather improbable possibility that the great French offensive in Lorraine would have become quite obvious before the *deployment of the Sixth and Seventh Armies were sufficiently complete*, which, eventually, would have made the very attack pointless. Rather it was *the deviation from the intent to attack. Things are the opposite way round* from what the *KW*[33] describes here and later!"[34]

If Mertz accused Rupprecht and Krafft of intending from the very beginning to "free themselves of the restrictions imposed on them by both situation and mission," and thereby intending to assume the offensive,[35] then he was wrong. For various reasons both Rupprecht and Krafft remained well within the framework of the *Aufmarschanweisung*, despite their undoubted preference for an offensive approach, for whatever different reasons.

The *Reichsarchiv* analysis justified the reinforcement of the left wing as a precaution against a possible French attack, hence the famous "watering down" of the Schlieffen Plan. Accordingly, Moltke thought a great French offensive in Lorraine was probable. Contrary to his predecessor, however, he was prepared to halt the advance of the right wing and to accept the intended decisive battle where the enemy offered it. In this case it naturally made sense to commit strong forces in the Imperial Territories from the very beginning.[36]

Given this perspective, it might be all too easy to conclude that the German senior command in the Imperial Territories ruined that nice plan by acting like a bull in a china shop, thus derailing the developing trap. Wolfgang Foerster replied to Krafft's objections that some of Moltke's notes during the war, as well as statements made by key officers of the Great General Staff or the OHL,[37] indicated the intent of fighting a decisive battle between Metz and Strasbourg. It is a fact that such deliberations were a part of the planning process. Erich Ludendorff, as a colonel in charge of the *Aufmarschabteilung* (Deployment Department) and over a long period Moltke's closest assistant, reported that in Moltke's numerous operational studies on a war in the west: "The leaders of the French army always attacked in Lorraine. General von Moltke was absolutely convinced that such an attack would occur in the casus belli."[38] In that case his intent was that "the army deployed in Lorraine should let the enemy advance farther into Lorraine so that the available [German] forces could launch an enveloping attack from Metz and from the direction of Strasbourg."[39] In a *Denkschrift* of 1913, Moltke even wrote that in case of a massive French advance on Lorraine the march through Belgium would lose its operational significance and Belgium would become a secondary theater of war.[40]

In the summer of 1915, after he had been relieved as chief of the General Staff, Moltke stated that there had been another operational intent for the left wing that completely deviated from the *Aufmarschanweisung* just noted: Whereas the First and Fifth Armies would swing through Metz–Diedenhofen to the south, the Sixth and Seventh Armies were to cross the Meuse between Nancy and Epinal[41] in order to rejoin with the Fifth Army south of Verdun.[42] Bavarian Crown Prince Rupprecht also heard rumors of such deliberations. On 19 November 1914 he wrote to Krafft: "Recently, Crown Prince Wilhelm told me that he had been astonished to hear from Tappen [the chief of the *Operationsabteilung* in 1914] on the occasion of a

Great General Staff prebriefing on the planned deployment in the case of war that the intent was to have the Sixth Army advance between Toul and Epinal."[43]

In 1925 the young Viennese historian Heinz Zatschek reached the same conclusion after corresponding with Tappen. As the *Aufmarschpläne* since 1910 did not foresee any transfer of the Seventh Army to the north, Zatschek concluded that at that time Moltke entertained the idea of fighting a decisive battle in Lorraine until achieving a breakthrough to the Moselle.[44] A report sent by Lieutenant General Karl Ritter von Wenninger (the then Bavarian military representative to OHL) to the Bavarian War Ministry two weeks after the beginning of the war indicates that the concept of a breakthrough was at least circulating among the members of the OHL staff: "The [Sixth] Army of His Royal Highness the Crown Prince of Bavaria, to which as already mentioned by phone the Seventh Army ([Josias von] Heeringen) has been assigned for coordination, is tasked with the subsequent mission of drawing and pinning down as many [enemy] forces as possible until a decision is reached in the north. If the opposing enemy lacks superiority, the army will thrust into the fortification gap between Toul and Epinal and continue the operational breakthrough by rolling up to the north."[45]

Considering that the available information about Moltke's "actual" operational intent in Lorraine, which also includes the *Aufmarschanweisung*, is so contradictory, one should rather doubt any such main intent existed at all. It seems that Moltke, contrary to the idea that surrounded the mystified original plan of his predecessor, had not been determined to carry out a predefined plan under any circumstances. Moltke, rather, was receptive to differing options for a western offensive.

Uncertainty

On 7 August 1914 the Sixth Army headquarters staff boarded a train in Munich. On 9 August at 0747 hours—as Krafft meticulously noted in his diary—they arrived at St. Avold where they were first quartered.[46] Whatever the intentions were of the senior staff, it first had to deal with the "frictions of war." Knowledge of the enemy situation, which was of paramount importance given the nature of the mission of the German forces in the Imperial Territories, was still not available. The German cavalry was unable to break through the French border guard. Aerial reconnaissance provided good intelligence on troop movements but not on stationary forces.[47] And the French did not move.

The *Aufmarschanweisung* provided for a maximum concentration of the Sixth and Seventh Armies, but it was impossible to accomplish that for the time being because of the independent will of the enemy. On 7 August, French troops had invaded southern Alsace. Seventh Army headquarters, with the concurrence of OHL, decided to launch a stiff counterattack against the invader. (Sixth Army headquarters had not yet arrived in the theater and only assumed the joint senior command on 10 August.) The Seventh Army, meanwhile, sent its two active army corps[48] to the Sundgau area. The intent of inflicting an extensive Cannae-like defeat on the French right at Mulhouse failed because the French left wing was anchored on the Vosges Mountains, where it was impossible to break through. Although the Germans succeeded in pushing the enemy back through a frontal battle,[49] their own forces paid a high price. As Krafft noted in his diary: "Both corps were highly overtaxed and will be exhausted for a number of days."[50] During their movement back to the north, elements of the XIV Army Corps were involved in combat in the Vosges, where the French tried to advance. Meanwhile, the XV Army Corps cancelled their railway transport without authorization when the allocated trains were seven hours late. XV Army Corps then marched on foot for most of the route.[51]

Despite the commitment of two army corps at Mulhouse, the resulting three hundred enemy troops and three guns captured was rather meager. The much smaller battle near Lagarde in Lorraine on 11 August had far better results, as Krafft noted with satisfaction.[52] But Krafft also noted the first indicators of tensions between Bavaria and Prussia: "Although the Bavarians[53] bore the brunt of the battle, the XXI Army Corps referred to it as their victory. War trophies captured by Bavarian cavalry and light infantry also were snatched away by Prussian troops during an unguarded moment."[54] The Prussians acted rather self-confidently. Lieutenant General Otto von Stetten, commander of the Bavarian cavalry division that had to coordinate with the XXI Army Corps to secure the border, had the impression that the Prussians felt themselves responsible for "bucking-up the dull Bavarians."

Some light, however, finally was cast on the enemy situation. An order of the French Second Army was found with a French brigadier general who had been killed at Lagarde. The order indicated that six French Army corps were assembled between Toul and Epinal.[55] On 13 August, Krafft calculated the strength of his direct opponents at some nine Army corps plus several reserve divisions. Thus, the German forces in the Imperial Territories were facing a numerically superior enemy.[56] And indeed, this picture was realistic. From the overall German point of view this was welcome intelligence, because the French Army had only twenty-one active army corps.

That meant that the Sixth and Seventh Armies were facing almost half of the French Army.

French War Plan XVII provided for two forceful advances into Germany: one on the right, between Metz and the Vosges, and the other on the left, north of the Verdun–Metz line.[57] The French, therefore, had (like the Germans) assembled two strong field armies between Toul–Nancy and Belfort. The first, in the south, was commanded by General Auguste Dubail, and the second, more to the north, was under the command of General Édouard de Castelnau. The southern army had been tasked with a mission similar to that of the Germans in the Imperial Territories. It was to contain the opposing forces and to prevent them from being committed in more important sectors of the theater.[58] To accomplish this mission, the French forces were to advance into the Imperial Territories from the south to the north, up to the level of Strasbourg, and from there support the attack to be launched later in Lorraine at the Rhine.[59]

That French scheme of maneuver fitted rather well with the German operational intent. The *Aufmarschanweisung* expressly anticipated surrendering southern Alsace. A perfunctory resistance, of course, had to be made, which led to the First Battle of Mulhouse, where the Seventh Army acted forcefully enough to nip the French ambitions in the bud. The theoretical readiness to give up territory for the sake of gaining operational advantage succumbed—for the first but not last time—to territorial ambitions. General Joseph Joffre, however, did not allow himself to be put off by this setback, nor by the obvious German main attack in Belgium. He ordered the planned offensive in Lorraine launched by the First and Second Armies, with the main effort on their internal wings. On 11 August, French operational planners designated 14 August as the start date for the offensive. The strictly defensive German approach was already beginning to unsettle the French.[60]

Sixth Army headquarters was unsettled as well. They still did not know what the French had planned. The basic assumption was that the French would have reached operational readiness by 11 August; however, by 13 August they still had not made any serious moves. Bavarian Crown Prince Rupprecht did not change his intent to attack: "An offensive solution to our mission seems desirable for seizing the initiative."[61] This intent could not be achieved, as he had to wait for the Seventh Army to arrive. Nonetheless, coordination with that army was rather difficult. Obviously General Heeringen found it hard to subordinate himself to a younger joint commander, and a Bavarian on top of that.

On 11 August, Sixth Army staff officer Major Rudolf von Xylander traveled to Seventh Army headquarters at Ensisheim to brief them on the intentions of the German senior commander in the Imperial Territories: "I got the overriding impression that General von Heeringen and his staff gave us the cold shoulder. . . . Even the army commander himself showed a profound aversion to subordinate [himself] to the Crown Prince of Bavaria." At Seventh Army headquarters they also boasted about having good direct communications with OHL.[62]

But even if the subordinate Seventh Army headquarters had been more cooperative and their component corps had been available, Rupprecht's intent to attack would have been hard to carry out. It seemed OHL was already pursuing other plans. On 12 August, Sixth Army headquarters received its first relevant instruction from OHL in Koblenz: "An advance of the Sixth and Seventh Armies *beyond* the Moselle between Metz and Frouard and the Meurthe is not in the interest of the Oberste Heeresleitung. An advance *against* this line is provided for in the *Aufmarschanweisungen* only under the circumstances noted. The destruction of Fort de Manonviller is desired as soon as the situation permits. Heavy howitzers are assigned to the Sixth Army. The army will deploy north of Metz in only a few days."[63]

This was a strange message. It deviated from the *Aufmarschanweisung*, which OHL had every right to do. But at the same time it appeared as an admonition to act within the framework of that instruction. Xylander saw this as an indication of "uncertainty ruling within OHL."[64] Obviously, the purpose of the telegram was to prevent the senior commander in the Imperial Territories from prematurely launching an offensive. It also can be regarded as the first indicator of the "*Sackidee*" (bag concept), the luring of the enemy into a Lorraine trap. Sixth Army headquarters interpreted the meaning of the OHL telegram to Seventh Army headquarters and the subordinate corps headquarters as follows: "The joint *mission of the forces in the Imperial Territories* is the security of the left flank of the army. . . . *Evasion of* the enemy should only be considered *if there is a vital necessity*. Currently, there are no indicators of such."

The reluctance of Sixth Army headquarters to withdraw is quite obvious from that message. Krafft and Rupprecht had one objective that was to play an important role throughout the entire campaign in Lorraine—the morale of the troops. In their opinion, every rearward movement would hurt that morale seriously.[65]

The *Aufmarschanweisung* did not say anything about deliberately allowing the French to move into Lorraine. However, the idea was in the air. Krafft himself had thought so when he made an "initial estimate of the situation," analyzing "*Fall B*" (Case B) of the *Aufmarschanweisung*. "If we manage to hold the line Metz–Nied–Saar–Pfalzburg–Donon–Molsheim–Strasbourg long enough, the conditions for shifting to the offensive will be favorable. We can assume that the enemy, once having come to a halt within that arc, will be seriously restricted in using his forces and will have great difficulties in fending off the attack from three sides. The objective of such an attack should be to destroy the enemy by means of an encirclement."[66]

Two days later some light seemed to have been cast on the French plans, although at the time the German forces in the Imperial Territories were still paralyzed as a result of the fighting at Mulhouse. According to a message retransmitted by Seventh Army headquarters, which it had received from the German military attaché in Bern, Switzerland, the Sixth and Seventh Armies faced twelve to fifteen French Army corps, a number that later would be increased to fifteen to eighteen.[67] Those indeed were the "superior forces" noted in the *Aufmarschanweisung* as a prerequisite for the second course of action. Sixth Army headquarters reacted promptly and announced an extensive withdrawal back to the line of Busendorf–Saarlouis–Saargemünd–Pfalzburg–Lützelburg.[68]

Thus another pocket was actually opened for the French into which they were to advance to destruction. On 14 August the French finally launched their much expected, even much desired advance. When the above-mentioned report from Switzerland reached OHL, it triggered a new instruction to the senior commander in the Imperial Territories. The war diary of the Sixth Army noted on 15 August: "Letter of *Generalquartiermeister* Stein to the chief of the General Staff of the Sixth Army. *Oberste Heeresleitung* wishes the Sixth Army to evade behind the Saar River above Saarbrücken."[69]

Stein's instruction also specified the allocation of mobile reserve units. The mobile capabilities of a large part of the *Ersatz* Army (Replacement Army) had been built up by the Great General Staff since 1910. By 1 April 1911, six and a half *Ersatz* divisions were available to OHL. But these conglomerate units lacked the stable internal coherence that, from the German perspective, was vital for the combat value of forces. Also, their equipment was far behind that of active units. Initially Moltke expected the *Ersatz* Army "not to conduct large operations but to put up strong resistance at suitable lines."[70] Such a secondary task seemed to be expected from them in Lorraine, where they were to assist in closing and holding the developing pocket.

The Fifth Army and the Fortress of Metz were also instructed to support the imminent great battle.[71] Things would have been well on track if the information that the mass of the French Army was about to enter Lorraine had been correct. This was, however, not the case. As early as 16 August the mirage was starting to dissolve. Early that day Tappen phoned Krafft and informed him that OHL no longer believed the French were assembling in significant strength between Toul and Epinal, and the probability of the French entering "the bag" had been reduced.[72]

The situation was fluid again, but important and far-reaching decisions had already been made. Even if the combat power of the *Ersatz* divisions was not particularly high, they were the only operational reserve Germany had at that point. After they had been staged in Lorraine, the relative weakness of the German Army would cause any reinforcements made in one sector to weaken the position in another sector.[73]

Between 13 and 16 August OHL's estimate of the enemy situation had twice changed significantly and triggered important dispositions of the German forces. Meanwhile, OHL expressed concern that the Sixth Army might withdraw too quickly, fears that Krafft was able to dispel.[74] The French advance that started on 14 August and the German defense baffled both sides. Joffre knew, of course, that it was dangerous to advance the French point between Metz and Strasbourg, and he therefore placed tight restrictions on his offensive.[75] The French advanced only in short bounds of some five kilometers each and then immediately dug in.[76] The war diary of the Sixth Army notes for 17 August: "Enemy quiet along the entire front. . . . Number of French corps and the hesitant attitude of the French are a strange contrast. Doubt as to whether the enemy seeks a decision here."[77]

Sixth Army headquarters evaluated the possibility that the French might well have the same mission as the Germans—just to fix the enemy by launching a demonstrative offensive. When Joffre was informed that the Germans had evacuated Saarburg, he was leery of German counterattacks and therefore ordered his forces to proceed cautiously beyond Saarburg.[78] The French suspected a trap.[79] Groener's 1927 conclusion that the Germans should have prodded the French into being more aggressive by withdrawing more rapidly[80] is far removed from the realities of those days in August 1914.

The Attack

In Hellimer, the new headquarters of Sixth Army, the advocates of an offensive now had the upper hand. The army's 16 August war diary entry indicates that the General Staff officer Ia recommended an attack with the inner wings of the Sixth and Seventh Armies for the next day.[81] That officer was Mertz, who later in 1932 publicly and harshly criticized the Sixth Army's offensive posture. As far as Sixth Army headquarters was concerned, the final decision had to be made by the chief of staff, who advocated an attack with limited objectives. "Only a short thrust would be required; a long pursuit deep into enemy territory would not be necessary." That would gain time for the offensive of the main forces.[82] OHL was not much help in the decision-making process. That evening they sent an instruction to Sixth Army headquarters that "was very much like an oracle." The task of the Sixth and Seventh Armies was to cover the left flank of the German Army. Furthermore, they were to proceed in accordance with the *Aufmarschanweisung*.[83] Thus, Krafft was back to the point where he had been on 2 August. He has three possible courses of action, from which he had to make a decision.

That order coincided with the visit of a liaison officer from Koblenz, Lieutenant Colonel Wilhelm von Dommes,[84] chief of the Political Division of OHL. Dommes expressly explained that he had not been tasked with bringing instructions, but rather with providing background. According to Dommes, OHL supported the idea that while the German forces in the Imperial Territories faced superior enemy forces, the French were about to reinforce their northern wing. The "bag" concept, therefore, had been abandoned. OHL wanted the Sixth and Seventh Armies to hold on to the Nied position and Metz to prevent the enemy from advancing into the German Army's left flank. Dommes expressed his doubts about the chance for a successful German offensive in the Imperial Territories.

Rupprecht admitted the disadvantages of an offensive, which would have to be conducted frontally. But he also thought the German heavy artillery added significant weight to the attack. Krafft argued that the permanent withdrawal would weaken the offensive spirit of the German forces. Rupprecht browbeat Dommes. He would not retreat to the Nied position voluntarily. Doing so would open a gap with the Seventh Army that the enemy could exploit. Nor would it be possible to hold the Breusch position. Unless he received a direct order from OHL to the contrary, he would attack: "Either they let me act, or they can issue definite orders."[85] According to Mertz, Rupprecht or Krafft emphasized that they "could not expect the Bavarian soldier to withdraw again from the enemy toward whom he felt superior."[86]

Krafft doubted the defense could be maintained along such an overextended line. But overall he considered the risk of an attack to be "smaller than the risks of evasion and passive defense over a long period. It will have a liberating effect on the mind of our troops when they are allowed to move forward against the enemy." Krafft associated factual rational arguments with the epochal conviction of the moral superiority of the offensive, as was typical of prewar thinking.

Dommes had not been able to persuade Sixth Army headquarters. He expressly left the decision to Rupprecht, as the latter noted in his diary. The parallels to the famous mission of OHL General Staff officer Lieutenant Colonel Richard Hentsch during the Battle of the Marne are obvious. The use of liaison officers as leadership instruments was OHL's usual method during the summer of 1914. The result of Dommes mission was unpleasant for both OHL and Sixth Army headquarters. An agreement on how to continue operations in the Imperial Territories had not been reached. Although OHL would not endorse the intent of Sixth Army, it refrained from enforcing its opinion through the chain of command.

To ensure that the attack order would not be countermanded from Koblenz, Krafft telephoned Quartermaster General (assistant chief of staff) Hermann von Stein the following day.[87] The latter is reported to have replied: "No, the *Heeresleitung* will not put a spoke in your wheels by prohibiting the attack. You will have to bear the responsibility. Make your decision in good conscience as you consider best. [Krafft] replied: 'It is made.'"[88] A report sent by Bavarian military representative von Wenninger to Munich on 19 August also gives the impression that OHL regarded the operations in Lorraine not from the perspective of the responsible command authority, but rather as an interested observer of a psychological drama. "Here, they assume that the Crown Prince accomplishes his task offensively, silently hoping, however, that the nerves of the commander will be strong enough to allow the enemy to reach Saarburg [the enemy was already there—author's note], and finally crush the enemy between two fronts."[89]

In 1922, General von Haeften told the *Reichsarchiv* that in November 1914 Moltke had called the halt of the Sixth Army's withdrawal movement an act of downright "disobedience."[90] Tappen, when requested to comment, replied that he had not heard of any prohibition on an attack, and thus there could be no talk of disobedience.[91] There was no basis for such strong words used by Mertz in his book to denounce the offensive orientation of his former superiors, who according to him spoke of "unshackling themselves from the constraints imposed by the Oberste Heeresleitung."[92] But OHL, in fact, had not even tried to shackle Sixth Army with such bonds.

Krafft was particularly affected by the criticism against the decision to attack made by Swiss military writer Eugen Bircher in 1927[93] that it had only been a "dynastic luxury battle."[94] In other words, the operation had not been conducted for military reasons but rather to enhance the prestige of the Bavarian Crown. Krafft was livid. For him, this was an accusation of "blatant treason." This perception, however, was a common one in the Prussian army, as evidenced by a report written by Mertz in 1928 for the *Reichsarchiv*.[95] He claimed to have known of the "widespread opinion that dynastic considerations had a *decisive* influence on the leadership of Sixth Army in Lorraine. At any rate, they did not play a role in the decision to attack on 20 August when I was present, neither in word nor in the smallest notion, and even less in the later endurance of the Sixth Army in Lorraine."[96]

It is at least possible that certain Bavarian—but not necessarily dynastic—reasons of state motivated the active posture of the Bavarian Army in the field. A corroborating indicator can be seen in the summary of Deuringer's description of the events in Lorraine, which had been read by Rupprecht and Krafft prior to publication. Deuringer said that considering the anticipated short duration of the war, the Bavarian troops could hardly be expected "to have been able to pride themselves only on a successful withdrawal!"[97] OHL would have been well advised to dispel such obvious concerns of the Bavarian Supreme Command with "definite orders" as demanded by Rupprecht.

At Sixth Army headquarters in Hellimer, the battle was anticipated with understandable apprehension. It was the first great battle of the war, and the initial situation was unfavorable because the attack clearly had to be made frontally. When the German offensive was launched on 20 August, the French were then in the process of advancing. Thus, there were two offensives on that day, which collided with each other. The battle developed as a "heated meeting engagement which . . . disintegrated into a number of isolated group combats. This resulted from the broad expansion of the operation in width, combined with the characteristics of the rugged Lorraine theater with its extended forests and sharp mountain ranges. Furthermore, the French attacks were faint and uncoordinated, while the German thrust had an enormous power and resoluteness."[98]

By the afternoon of 20 August the commander of the French Second Army was forced to order a withdrawal behind the border. The fortified position at Nancy offered a solid position.[99] The following day, the French First Army joined the withdrawal. In retrospect, the weak German resistance in the previous days resulted in the French perception that the enemy had consciously let them run into a strongly consolidated fortified line and then launched a counterstrike from that position.[100] For Joffre, the bad news came as a complete surprise. He had been convinced that the favorable correlation of forces would keep the French secure from a counterattack in Lorraine. The Second Army, however, had been severely treated and would need forty-eight hours to reconstitute, as the army commander reported on 21 August. General de Castelnau even considered abandoning Nancy, which for Joffre was out of the question for psychological reasons.[101] The Germans were not able to profit from that exigency since Krafft—being afraid of the deeper echelons of the French combat posture—had set only short-term objectives for the attack.

The day after the attack Moltke was still far from being angry with Sixth Army headquarters. According to Groener, Moltke assembled the officers of the General Staff that evening and, "deeply moved, proclaimed the 'great victory' of the Sixth and Seventh Armies in Lorraine. It was 'his' victory, which he had laid the foundations for in his *Kriegsspiele* [war games] and *Generalstabsreisen* [General Staff rides] of the previous years."[102]

Krafft wrote a report about the battle in which he interpreted the events as more or less a confirmation of prewar expectations. As he summarized his overall assessment: "The *Oberste Heeresleitung* may . . . look into the future with confidence."[103]

The Pursuit

OHL now had to make "meaningful decisions about the continuation of the operations in Lorraine and the further engagement of the armies committed there," as the official history prepared by the *Reichsarchiv* correctly states.[104] On 22 August, Krafft phoned Tappen to learn how to proceed. In a supplement written after the war and annexed to the diary of Crown Prince Rupprecht, Krafft described the phone call as if he had expressed the expectation that course of action three of the *Aufmarschanweisung* would occur: after reaching the Meurthe the shift to the defensive and redeployment of all available forces to the right bank of the Moselle. After consulting with Moltke, however, Tappen issued the instruction for "pursuit in the direction of Epinal." Krafft was dismayed: "I was disappointed with the decision and it raised my deep concern about the future. I could not but see this as a momentous deviation from Schlieffen's great operational plan."[105]

This conversation played a central role in Krafft's justification of his leadership in Lorraine.[106] Mertz pointed to inconsistencies in the narration of that phone call.[107] It was not included in the war diary of the Sixth Army, which is astonishing if one considers how Krafft was said to be in strong opposition to OHL. The fact that the Sixth Army headquarters had received a specific tasking from OHL, however, is indisputable. In a message to the *Reichsarchiv* Tappen confirmed the basic contents of the order,[108] which he also noted in his diary.[109] Later, Mertz raised a strong criticism of Krafft's obedience to orders. If he had in fact claimed to have realized the pernicious nature of the pursuit mission, it would have been not only his right but his duty to protest to OHL.[110] Krafft and Xylander countered that after the debate preceding the attack of 20 August, during which Sixth Army headquarters did not act contrary to an order but rather prevailed against the obviously different opinion of OHL, it would not have been possible to risk further friction with Koblenz, especially since the will of OHL was now clear in the form of an order.

After the war, critics advanced the argument that after the battle of 20 August would have been the time to scale back the German superiority of forces in the Imperial Territories and redeploy units via rail to the rear of the wheeling right wing.[111] The rail network and the available rolling stock reserves would have permitted a rapid and large-scale transport from the southern wing to the rear of the right wing of the German western army.[112] In August 1914 this concept apparently carried no weight with either Sixth Army headquarters or OHL. While Groener in his first book had criticized the fact that on 22 August the forces had been given a fatal order for pursuit, "instead of packing a considerable part into the readily available railway trains,"[113] he later changed his opinion and subscribed to Tappen's point of view as presented in the *Reichsarchiv* official history.[114] "Transporting the troops from Lorraine was no longer an option. The Belgian and French railways were still in the process of reconstruction and therefore unable to support such a mass transport in a short time. One had to agree with *Oberste Heeresleitung* in not wanting the forces to be made available from the Sixth and Seventh Armies to march from Aachen far behind the right wing without any operational purpose or task."[115]

In this context then, the question of why the corps to reinforce East Prussia had been withdrawn from the wheeling wing and not from the southern wing becomes much more interesting. Regardless, any forces withdrawn from the south would not have had any problems regarding transport. In 1934, Rupprecht cited a statement by Groener, which the latter was said to have made in Kiev in 1918. Reportedly, Groener in 1914 had recommended the transfer of a Bavarian army corps and the Bavarian reserve corps. "At General Headquarters, he was given the answer that it would not be possible to send Bavarians to East Prussia, since they [OHL] did not like the notion of East Prussia being liberated by Bavarians."[116]

Although OHL hoped for rapid progress in Lorraine after 22 August, the French resistance there stiffened. "It was called 'pursuit' by the Great General Staff, but for the troops the imminent battles could not have been farther removed from any kind of pursuit. They were as hard and difficult as the previous attacks had been."[117] The pursuit mission drew the Sixth and Seventh

Armies to the south. In the process, the right wing of those forces brushed along the French fortresses, ideal arterial gates for counterattacks. That right flank required strong security, at the cost of the forces committed to the "pursuit," which plodded along spiritlessly because of the general fatigue of the troops.[118] In Koblenz, they did not understand what actually happened.

> In the evening we received a message from OHL indicating now (that the initial concerns had been eliminated by our victory) the situation is perceived as much easier than it is. (People go from one extreme to the other). They now want a pursuit to the last man and horse. Captain [Bodo von] Harbou feels the necessity of noting that at Waterloo they would also have put a drummer on the horse![119]
>
> At the same time there is a letter by Wenninger who expresses great joy in the victory and also indicates that His Majesty entertains strongly sanguine hopes for the actions of the cavalry. He should see them!

On 24 August, the situation changed dramatically. Joffre had overcome his disappointment about the setback in Lorraine sufficiently to express a generally positive judgment on the course of the combat in that sector, where the French had succeeded in holding a significant part of the German forces. What mattered to him was not only holding their ground in Lorraine, but also continuing to hold down the Germans.[120] If they previously had believed that they would—even with great pain—follow after a defeated enemy, the French now made a completely surprising turn and attacked vigorously.

That attack immediately caused a crisis on the German side, which did not have any more reserves. The Sixth and Seventh Armies lay in Lorraine like an unbraided rope end and were not able to respond at first. The difficult situation became obvious at the French Fort de Manonviller, which was in a central position behind the German front line, preventing German use of vital roads. As soon as possible the Germans brought up the most powerful artillery they had available, including two batteries of the heaviest howitzers.[121] When the Bavarian II Army Corps became seriously engaged, the only thing the Sixth Army was able to offer was a categorical stand-and-fight order. Krafft even contemplated ordering a withdrawal, which was opposed by his staff. Those actions caused the troops considerable losses. Rupprecht, as a result, made several relevant observations in his diary that would be typical for military leaders in that war, and particularly during that phase of the war. While there was nobody who regretted the losses more, he also noted:

"Now no efforts should be spared to defeat the enemy decisively, thus avoiding much higher losses at a later time. That will certainly occur if the war lasts for a longer period and we do not succeed in achieving a decision in coordination with the other armies."[122] The high losses during the initial months of the war were not only the result of the inexperience of both forces and leaders, but also of the intent to end the war as soon as possible.

After several days, the French offensive petered out. The surrender of Manonviller on 27 August also contributed to stabilizing the situation. The German transport capabilities just behind the front improved considerably and forces were now free for deployment elsewhere. Nevertheless, the situation did not completely stabilize. Several times during the subsequent days the French supreme command confirmed the mission of the field armies on their right wing to contain German forces—and that meant to attack.[123] That objective also determined Krafft's actions, resulting in the strange situation that two armies attacking each other with maximum effort were united in the intent of not letting the other get away. In the meantime, however, another tasking had emerged for the German forces in the Imperial Territories, delivered by a messenger from OHL on the evening of 25 August. That point was the climax of the French offensive. The two German field armies were now ordered to cross the Moselle between Toul and Epinal.

Initially, that tasking was moot, since the general situation made it impossible to execute.[124] A few days later another OHL instruction ordered the bombardment of the "Position de Nancy." But that too was not possible, as Krafft noted in his diary: "That is something we are currently unable to do since we do not have the siege artillery!" The senior commander in the Imperial Territories now had two new taskings that were to determine the German actions there until the end of the battles in Lorraine. The first tasking was to pass through the Charmes Gap. The unfortified route along the Moselle had been named after a small town situated in the middle, between the large fortresses of Toul and Epinal. The second tasking was to attack the "Position de Nancy." That designation was a common "German Gallicism." The French called it something quite different. The Grand Couronné was a mountain range northeast of Nancy directly on the border of the German Reich, forming a natural protective shield. As part of their mobilization process, the French had reinforced the position according to plan.[125]

OHL, meanwhile, confirmed the oral instruction to cross the Moselle. In the *Allgemeine Anweisungen an die 1. bis 7. Armee für den Fortgang der Operationen* of 27 August,[126] the German forces in the Imperial Territories were initially tasked to repel the French advances in Lorraine and Upper

Alsace: "If the enemy withdraws, the Sixth Army, including the subordinate Higher Cavalry Command 3, will cross the Moselle between Toul and Epinal and advance in the general direction of Neufchâteau. The [Sixth] Army will then be responsible for the security of the left flank of the [German] Army. The line Nancy–Toul is to be closed, and sufficient security is to be ensured toward Epinal." In that case, the Sixth Army was to be reinforced by the two active corps of the Seventh Army while the latter would become independent and secure the area between Epinal and the Swiss border. The objective was to envelop the enemy, not only with the right wing but also with the left. But nothing like that happened because Sixth Army headquarters stuck to the condition "if the enemy withdraws." Obviously the enemy would not do so, hence there was no reason for crossing the Moselle. In addition, after several days of fierce combat and heavy losses, the forces were shattered and in urgent need of reconstitution, as the war diary of Sixth Army noted for 27 August.

Trench Warfare

During those days the combat in Lorraine assumed a new character, which soon came to define the war itself. Mobile warfare turned into trench warfare. The higher an echelon, the longer it took until they understood that this state was permanent and that it could not simply be overcome with the standard prewar tactics.[127] The overwhelming French artillery fire was the main thing emphasized in German descriptions of the fighting.[128] Prior to the war, the German artillery had focused on destroying the enemy's artillery,[129] but that now proved to be much more difficult than had been assumed. In the immediate prewar conflicts in Manchuria and in the Balkans the respective belligerents did not exploit the full ballistic potential of their guns, and that approach still prevailed in general military thought going into the war in 1914.[130] In general, the practical maximum ranges were expected to be three thousand to four thousand meters, or five thousand meters at best. The ballistic maximum ranges, such as the eight thousand meters for the French 75 mm field gun, were not exploited since the maximum range of the fire control equipment was sixty-five hundred meters.[131] But now that the mobile field operations had come to a standstill, the maximum effective ranges of the field pieces were increasingly required.

On 27 August, the commander of the French First Army, General Dubail, issued the order to dig in the trails of the guns to increase the elevation of the tubes to achieve the maximum effective ranges.[132] The French batteries were now generally positioned far away from the German artillery—too far—and it was also difficult to locate them. The French seemed to have the advantage, and they were already using aerial reconnaissance.[133] As soon as a French aircraft could be seen circling over a German battery, the French artillery fire would start falling within a half hour or less. Once a battery was acquired in this manner, the only thing it could do was march-order and abandon the position.[134] The French artillery generally reacted quickly and precisely. As the Germans later learned from captured documents, the effective French artillery fire was not only the result of good gun crew training, but also of the thorough tactical analysis the French had made of the border areas. The French artillery in Lorraine was especially well-equipped with heavy guns, in striking contrast to the other battlefields of the summer of 1914, where the German heavy artillery enjoyed unchallenged superiority.

The vicinity of the large fortresses, which characterized the military geographic situation in Lorraine, also facilitated the strength of the French heavy artillery there and shaped the character of the battles. Not merely concrete-covered barriers, those fortresses were also huge storage areas for war materiel of all kinds, mainly engineering equipment, artillery, and munitions. All that boded ill for any troops entering the force field of such concentrated annihilating power. Already in the first weeks of the war, both sides had opened their fortress depots to send the materiel stored there into the field. The relevant literature frequently indicates that the Germans in Lorraine fought against the French "fortress front." This term is somewhat misleading. The Germans, in fact, never entered the area of the fortifications of Toul or Epinal. They did, however, face the enormous resources provided by those bulwarks.

This also worked the other way, since the German fortresses were similarly equipped. The strongest fortress—Metz, minus Thionville—had 853 guns, 470 of which were heavy, with a stock of eight hundred thousand rounds of ammunition.[135] The Sixth Army had already "thoroughly plundered" the Bavarian fortress at Germersheim for the attack on 20 August.[136] A process that only a few weeks later became a routine logistics procedure was noted in the Seventh Army war diary in August 1914: "To provide XV Army Corps with effective armament for the fierce close battles, the governor of Strasbourg is ordered to send 1,500 hand grenades to Raon L'Etape."[137]

This also raises the question of whether the vast superiority of the French artillery mentioned in the German sources actually existed.[138] As the Bavarian crown prince later learned from the diary of a French officer, the French infantry did not feel their own artillery could support them adequately, and the infantry as a result suffered terrible losses from German artillery fire.[139] According to French general Georges Frédéric Herr, artillery commander of a French Army corps in 1914, the situation was the same everywhere: "In Lorraine, in the Ardennes, in Belgium . . . in 1914, our light artillery when marching in columns was often surprised by the fire of the long-range German artillery, reactively dashing into undulating covered and densely wooded terrain where it was difficult to maneuver and to establish communications. The firing range [of our light guns] cannot reach the enemy heavy artillery which in turn rains down shells on them and completely disrupts them."[140] While the Germans saw the superior firing range of the French guns as the reason for the unexpectedly long distances at which the artillery fight was prosecuted, Herr attributed it to the long range of the German heavy guns.[141] Herr's assessment is at odds with the German experience in Lorraine.[142] It can be assumed, therefore, that the German and French mutually exclusive evaluations of their respective artillery were functions of the peculiarity of positional warfare, where the effect of one's own long-range weapons is far less evident than those of the enemy.

In Lorraine, meanwhile, they prepared for that new kind of warfare. Sixth Army headquarters issued the relevant instructions, although a diary entry by Rupprecht indicates the difficulties they still had in identifying the new phenomenon: "I feel . . . compelled to point out to the corps that for the time being they should operate in the same way as they would for an attack against a fortress during that phase when it is necessary to conceal the deployment of the heavy artillery in protected firing positions. As a consequence, I recommend entrenching the infantry deeply; sparsely manning the firing trenches; dividing the infantry into three groups—security troops, sector reserves, and main reserves—as well as executing hasty counterattacks."[143] This, as Gebsattel ironically noted, "explained that the fortress warfare rightly existed."[144] The French command issued almost identical instructions.[145] In Lorraine, well-prepared field fortifications were erected on both sides. Several days later, Rupprecht noted with gratification that the infantry in the meantime had found a certain level of protection from artillery fire in the deep trenches.[146] Likewise, German patrols reported the "almost astonishing French digging."[147]

The Crossing of the Moselle and the Attack on the "Position de Nancy"

The respective army commands drew different conclusions from that situation. Joffre used the stabilized situation in Lorraine to shift troops from there to his left wing. He issued the first order to that effect to the Second Army on 30 August, and other orders followed in the subsequent days.[148] The Germans could not act similarly because their forces could not have been recommitted for weeks, owing to the transportation situation. But it was during this period that the campaign was expected to be decided. If they were to contribute, the units of the Sixth and Seventh Armies would have to fight in their current locations. Koblenz regarded the alleged inactivity of the German forces in the Imperial Territories with increasing apprehension, as Tappen noted in his diary on 28 August: "The slowness of the advance of the Sixth Army is hardly agreeable. They must either stand firm to fix a strong enemy or, if the enemy is weak, they should quickly cross the upper Moselle. Hopefully, the advance there will finally make progress."[149] In a telephone conversation with Tappen the following day, Krafft justified his hesitation, saying that the prerequisite for the attack, the withdrawal of the French, had not yet happened.[150] Tappen accepted that, but not so all the members of OHL. Moltke on 30 August vented his accumulated anger at the Bavarian military representative to OHL.[151] Affected as he was, Wenninger asked for an appointment the following day with the Prussian war minister, Lieutenant General Erich von Falkenhayn, who had just returned from Lorraine, where he also had visited Sixth Army headquarters. Falkenhayn shared Wenninger's view that the Sixth Army was too weak to force the crossing over the Moselle between two strong fortifications, and he therefore announced a new task for the forces on the German left wing.[152]

The day before, Sixth Army headquarters had received another visitor from OHL, whose visit was to have consequences. Major Max Bauer, the OHL staff officer responsible for heavy artillery, described the situation far differently than what Krafft was assuming. According to Bauer, OHL expected stronger French resistance to build up on the German wheel [right] flank. In order to break that resistance, as Krafft noted in his journal, the Sixth Army was to attack "the enemy's flank" through the "gap" between Toul and Epinal "and bring about the decision! That is a totally different assessment!"[153] For Krafft it meant a considerable complication of his task, since instead of pursuing a withdrawing enemy he had to repel him head-on. As a preparatory measure for that breakthrough, Bauer recommended seizing the "Position de Nancy" in order to reduce the area that the Sixth Army had to cover for its crossing of the Moselle. This was not an unreasonable suggestion. The question was whether the Sixth Army was capable of conquering that strongly fortified mountain range. In Bauer's opinion, three days would be sufficient to achieve that, and he provided the entire foot artillery reserve of Metz to support the operation.

Bauer had appeared very self-confident and he left the impression with Sixth Army headquarters that he was authorized to issue instructions on behalf of OHL. The following day, the senior commander in the Imperial Territories and his staff planned the action against the "Position de Nancy" with remarkable zeal. Unfortunately, the batteries that could be provided from Metz were largely without horses.[154] Therefore, the railway situation was vital for the organization of the attack, since the transport routes for the heavy equipment and the enormous fire requirement had to be kept as short as possible. Major General Otto Kreppel, commander of the Bavarian foot artillery brigade, distributed the batteries as Krafft did the corps so that "already before lunch the critical orders for bringing in the siege train could be issued."[155] In the event, realities on the ground were created that could not or would not be changed. A few hours later the situation changed again. On that day Sixth Army General Staff officer Rudolf von Xylander went to OHL, which had just relocated to Luxembourg. There he learned "quite by accident" that OHL saw no particular importance to the seizure of the "Position de Nancy."[156] Tappen now dictated those new instructions to Xylander that Falkenhayn had initiated. Accordingly, "it was essential" for the Sixth Army to contain the enemy at a strength level approximately equivalent to the combined strength of the Sixth and Seventh Armies. The attack on the "Position de Nancy" was specifically classified as "not necessary." It was merely necessary to establish strong security. The tasking to cross the Moselle remained, but Sixth Army was authorized to deviate from it if the river crossing attack could not be executed within the shortest time.

Sixth Army headquarters was finally allowed to leave French Lorraine. Tappen, however, imposed one additional restriction: "Careful consideration should be given to the possibility that the withdrawal would be too detrimental to the morale of the troops."

Quartermaster General von Stein, who had been present during the issuing of the orders, added his expectation that the Sixth Army would attack the bridgehead at Bayon, the French position in the Charmes Gap, on 2 December.[157] With this order OHL created as much ambiguity as possible. Groener spoke of a "Delphic oracle, the interpretation of which the senior command [in the Imperial Territories] did not succeed."[158]

The decision by Sixth Army headquarters to remain in position was based on several factors. Initially, they did not want to change the orders for the attack on the "Position de Nancy," which had already been issued only a few hours earlier. The conviction that a leader, if he wanted to retain the trust of his subordinates, had to stick to instructions once issued carried more weight with Krafft than the possibility of preventing a possible error. Krafft was not the only one thinking that way. When the kaiser wanted to halt the occupation of Luxembourg by the 16th Division after having received the 1 August telegram from Karl Max Fürst von Lichnowsky, the German ambassador in London, that raised hopes for the neutrality of France, Moltke refused to do so. His reasoning was that the cancellation of an action that had been prepared according to plan would "be immediately perceived by the troops as a sign of uncertainty."[159] Thus, the attack on the "Position de Nancy" was executed as planned. The operation would contain the French forces; it would improve the chances for an eventual breakthrough on the Moselle; and it used the assigned artillery, which could only be used where it could be moved by rail—and that was at Nancy.[160] There was no railway between Toul and Epinal, where the Sixth Army was to cross the Moselle. Without the attack there would have been no "gap" in the French fortification system.

The decision to withdraw had been made more difficult by OHL with their warning to consider the spirit of the troops. In so doing they had reinforced a point of great importance for Krafft, and for Rupprecht as well. A withdrawal after a fierce and costly battle could be taken as acknowledgment of defeat, which, in turn, was originally thought to have potentially disastrous consequences for the morale of the soldiers.[161] Krafft later generally criticized the instructions of OHL with the valid argument that a Supreme Army Command "must not leave the decision on an action that is crucial for the entire operation to the discretion of a subordinate command."[162] On 31 August, however, his opinion was different: "Our plan is almost in complete agreement with the wishes of OHL."[163]

The procedure for the following days seemed clear now. On the morning of 31 August Rupprecht and Krafft initiated the attack on the "Position de Nancy." The following day they discussed a combined attack on Nancy itself and across the Moselle.[164] That raised disagreements within the staff. Krafft was more in a hurry to launch the attack than Mertz and Xylander, who, considering the cautions from Luxembourg, preferred a more thorough artillery preparation. That afternoon at Sixth Army headquarters in Dieuze a theater-like scene played out. Four of the corps designated for the attack sent high-ranking representatives who argued against any hasty action. General Oskar von Xylander, the commanding general of I Bavarian Army Corps, argued against the attack on principle.[165] An open-mindedness to qualified objections from subordinates was an important element of German military culture. Krafft yielded to the arguments and postponed the attack, although only grudgingly. The interference of the subordinate commanding generals, he thought, must not become a rule, otherwise everybody would want to be involved in every issue.[166] A council of war must be avoided by any means.

The next day Krafft did something he should have done much earlier. He went to Luxembourg in person to consult directly with OHL. Again, OHL had a rather optimistic picture of the general situation. According to the accounts of Bauer and Rudolf von Xylander, Krafft had entertained the idea that the left wing units of the German Army were being required to intensify their efforts to get the right wing moving again. And now it seemed that the right wing was advancing rapidly. That, at least, was Tappen's opinion: "The general situation presents a rather favorable picture. The enemy is retreating everywhere. . . . On the western wing all advancing troops are marching at full speed. They promenade around France!" Krafft remained skeptical: "Ça va bien, pourvu que ça dure!" (That's fine as long as it lasts!)[167] He was pleased when Hentsch informed him that the Sixth and Seventh Armies faced strong French forces, stronger than they had assessed in Dieuze. That meant the superior enemy forces were operating in the Imperial Territories. The task to shackle the enemy, however, was not always practicable. As Krafft explained: "'If the enemy really wants to withdraw, then no God can stop him at the fortifications.' Since we bump against fortresses everywhere, the enemy can always hold the fortified sections with *inferior* force until the main forces have withdrawn."

There was agreement that a withdrawal of the Sixth Army was no longer under consideration because it would have to deploy behind the front and could not be committed for a longer period. Another factor was that the army would not actually have to run a major risk in making its attack: "The enemy must remain contained, but we should proceed carefully so as to not suffer a setback." In the next several days, maybe even by the next day, the envelopment by the German Army's right wing was expected to succeed. As Krafft noted in his diary, "We were, incidentally, in complete agreement."[168] Tappen, who had been Krafft's most important interlocutor at OHL, confirmed the sense of agreement in his own diary: "This morning General von Krafft, chief of Sixth Army, was here. Further actions of the Sixth and Seventh Armies were discussed in detail. They all concurred in their assessments of the situation."[169] After a period of confusion, it now seemed that OHL and the senior command in the Imperial Territories were acting in coordination.

The attack on the bridgehead at Bayon, the "Glacis of France,"[170] was postponed for the time being. It was now tied to the expected progress of the wheeling flank of the German Army. Meanwhile, the deployment of artillery toward Nancy continued forcefully. Within a few days the area had the most powerful concentration of heavy artillery the world had ever seen—272 guns in sixty-six batteries.[171] The actual attack began on 4 September with the costly advance of the infantry into the enemy's *Artillerieschutzstellung* (artillery security zone).

Before the forces on the German southern wing actually started to cross the Moselle, they advanced their right shoulder toward Nancy and the left near Epinal. The objective was the small town of Rambervillers. The Seventh Army had to fight its way through the eastern foothills of the Vosges, under extremely difficult terrain conditions. *Landwehr* units, several of which belonged in the Seventh Army, had difficulty fighting in the woody mountains,[172] in sharp contrast to the opposing French Chasseurs Alpines units that had been specifically trained and equipped for such terrain. Meanwhile, all the German units were greatly exhausted.[173]

The relationship with Seventh Army headquarters remained difficult. From the perspective of the senior command headquarters in the Imperial Territories it seemed that Heeringen and his staff were not cooperating. Seventh Army headquarters at Rambervillers was and remained unreachable. But the Seventh Army was dissatisfied with Sixth Army headquarters as well. The latter did not understand the particular difficulties of the terrain in the Vosges. Heeringen himself drove to Dieuze on 4 September to explain.[174] It was hard for Krafft to distinguish between the objective difficulties of the task and an allegedly passive resistance of the Seventh Army.

The splendid agreement between OHL and the German senior command in the Imperial Territories did not last long. At OHL the "last weeks' general Hallelujah spirit" was quite over, as the Bavarian military representative reported to Munich on 4 September. Assumptions were circulating that what was left of the German southern wing was weak rear guards supported by heavy artillery. The 36th Situation Report of the chief of the General Staff indicated the withdrawal of two French Army corps from the "area of Toul–Epinal in western direction."[175] That was exactly from where the German forces in the Imperial Territories were supposed to have contained the enemy forces, following them across the Moselle should they withdraw. But the fact that this did not happen led to a growing incomprehension and even to open irritation at OHL in the subsequent days. In the event, these reports indicated that the German forces in the south had not succeeded in depriving the French of their freedom of action in Lorraine.[176] The following day the Sixth and Seventh Armies were ordered to "advance as soon as possible to attack the Moselle [position] between Toul and Epinal, while securing against these fortresses."[177] Krafft, however, had the idea that it was not imperative to carry out the breakthrough in force, but rather to wait for the withdrawal of the French and then follow them.

Intelligence of the imminent arrival of British forces on the coast caused OHL the same day to form a new army in the north that was to operate under Colonel General von Heeringen and Seventh Army headquarters. The Sixth and Seventh Armies were to detach one corps each to form the new army. Doing so, of course, would reduce future operational capabilities. That afternoon Tappen informed Krafft of the OHL directive, which Krafft naturally did not receive enthusiastically: "To us, the whole matter is very bad indeed. (If that happens) we will not be able to avoid passivity." Prior to the inevitable weakening of the Sixth Army, Krafft thought it was necessary to achieve a "success by arms."[178]

On 5 September the Germans issued the first restrictions on ammunition expenditure. The firing of heavy howitzer (*Mörser*) rounds in support of field operations was specifically forbidden. The 210 mm heavy howitzer had originally been developed as a mobile weapon to be used in the field against enemy fortifications. Although those guns, with a range of 9,400 meters and shells weighing 120 kilograms, proved very effective in counterbattery operations against the French artillery,[179] such fire missions were no longer authorized. In the subsequent days the ammunition issue would become vitally important for the progress of operations. The French were experiencing munitions shortages as well. They already had resorted to using black powder as propellant and firing obsolete black powder projectiles.

For Sixth Army headquarters the attack in Lorraine thus became a fight against declining resources and against time. After the withdrawal of the XV Army Corps, Tappen then demanded the detachment of another corps. Krafft, meanwhile, complained about the "weak leadership" in several of his subordinate corps: "I do not have a single person [under my command] who would have the correct irrepressible urge for the attack.... And everybody is impressed with the enemy's heavy artillery. This would soon pass if appropriate action was taken." He conceded, however, that the prerequisites for an attack still had not been achieved: "the general situation is by far not suitable."[180] He was referring to the progress on the wheeling flank of the German Army.

As Krafft was dissatisfied with his subordinate corps, so was OHL in Luxembourg with the Sixth Army. The chief of *Feldmunitionswesen* [field ordnance], General Ludwig von Sieger, angrily left for Sixth Army headquarters to withdraw part of the heavy guns.[181] Upon reaching Dieuze, Sieger demanded the release of the 150 mm guns with shielded mounts that had come from Metz. He also withdrew the heavy howitzer ammunition and cancelled the already scarce 130 mm ammunition.[182] This caused particular problems because the heavy flat-trajectory guns were essential for counterbattery fire. Agreeing with Krafft's own artillery general, Sieger doubted the possibility of being able to reduce the Position de Nancy with the means available, and he supported the suspension of the attack that was no longer an option for Krafft.[183] It was now increasingly a question of prestige and of who would be responsible in the case of failure. In 1928, Metz quoted a member of OHL at the time, whose name he did not disclose: "It was my impression at the time that they [at Sixth Army headquarters] would have been happy if OHL had ordered the cancellation of the (breakthrough) plan. They then would not have had to bear the responsibility for the only correct, albeit depressing decision. They would have protested and then would have obeyed immediately—not without feeling inner relief."[184]

Krafft's diary shows that he did indeed entertain such thoughts: "The suspension of the attack is a serious moral setback for which *we cannot* take responsibility. Should it be inevitable . . . it would have to be clear that OHL issued such an order. They would have liked to convince me to support the lifting of the siege, in which case it would have been me who was responsible for the flip-flop. However, I did not swallow his [the chief of field ordnance's] bait. The responsibility for the whole idiocy of the on-again, off-again siege of the Position de Nancy lies solely with the OHL and their excellent desk officers."[185]

Thus, the situation in Lorraine hit rock bottom. The senior leadership had already lost their faith in the value of the attack near Nancy. They were afraid, however, to voice such and to come to the obvious conclusion. The willingness to take responsibility was obviously not greater in Luxembourg than it was in Dieuze. Even though OHL had realized the stagnation in Lorraine, they failed to end the situation through the chain of command. Instead, they hoped that Sixth Army headquarters would demand the termination of the operation. The primary concern at OHL, it seems, was "not to take the bait" of the other side. In the meantime, the German infantry bled to death at Nancy. Instead of ordering the formal end of the attack against the "Position de Nancy," OHL let it run out of steam by gradually withdrawing the artillery munitions, albeit without a clear policy: On 7 September they lifted the munitions restriction, only to renew it the following day.

Krafft at the time was under considerable pressure. For days he had been concerned that he would be held responsible for the possible failure of the Lorraine operation. On 2 September Crown Prince Rupprecht opined that the early commitment of the siege formations to attack the advance position of Nancy had been a mistake. Krafft was highly sensitive to what was an absolutely normal procedure—a critical assessment of a leadership decision: "I will soon have to defend myself vigorously. I do not want to be the scapegoat if things do not go as planned."[186] In the meantime, it looked very much like things were not going "as planned." It would be unfair, however, to explain Krafft's behavior only by his concern for his reputation, even if such was important to a man who harbored such strong ambitions as did the chief of staff of the Sixth Army. Like all general officers of his generation who had been educated and trained with a certain concept of warfare, Krafft had to overcome serious difficulties in accepting the situation of the real war. But there was little time for that, and in Lorraine the development of the situation was particularly serious. The XIV Army Corps did not make any progress, although on 5 September the I Bavarian Army Corps had fired one thousand heavy howitzer shells in support. By prewar standards, that was an enormous amount of ammunition. "This is a warfare that eludes comprehension. The eagerness to attack has declined alarmingly."[187] The unexpectedly slow progress at Nancy was a mystery to Krafft at that time: "A large artillery mass is committed against a field position. There is no equal enemy artillery, but nevertheless the enemy still holds his positions. Unbelievable! Can this be possible? This is contrary to everything that had been predicted during peacetime. (It is only possible because the infantry and their leaders do not take hold!)"[188] Krafft was frustrated: "This trench and fortress warfare is horrible!"[189]

In the same way that Krafft regarded the Sixth Army's subordinate leaders and troops as incompetent and weak, OHL in Luxembourg thought about Sixth Army headquarters. Krafft and Rupprecht learned that to their indignation on 8 September, when two liaison officers from OHL arrived in Dieuze. Lieutenant General Karl von Wenninger and Colonel Eugen Zoellner,[190] both Bavarian officers at OHL, "told many tales out of school about the mood in Luxembourg." According to their impressions, Luxembourg made no effort to develop a clear picture of the conditions in Lorraine. Rather, they thought that the "Sixth and Seventh Armies came to halt in front of nothing." It was only the report by former Seventh Army commander Heeringen in transit to his new assignment in Belgium that had provided some enlightenment. With bitterness, Krafft later wrote on the margin of his diary entry: "They simply did not believe us!—That is typical. They had to hear it from the Prussian [von Heeringen]!"[191] But Krafft himself was hardly more approachable than OHL when it came to objective advice about the insurmountable difficulties.

As Mertz complained in his diary: "The Chief simply does not acknowledge the difficulties in the forests. He thinks the troops just do not understand how to fight in the woods. . . . I tell him again and again that we cannot advance this way, but he thinks we *must* succeed."[192] The higher the echelon, the more difficult it was to accept the new kind of warfare.

Just the information on a new munitions restriction imposed by the chief of field ordnance had caused Rupprecht to consider resigning his command. A number of ammunition trains were transferred from the Sixth to the Fifth Army—in other words, from the Bavarian crown prince to the German crown prince. Rupprecht felt neutralized. Concerned about the fatal impression his resignation would make in Germany and abroad, Krafft advised Rupprecht against resigning and encouraged him to go to Luxembourg personally to obtain clarification. That would be a strong signal, since the successor to the crown of the second largest federal state carried a weight far beyond his military rank.

Shortly after Rupprecht's departure another visitor arrived at Dieuze from Luxembourg, Major Erich von Redern, the General Staff officer Ia of the Operations Division. Redern proclaimed a completely new approach to the stalled operations: "It would be preferable to break away from the enemy east of the Moselle, to withdraw the [Sixth] Army, to task part of it with the defense of the Metz–Strasbourg line, and to freely commit the remaining corps." There had been intelligence indicators of new troop landings in France; Hindus were reported to have landed in Southern France; a Siberian army corps was reported to have reached England via Archangel en route to France. German forces were needed to deal with all this. Apparently this marked the decisive turning point.

Krafft ordered the termination of the offensive action and instructed the chiefs of the subordinate army corps to assemble in Dieuze the following day.[193] But then a telegram received from Rupprecht threw everything in question. All attacks were to be suspended, except for the attack on Nancy. Krafft was stunned. What had happened? At OHL they had assumed Rupprecht had come to protest against Redern's directive. The fact that Rupprecht did not even know about it remained unexplained. It was a situation similar to the question of the extent of Bauer's authority in Dieuze a few days earlier. When [the Sixth Army staff] asked Luxembourg what was to be done, comply with Redern's directive or continue the attack on the Position de Nancy, they were told that Redern's directive was in force. They were authorized, however, to continue the attack on Nancy "with the most economical expenditure of required munitions."[194]

Thus the buck was passed back to Sixth Army headquarters, and not for the first time within the past weeks. But further action was discussed during a council of war that Krafft had first scheduled when the only issue seemed to be the solution of the technical issues of the withdrawal. Krafft advised Rupprecht to consider the recommendations of the corps chiefs of staff about the prospects of a continued attack on Nancy.[195] The chiefs did not favor continuation, and Rupprecht accordingly ordered a halt to the action. Right up until the end, the senior command authorities had not been able to express themselves clearly.

Thus ended the first major breakthrough attack of the First World War. It had been based on an improvised artillery mass, in part with obsolete guns, and even Krafft did not think it capable of success.[196] Although it had not seemed completely impossible to achieve that objective, it required far greater resources and time than initially expected. On the French side, the attack on the Grand Couronné was not perceived as a weak improvisation. Under heavy German artillery fire, a crisis occurred for the French on the second day. In order to save his army, de Castelnau considered withdrawing and prepared to evacuate the Grand Couronné.[197] Then, after a temporary period of stabilization, the situation escalated again on 7 September. In a telephone call to Joffre, de Castelnau recommended abandoning Nancy in order to prevent the collapse of his army. Joffre refused. During the Battle of the Marne he needed stability in Lorraine, and he therefore expressly ordered de Castelnau to hold for another forty-eight hours.[198] During those two days the Sixth Army halted its advance and then finally abandoned the attack. The First World War generation of military leaders would have seen this as a striking confirmation of their concept of war as a struggle of wills, with Joffre having the stronger will than his badly organized and erratic German opponents.

Joffre had major legitimate concerns about a withdrawal of his Second Army. If that were to happen, the French First Army would also have to abandon its positions. If the First Army followed the Second Army, there was the risk of losing Franche-Comté and of an envelopment of the entire French right wing. A withdrawal to the Epinal–Belfort line would have destroyed the front of the First and Second Armies.[199] During the entire Battle of the Marne to the north the situation in Lorraine was for Joffre "la source de graves preoccupations."[200] The battle in Lorraine, therefore, was not as useless as German military literature has since described. The secondary attack suggested by Major Bauer but not approved by OHL that was immediately executed by the Sixth Army had plunged the French defense of the Grand Couronné and the "Position de Nancy"—and thus the whole Moselle position—into a deep crisis. That fact, however, was not recognized.

Krafft and Rupprecht had been closer to the truth with their request to fight the matter out until a "success by arms" was achieved. This is not, however, to argue that after the failed Battle of the Marne the opportunity to still win the western campaign through the back door was missed in Lorraine. After their victory at the Marne the French again had the resources to control a crisis in the south, irrespective of the fact that German forces passing between the fortifications—the actual strength of which had not yet been determined—would only have been possible after substantially defeating the French in that sector. Admittedly, the center of gravity of the battle would have shifted to Lorraine for a certain period of time.

After the lost Battle of the Marne and the failure in Lorraine, the mood at OHL in Luxembourg was gloomy. Scapegoats were needed and they were found in Dieuze. The enlightenment of OHL by Heeringen's report about the combat situation in Lorraine did not last very long. Instead, the notion prevailed that "Sixth and Seventh Armies had been scorned by their enemy, that only weak [French] replacements were behind the heavy guns, and that all other [French] forces had been sent [north] to fight the [German] Second through Fifth Armies. It was quite openly acknowledged [at OHL] that the Bavarian crown prince was to be blamed for the whole crisis because he insisted that he was not able to attack where he should have attacked." As something of a punishment for this perceived failure, the decision was made to disband the Bavarian army: "The war minister openly said that the Sixth Army would have to be split up and its individual corps would be sent where reinforcement of the heavily fighting armies was necessary."[201]

In Luxembourg they did not or would not understand that since 2 September, the day when the alleged agreement was reached, Sixth Army headquarters and OHL had been thinking about two different operations. All the efforts in the Imperial Territories had been focused on the wings at Rambervillers and primarily near Nancy, to establish the prerequisites for crossing the Moselle into the alleged Charmes Gap. In Luxembourg, however, they did not understand why the central attack was not carried out. It seemed instead that only a monstrous cannonade took place, in which hardly any progress was made. In the opinion of OHL, the leadership of the Sixth Army had not really wanted to advance.

The problems in the coordination between OHL and Sixth Army headquarters cannot be fully explained by the technical communication problems, although they existed without a doubt and were rather grave during the initial days of Sixth Army headquarters in Lorraine. But after OHL moved from Berlin to Koblenz and then later to Luxembourg, communications improved considerably. The lack of a firm guiding influence from OHL is a characteristic feature throughout the campaign in Lorraine. After 16 August, when the issue was whether the German forces in the Imperial Territories were to continue their withdrawal or were to assume the offensive, the "instructions" given by Tappen and Stein to Major von Xylander on 31 August indicate that OHL practically relinquished its command responsibility. That is particularly obvious considering that the required decisions had effects far beyond the Lorraine sector. Regardless of the final evaluation of the leadership of the German senior command in the Imperial Territories, it has been clearly established that OHL had largely left them to their own devices during that period. In critical situations, the receipt of unclear instructions gives the impression that superior authority is trying to avoid its responsibility through downward delegation. This was how Krafft perceived the orders he received from OHL. "All orders formulated by Tappen indicate that [OHL] wants to take as little responsibility as possible. [The orders] all sound somewhat cryptic; caution is made at the expense of clarity."[202]

Sixth Army headquarters was not alone in feeling this obvious vacuum. After the war the *Reichsarchiv* felt compelled to ask Tappen for the reasons for this strange command style, to which not only Sixth Army was subject. Tappen explained the approach of the wheeling flank with the simplicity of the basic operational concept and the peacetime training of the General Staff. Moltke had deliberately held back on the assumption "that the [field] army commanders at the front would be able to assess the enemy situation more reliably than himself, far behind the front in Coblenz."[203] Moltke's concluding remarks on the occasion of his last General Staff ride prior to the war suggest that he saw with almost prophetic clarity the leadership problems challenging modern, widely deployed mass armies.[204] He was not, however, able to come up with a solution. In hindsight it is not possible to determine the extent to which the deliberate restraint of OHL influenced the stark German leadership crisis during the summer of 1914. The inadequate technical communication links and the lack of OHL liaison officers at the field army headquarters were also certainly contributing factors.[205] In the final analysis, the operations of the German Western Army in general, and the forces in Lorraine in particular, provided a classic example of the limits and dangers of the much-praised mission-type command (*Auftragsverfahren*).

One might wonder, then, what was the actual function of OHL, and who was actually in charge at OHL during those weeks in August and September.

The overall command of the operations should have rested with the chief of the General Staff of the Field Army, Colonel General von Moltke. The fact that he lacked the strength of character to fill this position is well-known, and was widely known even then. Commenting on the crisis over the command of the Eighth Army in the east, Hentsch said that Moltke had to be "encouraged like a sick horse."[206] Several days later Falkenhayn mentioned to the Bavarian military representative that the chief of the General Staff [Moltke] was "wrecked." That was one week prior to the Battle of the Marne.[207] Krafft's judgment on the most important man after Moltke, the head of the Operations Division (*Operationsabteilung*), was utterly devastating. He called Tappen a "completely unable paper shuffler who had obviously been employed by Ludendorff as a convenient and compliant aid to keep the seat warm."[208]

After the failure at the Marne, when OHL tried to make the Bavarians the scapegoat, Wenninger pointed to the "*Quadrifolium Operationen*, i.e., Tappen, Hentsch, Groener, and Dommes," as the center of the *Oberste Heeresleitung*.[209] Embittered by the anti-Bavarian attitude, he added regional affiliations, since none of those Wenninger considered really responsible was Bavarian: "The colloquium which discussed the operations were the Prussian Tappen, the Saxon Hentsch and the Württemberger Groener."[210] Bavarian Crown Prince Rupprecht also expressed a similar opinion at the time: "The last time I saw him [Moltke] seemed to me like a broken old man. A permanent war council was held by his staff with all the disadvantages involved. Anybody present spoke and asserted his influence.... Moreover, Falkenhayn increasingly brought his influence to bear. Most alarming was the conduct of junior staff officers who were given far-reaching powers, like Majors Tappen and especially Hentsch.[211] And Bauer, head of the Artillery Section, was a total dreamer who preferred to deal with operational and political issues. It is justifiable to speak of anarchy in disguise spreading in Moltke's staff."[212] The *Der Weltkrieg* official history produced by the *Reichsarchiv* also cautiously hints in this direction by referring to the strong ambitions of the Operations Division.[213] It does seem that OHL was governed by some kind of "war council" with vaguely defined responsibilities. Such a situation simply could not but increase the tendency toward ambiguous and compromising orders and instructions.

Quasi-historical and protocol constraints also mitigated against resolute orders. The organization of the Imperial German Army, owing to the federal structure of the Reich, became a source of friction in Lorraine and the Vosges. The Bavarians felt that the Prussians still had a certain distrust of their military capabilities. Thus, according to Rudolf von Xylander, Sixth

Army headquarters when dealing with OHL and the formally subordinate Seventh Army headquarters had to "show particular tact. This indeed was often significant as events played out."[214] Nevertheless, it seems that OHL—even when it was dissatisfied with the performance of Sixth Army—exhibited a restraint that was not solely a function of mission-type command, but rather consideration for the special status of the senior commander in the Imperial Territories, who was after all, the future Bavarian King. In contrast, Sixth Army headquarters certainly did not have the impression of being treated with certain benevolence. Rupprecht was already angry at being pushed by OHL after 22 August.[215] However, the growing discontent that spread after 27 August combined with the stagnation in Lorraine did not result in the more firm control by OHL one would have expected. Although trust was limited on both sides, that did not result in more direct dealings between the two. Without a doubt, the German Army in 1914 performed worst in the area of senior leadership, whereas prior to 1914 that was where their self-confidence had been the highest and where they believed themselves to be well-prepared through *Generalstabsreisen* and *Kriegsspiele*.

Concluding Remarks

The German operations in Lorraine and in the Vosges have almost universally been evaluated negatively. It started with the criticism of the "watering down" of the Schlieffen Plan by the reinforcement of the German left wing. That has frequently been criticized as a fatal deviation from Schlieffen's recipe for victory,[216] especially since increased strength on the left tended to encourage operations "reaching beyond the scope of the mission."[217] The *Aufmarschanweisung* was unambiguous in its intent to achieve a decision of the campaign with the right wing of the German Army, thus assigning the forces in the Imperial Territories a subordinate and supporting mission within the scope of the overall plan. It was and remained less clear, however, exactly how that mission should be accomplished. The 20 August decision by Sixth Army headquarters to conduct an offensive action in Lorraine had no support outside the immediate circle of the field army headquarters.[218] Müller, who was the last to thoroughly analyze the Lorraine operation, reached the conclusion that the decision to attack had been wrong and resulted in fatal consequences.[219]

Looking back from a distance of nearly two decades, Rupprecht himself questioned the timing at least of the attack.[220] But considered from the perspective of the situation during those days in August 1914, the decision to attack appears plausible. It is not even necessary to factor in the assumed secondary motives of the Bavarian high command. It is something of a game of chance for a strong group of forces to persist in withdrawing from an enemy whose strength and intentions are unclear and who exert little pressure to advance. It is especially so in the context of the general operation as intended by the Germans at that time. OHL did not want to take responsibility for that, and therefore laid it on Sixth Army headquarters. Rupprecht correctly called the attempt to lure the French into a bag "artificial and difficult to undertake."[221]

The French, of course, knew what the Germans intended. Prior to 1914, all European armies had thoroughly studied each other and the entire world was aware of the German operational concept of using flanking movements and envelopments if at all possible. The Germans likewise knew of the French intention of keeping the mass of their forces together behind a screen of advanced guards in order to conduct a unified and concentrated advance. The French would have been out of their senses if they had thrust into the open area between Metz and Strasbourg in some kind of an intoxicated frenzy. From a human point of view it is understandable, albeit unreasonable, that after his downfall Moltke came to believe that his opportunity for a Cannae-like victory had been ruined by the local leadership in Lorraine because they were not able to control their forces.[222] The fact is that the western operation in Lorraine during the summer of 1914 neither spoiled nor missed the opportunity to decide the overall German campaign in the west.

When the German attack ended it was too late to make a strategic realignment of forces. If the units of the Sixth and Seventh Armies were to contribute to the hoped-for rapid decision of the campaign, such could only be achieved if they remained active in Lorraine, regardless of whether or not the breakthrough at the Moselle was successful.[223] The situation at the time was no less spiritless than later in the war in Flanders, near Verdun, at the Somme, or at the Isonzo. It was the slowness of the tactical movements in this war that again and again robbed any local successes of great consequences and necessarily resulted in frontal attrition of the available forces and materiel. The bloody stagnation in Lorraine actually anticipated the general situation of the war that would become widespread several weeks later.

The path from mobile warfare via trench warfare to the beginnings of the battle of attrition that was already looming at Nancy became radically clear in Lorraine during the summer of 1914. The phenomenological uniqueness of the battles between Metz, Strasbourg, Epinal, and Toul indicates their importance in the history of warfare. The reason for this was that when the enormous stocks of war materiel stored in the large fortifications were committed to the field operations in Lorraine, the result was a destructive power on a scale that would not appear on other sectors of the front for several more months, when the construction of stable field fortifications became routine. The power provided from those French fortresses broke the August offensive of the Sixth and Seventh Armies. The fortresses were a base from which the defeated French corps could reconstitute and reorganize. Krafft after the war wrote that the first attempts to attack fortress-like field positions, such as happened at Nancy, should have received more attention at the time. Instead, the rapid success against the obsolete Belgian fortresses, which had been quickly destroyed by heavy howitzer fire, lulled the Germans into a false sense of power: "If they had drawn more clear conclusions [from the Lorraine experience], it could have deterred us from repeating a similar start [to operations] at Verdun, and saved us much valuable German blood."[224]

The angry reactions of the senior command staffs to the alleged inability of their subordinates, either the railings of Krafft against his corps or those of OHL about "the stupid Bavarians,"[225] are indicative of the widespread difficulty in understanding the new type of warfare. The staffs still pushed forward the mobilizing of all forces, just as they had learned to do before the war, but "under the completely new, never experienced technical conditions of the war. All in this situation acted without fully understanding the circumstances and the consequences of their actions. All are busy struggling in the dark with immense energy and basically never have any idea of what they are doing."[226]

The bloody consequences were horrible. The exact losses of German troops in the Imperial Territories were never established. Even Deuringer, who traced the battles in detail and had wide access to the war files of the Sixth Army and its subordinate Bavarian units, could only offer estimates. He assumed that the infantry, the force with the most personnel and the one that was more than any other subject to the effects of enemy weapons, suffered losses of some 60 percent of their strength.[227] Between Pont-à-Mousson and Markirch, the area where the heaviest fighting took place, the Germans committed some fifty infantry brigades totaling more than 300,000 soldiers. If Deuringer's assumption is correct, the German infantry lost more than 180,000 troops in that sector. The total and relative losses of cavalry and artillery were usually much lower and did not significantly change the overall toll. It is highly unlikely that the French losses differed considerably from those of the Germans. In total probably some 350,000 to 400,000 soldiers were injured or killed in the battles south of Metz during August and September 1914. From experience, 20 to 25 percent of the casualty total can be assumed to have been killed in action.

Notes

The title for this chapter is from *Tagebuch Krafft*, 7 September 1914, Bayerisches Hauptstaatsarchiv, Abt. IV Kriegsarchiv (Bayer. KA), Krafft papers 145.

1. Several years later, a "scenic reconstruction" was published as a book in which the above-mentioned phrase, however, is not included: Sebastian Haffner and Wolfgang Venohr, *Das Wunder an der Marne: Rekonstruktion der Entscheidungsschlacht des Ersten Weltkrieges* (Bergisch Gladbach, 1982).

2. Konrad Krafft von Dellmensingen, *Die Führung des Kronprinzen Rupprecht von Bayern auf dem linken deutschen Heeresflügel bis zur Schlacht in Lothringen im August 1914: Eine Entgegnung und zugleich eine Studie* (Berlin, 1925).

3. Wetzel was chief of the Operations Department of the Supreme Army Command from fall 1916 to September 1918.

4. [Georg] Wetzell, "Das Kriegswerk des Reichsarchivs: 'Der Weltkrieg 1914/18.' Kritische Betrachtungen zum I. Band: Die Grenzschlachten im Westen," *Wissen und Wehr* 6 (1925): 1–43, here page 17.

5. Konrad Krafft von Dellmensingen, *Das Oberkommando in den Reichslanden: Kritischer Streifzug durch die Studien des Generalleutnants a.D. Wilhelm Groener über den Weltkrieg* (Munich, 1931).

6. Wilhelm Groener, *Das Testament des Grafen Schlieffen: Operative Studien über den Weltkrieg* (Berlin, 1927), 15.

7. Wilhelm Groener, *Der Feldherr wider Willen* (Berlin, 1930), 16.

8. Up to 1931; on Mertz, cf. Markus Pöhlmann, *Kriegsgeschichte und Geschichtspolitik: Der Erste Weltkrieg. Die amtliche deutsche Militärgeschichtsschreibung 1914–1916* (Paderborn, 2002), 82–84.

9. Wetzell, "Das Kriegswerk des Reichsarchivs," 11.

10. Hermann Mertz von Quirnheim, *Der Führerwille in Entstehung und Durchführung: Erläutert an den Vorgängen beim Gemeinsamen Oberbefehl in den Reichslanden August bis September 1914* (Oldenburg, 1932).

11. Pöhlmann, *Kriegsgeschichte und Geschichtspolitik,* 291–295. Rupprecht's former staff still met for a headquarters reunion evening on 12 May 1949. Letter by Krafft to Rupprecht, 3 May 1949, Bayer. KA, Krafft papers 195.

12. Cf. Pöhlmann, *Kriegsgeschichte und Geschichtspolitik,* 284–321.

13. Thomas Müller, *Konrad Krafft von Dellmensingen (1862–1953): Porträt eines bayerischen Offiziers* (Munich, 2002), 296–373.

14. Bayer. KA, AOK 6, 369. The *Aufmarschanweisung* is handwritten; emphasis as in the original.

15. In that year the later, very controversial reinforcement of the German left wing was introduced for the first time. It was the last time that the planners had pro-

vided for a possible transfer of the Seventh Army to another part of the theater after the completed *Aufmarsch* or initial battles. Bundesarchiv/Militärarchiv (BA/MA), RH61/96.

16. *Tagebuch Krafft,* 2 August 1914, Bayer. KA, Krafft Papers 145.
17. Ibid.
18. Mertz, *Der Führerwille in Entstehung und Durchführung,* 25.
19. Ibid., 28.
20. Ibid.
21. Müller, *Konrad Krafft von Dellmensingen,* 308.
22. Karl Deuringer, *Die Schlacht in Lothringen und in den Vogesen: Die Feuertaufe der Bayerischen Armee,* ed. Bayerisches Kriegsarchiv, 2 vols. (Munich, 1929).
23. The Army Corps had to submit an annual status report. In the period when Rupprecht held the position of commanding general of I Army Corps (1906-1912) these reports were most elaborate. See, for example, the 1913 report, Bayer. KA, MKr. 2758.
24. Bayerisches Hauptstaatsarchiv, Abt. III Geheimes Hausarchiv (Bayer. GH), Nachlass Kronprinz Rupprecht 699. This paper is based on the original handwritten version of the diary. At the time, Rupprecht had not written it by himself but—as his introduction shows—he started to write only in January 1915.
25. Kronprinz Rupprecht von Bayern, *Mein Kriegstagebuch,* vol. 1, ed. Eugen von Frauenholz (Berlin, 1929).
26. Müller, *Konrad Krafft von Dellmensingen,* 290-295; cf. also the report of the Bavarian military representative in Berlin, Major General Karl Ritter von Wenninger, of 2 August 1914; these reports are published in Bernd F. Schulte, "Neue Dokumente zu Kriegsausbruch und Kriegsverlauf 1914," *Militärgeschichtliche Mitteilungen* 25 (1979): 123-185, here page 142.
27. Müller, *Konrad Krafft von Dellmensingen,* 295. On 31 July 1914 Krafft wrote in his diary: "My appointment to the (Army Supreme Command) Munich (Sixth Army) is certainly a concession (of Prussia) to Bavaria and evidence of trust for me as well." After the war he added the following remark: "During the centenary of 1813 on 18 October 1913 in Leipzig, when I expressed my doubts of whether it would be appropriate if in case of an emergency, under the agreements between Prussia and Bavaria, a commander and a chief [of staff] would come together who did not know each other well enough, General Moltke replied: 'Do you not think it understandable that Prussia thus secures its influence on the operations since it brought much weight to bear and bears a considerable share of responsibility.' Back then, I did not find it completely understandable. Prussia secures its influence mainly through the uniform training of the entire German general staff . . . and through the unconditional authority of the great headquarters! Moltke's point of view seemed to me rather Prussianly narrow-minded. I was astonished to find with him the general principal Prussian opinion: 'Only the Prussian is valuable and understands something.' This narrow-minded understanding of preeminence, the lack of trust, the bullheaded egoism and

the brutal and insensitive way in which the real 'Prussian' thinks himself entitled to let each non-Prussian feel his superiority, had done much damage and had to a considerable degree contributed to the later decline of spirit." Bayer. KA, Krafft papers 145.

28. Bayer. KA, Krafft papers 145.

29. Mertz, *Der Führerwille in Entstehung und Durchführung*, 32.

30. *Aufmarschanweisung*, Anlage 19b, Bayer. KA, AOK 6, 369.

31. *Der Weltkrieg 1914–1918*, vol. 1, *Die Grenzschlachten im Westen*, ed. Reichsarchiv (Berlin, 1925), 63f.; this is also supported by Wetzell, "Das Kriegswerk des Reichsarchivs," 10, 14.

32. Krafft, *Die Führung*, 5f.

33. "Kriegswerk" was Krafft's name for the *Reichsarchiv*'s official history, *Der Weltkrieg*.

34. "Notes on a New Edition of Volume I of the World War Opus," 8, Bayer. KA, Nachlass Krafft (Krafft papers) 186. This manuscript by Krafft of 14 February 1931 comprises a total of 146 pages.

35. Mertz, *Der Führerwille in Entstehung und Durchführung*, 25.

36. *Der Weltkrieg 1914–1918*, vol. 1, *Die Grenzschlachten im Westen*, ed. Reichsarchiv (Berlin, 1925), 63–65.

37. Hermann von Stein, Alfred von Waldersee, Ludendorff, Gerhard Tappen; *Bemerkungen zu den Aufgaben des Südflügels des deutschen Westheeres unter besonderer Berücksichtigung der Einstellung Moltkes zu ihnen*, no date, BA/MA, RH61/96.

38. Erich Ludendorff, *Mein militärischer Werdegang: Blätter der Erinnerung an unser stolzes Heer* (Munich, 1935), 125.

39. Ibid., 127. In a later comment on his diary entry of 16 August 1914, Krafft, too, mentioned, "The Lorraine trap verified and previously trained for in the *Grosse Generalstabsreisen* resulted in the 'big bag' formed by the Saar and *Niedstellung* with a consequent attack on both enemy flanks from the direction of Metz and Strasbourg." Bayer. KA, Nachlass Krafft 145.

40. Hans von Haeften an Tappen, 3 December 1923, BA/MA, Nachlass Tappen 56-2.

41. This means the Moselle.

42. "Moltke über den Rückzug an der Marne," in *Helmuth von Moltke 1848–1916: Dokumente zu seinem Leben und Wirken*, ed. Thomas Meyer, 3rd, largely extended new ed. of Helmuth von Moltke, *Erinnerungen, Briefe, Dokumente 1877–1916: Ein Bild vom Kriegsausbruch, erster Kriegführung und Persönlichkeit des ersten militärischen Führers des Krieges*, vol. 1, ed. Von Eliza von Moltke (Stuttgart, 1922; reprint, Basel, 1993), 352–359, here page 355; already Zatschek pointed to the limited significance of that belated statement by Moltke. Heinz Zatschek, "Moltke oder Schlieffen?" *Militärwissenschaftliche und technische Mitteilungen* 56 (1925): 337–345, 578–583, here page 345.

43. Bayer. KA, Nachlass Krafft (Krafft papers), 195.

44. Brief an Tappen, 15 March 1925, BA/MA, Nachlass Tappen 56-3.

45. Report dated 15 August 1914, Bayer. KA, Nachlass Krafft 187; Schulte, "Neue Dokumente zu Kriegsausbruch und Kriegsverlauf 1914," 145f. At that time it was not possible to speak of serious planning in this respect, as especially on that day the OHL hoped for a great decisive battle between Metz and Strasbourg. In 1932, the *Reichsarchiv* submitted Wenninger's report to Tappen for comment. The latter replied that he "did not have any knowledge" that already before the attack in Lorraine a plan had been pursued by either the OHL or a person close to it for a thrust between Toul and Epinal, BA/MA, Nachlass Tappen 56-5. He referred to his paper "'*Bis zur Marne 1914*,' which clearly expresses that the decision was made only after the Battle of Lorraine." Cf. Gerhard Tappen, *Bis zur Marne 1914: Beiträge zur Beurteilung der Kriegführung bis zum Abschluss der Marne-Schlacht* (Oldenburg, Berlin, 1920), 14f.

46. Bayer. KA, Nachlass Krafft 145.

47. Ibid., 10 August 1914.

48. XIV and XV Army Corps.

49. *Der Weltkrieg 1914–1918*, vol. 1, *Die Grenzschlachten im Westen*, ed. Reichsarchiv (Berlin, 1925), 160–168.

50. *Tagebuch Krafft*, 12 August 1914, Bayer. KA, Nachlass Krafft 145.

51. Ibid., 14 August 1914. On the transport of the two corps, cf. also *Der Weltkrieg 1914 bis 1918, Das deutsche Feldeisenbahnwesen*, vol. 1, *Die Eisenbahnen zu Kriegsbeginn*, ed. Reichsarchiv (Berlin, 1928), 102–105.

52. *Tagebuch Krafft*, 12 August 1914, Bayer. KA, Nachlass Krafft 145. Twenty-three hundred French soldiers were taken prisoner and eight guns were captured. *Der Weltkrieg 1914–1918*, vol. 1, *Die Grenzschlachten im Westen*, ed. Reichsarchiv (Berlin, 1925), 174.

53. The Bavarian Cavalry Division.

54. *Tagebuch Krafft*, 13 August 1914, Bayer. KA, Nachlass Krafft 145.

55. Deuringer, *Die Schlacht in Lothringen und in den Vogesen*, 1:62f.; Deuringer generally uses the German place names. He refers to the *Gefecht von Gerden*.

56. *Tagebuch Krafft*, 13 August 1914, Bayer. KA, Nachlass Krafft 145.

57. *Les Armées Françaises dans la Grande Guerre*, vol. 1, *La guerre de mouvement (opérations antérieures au 14 novembre 1914), Les préliminaires—la bataille des frontières, Annexes* (Paris: Ministère de la Guerre. État-major de l'armée–Service historique, 1922), 21.

58. Ibid., 20–25.

59. Ibid., 55; Joseph Joffre, *Mémoires du maréchal Joffre (1910–1917)* (Paris, 1932), 1:252.

60. *Les Armées Françaises dans la Grande Guerre*, 1:161–166.

61. Diary entry, 12 August 1914, Bayer. KA, Nachlass Rupprecht 699.

62. Rudolf von Xylander, *Deutsche Führung in Lothringen 1914: Wahrheit und Kriegsgeschichte* (Berlin, 1935), 34.

63. Bayer. KA, AOK 6, 369, Bund 48.

64. Xylander, *Deutsche Führung in Lothringen 1914*, 44.
65. Bayer. KA, AOK 6, 369, Bund 48, original emphasis.
66. Bayer. KA, Nachlass Krafft 145. In calculating the *Sackmanöver* (bag maneuver) after the war, Krafft reached a totally different conclusion: It is debatable whether the pincer arms would have been able to penetrate the strong flank security of the French, which the latter would have used to secure their entrance into the bag. Krafft, *Die Führung*, 25–47; also Krafft, *Das Oberkommando in den Reichslanden*, 22–26.
67. *Tagebuch Krafft*, 14 August 1914, Bayer. KA, Nachlass Krafft 145; *Tagebuch Rupprecht*, 14 August 1914, Bayer. GH, Nachlass Rupprecht 699.
68. Bayer. KA, AOK 6, 369, Bund 48.
69. Bayer. KA, AOK 6, 1.
70. *Der Weltkrieg 1914 bis 1918, Kriegsrüstung und Kriegswirtschaft*, Annexes to vol. 1, ed. Reichsarchiv (Berlin, 1930), letter of 20 August 1910 to the Kriegsministerium, 123–125, here page 124.
71. *Der Weltkrieg 1914–1918*, vol. 1, *Die Grenzschlachten im Westen*, ed. Reichsarchiv (Berlin, 1925), 201.
72. Ibid., 1:205.
73. Wilhelm Marx, *Die Marne—Deutschlands Schicksal? Ein Wort gegen die dramatische Geschichtsauffassung in der militärischen Literatur* (Berlin, 1932), 50.
74. *Der Weltkrieg 1914–1918*, vol. 1, *Die Grenzschlachten im Westen*, ed. Reichsarchiv (Berlin, 1925), 205.
75. Joffre, *Mémoires du maréchal Joffre*, 1:252.
76. *Tagebuch Rupprecht*, 17 August 1914, Bayer. GH, Nachlass Rupprecht 699.
77. Bayer. KA, AOK 6, 1.
78. Ibid., 188f., 199. Aircraft reconnaissance results indicated such counterattacks. Ibid., 184, 200.
79. Mertz, *Der Führerwille in Entstehung und Durchführung*, 183.
80. Groener, *Das Testament des Grafen Schlieffen*, 43f.
81. Bayer. KA, AOK 6, 1.
82. *Tagebuch Krafft*, 17 August 1914, Bayer. KA, Nachlass Krafft 145.
83. Ibid.
84. The description of the Dommes mission follows the diary entries of Rupprecht and Krafft on 17 August 1914 if not otherwise indicated.
85. Later, when the attack decision was criticized, that sentence would be used against Rupprecht and he would be accused of not having control over his forces. The intent to encircle the French in Lorraine was not carried out—wrote Moltke in summer 1915—as the leader of the Sixth Army declared "that he could not have his troops withdraw further without risking their moral cohesion." "Moltke über den Rückzug an der Marne," in *Helmuth von Moltke 1848–1916*, 355. Xylander tried to downplay the fact that Rupprecht had demanded an attack in deference to the morale of the troops. Xylander, *Deutsche Führung in Lothringen 1914*, 75.
86. Mertz, *Der Führerwille in Entstehung und Durchführung*, 63.

87. The OHL files name Tappen as the person Krafft talked to on the phone. Letter by Haeften to Tappen, 24 March 1922, BA/MA, Nachlass Tappen 56-2.

88. Description on a page attached to the *Tagebuch des Kronprinzen* of 18 August 1914. Frauenholz included it in the edition of the diaries of the crown prince. Kronprinz Rupprecht von Bayern, *Mein Kriegstagebuch*, 21; Rupprecht himself wrote Stein's answer in a cruder form: "We should do what we wanted," *Tagebuch* of 18 August 1914, Bayer. GH, Nachlass Rupprecht 699.

89. Bayer. KA, Nachlass Krafft 187.

90. Letter of 24 March 1922, BA/MA, Nachlass Tappen 56-2.

91. Letter of 28 March 1922, BA/MA, Nachlass Tappen 56-2.

92. Mertz, *Der Führerwille in Entstehung und Durchführung*, 26.

93. In a review of Groener's book *Das Testament des Grafen Schlieffen*, in *Allgemeine Schweizer Militärzeitschrift* 73 (1927): 95f.; additionally, Pöhlmann, *Kriegsgeschichte und Geschichtspolitik*, 302.

94. Ibid.

95. The occasion was the yet-to-be-described conduct of the former Major Max Bauer at Sixth Army headquarters in August 1914. Bauer later became famous as "Oberst Bauer" and close assistant of Ludendorff.

96. Dated 28 November 1928, page 6f.; a copy was sent to Krafft, Bayer. KA, Nachlass Krafft 188.

97. Deuringer, *Die Schlacht in Lothringen und in den Vogesen*, 2:850.

98. Ibid., 1:182.

99. *Les Armées Françaises dans la Grande Guerre*, 1:263.

100. Ibid., 1:267f.

101. Joffre, *Mémoires du maréchal Joffre*, 1:284f.

102. Groener, *Das Testament des Grafen Schlieffen*, 35.

103. Bayer. KA, Nachlass Krafft 72.

104. *Der Weltkrieg 1914–1918*, vol. 1, *Die Grenzschlachten im Westen*, ed. Reichsarchiv (Berlin, 1925), 302.

105. Bayer. GH, Nachlass Rupprecht 699, as noted for 22 August 1914; printed in Kronprinz Rupprecht von Bayern, *Mein Kriegstagebuch*, 38f. The *Reichsarchiv*, too, included Krafft's description. *Der Weltkrieg 1914–1918*, vol. 1, *Die Grenzschlachten im Westen*, ed. Reichsarchiv (Berlin, 1925), 568.

106. Deuringer, *Die Schlacht in Lothringen und in den Vogesen*, 2:374.

107. Mertz, *Der Führerwille in Entstehung und Durchführung*, 107f.; extensive reply in Xylander, *Deutsche Führung in Lothringen 1914*, 112–117.

108. *Der Weltkrieg 1914–1918*, vol. 1, *Die Grenzschlachten im Westen*, ed. Reichsarchiv (Berlin, 1925), 569.

109. "Further success by Sixth and Seventh Armies, which had been tasked with the pursuit in southern direction." Entry of 23 August 1914, BA/MA, Nachlass Tappen 56-1.

110. Mertz, *Der Führerwille in Entstehung und Durchführung*, 108–112. A few

years before, Mertz had vigorously defended Sixth Army headquarters against the criticism that it had not shown sufficient resolution against OHL. Expert opinion on the Bauer controversy, 20 November 1928, Bayer. KA, Nachlass Krafft 188.

111. Max Bauer, *Der grosse Krieg in Feld und Heimat: Erinnerungen und Betrachtungen* (Tübingen, 1922), 53.

112. *Der Weltkrieg 1914 bis 1918, Das deutsche Feldeisenbahnwesen*, vol. 1, *Die Eisenbahnen zu Kriegsbeginn*, ed. Reichsarchiv (Berlin, 1928), 4f, 41f, 110f.

113. Groener, *Das Testament des Grafen Schlieffen*, 42.

114. *Der Weltkrieg 1914-1918*, vol. 1, *Die Grenzschlachten im Westen*, ed. Reichsarchiv (Berlin, 1925), 569.

115. Groener, *Der Feldherr wider Willen*, 12. That does not mean that Groener approved of the order to pursue. Instead, he recommended a transfer of forces via Metz in the area of the Fifth Army as originally planned in the *Aufmarschanweisung*.

116. Letter to Krafft of 18 April 1934, Bayer. KA, Nachlass Krafft 195.

117. Berthold von Deimling, *Aus der alten in die neue Zeit* (Berlin, 1930), 183.

118. *Tagebuch Krafft*, 23 August 1914, Bayer. KA, Nachlass Krafft 145.

119. Allegedly, the following happened after the Battle of Waterloo: "When the fatigued infantry after a twenty-hour march was no longer able to follow [the defeated French], Gneisenau took the last drummer along on a carriage horse captured in Genappe. The drumbeats made the French believe that the enemy was on their heels." Hermann Müller-Bohn, *Die deutschen Befreiungskriege: Deutschlands Geschichte von 1806–1815*, vol. 2 (Berlin, 1901), 920. I owe the reference to that quote to Dr. Gerhard Bauer, Dresden.

120. *Les Armées Françaises dans la Grande Guerre*, 1:280.

121. On Manonviller and the siege, cf. Deuringer, *Die Schlacht in Lothringen und in den Vogesen*, 2:506–513. In the German armies only the Second and the Sixth Armies had heavy mortars in their organizational structure.

122. *Tagebuch Rupprecht*, entry of 17 August 1914, Bayer. GH, Nachlass Rupprecht 699.

123. *Les Armées Françaises dans la Grande Guerre*, vol. 2, *La manoeuvre en retraite et les préliminaires de la bataille de la Marne* (Paris, 1925), 355 (26 August 1914), 374 (28 August 1914), and 383f. (1 September 1914).

124. *Tagebuch Rupprecht*, 25 August 1914, Bayer. GH, Nachlass Rupprecht 699.

125. Joffre, *Mémoires du maréchal Joffre*, 1:252.

126. *Der Weltkrieg 1914–1918*, vol. 3, *Der Marne-Feldzug von der Sambre zur Marne* (Berlin, 1926), 7–10; the original signed by Moltke in the files of Sixth Army, Bayer. KA, AOK 6, 42.

127. *Tagebuch Krafft*, 30 August 1914, Bayer. KA, Nachlass Krafft 145.

128. For instance: Deuringer, *Die Schlacht in Lothringen und in den Vogesen*, 1:420–422, 1:431f., 1:434; Ludwig von Gebsattel, *Von Nancy bis zum Camp des Romains 1914: Nach amtlichen Unterlagen des Reichsarchivs, des Münchener Kriegsarchivs und Berichten von Mitkämpfern*, Schlachten des Weltkrieges, 6 (Berlin, 1926), 35, 38.

129. Dieter Storz, *Kriegsbild und Rüstung vor 1914: Europäische Landstreitkräfte vor dem Ersten Weltkrieg* (Herford, Berlin, Bonn, 1992), 187–190.

130. Ibid., 68f., 156.

131. Georges Frédéric Herr, *Die Artillerie in Vergangenheit, Gegenwart und Zukunft* (Charlottenburg, 1925), 16f.; cf. also Alfred Muther, *Das Gerät der leichten Artillerie vor, im und nach dem Weltkrieg*, vol. 1, *Feldgeschütze* (Berlin, 1925), 213–224.

132. *Les Armées Françaises dans la Grande Guerre*, 2:362.

133. In the opinion of Herr, only part of the army corps of the French Army used that method. Herr, *Die Artillerie in Vergangenheit, Gegenwart und Zukunft*, 45. Several of them were obviously in Lorraine in the summer of 1914.

134. *Tagebuch Rupprecht*, 27 August 1914, Bayer. GH, Nachlass Rupprecht 699; cf. also the war diary of the Seventh Army of 28 August 1914: "The firing precision of the French artillery is astonishing. The main reasons are the thorough reconnaissance by artillery and aircraft and the fact that the firing is observed by aircraft." Bayer. KA, AOK 6, 1.

135. Göldner, "Die Schwere Artillerie im Festungskriege," in *Das Ehrenbuch der Deutschen Schweren Artillerie*, vol. 2, ed. Franz Nikolaus Kaiser (Berlin, 1934), 57–71. In terms of mobility and rates of fire, many of these guns were obsolescent. Their ballistic capabilities, however, were still sufficient for the static conditions of fortress and trench warfare, and added to the overall firepower.

136. Krafft in a supplement to Rupprecht's diary entry of 19 August 1914, Bayer. KA, Nachlass Rupprecht 699.

137. *Kriegstagebuch der 7. Armee*, of 28 August 1914, Bayer. KA, AOK 6, 1.

138. "The impression cannot be denied that not only our field artillery is failing, but our foot artillery as well. Above all, we are lacking the organization of target acquisition and observation of concealed targets which can only be obtained from the height (artillery aviation, balloons and artillery metrology)." *Tagebuch Krafft*, 6 September 1914, Bayer. KA, Nachlass Krafft 145.

139. Diary entry, 7 September 1914, Bayer. KA, Nachlass Rupprecht 699.

140. Herr, *Die Artillerie in Vergangenheit, Gegenwart und Zukunft*, 40.

141. Ibid., 44.

142. Herr's personal experience is shaped by the events on the left wing of the French Army. This is reflected in his remark on the meagerness of the French heavy artillery, which was certainly not true for Lorraine. Ibid.

143. Bayer. GH, Nachlass Rupprecht 699.

144. Gebsattel, *Von Nancy bis zum Camp des Romains 1914*, 39.

145. *Les Armées Françaises dans la Grande Guerre*, 2:394.

146. *Tagebuch Rupprecht*, 4 September 1914, Bayer. GH, Nachlass Rupprecht 699.

147. Gebsattel, *Von Nancy bis zum Camp des Romains 1914*, 39.

148. *Les Armées Françaises dans la Grande Guerre*, 2:380, 382, 388. The German air reconnaissance realized this immediately, as indicated in the aviators' evening report in the war diary of Seventh Army on 30 August 1914; Bayer. KA, AOK 6, 1.

149. BA/MA, Nachlass Tappen 56-1.
150. *Tagebuch Krafft,* 29 August 1914, Bayer. KA, Nachlass Krafft 145.
151. Wenninger, journal entry dated 30 August 1914 and report dated 31 August 1914, in Schulte, "Neue Dokumente zu Kriegsausbruch und Kriegsverlauf 1914," 158, 160f.
152. Wenninger, report dated 31 August 1914, in ibid., 161.
153. *Tagebuch Krafft,* 30 August 1914, Bayer. KA, Nachlass Krafft 145.
154. The horse-drawn materiel had already been transferred to the Fifth Army.
155. *Tagebuch Krafft,* 31 August 1914, Bayer. KA, Nachlass Krafft 145.
156. Xylander, *Deutsche Führung in Lothringen 1914,* 153.
157. *Der Weltkrieg 1914–1918,* vol. 3, *Der Marne-Feldzug von der Sambre zur Marne* (Berlin, 1926), 287.
158. Groener, *Der Feldherr wider Willen,* 29.
159. Moltke, "Betrachtungen und Erinnerungen," in *Helmuth von Moltke 1848–1916,* 391–403, cited page 400.
160. Mertz, too, wrote later that he had been in favor of the attack on the mountainous position at Nancy. Mertz, *Der Führerwille in Entstehung und Durchführung,* 153.
161. In a subsequent remark in his diary Krafft admitted that he "had then been in error in various regards. I overestimated the adverse effects of a retreat. Later, when the withdrawal became a necessity, they did not occur, instead the rearward escape from the deadlocked situation had been perceived as a liberation." Krafft, diary entry of 31 August 1914, Bayer. KA, Nachlass Krafft 145.
162. Ibid.
163. *Tagebuch Krafft,* 31 August 1914, Bayer. KA, Nachlass Krafft 145.
164. Mertz got the impression that at that time Krafft considered the attack on the Charmes Gap to be more important than that on the "Position de Nancy." Mertz, *Der Führerwille in Entstehung und Durchführung,* 154.
165. This included the commanding generals of the *Ersatz* Corps, the I Bavarian Army Corps, and the Bavarian Reserve Corps; the III Bavarian Army Corps sent their chiefs.
166. *Tagebuch Krafft,* 1 September and 2 September 1914, Bayer. KA, Nachlass Krafft 145; *Tagebuch Rupprecht,* 1 September 1914, Bayer. GH, Nachlass Rupprecht 699.
167. *Tagebuch Krafft,* 2 September 1914, Bayer. KA, Nachlass Krafft 145.
168. Ibid.
169. Tagebucheintrag, 2 September 1914, BA/MA, Nachlass Tappen 56-1.
170. Mertz, *Der Führerwille in Entstehung und Durchführung,* 144.
171. Karl Deuringer, "Die Leistungen der Schweren Artillerie im Weltkriege: Im Verbande der 6. und 7. Armee," in *Das Ehrenbuch der Deutschen Schweren Artillerie,* vol. 1, ed. Franz Nikolaus Kaiser (Berlin, 1931), 148–155, here page 154f. The Japanese had only mustered 192 such guns against Port Arthur. *Erfahrungen aussereu-*

ropäischer Kriege neuester Zeit, T. 2: *Aus dem russisch-japanischen Kriege 1904 bis 1905*, vol. 1, *Port Arthur* (Berlin, 1906), 37.

172. *Kriegstagebuch der 7. Armee* of 2 September and 3 September 1914, Bayer. KA, AOK 6, 1.

173. Ibid., entry of 30 August 1914.

174. Ibid., entry of 4 September 1914. On these battles, cf. also Adolf Wild von Hohenborn, *Briefe und Tagebuchaufzeichnungen des preussischen Generals als Kriegsminister und Truppenführer im ersten Weltkrieg*, ed. Helmut Reichold, comp. Gerhard Granier (Boppard a.Rh., 1986), 15–18.

175. Bayer. KA, MKr. 1765.

176. *Der Weltkrieg 1914–1918*, vol. 3, *Der Marne-Feldzug von der Sambre zur Marne* (Berlin, 1926), 310.

177. *Der Weltkrieg 1914 bis 1918*, vol. 4, *Der Marne-Feldzug: Die Schlacht* (Berlin, 1926), 3f.

178. *Tagebuch Krafft*, 5 September 1914, Bayer. KA, Nachlass Krafft 145.

179. Ibid.

180. Ibid.

181. *Tagebuch Wenninger*, 6 September 1914, Bayer. KA, HS 2546.

182. *Tagebuch Rupprecht*, 6 September 1914, Bayer. GH, Nachlass Rupprecht 699.

183. *Tagebuch Krafft*, 6 September 1914, Bayer. KA, Nachlass Krafft 145.

184. Mertz, *Gutachten zur Bauerkontroverse*, 20 November 1928, 10, Bayer. KA, Nachlass Krafft 188.

185. *Tagebuch Krafft*, 6 September 1914, Bayer. KA, Nachlass Krafft 145.

186. Ibid., 2 September 1914.

187. Ibid., 5 September 1914. That morning information was received about the ban on the use of mortar ammunition for the purposes of the field war. Rupprecht was upset when he learned of the generous use in the evening. *Tagebuch Rupprecht*, 5 September 1914, Bayer. GH, Nachlass Rupprecht 699.

188. *Tagebuch Krafft*, 6 September 1914, Bayer. KA, Nachlass Krafft 145.

189. Ibid., 7 September 1914.

190. Assigned to the quartermaster.

191. *Tagebuch Krafft*, 8 September 1914, Bayer. KA, Nachlass Krafft 145.

192. Mertz, *Der Führerwille in Entstehung und Durchführung*, 171.

193. *Tagebuch Krafft*, 8 September 1914, Bayer. KA, Nachlass Krafft 145.

194. *Tagebuch Rupprecht*, 9 September 1914, Bayer. GH, Nachlass Rupprecht 699.

195. *Tagebuch Krafft*, 9 September 1914, Bayer. KA, Nachlass Krafft 145.

196. Ibid., 4 September 1914.

197. *Les Armées Françaises dans la Grande Guerre*, vol. 3, *La bataille de la Marne* (Paris, 1931), 1174.

198. Joffre, *Mémoires du maréchal Joffre*, 1:408.

199. Ibid., 1:407.

200. Ibid., 1:399.

201. *Tagebuch Wenninger,* 10 September 1914, Bayer. KA, HS 2546.

202. *Tagebuch Krafft,* 26 August 1914, Bayer. KA, Nachlass Krafft 145.

203. *Der Weltkrieg 1914–1918,* vol. 1, *Die Grenzschlachten im Westen,* ed. Reichsarchiv (Berlin, 1925), 258; Mertz, *Der Führerwille in Entstehung und Durchführung,* 69f.

204. Wolfgang Foerster, *Graf Schlieffen und der Weltkrieg,* 2nd rev. ed. (Berlin, 1925), 14–16.

205. An alleged reason was that the German Army did not have enough qualified General Staff officers to man the field army headquarters with liaison officers, on top of the many staffs to be mobilized. *Der Weltkrieg 1914–1918,* vol. 1, *Die Grenzschlachten im Westen,* ed. Reichsarchiv (Berlin, 1925), 1:180. This is a feeble argument, since there were only eight field armies.

206. *Tagebuch Wenninger,* 22 August 1914, Bayer. KA, HS 2546; Schulte, "Neue Dokumente zu Kriegsausbruch und Kriegsverlauf 1914," 156.

207. *Tagebuch Wenninger,* 30 August 1914, Bayer. KA, HS 2546; Schulte, "Neue Dokumente zu Kriegsausbruch und Kriegsverlauf 1914," 158. According to Krafft, "nobody who was familiar with the situation" could assume that Moltke would remain at the wheel. "You already got the picture of it during the *Generalstabsreise.*"

208. Subsequent addition to his diary entry of 12 August 1914, Bayer. KA, Nachlass Krafft 145.

209. *Tagebuch Wenninger,* 16 September 1914, cited in Schulte, "Neue Dokumente zu Kriegsausbruch und Kriegsverlauf 1914," 174.

210. *Tagebuch Wenninger,* 7 September 1914, cited in Schulte, "Neue Dokumente zu Kriegsausbruch und Kriegsverlauf 1914," 170.

211. Tappen and Hentsch were lieutenant colonels.

212. *Tagebuch Rupprecht,* 15 September 1914, Bayer. GH, Nachlass Rupprecht 699.

213. *Der Weltkrieg 1914–1918,* vol. 1, *Die Grenzschlachten im Westen,* ed. Reichsarchiv (Berlin, 1925), 179f.

214. Xylander, *Deutsche Führung in Lothringen 1914,* 27.

215. "I can't remember whether it was Major Redern or Major Bauer who pushed us so much on behalf of Moltke; however, I know that the words uttered indicated the unfounded accusation of a lack of energy which was even less justified since I attacked on the 20th despite all concerns of the army command! I have to admit that I felt hurt by those words." *Tagebuch Rupprecht,* 23 August 1914, Bayer. GH, Nachlass Rupprecht 699.

216. Karl von Einem, *Erinnerungen eines Soldaten 1853–1933,* 4th ed. (Leipzig, 1933), 175; Otto von Moser, *Ernsthafte Plaudereien über den Weltkrieg* (Stuttgart, 1925), 40; Hermann von Kuhl, *Der Weltkrieg 1914–1918: Dem deutschen Volke dargestellt,* 2 vols. (Berlin, 1929), 1:11f.; Groener, *Das Testament des Grafen Schlieffen,* 79f. At least there were also some who advocated this distribution of forces, like Ludendorff, *Mein militärischer Werdegang,* 128f.; Marx, *Die Marne—Deutschlands Schicksal?* 36f., 43; Wetzell, "Das Kriegswerk des Reichsarchivs," 10f.

217. Kuhl, *Der Weltkrieg 1914 bis 1918,* 1:12.

218. Karl Deuringer, chief of the Bavarian War Archives, Munich.
219. Müller, *Konrad Krafft von Dellmensingen*, 333.
220. "Looking back from a distance—after 17 years!—things sometimes appear differently from how they had been perceived at the moment. Thus—with the complete knowledge of the events—the question may remain whether the time when we launched the attack was not too early and whether it would not have been better to further withdraw from the enemy and thus lure him away from his fortifications." Letter from Rupprecht to Krafft of 8 June 1931, Bayer. KA, Nachlass Krafft 195. Cf. also Pöhlmann, *Kriegsgeschichte und Geschichtspolitik*, 309.
221. *Tagebuch Rupprecht*, 15 August 1914, Bayer. GH, Nachlass Rupprecht 699.
222. Ludendorff seconded Moltke in this by diagnosing a failure of the German local commanders. Ludendorff, *Mein militärischer Werdegang*, 129. Rupprecht was among the severest critics of the future *Erster Generalquartiermeister* and could not expect any kind of mercy from him.
223. Tappen, *Bis zur Marne 1914*, 14f.
224. Konrad Krafft von Dellmensingen, *Der Durchbruch: Studie an Hand der Vorgänge des Weltkrieges 1914–1918* (Hamburg, 1937), 29.
225. *Tagebuch Wenninger*, 7 September 1914, cited in Schulte, "Neue Dokumente zu Kriegsausbruch und Kriegsverlauf 1914," 169.
226. Haffner and Venohr, *Das Wunder an der Marne*, 16f.
227. Deuringer, *Die Schlacht in Lothringen und in den Vogesen*, 1:848.

Colonel General Helmuth von Moltke the Younger, chief of the Great General Staff at the start of World War I. (Bundesarchiv Image 146-2011-0065)

Crown Prince Rupprecht of Bavaria, shown here as a field marshal in late 1917 or early 1918. (Bundesarchiv Image 103-069-003)

Field Marshal Alfred Graf von Schlieffen, chief of the Great General Staff, 1891–1906. Picture taken after his retirement, about 1910–1913. (Bundesarchiv Image 183-R18084)

Former Crown Prince Rupprecht of Bavaria (right) talking with retired General of Infantry Erich Ludendorff (left), November 1924. (Bundesarchiv Image 102-00818)

Kaiser Maneuvers 1900. Kaiser Wilhelm II (forward right in the uniform of the Royal Mounted Jägers) conversing with Austria's Archduke Franz Ferdinand (left). Colonel General Alfred Graf von Schlieffen is in the background, far right. (Bundesarchiv Image 136-B0434)

Kaiser Wilhelm II with many of his principal World War I military and civilian advisers. Photo montage of various individual pictures taken between 1905 and 1917. Front row, sitting left to right: Crown Prince Rupprecht of Bavaria, Duke Albrecht of Württemberg, Kaiser Wilhelm II (in front of the table), Alexander von Kluck, Otto von Emmich, Gottlieb Graf von Haeseler, Paul von Hindenburg, Alfred von Tirpitz. Back row, standing left to right: Karl von Bülow, August von Mackensen, Helmuth von Moltke, Crown Prince Wilhelm of Prussia, Hermann von Francois, Erich Ludendorff, Erich von Falkenhayn, Karl von Einem, Hans von Beseler, Theobald von Bethmann Hollweg, Josias von Heeringen. (Bundesarchiv Image 146-2013-0086)

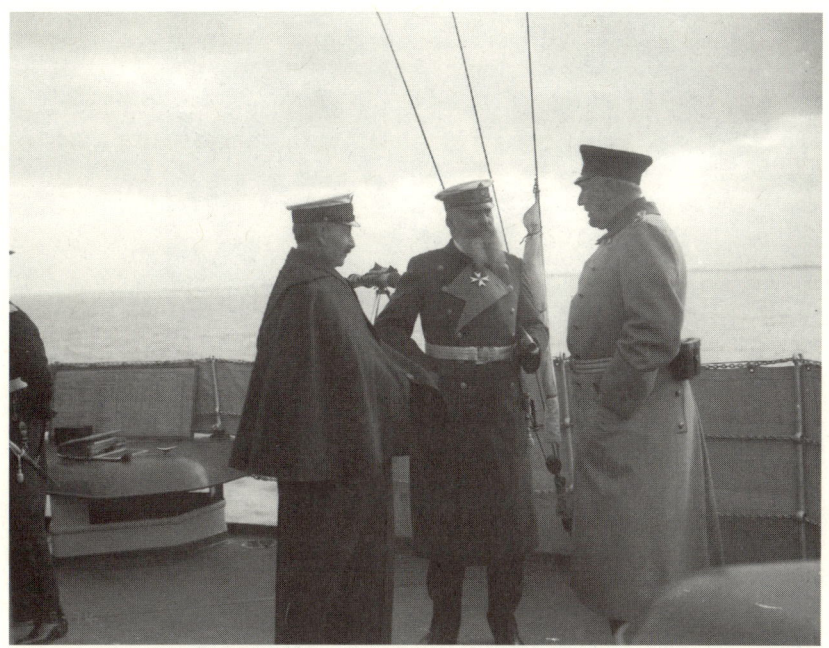

Left to right: Kaiser Wilhelm II, Grand Admiral Alfred von Tirpitz, and General of Infantry Helmuth von Moltke the Younger on board a ship. Photo taken sometime between 1900 and 1914. (Bundesarchiv Image 134-B2646)

Privy Councillor Friedrich von Holstein in his study. The picture was probably taken on 6 April 1906, the date of his retirement. (Bundesarchiv Image 183-S28606)

Theobald von Bethmann Hollweg sitting at a table during his last public appearance before the investigating committee of the Reichstag on 22 November 1919. (Bundesarchiv Image 146-2009-0045)

General of Artillery Konrad Krafft von Dellmensingen, chief of staff of Bavarian Crown Prince Rupprecht's Sixth Army during the Battle of Lorraine in 1914. Photo taken in 1917. (Bundesarchiv Image 183-R11612)

The Military Planning of the Austro-Hungarian Imperial and Royal Army and the Schlieffen Plan

Günther Kronenbitter

In the second half of the nineteenth century, the Habsburg monarchy, like the other Great Powers of continental Europe, underwent a process of systematization and perpetuation of the theoretical, administrative, and logistical preparations for war. As its primary institution for war planning, termed "specific war preparations" in experts' jargon, Austria-Hungary too relied on its General Staff. After the wars of the 1850s and 1860s had shown the need for reforms in the armed forces of the Danube Monarchy, the experimental phase of designing military leadership and planning structures came to an end and was replaced by a conscious orientation toward the Prussian model. Considering the complex constitutional situation of Austria-Hungary, its General Staff was of special importance for the cohesion of the land forces, even beyond preparations for war. In addition to the Royal and Imperial (*K.u.K.*) Army, which was controlled by the War Ministry in Vienna, the land forces included the Royal Hungarian *Honvédség* and the Imperial Royal *Landwehr*, both under the supervision of a Ministry of National Defense in Budapest and Vienna, respectively. Although war affairs after 1867 continued to be part of the mandate of the overall monarchy, these three land forces existed alongside each other. Since the General Staff coordinated the war preparations for all three components of the land forces and exercised the controls in planning, its competencies in the field of military affairs stretched far beyond the competencies of the War Ministry, which only controlled the *K.u.K.* Army and the navy.

Officially the chief of the General Staff was an "auxiliary appendage" of the War Minister. This, however, tells little about the position's real power structures and means of influence. While until 1906 the chief of the General Staff, Friedrich Graf von Beck-Rzikowsky, could leverage his close personal relationship with Emperor Franz Joseph, his successor, Franz Conrad von Hötzendorf, had to develop other ways to expand his influence. The chief of the General Staff had direct access to the emperor on all issues concerning war preparations. Conrad also was permitted to discuss matters of security policy directly with the foreign minister. He used that access to force upon both the foreign minister and the emperor his views on the difficult strategic position of Austria-Hungary, flooding them with speeches and *Denkschriften* (memorandums) on security issues.

Conrad maintained that the Habsburg Monarchy was surrounded by more potential enemies than it could possibly defend against with its limited military resources and those of its ally, the German Reich. Conrad's proposed solution to this political-military dilemma, which he advanced in ever-new versions, was to thin out the enemy's ranks by a succession of wars against individual neighbor states. To Conrad, such wars against Italy or Serbia were only the acceleration of what would be an inevitable passage at arms. The chief of the General Staff promoted preemptive war even when the foreign minister staunchly protested against such suggestions. When Conrad repeatedly overstepped his position by wide margins, he actually was suspended from office for a year during 1911–1912. In addition, the friction between Foreign Minister Alois Lexa von Aehrenthal and Conrad put a heavy strain for months on cooperation between the diplomatic and military leadership.[1]

The General Staff was organized into divisions. The core of the planning function—in terms of personnel strength, position in the workflow, and prestige—was the *Operationsbüro* (Operations Division), which coordinated the preparation of plans for mobilization, initial deployment, and operations during the early stages of a war. The Operations Division also was responsible for exercising the tactical and operational capabilities of the leadership and units. The other divisions performed the various preliminary work for the Operations Division. The railway was the most important means of transport for mobilization and initial deployment, and also for the execution of the operations plans. The General Staff, therefore, had its own *Eisenbahnbüro* (Railway Division). Shortly before 1914 there was a realization that the subsistence and field transportation systems also required thorough and centralized planning. The *Etappenbüros* (Supply Divisions) were therefore established in 1909, along with the *Landesbeschreibungsbüro* (Area Studies Division), which performed the crucial tasks of collecting and compiling topographic, transportation, and economic-geographical information, predominantly in the form of maps. But that division largely lost its justification for existence during periods of easy access to detailed information from the various areas, and its abolition was therefore the subject of heated discussion shortly before 1914.

During the nineteenth century information on budgets, force levels, organization, weapons, logistics, and garrisons of the other European states became increasingly available through public sources. The developing detailed and specialized journalism and the media coverage in the daily press about parliamentary decision-making and the legal and budgetary conditions of the military organizations in many countries made it easier to assess the relative strength ratios of the armies of the European Great Powers. Gathering intelligence on the military situation abroad was the task of the General Staff's *Evidenzbüro* (Intelligence Division), which was organized into functional groups. Most of the groups collected intelligence on one particular state. Military espionage and counterespionage were among the tasks of the Intelligence Division's *Kundschaftsgruppe* (Reconnaissance Group). The Austro-Hungarian organization of information collecting and processing differed greatly from the structures of the Great General Staff in Berlin. There, espionage was the task of *Sektion IIIb,* while the other information collection tasks were integrated into operational planning. The Germans had no direct equivalent to the Austrian *Evidenzbüro*. There had been serious consideration given to abolishing the *Evidenzbüro* and restructuring the Austrian General Staff based on the German model, but such reorganization was not initiated prior to the outbreak of war in 1914.

Despite the relatively important position of the *Evidenzbüro,* the chief of the General Staff, his deputy, and the Operations Division were the central actors in the planning process. They set the guidelines for the information collecting by the Area Studies Division, the Railway Division, and the Intelligence Division. The individual groups within the Operations Division worked out the plans for mobilization, initial deployment, and operations, which were then submitted to the chief of the General Staff by the chief of the Operations Division.[2] The groups of the Operations Division dealt with specific war scenarios, the *"Fälle"* (cases). These war scenarios were designated by the initial of the operational area, such as *Fall R* (for Russia), *Fall I* (for Italy), or *Fall B* (for the Balkans). It was also common practice to name the plans after the color of the paper they were printed on. Apart from the

"Blue" mobilization against Russia, there was the "Red" one against Italy. For wars against Serbia and/or Montenegro, the General Staff officers distinguished between the "Brown" mobilization, which only consisted of a defensive increase of the troop levels (in the XV or the XV and XVI Corps areas) in Dalmatia, Bosnia, and Herzegovina, and the "Yellow" mobilization, which had the options for offensive operations and the commitment of additional corps.[3]

What were necessary to determine the specific preparations for each war scenario were the force levels, the order of battle, the assembly areas for initial deployment, the type of deployment and its security, the command structures, and the provision of the units with the required equipment. Also prepared were detailed instructions for the corps commanders and the regional commanders. Graphical schematics of the deployment and an index of directives on the measures to be executed in the deployment areas were compiled in "*cahiers*" (quick reference files). The alerting instructions, the order of battle, or "*Kriegs-Ordre de bataille,*" and the initial deployment plans for each war scenario had to be completed by autumn and approved by the emperor. Only then could the Railway Division begin to plan the rail transport, the most important aspect of the "*Instradierung*" (mobilization). Until the spring there was time to determine the mobilization stations and the deployment readiness dates and to establish the transport and movement plans for mobilization and the initial deployment movements.

In contrast to the German Reich, the objective of Austria-Hungary was to achieve the highest possible flexibility for the various war scenarios and their combinations. Considering the political situation of the Habsburg Monarchy, nearly every neighbor to the south and east was a potential enemy. Italy, a Triple Alliance partner, was considered unreliable. In addition, doubts increased in the final prewar years about whether Romania would meet its alliance obligations in the event of a war with Russia. While the relationship with Germany was not free of friction, the loyalty of the German Reich to the alliance was unquestioned.[4] Apart from *Fall I*, *Fall B*, and *Fall R*, consideration also had to be given to the possibility of combined war scenarios. There was no shortage of political imponderables and military risks. But the assessment of the strategic situation predominately dictated preparations for a war against one enemy, which would turn into a multifront war after the start of deployment. Under Conrad's leadership, the required planning efforts were reviewed. In June 1909 the chief of the General Staff stated in his outline for the deployment planning for the following year the assumption of dealing with more than one enemy in the event of war. The Habsburg Monarchy would, however, be able to count on allies in any event of a war between Great Powers:

> Considering the complex political neighborhood relations of the Monarchy, the most varied combinations of this constellation are conceivable;—it is not feasible to work out for each of these combinations an individually complete deployment plan purely designed for the respective case, to include a complete mobilization schedule. The consequence, therefore, must be to focus on the most likely scenarios, work out the plans for them, but make them flexible—or better put, "adaptable," in such a way that if that scenario materializes the necessary steps can be initiated and executed without disrupting the general preparations. The basis for this approach is primarily a decentralized mobilization, relatively independent for the individual army corps and the special units.[5]

It was exactly this fundamental reorganization that the *K.u.K.* Army had been implementing since the end of 1908. In a contingency war directive that Conrad sent to the Railway Department, the land forces were organized into deployment echelons, and then the mobilization was decentralized at a later point. Apart from the "Minimum Group B" for the security of the southeastern areas of the Habsburg Monarchy, the army was divided into A and B Echelons, which should be transported consecutively into their initial deployment areas, while C Echelon was initially not deployed to the battle line. B Echelon, as the flexible element, was tasked with facilitating the transition to a multifront war. The assembly of the individual echelons had to be scheduled in such a chronological manner as to prevent chaos on the railroad lines and at the rail centers during the transition phase from one war scenario to the other. According to the judgment of the contemporary experts, the exercise of battalion command and control functions during well-rehearsed General Staff war gaming would enhance the combat efficiency of the units. The peacetime "*Ordre de bataille,*" therefore, had to be as close as possible to the wartime order of battle.

Based on the experiences of the 1866 and 1870 wars, a high mobilization tempo was vital. That required the close proximity of the "*Ergänzungsbezirke*" (recruiting districts) and the units' garrison locations. Despite political concerns about the repercussions to the internal security of the multiethnic empire, the *K.u.K.* Army adopted the territorial augmentation scheme in 1889. The one exception was in Bosnia-Herzegovina, where concerns still lingered about the troops' reliability—at least for the Bohemian units. That somewhat complicated the planning process of the echelon deployment schemes. Conrad's instruction not to go into too much detail in the planning saved the Operations Division and especially the Railway Division a great deal of work. The chief of the General Staff generally tried to avoid overburdening his personnel.[6]

The great disadvantage of the echelon-based deployment system was that the units of B Echelon were deployed with artificial delay. That was the price to be paid for an initial deployment organization designed to facilitate the transition to a multifront war. What was also urgently necessary was the exact timing of that echelon's deployment for correctly scheduling the decision to shift to a different scenario. The schedules for the individual echelons had to be determined exactly for the different war scenarios. Consequently, the plans were both flexible and rigid at the same time—flexible in so far as the various war scenarios were concerned, but rigid in the echelon structure and the deadline for the transition between the war scenarios.

The political sensitivity of the German war plans was the result of the lack of alternatives to the "France first" concept advanced by Alfred von Schlieffen and Helmuth von Moltke the Younger, with all its implications for the schedule and direction of operations of the German Army in the field. The flaw in the Habsburg Monarchy's planning was the necessity of basing the deployment decision on the B Echelon schedules, which reduced the originally intended flexibility. Without expansion of the armed forces, in particular the formation of a reserve force, no plan would provide a remedy for the strategic requirements of Austria-Hungary. In the summer of 1914 the limitations of the Railway and Operations Divisions' war preparations became strikingly apparent. The divergence between the politically favored delay in redirecting B Echelon toward the northeast and the deadline constraints of the initial deployment plans could only be resolved if one was ultimately prepared to take extreme risks, as Conrad was in late July 1914. The extent of the problems actually involved in the General Staff's war plans, however, remained unknown by most decision-makers until into the first weeks of war.

Within the General Staff, both the Operations Division and the chief of the General Staff exercised only fragmentary control over the execution of the initial deployment plans by the railway experts. One reason for this may have been Conrad's ambition to shape the security policy that took up too many working resources. There was no external control of the General Staff's planning performance in any way. The War Ministry hardly interfered in operational planning at all. The 5th Branch of the War Ministry, which dealt with deployment strategy issues, cooperated with the Operations Division without much conflict, perhaps partly owing to the close personal ties between the members of the two organizations. The emperor himself did not exert any noteworthy influence on the planning process. Although the initial deployment was submitted to and had to be approved by him, Franz Joseph did not interfere with the plans. He gave free rein to his notorious addiction to details about the external appearances of his armies, but as a military leader he was once bitten, twice shy. After the 1859 debacle, he did not want to play the future commander and he initially relinquished the function of commanding general to Archduke Albrecht, the victor of Custozza. In General Friedrich Graf von Beck-Rzikowsky, His Majesty's Military Chancellery temporarily had an influential and ambitious officer as its chief. But after Beck left to become chief of the General Staff in 1881, the Chancellery lost much of its former significance, apart from personnel policy responsibilities. In 1914 there was no one on the senior staff of the Military Chancellery with any real operational expertise.

The same was true for Archduke Franz Ferdinand, who after Crown Prince Rudolf's suicide became—first de facto and then officially—the successor to the throne. Franz Ferdinand's difficult personality was not a good match with his position as successor to the throne. Not willing to restrain himself until assuming the throne, he tried to assert his political ideas by force. Franz Ferdinand's aim was to strengthen the role of the Crown, certainly not only because he longed for a scope of action, but also because he was convinced that only fundamental and swift changes would be able to save the Habsburg Empire from disintegration. Thus, he would not flinch from openly or covertly attacking the governments in Budapest and Vienna, as well as the common ministers, when he believed this was in the best interest of the House of Habsburg. He was not impressed by the fact that the political leaders had been appointed by his uncle Franz Joseph.

It was only in the military that Franz Ferdinand really had an official function. He had various control tasks and was appointed Inspector General of the Army in 1913. His Military Chancellery served him as the organizational backbone for his political actions, even outside of the scope of the armed forces. The leaders of that Chancellery were mostly General Staff officers who had the necessary expertise to provide informed opinions on the operations plans. The heir apparent paid intense attention to personnel policy and the expansion of the navy, and he cared about the traditions and cohesion of the army. But he was neither willing nor able personally to subject the planning process of the General Staff to close scrutiny, despite the fact that the initial deployment plans were submitted to him. Colonel Alexander Brosch von Aarenau, the long-standing chief of the Military Chancellery, did try to influence the plans.

Thus, within the military structure there was no one (including the monarch and the heir apparent) who could seriously challenge the planning competence of the General Staff. Nor was any interference by the civilian heads of the Danube Monarchy to be expected. The information flow between the Foreign Ministry and the General Staff was more robust than might have seemed likely, considering the divergences between Foreign Minister Aehrenthal and Conrad. The military agreements with the German Great General Staff of 1908–1909 were known to the foreign minister, and the annual *Denkschriften* of the chief of the General Staff contained references to war planning, similar to many other of Conrad's speeches and *Denkschriften*. Designing the initial deployment strategy, however, remained a strictly military matter.

Franz Joseph's concept of compartmentalized competencies, the social distance between diplomats and military functionaries, and the disagreements of the top representatives of both institutions all impeded any debate on the deployment and operational plans. Such, however, was consistent with the contemporary concepts of military professionalization, as promoted by the other Great Powers. Accordingly, a uniform plan for all components of the land forces within the Habsburg Empire was sufficient and appropriate. During a crisis situation the war minister and the chief of the General Staff informed the Common Council of Ministers, the highest body for coordinating the Dual Monarchy's politics, about the individual aspects of the initial deployment. There is no documentary evidence, however, that such consultation was associated with political control of the concrete war preparations. Only the prime minister of Hungary, István Tisza, showed some intention in 1913–1914 to subject the plans of the General Staff to a critical examination.

Even as late as the July Crisis of 1914 there was no political control over the operational planning process. Formally, the monarch was the head of the civilian as well as the military decision-making apparatus. The emperor, however, disapproved of any further association of the two spheres and he did nothing to enforce any attempt to control the General Staff's planning process from within the military organization. Franz Ferdinand was far too occupied with the establishment of his "counter-government" at Belvedere to be able to assume this role. Similar to the German Reich, the dynastic head of the Austro-Hungarian monarchy did not function as a check on the narrower military biases of the General Staff.

Conrad's energetic efforts to increase substantially the combat readiness of the land forces produced results, although the start of a massive armament increase was only triggered by the 1912–1913 crises. The training of future officers, the troop exercises, General Staff rides, and war games all underwent reform, and personnel policy was rigorously adapted to the anticipated requirements of a coming war. Pride in the improvements, such as for the new maneuver schemes, and frustration over the lack of the politicians' understanding of the requirements of war went hand in hand for many General Staff officers.

True enough, there were feuds between individual cliques within the General Staff, but such squabbles were mainly about career issues and institutional rivalries between divisions or groups. Only in individual cases was there fundamental criticism of Conrad's concepts and his resulting war plans. One such criticism came from Alfred Krauss, who for several years was deeply involved with the logistical issues. He did not think much of the feasibility of the operational plans, which he thought took insufficient account of the physical resilience of the forces, the availability of supplies, and the geographical conditions in the operational areas. Despite the isolated criticism expressed by individuals like Krauss, a close reading of the letters and memoirs of many of the General Staff officers gives the impression that a new and stronger sense of institutional self-esteem blossomed under Conrad's leadership. That was reflected in the increased standing of the General Staff within the military organization similar to the Prussian model, as well as Conrad's active involvement in security policy issues.

That new sense of self-esteem, however, was dealt a heavy blow shortly before the start of World War I when the former chief of the Reconnaissance Group in the Intelligence Department, Colonel Alfred Redl, was convicted of espionage in 1913. Along with others, Redl had disclosed information on the *K.u.K.* Army's network of agents in Russia to the Czarist Empire's counterespionage operatives. Despite this debacle and the hardly less catastrophic consequences of the cost-cutting measures implemented between 1903 and 1906, the Intelligence Department succeeded in drawing a quite accurate picture of Russia's war preparations. Much could be deduced from the expansion of the rail network and centers in western Russia. Comparing the capacities of their own railway lines toward the northeast provided an important basis for evaluating the scope of action available to the two military commands. Together with the conditions of the natural environment and the available military resources, this approach consequently provided the foundation for Austria-Hungary's own war planning process. The condition of the Russian fortresses provided additional indicators of the Czarist Empire's intent. Since 1908, however, the principal question had been if and to what extent a redeployment of the Russian mobilized force could be expected. The neglect of the fortresses in the west of Russia and the significantly increased transport capacity of many of the deployment routes suggested the conclusion that Russia would evacuate large parts of Congress Poland. By accelerating the mobilization process the Russian Army increasingly succeeded in reducing Austria-Hungary's head start. The redeployment of the initial deployment was therefore not a sign of weakness, but of the increasing strength of Russia. More than ever there was the danger that the Russian Army might first withdraw into their own interior and thus evade a military decision. The least predictable element was the center of the main effort that the Russian deployment would establish. It was possible that the main body of the available forces would initially turn either against the Habsburg Monarchy or against Germany. The answer to that question was partly decisive in shaping the coalition's concept of warfare in the east.

By the year 1914 the mutual defense coordination between the land forces of the Danube Monarchy and the German Reich had only been established in rough outline.[7] Apart from the chiefs of the General Staffs in Berlin and in Vienna, who since 1882 had repeatedly made agreements about warfare against Russia, the two military intelligence services also cooperated regularly and rather closely. As was natural among allies, there was an exchange of information on the war preparations of potential enemies and the sharing of helpful counterespionage details. What was deemed necessary for the mutual defense preparations of the Triple Alliance was discussed at the expert level, especially the transport of Italian forces through Austria to the western front of Germany. No detailed agreements were needed for the war against Russia, since it had been determined in 1895 already that the German *Ostheer* would deploy mainly in East Prussia. The direct contact of German and Austro-Hungarian forces, therefore, would be limited to the Silesian-Galician border region or to the adjacent regions of Congress Poland, respectively. Since the initial military decisions were expected to be achieved farther to the east, it was thought unnecessary to plan for large-scale combined operations.[8] The factual level of information sharing and cooperation was limited to what was expected for the event of war and the contemporary notions of sovereignty. The Habsburg Monarchy, as the undoubtedly weaker military partner, paid much closer attention to preventing the alliance from imposing an unavoidable dependence on Germany in security policy matters. Up to 1914, combined exercises were not among the essential military requirements in the opinion of either Vienna or Berlin. Nor were arrangements for the establishment of a combined command for the eastern front.⁹

Such coordination as might be required between the operations of the two allies was overseen by the two chiefs of the General Staffs. The *K.u.K.* Army counted on the assumption that, thanks to their faster mobilization compared to the Russians, they would initially achieve a favorable force ratio in the area of operations that would facilitate offensive action. This implied, however, placing the focus of the deployment not too far into eastern Galicia. The transportation routes there were still inadequate, despite all of the railway projects that had been carried out.

The Germans, who would deploy even more rapidly, had been planning their operations largely independently from their allies' operational objectives since the mid-1890s. Schlieffen, the chief of the Great General Staff, had tasked the German elements deploying east of the Vistula River in the event of war with defending the area, but he did not exclude a possible withdrawal from East Prussia if the overall situation warranted such. He let his colleague in Vienna know that in such a scenario an attack on the Russian Neman Army would have priority. Beck, who at the time was still chief of the General Staff in Vienna, accepted this without complaint. But he expected from the remaining German forces that "despite their initial secondary task, [they would] also act as offensively as possible without hesitation in order to contain directly the Russian forces at the Narew River. The more efficient this containment is, the faster our offensive can advance and the sooner our offensive will impact the relief of the German Army."¹⁰

Beck pointed out that the head start against the slower deploying Russians would be the decisive factor for the successful completion of the initial operations. It was, therefore, essential to ensure that the alliance's offensive operations "do not encounter an already advanced posture of adverse forces and assets . . . which actually might occur in the case of the two allies Germany and Austria-Hungary deciding only upon imminent threat of war whether or not to invoke mutual defense, thus halting the German offensive until after such decision."¹¹ Beck, however, did not receive any clarification regarding the *casus foederis*. This situation would only change when a new round of consultations began between the chiefs of the General Staffs in Berlin and Vienna during the Bosnian crisis in 1908–1909.¹²

After assuming office in 1906, Conrad was in no hurry to plan an alliance war against Russia. It suited his political priorities to make new plans first for a deployment against Italy. In doing so he could fall back to his own previous work. As a brigade and divisional commander he had dealt intimately with the southwestern theater. The war against the Czarist Empire remained the actual challenge for the Operations Division. The army of the Habsburg Empire could not fall back upon experience. Nor did the force ratios offer any real optimism in the planning for a campaign against Russia. The agreements with Germany from the mid-1890s on offered at least a basis for Austria-Hungary's own war preparations.

The changes made during the new chief of the General Staff's first years in office were therefore not too dramatic. After the 1904 Russian defeat in the Russo-Japanese War, the revision of the plans for *Fall R* did not appear urgent, and Conrad thus felt safe in following his own list of priorities. The chief of the General Staff, however, knew full well that a war against Italy or Serbia could bring Russia to the scene, thus posing an existential threat to the Danube Monarchy. It is telling that it was in this context that the deployment against Russia was finally discussed from a new and principal perspective.

Summing up the plans for a war against Russia in 1907, the later head of the Operations Division, Joseph Metzger, pointed out that considering the German return to the old concept of assembling their *Ostheer* east of the lower Vistula and subsequently advancing toward the Narew River in Austria-Hungary, there was widespread belief that a swift offensive by the Austro-Hungarian Third Army against Rovno and by the First and Second Armies between the Bug River and the Vistula would be the best solution to the strategic problem. Even though the initial deployment plans for 1907–1908 were shaped by this basic idea, alternatives had been considered for several years. One potential option was to have only the First Army, consisting of five corps, advance between the Bug and Vistula, and instead direct the offensive main effort against Rovno with the Third and Second Armies (in other words, with nine instead of only six corps).[13]

The chief of the General Staff did not think much of such a shifting of the main efforts, at least not in the very probable case of French intervention. Conrad was not interested in a war between the Habsburg Monarchy and the Czarist Empire, but he definitely was interested in launching an attack on Italy or Serbia. He therefore concerned himself with the combination of the two war options, *Fall R* and *Fall I* or *Fall B,* respectively. It is probable that Conrad was influenced by his political preferences when he represented the attack on the weaker enemy as the priority course of action.

First, Conrad had to assert his theory within the General Staff. In a *Denkschrift* dated April 1908 he tried to prove that initially an attack should be launched on Italy, then against Russia. Only in the case of an offensive along the Warsaw–Brest line would the Russians be forced to accept engagement, while an attack in Podolia-Wolhynia toward Rovno would allow the czar's army to evade. "When Germany wants to conduct its main attack first against Russia and then against France, only then could the Monarchy consider seeking a decision against Russia first and then against Italy . . . , [the exception would be] if Germany in this situation would also turn such a powerful force against Russia [so] that the latter's forces concentrated in Poland, Lithuania and at the Neman River would be contained there."[14]

The Operations Division did not agree, but recommended instead changing the distribution of forces so that forty instead of thirty-five infantry divisions would be available against Russia in case of a northeast main attack. The Operations Division doubted the possibility that redeployment from the southwestern to the northeastern theater could be completed before the Russians had advanced to Vienna and Budapest. They offered the comparison that the Rovno–Lutsk line could be reached with twenty-four infantry divisions by the thirtieth mobilization day, still leaving three corps for the area between the Vistula and Bug Rivers, and two corps for the right wing. Conrad emphasized in his marginal note that this might result in attacking a gaping void, particularly considering information suggesting a withdrawn Russian deployment.[15]

This debate about strategic priorities and possible directions of operation was closely connected to the political discussion about Austria-Hungary's Balkans policy. After the failure of the Sandžak railway project, Conrad tried in vain to win over the monarch and the foreign minister to his concept of an offensive war against Italy, despite the changed international situation. In a discussion with Foreign Minister Aehrenthal the chief of the General Staff emphasized that he would only want to augment personnel strength in the south Slavic areas for securing the southeastern border, but apart from that, all forces should be held ready for an attack against Italy. Now Conrad needed clear information about the current state of German war plans. In April and May 1908 his requests to be allowed to have direct contact with Schlieffen's successor Moltke were still rebuffed by Aehrenthal. The Bosnian Crisis made the foreign minister change his mind in December. However, he underestimated Conrad's persistent interest in the preparation of a war against Italy.

Over the following years the exchange of letters between Conrad and Moltke, beginning in January 1909, became the basis of the limited efforts by the General Staffs in Vienna and Berlin to coordinate their war planning. Conrad also finally obtained from Moltke the very clarification regarding the *casus foederis* that Beck had vainly sought in 1897. Nonetheless, it is essential to remember that the major motivation of the Austro-Hungarian chief of the General Staff was initially his freedom to plan his favorite war scenario in such a way that the first offensive attack would be conducted in the southwest. For this, it was absolutely necessary that Germany back Austria-Hungary against Russia. As became apparent later, an unmistakable attitude on the part of Austria-Hungary's ally would be sufficient to bring the still militarily weakened Russia to its knees. In contrast, an attack on Serbia with German backing, as Moltke offered to his colleague in mid-January, appeared only as a second-best solution. In the case of such action eventually resulting in a war against Russia, the Austro-Hungarian chief of the General Staff saw good chances for the *Fall R* option ending victoriously in an already ongoing deployment into the Balkans.[16]

Moltke allowed Conrad insight into the basic principles of the German war planning process. If the concept "*Schlieffenplan*" is predominantly defined as a strategic principle which determines that in the event of a war between the Great Powers, France will be attacked with the vast majority of the German land forces while a small number of forces will be committed in limited offensive operations in the east, and then after the decision of the campaign in the west the then available forces will be deployed in an offensive against Russia, then the General Staff in Vienna had known the "Schlieffen Plan" since 1909. The German Great General Staff, however, held closely and did not share the deployment plans and tactical schemes for the west, no matter whether they were developed under Schlieffen or under Moltke. Such indeed was consistent with the character of the alliance and cannot be regarded as a special affront to Conrad and his subordinates. The chief of the *K.u.K.* General Staff accepted this as well as the task allocation, which, given the German strategy, was imperative in the case of war on the eastern front.

Austria-Hungary's task initially would be to serve as a buffer for an estimated forty days against Russia. The small German Eastern Army of thirteen divisions could initially tie down only as many Russian forces as possible, thus partially relieving the pressure on the allies. The framework of the coordination was now clear. Germany needed the offensive of the *K.u.K.* Army in order to prevent the Russians from advancing toward the west, while the chances of success of the Austro-Hungarian operations also depended on how many Russian forces could be contained by the German *Ostheer*. Both allies, therefore, had to try to induce their respective partners to conduct vigorous offensives on the eastern front. When Conrad hinted that redeployment of the initial deployment in Galicia might be reasonable, considering that the center of the German main effort would be in the west, the chief of the German General Staff promised an offensive advance against the

Narev Army, as Beck had recommended years earlier. Conrad, in turn, now offered to thrust forward between the Bug and Vistula Rivers to the north, thus emphasizing the urgent necessity of a German attack on the Russian Narev Army.

The agreements of the following years, resuming the exchange of letters of 1909, were imperatively characterized by the two chiefs of the General Staffs promising each other more than they consequently could deliver. This resulted from the logical assumptions upon which the agreements of 1909 were based. The mutual disappointments of the two allies and the frictions between the middle powers during the early stages of the war were not the only consequences of the basic pattern of the agreements.[17] These agreements of 1909 even remained in force when in 1911 Conrad was forced out of office for approximately a year and was replaced by General of Infantry Blasius Schemua, who expressly referenced the written agreements between Conrad and Moltke and declared them to be binding. "In this sense," he wrote in May 1912, "I take the liberty of notifying Your Excellency that the directives given me regarding the preparation of the case of war 'R' for the year 1913–1914 envision the quickest deployment of the left wing of our own army—as before—in central eastern Galicia in order to launch the offensive immediately from this wing. This swift offensive against the left wing of the Russian main force thrown against Austria-Hungary will be the more decisive for the common goal of the allied armies the less the Russians are allowed to move to the south [their] forces originally intended against Germany."

Considering the strength of the forces and the schedule for the Narev offensive, Schemua tried to obtain a definite statement from Moltke. "True, the circumstances have changed, in part because of the assumed withdrawn Russian deployment; but I still believe for the future on being able to count on the offensive Your Excellency agreed upon with my predecessor in office, i.e., German forces—in the case of war R+F against G and AH—advancing against the Narev, and the more so, as Your Excellency expressed with regard to the talks in Berlin that G would in the future presumably enter into the offensive with more than the thirteen infantry and two cavalry divisions, as originally agreed upon in the previous written agreements."[18]

There was no response from Moltke, although the Austro-Hungarian chief of the General Staff requested one.[19] Moltke, however, raised Schemua's hopes in November, when the conflict between the Habsburg Monarchy and Russia became more and more acute, by promising additional German forces in the east. Schemua's summarized account of the discussion indicates that one of the chief of the German General Staff's key objectives was to pacify his ally. Initially, Moltke emphasized the strategic priorities for the event of a war between the Great Powers, priorities that had already been known to Vienna for a long time. It would be "naturally the foremost intention to defeat the enemy to the west, which he hopes to achieve within four to five weeks, and then commit the force surplus against the east. To my objection that this short period appeared very doubtful to me and the strength of force initially committed in the cast appeared rather low, Moltke responded that he could possibly commit there further divisions formed from replacements, whose operational readiness, however, should be expected a little bit later."[20]

Moltke's vague promises were an attempt at inspiring trust and encouraging the Austro-Hungarian chief of the General Staff to offensive action. Since 1909 both sides repeatedly had endeavored to dispel all doubts about the binding character of the promises, irrespective of the significant changes in the strategic situation. In addition to the alliance relations with Italy and Romania, the armament efforts of the Czarist Empire and especially the anticipated withdrawn Russian deployment carried particularly great weight. As an innovation, the German Great General Staff had introduced into the 1909–1910 *Aufmarschanweisungen* (Deployment Directives) the plans for a *Grosser Ostaufmarsch* (Deployment Plan for the East) for the event of war only against Russia. Doubts remained, however, about a swift decision of the war in the east, particularly given the risk of the Russian forces withdrawing into their own interior. After only a few years the *Grosser Ostaufmarsch* vanished again from the *Aufmarschanweisungen*. For 1913–1914 only one deployment alternative was included, with the center of the main effort in the west. Not only was a war against Russia without immediate French intervention an extremely unlikely scenario, it also raised operational and strategic problems. Hence, Moltke's decision to drop the option of a *Grosser Ostaufmarsch* appears hardly dramatic, considering that this option had been introduced to the deployment plans only shortly before.[21]

This step by Moltke at least suited the political climate and the coordination problems of the allies' war planning process for the east. Thus, Conrad in 1911 rejected the proposal by the German Great General Staff to attack with the right wing of the *K.u.K.* Army in order to force the Russian Army toward the Pripyat Marshes, thus preventing their withdrawal into the Russian interior. The reasons Conrad stated were the threat to his own lines of communication in Galicia and the risk of flank envelopment. Moltke's concern that the Russians could withdraw into their own interior, therefore, remained. In contrast, Conrad obviously feared that the Germans would not muster enough vigor in their promised attack on the Narev Army. He pointed out that the *K.u.K.* Army continued to count on the *Nordstoss* (Northern Thrust) with the left wing between the Bug and Vistula Rivers.[22] And although that was the truth, it was not the whole truth, because the *Nordstoss* served to protect the flanks and should result in the *Aufschwenken* (Opening Up) of the front toward Lutsk and Dubno. The insisted-upon German Narev offensive could only expect very limited support from the *K.u.K.* Army. Conrad, however, continued to insist with all decisiveness on this offensive as late as 1914, and he believed that Alfred Graf Waldersee, Moltke's *Oberquartiermeister I* (senior quartermaster), had assured him of a German thrust northeast past Warsaw toward Siedlce. When this operation did not take place at the outbreak of war in 1914, Conrad saw it as a main reason for the setbacks his army suffered in Galicia. During the period between the two world wars the *Stoss auf Siedlce* (Siedlce Thrust) remained a controversial issue in German and Austrian military writings.[23]

A closer examination of the sources and the military situation of 1914 reveals that the instructions for the commanding general of the German Eighth Army in East Prussia did not conform to Moltke's pronouncements. Considering the relative strength ratios, however, those instructions were consistent with the general idea of the agreements. The objective was to tie down as many units of the Russian Army as possible in order to relieve the Austro-Hungarian front, although an attack on the Narev Army was not necessarily the only way to achieve that. Regardless, in the case of a massive Russian offensive operation against eastern Prussia, "an offensive move into Russia by the Eighth Army will be the only way to tie down strong Russian forces and prevent them from reinforcing those elements committed against Austria. The general situation must dictate the direction of this offensive. If, in due consideration of the Russian forces situated farther north, an offensive toward the southeast past Warsaw becomes possible, then it must be understood that the Narev River and the fortifications of Pultusk, Ostrolenka, and Razan will offer no insurmountable obstacles. Combined action with the Austrian Army must be considered for all such offensive movements of the Eighth Army."[24]

This sounded more cautious, pragmatic, and flexible than Conrad would have wished, but the instruction itself as well as the German *Ostheer*'s operations in 1914 at least aimed at fixing as many Russian forces as possible. Not only the General Staff in Berlin, but the General Staff in Vienna as well did not always put all their cards on the table. Foreign Minister Schemua, for example, withheld from the German Great General Staff the plans for withdrawing the East Galician deployment to the San and Dniester Rivers in the case that Russia had a head start in mobilization.[25]

The sequence of crises in 1912–1913 triggered a robust military cooperation, but did not change the fact that close coordination during the initial offensive of a war against Russia was still not precisely planned. As with the agreements of the Entente, the one between Germany and Austria-Hungary remained vague. The pessimistic assessment of the strategic situation faced by the two allies in the early summer of 1914, which was shared by both chiefs of the General Staff, did not result in a critical analysis of the war plans and the striking powers of the other ally. Instead, the Austro-Hungarian chief of the General Staff relied on Germany being capable of decisively defeating France's army within a few weeks, and Moltke did not doubt the K.u.K. Army's capability of containing a Russian attack. As it soon turned out, that was a fatal mistake on the part of both chiefs.[26]

Notes

1. On the General Staff before World War I, cf. Günther Kronenbitter, *"Krieg im Frieden": Die Führung der k.u.k. Armee und die Grossmachtpolitik Österreich-Ungarns 1906–1914* (Munich, 2003).

2. [Franz] Conrad von Hötzendorf, *Aus meiner Dienstzeit 1906–1918*, vol. 1, *Die Zeit der Annexionskrise 1906–1909* (Vienna, Leipzig, Munich, 1921), 364–366.

3. Kronenbitter, *"Krieg im Frieden,"* 605.

4. Ibid., 277–292. Cf. also the literature mentioned on 277f., notes 213 and 219.

5. Conrad, *Denkschrift,* 6 June 1909, Österreichisches Staatsarchiv, Abteilung Kriegsarchiv (KA), Generalstab (Gstb) Operationsbüro (OpB), Karton 742.

6. On the military planning process of Austria-Hungary, cf. Diether Degreif, *Operative Planungen des k.u.k. Generalstabes für einen Krieg in der Zeit vor 1914 (1880–1914)* (Wiesbaden, 1985); Hans Jürgen Pantenius, *Der Angriffsgedanke gegen Italien bei Conrad von Hötzendorf: Ein Beitrag zur Koalitionskriegsführung,* 2 vols. (Cologne, Vienna, 1984); Graydon A. Tunstall Jr., *Planning for War against Russia and Serbia: Austro-Hungarian and German Military Strategies, 1871–1914* (New York, 1993).

7. Cf. Kronenbitter, *"Krieg im Frieden,"* 293f., annotations 309–314.

8. Tunstall, *Planning for War against Russia and Serbia,* 39–54.

9. Kronenbitter, *"Krieg im Frieden,"* 277–314.

10. Beck to Schönburg-Hartenstein, 20 January 1897, Österreichisches Staatsarchiv, KA, Gstb Militärattaché Berlin, Karton 11.

11. Ibid.

12. Cf. Tunstall, *Planning for War against Russia and Serbia,* 55–135; Kronenbitter, *"Krieg im Frieden,"* 334–454; Samuel R. Williamson Jr., *Austria-Hungary and the*

Origins of the First World War (Basingstoke, London, 1991), 58–189. Cf. also the literature mentioned in Kronenbitter, *"Krieg im Frieden,"* 296, note 319.

13. Joseph Metzger, *Zusammenstellung* [1907], Österreichisches Staatsarchiv, KA, Gstb OpB, Karton 685.

14. Conrad, *Aus meiner Dienstzeit 1906–1918*, 1:586.

15. Operationsbüro (Krauss), Bemerkungen zur Denkschrift Conrads, Österreichisches Staatsarchiv, KA, Gstb OpB, Karton 742.

16. Kronenbitter, *"Krieg im Frieden,"* 333–348.

17. Cf: Conrad, *Aus meiner Dienstzeit 1906–1918*, 1:369–406, 631–634; Degreif, *Operative Planungen des k.u.k. Generalstabes für einen Krieg in der Zeit vor 1914*, 128–133; Günther Kronenbitter, "Falsch verbunden? Die Militärallianz zwischen Österreich-Ungarn und Deutschland 1906–1914," in *Österreichische Militärische Zeitschrift* 6 (2000): 743–754; Norman Stone, "Moltke-Conrad: Relations between the Austro-Hungarian and the German General Staffs, 1909–1914," in *Historical Journal* 9 (1966): 201–228; Tunstall, *Planning for War against Russia and Serbia*, 64–78.

18. Schemua to Moltke, 7 May 1912, Draft, Österreichisches Staatsarchiv, KA, Gstb OpB, Karton 737.

19. Karl Freiherr von Bienerth to Schemua, 18 June 1912 and 2 July 1912, Österreichisches Staatsarchiv, KA, Gstb OpB, Karton 737.

20. Schemua, Bericht über meinen Aufenthalt in Berlin am 22. [November 1912], Österreichisches Staatsarchiv, KA, Gstb OpB, Karton 737.

21. *Aufmarschanweisungen* for the years 1893–1894 to 1914–1915, Bundesarchiv/Militärarchiv (BA/MA), RH61/96.

22. Christophori, Auszüge aus der Korrespondenz Moltke, Österreichisches Staatsarchiv, KA, Gstb OpB, Karton 737; Tunstall, *Planning for War against Russia and Serbia*, 87–92.

23. Günther Kronenbitter, "Waffenbrüder: Der Koalitionskrieg der Mittelmächte 1914–1918 und das Selbstbild zweier Militäreliten," in *Mythen und Legenden in der Geschichte*, ed. Volker Dotterweich (Munich, 2004), 157–186, here pages 158–168.

24. *Aufmarschanweisungen* for the years 1893–1894 to 1914–1915, BA/MA, RH61/96.

25. Degreif, *Operative Planungen des k.u.k. Generalstabes für einen Krieg in der Zeit vor 1914*, 165–170; Kronenbitter, *"Krieg im Frieden,"* 297f.

26. Kronenbitter, *"Krieg im Frieden,"* 452–454, 499–515.

French Plan XVII
The Interdependence between Foreign Policy and Military Planning during the Final Years before the Outbreak of the Great War

Stefan Schmidt

Ever since the operational intentions of the European powers during the final run-up to 1914 became the subject of intensive scrutiny by historians, the Schlieffen Plan has been the focus of interest and criticism.[1] This plan, developed by German chief of the General Staff Count Alfred von Schlieffen between the years 1892 and 1905, and despite all the subsequent modification by his successor, Helmuth von Moltke (the Younger), remained valid as the strategy of the German Reich at the outbreak of the war. Schlieffen was initially criticized for his plan to invade Belgian territory, which many believed was the major reason for Great Britain's entry into the war and Germany's final defeat.[2] Later historical criticism, however, recast his plan as only one of those elements of Germany's overall situation during the July Crisis of 1914, during which a major war seemed an acceptable alternative if the aggressive foreign policy to "break up the British, French and Russian ententes" failed.[3] The specific intent of this plan was to divide the war against a coalition of the Great Powers into several fragmented efforts, and therefore concentrate the major German offensive strength against France initially. As a direct result, however, Germany was especially sensitive to any increase in Russia's power. When this strategy finally threatened to become obsolete, Germany was encouraged to take the final step in July 1914.[4]

The recent thesis on the Schlieffen Plan advanced by Terence Zuber[5] has resulted in less agreement than criticism.[6] Nonetheless, if we compare the research done on the strategic plans of the other continental European powers with that done on Germany's over the past half-century, it becomes apparent that comparatively little is known about the strategic ideas upon which they were based, and virtually nothing about their implications for foreign policy.[7] Because the question of what political consequences might have resulted from the planning for a major war remains to be thoroughly researched, the question of the extent to which Germany's strategic concept was singularly national or was the European norm must also remain open.

We shall, therefore, be examining the strategic planning of that country which, according to Gerhard Ritter, was intended to be the victim of Schlieffen's Cannae on a gigantic scale.[8] Our focus will center on the questions of which factors the French General Staff thought would determine France's triumph or defeat in the case of war, the relationship between these factors and the resources available to France, and what consequences the military leadership's grand strategy might have caused for the country's foreign policy. This method seems appropriate, because looking at the picture that the French General Staff had of Germany's operational intentions does not really help in answering the question of whether the Schlieffen Plan was one of the biggest errors in history. Zuber's thesis is too detailed in the posited degree of foreknowledge about German planning, while the information actually available to the French General Staff about the German intentions was too inexact.

It was, indeed, considered certain knowledge that in a major war the German Reich would be forced to open hostilities with an unrestricted general offensive using every available resource to achieve an annihilating victory over one of its opponents. Under the given circumstances, such could only be achieved in the west. Nevertheless, the French General Staff was unable to do more than formulate a series of hypotheses of varying probability about the specific German operational plans.[9] Since the French General Staff had no knowledge of its German opponent's exact intentions, it based its assumptions on a detailed study of the strategic railway network and fortresses in Lorraine. From this analysis the French concluded that the considerable sums that had been invested in expanding Germany's military infrastructure in the Aachen–Trier area and on the Metz–Thionville fortifications only made sense in the context of an incursion into Belgian territory.[10]

Based on this deduction, Plan XVII, the plan in force when war began and which itself was a modified version of Plan XVI of 1907–1908, foresaw a shift of the strategic concentration by stages northward and an extension of the French left wing as far as Mézières.[11] This posture alone, stretching only as far as the banks of the Meuse, reveals clearly that the French General Staff did not foresee the dimensions of the German offensive through Belgium. The French were certain that only negligible German forces would cross the Meuse.[12] The assumption that Germany would not commit pure reserve units in its front line was particularly responsible for that error of judgment and the conclusion that crossing the Meuse would cause the German lines to be overextended.[13] The French General Staff did indeed have in its possession German documents, compromised in 1913, which indicated that the reserve units would be committed right from the very start of war alongside and for the same tasks as the regular units. But since their own opinion was that such units would be of limited combat value, the French General Staff was unwilling to concede that the opposing military leadership might see the matter differently. This last point serves as a caveat that the mere study of whatever concepts the French General Staff had about German intentions might have more to say about its own strategic thinking than about its opponent's. A more fundamental criticism of this approach would be that French assumptions about what Germany might or might not do can shed no light on what they actually did or did not, since the French were not in possession of the pertinent documents.

We can nevertheless be certain that with the nomination of Joseph Joffre to the office of chief of the General Staff on 28 July 1911 a new chapter opened in the history of French military planning.[14] Although the German General Staff's plans for the opening phase of military hostilities meant that time simply had to be working in France's favor, under Joffre's leadership France abandoned its decade-old maxim of standing on the defensive in favor of attacking at all costs. In doing so, France like the rest of Europe succumbed to a phenomenon that had gradually taken hold and that has been called by historians the "Cult of the Offensive."[15]

The concept of drawing out the decisive confrontation backed up by the fortified line Verdun–Toul–Epinal–Belfort would give the allies the time required to organize a simultaneous offensive and thus deny the Germans the advantage of interior lines, upon which so much of their strategic calculus relied. General Édouard de Castelnau,[16] appointed first deputy chief of staff in 1911 by Joffre and his closest collaborator until 1913, wrote in a strategic memorandum: "By delaying the moment of the initial confrontations we approach the moment when Russian forces will be in a position to mass on the eastern German frontier, while ensuring the timely support from the British Expeditionary Corps. We will also be confounding the plans of the enemy, who certainly intends to knock us out as early as possible. [The German intent is] not only to make it impossible for the British Army to intervene, but also to free up part of their forces and redeploy them to the East Prussian theater."[17]

In his memoirs, Joffre condemned this plan with undisguised contempt: "In this scenario the French Army would initially play the role of a security force for the Triple Entente."[18] Whatever might be the advantage from the defensive in any given situation, that advantage was considered too small and therefore was not to be countenanced.[19] France would not conform to Russian requirements, rather Russia was expected to bow to those of France. And the concept of military action in war took a new turn as the French chief of the General Staff had it written into the general directives in 1914: "It is the Commander in Chief's absolute intent to attack the German armies with all forces available."[20]

Even though this change involved a series of challenges for French foreign policy, upon which they would have significant influence, the reorientation of strategic planning was greeted by unconditional approval from political leaders. The meeting of the *Conseil supérieur de la défense nationale* (CSDN) on 9 January 1912 adopted the decision to concentrate all of the active forces against Germany, and thus laid the foundation for the *offensive à outrance*. The official minutes noted: "The President was gratified to note that defensive planning, which amounted to an admission of inferiority on our part, had been abandoned. We are now determined to confront the enemy head-on, without reservation. The offense is suited to the temper of our soldiers and will ensure that victory will be ours."[21]

An initial perquisite, which the General Staff viewed as not only militarily but also politically relevant for any headlong attack against Germany, was that France would have to deploy numerically superior forces right from the onset of hostilities. The overview of the strategic situation presented at the opening of the decisive meeting of the CSDN made clear that only numerical superiority would allow France "to seize the offensive and take the war into the enemy's country."[22] Numerical calculations of the correlation of forces were accompanied by the fundamental questions of what support might be expected in case of war, which of the powers would be France's friends or foes, and which states would remain neutral?

An analysis of the overall diplomatic situation was placed on the agenda by the General Staff as early as 3 July 1911. On that day it forwarded a note to the minister of war in which it formulated a series of questions. Some were very detailed, concerning France's position in the international political system, the answers to which would serve as the basis for strategic planning. In taking this step, the military leadership initiated a discussion that had been prepared in direct consultations between the General Staff and the Foreign Ministry, and was finalized during the deliberations of the CSDN. There were two powers about whose stance in the case of war clarity was especially sought—Italy and Great Britain.

In the case of Italy, it should be recalled that the relations between the two nations in the event of a war involving one of the two were governed by a secret agreement signed in 1902. That agreement bound both powers to strict neutrality under certain specific conditions.[23] It is certain that France's military and political leaders were in fundamental agreement on their assessment of whether or not Italy would stand by Germany and Austria-Hungary in the event of war. Although the arguments presented differed slightly in detail, the assembled members of the CSDN agreed on 9 January that "Italy . . . would probably remain neutral."[24] This highest body for strategic issues expected, however, that the "Least of the Great Powers"[25] would intervene if one side faced defeat, in order to participate in the division of the spoils.[26] With that assessment early in 1912, Italy's probable course of action in the event of war was reduced to a formula. French president Raymond Poincaré agreed with it completely during the months leading to the outbreak of war.

In November 1912 the Russian ambassador in Paris, Aleksandr Petrovich Izvol'skiy, wrote a private letter to Foreign Minister Sergey Dmitriyevich Sazonov. Izvol'skiy summarized his impressions of the series of talks he had held with the French president and foreign minister about Italy's position in the case of an escalation of the military conflicts in the Balkans, which had been ongoing since October.[27] "The general belief here is that neither the Triple Entente nor the Triple Alliance will be able to count on Italy's loyalty, and that the Italian government will make every effort to preserve the peace. Should, however, war come, [Italy] will initially assume a waiting posture, and later join whichever side victory seems to favor."[28]

A key reason that the discussions about the possibility that Italy might intervene in case of war were not an issue of dispute between military and diplomatic decision makers was the French General Staff's belief that even a miscalculation of Italy's intentions would not have any serious consequences. For even if contrary to all expectation France's southern neighbor decided on an immediate intervention at Germany's side, the secret agreement of 1902 would have born fruit nonetheless. This was because since the signing of the agreement Italy had refrained from concentrating its forces or building up its military infrastructure along its border with France.[29] Another indicator was that the Italian expeditionary force sent to Africa in September 1911 was assembled from units withdrawn from the border with France, while the units deployed along the border with the Habsburg Monarchy remained in position.[30]

The reduced size of the Italian border forces and the inadequate military infrastructure would necessarily lead to a relatively slow mobilization and concentration. In the assessment of the French General Staff, that factor together with the extremely favorable defensive alpine terrain obviated any possibility for Italy to attack effectively early in a military conflict.[31] "According to the military," as the Russian ambassador reported following a conversation with Poincaré, "the fate of the war will be decided before Italy has time to concentrate serious forces against France."[32]

During the discussions on the issue of Italy's neutrality, a factor emerged that would have momentous repercussions for France's relations with Russia. The decision makers came to see the principal significance of an agreement no longer for its political value, but rather for its effect on the military balance of power. This is particularly apparent in Poincaré's reply to a report by the French ambassador in Rome, in which the diplomat reiterated the importance of the secret neutrality agreement of 1902, emphasizing that the signing of the agreement had prevented the Triple Alliance from developing into an instrument of power politics with an offensive character.[33] Poincaré replied, correcting his ambassador: "I value the military effects of this pact even more than its diplomatic results. It is a proven point that for the past ten years the defense of our Alpine border has required only simple measures from us. Our options on the northeastern frontier have accordingly become much greater."[34] The French president expressed himself similarly to the Russian ambassador some six months later. Interpreting Poincaré's comments on the 1902 agreement, Izvol'skiy wrote, "For France, the value of this treaty lies not in this wording or that, but rather in [the fact] that since it was signed Italy really has foregone all defensive and offensive measures along the border with France, transferring all of its preparations to the border with Austria."[35] His exact words to the diplomat were: "For France, [the agreement's] practical benefit was that the military position along the Italian borders could be kept weaker, enabling [France] to direct all of its forces and preparations against Germany."[36] Clearly, then, the political character of the agreement gradually faded in contrast to its military consequences. As Poincaré saw it, its function was no longer preserving peace, but preparation for military victory. This phenomenon that first emerged concerning Italy would later be confirmed in the agreements between France and Russia.

Even considering that an Italian intervention was no significant distraction for the French General Staff's planned *offensive à outrance,* closer study of its calculations reveals that France's numerical superiority was only moderate, even assuming a total concentration of all of its forces. When putting the numbers submitted to the CSDN at its deciding meeting of 9 January 1912 in relation to one another, the French advantage amounted to only 1.07-to-1 or 1.08-to-1.[37] This narrow margin diminishes even more when considering the force composition of the units that would be facing each other in an actual war. The General Staff's calculations as presented to the Council assumed that Germany would counter France's 585 regular battalions and 314 reserve battalions by committing 591 and 250, respectively. As things stood, the numerical superiority of France's forces lay exclusively in a larger number of reserve units, and was therefore anything but a comfortable margin.[38] This was even more so considering that the general consensus among military leaders was that "the value of reserve troops at the opening of a conflict was practically equal to zero."[39] The force-ratio superiority calculated early in 1912—meager as it was—was not a sufficient basis for an *offensive à outrance,* and considering that reality, France's alliances gained supreme importance.

The achievement of a significant numerical superiority was only possible with the intervention of Britain or Russia. The possibilities that France would be augmented by the British Expeditionary Force (BEF), whose strength was established at 150,000 troops by the military convention of 10–21 July 1911, or that Russia would succeed in tying down a German force through a relentless attack were key assumptions of early 1912.[40] In its arguments upon which the deliberations of the CSDN on 9 January 1912 were based, the General Staff conceded indirectly that the total concentration of every regular unit would be insufficient for military success.[41] As the General Staff noted, "In this way we would have a numerical superiority, *for which cooperation with the British Army might be an absolute necessity.*"[42] The same held true for any Russian intervention. Should that ally, attacking quickly and unreservedly, be able to tie down twelve instead of six regular German divisions in East Prussia, it would amount to the numerical equivalent of the BEF. As French chief of the General Staff Auguste Dubail[43] characterized the situation at the meeting of the CSDN: "The result would be satisfactory to us in every respect, and would even exceed our expectations."[44]

Considering the foreign policy implications of this numerical standoff, it seems paradoxical that the strategy that was supposed to ensure France's military triumph should at the same time be a source of political weakness. The discrepancy between the demands of strategy and the military realities could have no other result than increased consideration for and closer ties to the allies, with a concomitant loss of valuable Great Power autonomy. Indeed, the possibility of such supportive moves by the British or Russians would give back to France some room for maneuver, but both British and Russian intervention involved certain problems. Both options were only available under specific conditions. Furthermore, they might conflict with one another to a certain extent, or even be subverted by the implications of France's own strategic planning.[45]

In the case of the British, it should be recalled that the treaty Great Britain and France had signed to address the contingency of the military escalation of an international crisis was much more recent than the agreements made with Russia or Italy, and it also had a totally different quality.[46] It was neither an alliance nor a neutrality agreement, nor a nonaggression pact. In stark contrast to the military convention France had with Russia or the agreement binding between France and Italy, the Entente Cordiale was not a formal promise of support, and it did not stipulate any conditions under which the two nations would be obligated to remain neutral, or to render mutual military assistance.[47] When the Great War broke out, the relations between Britain and France were governed by a series of colonial agreements, a naval and military convention, and the famous exchange of letters between Foreign Secretary Sir Edward Grey and France's Ambassador Paul Cambon in November 1912, in which consultations were promised in the event that an international crisis presented an acute threat to European peace. "Uncommitted to act" was the trenchant way the content of these letters was described by Samuel Williamson, one of the leading experts on Anglo-French relations in the final decade prior to the outbreak of the war: "The two governments committed themselves to consult each other."[48]

That the British foreign secretary did not consider the existing military arrangements between the two nations or the correspondence between Grey and Cambon to imply any obligation of support was made plain to French representatives on various occasions. In December 1912 Poincaré, anticipating the cascade of military interventions that just two years later was to result in the outbreak of war,[49] inquired as to Great Britain's intentions in the event that the Balkan conflict might escalate militarily. Grey replied to the French ambassador, "Much would depend upon how the war broke out. If Serbia provoked Austria and gave her just cause of resentment, feeling would be different from what it would be if Austria was clearly aggressive. I do not think that public opinion could take things seriously unless Germany moved. And if things did become serious, I think that public opinion would first require an attempt to secure that Germany, France and England keep out of the trouble."[50]

Although the British foreign secretary's reply might not have satisfied Poincaré under the given circumstances, Grey did give a clear signal about the conditions under which France might count on a British military intervention. The most important factor in the event of war would be whether public opinion in Great Britain favored a military intervention, and therefore much would depend on which side was seen as the aggressor. Considering the British foreign secretary's unambiguous statements, France could not fail to be certain about the conditions under which Great Britain would render military support. Neither France's representative in London nor its decision makers in Paris labored under any illusions in that respect. During a private conversation between Cambon and British ambassador Sir Francis Bertie on 24 April 1914, Bertie stated that Great Britain would not be able to give any formal promise of assistance "unless at the time when trouble arrived public sentiment in England was prepared to undertake a war."[51] Poincaré had already complained to the Russian emissary in December 1912 that "the cabinet in London always answers that [a declaration of war] would depend upon the circumstances, and that the question of war or peace would depend upon the public opinion."[52] The French president assigned such importance to public opinion in Great Britain that he once told the Russian ambassador that not even the conclusion of an alliance would be sufficient to guarantee Britain's entry into a war, because "at the decisive moment the English government would decide only what the will of the English nation dictates."[53] That may have been somewhat of an exaggeration, but it was not inaccurate in principle.

No less significant might be the fact that by the summer of 1913 Poincaré had gained a very favorable impression of the climate of British public opinion. At the end of his state visit he told Great Britain's ambassador he was convinced that "the Entente had been thoroughly adopted by the people of England."[54] Using much the same words he had spoken almost one year before to Izvol'skiy, he noted that this was "a much more satisfactory and reliable bond between the two countries than any formal treaty engagement."[55] However, it was not the British public's favorable attitude toward France alone that allowed the French political leaders to look hopefully to the future decisions that Great Britain would make in the event of war. They were also convinced that Britain's foreign policies were oriented on balance-of-power principles, which were a certain guarantee that Britain would intervene.

During a conversation with French premier Gaston Doumergue, Great Britain's foreign minister admitted relatively candidly that Britain considered the continued existence of France as a Great Power as an indispensable element of the balance-of-power system. Grey fully understood that in the final event the question of whether or not Britain would enter into a war would be decided by the attitude of the public. However, he linked public opinion directly to the concept of balance-of-power. In April 1914, for example, he stated that in the event of a German attack on Russia, "Great Britain would be inclined to say that, though Germany might have successes at first, Russia's resources were so great that in the long run Germany would be exhausted without our helping Russia."[56] Regarding France, however, the matter stood differently. "Public opinion," Doumergue noted in his record of the conversation, "is less certain that a surprised France would be capable of resistance. For that reason, England would intervene in the case that France is unjustly attacked."[57]

In his dispatches for the years 1911 and 1912, the British ambassador also noted that the cabinet believed that in the event of a military conflict Great Britain would in its own interest be tied to France.[58] And Izvol'skiy noted in a secret memo to Foreign Minister Sazonov in December 1912 that Poincaré too would tend toward the assumption "that the inexorable progress of events would lead the British government toward an armed intervention against Germany."[59] In the spring of 1913 Paris even believed that "the tone and kind of assurances that the French government is hearing from the cabinet in London" would "allow France in the current political situation to expect military assistance from England, should it come to war with Germany."[60]

All in all, it seems clear that the French political and military leaders were guardedly optimistic about the British decision in the event of war.[61] They were, however, well aware of the fact that Great Britain's actions could not be foreseen for every eventuality, and that it was in fact impossible given the paramount importance the British assigned to the element of public opinion for British policy in the event of war. Where "British interests" were not immediately involved, and if the issue of who bore the blame as the aggressor was in question, then Britain's position could not be predicted with precision. That notwithstanding, and also from the military perspective, the island nation was not completely reliable as a French ally.

Abstracting from the conditions we have already discussed for entering into a war, and proceeding from the proposition that Britain would intervene militarily, neither France's military nor its political leaders could tell for certain whether the British cabinet would actually deploy the BEF to the Continent. And even if that did happen, it was not at all certain that the British contingent would arrive in time and in full strength. True, the military conventions and the details for their implementation had been worked out in all the necessary details for transporting and concentrating the British divisions. But as we have already noted, these arrangements would not automatically come into force, even in the case of coalition warfare. During the negotiations leading up to the final exchange of notes between Grey and Cambon, France had sought without success to establish just such a kind of automatic mechanism.[62] Thus, the final text of the exchange of notes read: "If these measures involve action, the plans of the General Staffs will at once be taken into consideration, and the governments will then decide what effect should be given to them."[63] It could, of course, be argued that in case of a war coalition the British cabinet would do everything in its power to ensure the triumph of the alliance, and consequently that France—trusting to the power of necessity—had reasonable grounds for hope that Great Britain would not improvise at the moment of decision, but rather would fall back on that which was firmly established in the military conventions. This in fact was already the case for the maritime arrangements, but not for the British Expeditionary Force itself.[64] Thus, the French worried that the valuable time they did not have might be lost at the decisive moment. As early as August 1911 Joffre had emphatically stated to the British military attaché that the expeditionary force "would have to be sent early in the day. Its intervention, for instance, on the 18th day of the French mobilization might not prove a bit too soon."[65]

The British General Staff's director of military operations, reflecting on just this question, reported to the responsible undersecretary in the Foreign Office that "he found some doubts in the minds of the military men as to what would be our attitude, whether we should really in the case of conflict give them any material assistance on land, and whether indeed, such assistance would be efficient and above all timely."[66] Apprehensions of this kind were responsible for the insertion in 1913 of an explanatory remark in the introductory section of Plan XVII—the *Bases du Plan*. Referring to the periodically recurring fears about a German invasion on the part of the British public: "One might well ask whether the British government would agree to send all available British forces to the Continent. Some know-it-alls in England have already spoken out against any such plan. For that reason we should take the precaution of not including British forces in our plans of operations."[67]

The fears that the British expeditionary corps might arrive late and understrength were shared by the French political leadership. The British ambassador reported to his prime minister that Poincaré had explained to him more than once that "English support to be effective must come within a few days, and the French authorities thought that there might be protracted discussions and valuable time lost in considering whether the *casus foederis* had arisen."⁶⁸ Although Canadian historian Roy A. Prete has maintained otherwise, it clearly was not the case that French politicians and military leaders had any illusions that "British mobilization would be simultaneous with that of the French, and that dispatch of the B.E.F. would follow automatically."⁶⁹ The issue of whether the British Empire would enter into a war for certain remained imponderable, but it was merely one of two reasons why Russia's strategic plans played such a significant role in the French General Staff's military calculus.

Historians recognized early on the significant weight Russia's offensive had for France's military success, albeit from a different perspective. In his doctoral dissertation, Gerd Krumeich advanced the theory that under British influence France after 1912 was compelled to concentrate its strategic planning "for lack of an alternative" on an offensive in Lorraine, and that the resulting "unfavorable starting position" could only be "improved" by a Russian offensive to tie down significant German forces in East Prussia.⁷⁰

Once the French General Staff had decided to begin a war with Germany with an *offensive à outrance,* it found itself confronted with the fact that the chances of success for such an endeavor were unequally distributed on the map of Europe. From the military perspective Alsace can be regarded as a narrow corridor bounded on the north by the Strassbourg–Molsheim fortress system and on the east by the upper course of the Rhine. For that reason it could never be more than a "theater for secondary and limited operations."⁷¹

Better, but by no means more advantageous, was the situation in Lorraine. There the mighty Metz–Thionville German fortress system blocked the approach to the Reich, and unfavorably bisected the area in two narrow corridors, permitting attacks by limited forces only.⁷² Under such conditions any offensive would amount to a frontal assault on a fortress, the flanks of which additionally might be threatened by German offensives that could be mounted from Metz and Strasbourg. The risks associated with such an attack stood in no relation to the consequences of any foreseeable victory. A military victory in Lorraine would not cut the German armies off from their lines of communication, which ran from the western provinces to the Reich's Prussian center of gravity.

Summarizing the General Staff's strategic studies during a secret meeting of the principal military and political decision makers at the Foreign Ministry on 21 February 1912, Joffre concluded: "Neither in Alsace nor in Lorraine can we find the right terrain for a decisive offensive. The situation would be much more favorable if we could extend our left flank into the Grand Duchy of Luxemburg and to Belgium."⁷³ Enthusiastically weighing the option of invading the neutral countries, the chief of the General Staff concluded: "On that side we could bring all of our resources to bear; we could bypass on the north the fortress systems our opponents have built with such effort, which would then be useless. Should we meet with success, our armies will throw the German masses back on southern Germany by directly threatening their main avenue of retreat to Mainz and Berlin. Finally, violating Belgian neutrality will give us the opportunity to allow the disembarked British expeditionary army to participate effectively in our operations. Their support gives us clear numerical superiority over our opponent."⁷⁴

That meeting in 1912 was not the first time that the General Staff had briefed the civilian leadership about the much lesser risks and greater chances for success involved with an offensive through neutral territory.⁷⁵ No sooner had the CSDN met on 11 October 1911 for initial discussions about the political framework for strategic planning than Joffre had declared that from a military perspective France had "the greatest interest"⁷⁶ in invading Luxembourg and Belgium. When reaching a decision, however, the responsible political leaders finally rejected the course of action of invading Belgium immediately upon the outbreak of hostilities. There were, however, some contrary voices in the cabinet.

The reasons for the French position were neither moral nor legal. The political leadership had no reservations about offering Luxembourg's territory for the use of the General Staff. "It is obvious," Foreign Minister Justin de Selves told the CSDN on 20 October 1911, "that a French invasion of Luxemburg territory, whose neutrality has been guaranteed by treaty, would be in violation of the law. However, the case at hand has nothing to do with discussing a point of international jurisprudence. The government of the Grand Duchy subordinates itself to German policy; therefore, our armies may indeed violate Luxemburg territory."⁷⁷ Accordingly, it would be the political balance that would decide the course of action in the event of war, and it was the considerations of British opinion that dictated that the territorial integrity of Belgium be respected.

The Foreign Ministry's reply to a long General Staff memorandum on the diplomatic situation in October 1911 was categorical: "The British government's constant concern for Belgium's neutrality would oblige us in case of war with Germany to do nothing that might be construed as a violation of that neutrality."⁷⁸ Respecting British sensibilities, the CSDN decided at that crucial meeting that only violation of Belgian neutrality by Germany would serve as justification for France to follow suit.⁷⁹

The fact that the highest French strategic authority applied this limitation to the question of the integrity of Belgian territory was, however, of little concern to Joffre. The General Staff considered it a fact that in the event of a war against a coalition of enemies Germany would first seek military victory over France, and most probably would invade Belgium to achieve that objective. That notwithstanding, the violation of Belgian neutrality by Germany, which was considered highly probable, was held not to be sufficient grounds to justify an immediate French invasion at the early stage of the military conflict. The General Staff's analyses were based on the assumption that Germany would not launch an invasion of Belgium until it completed the concentration of its forces.[80] By that time, France would have already had to decide on what direction its offensive would take, since the strategic concentration of its own forces was supposed to begin on the fourth day of mobilization.[81] For that reason Joffre declared at the CSDN meeting on 9 January 1912 that the Foreign Ministry would need to determine definitively Great Britain's position by that date. Foreign Minister de Selves could only give the seemingly helpless reply that the diplomats would do their best.[82]

The heated debate between the decision makers over the issue of whether Belgium's neutrality would have to be violated right at the outset of the conflict was not one strictly between the military and political leaderships. In 1912 there were indeed some in the political camp, among them Navy Minister Théophile Delcassé and Minister of War Alexandre Millerand, who favored an immediate invasion of Belgium, while the General Staff on the other hand was by no means blind to the consequences such a course of action might entail. The ultimate reason why the military and political *raison d'état* did not square off irreconcilably and why the General Staff did not simply ignore its political restrictions and tie its plan irrevocably to an immediate invasion of Belgian territory, thus presenting its political leadership in the end with a *fait accompli,* was that it could not afford to sacrifice the chances for a British intervention to the opportunities involved in the invasion of Belgium. Opinions differed about what Britain's interests were exactly, and about how durable the Anglo-French relationship was; but there was no argument that those factors would be crucial.[83] The consensus in effect left the determination of the direction the French offensive would take up to Great Britain, and the British Empire was unwilling to give France carte blanche for any such invasion.[84]

But this was not the reason why the General Staff decided, "for lack of an alternative," on an offensive in Lorraine.[85] When he initiated studies for the new military plan in August 1911, Joffre told the General Staff to consider an offensive through Belgium as a possible variant to an attack in Lorraine.[86] The resulting studies came to the conclusion that the strategic concentrations leading up to the one offensive or the other did not differ significantly, and that an invasion of Belgian territory under any scenario would require a supporting attack in Lorraine.[87] Hence, when the war broke out France's Plan XVII had a variable set of options for the initial deployment of its forces, providing for both an offensive in Belgium and an attack in Lorraine.

In the former case the main body of forces would advance on Trier, while simultaneous attacks in Lorraine fixed the German forces on the southern sector of the front. In the latter case the attack would be either toward Château-Salins and Sarrebourg, with the objective of breaking through the center of the front, or by means of concentric attacks through Luxembourg in the north and the Château-Salins corridor in the south to encircle part of the German forces in the Metz area.[88]

Should, however, France be compelled to launch its *offensive à outrance* in Lorraine—and as things stood such was to be feared—it would not be in its power to deny Germany the means for continuing the military struggle. Such an attack held no promise of decisive victory, only of a limited tactical success, the final outcome of which other powers would then decide. In his study of Joffre's strategic thinking, French historian Guy Pedroncini noted with surprise, but without indeed inquiring further into its diplomatic consequences: "He issued Plan XVII even though he himself... had already shown the ineffectiveness of the strategic solutions it contained."[89]

The main grounds for Joffre's decision must be sought in the moral significance of any British intervention. As Ferdinand Foch replied to the director of military operations of the British General Staff's question on how large a British force would have to be in order to be useful, "One single private soldier, and we would take good care to see that he was killed."[90] An additional factor was the importance that the military and political leadership attached to the British Royal Navy. Far from disregarding the value of the British fleet, Castelnau thought that "the French, even if they suffer reverses, must win in the end provided that England will aid by closing the sea approaches to Germany. In such case Germany must be starved out in four months."[91] On 30 July 1914, Poincaré told the British ambassador that "Germany... would not run the risk of having her sea-borne trade destroyed and of being starved by the British fleet."[92]

Although it is unclear what calculations formed the basis for Castelnau's and Poincaré's assessments—I am unaware of any study on the possible effects of a British blockade on the German Reich—this statement by a member of the General Staff and one of the president's closest advisers seems by no means incredible. It is certain, for instance, that the Russian leaders believed that the British fleet would be a deadly instrument in a military conflict. Considered from this perspective, the rejection of any violation of Belgian neutrality can be seen as an insurance policy. Such insurance, however, cannot be interpreted to mean that France was taking preventative measures in the event that the military struggle turned into a prolonged one. Castelnau's estimate that the British fleet would be able to starve out the enemy within four months' time and Poincaré's remark that "the fate of the struggle will be decided before Italy can concentrate its forces against France"[93] indicate the belief that any war would be a long one.

Indeed, modern research might well dispute the theory that Europe prior to the outbreak of the Great War had fallen under the illusion that war would be brief, particularly through the study of Germany's case.[94] In France's case, nevertheless, such remains valid without reservation. Although its military and political leaders were quite convinced that a future war would amount to an existential struggle between nations, that realization, however paradoxical it might seem, did not lead to the conclusion that a military conflict between the Great Powers would draw out over a long period of time. On the contrary, the director of the *École supérieur de la guerre*, Ferdinand Foch, was convinced that modern "total war"[95] between nation states would impinge so drastically on public life that the belligerent states would soon be forced to make peace, should total victory not quickly be won on the battlefield.

But France, which had abjured the invasion of Belgian territory and which could field only an insufficient numerical superiority of forces, could hardly expect to achieve such an overwhelming military victory as to render its enemy incapable of continuing the struggle. This was especially so considering the imponderability of whether Britain would enter a war, unless France's Russian ally were to decide on a determined attack of its own.

The importance of the Russia factor for France's military calculus arising from the premise of an *offensive à outrance* goes far to explain the intensity with which Joffre's staff studied and analyzed the intentions both of Germany and Russia in the event of a confrontation. A study of the map of East Prussia led the French General Staff to the sobering conclusion that the military topography of that province lent itself extraordinarily well to a German delaying action. In the opinion of the military leadership, a number of geographical factors augmented by systematic fortification had turned the region into a labyrinth that not only could be defended by modest forces against a largely superior attacker,[96] but whose western exits were also sealed almost hermetically by the Vistula River.[97]

The French General Staff thus concluded that only an attack between Thorn and Posen held the promise of a decisive victory. Any Russian offensive that succeeded in bypassing the fortress of Thorn would bring about the loss of the Vistula River line, and with it the last German line of resistance. In its study the General Staff elaborated, "The decisive result, which the Russians must achieve as quickly as possible, is not the conquest of East Prussia, but rather an earliest possible success in the neighborhood of Thorn . . . , which would have vital consequences in military and morale terms. Operations have value only when they contribute to the success of this important [campaign]."[98]

These last remarks constitute the basic outline of a military plan that France urged upon its Russian ally insistently during the final years leading up to the outbreak of the Great War. "The question of the way in which our offensive should be carried into German territory was always a central issue on the conference agendas and was regarded with extreme attention by our [French] allies," recalled the Russian quartermaster general, Yuri Danilov, after the war. "The French took every opportunity to emphasize the need for our offensive to be directed against the center of the enemy's country in order to reach Germany's critical areas."[99]

The strategic plans of its Russian ally, however, were apparently not to France's liking. In the event of a military confrontation, the modification of Russia's old Plan 19 projected the concentration of twenty-eight corps from Russia's European military districts. The plan also had variants designated by the Russian General Staff "A" for Austria and "G" for Germany, but Variant G was to be implemented only in the unlikely event of Germany concentrating at the very outbreak of hostilities a force of significantly more than twenty-five divisions in the east. Under Variant A, however, the group of forces directed against Germany was to consist of only nine corps in two field armies.[100]

In terms of numerical relationships, that meant that at the outbreak of hostilities Russia would commit only about a third of its available forces in Europe against Germany, while deploying more than half of their forces against the Habsburg Monarchy. It is important to remember, however, that Austria-Hungary would be concentrating the greatest portion of its troops against Russia, and therefore was the most dangerous opponent during the opening phase of hostilities.[101] This fact notwithstanding, the correlation of forces gives clear indication of the intentions of France's Russian ally during the final years prior to the outbreak of the Great War: While the group of forces opposite Germany would be attacking north and south of the Masurian Lakes to seize East Prussia up to the Vistula, a simultaneous general offensive would be launched against Austria-Hungary.[102] Although the invasion of East Prussia might seem an enormous undertaking, it was only a limited economy of force effort compared with the gigantic maneuvers with which Russia intended to envelop the armies of Austria-Hungary. The supporting effort against Germany was subsidiary to the primary objective of bringing about the annihilating defeat of Austria-Hungary, Russia's hated rival. We can see, then, that the Russian General Staff's reading of the military conventions followed a logic of its own, which left ample room for interpretation, even in the case of the stipulation that "the defeat of the German armies remains the first and foremost objective of the allied armies, whatever the circumstances might be."[103]

Knowing full well that its own strategic plans would hardly satisfy France's wishes, what the Russian General Staff revealed to the French decision makers matched reality only in part. Remarkably, Russia did not inform its French ally about its new strategic plans until 1913, even though those plans had already gone into effect before the General Staff conference of 1912. Additionally, and much a cause for concern, was the fact that the czar's chief of the General Staff led his French colleague astray about the strength of the forces Russia planned to commit against Germany.[104]

That notwithstanding, the important point for the purposes of this study is that France, regardless of whether or not it was deceived by Russia about the strategic concentration of its forces, was at least aware that Russia at the outbreak of hostilities had no intention whatsoever of launching an offensive action to deprive Germany of its means to continue the war. In December 1913, after thorough study of Russia's strategic planning, Joffre's staff concluded, "In the protocol for 1913 the objective of the Russian offensive is described as follows: 'either to defeat the enemy forces concentrated in East Prussia or to advance on Berlin along an axis south of that province, should the concentration of German forces take place on the left bank of the Vistula.' The Russian plan does not, however, seem to be directed toward these two objectives. In reality, its intention is clearly and exclusively the invasion of East Prussia."[105] The realization that the Russian concentration would not result in an attack offering any promise of a decisive success against Germany was sobering enough for the French. And even beyond that, the study's criticism of the way in which the attack on East Prussia was to be executed was devastating.[106]

What the study explained in detail, and another study in June 1914 confirmed,[107] had been apparent to Joffre since the final prewar conference, which led to his objections. The Russian military attaché, who was present at the conference, recorded in his memoirs that as the Russian chief of the General Staff began to present his plans for the invasion of East Prussia, "Joffre, waving his pudgy hand over the outspread map of our western borders, instead of approving the plan of attack, tried to convince Zhilinskiy of the dangers of an invasion of East Prussia." As Joffre declared repeatedly, "This direction is for us the least favorable. *C'est un guet-apens*" (It is a trap).[108]

Thus, France's Russian ally only intended to conduct a limited offensive against the common enemy, which under favorable circumstances might indeed inflict a partial defeat on Germany, but without striking a decisive blow. That was the kernel of truth behind the French apprehensions, poignantly reflected in the contemporary sources. At the moment of truth, Russia might march against Austria-Hungary only.

One exact piece of evidence for that fear is the stubbornness with which Joffre in the final years leading up to the Great War and right into the July Crisis of 1914 sought to draw attention to what he saw as that clear truth. During both of the General Staff conferences of 1912 and 1913 he attempted to remind his Russian colleague that defeat for Germany would be defeat for Austria-Hungary, and would cause the latter to sink into insignificance. It was, therefore, the destruction of the German armies "which must be sought at any cost,"[109] and "right from the start of operations."[110] Right up to the July Crisis of 1914 Joffre continued to insist that the Russian attack "be directed in the first instance against Germany," and not "against Austria."[111]

Consistent with these demands, French minister of war Adolphe Messimy argued with the Russian military attaché on 31 July that Austria-Hungary would only be able to play a bit part in the approaching war, and thus could be treated as a *quantité négligeable*.[112] The war minister's memoirs, from which this quote is taken, document that these thoughts did not express the fears of the military leaders alone, but those of the political leadership as well.[113] In memoirs Messimy noted: "From 31 July until my resignation, and in complete consensus with the Foreign Minister and the President of the Republic, I never tired in giving the Russian military attaché to understand that fundamental strategic considerations and common sense dictated that offensive action be directed against Germany as the principal and sole opponent."[114]

Seen in this light, the statements made in 1936 to historian Pierre Renouvin by Maurice Paléologue no longer appear as the self-justifying fabrications of an ambassador whom historians even *ante mortem* were accusing of having failed to warn France's Russian ally prior to its general mobilization in July 1914, despite explicit instructions from his government to do so.[115] Rather, his statements appear as a telling expression of the anxieties that the French decision makers shared. Summarizing Paléologue's statements, Renouvin wrote: "The biggest concern, not only in military circles but of the French government as well, was Russia's assurance that in case of a German attack it would move quickly against Germany—and not against Austria-Hungary. For the French government this was an issue of such central importance that Paléologue, when he was about to leave for St. Petersburg to take up his post as ambassador, was advised by Poincaré and Doumergue to take along a copy of the record of the conference of 21 February 1912 and to show it to the Russian minister."[116]

With this coy reference to the secret meeting of key military and political decision makers on 21 February, the former diplomat revealed to the historian the extraordinary significance of the question of whether Russia would go primarily against the Habsburg Monarchy when the time came. It was at that meeting that the French made the decision to refrain from invading Belgian territory immediately at the outset of hostilities. Joffre characterized the presumably only remaining option with the words, "Neither in Alsace nor in Lorraine will we find terrain suitable for a decisive offensive."[117]

The question of which of France's enemies its Russian ally would attempt to direct its first decisive blow against was not the only one that France focused on. What is also important to note in this connection is that it was a known fact that any Russian attack on Germany would depend upon a military infrastructure that was not or was only partially existent when the Great War began. Studying its ally's plans for the strategic concentration of its forces, the French General Staff in 1913 came to the conclusion that for the moment Russia would not be able to carry through its concentration of forces as required. "Is Russia currently able to implement a plan of this kind? We do not believe so. . . . The shift of the center of gravity westward can happen only after the expansion of the Polish rail network."[118]

The French General Staff thought that the necessary shifting of the center of gravity of the strategic concentration would have to be facilitated by an expansion of the Russian railway system, hence the references to the enormous expansion of Russia's military infrastructure that Joffre included in the protocols to the military conventions of 1912 and 1913. By building a network with a total length of more than five thousand kilometers, the center of the Russian troop concentration could be moved westward, and the time required for mobilization reduced overall.[119] That would make it possible for Russia to bring its numerical superiority to bear sooner.[120] With the expansion of the Russian strategic railway network, France sought nothing less than depriving Germany of the ability to project force outside of its own territory; and at its heart lay nothing less than the wish for an absolute security that, should it ever become a reality, would necessarily and fundamentally change the balance of power within the concert of nations.

Considering its modest demands for 1912, the French General Staff argued, "The mere existence of the possibility that the time interval between the initiation of operations by Russian and French forces might be reduced would force Germany *to abandon* all thoughts of conducting its operations along interior lines. Moreover, Germany would be compelled to face its enemies simultaneously on both fronts, and consequently to divide its forces at the price of all expectation of success."[121] This carefully formulated description of the consequences of expanding Russia's military infrastructure found its way into the memorandum that the General Staff prepared for President Poincaré's trip to Russia in August 1912, an amended version of which the Foreign Ministry at the Quai d'Orsay sent to its new ambassador to St. Petersburg in March 1913.[122] Delcassé reported from the Russian capital to Foreign Minister Stéphan Pichon in retrospect, "Since that day I have been following events as they unfold to discover more about their possible consequences, and have been emphasizing incessantly the need to have at the earliest possible date the service of an instrument, by means of which the Russian Army might be able to take the offensive at the same time as ours, forcing the Germans to split their forces."[123]

Ironically, it was the French ambassador, whose primary mission was to force the expansion of Russia's military infrastructure so that it could threaten Germany with a fatal attack, who predicted a preemptive war by Germany. The former navy minister in Poincaré's cabinet was already convinced by April 1913 "that Germany cannot afford to wait; that she will not be able to bear the strain; that her position will be worse in a few years' time than it is now; and that . . . if war cannot be averted, she would sooner face it at once."[124]

Delcassé declared to the British ambassador almost apodictically that "Germany would strike before Russia was ready and discover a pretext for war whenever she found a weak place in Russia's armor. [Delcassé] assured me that he knew this as a fact."[125] This opinion alone would hardly have won Delcassé the solid support of his British colleague.[126] In the final months preceding the outbreak of hostilities other French officials recognized the danger that Germany would strike first. It was at this time that Poincaré confided to the editor in chief of *Matin*: "It is not only that the kaiser and Germany feel hatred toward France, they are afraid of Russia. They know that a huge conglomeration is growing closer together every day; they want to attack and destroy it, before it can reach its fullest strength."[127]

What we have already seen confirmed in the treaty between France and Italy for the eventuality of a military conflict applies equally and particularly to the growth of Russia's power. It would appear that during the final years preceding the outbreak of the Great War the focus on military factors had thrust other considerations into the background, and even from sight. The strident French demands and offers of support for the expansion of Russia's military infrastructure mirror what American historian Paul W. Schroeder once observed as the cause for the partial collapse of the Ottoman Empire and the resultant reorganization of the Balkans. "[No] government addressed itself to the most obvious and critical question of all: how was this new, crucial development to be managed? How, that is, could it be harmonized with the overall European balance, incorporated into the prevailing international system, without raising the already fearful strains upon that system to the point of explosion? No one thought of this problem or suggested doing anything about it."[128]

The key figures among France's military and political leadership knew that Germany's position during the final prewar years was growing precarious because of the growth of Russian power and the decline of Austria-Hungary's, and that the key decision makers among the leadership of the German Reich were watching those developments with growing anxiety and might even seek to counter them through military means. The French, however, drew no conclusions from that knowledge. Instead of thinking in terms of the overall context of the European political system and attempting to make Germany's situation more tolerable through concessions in the areas of arms industry or cooperation outside of existing alliances, France not only promoted the growth of Russia's power with every means at its disposal, it also sought to deprive Germany of the ability to attack while making every effort to avoid the slightest disagreement with its Russian ally. Before his departure to assume his new position in St. Petersburg, Delcassé was heard to say during a conversation with the political director of the Foreign Ministry, "As far as that diplomatic silliness goes, that old blather about the European balance of power, I'm going to pay as little attention to it as possible: it's all just empty talk."[129]

This chapter has sought to clarify one of the reasons responsible for the loss of the ability to think in the overall context of the European System. One must consider the fact that the French war planning during the final years prior to the outbreak of the Great War, in which the word "defensive" was largely considered synonymous with defeat, had maneuvered the country into a strategic position whose primary characteristics were a visible discrepancy between what France could accomplish on its own and what it would need to assure a military victory. Considering that the *offensive à outrance* against Germany required a numerical superiority that France could not generate on its own, and the fact that the contemplated invasion of Belgian territory right at the outbreak of hostilities had to be abandoned out of consideration for British sensibilities and a vague prospect of British intervention, there was little room left for concessions. Thus, a plan initially conceived to guarantee the French military victory led to greater insecurity and accentuated the security dilemma, which during the July Crisis of 1914 led the Great Powers to seek their salvation no longer in peace, but in war.

Notes

1. Cf. the introductory remarks in Paul M. Kennedy, ed., *The War Plans of the Great Powers, 1880–1914* (Boston, 1979), 3ff.

2. Cf. Gerhard Ritter, *Der Schlieffenplan: Kritik eines Mythos* (Munich, 1956), passim, esp. 93; Leonard C. F. Turner, "The Significance of the Schlieffen Plan," in Kennedy, ed., *The War Plans of the Great Powers*, 199–221, see 204.

3. Klaus Hildebrand, *Das vergangene Reich: Deutsche Aussenpolitik von Bismarck bis Hitler*, 2nd ed. (Stuttgart, 1996), 304.

4. Cf. the discussions in Stig Förster, "Dreams and Nightmares: German Military Leadership and the Images of Future Warfare, 1871–1914," in *Anticipating Total War: The German and American Experiences 1871–1914*, ed. Manfred F. Boemeke, Roger Chickering, and Stig Förster (Cambridge, New York, Melbourne, 1999), 343–376, cf. page 346; Stig Förster, "Im Reich des Absurden: Die Ursachen des Ersten Weltkrieges," in *Wie Kriege entstehen: Zum historischen Hintergrund von Staatenkonflikten*, ed. Bernd Wegner, Krieg in der Geschichte, 4 (Munich, Vienna, Zurich, 2000), 211–252, cf. page 248ff.

5. Cf. the groundbreaking study by Terence Zuber, "The Schlieffen Plan Reconsidered," *War in History* 6 (1999): 262–305, and Terence Zuber, *Inventing the Schlieffen Plan: German War Planning, 1871–1914* (Oxford, New York, 2003). Cf. also Terence Zuber, "Terence Holmes Reinvents the Schlieffen Plan," *War in History* 8 (2001): 468–476.

6. Cf. especially Terence Holmes, "The Reluctant March on Paris: A Reply to Terence Zuber's 'The Schlieffen Plan Reconsidered,'" *War in History* 8 (2001): 208–

232, Terence Holmes, "The Real Thing: A Reply to Terence Zuber's 'Terence Holmes Reinvents the Schlieffen Plan,'" *War in History* 9 (2002): 111–120, and Robert T. Foley, "The Origins of the Schlieffen Plan," *War in History* 10 (2003): 222–232.

    7. It is, for example, no easy thing to gain a well-founded overview of Russian strategic planning during the final years prior to the outbreak of the war. The most extensive study based on Russian archival material on the subject is only available in Russian. Cf. A. M. Zayontchkovskiy, *Podgotovka Rossii k imperialističeskoj vojne: Plany vojny* (Moscow, 1926). Around ten years after Zayontchkovskiy, a former teacher at the Russian General Staff Academy published a helpful article on Russian war plans. See Nikolay N. Golovin, "The Russian War Plan of 1914," *Slavonic and East European Review* 14 (1936): 564–584. See also Nikolay N. Golovin, *The Russian Army in the World War* (New Haven, 1931), and Nikolay N. Golovin, *The Russian Campaign of 1914: The Beginning of the War and Operations in East Prussia* (Fort Leavenworth, Kans., 1938). A more recent study has appeared from the pen of political scientist Jack Snyder: *The Ideology of the Offensive: Military Decision Making and the Disaster of 1914* (London, Ithaca, 1984). Snyder's book has the advantage of paying special attention to Russian research, and thus making it accessible to the researcher, but it is not founded on any knowledge of the archival material. Of the more recent works, only that of William C. Fuller Jr. is based on such material. Cf. William C. Fuller Jr., *Strategy and Power in Russia 1600–1914* (New York, 1992), passim. Some additional interesting discussions may be found in Bruce W. Menning, *Bayonets before Bullets: The Russian Imperial Army, 1861–1914* (Bloomington, Indianapolis, 1992), 240–252. In the case of the French, see the literature cited in this article.

    8. Cf. Ritter, *Der Schlieffenplan*.

    9. Cf. Note sur la concentration, February 1912, Service Historique de l'Armée de Terre (SHA), Vincennes, France, 7N1771, and the section: "Concentration et condition d'entrée en action des armées allemandes," in *Étude du plan d'opérations contre l'Allemagne*, SHA, 7N1771. See also: Note sur les chemins de fer, May 1914, SHA, 7N1771, and Mobilisation et concentration, June 1914, SHA, 7N1771.

    10. Cf. the chief of the General Staff's instructive remarks in his memoirs. Joseph Joffre, *Mémoires du Maréchal Joffre (1910–1917)* (Paris, 1932), 1:115ff.

    11. Cf. Mémoire sur les modifications à apporter au Plan XVI, May 1911, SHA, 7N1784. See also Édouard de Castelnau and Alexandre Millerand, 24 October 1912, SHA, 7N1785. This document is a General Staff report explaining the reasons for the need to draw up a new plan. Cf. Bases du Plan. Conseil Supérieur de la Guerre (CSG), 18 March 1913, SHA, 1N11, CXLIII, fol. 2.

    12. The belief that Belgium would indeed put up resistance to a total invasion but might acquiesce to a partial one led the General Staff to this idea. Also, Belgium might even seek to exploit the latter eventuality by picking an auspicious moment to attack the losing power in the hopes of participating in the division of its riches and territories. See the discussion on Belgium's position in case of war in Description sommaire du théâtre d'opération du Nord-Est d'une part et d'autre de la fron-

tière, SHA, 7N1784. Cf. also the undated and untitled campaign memorandum, SHA, 7N1784. See also Étude du plan d'opérations contre l'Allemagne, SHA, 7N1771.

13. The chief of the 2nd Department of the General Staff, Charles Dupont, admitted later in his memoirs: "I must honestly admit that we thought the Germans would not cross the line of the Meuse and the Sambre." Mémoires du Général Dupont, SHA, Dupont papers, 1T526, fol. 59.

14. A biography of this chief of Staff that would meet academic standards remains a desideratum of historical research. Indeed, Arthur Conte published a narrative biography entitled *Joffre* in 1991. But the work contains neither a list of archival documents, sources and published works used, nor a single footnote. See Arthur Conte, *Joffre* (Paris, 1991). For the earlier research see Raymond Recouly, *Joffre*, 52. ed. (Paris, 1931), and Pierre Varillon, *Joffre* (Paris, 1955), a work with hagiographic tendencies.

15. See Stephan van Evera, "The Cult of the Offensive and the Origins of the First World War," in *Military Strategy and the Origins of the First World War: An International Security Reader*, 2nd ed., ed. Steven E. Miller, Sean M. Lynn-Jones, and Stephan van Evera (Princeton, 1991), 59–108.

16. De Castelnau headed the General Staff's 2nd (Military Intelligence), 3rd (Operations), and 4th (Logistics) Bureaus in preparing the groundwork for Plan XVII.

17. Mémoire pour servir a l'établissement d'un plan de guerre, SHA, Nachlass Castelnau, 1K795/5. Castelnau began writing this memorandum after assuming command of the Second Army in December 1913. His initial intention probably was to make sure of the forces under his command in the current strategic situation. But having taken up his pen, Castelnau's memorandum grew to encompass a global appreciation of the available strategic options. See Yves Gras, *Castelnau ou l'art de commander (1851–1944)* (Paris, 1990), 139ff. In his memorandum, Castelnau finally rejects the option cited here.

18. Joffre, *Mémoires du Maréchal Joffre*, 1:252.

19. Various explanations have been offered for this change of mind. Early studies already sought to explain it as the result of an immanent evolution of strategic thought, and this thesis continues to find followers among modern researchers. See Basil H. Liddel Hart, "French Military Ideas before the First World War," in *A Century of Conflict, 1850–1950: Essays for A.J.P. Taylor,* ed. Martin Gilbert (London, 1966), 133–148; Michael Howard, "Men against Fire: Expectation of War in 1914," in Miller et al., ed., *Military Strategy and the Origins of the First World War,* 3–19, esp. pages 16–18. Military historian Douglas Porch has offered an alternative explanation for this change in French strategic thinking: that the new doctrine was intended to compensate for deficiencies in the army's materiel. Seen from this perspective, the *offensive à outrance* can be considered less a brave attack than a forlorn hope. See Douglas Porch, "Clausewitz and the French, 1871–1914," *Journal of Strategic Studies* 9 (1986): 287–302, cf. pages 297ff.: "The doctrine of the offensive, based on the superiority of Gallic 'moral force' . . . provided a durable tactical law. The only way to cope with

the new technical developments despite poor French resources was to rely on the patriotic audacity, the historic élan, of French soldiers." See also Douglas Porch, "The French Army and the Spirit of the Offensive, 1900-1914," in *War and Society: A Yearbook of Military History*, ed. Brian Bond and Ian Roy (New York, 1975), 117-143, cf. pages 136ff.; Douglas Porch, *The March to the Marne: The French Army 1871-1914* (Cambridge, 1981), 214ff. Placing more emphasis on the social context of military thinking, Snyder interpreted the new primacy of the unlimited attack as an attempt to defend France's military institutions from political influence. See Snyder, *The Ideology of the Offensive*, 46-106.

20. "Directives générales," in *Les Armées Françaises dans la Grande Guerre*, vol. 1, *Annexes* (Paris: Ministère de la Guerre. État-major de l'armée—Service historique, 1922), Annex 8, page 21.

21. Procès-verbal, CSDN, 9 January 1912, SHA, 2N1, VI/38. See also cable from Major Detlof von Winterfeldt, military attaché in Paris, 11 May 1912, in *Die Grosse Politik der Europäischen Kabinette 1871-1914: Sammlung der Diplomatischen Akten des Auswärtigen Amtes*, vol. 31, *Das Scheitern der Haldane-Mission und ihre Rückwirkung auf die Tripelentente 1911-1912*, ed. Johannes Lepsius, Albrecht Mendelssohn Bartholdy, and Friedrich Thimme (Berlin, 1927), doc. 11522.

22. Note de présentation, CSDN, 9 January 1912, SHA, 2N1, VI/36. In its final, 1913 version the Franco-Russian military convention pointed out that "it is decisive that a clear numerical superiority of the French Army over the German forces in the west can actually be achieved." Procès-verbal des entretiens du mois d'août 1913 entre les chefs d'état-major des armées française et russe, in *Documents Diplomatiques Français*, ed. par Ministère des Affaires Étrangères, Commission de publications des documents relatifs aux origines de la guerre de 1914, series 3, vol. 8, no. 79 (Paris, 1947). In his memoirs Joffre ascribed the defensive orientation of strategic planning in the previous decades to calculations based on the assumption that France's forces would be "numerically inferior." Joffre, *Mémoires du Maréchal Joffre*, 1:22, 26ff.

23. See the text of the agreement in *Documents Diplomatiques Français*, series 2, vol. 2, no. 389.

24. Note de présentation, CSDN, 9 January 1912, SHA, 2N1.

25. This is a reference to the title of Richard Bosworth's study of Italy's foreign policy prior to the First World War. See Richard J. B. Bosworth, *Italy: The Least of the Great Powers: Italian Foreign Policy before the First World War* (London, 1979).

26. Cf. Note de présentation, CSDN, 9 January 1912, SHA, 2N1.

27. Izvol'skiy to Sazonov, letter of 9 November 1912, in *Die Internationalen Beziehungen im Zeitalter des Imperialismus: Dokumente aus den Archiven der zarischen und provisorischen Regierung*, ed. von der Kommission beim Zentralexekutivkomitee der Sowjetregierung unter dem Vorsitz von Michail N. Pokrovskiy. Namens der Deutschen Gesellschaft zum Studium Osteuropas, ed. von Otto Hoetzsch, series 3, vol. 4.1, no. 201 (Berlin, 1942). See also Izvol'skiy to Sazonov, letter of 20 November 1912, in ibid., no. 300; Izvol'skiy to Sazonov, letter of 21 November 1912, in ibid., no.

309; Izvol'skiy to Sazonov, letter of 25 November 1912, in ibid., no. 339; Izvol'skiy to Sazonov, letter of 5 December 1912, in *Der Diplomatische Schriftwechsel Iswolskis 1911–1914: Aus den Geheimakten der russischen Archive,* in *Auftrag des Deutschen Auswärtigen Amtes in deutscher Übertragung,* vol. 2, 3rd. ed., ed. von Friedrich Stiewe (Berlin, 1926), doc. 606.

28. Quote from Izvol'skiy to Sazonov, letter of 5 December 1912, in *Der Diplomatische Schriftwechsel Iswolskis,* doc. 608.

29. See Note indiquant les points relatifs à la situation extérieure à élucider dans la Conférence du 16 octobre 1911, SHA, 2N1, V/32. See also Camille Barrère to Poincaré, letter of 30 March 1912, in *Documents Diplomatiques Français,* series 3, vol. 2, no. 280. See also the detailed memorandum of the military attaché de Gondrecourt in ibid., appendix.

30. See Note de présentation, CSDN, 9 January 1912, SHA, 2N1. See also Izvol'skiy to Sazonov, letter of 12 September 1912, in *Der Diplomatische Schriftwechsel Iswolskis,* doc. 429. See also the chapter "Influence de l'Occupation actuelle de la Libye," in Situation sur le pied de Guerre des principales armées européennes, 10 November 1913, SHA, 7N1771. See also Autriche et Italie, June 1914, SHA, 7N1771.

31. The assessment of the strategic situation presented at the opening of the CSDN meeting on 9 January 1912 calculated that Italy would only be able to concentrate six active corps along the border with France at the outset of a military conflict, and would not be able to open a limited offensive before the eighteenth day at the earliest. The General Staff concluded from this that "an Italian intervention would come too late to have any influence on the first major battles." Note de présentation, CSDN, 9 January 1912, SHA, 2N1. Cf. on the same subject the letter from Nostitz to Yakov Grigor'evich Zhilinskiy, 17 January 1912, in *Der Diplomatische Schriftwechsel Iswolskis,* doc. 460.

32. Izvol'skiy to Sazonov, letter of 5 December 1912, in *Der Diplomatische Schriftwechsel Iswolskis,* doc. 608.

33. See also Camille Barrère to Poincaré, letter of 10 March 1912, in *Documents Diplomatiques Français,* series 3, vol. 2, no. 181. The published files contain a slightly abbreviated version of this document. The original can be found in Archives Ministère des Affaires Étrangères (MAE), NS Italie 22, fol. 60/2–61.

34. Poincaré to Barrère, 18 March 1912, in *Documents Diplomatiques Français,* series 3, vol. 2, no. 218. Cf. also the memoirs of the first secretary in the French embassy in Rome: Jules Laroche, *Quinze ans à Rome avec Camille Barrère (1898–1913)* (Paris, 1948), 270ff. A little later, Poincaré expressed himself in the same vein to the Russian ambassador. See Izvol'skiy to Sazonov, letter of 6 June 1912, in *Der Diplomatische Schriftwechsel Iswolskis,* doc. 316.

35. Izvol'skiy to Sazonov, 5 December 1912, in *Der Diplomatische Schriftwechsel Iswolskis,* doc. 606. Cf. Izvol'skiy to Sazonov, letter of 5 December 1912, in ibid., doc. 608.

36. Ibid. Cf. the report of the British ambassador for the year 1912: Francis L. Bertie, "Annual Report France 1912," 1 August 1913, in *British Documents on Foreign Af-*

fairs: Reports and Papers from the Foreign Office Confidential Print, Series F: Europe, ed. David Stevenson and John F. Keiger, vol. 13 (France) (London, 1989), doc. 108.

37. In the annexes to this memorandum, the General Staff calculated that the 900,000 "rifles" of France would be faced by 830,000 to 840,000 German. See Indications sur les forces militaires de la France, de ses alliés et des petits États neutres, CSDN, 9 January 1912, SHA, 2N1, VI/36, and Indications sur les forces militaires de l'Allemagne et de ses alliés, CSDN, 9 January 1912, SHA, 2N1, VI/36.

38. See the table in Indications sur les forces militaires de l'Allemagne et de ses alliés, CSDN, 9 January 1912, SHA, 2N1, VI/36. Cf. the comments by the chief of the General Staff at a meeting in the Foreign Ministry on 12 October 1912. Although his figure regarding active formations generally matched his calculations for the CSDN, he gave the number of 362 reserve battalions. See Comparaison des forces qui pourraient se trouver en présence sur le théâtre du Nord-Est en cas de conflit avec l'Allemagne, CSDN, 19 October 1912, SHA, 2N1 VII. See also the calculations made by Joffre and Castelnau approximately one year previously at a conversation with the director of military operations of the British General Staff. [Henry] Wilson diaries, Imperial War Museum, DS/MISC/80 (29 November 1911).

39. Quoted in Procès-verbal de la Séance, CSG, 18 April 1913, SHA, 1N11, CX-LIII. The quote reflects a comment by the later commanding general of the Armée d'Alsace, Paul Marie Pau. Opinions to the contrary found no majority among military decision makers in the final years prior to the outbreak of the Great War. When designated Generalissimo Victor Constant Michel submitted a new strategic plan to the CSG in the spring of 1911, which foresaw extensive use of France's reserve formations, the Council rejected it, leading to Michel's subsequent dismissal. Cf. Jean Fabry, *Joffre et son destin: La Marne, Verdun, la Somme, l'Amérique,* 2nd ed. (Paris, 1931), 177ff.; Jan Karl Tanenbaum, *Général Maurice Sarrail (1856–1929): The French Army and Left-Wing Politics* (Chapel Hill, 1975), 27ff.

40. "If France does not permit itself to be distracted by secondary considerations it can throw just as many active battalions, and more and more reserve battalions, into the main battle than its enemy. This superiority will be even greater if Russia can bind a larger number of forces on the border to Poland through an energetic offensive, and, above all, if England sends its entire expeditionary army to the continent as intended." Note de présentation, CSDN, 9 January 1912, SHA, 2N1. See also the chief of the General Staff's remarks on 12 October 1912: "with few exceptions our active forces are equal to the corresponding German forces. If English troops participate in our Armies' operations, the forces of France and England would have clear superiority over the German forces." Comparaison des forces qui pourraient se trouver en présence sur le théâtre du Nord-Est en cas de conflit avec l'Allemagne, CSDN, 19 October 1912, SHA, 2N1.

41. Consequently, there is not justification for the opinion that "[the] experts in the French Army . . . had, on the basis of numerous assessments of Britain's situation, come to a general agreement that the British would play a decidedly limited role in

any combined military operations for the defense of France." See Patricia Elisabeth Prestwich, *French Attitudes towards Britain: 1911-1914* (Stanford, 1973), 284.

42. Note de présentation, CSDN, 9 January 1912, SHA, 2N1 (author's emphasis). Cf. Joffre's admission to the British military attaché in August 1911: "The new chief attaches the very greatest importance to the co-operation of a British expeditionary force, which . . . falling on the right flank of the German advance, might produce great, and even decisive, results." Quoted in: Fairholme correspondence with Bertie, 24 August 1911, in *British Documents on Foreign Affairs*. Cf. in this regard the remarks made in the Bases du Plan, in which the British expeditionary corps is called "an enormous reinforcement." Bases du Plan, CSG, 18 March 1913, SHA, 1N11, CXLIII, fol. 5.

43. Dubail held office as "Chef de l'État major de l'armée" until its abolition on 20 January 1912.

44. Procès-verbal, CSDN, 9 January 1912, SHA, 2N1. See also Dubail's additional remarks in Procès-verbal des entretiens du mois d'août 18 entre les chefs d'état-major des armées française et russe, in *Documents Diplomatiques Français,* series 2, vol. 14, no. 232. See also *Mémoires du Maréchal Joffre,* 1:26: "the best way to free ourselves from a purely defensive posture would be intensive efforts on the part of our allies."

45. Note should be made of the diverging interests within the Triple Entente. In a situation in which France would go to war for Russia but not Russia for France, that meant that if Russia was completely ready to take the field, the interests of Great Britain would have only marginal influence. This is shown for instance by the fact that in November 1912 the British ambassador, in a conversation with the French premier, was convinced that the British public would not go to war to extend Serbia's territory to the Adriatic. Cf. Bertie to Edward Grey, 26 November 1912, in *British Documents on the Origins of the War, 1898-1914,* ed. G. P. Gooch and Harold Temperley, vol. 9, part 2 (London, 1938), doc. 200. See also Paul Cambon to Poincaré, letter of 4 December 1912, in *Documents Diplomatiques Français,* series 3, vol. 4, no. 622. In this telegram the ambassador reports that the permanent undersecretary in the Foreign Office, Arthur Nicolson, had said that "in the Commons, where no one gives much thought to the Austro-Serbian conflict . . . even a limited conflict between Germany, Austria-Hungary and Russia would be met with indifference." Cf. Poincaré's memoirs, which give witness to similar sentiments as late as April 1913. See Raymond Poincaré, *Au service de la France: Neuf années de Souvenirs,* vol. 3, *L'Europe sous les armes* (Paris, 1926), 169ff. Much more optimistic though much less accurate was the estimate of the director of military operations on the British General Staff. To the French military attaché, he declared: "The Balkans is currently much in favor with the British public, and the Government is well aware of that. For the British public the current Serbian question is of considerably greater interest than the question of Morocco." De la Panouse to Millerand, 13 November 1912, SHA, 7N1227. As late as during the July Crisis the British ambassador reported to the attorney general, who was acting as head of the Foreign Office: "I felt sure that public opinion in England

would not sanction a war in support of Russia if she, as a protector of Slavs, picked a quarrel with Austria over Austro-Serbian difficulty." Bertie to Grey, 25 July 1914, in *British Documents on the Origins of the War,* doc. 129. See also Francis L. Bertie, *The Diary of Lord Bertie of Thame 1914-1918,* vol. 1, ed. Lady Algernon G. Lennox (London, 1924), 1 (26 July 1914). To a reporter of the newspaper *Figaro* on 25 July 1914 Bertie expressed the following words: "Are you French truly interested in Serbia? We certainly are not." Recouly, *Joffre,* 9.

46. For the following see Christel Gade, *Gleichgewichtspolitik oder Bündnispflege? Maximen britischer Aussenpolitik (1909-1914)* Veröffentlichungen des Deutschen Historischen Instituts London, 40 (Göttingen, Zurich, 1997), 158-164, and the seminal work by Samuel R. Williamson Jr., *The Politics of Grand Strategy: Britain and France Prepare for War. 1904-1914* (Cambridge, 1969), 264-299.

47. On the difference between alliances and ententes, see Robert A. Cann, "Alliances versus Ententes," *World Politics* 28 (1976): 611-621, cf. pages 611ff., and Rudolf Kjellén, *Dreibund und Dreiverband: Die diplomatische Vorgeschichte des Weltkrieges* (München, 1921), 9.

48. Williamson, *The Politics of Grand Strategy,* 298.

49. The exact wording of the question the ambassador was directed to ask the British foreign secretary was, "If Austria were to attack Serbia, and Russia see itself impelled to come to Serbia's defense, if then Germany were to intervene to defend Austria against Russia, and if then France were to be compelled to support Russia, how then would the British government react?" Poincaré to Cambon, 3 December 1912, in *Documents Diplomatiques Français,* series 3, vol. 4, no. 612.

50. Poincaré to Bertie, 4 December 1912, in *British Documents on the Origins of the War,* vol. 9, no. 2, doc. 328. Similar instructions went out to the British ambassador to Russia. Cf. Grey to George William Buchanan, 17 February 1913, in ibid., doc. 626. The French ambassador's reply was somewhat more brief. Cambon cabled Poincaré, reporting, "He replied that the time to consider such an eventuality had not yet arrived, and that the government's position would depend upon the disposition in both Houses and on public opinion, whereby public opinion would again be governed by how and why the conflict arose." Paul Cambon to Poincaré, 4 December 1912, in *Documents Diplomatiques Français,* series 3, vol. 4, no. 622. That this dispatch nevertheless contained more or less the exact words of the reply is shown by the dispatch of the Russian ambassador. See Izvol'skiy to Sazonov, 5 December 1912, in *Der Diplomatische Schriftwechsel Iswolskis,* doc. 606.

51. Memorandum, 24 April 1914, Public Record Office (PRO), Nachlass Bertie, FO 800/166, fol. 65.

52. Izvol'skiy to Sazonov, 5 December 1912, in *Der Diplomatische Schriftwechsel Iswolskis,* 608.

53. Izvol'skiy to Sazonov, 6 June 1912, in *Der Diplomatische Schriftwechsel Iswolskis,* doc. 318.

54. Bertie to Grey, 25 July 1913, PRO, Nachlass Grey, FO 800/54, fol. 252.

55. Ibid., fol. 253. Cf. Izvol'skiy to Sazonov, 5 December 1912, in *Der Diplomatische Schriftwechsel Iswolskis,* doc. 608.

56. Grey to Bertie, 1 May 1914, in *British Documents on the Origins of the War,* vol. 10, part 2 (London, 1936), doc. 541.

57. Note du Ministre: Conversation, au ministère des Affaires étrangères entre Sir Edward Grey et M. Gaston Doumergue, en présence de M. Paul Cambon, Sir William Tyrell, M. de Margerie, 24 April 1914, in *Documents Diplomatiques Français,* séries 3, vol. 10, no. 155.

58. Bertie, "Annual Report France 1911," 31 December 1912 [*sic*], in *British Documents on Foreign Affairs,* doc. 76; Bertie, "Annual Report France 1912," 1 August 1913, in ibid., doc. 108. Cf. Prestwich, *French Attitudes towards Britain,* 257ff.

59. Quote in Izvol'skiy to Sazonov, 5 December 1912, in *Der Diplomatische Schriftwechsel Iswolskis,* doc. 608. See also Izvol'skiy to Sazonov, 18 March 1912, in *Der Diplomatische Schriftwechsel Iswolskis,* Reihe 1, vol. 2, doc. 42. Cf. also Poincaré's remarks to the Belgian ambassador in June 1912, which may be consulted in the Belgian national archives: Marie-Thérèse Bitsch, *La Belgique entre la France et l'Allemagne, 1905–1914* (Paris, 1994), 457ff. Poincaré was still advancing similar arguments on 30 July 1914. Speaking with the British ambassador, he stated: "If war broke out between Russia and Austria, and Germany came to the assistance of Austria, France would be bound by her treaty engagements to aid Russia. There would be a general war on the Continent in which England would inevitably be involved in the curse of it for the protection of interests vital to her position." Bertie to Grey, 30 July 1914, PRO, FO 146/4382. This document is the draft of a letter to Grey found in the archives of the British embassy in Paris. Cf. Raymond Poincaré, *Au Service de la France,* vol. 1, *Le lendemain d'Agadir* (Paris, 1926), 178, 188ff. For Cambon's assessment, see Aleksandr Konstantinovich Benckendorff to Sazonov, 25 February 1913, in *Graf Benckendorffs Diplomatischer Schriftwechsel: Neue, stark vermehrte Aufl. der Diplomatischen Aktenstücke zur Geschichte der Ententepolitik der Vorkriegsjahre,* vol. 3, ed. von Benno von Siebert (Berlin, Leipzig, 1928), doc. 896. See also postwar statements by Cambon to Raymond Recouly: "That England sooner or later would have to intervene in the Franco-German conflict I had no doubt whatsoever." Raymond Recouly, *Les Heures tragiques d'avant-guerre* (Paris, [1921]), 44. For Paléologue's assessment, see Maurice Paléologue, *Au Quai d'Orsay à la veille de la tourmente: Journal 1913–1914* (Paris, 1947), 28 (for 4 February 1913).

60. Izvol'skiy to Sazonov, 27 February 1913, in *Der Diplomatische Schriftwechsel Iswolskis,* vol. 3 (Berlin, 1926), doc. 747.

61. Cf. the concurring opinion of John F. V. Keiger, *Raymond Poincaré* (Cambridge, 1997), 143ff.

62. Cf. the British ambassador's notes on his trip to London on 25 July 1912, PRO, Nachlass Bertie, 800/165, fol. 154ff. See there his description of the French demands. Bertie to Grey, 13 August 1912, PRO, Bertie papers, 800/165, fol. 154ff.

63. Grey to Cambon, 22 November 1912, in *British Documents on the Origins of*

the War, vol. 10, part 2, doc. 416. Cf. also Cambon to Grey, 23 November 1912, in ibid., doc. 417.

64. Bases du Plan, CSG, 18 March 1913, SHA, 1N11.

65. Fairholme to Bertie, 24 August 1911, in *British Documents on Foreign Affairs,* doc. 70. Although the military convention had been signed but a month before, the chief of Staff in his conversation with the military attaché made no secret of his doubts about whether the British cabinet would in fact be prepared to commit the Expeditionary Force to the Continent in its entirety. The General Staff prepared its own study of at which point in time and in what strength the British Expeditionary Force would arrive. Cf. La coopération militaire anglaise, 15 May 1912, SHA, 7N1227.

66. Nicolson to Grey, 24 February 1913, in *British Documents on the Origins of the War,* vol. 9, part 2, doc. 656.

67. Bases du Plan, CSG, 18 March 1913, SHA, 1N11. The memorandum "La coopération militaire anglaise" contains a similar assessment: "It might be that the government, despite otherwise favorable circumstances, will only dispatch four divisions at first, in order to pacify certain sections of the public." La coopération militaire anglaise, 15 May 1912, SHA, 7N1227.

68. Memorandum, 23 June 1913, PRO, Bertie papers, FO 800/166, fol. 43. These were the records of a conversation that the ambassador had on that date with the British foreign secretary. Cf. also: Memorandum, 3 July 1913, PRO, Bertie papers, 800/166, fol. 46. In his annual report for 1913, Bertie remarked: "many people in France, and Military authorities... fear that if war should break out without much preliminary warning British Military aid might not arrive in time or be numerically sufficient to stay a German invasion of France by land, and that in the absence of adequate British Military aid the useful assistance of England would be limited to dealing with the German navy and the cutting off of supplies to Germany by sea." Bertie, "Annual Report France 1912," 1 August 1913, in *British Documents on Foreign Affairs,* doc. 108. That the "many people" so vaguely circumscribed here referred in fact also to the cabinet and to Premier Poincaré is made clear through other references in the ambassador's papers quoted here.

69. Roy A. Prete, "French Strategic Planning and the Deployment of the B.E.F. in 1914," *Canadian Journal of History* 24 (1989): 42–62, esp. 61.

70. Gerd Krumeich, *Aufrüstung und Innenpolitik in Frankreich vor dem Ersten Weltkrieg: Die Einführung der dreijährigen Dienstpflicht 1913–1914* (Wiesbaden, 1980), 22ff. Cf. also Gerd Krumeich, "A propos de la politique d'armement de la France avant la Première Guerre mondiale," *Revue d'Histoire moderne* 29 (1982): 662–672, cf. page 667.

71. Description sommaire du théatre du Nord-Est de part et d'autre des frontières, SHA, 7N1784. On the chances and risks of an offensive in Alsace, see also the memorandum prepared by the 3rd Bureau of the General Staff: Mémoire sur les modifications à apporter au Plan XVI, May 1911, SHA, 7N1784, and Joffre's comments of 21 February 1912. Cf. Conférence tenue au Ministère des Affaires Étrangères, Minute, CSDN, 21 February 1912, SHA, 2N1, VI/39.

72. The General Staff calculated that a maximum of eleven corps might be employed in such an offensive. Cf. Mémoire sur les modifications à apporter au Plan XVI, May 1911, SHA, 7N1784.

73. SHA, 2N1/VII. This document constitutes the detailed minutes, possibly even the typed manuscript, of the chief of staff's remarks on 21 February 1912. In the minutes of this meeting Joffre's conclusions were mitigated somewhat by the insertion of the word "immediately." Cf. Conférence tenue au Ministère des Affaires Étrangère, Minute, 21 February 1912, SHA, 2N1, VI/39. Present at this meeting were, besides Poincaré, Joffre, and Maurice Paléologue, Navy Minister Théophile Delcassé, Army Minister Alexandre Millerand, and Chief of Naval Staff Vice Admiral Jacques Aubert.

74. SHA, 2N1/VII. On the chances for an invasion of Belgian territory, see also the untitled and undated campaign memorandum, SHA, 7N1784. From an annotation on page 20 of this document it can be seen that parts of this long memorandum found entry into the study filed under: "Files concerning Variant I of Plan XVI." The memorandum must have been written in the second half of 1911.

75. The official minutes of the meeting record: "General Joffre concludes that it would be very advantageous in any event if our armies were to be permitted to cross Belgian territory south of the line Namur-Liège." Conférence tenue au Ministère des Affaires Étrangères, Minute, 21 February 1912, SHA, 2N1, VI/39.

76. Quoted from Procès-verbal, CSDN, 11 October 1911, SHA, 2N1, V/29.

77. Procès-verbal, CSDN, 9 January 1912, SHA, 2N1. The answering note of 20 October 1911 from the Foreign Ministry in response to the General Staff's memorandum on the diplomatic situation states with regard to Luxembourg: "The neutral status of the Grand Duchy of Luxemburg can be regarded quite differently to that of Belgium. Great Britain is in no way interested in upholding the Treaty of 1867 in its entirety. . . . Under these circumstances France could in case of war make any disposition over the Grand Duchy the situation might require." Note, Neutralité belge, CSDN, 20 October 1912, SHA, 2N1, V/34.

78. Note, Neutralité belge, CSDN, 20 October 1912, SHA, 2N1, V/34/3.

79. Procès-verbal, CSDN, 9 January 1912, SHA, 2N1. On the British position on this issue, see also Williamson, *The Politics of Grand Strategy*, 214–218.

80. The "Mémoire sur les modifications à apporter au Plan XVI" declared categorically, "The only report so significant as to form the basis of a definitive overall decision on the concentration [of our troops], and which we can be certain of getting, is the report that Belgian territory has been violated. But this violation will with certainty not occur prior to the concentration [of the armies], when the armies begin their offensive . . . the Germans will carefully avoid crossing the Belgian frontier until the day when their armies are ready to continue their offensive without any interruption." Mémoire sur les modifications à apporter au Plan XVI, May 1911, SHA, 7N1784.

81. Cf. Note au sujet de plan, 29 August 1911, SHA, 7N1763, and Bases du Plan, CSG, 18 March 1913, SHA, 1N11, CXLIII, fol. 50ff.

82. Cf. Procès-verbal, CSDN, 9 January 1912, SHA, 2N1.

83. Joffre, for instance, argued in this vein: "Since the British government seeks ends that can be met only through the total defeat of the common enemy it will in the final event scarcely have any scruples about the choice of means." Conférence tenue au Ministère des Affaires Étrangères, Minute, CSDN, 9 January 1912, SHA, 2N1, VI/39. The chief of staff's words were almost verbatim those spoken by Navy Minister Delcassé at the CSDN meeting on 9 January 1912. Cf. Procès-verbal, CSDN, 9 January 1912, SHA, 2N1.

84. Cf. *Mémoires du Maréchal Joffre*, 1:125ff. See also Cambon to Poincaré, 21 March 1912, in *Documents Diplomatiques Français*, series 3, vol. 2, no. 240. See also Poincaré to Cambon, 28 March 1912, in ibid., no. 269, and Cambon to Fleurieu, 3 April 1912, in ibid., no. 295.

85. Krumeich, *Aufrüstung und Innenpolitik*, 22.

86. Cf. Note au sujet de plan, 29 August 1911, SHA, 7N1763.

87. See the undated and untitled campaign memorandum, SHA, 7N1771, and Joffre's instructive comments in the chapter "Le plan XVII.—Idées qui ont servi de base au plan de concentration" in his memoires. Joffre, *Mémoires du Maréchal Joffre*, 1:141–162. Cf. the alternative view in the article by Robert Doughty, who sees alliance considerations as the motive for the offensive in Alsace and Lorraine. Robert A. Doughty, "French Strategy in 1914: Joffre's Own," *Journal of Military History* 67 (2003): 427–454, cf. pages 453ff.

88. Cf. Joffre, *Mémoires du Maréchal Joffre*, 1:145–161.

89. Guy Pedroncini, "Stratégie et relations Internationales: La séance du 9 janvier du Conseil Supérieur de la Défense nationale," *Revue d'histoire diplomatique* 91 (1977): 143–158, cf. page 143. See also Guy Pedroncini, "Influence de la neutralité belge et luxembourgeoise sur la stratégie française: Le plan XVII," in *Les relations franco-luxembourgeoises de Louis XIV à R. Schuman:* Actes du Colloque de *Luxembourg (17–19 novembre 1977),* ed. Raymond Poidevin and Gilbert Trausch (Metz, 1978), 185–197.

90. Henry Wilson, *Field-Marshal Sir Henry Wilson: His Life and Diaries,* vol. 1, ed. Charles E. Callwell (London, 1927), 78ff. In their conversations with the director of military operations, Castelnau and Joffre also emphasized that his country's declaration of war would have high moral value for France. Ibid., 122. The British ambassador in Paris argued along the same lines, emphasizing in a conversation with his foreign secretary "the moral forces which would be given to the French people by the feeling that England was with them." Memorandum, 25 July 1912, PRO, Nachlass Bertie, FO 800/165, fol. 152.

91. Bertie to Grey, 4 August 1914, PRO, Nachlass Bertie, FO 800/166, fol. 92. See also the draft of this telegram dated 3 August 1914, PRO, Bertie Papers, FO 800/166, fol. 91.

92. Bertie to Grey, 30 July 1914, in *British Documents on the Origins of the War,* vol. 11, doc. 373.

93. Izvol'skiy to Sazonov, 5 December 1912, in *Der Diplomatische Schriftwechsel Iswolskis,* vol. 2, doc. 608.

94. Cf. in particular Stig Förster, "Der deutsche Generalstab und die Illusion des kurzen Krieges, 1871–1914: Metakritik eines Mythos," *Militärgeschichtliche Mitteilungen* 54 (1995): 61–95. See also Förster, "Dreams and Nightmares," 343–376. For the chief of the German General Staff, see Annika Mombauer, *Helmuth von Moltke and the Origins of the First World War* (Cambridge, 2001), 95ff. Another brief survey studded with his own observations has been submitted by Holger H. Herwig: "Germany and the 'Short-War' Illusion: Towards a New Interpretation?" *Journal of Military History* 66 (2002): 681–694.

95. Ferdinand Foch, *Des principes de la guerre,* ed. André Martel (Paris, 1996), 115–120, 130–132.

96. On the study of East Prussia's terrain, see Au sujet de la valeur de la coopération russe, December 1911, SHA, 7N1538. See also the section "Description sommaire du théâtre d'opérations" in Note sur le plan russe de 1913, December 1913, SHA, 7N1771. The most exhaustive treatment of this subject is Étude relative à l'importance, à la répartition et à l'emploi des forces allemandes sur le théâtre d'opérations russo-allemandes, May 1914, SHA, 7N1538.

97. On the military significance of the Vistula River line, see Au sujet de la valeur de la coopération russe, December 1911, SHA, 7N1538, and Étude relative à l'importance, à la répartition et à l'emploi des forces allemandes sur le théâtre d'opérations russo-allemandes, May 1914, SHA, 7N1538.

98. Quoted in Étude relative à l'importance, à la répartition et à l'emploi des forces allemandes sur le théâtre d'opérations russo-allemandes, May 1914, SHA, 7N1538. As early as 1908 the chief of the Russian General Staff told the French military attaché: "An offensive from the Memel River to the tip of East Prussia could be carried out very quickly, but that kind of operation . . . would hardly do Germany any damage while not promising any serious result. Likewise, an offensive launched over the Narew River along the axis Lomsza-Allenstein would also not lead to any decisive result. Only the axis Warsaw-Berlin would cause the Germans any worries." Moulin to Piquart, 2 September 1908, in *Documents Diplomatiques Français,* series 2, vol. 11, no. 442.

99. Youri Danilov, *La Russie dans la Guerre Mondiale (1914–1917)* (Paris, 1927), 117. Cf. the Russian minister of war's similar statements in Wladimir A. Suchomlinow, *Erinnerungen* (Berlin, 1924), 243.

100. Cf. Golovin, "Russian War Plan," 374–376; Snyder, *The Ideology of the Offensive,* 179–184. With the intention of accelerating the offensive against Germany and Austria-Hungary, the modifications to Plan 19 were reviewed once again in 1913. In order to shorten the time needed for the strategic concentration of forces, the divisions that would not arrive at the western frontier until an advanced stage of the conflict were no longer allocated to the attacking contingent, but assigned rather to the strategic reserve. Important in this context, however, is that Plan 20, which would not

have taken effect until the second half of 1914, foresaw neither a redistribution of the contingent between the northwestern and southern groups of forces, nor any fundamental change to strategic intentions. See Snyder, *The Ideology of the Offensive*, 183ff.

101. Cf. the remarks of the chief of the Russian General Staff in Procès-verbal de l'entretien du 13 juillet 1912 entre les Chefs d'États-major des Armées française et russe, in *Documents Diplomatiques Français*, series 3, vol. 3, no. 200.

102. Cf. Golovin, "Russian War Plan," 575 et. seq.; Snyder, *The Ideology of the Offensive*, 179 et. seq.

103. Quoted in Procès-verbal de l'entretien du 13 juillet 1912 entre les Chefs d'États-major des Armées française et russe, in *Documents Diplomatiques Français*, series 3, vol. 3, no. 200.

104. Cf. the handwritten notes: Renseignements donnés par le Général Gilinski au G[énér]al Joffre dans la conférence préliminaire du 20–12 août 1913, SHA, 7N1535. This fact went long unrecognized by historians. See Frank M. Laney, "The Military Implementation of the Franco-Russian Alliance 1890–1914" (Ph.D. diss., University of Virginia, 1954), 325ff. The study by Finnish historian Pertti Luntinen already leaves out the 1913 General Staff conference. Pertti Luntinen, *French Information on the Russian War Plans, 1880–1914*, Studia Historica, 17 (Helsinki, 1984).

105. Note sur le plan russe de 1913, December 1913, SHA, 7N1771.

106. Ibid.

107. Note pour le 3e Bureau (avant propos pour le plan), 12 June 1914, SHA, 7N1771.

108. Quoted in Alexej A. Ignatjew, *Fünfzig Jahre in Reih und Glied* (Berlin, 1956), 269.

109. Procès-verbal de l'entretien du 13 juillet 1912 entre les Chefs d'États-major des Armées française et russe, in *Documents Diplomatiques Français*, series 3, vol. 3, no. 200.

110. Procès-verbal des entretiens du mois d'août 1913 entre les chefs d'état-major des armées française et russe, in *Documents Diplomatiques Français*, series 3, vol. 8, no. 79. Cf. Poincaré's similar statements in his memoirs, where in regard to the consultations in 1912 we read: "The minutes of the talks . . . show in any case clearly that an outbreak of hostilities would upset the General Staff in several respects. General Joffre feared that should it come to a world conflagration Russia would deploy too large a part of its armies against Austria, and would not give us adequate support against Germany." Poincaré, *Au Service de la France*, vol. 2, *Les Balkans en feu* (Paris, 1926), 87.

111. L'Accélération de l'Offensive russe, Archives Nationales (AN), Messimy papers, 509 AP 6, fol. 8. See also Adolphe Messimy, *Mes souvenirs* (Paris, 1937), 202ff.

112. L'Accélération de l'Offensive russe, AN, Messimy papers, 509 AP 6, fol. 7. Cf. Izvol'skiy to Sazonov, letter of 31 July 1914, in *Der Diplomatische Schriftwechsel Iswolskis*, Reihe 1, vol. 5, doc. 356. Also, ibid., doc. 451.

113. When the Russian minister of finance informed Poincaré in 1912 that the first steps had already been taken to satisfy the demands of the French General Staff, informing him in this connection additionally about the expansion of a railroad line for

the concentration of troops against Austria-Hungary, Poincaré's reply was that it was much more urgent to accelerate the concentration of Russia's forces against Germany. Poincaré further stressed that "The outcome of the war will probably be decided on the German frontier." Notes de M. Poincaré sur ses entretiens de Saint-Pétersbourg, August 1912, in *Documents Diplomatiques Français,* series 3, vol. 3, no. 264. It seems, therefore, that it was, as Poincaré in his memoirs would have us believe, not only military men who feared that "in a world conflagration Russia would deploy too large a part of its armies against Austria, and not give us adequate support against Germany." Quoted in Poincaré, *Au Service de la France,* 2:87. See also Sazonov to Nicolas II, 17 August 1912, in *Der Diplomatische Schriftwechsel Iswolskis,* vol. 2, doc. 401.

114. L'Accélération de l'Offensive russe, AN, Messimy papers, 509 AP 6, fol. 7. See also Ignatjew, *Fünfzig Jahre in Reih und Glied,* 319. See also Adolphe Messimy, *Mes souvenirs,* 180ff.

115. See esp. Pierre Renouvin, *Les origines immédiates de la guerre: 28 juin–4 août,* 2nd ed. (Paris, 1927), 188–190, and Pierre Renouvin, "La politique française," *Le Monde,* 30 July 1964, 6.

116. René Girault, "Maurice Paléologue répond à Pierre Renouvin," *Matériaux pour l'histoire de notre temps* 47 (1997): 58–64, page 61.

117. Conférence tenue au Ministère des Affaires Étrangères, CSDN, 9 January 1912, SHA, 2N1, VI/39.

118. Note sur le plan russe de 1913, December 1913, SHA, 7N1771.

119. Cf. Gunther Frantz, "Das strategische Eisenbahnnetz Russlands 1914 unter besonderer Berücksichtigung des Bündnisses mit Frankreich," *Berliner Monatshefte* 8 (1930): 259–280, pages 264 and 270–272. In 1910 Russia had already conducted a thorough reform of its mobilization and concentration processes. Previously, a major portion of its active components were stationed in Poland, so that on the outbreak of hostilities reservists had to be transported to their units. Now Russia went over to the principle of territorial mobilization used by most European Great Powers. Under the reform the active contingents were stationed in the regions from which they received their reservists upon mobilization. Considering the varying density of the population, that meant a considerable part of the active formations was transferred to the Russian interior and would need to be transported over long distances in case of hostilities. Accordingly, the time required to complete the strategic concentration of forces was considerably extended. Cf. Snyder, *Ideology of the Offensive,* 171ff.; Fuller, *Strategy and Power in Russia,* 427–432.

120. Note sur l'action militaire de la Russie en Europe, August 1912, SHA, 7N1538.

121. Quoted in Améliorations possibles du réseau ferré, SHA, 7N1538. Joffre admitted as much in his memoirs: "With this common declaration of the will to take the offensive, the German plan—such as we conceived it to be—was brought to failure by causing our enemy to change the distribution of its troops and perhaps even to drop the concept of taking the offensive against us at the outset of hostilities, once again upsetting their plan." Joffre, *Mémoires du Maréchal Joffre,* 1:27.

122. This was the "Note sur l'action militaire de la Russie en Europe," which closed with the words: "Implementation as described above would have the additional advantage of shifting German attention to the ongoing work on the Russian railways and possibly move them to modify their intentions and especially the distribution of their forces." Quoted in Note sur l'action militaire de la Russie en Europe, August 1912, SHA, 7N1538.

123. Delcassé to Pichon, 1 August 1913, in *Documents Diplomatiques Français*, series 3, vol. 7, no. 513.

124. Buchanan to Nicolson, 11 April 1913, PRO, Nicolson papers, FO 800/365, fol. 42ff.

125. Ibid. Cf. also Buchanan to Grey, 9 April 1913, in *British Documents on the Origins of the War*, vol. 9, part 2, doc. 820. "He [Delcassé] takes a very serious view of Germany's present attitude. He looked he said at the facts. Rate of taxation in Germany was far higher than in France and her economic condition was not so good. She could not therefore bear for long the strain of the new taxes necessitated by her increased armament. She knew moreover that in two or three years, the Balkan states would be far stronger than at present. She would therefore prefer not to postpone the evil days."

126. Cf. Buchanan and Grey, 18 March 1914, in *British Documents on the Origins of the War*, vol. 10, part 2, doc. 528; Buchanan to Nicolson, 19 March 1914, in ibid., doc. 529. Buchanan returned to this line of thought repeatedly over the following months, revealing to his Italian colleague as late as 21 July his fears that Germany would use the crisis to launch a preventive war against Russia. See Carlotti to Antonio San Giuliano, 22 July 1914, in *I Documenti Diplomatici italiani*, ed. per Ministero degli affari esteri, Commissione per la publicazione dei documenti diplomatici (Rome, 1964), series 4, vol. 12, doc. 406.

127. Stéphane Lauzanne, *Les hommes que j'ai vus: Souvenirs d'un journaliste* (Paris, 1920), 56.

128. Quoted in Paul W. Schroeder, "Rumania and the Great Powers before 1914," *Rumanian Studies* 3 (1973–1975): 3–19, page 19.

129. See Paléologue, *Au Quai d'Orsay à la veille de la tourmente*, 79.

Russian Forces and the German Buildup at the Outbreak of World War I

Jan Kusber

In a concise overview of World War I historiography, Gerhard Hirschfeld recently noted a turn toward a cultural historical interpretation of the war events between 1914 and 1918 and the intertwined military and civilian lives of the states and their peoples.[1] One could justifiably say that the research on the war as war experience has become the focus of current scholarly discourse.[2] And this seems to have shifted the detailed reconstruction of the outbreak of war and the sequence of events into the background, even though there still are a vast number of themes regarding the eastern front and the Czarist Empire that are worth some research. During the period of the ninetieth anniversary of the outbreak of war, the historiography on Russia in the "*Weltenbrand*" (universal conflagration) produced publications providing a fresh perspective on World War I, far removed from the traditional Soviet interpretation that offered the somewhat conflicting concepts of an imperialistic war and heroic Russian battle leaders striving hard to defend their country.[3] Altogether, it became apparent that there are some reasons in favor of considering that World War I was for the Czarist Empire an integral part of the revolutionary process that, beyond the epochal year of 1917, led to the totalitarian Soviet experiment.[4]

At first glance it seems all this has little to do with the concise description of the readiness of the Russian forces for war and their orientation toward the German war planning scenarios that are the subject of this anthology. It is, however, a part of the broader reemerging discussions of varying intensity on the issue of the paths that led to World War I. This topic also contributes to finding an explanation for the structural weakness of the Czarist Empire as a whole. It is the military at all levels of command as a social subsystem. It shows that the circles of leaders, both political and military, suffered from significant communication and decision-making problems, which were not solely the result of the 1914 July Crisis, but rather were structurally inherent in the national constitution. The military and civilian leadership did not succeed in countering with coherent plans the "German threat," as perceived by large segments of the public and the government.[5]

The arguments exchanged by the various factions and individuals and the emphasis on a decision for either a partial or a full mobilization of the Russian Army were less a consequence of the German deployment than of the mobilization of the Austro-Hungarian forces on the southeastern front. That decision, ultimately left to the insecure Nicholas II, is a striking example of what has been described by Anglo-American research as the absence of "united government."[6] The Russian war minister Vladimir A. Sukhomlinov and his navy counterpart, Ivan K. Grigorovič, emphasized officially and also vis-à-vis the czar that not only were the Russian forces equipped for war with the Central Powers, but also they were strategically and tactically ready for it. Pandering to mighty public opinion, Sukhomlinov in March 1914 thus wrote a newspaper article with the title "Russia Wishes for Peace, but Is Ready for War." Three months later he followed up with a further contribution titled defiantly "Russia Is Ready,"[7] well knowing that this was not the fact.

The purpose of the following examination is to determine why this was not the fact. First, we will examine a few general points about the development of Russian forces following their defeat in the Russo-Japanese War and after their looming and almost complete self-disbandment at the end of the revolution year of 1905. Second, we will develop an outline of what the Russian Army knew about the armaments and strategies of the Central Powers. Finally, we will examine the conclusions drawn for the planning process. The starting point will be a thesis that has already been suggested by Norman Stone—that there were no unsolvable materiel, personnel, or infrastructure problems that the Russian forces had to face.[8]

The Russian Forces after 1905

The Russo-Japanese War of 1904–1905 clearly exposed the infrastructure and logistical deficiencies of the Czarist Empire's military to its army and navy leaders. The mobilizations and force deployments to the Far East had been conducted far too slowly. The mobilization plans had focused on the west since the time of War Minister Petr S. Vannovskiy in the 1890s, or upon conclusion of the Franco-Russian military conventions at the latest.[9] From the military perspective of that period the German Reich was identified first and foremost as the enemy, while Austria-Hungary only came second. In terms of foreign policy objectives, however, the opposite was true, as the Bosnian Crisis and the Balkan Wars should show. The Russian military leaders advised the foreign policy leadership to exercise reserve after the defeat by Japan. After all, the years 1904 and 1905 had seen the destruction of nearly the entire Russian Pacific and Baltic Sea Fleets.

The failure of the officer corps in the war and the mass phenomenon of mutinies occurring at the end of 1905, as if foreshadowing the end of the Romanov dynasty, were the facts that dominated the discussion of the problems in the initial years following the war and the revolution. The reformist war minister Aleksandr F. Rödiger, who served from 1905 to 1909, shared the opinion voiced by influential writers and critics that the officer corps and the generals above all should be subject to an evaluation and a reorientation of their leadership abilities.[10] The power of resistance to change, however, is apparent in the Russian unwillingness to draw conclusions from the failures in war and revolution, conclusions that might have threatened the very foundations of the armed forces.[11]

The majority of the generals, including the grand dukes under the leadership of the popular and ultraconservative Nicholas Nikolaevich, sabotaged Rödiger's reforms intended to improve the military leadership. They did so from their positions on the Council of State Defense,[12] originally established in 1905 to achieve a structural harmonization. The war minister failed in 1909, and when the Council of State Defense was dissolved that same year, his successor, Sukhomlinov, focused on equipping the army and making the mobilization process more efficient.[13] There were no fundamental reforms of officer training. This is worth noting insofar as it illustrates a basic problem of the Russian military that was central to the discussions about armament schemes, about the threat potentials of the Central Powers, and about the resulting mobilization scenarios. The officer corps and the generals lacked an overarching identity and frame of reference, and that prevented agreement on factual issues.[14]

In part, the fault lines ran across the General Staff and the War Ministry. Suggestions made by Quartermaster General Yuri N. Danilov,[15] for example, were regarded with suspicion because his liberal outlook gave him a reputation of being a "peasant revolutionary." Basic positions like that of Grand Duke Nicholas prevented any consequent planning against Germany as the major enemy, since a number of Russian officers were very pro-German, in contrast to large segments of the population.[16]

Finally, it must be noted that the lack of group identity and the formation of shared opinions mirrored the reality of civilian life. During the Balkans Wars the Russian military attaché in France criticized the public in Russia for having no interest in things military, contrary to the populations of France, Germany, and Great Britain. Since the disaster with Japan, the public was indeed in an extremely civilianized mood, with only a weakly developed interest in naval matters, although Nicholas II was enthusiastic about the navy and supported the fleet armament programs.

There were hardly any informed writers in Russia who were willing to address the military services or to discuss deployment scenarios in any depth. Memoirs about the war with Japan only dealt retrospectively with the trauma of defeat.[17]

The Russian Army was nothing to be proud of, and the officers' failure had contributed to this as well as the hated use of the military as a police force, which remained necessary after the 1905 revolution. This poor appreciation of the military as compared to that in other European states did not, however, parallel a moderation of Russian nationalism when it came to articulating foreign policy requirements.[18]

Sukhomlinov publicly avoided these two opposing currents. Instead, he focused on armament and equipment matters in close cooperation with the various factions that formed a considerable pressure group in the Duma. He therefore circumnavigated the clashing interests of the grand dukes, the members of the General Staff, the guard officers, and the various other special interests. In doing so he had significantly less leverage available than did his navy counterpart, who could rely on resources that even surpassed German fleet spending in 1913 and 1914.[19] That, of course, was a function of the requirement to replace the losses of the Far East battles of 1904 and 1905. Sukhomlinov's efforts to better equip the army with mobile artillery, machine guns, and sufficient ammunition were retarded not only by the corruption of which he was accused, but also by two basic assumptions that were shared largely by the generals.[20]

First, a significant part of the artillery budget was used for the Russian fortification system in Polish–White Russian territory that had been extended in the 1880s. The value of those fortifications, however, was more than questionable under the changed conditions of warfare. It was the commanders of the military districts of Kiev and Warsaw who insisted on the continued utility of the fortifications and who opposed the reduction of the fortresses when the issue was first brought up in 1908. Victory in that debate was the result of the vested interests of the regional army rulers in combination with those of the regional civilian powers.[21]

Second, most of the higher-ranking officers were inclined to await the outcome of the "Great Scheme," introduced in 1913–1914 and projected to produce results in four years' time. Only then could offensive action be taken. Nonetheless, the majority of the generals acted on the assumption of a brief military confrontation.[22] The enemies to the west were close and would also seek a swift decision. While during the discussions after 1910 some military leaders, like General Danilov, stressed the lessons of the slow deployment to the Far East against Japan, the majority emphasized the better railway network in the west. Warning voices of the civilians were hardly listened to, although State Council member Petr G. Durnovo warned in a memorandum[23] of a long war that would lead to the overthrow of the czarist regime. Therefore, the stocks of shells and ammunition for the Russian Army's heterogeneous arsenal of guns and small arms was only projected for a confrontation lasting some months.

These basic assumptions, shared by the majority, did not mean that Russia tended to underestimate its enemy—at least not entirely. The German Army especially was a much-feared opponent. Its organizational and strategic-tactical orientation was the opposite of the Russian Army's. The combat power of the Austro-Hungarian Army was generally estimated to be lower, and not a few of the Russian generals anticipated the collapse of Austria-Hungary's multiethnic empire.

Enemy Intelligence

According to historian William Fuller, what the Russian military leadership lacked was an effective military intelligence service that could collect and process sufficiently detailed intelligence on strategic-tactical plans, force strengths, and the equipment of all potential opponents.[24] There also was a problem with the collation of the information collected from the various sources. Primarily it was the diplomats and especially the military attachés of the embassies who tried to collect information.

This process worked much better for the Russians in Austria-Hungary than it did in Germany, where after World War I there was sometimes unjustified mention of the country swarming with Russian spies. In the Dual Monarchy, on the other hand, it was possible for the Russians at least from 1905 on to smuggle out relevant information on Austrian mobilization and deployment plans via Colonel Alfred Redl, known to the broader public since István Szábo's film. The damage done by Redl is a question of perspective. It was surely larger than the Austrians would admit after Redl's compromise in 1913, but actually smaller than the Russian military leadership thought.[25]

Because the Austrian deployment plans as of 1913 were known, the Russians thought they could afford to underestimate that enemy, while they had only very vague ideas about the plans of their German opponents. The deliberations in the internal *Sborniki* (journal of the Russian General Staff, analyzed by William Fuller) discussed the possible offensive orientation of the German Army against Russia, particularly in East Prussia, but the developing picture was one of ambiguous views. The deliberations mainly leave the impression of being based on secondhand information from printed and other "open source" material.

Another major asset of Russian military intelligence collection was the reconnaissance conducted by the military districts bordering on the Central Powers. The effectiveness of border surveillance conducted by the Kiev Military District produced a high density of information about the Austro-Hungarian deployment plans in Galicia that was greater than that on the German troop deployment in East Prussia. The information from the Kiev sector was also superior to that collected in *Polonia maior*, which was the responsibility of the military districts of Warsaw and St. Petersburg. As a result of the scarcity of information, the Russian military leadership increasingly assumed that the German *Erstschlag* (first strike) would be directed against France.

This assessment by the Russian generals was reinforced by the Russian-French General Staff consultations conducted annually since 1910.[26] While the St. Petersburg military leadership did not think that the consultations ran smoothly, they were nonetheless very informative for Russian interests.[27] During the 1913 conference, General Joseph Joffre was not willing to explain the French operational plans in detail, and that resulted in protracted discussions about who would be Russia's main opponent. The necessity of a significant Russian relief offensive in the east in the event of a German advance against France was acknowledged by the Russian representatives, who at the same time were no more communicative about their own strategic plans than were the French.

Given the difficulties in information collecting, combined with the extent to which even after 1905 governance was centered on the czar, it was a matter of course that any intelligence gains about the military forces of the Central Powers were not necessarily shared with the civilian leadership of the St. Petersburg government. During the Balkans Wars of 1912–1913, Prime Minister Vladimir N. Kokovtsov was informed only very late and indirectly of the War Ministry's assessments of the strength of the Ottoman Empire or the Central Powers. When the prime minister complained to the czar, Nicholas II backed his war minister, who regarded Kokovtsov's demands for military intelligence information as impertinence and an intrusion into his own portfolio.[28] Even in June and July 1914, during deliberations on whether and how Belgrade should be supported against Vienna, Foreign Minister Sergey D. Sazonov believed that he was being provided with insufficient information by the military about their readiness for war and the deployment plans of the potential opponents.[29]

All in all, the Russian assessment in 1914 was that the German main effort would be against France, but that Germany could easily reinforce its army corps in the east. Considering Germany's superior mobilization speed, the presumed offensive posture of the German Army, and German effectiveness, the German threat could only be countered by a strong superiority in numbers. The Austrian enemy was considered weaker, a colossus on clay feet. In any event, those two assumptions required an early mobilization of the forces to achieve quantitative superiority as rapidly as possible.[30]

Mobilization Scenarios

Even after the conclusion of the Russian-French military conventions there initially was no change in the defensive orientation of the Russian deployment plans.[31] The revised mobilization Plan 18 of 1906 provided for an assembly of the mobilizing forces northeast of the Neman River and east of the middle Vistula. According to those plans, Russian Poland south of the Vistula would be abandoned and the previously noted fortifications that ran in a chain along the border with the German Empire and Austria-Hungary would serve as bulwarks that should screen the mobilization process. The mobilized divisions and battalions were reasonably equally deployed into three main concentrations—the Neman, the middle Vistula, and the Galician border—with the reserve concentrated near Brest–Litovsk. That disposition should keep open the option of turning the main effort against either Austria or Germany, or both. Under that plan, completion of the mobilization was projected for no later than forty-five days following the initial order.

But at least since the Bosnian Crisis this defensive disposition, in particular against Germany, faced internal criticism. This, combined with the demands of the French, had been taken into account by War Minister Sukhomlinov and Quartermaster General Danilov in their draft of Plan 19, which they submitted in 1910.

Plan 19 was based on the assumption that Russia must not limit itself to defensive action, but rather should shift to the offensive as soon as possible. Such, however, could not be done from the Vistula positions (Russian Poland), but only from the flanks. Accordingly, Russia had to decide between an attack on Galicia or on East Prussia. The French, of course, urged the German option, but that still remained in dispute even after approval of Plan 19.

Plan 19 introduced a different approach to mobilization. Until recently the Russians had planned to call up the reserves in such a manner as to ensure an ethnic mixture of the multiethnic empire's soldiers. This was particularly important for the western *Gubernias* to address the Greater Russian fears of ethnically homogeneous units that might add to the ferment for national resistance and self-awareness. But Sukhomlinov now wanted to return to the territorial principle, as originally planned when universal conscription was introduced in 1874. Sukhomlinov's objective was to accelerate the mobilization tempo by reducing the travel distances to the assembly areas.[32]

Sukhomlinov thought this was the suitable strategy to comply with French demands for a significant relief operation[33] within fifteen days after the expected outbreak of hostilities in Luxembourg, Belgium, and Lorraine. However, the influential commanders of the military districts, who had to deal with the military-civilian interactions among their units, put up massive resistance against the territorial principle. To the commanders, the largely homogeneous Polish, Jewish, or Ukrainian units did not appear loyal enough, either internally or externally. Powerful members of the General Staff as well as the grand dukes supported the military district commanders. What Sukhomlinov finally achieved, therefore, was a combination between the territorial principle and the principle of placing as much distance as possible between the point of mobilization and the point of deployment. In other words, the system was a combination of bringing in reservists from regions close to the border and drawing them from central Russia and even Siberia.[34] For partial and general mobilization, the options for the combination of reservist units were different, and therefore exclusive of each other. That fact would play a significant role in the question of whether to respond to the Austrian bombardment of Belgrade with a partial or a general mobilization.

After 1912, two-fifths of the Russian Army was based in Russian Poland. As preparatory measures prior to the actual mobilization, the last three reserve age groups in the areas west of the Vistula were ordered to be drafted. Parallel to this, an amended Plan 19 went into effect in May that same year, betraying the eventual indecisiveness of the Russian military leadership. The revised plan included an Option A directed against Austria and an Option G targeted against Germany. The intent was to achieve a force ratio superiority of at least 20 percent on both fronts in order to be able to take the offensive in the southwest as well as the northwest.[35] The plan was based on being able to attack East Prussia on mobilization day plus sixteen, and on twenty-five to thirty days to invade Galicia. This modified Plan 19 was exercised during extensive maneuvers in 1913, although the mobilization tempo was tested neither there nor in a simulated war game in 1914, during which the generals and commanders sitting in a wing of the St. Petersburg Winter Palace conveniently played the interaction of the *Stavka*, the army-level command, and the field headquarters to be established. The gap in the real-time communications with the middle Vistula was not a factor.[36]

During a meeting in the presence of the czar of the cabinet with several members of the State Council and with the General Staff on 24–25 July 1914, the pros and cons of partial mobilization or general mobilization were finally discussed in a charged atmosphere. Considering the now generally expected war, nearly all the ministers and generals argued for a swift general mobilization—only Nicholas himself had a different opinion—in order to gain a head start and be ready to attack at the borders with East Prussia and Galicia when the Central Powers' declaration of war arrived. Nicholas terminated the two-day meeting without making a decision.[37]

Germany's so-called Schlieffen Plan was based on the assumption that the Russian mobilization would be slow and that it would be sufficient to leave some second-rate divisions in East Prussia as a defense measure against the Russians until France was defeated. Although the Russians were not familiar in detail with the modified German plans, they knew that they had to mobilize quickly, if for no other reason than in response to the continuing insistence of their French allies. The consequences were the increased railway construction in the western *Gubernias*, partially financed by French bonds,[38] and the massive production of locomotives and rolling stock that, according to the "Great Scheme of 1914," should peak only in 1917. There are parallels here with the efforts to arm the Russian fleet.[39]

When the Russian Second Army crossed the border into East Prussia, leading to the battles of August 1914,[40] their handicap was neither the poor training of the soldiers nor a lack of guns and ammunition, but rather irresolute leadership at the level of the higher officer ranks combined with poor coordination and communications. For the approximately 150,000 advancing soldiers there were only twenty-five telephones, a broken telegraph system, ten motor cars, and four defective motorcycles. What aircraft they had were nonoperational because of maintenance problems. The observation of enemy movements and the communications with the rearward echelons could only be accomplished with horse-mounted messengers.[41] Thus, the problems arising from the largely neglected reforms in officer training and the outdated communications systems were evident right at the beginning of the war—and would increase throughout the following war years.

On 29 July 1914 Russian foreign minister Sergey Sazonov had the following cabled to Aleksandr P. Izvol'skiy, the Russian ambassador to Paris, who had been Sazonov's predecessor in office: "The German ambassador informed me today that his government has decided to mobilize if Russia does not halt its military preparations. We have done this only because of the mobilization of Austria-Hungary that has already begun and as a result of the current lack of willingness by Austria-Hungary to respond to any means for a peaceful solution of its conflict with Serbia. Since it is impossible for us to accommodate the wishes of Germany, we can do nothing else but to accelerate our own armament build-up, and reckon with the probable inevitability of war."[42]

This cable accurately describes the perception of the situation, by not only the Russian diplomats but also the military leadership. Both saw themselves being driven. From a national perspective, the Russian general mobilization seemed a defense measure necessary to compensate, at least to some degree, for the assumed higher tempo of the German mobilization. In the discussions on both the civilian and the military leadership levels there was agreement that the transition to offensive action after completion of the general mobilization was not mandatory, despite the fact that such was repeatedly claimed by postwar German writers, including Gunther Franz.[43] The intent of those writers was to assign to Russia a considerable share of the collective guilt for the outbreak of the "great seminal catastrophe of [the twentieth] century."

Throughout July 1914 perceptions and expectations affected decisively the reactions of all sides. The Czarist Empire deployed its forces along its borders in order to have the option of attacking Germany or Austria-Hungary individually or simultaneously, depending on political developments. Those, of course, were dictated by the workings of the alliance. In the end, the thwarting of the German offensive against France was the main reason that the Russian attacks against East Prussia and Galicia were conducted concurrently. The Russians also firmly counted on the assumption that the Germans would violate the neutrality of Luxembourg and Belgium. The exact details were not known, but they were of no importance for the actions Russia had to take.

During the meetings between the Russian and French General Staffs between 1912 and 1914, the French never tired of demanding the Russian relief operation against East Prussia, and from there a deep invasion into the Reich. The Russians complied with the French request on the day of Germany's declaration of war, although the German enemy, in contrast to Austria-Hungary, was considered undefeatable by most of the Russian generals.

The first months of war seemed to confirm those expectations. After the unexpectedly rapid mobilization and a successful incursion into East Prussia, the Second Army under the command of General Aleksandr V. Samsonov was annihilated at the Battle of Tannenberg at the end of August. The Russian First Army under General Paul Edler von Rennenkampf was forced to withdraw across the Nemen after it suffered a decisive defeat. But at least the German leadership was forced to concentrate additional forces to reinforce East Prussia's defense, and those forces were lacking later in the west at the First Battle of the Marne.[44]

Against Austria-Hungary, meanwhile, the popular but inexperienced Grand Duke Nicholas Nikolaevich was able to wrest Galicia and Bukovina from the K.u.K. Army and march into Lwow.[45] As a result, the Russian generals increasingly criticized the division of the offensive forces, arguing that a swift victory would have been possible if they had concentrated on the Habsburg Monarchy.

Despite the few earlier voices of caution noted above, all the Russian mobilization schemes were based on a war that should last three months, six at the most. Since the development of a uniform military doctrine was already too much for the leadership of the Czarist Empire, because of the many different conflicting interests, the short war assumption was even more necessary, considering the command structure and organization of a total war. Putting approximately 5 million soldiers into the field after mobilization required additional waves of reservists and the commitment of the entire civilian society. The result was what Peter Gatrell called, "a whole Empire walking," which significantly contributed not only to the collapse of the war fronts against the external enemies, but also to the failure of the internal power structures.[46] Thus, the debates of the military leadership about tactical and strategic options during the years 1912 to 1914 strikingly exposed the structural faults of the Czarist Empire.

Notes

1. Gerhard Hirschfeld, "Der Erste Weltkrieg in der deutschen und internationalen Geschichtsschreibung," in *Aus Politik und Zeitgeschichte: Beilage zur Wochenzeitung "Das Parlament,"* B 28–30/2004, pages 3–12.

2. Cf. the main chapter "Gesellschaft im Krieg," in *Enzyklopädie Erster Weltkrieg*, 2nd ed., ed. Gerhard Hirschfeld, Gerd Krumeich, and Irina Renz (Paderborn, 2004). As examples for Russia, cf. Scott M. Kenworthy, "The Mobilization of Piety: Monasticism and the Great War in Russia, 1914-1916," in *Jahrbücher für Geschichte Osteuropas* 52, no. 3 (2004): 388-401; Dietrich Beyrau, "Projektionen, Imaginationen und Visionen im Ersten Weltkrieg: Die orthodoxen Militärgeistlichen im Einsatz für Glauben, Zar und Vaterland," in *Jahrbücher für Geschichte Osteuropas* 52, no. 3 (2004): 402-420.

3. For the older Soviet historiography, see Karl Heinz Schlarp, *Ursachen und Entstehung des Ersten Weltkrieges im Lichte der sowjetischen Geschichtsschreibung*, Darstellungen zur auswärtigen Politik, 10 (Hamburg, 1971). Cf. also the difficult reorientation of the journal *Voenno-istoričeskij žurnal*.

4. Peter Holquist, *Making War, Forging Revolution: Russia's Continuum of Crisis 1914-1921* (Cambridge, Mass., London, 2002); Josh Sanborn, "The Mobilization of 1914 and the Question of the Russian Nation: A Reexamination," *Slavic Review* 59, no. 2 (2000): 267-289. See also the description of the military level based on the writings of the Russian General Aleksej A. Brusilov in Orlando Figes, *Die Tragödie eines Volkes: Die Epoche der russischen Revolution 1891 bis 1924* (Berlin, 1998).

5. For this, cf. Uwe Liszkowski, *Zwischen Liberalismus und Imperialismus: Die zaristische Aussenpolitik vor dem Ersten Weltkrieg im Urteil Miljkovs und der Kadettenpartei 1905-1914*, Kieler Historische Studien, 18 (Stuttgart, 1974), in particular pages 229-334.

6. As, for example, by David McLaren MacDonald, *United Government and Foreign Policy in Russia 1900-1914* (Cambridge, Mass., 1992).

7. Horst Günther Linke, *Das zarische Russland und der Erste Weltkrieg: Diplomatie und Kriegsziele* (Munich, 1982), 31.

8. Norman Stone, *The Eastern Front* (New York, 1975), 12f.

9. For a comprehensive overview, cf.: George F. Kennan, *The Fateful Alliance: France, Russia, and the Coming of the First World War* (New York, 1985).

10. Jan Kusber, *Krieg und Revolution in Russland: Das Militär im Verhältnis zu Wirtschaft, Autokratie und Gesellschaft*, Quellen und Studien zur Geschichte des östlichen Europa, 47 (Stuttgart, 1997), 239-241.

11. John Bushnell, "The Tsarist Officer Corps, 1881-1914: Customs, Duties, Inefficiency," *American Historical Review* 86, no. 4 (1981): 753-780; Peter Kenez, "A Profile of the Prerevolutionary Officer Corps," *California Slavic Studies* 7 (1973): 121-158.

12. Michael Perrins, "The Council of State Defense 1905-1909: A Study in Russian Bureaucratic Politics," *Slavonic and East European Review* 58, no. 3 (1980): 370-398.

13. Wladimir A. Suchomlinow, *Erinnerungen* (Berlin, 1924).

14. Carl Van Dyke, *Russian Imperial Military Doctrine and Education, 1832-1914*, Contributions in Military Studies, 105 (New York, 1990).

15. Yuri Daniloff, *Dem Zusammenbruch entgegen: Ein Abschnitt aus der letzten Epoche der russischen Monarchie* (Hanover, 1928); Yuri Daniloff, *Grossfürst Nikolai*

Nikolajewitsch: Sein Leben und Wirken (Berlin, 1930); cf. also the evaluations in A. I. Denikin, *Staraja armija*, vol. 1.2 (Paris, 1929–1931), particularly in the second volume, and the records of the deputy war minister in A. A. Polivanov, *Iz dnevnikov i vospominanij po dol'žnosti voennogo ministra i ego pomoščnika, 1907–1916* (Moscow, 1924).

16. Cf. a detailed outline of these conflicts: Walter Thomas Wilfong, "Rebuilding the Russian Army, 1904–1914: The Question of a Comprehensive Plan for National Defense" (Ph.D. diss., University of Indiana, 1977).

17. Jan Kusber, "Der russisch-japanische Krieg 1904–1905 in Publizistik und Historiographie: Anmerkungen zur Literatur über den 'kleinen siegreichen Krieg,'" *Jahrbücher für Geschichte Osteuropas* 42, no. 2 (1994): 217–234.

18. Dominic B. Lieven, *Russia and the Origins of the First World War* (London, 1983), 118–136, and also the work of Liszkowski, *Zwischen Liberalismus und Imperialismus*, passim.

19. Peter Gatrell, *Government, Industry and Rearmament in Russia, 1900–1914: The Last Argument of Tsarism*, Russian, Soviet and Post-Soviet Studies, 92 (Cambridge, 1994), 277–317.

20. On the respective share of the state budget, see W. M. Pintner, "The Burden of Defense in Imperial Russia, 1725–1914," *Russian Review* 43 (1984): 231–259, here pages 253–259.

21. See A. A. Kersnovskij, *Istorija russkoj armii*, vol. 3, *1881–1915* (1935; reprint, Moscow 1994).

22. I. I. Rostunov, *Russkij front pervoj mirovoj vojny* (Moscow, 1976), 58f.

23. Dittmar Dahlmann, "Russland," in *Enzyklopädie Erster Weltkrieg*, 87–96, here page 89.

24. See William C. Fuller, "The Russian Empire," in *Knowing One's Enemies: Intelligence Assessment before the Two World Wars*, ed. Ernest R. May (Princeton, 1984), 98–126.

25. Hew Strachan, *The First World War*, vol. 1, *To Arms* (Oxford, 2001), 291f., 308.

26. Lieven, *Russia and the Origins of the First World War*, 116–118.

27. William C. Fuller Jr., *Strategy and Power in Russia 1600–1914* (New York, 1992), 433–441.

28. V. N. Kokovtsov, *Out of My Past* (Stanford, 1935), 346.

29. I. V. Bestužev, "Bor'ba v Rossii po voprosam vnešnej politiki nakanune pervoj mirovoj vojny (1910–1914)," *Istoričeskie zapiski* 80 (1965): 44–85, here page 63f.

30. S. K. Dobrorol'skij, *Mobilizacija russkoj armii v 1914: Podgotovka i vypolnenie* (Moscow, 1929); cf. also the evaluations in W. Barnes Steveni, *The Russian Army from Within* (New York, 1914); W. Bruce Lincoln, *Passage through Armageddon: The Russians in War and Revolution, 1914–1918* (New York, 1986).

31. On the French objectives regarding the Russian military planning after the Russo-Japanese War, see D. W. Spring, "Russia and the Franco-Russian Alliance, 1905–1914: Dependence or Independence," *Slavonic and East European Review* 66 (1988): 564–592.

32. For a concise view on this, see Nikolaus Katzer, "Russische Regierung und Militär zwischen Krimkriegstrauma und imperialer Expansion," in *Das Militär und der Aufbruch in die Moderne 1860 bis 1890: Armeen, Marinen und der Wandel von Politik, Gesellschaft und Wirtschaft in Europa, den USA sowie Japan*, ed. Michael Epkenhans and Gerhard P. Gross, Beiträge zur Militärgeschichte, 60 (Munich, 2003), 51–74, here pages 53–58.

33. Pertti Luntinen, *French Information on the Russian War Plans 1880–1914*, Studia Historica, 17 (Helsinki, 1984).

34. N. N. Golovin, *Voennaja usilja Rossii v mirovoj vojne* (Paris, 1939), 46–48.

35. Stephen J. Cimbala, "Steering through Rapids: Russian Mobilization and World War I," *Journal of Slavic Military Studies* 9 (1996): 376–398. On the focal point of the German planning process, see Dennis A. Showalter, "The Eastern Front and German-Military Planning, 1871–1914: Some Observations," *East European Quarterly* 15 (1981): 163–180.

36. Bruce W. Menning, *Bayonets before Bullets: The Russian Imperial Army, 1861–1914* (Bloomington, Indianapolis, 1992), 239–255; A. N. Suvorov, "Voennaja igra staršich voennych načal'nikov v aprele 1914 goda," *Voenno istoričeskij sbornik* 1 (1919): 9–11.

37. Dominic B. Lieven, *Nicholas II: Twilight of the Empire* (New York, 1993), 200–203.

38. D. N. Collins, "The Franco-Russian Alliance and Russian Railways, 1891–1914," *Historical Journal* 16, no. 4 (1973): 777–788.

39. On this in detail, see Kornej F. Šacillo, *Rossija pered pervoj mirovoj vojnoj: (Vooružennye sily carizma v 1905–1914 gg.)* (Moscow, 1974); Kornej F. Šacillo, *Russkij imperializm i razvitie flota nakanune pervoj mirovoj vojny (1906–1914)* (Moscow, 1968); L. G. Beskrovnyj, *Armija i flot Rossii v načale XX v. Očerki voenno-ėkonomičeskogo potenciala* (Moscow, 1986).

40. As Solzhenitsyn titled his novel on this subject: Alexander Solzhenitsyn, *August 1914* (New York, 1972).

41. Stone, *The Eastern Front*, 50.

42. S. D. Sasonoff, *Sechs schwere Jahre* (Berlin, 1927), 239f.; in English: Sergei Dimitrievich Sazonov, *Fateful Years, 1909–1916: The Reminiscences of Serge Sazonov* (New York, 1928; reprint, New York, 1971), xxxf.

43. Gunther Frantz, *Russlands Eintritt in den Weltkrieg: Der Ausbau der russischen Wehrmacht und ihr Einsatz bei Kriegsausbruch* (Berlin, 1924).

44. On this in detail, see Dennis A. Showalter, *Tannenberg: Clash of Empires* (Hamden, 1990).

45. Strachan, *The First World War*, 1:347–356.

46. Peter Gatrell, *A Whole Empire Walking: Refugees in Russia during World War I* (Bloomington, 1999); cf. also Eric Lohr, "The Russian Army and the Jews: Mass Deportations, Hostages and Violence during World War I," *Russian Review* 60 (2001): 404–419.

The Southern Envelopment
Switzerland's Role in the Schlieffen and Moltke Plans

Hans Rudolf Fuhrer and Michael Olsansky

"We have to admit that we owe our country's preservation in the World War not only to divine providence, but more especially to the simple circumstance that both warring parties were in equal measure interested in preserving Switzerland's neutrality."[1]

These were the words of Theophil Sprecher von Bernegg, chief of the Swiss General Staff, in his famous speech to the Bern Officers' Association in 1927. Renowned Swiss historians have reached similar conclusions in their evaluation of the events while at the same time emphasizing the importance of military border protection.[2] It is, therefore, little wonder that World War I is known in Swiss history as the "Border Occupation of 1914–1918." Two recent broad studies dealing with the problems of the Swiss Army in World War I correct this one-sided picture in several respects.[3]

"*Nolite Tangere*": Switzerland as a Non-Objective of German War Planning

The findings of the research are unanimous. Unlike the French General Staff during the second winter of the war, the Central Powers at no time during the First World War contemplated any form of aggressive actions directed toward a neutral Switzerland. Even the southernmost planning variants based on attacks on the Belfort fortifications gave no indication or showed any intentions of violating Swiss territory.

The fact that the symposium "The Schlieffen Plan: Reality and Myth of German Deployment Plans in the West before 1914 in an International Context," conducted by the German Military History Research Institute, did not address the problem of a possible envelopment of the French front via the left wing is sufficient reason to take an in-depth look into this historical point. In doing so, however, our intention is not merely to accept the thesis that a violation of neutral Swiss territory had never been considered seriously in pre-1914 German war planning.[4]

Those who have knowledge of the Schlieffen and Moltke Plans may not, however, be surprised at the lack of a "Plan South." Perhaps those who have focused extensively on the right wing would explain such an omission by arguing that there was no necessity to even consider an attack via the left wing. However, the task of the chiefs of the General Staff like Alfred von Schlieffen and Helmuth Moltke would have been to consider any possible scenarios for a war against France.

Hence, the urgent question arises as to why a southern option had not even received a minimal amount of attention. Why, for many years, was the obvious plan of the German General Staff simply to envelop the French fortification line of Belfort–Verdun from the territory of politically neutral Belgium, while completely ignoring considerations of the operational option of going though neutral Switzerland? Why was there broad agreement throughout the ranks of the German General Staff that the violation of Belgian neutrality, with the consequence of the probable entry of Great Britain into the war in support of the Entente, was necessary and justifiable under international law?[5] Why was the violation of Swiss neutrality in achieving the same objective never given serious consideration?

Few historians to date have dealt with these questions. For the most part their answers do not go any farther than military-geographic or technical aspects, which are dealt with rather sparingly. Annika Mombauer writes: "Moving through Switzerland would have been impractical."[6] Indeed, it was impractical. Jehuda Wallach wrote: "As we well know, the solution chosen was to the detriment of a neutral country. There were two options: Switzerland on the French right flank or Belgium on the left flank. Topographic considerations led to the violation of Belgian neutrality."[7]

On closer examination, however, these explanations alone are not fully convincing. Indeed, the Jura mountain range in the northwest of Switzerland is quite impractical for conducting large-scale military operations. But for the German Reich and its armed forces the probability of Great Britain entering into the war upon the violation of Belgian neutrality could hardly have been described as being the least bit more practical. While a southern envelopment would have required the German Army to get through two Jura passes, as well as Swiss border defenses, the northern envelopment required it to take the strongly manned Belgian fortresses near Liège. It is the better transport routes in the north that have repeatedly been given as the reason why the northern envelopment was the favored option. Yet there was no guarantee that the German Army could, in sufficient time, have taken control of the Belgian railroad system undestroyed, which was a vital condition for the campaign to succeed.[8]

The general absence of a plan for the southern envelopment is surprising enough. But German planning reservations that firmly excluded Swiss national territory when planning for potential troop movements by its Triple Alliance partner Italy during the run-up to the First World War are even more perplexing. Those forces could have been deployed to reinforce the German Army to the south of the German-French front against the Gate of Burgundy or the Western Alps.

All these unanswered questions, inconsistencies, and contradictions lead to the key question of why the German Army command under the leadership of Schlieffen and Moltke considered Switzerland untouchable, or *nolite tangere*. To provide an adequate answer, the following supporting questions must be addressed:

- Are there really no indications as to whether or not, or to what degree, the problem of the southern envelopment might have been discussed by the German General Staff prior to the war?
- How did Switzerland assess its own situation with regard to the threat of a European war? How did it prepare for this possible eventuality?
- How did cooperation with Germany's Italian alliance partner develop up to the outbreak of the war, considering the possibility of troop movements through Switzerland?
- Was it simply for military-geographical or technical reasons that Swiss neutrality was respected?

The Envelopment via the Left Wing

The limited number of available sources resulting from the loss of essential files during the latter days of World War II is a known fact. It is, therefore, necessary to assemble in summary the few remaining pieces of information in order to develop as accurate a picture as possible.

An Interpretation by the German Reichsarchiv

Despite all doubts about the historical objectivity of the *Reichsarchiv*, the institution's work on the German deployment plans are still of great significance and will be examined first.[9] In Schlieffen's *Denkschrift* (Memorandum) of December 1905 the following passage is relevant to the problem at hand: "By all means the attempt should be made to attack the left wing of the French in order to push them eastward against the Moselle fortifications, the Jura mountain range, and Switzerland. The French Army must be destroyed."[10]

The role of Switzerland as a barrier against which the French Army could be pushed seems clear. Swiss neutrality in general and the Swiss Army in particular were elements of that barrier, which was instrumental to the destruction of the enemy's army. It can, therefore, be assumed that an envelopment from the left would have rendered void the concept of total annihilation, and hence a speedy ending of the war.

Further Studies by the German Reichsarchiv

The possibility of Switzerland's neutrality being violated by the French was the subject of a March 1888 memorandum by Field Marshal Helmuth Graf von Moltke the Elder. Schlieffen, in his Memorandum of October 1898, described the possibility of a southern envelopment of the German left wing along the Rhine front as the enemy's most dangerous course of action. Schlieffen, therefore, examined the operational option of requesting Italian support for a push through the southern flank via the Gate of Burgundy; or in the event that the French launched their initial attack out of Lorraine, a push into their flank from the south. Most significantly for our discussion, Schlieffen noted that such an operation should not be launched via Switzerland, "where an army ready to go to war would have to be defeated and the fortified Jura passes overcome, only to engage in combat with the French under most adverse circumstances." Hence, he reasoned that only an envelopment in the north would make any real sense, "through Luxembourg, which had no army at all, and the weak Belgian army which was expected to retreat into its fortifications." Moreover, the operation would be "easier and more effective ... as it would directly hit the enemy's fallback line." This confirms the above thesis.[11]

Schlieffen also assumed his French opponents would reach a similar assessment of the violation of Swiss neutrality. In his Memorandum of

December 1905 he wrote: "If the enemy were to enter Switzerland, this would provide us with an ally that we are in great need of, and which would help tie down part of the enemy forces."[12]

One of the main reasons why Colonel General Helmuth von Moltke the Younger in his final deployment instructions reinforced the German left wing was his intention to "stop any enemy advancement from Belfort to Upper Alsace."[13] Hence, the French option of launching an offensive exclusively through its own territory was seriously considered at one point. This meant that the Swiss power of resistance that provided flank protection in the south was vital to both warring parties.

A Selection of Additional German Sources

The compendium *Organisation des Nachrichtendienstes von 1906* is also significant to our inquiry.[14] The German General Staff's 9th Department dealt with intelligence on Austria-Hungary, Italy, and Switzerland, with Austria-Hungary being an alliance partner.

Equally revealing is the justification for the invasion of Belgium that Major General Wilhelm von Dommes zu Handen offered to the commission negotiating the peace in January 1919.[15] Dommes was of the opinion that the German General Staff had no doubt that in the event of a German offensive a support agreement existed between France and Great Britain on the one hand, and Belgium on the other hand. On several occasions during peacetime there had been indications of cooperation in various fields. The Germans, therefore, observed with growing concern the fact that Belgium was augmenting its army. In 1907 Belgian peacetime strength was forty-seven thousand troops, with 19 percent of those being drafted recruits. In 1914 Belgian strength stood at a total of fifty-eight thousand troops, 49 percent of which were recruits. What is striking is the different German assessment of the Belgian and Swiss rearmament processes.

Germany registered objections to British officers conducting reconnaissance of the Belgian coast, particularly the port of Zeebrugge and the fortifications in the Antwerp area; and also reconnaissance of the Belgian road network by French officers, most likely for the purpose of flanking the presumed German right wing.[16] Moreover, the Belgian military attaché Collin revealed to his German counterpart, Major Detlof von Winterfeldt, that in the event of war French troops would march into Belgium even if the Belgian government had not made any such request. Dommes concluded from all these indications that Belgium had abandoned the principle of neutrality and thus sided with the Entente. Similar allegations against Switzerland were not made, however.

French Troop Movements through Switzerland?

Between 1875 and 1914 the French General Staff prepared seventeen operational plans.[17] Ever since Plan III the French General Staff had been expecting the German Reich to violate Belgium's neutrality, and they therefore planned their own counteroffensives to be launched through Belgian territory. In that event, General Victor Constant Michel, vice president of the war council, projected the deployment of forty army corps.[18] The final version of Plan XVII was based on the assumption that the Germans would launch their main thrust across southern Belgium and Luxembourg. Marshal Joseph Joffre wrote in his memoirs that by studying the German railroad network, the war games of the Great General Staff had become known. Publications by Friedrich von Bernhardi and Ludwig Freiherr von Falkenhausen, as well as the solely defensive German preparations in the south, also indicated that the Germans did not plan to attack across Swiss soil, but were far more likely to attack in the north, or even through southern Belgium.[19]

When the French compared the relative strengths of the national defenses of Belgium with Switzerland, they clearly thought the Swiss to be stronger. Despite the nominal Belgian strength of 340,000 troops,[20] the French assumed that the Belgians would withdraw to a fortified redoubt in the area of Antwerp as they came under threat from all directions. This move would open the axes of advance toward France. The marginal Swiss force of 212,000 was then expected to provide effective flank protection.

According to the analysis by the French General Staff: "All in all, the combat-ready Swiss Army with its solid core of well-trained soldiers and state-of-the-art equipment is capable of defending Swiss territory."[21] However, the French planning bodies were troubled by repeated reports suggesting that the strong German and Austrian influence on the Swiss General Staff might threaten the possibility of a tactical envelopment of Belfort by German forces. If that were to occur, would, as Joffre suspected, Switzerland use all its strength or "only half its strength" to defend itself? Joffre was not really alarmed,[22] but the intelligence order of 28 May 1914 included all the elements required for a continuous surveillance of the sector from which the threat of an envelopment could emerge.

Commandant Gaston Léonce Edouard Pageot, the French military attaché in Bern, assured the Swiss Federal Council as well as the chief of the

General Staff in July 1914 that France would "fully" respect the neutrality of Switzerland. He enquired what Switzerland intended to do to secure the German Reichbahn's Badische Bahnhof railroad station in Basel as well as how it intended to defend the Ajoie region in the event of a German attack.[23] The reply by Councillor Camille Decoppet, minister of defense, was clear and blunt: Switzerland is convinced that Germany will respect Swiss neutrality, "since it [is] aware of Switzerland's determination to resist a German attack with its full force."[24]

Basel continued to be important to the French General Staff.[25] Of primary interest, however, were German troop movements across the Rhine River bridges and troop concentrations on the right bank. A report indicating that German troops had disembarked at the Badische Bahnhof railroad station in Basel would have immediately triggered French countermeasures.

On 4 August 1914 at 0845 hours another hypothetical threat vanished when "Italy officially declared its full neutrality."[26] At the same time, however, the intelligence order issued that day required continued surveillance of the Great St. Bernhard, Simplon, Gotthard, and Brenner mountain passes, "in order to prevent any Italian offensive from being launched via Switzerland, or Italian troops being moved north to Germany."[27] This is a key point to which we will return.

The French General Staff feared the possibility of false German reports that might deceive the French into being the first to violate neutral Belgian territory.[28] The detailed orders issued to the VII Army Corps at the Burgundy Gate shows that corresponding instructions existed about Swiss neutrality.[29]

As an interim assessment we have established that the German General Staff most likely did not consider seriously the southern envelopment option. The military reasons for this decision were primarily operational, since only a northern envelopment would have held the promise of a quick success. Considering Dommes's weak arguments presented to justify the infringement of Belgian neutrality, we can conclude that it would have been far more difficult to justify a violation of Swiss neutrality. It can also be taken as a certainty that the French had neither during their prewar preparation or the initial phases of the war prepared any proper plans for a southern envelopment of the western front.

The Deliberations of the Swiss General Staff

It is quite clear that neither the Swiss Federal Council nor the General Staff had any knowledge of the concepts or plans of any of the other countries'

General Staffs at the time when they were contemplating how to avert the imminent threat of the forthcoming war. Prior to World War I all of Switzerland's neighboring countries, as well as Great Britain, Russia, and the United States, had military attachés accredited in Switzerland. The work of the Swiss intelligence service, however, was utterly inadequate. Up until 1936 the Swiss did not have military attachés assigned to their embassies. Although the Swiss embassies were required to compile military reports, the quality varied and depended very much on the interests and competence of the individual diplomats. In fact, the Swiss intelligence service was basically a one-man enterprise in the person of *Oberstkorpskommandant* Theophil Sprecher, chief of the General Staff as of 1 May 1905.

Sprecher's Memorandum of December 1906

On 15 February 1906, Sprecher gave his first detailed briefing on his operational ideas to the National Defense Commission.[30] Primarily for reasons of expediency, he recommended the formation of a neutral uniformed protective force that could be committed in any conceivable scenario. Transport required for an actual deployment would have to be organized to fit the situation and intent of the commanding general of the forces. Sprecher accepted the idea of a time delay because he wanted to avoid under any circumstances a situation where preconceived opinions and existing plans would have prevented the commanding general, who had yet to be designated, from acting as the situation required. Sprecher's first memorandum, *Die militärpolitische Lage der Schweiz und die Aufmärsche der schweizerischen Armee* (The Military-Political Situation in Switzerland and Deployment of the Swiss Army), of December 1906, was classified as a secret document, drawn up in only one copy, and consisting of eighteen pages.[31]

This threat analysis is proof of a clear, analytical, and realistic assessment of the situation. Sprecher considered the competition between the Triple Alliance (Germany, Austria-Hungary, and Italy) on the one hand, and the Dual Alliance (France and Russia) on the other hand as the driving factor in European politics up until the year 1900. He noted that Great Britain had been of only limited significance, even though it had always been obvious "that Italy with its almost totally unguarded coastline and trade ports and its rather weak fleet would never take part in a European war against the wishes of Great Britain." By contrast, France would take up arms as soon as Germany had been isolated and the participation of Great Britain had been secured.

Italy would hesitate and only act as it deemed appropriate, depending on the course of the battle and the position of Russia. The casus belli with Austria could easily be achieved, since a sufficient number of contentious issues already existed. Sprecher inferred that: "Even though war must not necessarily emanate from these circumstances, it is highly likely that sooner or later it will emanate from these very circumstances. How would Switzerland be affected by this forthcoming war? . . . I would rule out the idea that Germany would violate our territory of its own initiative, the simple reason being that such a move would have rather more disadvantages than advantages with respect to German operations." Nor could he see any desire for annexation on the part of either the German Reich or the Austro-Hungarians. It was not seen as reasonable that a monarchy with such a long tradition would annex a democracy. On the contrary, a strong Switzerland would be in the interests of the German Reich.

Sprecher did not rule out but considered it unlikely that France would attempt to annex Swiss territory, particularly Geneva or the Wallis. In any case, a French push would have to be expected through central Switzerland should a German-Franco war in the north stall and turn into a stalemate. In addition, Italy's desire to pursue its own annexationist goals could possibly trigger a French attack. In the event of an Italian attack, however, Austrian assistance could be expected. Sprecher drew the following conclusions from the threat situation at that time:

- The primary threat came from the west: France.
- A secondary threat was expected from the south: Italy.
- The most likely scenario was a war between Germany and France, and Austria against Italy, without Switzerland being threatened or involved.

Sprecher concluded his memorandum with a reference to "foreign assistance," a sensitive issue in the context of the Swiss policy of neutrality. What should Switzerland do if it had to defend itself? Should it look to an ally, or should it defend itself on its own? Should it seek an alliance with the manifestly stronger side, or act on a matter of principle with the enemy of the aggressor?

Sprecher rejected outright the option of an alliance with the strongest, something his predecessor, Arnold Keller, had judged to be the wiser course of action. Sprecher declared that an alliance with the primary opponent of the invader was the dictate of the moment, and that it would be "folly to hold back." Thus his decision about the then-precarious situation was in favor of the party that generally decided on foreign assistance. In the case of a defensive war Sprecher prepared a draft alliance agreement that he called "*Puncta-*

tions," just as Keller had previously. The draft was meant to provide the basis for a military link-up with the German Reich, with the potential addressee being Moltke. The draft was drawn up in the form of a simple checklist based on the same criteria and governed three major points: purpose, duration, and obligations.[32]

The complete version of the 1906 memorandum was submitted to the chief of the Military Department, Federal Councillor Eduard Müller, and the Federal president, Federal Councillor Ludwig Forrer. The comments Forrer attached to the memo indicate that he not only accepted Sprecher's basic ideas, but he even strengthened certain aspects. Forrer wrote: "In the event [of a war with France] we must see to it that everything is done to secure the French regions to the south and northwest of Geneva as the prize for victory." Sprecher, however, categorically rejected that demand.[33]

The February 1912 Memorandum

Sprecher's operational assessments of 1912 do not contain any fundamentally new ideas.[34] Based on the current situation, Sprecher assessed a threat by Germany as a "continued unlikely occurrence," and any such threat by Austria-Hungary as an "impossible occurrence."[35] His arguments were more or less based on a cost-benefit calculation. Germany would commit its strategic reserves in far less adverse terrain such as the northwest, but not in the southwest. Since circumstances had previously forced Austria to adopt a defensive posture vis-à-vis Italy, why then should it want to extend its front? Only if Italy won major victories against Austria would it start an offensive against Switzerland.

Its policy of neutrality committed Switzerland to remain strategically defensive. Therefore, only the violation of Swiss neutrality could create new realities. In any event, Switzerland was bound to wait until one of the potential enemies made a move. In any conceivable war in Europe, Switzerland would have to deploy its entire army. The strategic objective had to be to forestall any ideas its warring neighbors might entertain about violating Swiss borders. That would require the preparation in peacetime of three key factors:

- An efficient intelligence service.[36]
- A basic plan for the provision of an army—in other words, of a force potential for the protection of Swiss neutrality that was not directed against any of the neighboring states.
- Plans for the fortification of key areas of potential battles.

Furthermore, all conceivable arrangements would have to be made to ensure that Switzerland would not have to face the enemy on its own. Such a course of action had been possible in earlier times when the Swiss people defended themselves against mercenary troops. In modern warfare, however, where nation confronts nation in wars of mass armies, a smaller nation would be unable to persevere. Sprecher's intent was to halt any French attack (Deployment I) with the support of the Germans. The two Swiss divisions in the west would be tasked with conducting a sustained delaying action, thus securing the time needed for the deployment of the rest of the army behind the middle Aare. In an Italo-Austrian war (Deployment II), only the two mountain brigades (Mountain Brigade 18 in the Graubünden canton and Mountain Brigade 15 in Tessin) would initially be capable of preventing any Italian incursion. Depending on how the situation developed, additional forces could then be committed. The third scenario of concentric attacks by France and Italy (Deployment III) would unleash the dreaded war on two fronts. Yet the only additional precaution that Sprecher considered necessary was the shifting of the main effort to the southern front.

The early August 1914 writings of Theophil Sprecher served as the foundation upon which the Swiss Army Command based its operational considerations. These were adopted in an almost unaltered form by General Ulrich Wille, the supreme commander of the army, elected by Parliament.

The Intelligence Service Contacts

On 19 March 1921, the socialist daily *Berner Tagwacht,* under the lurid headline "Habsburg's Covert Attacks on Swiss Neutrality," was the first to inform the wider public about the alleged "secret negotiations" between Sprecher and the Central Powers.[37] Understandably, this explosive revelation immediately after World War I grew into what became known as the Sprecher Affair.

Recent studies on this subject show that Sprecher acted in keeping with his threat analyses of 1906 and 1912, and that all the measures he took to counter a potential attack were legitimate.[38] His main concern was to ensure that key information about imminent operations was received in time. To that end he received the assistance of the General Staffs of the Central Powers, which wanted to make certain that Switzerland remained neutral in the event of a European war and maintained its full defensive readiness in the event of an attack.

On 15 June 1907, the chief of the Intelligence Office (*Evidenzbüro*) in the Austrian General Staff, Colonel Eugen Hordlicka, had a confidential meeting with Sprecher. The latter subsequently reported to the chief of the Austrian General Staff, Franz Graf Conrad von Hötzendorf, that there was general agreement about the potential threat to Switzerland and Austria from the annexationist policy being pursued by Italy.[39] Sprecher, according to Hordlicka, explained that in the event of a violation of its neutrality by Italy, Switzerland would immediately side with Austria and take offensive action against Milan. Moreover, they also agreed upon an exchange of intelligence on Italy.

There is controversy as to the content of this conversation. It is unlikely that Sprecher actually said that much.[40] He most definitely did give Conrad a clear indication that the passage of Italian troops through Switzerland would be fiercely opposed and that Switzerland would not merely remain on the defensive. But neither an alliance with Austria nor an automatic association was implied. The establishment of the post of Austro-Hungarian military attaché and the resulting exchanges of intelligence, however, were the obvious results of this conversation.[41]

For the same purpose and at the same time, Sprecher held preliminary consultations with the chief of the German Great General Staff, Helmuth von Moltke, on the formation of an alliance in the event that Switzerland should be forced to defend itself.[42] Sprecher's assessment of the situation in 1906 served as the basis for this understanding. Moltke took the initiative, using the opportunity provided by Sprecher's attendance at the annual German Kaiser Maneuvers.[43] When the war broke out, Moltke on several occasions invoked this drafted treaty and considered it to be the equivalent of a valid agreement. In 1912, however, the French ambassador in Bern offered a more prudent assessment of Sprecher's contacts. He wrote to Raymond Poincaré: "My personal opinion is that this information is somewhat exaggerated. I consider a secret agreement between Switzerland and Austria directed against Italy as equally unlikely as an agreement between Switzerland and Germany that is directed against France. Highly likely, albeit in no way certain, is the exchange of views between the Swiss General Staff and the Austro-Hungarian General Staff, with the assurance by the Swiss government to its neighbors in the east to counter immediately and with full force any Italian attempt to use the roads leading through Swiss territory for an invasion of Tyrol."[44]

In his letter in his own defense to Federal Councillor Karl Scheurer on 22 March 1921, Sprecher emphasized that "neither the German nor the Austrian General Staffs had ever contemplated during their discussions a war scenario other than a defensive situation in the event of an enemy attack. Yet, they also clearly assured me that considering Switzerland's determination to protect its territory arduously, they would never include the invasion of our territory in their defensive planning unless the Swiss government submitted an explicit request for military assistance. As the Federal Council is aware, the written understandings reached with France during the war included a similar assurance by the French state, offered forthrightly and without reservation."[45]

Although France only offered that binding assurance in 1916, and not quite as readily as maintained by Sprecher, the statement is basically correct. All these circumstances must be taken into account if the controversy surrounding Sprecher's "foreign contacts" is to be seen in its correct light. To understand why he pursued the tentative statements made by Moltke, one must look at his threat analysis. Those who interpret the threat in a different way must of necessity arrive at different conclusions.

The Kaiser Maneuvers of 1912

Swiss officers were almost always welcomed by the armies of the neighboring states.[46] The respective host countries kept very few secrets from the Swiss. Cultural diversity has always been quite an advantage to Switzerland. German-Swiss citizens, such as Wille, Sprecher, Gertsch, or Karl Egli, were on particularly good terms with their German counterparts. Sprecher also had very good relations with Austria-Hungary. The French-Swiss officers, such as Alfred Audéoud, Bornand, Edouard Secrétan, or Chavannes, had easy access to the French.

There was generally less interest in paying return visits to Switzerland. There were, however, multiple occasions when officers of the two major alliance blocs wanted to familiarize themselves with the Swiss Army. Of special interest were the training courses of the medical services, of the Military Science Department at the Swiss Federal Institute of Technology in Zurich, and of the Marksmanship School at Walenstadt. Major maneuvers also regularly attracted an audience of illustrious international guests. On the occasion of a state visit and with large crowds in attendance, Kaiser Wilhelm II was present at a maneuver of the III Army Corps directed by Wille in eastern Switzerland. Contrary to expectations, no difficulties occurred during the visit. The kaiser was sometimes given an enthusiastic welcome in both the city of Zurich and in the countryside.

Against this background, Federal President Ludwig Forrer used the opportunity of his welcome speech to highlight the untroubled friendly relations between Switzerland and its neighboring nations, in particular the German Reich. Yet he also made a highly political statement: "We have the clear intent to protect our independence, our most precious asset, against any attack and to maintain our neutrality vis-à-vis anyone who does not respect it. A necessary and appropriate means of doing so is to maintain an effective and dexterous army."[47]

The kaiser appeared to have understood the message and after his maneuver visit he replied to his host: "To see that today's Swiss citizens, conscious of their glorious history, follow in their ancestors' footsteps as capable soldiers has greatly pleased my soldier's heart. The two days of the maneuver have made me realize that the Swiss Army shows an eager commitment all around, and that Swiss soldiers willingly accept great exertions for the love of their country, and that the Swiss Army is borne by the love of all Swiss citizens."[48]

While on the one hand the words of Kaiser Wilhelm II show his attempt at good neighborly relations with Switzerland, there is no denying their real military context, considering the primary intent behind his state visit. The actual purpose of the visit was to provide the "Kaiser and his senior officers with the opportunity to familiarize themselves with the effectiveness of the Swiss Army in military terms. It was vital to the German Army Command that in the event of a war with France the German left flank would be covered by the assurance that Swiss neutrality could be relied upon."[49] Taking the words of Wilhelm II as a benchmark, the German Army Command appeared to be satisfied with "its left flank."

Ante Portas

In his Bern speech of 1927, Sprecher for the first time admitted publicly that the kaiser's visit had provided him with the opportunity to hold intensive discussions with Moltke, and that the latter had informed him of the intentions of the German Army Command. Moltke had expressed his belief that Switzerland was serious about the protection of its neutrality and that it had the effective capabilities to ensure that security. Especially concerning Swiss neutrality, Moltke had promised that Swiss territory would be respected. In agreement with the Federal Council, Sprecher had affirmed that "Switzerland would not tolerate the invasion of its territory by any country, and would use its full force to defend itself."[50] Switzerland would initially be fighting on its own, and should the Federal Council or the commanding general of the field forces demand such, it would fight with the support of the aggressor's enemy. Moltke is said to have spontaneously answered: "I fear the French will not harm you." Despite this assessment, however, Moltke was willing to provide Switzerland with the key reports necessary to facilitate its timely mobilization.

As agreed, Sprecher on 29 July 1914 received a first warning message from Moltke: "My dear colleague, the situation is more than ever coming to a head, and the onset of the big and long-awaited drama may be imminent. What is the status of the situation? Will our agreements still be valid? Or are you of a different opinion now? I am curious to know whether you will be an actor or an audience. My *ante portas* assurance is still valid.[51] The maneuvers we had planned for the fall will presumably be brought forward and be conducted on a larger scale than intended, and blanks will definitely not be used. In any case I shall remain your well-disposed friend, Moltke."[52]

The *Ante Portas* telegram actually did arrive at Sprecher's private address in Bern on 31 July. Having been given this assurance, the chief of the Swiss General Staff then succeeded in convincing the reluctant Federal Council that the mobilization order for the entire army should be issued on 1 August.

On 2 August another important telegram reached the Swiss federal president. Minister Alfred de Claparède, the Swiss ambassador in Berlin, had been received by Moltke. The latter had assured him that "not a single German soldier shall set foot on Swiss territory, and not one inch of [your] country shall be occupied by German troops."[53] The German Reich considered Switzerland a friendly country and would be as accommodating as possible to ensure logistical support. Regrettably, Moltke could not give the same assurances for France. Recent reports from Upper Alsace suggested a possible violation of Swiss neutrality by French forces. Moltke linked this confidential information with an explicit offer of support by German forces in the event of a French attack.

When, in his 29 July message, Moltke mentioned to Sprecher that he was curious to know whether Switzerland in the event of war would be an actor or an audience and hinted at the alleged concentration of French troops along the Swiss border, he advanced unambiguous offers to his Swiss colleague. A telegram Moltke sent to the chief of the Foreign Office on 3 August 1914 reveals that he was serious about his offer, and that the agreement he had drafted with Sprecher in 1907 concerning a possible alliance was of great importance to him.[54] This document contained crucial statements Moltke made about his attitude toward Switzerland at the outbreak of the war. In response to the report that Switzerland had mobilized its troops and now feared the possible violation of its neutrality by French forces that had deployed along its western border, Moltke added precise instructions to the Foreign Office on how it should deal with Switzerland and upon which previous discussions its actions should be based. "It will be of great advantage to assure Switzerland that Germany would be willing to ensure Swiss neutrality by providing military assistance. In preparation for this eventuality, an alliance agreement with His Majesty has been drafted, single identical copies of which are in my hands and in the possession of the Swiss General Staff. The agreement under which the Swiss Army in its entirety will be placed under the [operational] control of the German Army Command needs only to be ratified and exchanged."

All of Moltke's statements indicate that he had accorded Switzerland only two possible roles in the great European struggle—as a small neutral state capable of defending itself, and as a friend of the German Reich. Switzerland would either provide the flank protection in the south for the German front, or it would enter the war as a German ally. Quite obviously the two chiefs of the respective General Staffs interpreted the agreements very differently. While Moltke obviously considered the mutual defense scenario a mere technicality, his Swiss colleague Sprecher did not share that opinion for the lack of the crucial criterion, a French attack on Switzerland. Moltke's attitude is a clear indication of the enormous importance the chief of the German General Staff attached to the agreements. This assessment also attests to Moltke's misjudgment of the political power structure in Switzerland, where only the national government had the authority to sign any alliance agreement.

Italian Troop Movements through Switzerland?

Of the Triple Alliance partners[55] the Kingdom of Italy was the most interested in the Swiss territory. Even before the conclusion of the agreement in May 1882, Italy was especially interested in the operational axis. As early as July 1876, the Italian General Staff considered conducting a joint operation with German forces against France as a means to eliminating Italy's most dangerous rival in the Mediterranean. For obvious reasons, the deployment of Italian forces to Alsace via the Swiss mountain passes was considered a viable course of action.[56]

Upon the establishment of the Triple Alliance, Italy consolidated the western option. France responded by reinforcing its border fortifications in the western Alps. This forced the Swiss to react. The establishment of fortifications along the Alpine crossings was intensely discussed in Swiss Army circles in the 1880s, as a means of countering the effects of the obvious or assumed French and Italian rivalry.

The Convention of 28 January 1888

The review of the Triple Alliance after its initial five-year period resulted in a shift in its emphasis. The tensions with Russia and the threat of a two-front war prompted the German Army Command to explore increasingly the options of Italian military assistance. At that moment in late December 1887 the Italian prime minister, Francesco Crispi, dispatched two General Staff officers to Berlin for discussions on the degree of cooperation in the event of a war with France.[57] The German side assigned Schlieffen, then a major general, to conduct the negotiations. The January 1888 convention, a fifty-two-page document, provided for the first time for the movement of Italian forces to the Upper Rhine. Three railroad routes were designated for the operation, and they all meticulously respected the Swiss borders.

- Cormons–Graz–Vienna (alternative route: Pragerhof–Kanizsa–Wiener Neustadt)–Wels–Passau[58]–Regensburg–Nuremberg–Heilbronn–Bruchsal–Germersheim–Strasbourg.
- Pontebba–Villach–Selzthal–Bischofshofen–Salzburg–Munich–Augsburg–Nördlingen–Stuttgart–Karlsruhe or Appenweier–Strasbourg–Schlettstadt.
- Ala–Innsbruck–Kufstein–Munich–Ulm–Radolfszell–Singen–Offenburg–Freiburg–Colmar.

The route from Innsbruck via Arlberg to Lindau and then to Ulm remained an option. The technical details were also identified.

In the event of a *casus foederis* the partners of the Triple Alliance counted on reinforcement by a maximum of six Italian corps and three cavalry divisions, all deployed in the south of Germany.[59] There was some concern that the slow pace of the Italian mobilization and the long-distance railroad movements would result in a time-consuming deployment. Germany did not expect to receive immediate assistance. Moreover, the Great General Staff doubted whether the assistance would ever materialize. This was because in the event that either the British or French navy threatened the Italian coastline the majority of the Italian forces would most likely remain within their country. Based on these assumptions, Italy would only be able to pin down a small number of French forces at best. Germany on its own would have to defeat the majority of the enemy forces.

The Convention of 1888 shows beyond doubt that the Triple Alliance had planned to move approximately two hundred thousand troops of the Italian Third Army to southern Germany solely through Austrian territory. The Austro-Hungarian Empire, however, had insisted on authorizing the transit requests on a case by case basis. Transiting through Switzerland was not considered by either the German or Austro-Hungarian General Staffs, and remained solely an Italian option.

Italy's Contingency Plans

One year after the Convention of 1888 was concluded with the two other partners of the Triple Alliance, Italian military planning staffs initiated a fresh review of the option of moving five to six army corps to southern Germany via Switzerland.[60] The basic assumption of the Italian General Staff was that the war would be conducted by the German Reich and Italy against France only. Austria and Russia would remain neutral in the conflict. That meant that Italian troop movements through the eastern Alps might not be possible. A further assumption was that Switzerland, apart from verbal protests, would not put up any resistance if Italian troops were merely passing through in a northerly direction. The Italian plans, however, were not accepted by the German side. Among others, Herbert Graf von Bismarck, state secretary in the Foreign Office, was strongly opposed to any such considerations.[61]

Review of the Agreements of 1890–1914[62]

The 4 May 1898 Convention[63] on the movement of Italian forces to southern Germany is limited to that topic only. Five corps and two cavalry divisions were to move through Austria and assemble on the right bank of the Rhine River between the seventh and twelfth day of the operation. The assembly point of the cavalry was established between Ottenheim and Kappel, in the region of Breisach. The two mobile divisions would then deploy immediately to the Saarburg area and Alsace (Colmar–Munster). The first two corps arriving between the fourteenth and twentieth mobilization days were to launch an attack from their deployment areas toward either Colmar–Munster or Schlettstatt–Markirch. Once the three remaining corps arrived in the Offenburg–Emmendingen–Freiburg–Breisach area between the sixteenth and twenty-eighth mobilization days, they would be held in reserve for commitment as the situation required. Along with the reviews, the chief of the Italian General Staff, General Tancredi Saletta, in 1898 ordered the preparation of a detailed plan that in the event of a German-Italian-French war would, if required, move Italian forces through Switzerland into Germany, thus violating Swiss neutrality.[64]

The chief of the German General Staff, Alfred von Schlieffen, had no confidence in the Italian plans. Writing in October 1898, he doubted "that Italy was able to do anything that would be of tangible use to us. If France were to leave behind two army corps with its reserve formations on the Alpine border, that would be the only advantage that we would likely get out of the alliance with Italy in the event of a war."[65]

On 21 December 1912 the Agreement of 28 January 1888 was voided. In a letter to the chief of the German General Staff, his Italian counterpart, General Alberto Pollio, wrote that under the current political circumstances Italy no longer was in a position to deploy its Third Army to Germany, not even a scaled-back force. Considering the turmoil in North Africa and the Balkans, that statement was not really surprising. It simply confirmed Schlieffen's assessment of 1898. The Italian government, however, renewed its assurance to its two partners in the Triple Alliance that in the event of war it would mobilize its entire land and naval forces. The Italian troops would attempt "to launch an intensive attack through the Alps in order to hold back the French forces or to pin down elements thereof on a large scale; or alternatively, land on the French coast in the shortest time possible in order to inflict as much damage as possible on the French in a concerted action by naval and land forces."[66]

At a conference held on 19 and 20 December 1913, the Italians reasserted their willingness to provide, as previously offered, at least three Italian corps and two cavalry divisions for a joint attack against France.[67] But the two parties agreed in mid-April 1914 to postpone the discussions on the details of their new cooperation until October 1914, when Italy would convene a meeting. That meeting, of course, never happened.[68]

As Moltke pointed out to Conrad, the fact that Italy had again clarified its position necessitated the consideration of two concrete consequences. On the one hand, Austria would now be able to deploy its entire force against Russia without having to leave security forces along the Italian border. On the other hand, the shortfall of Italian corps on the western front would have no implications for the deployment of German forces against Russia. Moltke wrote: "The forces to be deployed against France will not be reinforced at the expense of those forces that will be deployed against Russia. I hope to bring the operations to a successful conclusion with the disposition of forces as planned."[69] As it turned out later, Moltke's assumption was one of many inaccuracies and misunderstandings that carried disastrous consequences for the Central Powers' execution of the war in the fall of 1914.[70]

Summarizing to this point, it can be said that all the Italian plans for a passage through Switzerland, be it via the Wallis or the Buendner Passes, were merely rough operational outlines. The Germans in particular never fully supported such an operation. All relevant planning had been based on using only Austrian rail routes. It is, therefore, an untenable conclusion that the German protests of innocence during the period between the two world wars were meant to conceal their true intents.[71]

Other than Military Reasons for Systematically Excluding Switzerland from the German Attack Plans

Our observations so far lead to a very interesting revelation. Up until 1914, the German Army Command, and therefore Schlieffen and Moltke, seemed not to consider: (a) an attack on Switzerland, (b) the launching of an offensive against France via Switzerland, or (c) the demand that Switzerland authorize the passage of Italian troop movements to the German-French southern front. Within the German General Staff there was, consciously or unconsciously, a predisposition to assume an attitude of strict nonaggression toward Switzerland. The absoluteness of this attitude is surprising, and we will examine it further. The focus will be on the reasons beyond the operational military spectrum that motivated the German Army Command never to consider a southern envelopment, or any similar operation. The authors of this chapter wish to point out that we believe it unlikely that the German Army Command during the period prior to the outbreak of the war in 1914 took into consideration any fundamental financial or economic criteria that might have influenced their general decision to spare Switzerland. Such motives, of course, have been attributed to Germany's policy of preserving the integrity of Switzerland during World War II. There are no sources worth mentioning that support such a premise. In the German Reich prior to 1914, war plans were exclusively the responsibility of the Great General Staff. Apparently the political leadership, for whom economic factors might have played a greater role in their policy toward Switzerland, could only take cognizance of—but not exert any significant influence on—the military planning of the General Staff.[72] Since the politicians had no say in the military war plans, and the General Staff was thinking mainly in military terms when drawing up their plans, there arises the question of what other possible motives could have prompted the German Army leadership to rule out absolutely a southern envelopment via Switzerland, or the coercion of that country into granting the right of passage. There are two plausible explanations that can be considered together or separately, but which in the context of this chapter will only be touched upon, and therefore cannot lay claim to being a proper thesis.

"Tribal Kinship"—A Hindrance?

Following the state visit by Wilhelm II in the late summer of 1912, the German ambassador in Bern forwarded a detailed report on the kaiser's stay to Imperial Chancellor Theobald von Bethmann Hollweg. In his personal comments the German ambassador gave an enthusiastic appraisal of the visit and ascribed his reaction to the allegedly generally pro-German mood that prevailed in Switzerland.[73] The elaborations of the German ambassador in Bern support the assumption that the German Army leadership and the German elites regarded the Swiss people as a whole, and especially the German-Swiss, as being "German," or at least closely related to the Germans. They therefore, consciously or unconsciously, considered absurd any attack by the German military on Switzerland. That even the kaiser's mind worked in such ethnic categories can be seen in remarks he made about the "Germanic English people."[74] Since the kaiser considered the English-speaking British as kin, how would he then regard the German-speaking German-Swiss? Did the kaiser have a view of the world in which the Swiss and the German elites were such close kin that a military attack on the Swiss was unthinkable? Was it not the kaiser's intent to focus "all his political aspirations and thoughts" on "joining together all Germanic tribes in the world, above all those in Europe, into a yet stronger union"?[75]

This attempt at explaining the then-prevailing mentality in historic terms focuses on how Switzerland and the Swiss were perceived by the German government and military leaders prior to World War I. Since military leaders such as Moltke and Schlieffen rarely commented on this matter, the fundamental aspects of the German state of mind toward their Helvetic neighbors can be seen only through the statements of other decision makers.

It became apparent on several occasions that Kaiser Wilhelm II had a positive image of the Swiss and was in general amicably inclined toward Switzerland.[76] When around the turn of the century leading military and political circles in Switzerland were discussing the merits of entering into alliances in the event of a European war,[77] actions that would have resulted in direct connections with either the German Reich or the Habsburg Monarchy, the German kaiser tellingly remarked: "Very well, the utmost care should be applied to this delicate plant."[78] Such thinking was apparently widespread throughout influential circles in Germany, and every indication of Germanophilia by the Swiss was noted with appreciation.

It is essential to remember here that the widely discussed question of just how Germanophile or German the Swiss people and their leading military and political circles actually were prior to World War I is of relatively minor interest. Rather, the main point is how Germanophile or German the Swiss were *perceived to be* by the political and military leadership in Germany. It appears that the Pan-German League, which had close links with the leading circles in Germany, played an important role in shaping the image the Germans had of Switzerland.[79] For the representatives of the Pan-German League that gained especially considerable influence within the German colony in Switzerland, Germanism reflected a trans-border outlook on life, and was therefore not tied to holding German nationality.[80] Consequently, the League's focus of attention was on the situation of the German-speaking peoples and language families of Europe and the preservation of "Germanism."[81] With this in mind, the Pan-German League in 1903 changed its objectives on the occasion of the League Day held in the German town of Plauen. From then on the League considered one of its main objectives to be the "vitalization of the German national attitude, especially through the awareness and promotion of the racial and cultural solidarity of all sections of the Germanic people" and "the preservation of German folklore in Europe and overseas support for the latter in the parts of the world where its survival is under threat."[82]

Before the outbreak of World War I approximately 220,000 German nationals lived in Switzerland, the majority in the cities of Zurich and Basel.[83] In 1906 the chairman of the Pan-German League, the economist Ernst Hasse, made the following comment on the German expatriates: "The most important and worthwhile task of current and future German statecraft will be to make the German expatriates living along our borders into repatriates, that is to achieve their integration at the national level within the framework of German border policies.... The best settlement colonies that Germany can obtain are not those in the remote parts of the world, but those located in Europe along the borders of the German Reich. They need not be acquired and populated. We only should hold onto and revitalize with German blood and organize at the state level what was once won with German blood and through German nationhood."[84] Or as Max Mittler laconically commented, "the Swiss had the opportunity to become 'German repatriates.'"[85] In the same speech, however, Hasse had some reassuring words for the Swiss: "Incidentally, the huge number of Germans that immigrate to Switzerland constitutes the best reassurance for the preservation of Germanism in Switzerland, without the necessity for German border policies to safeguard that situation through the use of armed force." Therefore, the question seems justified as to whether in the perception of the Pan-German League there was actually a distinction between Germans living in Switzerland and the German-Swiss.

According to Klaus Urner, the ideological nationalist ideas of the Pan-Germans went so far as to consider resolutely the German-speaking Swiss as Germans, and to place them and not the German citizens living in Switzerland at the center of all efforts taken to strengthen Germanism in Switzerland.[86] It may well be assumed that these Pan-German patterns of thought largely coincided with those adopted by the leading military and political circles of the German Reich. The Pan-German nationalist way of thinking obviously had a strong influence on society during the latter period of the Wilhelmine era in general, and the leading German military circles in particular.[87] On the occasion of his state visit in 1912 Kaiser Wilhelm II did express his full approval of and great respect for a politically independent Switzerland during an official reception on 6 September. However, he also emphasized the intellectual, cultural, and social commonalities shared by Switzerland and the German Reich. "A large part of Switzerland adheres to the German intellectual and emotional mentality, and the exchange of intellectual and material goods between Switzerland and Germany is indeed as extensive as it is natural." And he concluded: "For nearly twenty-five years I have been a close friend of Switzerland, and for my part it shall remain that way."[88]

From today's perspective it is naturally very difficult to judge how the German public then would have reacted to a southern envelopment, which would have amounted to a military attack on Switzerland by the *Kaiserheer* (Imperial Army). There are, however, good reasons to assume that a war-like confrontation between the two "Alemannic neighbor nations" would have been unpopular in Germany. Considering the mood prevailing on the Prussian home front during the Prussian-Austrian War of 1866, it does not appear absurd to assume that the German military command would have to have been prepared for political protests at home in the event of an attack on Switzerland.[89] Yet the German military command was intent on avoiding domestic protest against the war, and therefore took great care not to alienate public support.[90]

Switzerland's Self-Defense Capability—A Hindrance?

There is another traditional pattern of thought that exists beyond Swiss borders and appears likewise to have influenced the German military command's deliberations. It is obvious that the German Army Command had throughout the years kept alive the image of "the Swiss mountain people with the ability to defend themselves." In 1898 Schlieffen spoke of the Swiss Army ready to go to war, a notion from which he concluded that a flank attack in the south would be highly inadvisable. In 1905 Schlieffen went even a step farther and wrote in his *Denkschrift* (Memorandum) as previously noted that a French attack on southern Germany via Switzerland would almost be desirable, since Germany then would acquire a much-needed ally who would pin down part of the French Army.

It may on the face of it be difficult to believe that the chief of the General Staff of the large German Imperial Army would actually have considered the small-numbered and under-equipped Swiss Army an essential ally.[91] Yet a basic, somewhat unreflective pattern of thought that associated Switzerland with terms such as "ability of self-defense" and "tradition of warriors" is recognizable. In his previously noted speech in Bern on 6 September 1912, Kaiser Wilhelm II said: "Since time immemorial the inhabitants of the Swiss mountains have been effective and robust fighters. When toward the latter days of the Middle Ages the glory of knighthood was fading, the brave Swiss became the role model for the creation, equipment, and training of the Landsknechts, which were the first German foot soldiers. For it is well known that the Swiss infantry won glorious victories on many battlefields."[92]

To summarize to this point, we can say that the basic patterns of prevailing thought about Switzerland among German military leaders contained elements of the cluster of motivations that caused those in the leading circles and the kaiser to refrain from seriously contemplating an attack on France launched by crossing Swiss territory. Nationalist patterns of thought and strongly felt sociocultural ties reinforced by traditional images of truculent medieval Swiss warriors played a part in avoiding any consideration of armed conflict with Switzerland. Apparently the Germans entertained no comparable thoughts about Belgium.

The scope of this chapter allows only a thesis-like summary of these points, while a detailed examination remains a research requirement. The theses presented here, however, appear to stand up to the initial examinations. Hence, it is appropriate once again to refer to the German ambassador in Bern, who in his report of 9 September 1912 to Bethmann Hollweg concluded: "The visit His Majesty paid to Switzerland on the occasion of the maneuvers made evident and further strengthened the ties of amicable trust that exist between His Majesty and the Swiss Army, as well as the Swiss people. While these ties will have positive effects in times of peace, they will bear excellent fruit in the form of the Swiss 'Watch in the Jura Mountains' in the event of a Franco-German war."[93]

Assessment

The preparation and execution of the Schlieffen-Moltke Plan make it appear most unlikely, despite the existence of only a few sources, that before the war Germany had ever planned to violate Swiss territory. This conclusion is supported by at least three reasons: one military, the second political, and the third sociocultural.

- The unfavorable military cost-benefit calculation for a southern envelopment of the western front owing to the Swiss army's border defenses, the adverse terrain, the awkwardly eccentric direction of attack that would prevent the swift destruction of the French and British forces, and the dubious nature of the agreed-upon Italian support were instrumental factors in the decision against a southern envelopment. Moltke reckoned that Switzerland would adopt a sympathetically neutral attitude because of the personal understandings he had reached with the chief of the Swiss General Staff, Sprecher. Moltke particularly relied on the jointly drafted alliance covenant. He hoped that Switzerland would voluntarily enter the war on the side of the Central Powers, which would be the best-case scenario for Germany.
- Berlin had no doubts about Swiss neutrality and its sustainable defensive capability to counter any aggressor. Respecting Swiss neutrality in August 1914 was in the best interest of all parties. None of the parties involved in World War I could afford to drive Switzerland into the arms of the enemy. This realization, however, did not by any means prevent them from conducting a brutal economic war against that neutral country.[94]
- This study has shown definitively that the friendly relations between the Central Powers and the German-Swiss majority in Switzerland played a key part in Germany's refraining from planning an attack on its neighbor. In general, both sides were well disposed toward each other. This factor appears to be very important and has previously been given insufficient attention.

To highlight the special importance of the attitude that the leading German politicians had assumed toward Switzerland before the beginning of World

War I, and to show, while consciously risking a slight exaggeration, how far any military intervention in Switzerland was from their intentions in 1914, we can juxtapose a statement from World War II against one from the World War I period. In an assessment of the importance of Switzerland in terms of military operations during World War II, Colonel General Franz Halder during the early postwar days offered the following dry comment: "The thought that advantages could be gained by exploiting the northern parts of Switzerland as an operating theater for a major envelopment operation is absurd. If Switzerland were to defend its territory with military means, it could indeed be forced to clear the northern Swiss lowlands for an operation that was to be conducted either in the east-west or in the opposite direction. Yet, under these circumstances, the assault troops would never have had the operational freedom to conduct a breakthrough in this area. Withdrawing the defense of Swiss territory into the Swiss mountains would have forced any aggressor to allocate strong forces to secure the southern flank to an extent that such a military undertaking ... would have meant an irresponsible dissipation of forces."[95]

The prevailing tone during the summer of 1914 was completely different. On 3 August the chief of the Swiss General Staff, Sprecher, received a cordial letter from his German counterpart, Moltke, who wrote the following amicable words: "The die is cast. It becomes ever more apparent that the outrageous war forced upon us by our enemies and toward which they have systemically and continuously worked, has one objective: the destruction of Germany. But the Germanic race is sound.... With trust in God, we will face the outcome. It is still uncertain how hostilities will evolve. You know that we would appreciate fighting alongside the brave Swiss forces."[96]

Notes

1. Theophil Sprecher von Bernegg, *Fragen der Schweizerischen Landesverteidigung nach den Erfahrungen in der Zeit des Weltkrieges* (Zurich, 1928), 30.

2. In 1938 Edgar Bonjour wrote: "The strategic location of Switzerland exposes the country to a high degree to the danger of an enemy passage through its territory in the event of an outbreak of a central European war. Every combat unit would be tempted to threaten the enemy through the Confederation's territory from the flanks and the rear. If the Swiss border is not heavily guarded, self-preservation would force the warring parties to a military operation or at least to take precautionary measures in Switzerland to cover their exposed flanks and to get ahead of the enemy." Edgar Bonjour et al., *Geschichte der Schweiz* (Zurich, 1938), 634. (English translation: *A Short History of Switzerland* [Oxford, 1952].)

3. Hans Rudolf Fuhrer, *Die Schweizer Armee im Ersten Weltkrieg: Bedrohung,*

Landesverteidigung und Landesbefestigung, 3rd ed. (Zurich, 2003); Hans Rudolf Fuhrer, *General Ulrich Wille: Vorbild den einen—Feindbild den andern* (Zurich, 2003).

4. *Enzyklopädie Erster Weltkrieg,* ed. Gerhard Hirschfeld, Gerd Krumeich, and Irina Renz (Paderborn, 2003), 826f.

5. Holger Afflerbach, "Die militärische Planung des Deutschen Reiches im Ersten Weltkrieg," in *Der Erste Weltkrieg: Wirkung, Wahrnehmung, Analyse,* ed. Wolfgang Michalka (Munich: Military History Research Institute, 1994), 280–318, specifically page 282. Including, in this respect: Martin Raschke, *Der politisierende Generalstab: Die friderizianischen Kriege in der amtlichen deutschen Militärgeschichtsschreibung 1890 bis 1914,* Einzelschriften zur Militärgeschichte, 36 (Freiburg i.Br., 1993).

6. Cf. in particular the work by Annika Mombauer: *Helmuth Moltke and the Origins of the First World War* (Cambridge, 2001), 76.

7. Jehuda L. Wallach, *Das Dogma der Vernichtungsschlacht: Die Lehren von Clausewitz und Schlieffen und ihre Wirkungen in zwei Weltkriegen* (Frankfurt a.M., 1967), 89.

8. Ibid., 142f.

9. Cf. *Der Weltkrieg 1914–1918,* vol. 1, *Die Grenzschlachten im Westen,* ed. Reichsarchiv (Berlin, 1925), 49–65.

10. Ibid., 58.

11. Wilhelm Dieckmann, "Der Schlieffenplan," unpublished manuscript, Bundesarchiv/Militärarchiv (Federal Archives, Military Division—BA/MA), W10/50220. The preliminary work for the German *Reichsarchiv* includes some interesting additions, especially as the work helped preserve original documents. Citations by Schlieffen have been quoted from this study.

12. *Der Weltkrieg 1914–1918,* vol. 1, *Die Grenzschlachten im Westen,* ed. Reichsarchiv (Berlin, 1925), 60.

13. Cf. Gerhard Ritter, *Der Schlieffenplan: Kritik eines Mythos* (Munich, 1956).

14. Reference material on all countries worldwide, 1906, BA/MA, N 78/24.

15. "Gründe für die Entstehung und den Einmarsch in Belgien," expert statement by Major General von Dommes, BA/MA, N 78/34.

16. When Lieutenant Colonel Picard fell ill in Namur, the General Staff rides in 1913 (headed by General Tauflier) were compromised.

17. Cf. *Les Armées Françaises dans la Grande Guerre* (AFGG), vol. 1, *La guerre de mouvement (opérations antérieures au 14 novembre 1914)* (Paris: Ministère de la Guerre. État-major de l'armée-Service historique, 1922).

18. Michel, "Concentration et plan d'opérations, 10 février 1911" (written in July 1910), in AFGG, vol. 1, *Annexe,* no. 3, pages 7–11.

19. Joseph Joffre, *Mémoires du Maréchal Joffre (1910–1917)* (Paris, 1932), 1:20f.

20. 150,000 army, 130,000 troops at the fortifications, and 60,000 support troops.

21. AFGG, vol. 1, *Annexe,* no. 10, page 49. Original quotation: "En somme, l'armée suisse sur pied de guerre, comprend un noyau solide d'hommes exercés et pourvu d'un matériel moderne, représentait une force susceptible de faire respecter le territoire de la Confédération helvétique."

22. Étude du Plan d'opération contre l'Allemagne, Service Historique de l'Armée de Terre, 7N1771. Dossier: "Renseignements sur les plans d'opération et de concentration des Armées Étrangères." Cf. Adolf Lacher, *Die Schweiz und Frankreich vor dem Ersten Weltkrieg* (Basel, Stuttgart, 1967), 180.

23. "Pageot an Affaires Étrangères/Cabinet du Ministre de la Guerre, 28.7.1914," 1745, in AFGG, vol. 1, *Annexe*, no. 13, page 52.

24. Original quotation: "sachant la Suisse résolue à s'y opposer avec toutes ses forces."

25. "Will Switzerland mobilize its forces? Will the Swiss move forces to Basel and monitor the French and German borders?" AFGG, vol. 1, *Annexe*, no. 10, page 41.

26. Original quotation: "L'Italie a fait une déclaration officielle de neutralité complète."

27. "Théâtre d'opérations des côtes et de Russie: Coopération éventuelle à l'offensive allemande des Italiens et des Autrichiens. Pays neutres. 4.8.1914, 1630," in AFGG, vol. 1, *Annexe*, no. 10, pages 48ff., original quotation: "afin d'éventer toute offensive italienne par la Suisse, ou tout transport de troupes italiennes vers l'Allemagne du Nord."

28. Joffre therefore issued the unambiguous order: "Until ordered on the contrary, our troops are strictly and explicitly forbidden to penetrate Belgian territory, be it even just patrols or single troopers. Likewise, aircraft are strictly and explicitly forbidden to pass [over] Belgian territory." AFGG, vol. 1, *Annexe*, no. 10, page 49.

29. In his order to the First Army of 4 August 1914 at 1630 hours Joffre wrote: "There will be no attack attempted on the Basel railway station. The St Louis railway station and the Hüningen bridge may be destroyed should the army commander consider this necessary. In that case he would have to obtain a new order from the supreme commander. The 155 mm artillery may take part in the operation."

30. Sprecher an Landesverteidigungskommission (LVK), Mobilmachung und Aufmärsche, 15.2.1906, Bundesarchiv Bern (BAr), E 27/12759 B. Cf. Hans Rapold, *Der Schweizerische Generalstab = L'état-major Général Suisse*, vol. 5, *Zeit der Bewährung? Die Epoche um den Ersten Weltkrieg 1907–1924* (Basel, Frankfurt a.M., 1988), 122.

31. Sprecher, Memorial: Die militärpolitische Lage der Schweiz und die Aufmärsche der schweizerischen Armee, Dezember 1906, BAr, E 27/12761. Cf. Fuhrer, *Die Schweizer Armee im Ersten Weltkrieg*, 59ff.; Rapold, *Der Schweizerische Generalstab*, 122f.; Daniel Sprecher, *Generalstabschef Theophil Sprecher von Bernegg: Eine kritische Biographie* (Zurich, 2000), 123f.

32. According to Sprecher the following three fundamental issues and their subtasks had to be clarified in the event of an attack: 1. Purpose: the engagement of the common enemy and a peace agreement on terms as favorable as possible; 2. Duration: the conduct of operations up to the peace agreement; 3. Obligations: the deployment of the entire army, assignment of commanders to our army, the reciprocal exchange of liaison officers as authorized military representatives to foreign supreme commands, the deployment of the Swiss Army within and possibly also out-

side Swiss territory, the demarcation of a defense line, the immediate dispatch of auxiliary forces, the designation of a Swiss redoubt (St. Gotthard and St. Maurice shall always remain Swiss), the organization of logistics, and the agreement on diplomatic assistance in the process of concluding a peace agreement.

33. Secret handwritten letter from Sprecher to Federal Councillor Forrer, 23 January 1907, BAr, E 27/12761. Cf. Rapold, *Der Schweizerische Generalstab,* 123.

34. Fuhrer, *Die Schweizer Armee im Ersten Weltkrieg,* 64–68.

35. "Any border violations on the part of Austria should be considered as quasi-impossible, and as highly unlikely any such violations on the part of Germany."

36. Sprecher was convinced that a nation with a mobilization army needed a reliably working intelligence service to be ready in due time. Such a service would have to be already established in peacetime.

37. *Berner Tagwacht* of 19 and 23 March and 6 April 1921. The reporting was based on a letter by the *K.u.K.*'s Colonel Hordlicka addressed to Conrad. Cf. Edgar Bonjour, *Geschichte der Schweizerischen Neutralität: Vier Jahrhunderte eidgenössische Aussenpolitik,* 4th rev. ed., vol. 2 (Basel, 1970), 101ff.

38. Cf. Fuhrer, *Die Schweizer Armee im Ersten Weltkrieg*; Sprecher, *Generalstabschef Theophil Sprecher von Bernegg.*

39. Cf. Sprecher, *Generalstabschef Theophil Sprecher von Bernegg,* 195f.

40. On several occasions Italian diplomats had mentioned Sprecher's Austrian contacts vis-à-vis the Swiss government. It was Federal Councillor Ludwig Forrer who vehemently defended Sprecher by saying that he was not a "talkative individual," and that contacts with Austrian generals "are conceivable, but absolutely irrelevant." Notes by the vice president of the Federal Council, Ludwig Forrer, on a conversation he had with the former Italian prime minister, Luigi Luzzatti, on 4 August 1911, in *Diplomatische Dokumente der Schweiz 1848–1945,* vol. 5, *1904–1914,* ed. Herbert Lüthy and Georg Kreis (Bern, 1983), file 292, page 646f.

41. Cf. Peter Schubert, *Die Tätigkeit des k.u.k. Militärattachés in Bern* (Osnabrück, 1980).

42. For the General Staff agreements of the prewar period, see Rapold, *Der Schweizerische Generalstab,* 158ff.

43. Otto Freiherr von Berlepsch reported this fact to Conrad in June 1908. Sprecher deemed the violation of Swiss neutrality an event so unlikely that he also entered into negotiations with the German General Staff. Schubert, *Die Tätigkeit des k.u.k. Militärattachés in Bern,* 7.

44. Jean-Baptiste Paul Beau to Poincaré, 3 March 1912 (kindly made available by Frau Martina Wille).

45. Sprecher to Scheurer on 22 March 1921, BAr, E 27/12837. Cf. Sprecher, *Generalstabschef Theophil Sprecher von Bernegg,* 201f.

46. Cf. BAr, E 27/7417, 1–3, and Rapold, *Der Schweizerische Generalstab,* 116.

47. In *Diplomatische Dokumente der Schweiz 1848–1945,* vol. 5, file 327, page 704.

48. Ibid., page 705.

49. Sprecher, *Fragen der Schweizerischen Landesverteidigung nach den Erfahrungen in der Zeit des Weltkrieges*, 8. Cf. Sprecher, *Generalstabschef Theophil Sprecher von Bernegg*, 271.

50. Sprecher, *Fragen der Schweizerischen Landesverteidigung nach den Erfahrungen in der Zeit des Weltkrieges*, 8.

51. This arrangement was made on the occasion of the kaiser's visit. The *Ante Portas* key report referred to the imminent outbreak of war.

52. Moltke to Sprecher, 29 July 1914, Sprecher Archives, Maienfeld, first published in Fuhrer, *Die Schweizer Armee im Ersten Weltkrieg*, 116. Cf. Sprecher, *Generalstabschef Theophil Sprecher von Bernegg*, 307.

53. De Claparède to [Arthur] Hoffmann, 2 August 1914, in *Diplomatische Dokumente der Schweiz 1848–1945*, vol. 6, page 24.

54. Copy of the telegram dated 3 August 1914 in Persönliche Dokumente, Sprecher Archives, Maienfeld.

55. Triple Alliance: Holger Afflerbach, *Der Dreibund: Europäische Grossmacht und Allianzpolitik vor dem ersten Weltkrieg* (Vienna, 2002).

56. Cf. Hans Eberhart, "Zwischen Glaubwürdigkeit und Unberechenbarkeit: Politisch-militärische Aspekte der schweizerisch-italienischen Beziehungen 1861–1915" (Ph.D. diss., University of Zurich, 1985), 60ff.; Alberto Rovighi, *Un secolo di relazioni militari tra Italia e Svizzera 1851–1961* (Rome, 1987), 218.

57. Afflerbach, *Der Dreibund*, 266f. Further technical arrangements followed soon in the spring of the same year. Copy of the arrangements, 14 April 1888, with an addendum dated 31 October 1891, Österreichisches Staatsarchiv, Abteilung Kriegsarchiv (KA), Generalstab Operationsbüro (Gstb OpB) 747, pages 114–138. Cf. Eberhart, "Zwischen Glaubwürdigkeit und Unberechenbarkeit," 64; Rovighi, *Un secolo di relazioni militari tra Italia e Svizzera*, 91. The arrangements are outlined in both studies. The document held at the Kriegsarchiv (War Archives) in Vienna appears to be unknown.

58. Passau, Salzburg, and Kufstein were the places at which the German Railway Administration assumed control.

59. Within four days of the mobilization, railway routes 2 and 3 were operational, and within nine days railway route 1 was running. The movement plans were as follows: from Cormons 225 trains for two army corps; from Pontebba 192 trains for 1½ army corps and one cavalry division; from Ala 206 trains for 1½ army corps and one cavalry division.

60. The strength of the Italian corps corresponded approximately with that of the formations that were to be moved through Austria under the convention of 1888. The agreement also provided for three movement routes: Novara–Arona–Domodossola–Simplon–Brig–Lake Geneva or Jura; Milano–Como–Airolo–Gotthard–Arth–Goldau–Rhine or Bern–Lake Geneva or Jura; Bergamo–Colico–Chiavenna–Splügen–Rhine Valley.

61. Johannes Lepsius, Albrecht Mendelssohn Bartholdy, and Friedrich Thimme, eds., *Die Grosse Politik der Europäischen Kabinette 1871–1914: Sammlung der Diplo-*

matischen Akten des Auswärtigen Amtes, vol. 4, *Die Dreibundmächte und England* (Berlin, 1922), doc. 841, page 225.

62. Cf. Conventions of 12 October 1893, 4 May 1898, 15 May 1903, 14 June 1907, 27 November 1909, 8 July 1911, 18 February 1912, 19–20 December 1913, 4 February 1914, as amended as of 10 April 1914, Österreichisches Staatsarchiv, KA, Gstb OpB, sheet 1-594.

63. Konvention betr. Transport königlich italienischer Truppen durch Österreich-Ungarn und Süddeutschland nach dem Oberrhein (Convention Governing the Movement of Royal Italian Forces through Austria-Hungary and Southern Germany to the Upper Rhine), ibid., box 737.

64. Afflerbach, *Der Dreibund,* 519.

65. Dieckmann, "Der Schlieffenplan," BA/MA, W10/50220.

66. Pollio to Moltke, 21 December 1912, Österreichisches Staatsarchiv, KA, Gstb OpB, pages 437–562.

67. Transport der für den mitteleuropäischen Kriegsschauplatz bestimmten italienischen Streitkräfte im Dreibundkriege (Movement of the Italian Armed Forces Earmarked for the Central European Theater of War in a Triple Alliance War), minutes of the meetings held on 19 and 20 December 1913, ibid., microfilm 544.

68. Agreements of 4 February 1914, Colonel Johann Straub, Lieutenant Colonel Wilhelm Groener, and Lieutenant Giulio Fiastri, as amended on 10 April 1914, ibid., 595–664.

69. Moltke to Conrad, 2 January 1913, ibid., 437–562.

70. Cf. Diether Degreif, *Operative Planungen des k.u.k. Generalstabes für einen Krieg in der Zeit vor 1914 (1880–1914)* (Wiesbaden, 1985); Gerhard Ritter, "Die Zusammenarbeit der Generalstäbe Deutschlands und Österreich-Ungarns vor dem ersten Weltkrieg," in *Zur Geschichte und Problematik der Demokratie, Festgabe für Hans Herzfeld* (Berlin, 1958), 523–549; Norman Stone, "Moltke-Conrad: Relations between the Austro-Hungarian and the German General Staffs, 1909–1914," *Historical Journal* 9 (1966): 201–228.

71. Cf. Eberhart, "Zwischen Glaubwürdigkeit und Unberechenbarkeit," 13.

72. *Enzyklopädie Erster Weltkrieg,* 819. Cf. John C. G. Röhl, *Kaiser, Hof und Staat: Wilhelm II. und die deutsche Politik* (Nördlingen, 2002), 180.

73. Depesche Nr. 52 der Kaiserlich Deutschen Gesandtschaft (Dispatch to Bethmann Hollweg, dated 9 September 1912), copy in the possession of the Military Academy, Zurich. We thank the German embassy in Bern for the files that were retrieved by chance.

74. "Hence, the Germanic English would fight 'with the French and Russians' against their kin." Röhl, *Kaiser, Hof und Staat,* 188.

75. Röhl, *Kaiser, Hof und Staat,* 212. See also: Klaus Urner, *Die Deutschen in der Schweiz: Von den Anfängen der Kolonienbildung bis zum Ausbruch des Ersten Weltkrieges* (Frauenfeld, 1976), chapter 3.1, "Deutschschweizer oder Deutsche? Ursprünge einer Existenzfrage."

76. Max Mittler, *Der Weg zum Ersten Weltkrieg: Wie neutral war die Schweiz? Kleinstaat und europäischer Imperialismus* (Zurich, 2003), 328.

77. Cf. Sprecher, *Generalstabschef Theophil Sprecher von Bernegg,* 163ff.

78. Bonjour, *Geschichte der Schweizerischen Neutralität,* 76.

79. Röhl, *Kaiser, Hof und Staat,* 193f.; Rainer Hering, *Konstruierte Nation: Der Alldeutsche Verband 1890 bis 1939* (Hamburg, 2003), 128.

80. Mittler, *Der Weg zum Ersten Weltkrieg: Wie neutral war die Schweiz?,* page 342; "Zur Geschichte der deutschen Kolonie in der Schweiz," in Urner, *Die Deutschen in der Schweiz.*

81. Michael Peters, *Der Alldeutsche Verband am Vorabend des Ersten Weltkrieges (1908–1914)* (Frankfurt a.M., 1992), 15.

82. Hering, *Konstruierte Nation,* 124. The founding assembly of the All-German Union (Alldeutscher Verband) on 9 April 1891 had similar objectives on its agenda. Cf. Peters, *Der Alldeutsche Verband am Vorabend des Ersten Weltkrieges,* 19.

83. Bonjour, *Geschichte der Schweizerischen Neutralität,* 147.

84. Ernst Hasse, *Deutsche Grenzpolitik* (Munich, 1906), 169ff.

85. Mittler, *Der Weg zum Ersten Weltkrieg,* 333.

86. Urner, *Die Deutschen in der Schweiz,* 68ff.

87. Hering, *Konstruierte Nation,* 171, 180ff.

88. Speeches by the Chairman of the Political Department, Ludwig Forrer, and the Kaiser on the occasion of the visit by the German Kaiser Wilhelm II, on 6 September 1912, in *Diplomatische Dokumente der Schweiz 1848–1945,* vol. 5, file 327, page 704f.

89. Cf. Thomas Nipperdey, *Deutsche Geschichte 1800–1866: Bürgerwelt und starker Staat* (Munich, 1983), 782. "The imminent war [against the Habsburg monarchy] was unpopular. Public meetings and proclamations denouncing the fratricidal war took place everywhere, even in Prussia there was no enthusiasm for a war." We would like to thank Dr. Peter Mertens for this information.

90. Holger Afflerbach, *Falkenhayn: Politisches Denken und Handeln im Kaiserreich* (Munich, 1994), 157.

91. For a negative Swiss assessment of their own military capabilities at the beginning of World War I, see Fuhrer, *Die Schweizer Armee im Ersten Weltkrieg,* 526.

92. Speeches by the Chairman of the Political Department, Ludwig Forrer, and the Kaiser on the occasion of the visit by the German Kaiser Wilhelm II, on 6 September 1912, in *Diplomatische Dokumente der Schweiz 1848–1945,* vol. 5, file 327, page 704f.

93. Dispatch No. 52 by the Kaiserlich Deutschen Gesandtschaft, dated 9 September 1912, to Bethmann Hollweg.

94. Hans Rudolf Fuhrer, "Lehren aus der Geschichte: Die Fehler der schweizerischen Wirtschaftspolitik im Ersten Weltkrieg," International Conference for Military History, Rabat, Morocco, 2004.

95. Halder to Noack (BA/MA), 14 November 1952, cited in Hans Rudolf Fuhrer, *Spionage gegen die Schweiz: Die geheimen deutschen Nachrichtendienste gegen die Schweiz im Zweiten Weltkrieg 1939–1945* (Frauenfeld, 1982), 136, n. 23.

96. Fuhrer, *Die Schweizer Armee im Ersten Weltkrieg,* 118.

The British Army, Its General Staff, and the Continental Commitment, 1904–1914

Hew Strachan

After the First World War, Lord Haldane, anxious to refurbish his reputation as secretary of state for war between 1905 and 1912, published a self-justificatory memoir, *Before the War* (1920). His army reforms were, he claimed, an integrated whole, unified by a single strategic conception. That conception was "how to mobilize at a place of assembly to be opposite the Belgian frontier, a force calculated as adequate . . . to make up for the inadequacy of the French armies."[1] This was the Continental commitment, and its origins were dated to January 1906, the moment in the First Morocco Crisis when the foreign secretary, Sir Edward Grey, impressed upon the War Office the need to bolster French resolve by demonstrating Britain's readiness to provide military support. Joint staff talks began in December 1905 and continued until May 1906.[2]

Haldane's claim was both a vindication and an accusation. If it was substantiated, he was the man who had presciently prepared the British Army for the greatest war in which it had ever been engaged. But at the same time he exposed his country to A.J.P. Taylor's charge that in 1914 the foreign policies of the European powers had been hijacked by General Staff planning, with the result that Europe had gone "to war by railway timetable." In any literal sense that statement—untrue even for Germany and Austria-Hungary—was inapplicable to Britain. But what was true was that both the cabinet and Parliament had assumed on 2 and 3 August 1914 that Britain's principal effort in the war on which they were about to embark would be maritime. The argument that Britain's policy in the event of war was determined by the army's notion of strategy was not without foundation.

Haldane's interpretation and chronology were accepted by the first generation of scholars to have access to the papers, Nicholas d'Ombrain and J. McDermott.[3] The former believed that the Royal Navy had ceased to exercise its preponderance over the Committee of Imperial Defence in 1905–1906, and that thereafter the army's General Staff had usurped the policy-making function of both. Relieved of the threat of a Russian attack on India, first because such an invasion was logistically impossible and second—after 1907—because of the diplomatic settlement between the two powers, the army had latched onto Germany as the justification for its existence. For d'Ombrain the Anglo-French staff talks in 1905–1906 did at least provide a policy-making pivot for an argument that was largely driven by bureaucratic politics. McDermott took this point even further than d'Ombrain. He contended that the shift from expecting to fight Russia in India to planning a war with Germany in Europe had begun in 1904, even before the First Morocco Crisis.

McDermott published his article in 1974. In the same year John Gooch's *The Plans of War: The General Staff and British Military Strategy c. 1900–1916* not only examined the creation of the General Staff as an institution but also drew attention to those of its plans that were never implemented as well as those that were. Gooch abandoned McDermott's vocabulary of revolution for that of gradualism, dubbing the period 1902–1907 as one of "strategic reorientation." For him 1910, not 1906, let alone 1904, was when this process of change hardened. In August of that year Sir Henry Wilson was appointed director of military operations. "Wilson's drive, enthusiasm and complete conviction about the necessity to render effective land support to France were to provide the stimulus to move military strategy on from the period of consideration and of deciding between alternatives to that of detailed planning for action."[4] In the foreword to his collection of essays, *The Prospect of War* (1981), Gooch was even more forthright in condemning the work of d'Ombrain and McDermott.[5]

Edward Spiers's study of Haldane as an army reformer, published in 1980, endorsed Gooch's view. Spiers dismissed Haldane's claim that he had set about the creation of a British Expeditionary Force (BEF) in 1906 with a view to fulfilling the army's continental commitment in 1914. The BEF, Spiers insisted, was a force designed for intervention anywhere in the world, not just in Europe. It was the solution to a long-standing dilemma: the pressure to scatter British regular forces around the empire in penny packets as opposed to the need to create a central strategic reserve. At least until 1907 and the Anglo-Russian entente, and even implicitly thereafter, the continent for which the BEF seemed to be destined was Asia, not Europe, and its putative opponent Russia rather than Germany. Spiers, like Gooch, pinpointed Henry Wilson's arrival as director of military operations in August 1910 as the moment of change.[6]

Gooch and Spiers were making explicit a claim bruited from the moment Charles Callwell published his revealing and in some ways indiscreet biography of Wilson in 1927. Callwell had quoted freely from Wilson's diaries. A passionate man, a Unionist and a Francophile, Wilson was indeed a forceful advocate of the continental commitment as it came to be implemented—that is to say, direct support for the French Army with its implicit subordination of the BEF to French suzerainty, rather than an independent British operation in Belgium based on Antwerp. One of the first academic scholars in the field, J. E. Tyler, in *The British Army and the Continent 1904–1914* (1938), had accepted elements of the Haldane argument by beginning his study with the plans of 1906, but had pointed out that two continental options rather than one were in play between 1906 and 1910, and that what Wilson had achieved was a definite commitment to France rather than to Belgium as the basis for General Staff planning. Tyler declared that Wilson's enthusiasm for France "verged on the fanatical."[7]

For Tyler, as for Gooch and Spiers, the meeting of the subcommittee of the Committee of Imperial Defence (CID) on 23 August 1911 was when the French version of the continental commitment was accepted as British strategy. Asked to present the army's mobilization plans in the midst of the Second Morocco Crisis, Henry Wilson displayed his familiarity with French thinking while dismissing the Belgian option. Moreover, he left his naval opposite number reeling. The exposition of the First Sea Lord, Sir Arthur Wilson, was—according to Henry Wilson himself—"pitiful."[8] Gooch described the meeting as a "victory" for Wilson. The prime minister, Herbert Asquith, committed Britain to a military rather than a naval strategy, with the result that the latter was no longer an option when war broke out in 1914.[9]

That was not the conclusion of Maurice Hankey, the secretary of the CID, who wrote to the former First Sea Lord, Sir John "Jackie" Fisher, on the day following the meeting of 23 August 1911: "The great point is that no decision was arrived at."[10] D'Ombrain pointed out that Asquith had assured Reginald McKenna, the First Lord of the Admiralty, that he personally opposed a continental strategy, and that it was only a suggestion, not a settled policy.[11] The CID's attention between 1911 and 1914 was focused not on the BEF and its possible deployment, but on the Royal Navy, blockade, and home defense.[12] The only clear outcomes from its meeting on 23 August were the replacement of McKenna as First Lord of the Admiralty by Winston Churchill, and the latter's brief to create a naval General Staff. Henry Wilson's performance had scotched the navy's lingering advocacy of amphibious warfare, but it had done so at the price of reinvigorating the search for a more effective naval strategy. It was the 1912 Anglo-French Naval Agreement, not the army staff talks, that provided France with leverage over Britain in the July Crisis of 1914. On 1 August 1914 the cabinet was proposing not to send the BEF to France, and when Grey addressed the House of Commons two days later he assumed that Britain's role in the coming war would be maritime. Even on 5 and 6 August, when a rump Committee of Imperial Defence met to discuss British strategy, the key decisions regarding the employment of the BEF—whether it was to go to Belgium or to France, and whether it was to take its full complement—were all reopened.[13]

The basis for seeing 23 August 1911 as pivotal is Henry Wilson's own version of events. But, as Wilson himself realized, his very advocacy of the commitment to France jeopardized not only his own position but also the strategy that he represented. The "peace party of the cabinet," he wrote in his diary on 16 November 1911, "are calling for my head. Dirty ignorant curs. They think I forced the pace during the crisis, & they quote all my teaching at the S.C. [Staff College] as evidence of my villainy."[14] Significant here is Wilson's branding of those who opposed him as the "peace party." He named John Morley, Lord Crewe, Lewis Harcourt, and Reginald McKenna, but of these only Morley would resign at the beginning of August 1914. The others, notably McKenna, represented not so much a policy of peace per se, but an alternative strategy. McKenna had worked hand in glove with Jackie Fisher to overhaul the capabilities of the Royal Navy, and in the climate of Edwardian Britain few would describe him as a pacifist. Wilson's opponents were less the "peace party" and more those who adumbrated other ways of fighting a European war should one occur. The paradox of Wilson's performance on 23 August was that he persuaded some cabinet ministers to adopt a continental strategy that involved the deployment in Europe of an army still structured for colonial operations. His glibness convinced them that six divisions could swing the balance, and so it was not only the Belgian option but also the issues of conscription, operational doctrine, and higher command that were conveniently ignored.

The General Staff was a new creation; it was not the capital body identified by Dallas D. Irvine.[15] Its chief had to compete with preexisting peers, like the adjutant general and quartermaster general. Nor was Henry Wilson its sole spokesman. As his diaries make clear, his vituperation was not reserved solely for the "Little Englanders" within the Liberal government. It embraced many of his professional colleagues and superiors—including Horatio Kitchener and Sir John French. Institutionally the army was not a monolith, a point the "Curragh Mutiny" was both to prove and to deepen. In 1914 the armies of France and Germany were focused (at least in so far as external enemies were concerned) on a possible war against each other to be fought on their joint frontier or in Belgium, and had prepared themselves accordingly. Within Britain elements of the General Staff had given such an eventuality very serious consideration over a decade, but the schemes that had resulted had not permeated the army institutionally, and had failed to change either its ethos or its structure.

The debate about when the British General Staff adopted continentalism is important, and will be considered in the second section of this chapter. But, whatever the difference in dating—1904 or 1906 or 1910 or 1911—its decision to do so had not become the basis of national policy by 1914. A far more significant issue is the fact that Britain condoned the General Staff's continentalism without willing the means to the ends. The General Staff accepted a plan for war in Europe without managing to create a European army.

Henry Wilson had plenty of enemies within the army. His politicking and scheming alienated those who took a more conventional view of civil-military relations. But self-evidently he also had friends. His final elevation, to become chief of the Imperial General Staff in 1918 and a field marshal, can of course be attributed to the patronage of politicians. But the fact that he was appointed director of military operations in 1910 and that he held that post throughout the ensuing four years shows that he also enjoyed the support of some soldiers. Wilson was at the center of controversy in 1910–1914—not only because of the CID meeting of 23 August 1911, but also because of the "Currragh Mutiny" of March 1914—and yet he did not change his spots in that time. His francophilia and his relish for political intervention were both proven by 1910. He became director of military operations because of these attributes, not in spite of them. Wilson was not sui generis, nor was his brand of continentalism.[16]

At the broadest level every thinking and literate soldier in the late Victorian army was European in outlook. Military history and military theory venerated the examples of Napoleon and Moltke, not of the Afghans and Zulus. J. F. Maurice has been dubbed "the second pen" of Sir Garnet Wolseley: he was a member of the latter's "ring" that established itself as a prototype field staff for the successful execution of colonial operations. In 1891 he published as a separate volume his essay "War," originally written as an entry for *Encyclopedia Britannica*. To it he added "an essay on military literature and a list of books." Maurice's departure point for the examination of modern war was the campaigns of 1866 and 1870, and the works he recommended were predominantly French and German. A short section of his bibliography was devoted to "minor British wars since 1815," and included his own account of the 1882 Egyptian Campaign, but—like other British military writers—his actual discussion of colonial warfare was severely restricted. A page on the "method peculiar to campaigns in uncivilized countries" was largely confined to their logistical difficulties.[17]

Theoretically Wolseley's army was posted on the Rhine, but its practice and its strategic assumptions remained firmly imperial. The Stanhope Memorandum of 1888 considered the dispatch of forces to the continent the remotest of all possible contingencies.[18] Wolseley, as commander in chief of the army between 1895 and 1900, devoted much attention to its capacity for rapid mobilization, but the expeditions that he had in mind were to Africa rather than to Europe.

In 1899 that ability was tested on exactly those terms that Wolseley had anticipated. The Boer War exposed many deficiencies in the army. The reforming efforts that followed were therefore intended to render the army better able to fight a similar war should one occur, not a war on the European continent. And yet by late 1904 a change had taken place. In January 1905 James M. Grierson, the director of military operations, ordered a strategic war game to be conducted in April and May, whose assumption was that Germany had violated Belgian neutrality in the course of a war with France. The foundations of the Stanhope Memorandum had been significantly modified, if not overthrown. The explanations for the change are both bureaucratic and personal.

The bureaucratic argument has been rehearsed by McDermott, and its key point is that it links the intellectual foundations of British military thought to the final establishment of a General Staff in 1904–1906. Henry Campbell-Bannerman had used the platform of the Hartington Commission in 1890 to oppose the creation of a General Staff for fear that such a body would prepare for a continental war, and so enlarge British military policy.[19] Those within the army who opposed the establishment of a General Staff did so for reasons that were the corollary of Campbell-Bannerman's: in peacetime a staff needed to plan, and it would tend to concentrate on the single but remote scenario of a big war rather than on the day-to-day immediacies of unpredictable but relatively minor imperial crises. Both lines of criticism were not without foundation. When the decision to create a General Staff was promulgated, Britain's forces did indeed take on the trappings of a continental army. In 1905 the War Office published a translation of Paul Bronsart von Schellendorff's *The Duties of the General Staff*, and that remained the principal official publication on the subject until the outbreak of the First World War. The role model, therefore, was Germany. And yet the planning assumptions that framed the professional mission of the German General Staff were very different from those of Britain. Germany's most likely threat was war on its own frontiers. In Bronsart von Schellendorff's volume of 567 pages, only seven were devoted to cooperation between the army and navy, and a further seven to colonial warfare.

The British assumption of the German model was in some ways unremarkable. The idea of a General Staff had been promoted by the military commentator and academic Spenser Wilkinson in *The Brain of an Army*, "a popular account of the German General Staff," published in 1890. In his preface Wilkinson quoted the words of another member of the Wolseley ring, Henry Brackenbury. In his evidence to the select committee on the army and navy estimates in 1887, Brackenbury had described the German General Staff as "the keystone of the whole system of German military organization . . . the cause of the great efficiency of the German army . . . acting as the powerful brain of the military body, to the designs of which brain the whole body is made to work."[20] Wilkinson's book went on to describe the history and characteristics of the Prussian General Staff against the background of the wars of 1866 and 1870.

The Wolseley "ring" was therefore happy to live with a contradiction. Their own battlefield experience was colonial, but their model for a General Staff—whose formation they supported—was continental. Maurice's strategies in the event of war with a European power embraced amphibious operations and a continental alliance. This was what Basil H. Liddell Hart would later call "the British way in warfare." It was not continentalism as it would be defined in the run-up to, let alone the aftermath of, the First World War, but it was the nearest that late Victorian military thinkers came to it. And many did not. Maurice criticized *Imperial Defence* (1892), written by Wilkinson in conjunction with Sir Charles Dilke, for its rejection of a European alliance. Wilkinson believed that the Royal Navy would be Britain's primary arm in a European war. He favored a "forward" policy in India against Russia, and this therefore was the scenario in which a General Staff modeled on European lines was likely to find service. But the key point, common across the spectrum of military thought, was that before 1900 advocacy of a General Staff did not of itself presuppose the deployment of a British army on the Continent. To understand this development, the weight of explanation needs to shift from structures to personalities.

Wilkinson's own military career was confined to the volunteers: his experience, such as it was, related to home defense, not colonial conquest. Moreover, his writings as a military historian focused on France and Germany, on Napoleon and Moltke. In 1899 he castigated Wolseley for the setbacks in South Africa. By then his interest in the defense of India had already resulted in a close relationship with Wolseley's great rival, Lord Roberts. Like that of Wolseley, Roberts's focus in the early 1890s was on the empire, albeit in India rather than Africa. But, unlike Wolseley, Roberts saw the ultimate enemy as likely to be a major European army. The threat to India was Russia.

The personal conversion that is at the heart of the British General Staff's espousal of continentalism between 1900 and 1905 is that of Roberts. A man whose reputation was founded on India, and made at the head of a predominantly sepoy army, became the advocate of preparedness against Germany and of conscription within Britain. His friendship with Wilkinson was perhaps one factor in effecting this change. Eyre Crowe, the most trenchant harbinger of the German threat among Foreign Office clerks, was Wilkinson's brother-in-law, and the arguments in Crowe's memorandum of 1 January 1907 on British relations with Germany were a summary of those already published by Wilkinson.[21] In 1904–1905 Roberts moved from being the army's last commander in chief, via the Committee of Imperial Defence, to becoming the president of the National Service League. His influence in the senior echelons of the army was still pivotal in 1914, in the Curragh crisis. With one rising officer above all he had a particularly close relationship: for Henry Wilson, Roberts was always simply "The Chief."

Wilson was only the most voluble, not the most important, army advocate of continentalism. His diary entry for 28 October 1904 still sees France and Russia as Britain's putative enemies, and the volume for the following year, 1905, is devoid of references to the diplomatic and wider strategic context in which his enthusiasm for the General Staff might be set. Others both anticipated him and were more adroit in their political handling.

Preeminent was J. M. Grierson, the General Staff's first ever director of military operations. Like other serious students of his profession, Grierson was a long-standing admirer of the German Army, so much so that in 1890 one German officer said of him that he was "almost as well known at Berlin as at Woolwich."[22] As a gunner he had received his military education at the Royal Military Academy at Woolwich, where the bracket above his bed held a statuette of Moltke. In 1897 he published anonymously, first in German and then—two years later—in English, a study of the British Army, presciently bound in khaki. *The British Army* is virtually devoid of any other anticipatory quality: it is a description of the army as it was on the eve of the South African War, not as it might become in its aftermath. Its assumptions are Wolseleyan. And yet the color illustrations betray the continental influences operating on Grierson, for they are the work not of Richard Simkin or Harry Payne, the fashionable military artists of the day, but of the German illustrator of uniform, Richard Knötel.

In 1896 Grierson went to Berlin as Britain's military attaché. His experiences over the ensuing four years ended his love affair with the German Army. The Anglophobic tirades of its officers, and particularly of the kaiser, convinced him that war between the two countries was likely.[23] In 1900 he was relieved to be appointed to Lord Roberts's staff in South Africa. The move showed how permeable both the "rings" of the late Victorian army were. Grierson never ceased to regard Wolseley as "the best soldier of my time."[24] His first campaign had been Egypt in 1882, and he had served Henry Brackenbury in the Intelligence Division thereafter. But like Henry Wilson (to whom he handed over the quartermaster general's department in South Africa), he called Roberts "The Chief."[25] Grierson's hopes that Britain would create its own General Staff had been stoked by the Hartington Commission in 1890. The lessons that he drew from the South African War began with the staff question: "We must have big annual manoeuvres," he wrote from Pretoria on 7 July 1900, "and have our staffs properly trained. We don't seem to grasp anything higher than a division. And we must have 'staff journeys' to teach the control of armies in the field. If we take the field with a force the size of this one against a European enemy and continue in our present happy-go-lucky style of staffing and staff work we shall come to most awful grief. There is no system about it, and without a system a large army cannot be properly handled."[26]

Therefore, by 1900, well before the Anglo-French entente and its ensuing staff conversations, Grierson was both anticipating war between Britain and Germany and talking about the creation of a British Army organized and staffed on European lines. The two elements of continentalism had converged.

Grierson's patronage swept up Lieutenant Colonel William Robertson. Robertson was another product of Brackenbury's Intelligence Division who had served on Roberts's staff in South Africa. In 1900 he was appointed head of the foreign section of the Intelligence Division—part of the Directorate

General of Mobilisation and Intelligence. In his memoirs, Robertson wrote of this period of his life that "it is not possible, and should not be necessary to try, to prepare at one and the same time for half-a-dozen different wars." His conclusion, therefore, was that "soldiers charged with the duty of preparation aim at making ready for the greatest and the most probable war in which their army may become engaged."[27] Herein were the intellectual origins of the shift from continentalism as method to continentalism as strategy.

In 1898 Robertson had written an essay at the Staff College for his mentor, G.F.R. Henderson, in which he declared that "conflict with Russia must come sooner or later."[28] For a man who had passed most of his commissioned service in India, such views were no more than orthodoxy. But by 1902 he was penning a paper destined for Roberts's desk in which he challenged the assumption that a continental war meant a war in Asia against Russia. "It is not an exaggeration to say," he wrote, "that in no other European country is hatred of England so general or so deeply-rooted as in Germany." The greater security need was to preserve the balance of power in Europe, "and in playing it at the present time we should recollect that a new preponderance is now growing of which the centre of gravity is Berlin."[29]

Robertson had never been nearer Germany than a tour of the 1870 battlefields in the Meuse valley. His conversion to anti-Germanism was in part the result of his rejection of the feasibility of a Russian invasion of India. He needed to find another enemy who could become the focus for the army's peacetime preparations. But it is not fanciful to see the influence of Grierson on Robertson. Grierson employed Robertson as the commander of the German force in his 1905 staff ride. In the same year the two of them visited the Franco-German frontier. In January 1906 Grierson drew up a memorandum—which, significantly, is to be found in the Robertson papers—on possible contingencies in which military forces might be deployed overseas. It envisaged six scenarios, one of which, a war with France against Germany, was deemed "possible." In such circumstances, after an initial commitment of at least four cavalry brigades and three army corps, "it might be desirable to send troops to an unlimited extent."[30] In a lecture given apparently in about 1906 on "the true standard of our military needs," Robertson declared, "that standard must be looked for nearer home, if the *entente cordiale* is to be regarded as having any meaning, and if we are to hope for its continuance."[31]

Robertson had little truck with Henry Wilson, who is not even mentioned in his autobiography, *From Private to Field Marshal*. But even allowing for personal animus, it is clear that the grooves along which Wilson traveled as director of military operations after 1910 were not his own, but were set earlier and by others. Grierson it was (and here Robertson was explicit) who believed "that the only policy consistent with the interests of the Empire was an active alliance with France and Belgium," and who "did more than any other officer of his time to establish good relations between the French and British and armies."[32]

To argue that the momentum of continentalism was lost because the Anglo-French staff talks were suspended between 1906 and 1910 ignores two points. The first concerns continuity. Grierson's successor as director of military operations, Sir J. Spencer Ewart, also saw war with Germany as a matter of time and therefore sustained contacts with the French. He kept warm both continentalism as a strategy and the chair of the director of military operations as its focus.[33] The second concerns the conclusions of the subcommittee of the Committee of Imperial Defence set up to examine "the military needs of the empire" in 1908. It included within its brief situations "in which the British Army might be called upon to operate either alone or with other powers." In 1909 that subcommittee approved the General Staff's plan to send an army to France. Admittedly, it simultaneously asked for plans for expeditionary forces to Belgium and Holland, and it stressed that no decision had been taken with regard to a single continental strategy, or indeed to any continental commitment. But Sir William Nicholson, the chief of the Imperial General Staff between 1908 and 1912, argued that the 23 August 1911 debate was a storm in a teacup because the continental strategy had been settled two years previously.[34]

The limitations of Wilson's achievement in 1910–1911 can be further appreciated by shifting the focus from London to Delhi. In 1902 Robertson's most pressing need was to undermine the legacy of Roberts's determination that Britain's principal military threat lay on the northwest frontier of India. In due course Roberts himself was converted, but Roberts's legacy had in the interim found a doughty advocate in Lord Kitchener, as commander in chief in India from 1902 to 1909. Realists involved in military planning reckoned that a Russian invasion through Afghanistan was a logistical impossibility— a conclusion reached by the Russians as long before as the late 1880s.[35] But in the end neither logistics nor diplomacy could shift the assumptions of the Indian Army. The 1902 Anglo-Japanese Agreement provided scant relief to planners in either India or Britain. For the former, there was the impossibility of Japan deploying troops on the northwest frontier; for the latter, as Grierson observed in 1905, the agreement was irrelevant as the threat from Germany was greater than that from Russia.[36] The 1907 Anglo-Russian Agreement might have made more difference, but it did not. Douglas Haig was appointed chief of the Indian General Staff in 1909. Fresh from working as director of staff duties under Haldane, Haig was determined to integrate the Indian Army with the BEF concept. He instituted a close study of German Army organization and looked at the possibility of sending an Indian expeditionary force to Europe in the event of war. The viceroy, Hardinge, blocked Haig, and ordered his plans destroyed. It was the discovery of the Indian schemes that alerted the cabinet to the machinations of Henry Wilson in October 1911.[37] The 1912 Army in India Committee concluded that India should not be called upon to maintain troops specifically for war outside the subcontinent. Instead, its army should be geared for the needs of internal security and frontier warfare. In 1914, if the Indian Army had any European army in its sights, that enemy was still Russia—by now Britain's ally. Its equipment was—according to the Mesopotamia Commission in 1917—less appropriate for war against a European opponent in 1914 than it had been before the South African War. In the event, India did of course send four expeditionary forces overseas when war broke out; every one of them was improvised and all of them suffered accordingly.[38]

The sorry tale of Indian planning makes two key points relevant to the argument that centers on Henry Wilson and the CID meeting of 23 August 1911. The first relates to personalities. Douglas Haig set about "trying to do a Wilson" before Wilson had become director of military operations. In other words, he, like Grierson and Robertson, anticipated Wilson because continentalism was established in British General Staff thought before 1910. The second is institutional. The writ of the British General Staff did not extend very far. It never established control over its partners in India before the First World War. From the perspective of Delhi, none of 1904, 1906, 1910, or 1911 denotes any development of significance in relation to strategy. A total of fifty-three infantry battalions served in India at some point in 1913.[39] This was where active service was most likely to be found, and it was where ambitious but impoverished subalterns wished to be posted. And yet continentalism had not entered the intellectual horizons of the army in which they served. This was not because the War Office General Staff was not continentalized, but because the General Staff was not the dominant force within the British Army.

The status of the General Staff within Wihelmine Germany has been much exaggerated. In peacetime its chief often had to play second fiddle to the Prussian war minister; the latter, not the former, had a greater say in the establishment and size of the army. The training of the army, by which its ideas on war achieved a degree of universality, was in the hands not of the General Staff but of the individual commanders of corps districts. Nonetheless, it is to the German General Staff that military thought, before the First World War as still today, is indebted for the idea of a capital General Staff—an institution that provides the leading ideas that animate the army as a whole and whose intellectual coherence creates an institutional and politically independent identity. For all intents and purposes Britain has never possessed such a staff. Before 1914 some reformers aspired for it to do so, but three major obstacles stood in their path.

First, the status of the German General Staff had been hallowed by victory: the wars of unification had vested the General Staff with a degree of independence that it had not enjoyed before 1866. In 1914 the British staff had no such legacy on which to draw; after 1918 it would be branded with responsibility for the nature of the First World War, and so advocates of the General Staff idea (preeminently William Robertson) could be pilloried by such influential critics as Basil Liddell Hart.[40]

Second, the British supporters of a General Staff often misunderstood the model on which they were basing their designs. They believed that the German General Staff was the author of doctrine, and that it was doctrine that gave the staff its dominant and unifying role in the army. They therefore argued that the job of the General Staff was first to develop doctrine and then to teach it.[41] But doctrine was not the German General Staff's method of instruction: it taught by way of concrete examples. Throughout the twentieth century the British Army tended to impute to the German General Staff a more cerebral and more principled approach to the study of war than it did in fact implement. German staff training concentrated on practicalities more than theories.

The confusion arose because the German Army's strategic problem—the defense of its western and eastern frontiers—was clear-cut. This was the third obstacle to Britain's comprehension of the German General Staff idea. The German General Staff seemed to have a single doctrine because its grand strategy was simple. It developed a number of operational possibilities, but it did so within a much narrower policy framework than that which could ever be embraced by the British General Staff. The latter's call for continentalism was in many ways a summons for simplification. Wiser heads knew that the world—and Britain's role in it—demanded political flexibility, and hence greater complexity.

Grierson's memorandum of January 1906, which deemed war in alliance with France against Germany as "possible," listed five further scenarios for war. Two—war with France and war with the United States—were reckoned to be "improbable"; one, war with Russia, became less likely after 1907 but never went off the agenda in India; and two, a Boer rising in South Africa and a general category of "small wars," were the baggage of empire that the European alliances were designed to alleviate but that they could never remove. The drift of Grierson's memorandum was of course to minimize all but the German threat. He could not however discount the danger outside Europe, and indeed one could prompt the other: in 1914 the Boers did rebel after war broke out against Germany. He thought that most small wars could be conducted with the army still on a peace footing, but some more serious dangers, such as conflict with China, or mutiny in the Egyptian army, or a rising in the Sudan, would need a greater effort. The trouble was that Britain was never sufficiently at peace between 1870 and 1914 for its army to concentrate exclusively on the threat in Europe.[42]

Planning for these colonial contingencies was not primarily a function of operational thought. The tasks were administrative and logistical; the issues were medical, cartographical, and calorific. Thus, as an imperial power, Britain needed a staff that put as much weight on administration as on command. This was the nub of the deeply divisive debates between 1904, when the scheme for a General Staff was promulgated, and 1906, by which time it was put in place. Henry Wilson, for example, was terrified that the adjutant general would "put a very senior officer in as head of Administrative Staff & a junior as General Staff."[43] This did not happen, but the result was still a compromise. The first chief of the General Staff, Sir Neville Lyttelton, lacked the authority to establish the supremacy of the new office. It did not become the dominant appointment in the army, the putative commander in chief in the field, or the country's principal adviser, but more a *primus inter pares*. It was squeezed from above and below, as well as from the sides.

On top was the Committee for Imperial Defence. The broader policy context, which so trammeled the General Staff's demand for simplification, was precisely why the Committee of Imperial Defence had been created. Its principal instigator, Lord Esher, favored a maritime strategy, and had envisaged that the CID would embrace naval and political as well as military dimensions and so would develop into a department that would itself "fulfill the main functions of a General Staff." Esher had seen the General Staff of the army as an intelligence division locking into this wider framework. Instead, by 1906, he was damning it as a "Frankenstein," usurping functions for which it had not been designed and perverting Britain's strategy in the process.[44] If Britain had created a capital staff before 1914, it would have grown from the CID, not from within the War Office. The fact that the CID never developed as Esher hoped it might should not obscure the fact that formally the army's General Staff, however powerful it became, was ultimately a subordinate organization in planning terms.

To the sides were the administrative aspects of staff work, kept separate and answerable to departments of much greater antiquity and well-established status. Manpower and discipline were subordinated to the adjutant general, and logistical and material matters to the quartermaster general.[45] This divided structure was repeated in field formations. The commander of an expeditionary force had not one principal adviser, as was the case in the German Army, but three—the chief of staff, tasked with operations and intelligence; the adjutant general (or A Branch), responsible for men and their needs; and the quartermaster general (or Q Branch), charged with supplies, movements, and accommodation. The field commander therefore had a dual function: the conduct of operations and the coordination of the administrative and fighting branches of his headquarters.

At the conference of General Staff officers held in Camberley in January 1909, the consequences of the split were made explicit by Colonel John P. Du Cane. He reckoned that, with its attention now "concentrated on Northern Europe," ". . . the center of gravity in which the British may be called upon to conduct warlike operations has changed in recent years." He pointed out, however, that the regulations for supply did not seem to contemplate war on the continent of Europe. Du Cane attributed this division to the organizational separation of the General Staff from the quartermaster general's department.[46] Du Cane's point was well made. The split was enshrined in the *Field Service Regulations* promulgated in 1909. It meant that Henry Wilson's presentation to the CID on 23 August 1911 was largely a paper exercise. Wilson's task was mobilization and deployment, the stuff of administration, not of the conduct of operations in the field. Its implementation was therefore not in his hands as director of military operations, but in those of the adjutant general's and quartermaster general's departments. The former was responsible for the call-up of personnel, the latter for remounts, railways, and supplies—not only of food but also of fuel.[47]

In Germany all these functions were subordinated to the chief of the General Staff; in Britain they depended on cooperation between departments. Between 1912 and 1914 Sir John Cowans, as quartermaster general, gave Wilson that cooperation.[48] Similarly in 1914 itself, when mobile warfare revealed the total impracticality of the administrative-operational divide, the situation was saved when Robertson, then the quartermaster general in the BEF, subordinated himself to the chief of the General Staff.[49] But Sir Ian Hamilton, as adjutant general in 1910, effectively withheld that cooperation. In *Compulsory Service*, published as a refutation of the arguments for national service, Hamilton openly rejected a continental strategy: for him command of the sea was the pivot of national defense, the army was the navy's projectile, and its organization should be framed to meet the needs of imperial defense and of joint warfare in the event of European war.

The fact that the theoretical separation of responsibilities was not practicable had already become evident before the war. Henry Wilson, then commandant of the Staff College, had responded to Du Cane's challenge by pointing out that the staff rides of both 1907 and 1908 had focused on supply. He was right. The objective of the 1908 exercise, centered on operations in a "neutral country between Scotland and Holland" (and therefore further evidence of "continentalism" before 1910–1911), was to test the lines of communication and maintenance services, not to explore the operational or strategic framework. Staff work was therefore increasingly interpreted as confined to administrative aspects.[50]

Henry Rawlinson reflected this concern at the General Staff conference of January 1908, when he urged the Staff College not to forget that its tasks should include training for command in war, not just for the exercise of administrative duties.[51] But that was by no means received wisdom. Just as General Staff duties were meant to be distanced from administration, so they were also deemed to be distanced from the frictions of command. The chief of staff might head the most significant of the three administrative branches of a field headquarters, but he was in no sense a surrogate commander. "There is an essential distinction," wrote Colonel Hubert Foster in 1911 in a work designed to supplement and popularize the *Field Service Regulations* of 1909, "between the action of *Commanders* and that of *Staff Officers* however capable. It is true that Staff Officers are not mere clerks or messengers." "But it is outside the scope of the Staff to interfere with the exercise of Command. . . . Only one man can command."[52] Foster's own treatment of *Staff Work*, published in the following year, was principally concerned with administration and devoted nearly half its length to the movement of troops.

Thus neither the Staff College nor service in staff appointments was necessarily an avenue to high command. This too was a consequence of the 1904–1906 debate. Those who had intended the General Staff to be an elite had been defeated by those who favored a more open body, whose corporate identity derived not from the existence of a series of posts designated as those of the General Staff but solely from its members having passed through the

Staff College and thus having acquired eligibility for (but not exclusive rights over) staff appointments.[53] Many jobs that might be deemed staff posts were not held by Staff College graduates.

The exercise of higher command in a pre-1914 European army was focused at the level of the corps. But in the British Army Aldershot was the only area where two or more divisions could be assembled for maneuvers, and therefore the only command in which the training of a corps was possible.[54] The Army Council discussed whether or not to create the corps as a command with a permanent staff in 1906, but rejected the idea in favor of large divisions, of three brigades rather than two. The decision was driven by rejection of continentalism. Sir William Nicholson, then the quartermaster general, feared that the adoption of corps command would be tantamount to preparing the army for one contingency only. The fact that the BEF was structured around the division, not the corps, so that its organization was compatible with that of the Indian Army, was clear evidence of the strict limits placed around the penetration of General Staff–inspired continentalism.[55]

The effect was to vitiate yet further the training of British commanders for European warfare. Having separated staff duties and staff training from preparation for the exercise of command, the prewar army now ensured that higher command itself would not be a subject for serious study. At the General Staff conference in January 1908, Haig spoke of the impossibility of one man commanding six divisions (the anticipated size of the BEF) in the field.[56] Nonetheless, the *Field Service Regulations* of 1909, for which he is given principal credit, established the division as the highest subordinate field command. Moreover, a survey in 1908 suggested that even at this level there was little by way of common practice. The keynote in divisional training within the home commands was decentralization. Units were judged by results rather than the application of common methods. Training was one of the key prerogatives of command, and therefore was in the hands of individual divisional generals and their enthusiasms, rather than of staff officers schooled in shared modes of thought.[57]

Command expertise was acquired by practice. The principle of instruction through allowing officers to exercise command in the rank higher than their current one was not widely accepted. Moreover, in the pre-1914 army, the command in which most officers honed their leadership skills was not as high as the all-arms division, but was the single-arm, single-battalion regiment.

The ethos of the Victorian army, determined by its dispersal overseas in colonial garrisoning, was mediated through the regiment. The creation of the

General Staff presented a challenge to the regiment's dominance, which the Army Council attempted to defuse by declaring in December 1906 that nothing in the creation of the General Staff was "intended to relieve [regimental] Commanding Officers of their prime responsibility for the efficiency and proficiency of their officers in educational and professional respects."[58] The note of protest was significant: the General Staff was fighting for acceptance.

For most regimental commanding officers the existence of the General Staff remained in many ways a dead letter. The creation of the BEF and the acceptance of the continental commitment (regardless of whether the latter preceded or followed the former) ought to have resulted in a redistribution of infantry battalions away from the imperial periphery and toward Britain itself. This would have had two effects. First, it would have brought more battalions within the purview of the General Staff, with its physical concentration in Camberley, London, and Aldershot. Second, it would of course have created immediately available reinforcements should an expeditionary force be sent to Europe. But what is striking about the distribution of the infantry battalions between 1870 and 1914 is the evenness of the pattern. For all the dire warnings of imminent collapse, the so-called Cardwell system of linked battalions proved remarkably resilient. Grierson was right: most small wars could be accommodated within the peacetime pattern, because they were of a scale where one or two regular battalions supplemented by locally raised units would suffice. Only twice did the system bend and even buckle—during the 1882 Egyptian War and during the South African War. The abandonment of the Stanhope Memorandum and the diplomatic realignments of 1904–1907 produced no change in the pattern of regimental postings. Nor did Wilson's alleged triumph in the CID. In July 1914 the infantry battalions of the regular army were as firmly wedded to the distribution of imperial garrisoning as they had been twenty or thirty years previously. The continentalism of the General Staff not only failed to move laterally, to the adjutant general's and quartermaster general's departments, it also failed to percolate downward to the parts of the army that were responsible for the actual business of fighting.[59]

The continentalism of the General Staff therefore had to balance its own expectations of future war with the reality of the army's current practices and commitments. Herein was the reason for the British General Staff's rejection of the German pattern of training and instruction through specific examples, through case studies and staff rides. In January 1911, junior officers asked that the General Staff consider sanctioning a book on applied tactics. If Henry Wilson's focus on France really had provided the leading idea around which the army as a whole could have been shaped, there would have been no harm and much merit in the scheme. Significantly, the precedent cited by Captain C.A.L. Yates in making the case was German. However, the General Staff response was unequivocal: "We must remember that our officers must be prepared to fight in every country on the globe. Arrangements that are desirable in England, or even on the continent of Europe, will be very different from those which will be necessary in South Africa, or on the North-Western Frontier of India."[60]

Therefore the British Army studied war through the medium of principles. William Robertson may have wanted to concentrate Britain's planning effort on a single contingency, but even he would not depart from the idea that training should be by way of general principles.[61] For him, as for Douglas Haig, this was what a General Staff was for—to enunciate general principles, on the basis of which officers should work out responses adapted to individual circumstances.[62]

The promulgation of general principles in war was hardly a new approach to military theory. Their origins lay in the Enlightenment's search for universal rules for most human activity, and they had found their embodiment in Jomini. But it was the British Army that used principles as a substitute for doctrine, and that ensured their high priority in twentieth-century military thought.[63] They were embodied in the *Field Service Regulations*, drawn up under the supervision of Douglas Haig while he was director of staff duties, and published in 1909. They reflected ideas that Haig had formulated in 1896–1897 while at the Staff College and against the background of colonial warfare, and they included a chapter on warfare against an uncivilized enemy.[64] The criticism voiced by the military correspondent of the *Times*, Charles à Court Repington, that they should have been more directly geared to the specific application of British troops in a European war, was not without foundation: indeed it went to the nub of the dilemma that the General Staff's continentalism exposed.[65] But Haig defended the line he had taken both on general and on specific grounds. The former embraced the refrain of every military commentator since G.F.R. Henderson: to go farther than general principles and espouse specific doctrines ran the risk that the army would find itself fighting the wrong sort of war. The latter rebutted the notion that, because the principles were therefore as applicable outside Europe as within it, they were somehow invalid. Haig was clear that the *Field Service Regulations* were geared for the eventuality of major war, and when the First World War broke out he continued to see them as his benchmark. They remained applicable right through to 1918.[66]

By then continentalism had transformed the character of the British Army. It had ceased to be a small, regular, professional force, and had become a conscripted citizen army. National service, even more than the system of higher command, or the patterns of military doctrine, was the key denominator in European warfare.

The General Staff advocates of continentalism were fully aware of this. In January 1906, Grierson, in sketching out the pattern of possible support for France in a war against Germany, spoke of sending "troops to an unlimited extent."[67] Robertson, writing at around the same time, was more specific. Britain needed to put in the field "a contingent of at least the same proportionate strength as those we supplied when fighting in alliance with other Powers in a similar cause a hundred years ago." He wanted to be able to move one hundred thousand men to the continent within fourteen days, and to have at least five hundred thousand ready for instant employment. The corollary of a continentalist scheme was a continental army: "any scheme for the creation of a National Army," he warned, "must be based on European and not on Asiatic conditions, otherwise it may prove to be both worthless and disastrous."[68]

Henry Wilson was of course as firm an advocate of compulsory service as his mentor, Lord Roberts. But he was slower than Robertson to put it in a specifically European context. Not only publicly but also privately both Wilson and Roberts tended to justify the need for conscription in terms of home defense or of the empire rather than of the manpower needs of a British Army on the continent.[69] But by 12 September 1911 Wilson too had squared this particular circle, cornering Lloyd George and linking in a single package the need for a friendly Belgium, for mobilization that was simultaneous with that of France, and for conscription in peacetime.[70]

In this conversation Lloyd George was, according to Wilson, "quite in favour of war now." Wilson himself, however, seems to have been entirely reactive in terms of the international situation. To construct a conspiracy theory from Wilson's diary—that he sought to use either the Morocco Crisis to argue for preventive war, or that he was anxious for European war in itself—would be an uphill struggle. Not even the 1914 July Crisis itself seems to have caused Wilson to leap from the advocacy of a firm commitment to France if war broke out to an expectation that a continental strategy predetermined Britain's policy. As an Ulsterman, Wilson's own sights in July were focused on Ireland. On 27 July he thought there would not be war, and when on 30 July he concluded that war was inevitable his diary entry smacks of resignation rather than jubilation. However tendentious the conclusions of the

CID meeting of 23 August 1911, they can hardly be made to carry the weight of interpretation and expectation now loaded on the so-called war council of 8 December 1912 in Germany.

The burden of this chapter has been to deemphasize the place of the meeting of 23 August 1911 in Britain's preparations for the First World War, and by extension to reduce the role that Henry Wilson ascribed to himself and to which others have also subscribed. Wilson's intervention did not inaugurate continentalism in British General Staff thinking; instead it gave a push toward that continentalism taking a French rather than a Belgian form, but that in itself was as much the product of Belgium's own decision to distance itself from Britain and to reaffirm its neutrality. Moreover, that preference for rapid military support to France was not the basis for consistent British policy between 1911 and 1914. As J. E. Tyler recognized long ago, Wilson's intervention generated as much confusion as it did certainty. He strapped British strategy to French planning, but he did so before he knew in detail what France's plans were. He managed it by arguing that six divisions could have a decisive effect. However, as the debate in August 1914 revealed, the old assumptions—that only four divisions would go to the continent and that two would be held back for home defense—were not thereby superseded.[71]

In 1914 the BEF suffered a shattering defeat. The army survived, but it did so by effectively reverting to the idea of a limited liability on the continent of Europe—at least until 1916.[72] It had no option, for the General Staff had embraced a continental strategy without creating a continental army. That was true organizationally and doctrinally, but it was above all true in terms of recruitment. Britain had no other option from the autumn of 1914 than to mark time, for it now had to create the mass army that its strategy demanded of it.

The legacy of the decade 1904–1914 extended far beyond the opening years of the First World War. The General Staff would continue to see continental warfare as the gold standard both in the interwar period and in the later stages of the Cold War, but it persisted in doing so despite the fact that it did not have the manpower resources of a truly European army. Moreover, the institutional weakness of the General Staff within the British Army was also not eradicated. Robertson, and his successors, worked to establish a capital General Staff within Britain in the 1920s, but they were undermined both by those who equated such thinking with continentalism (like Liddell Hart) and by those who continued to see the regiment as the army's true center of gravity. And, finally, this delegation of authority to the periphery consistently undermined efforts to create doctrine that was truly continentalist in its thrust. Tied to colonial campaigning and to counterinsurgency, the British Army sought an approach to war that could be universal: the upshot was a preference for general principles, and a rejection of specifics. In espousing a theoretical approach that was one stage removed from the particular the British Army allowed its subordinate formations to produce solutions that were peculiar to themselves and that lacked the imprint of a General Staff mentality.

Notes

1. Edward M. Spiers, *Haldane: An Army Reformer* (Edinburgh: Edinburgh Univ. Press, 1980), 22.

2. Samuel R. Williamson, *The Politics of Grand Strategy: Britain and France Prepare for War, 1904–1914* (Cambridge, Mass.: Harvard Univ. Press, 1969), 60–88.

3. Nicholas d'Ombrain, *War Machinery and High Policy: Defence Administration in Peacetime Britain 1902–1914* (London: Oxford Univ. Press, 1973); J. McDermott, "The Revolution in British Military Thinking from the Boer War to the Moroccan Crisis," *Canadian Journal of History* 9 (1974), reprinted in Paul Kennedy, ed., *The War Plans of the Great Powers 1880–1914* (Boston: Allen and Unwin, 1979).

4. John Gooch, *The Plans of War: The General Staff and British Military Strategy c. 1900–1916* (London: Routledge and Kegan Paul, 1974), 289.

5. John Gooch, ed., *The Prospect of War: Studies in British Defence Policy 1847–1942* (London: Frank Cass, 1981), vii–viii; see also 105–112.

6. Spiers, *Haldane,* 81–83, 154.

7. J. E. Tyler, *The British Army and the Continent 1904–1914* (London: Arnold, 1938), 97.

8. Henry Wilson diary, 23 August 1911, Imperial War Museum, DS/MISC/80, reel 4.

9. Gooch, *The Plans of War,* 292–295.

10. Keith Wilson, "Hankey's Appendix: Some Admiralty Maneuvers during and after the Agadir Crisis," *War in History* 1 (1994): 81–97.

11. D'Ombrain, *War Machinery and High Policy,* 259.

12. Avner Offer, *The First World War: An Agrarian Interpretation* (Oxford: Oxford Univ. Press, 1989), 242–243, 291–309. D'Ombrain takes the line that the CID was increasingly preoccupied with technical questions only.

13. Williamson, *The Politics of Grand Strategy,* 353–370.

14. Wilson diary, 16 November 1911.

15. Dallas D. Irvine, "The Origin of Capital Staffs," *Journal of Modern History* 10 (1938): 161–179.

16. Brian Bond, *The Victorian Army and the Staff College, 1854–1914* (London: Methuen, 1972), esp. 251.

17. F. Maurice, *War* (London: Macmillan, 1891), 41; see also Jay Luvaas, *The Education of an Army: British Military Thought 1815–1940* (London: Cassell, 1965).

18. Ian Beckett, "The Stanhope Memorandum," *Bulletin of the Institute of Historical Research* 57 (1984): 240–247.

19. Tyler, *The British Army and the Continent,* 12–13; also W. S. Hamer, *The British Army: Civil-Military Relations 1885–1905* (London: Oxford Univ. Press, 1970).

20. Spenser Wilkinson, *The Brain of an Army* (London: Macmillan, 1890), v.

21. Luvaas, *The Education of an Army,* 275.

22. D. S. Macdiarmid, *The Life of Lieutenant-General Sir James Moncrieff Grierson* (London: Constable, 1923), 87.

23. Ibid., 115, 130–134.

24. Ibid., 250, see also 19, 47, 62–63.

25. Ibid., 165.

26. Ibid., 271, see also 82.

27. William Robertson, *From Private to Field Marshal* (London: Constable, 1921), 132. Obviously, this is not a contemporary reference, but see his observations in a lecture of 1913, Robertson papers, Liddell Hart Centre for Military Archives, King's College London, 1/3/5.

28. Robertson papers, L.H.C.M.A., 1/2/1, page 6.

29. Ibid., 1/2/4, pages 3, 9.

30. Ibid., 1/2/6, pages 6–7.

31. Ibid., 1/2/9.

32. Robertson, *From Private to Field Marshal,* 139–140.

33. D'Ombrain, *War Machinery and High Policy,* 89–94, 149–150.

34. Ibid., 97–102.

35. Alexander Graham Marshall, "'Dar al-Harb: The Russian General Staff and the Asiatic Frontier, 1860–1917." Master's diss., University of Glasgow, 2001.

36. G. P. Gooch and Harold Temperley, eds., *British Documents on the Origins of the War, 1898–1914* (London: H.M.S.O.), 4:127.

37. Tyler, *The British Army and the Continent,* 140; see also G. J. De Groot, *Douglas Haig, 1861–1928* (London: Unwin Hyman, 1928), 136–137.

38. This paragraph has benefited from my supervision of the Glasgow University M.Phil. thesis of Ben Gillon. See De Groot, *Douglas Haig,* 133–139; George MacMunn, *Behind the Scenes in Many Wars* (London: J. Murray, 1930), 81–87; F. J. Moberly, *Military Operations: The Campaign in Mesopotamia* (London: H.M.S.O., 1923–1927), 1:73.

39. This paragraph draws on the painstaking but unpublished work of Corinne Mahaffey plotting the movement of infantry battalions between 1870 and 1914.

40. William Robertson, *Soldiers and Statesmen* (London: Cassell, 1926); Basil Liddell Hart, *The Real War* (Boston: Little, Brown, 1930).

41. Shelford Bidwell and Dominick Graham, *Fire-Power: British Army Weapons and Theories of War 1904–1945* (London: Allen and Unwin, 1982), 1–4.

42. J. M. Grierson, "Memorandum upon the Military Forces Required for Over-Sea Warfare," 4 January 1906, Robertson Papers, L.H.C.M.A., 1/2/6, pages 7, 12.

43. Wilson diary, 14 October 1904, Imperial War Museum, DS/MISC/80, reel 3.
44. D' Ombrain, *War Machinery and High Policy,* 89–94, 149–150.
45. Gooch, *The Plans of War,* 80–82, 99–103.
46. "Report on a Conference of General Staff Officers at the Staff College," 21 January 1909, Haig Papers, National Library of Scotland, Acc 3155/81, pages 69–70.
47. General Staff, War Office, *Field Service Regulations, Part II: Organization and Administration* (London: H.M.S.O., 1909), 38–41.
48. Desmond Chapman-Huston and Owen Rutter, *General Sir John Cowans, G.C.B.: The Quartermaster-General of the Great War,* 2 vols. (London: Hutchinson, 1924), 1:250–258, 263–274; see also Tyler, *The British Army and the Continent,* 149.
49. Ian Malcolm Brown, *British Logistics on the Western Front, 1914–1919* (Westport, Conn.: Praeger, 1998), 41–75; see also Roberston, *From Private to Field Marshal,* 197–201.
50. "Report on a Staff Tour Held by the Chief of the General Staff. 26th to 30th October, 1908," Haig Papers, National Library of Scotland, Acc 3155/77, pages 5, 9.
51. "Report on a Conference of General Staff Officers at the Staff College," 10 January 1908, Haig Papers, National Library of Scotland, Acc 3155/81, page 36.
52. Hubert Foster, *Organization: How Armies Are Formed for War* (London: Hugh Rees, 1911), 246.
53. Gooch, *The Plans of War,* 98–99, 107–108.
54. "Report on a Conference of General Staff Officers at the Staff College," 8 January 1908, Haig Papers, National Library of Scotland, Acc 3155/81, pages 17, 25.
55. Gooch, *The Prospect of War,* 108–109; see also Andrew Simpson, "The Operational Role of British Corps Command on the Western Front, 1914–18" (Ph.D. thesis, University of London, 2001), 20–23.
56. "Report on a Conference of General Staff Officers at the Staff College," 8 January 1908, Haig Papers, National Library of Scotland, Acc 3155/81, page 25.
57. Ibid., 7 January 1908, pages 5–13.
58. Ibid., 10 January 1908, page 31.
59. Based on the research of Corinne Mahaffey.
60. Major-General E. S. May, in "Report of a Conference of General Staff Officers at the Staff College," 9 January 1911, Haig Papers, National Library of Scotland, Acc 3155/81, page 7.
61. "Remarks on a Visit to Battlefields 1912," Robertson Papers, L.H.C.M.A., 1/2/12; see also "Notes on Strategy by Colonel Henderson Campbell for use of Students at the Staff College," Robertson Papers, L.H.C.M.A., 1/2/10.
62. "Report of a Conference of General Staff Officers," 7 January 1908 and 10 January 1908, Haig Papers, National Library of Scotland, Acc 3155/81, pages 5, 46.
63. John I. Hyer, *The Quest for Victory: The History and Principles of War* (Westport, Conn.: Praeger, 1982).
64. Albert Palazzo, *Seeking Victory on the Western Front: The British Army and Chemical Warfare in World War I* (Lincoln: Univ. of Nebraska Press, 2000), 17–20.

65. De Groot, *Douglas Haig*, 136.

66. Palazzo, *Seeking Victory on the Western Front*, 8–10, 23–24; Simpson, "The Operational Role of British Corps Command on the Western Front," 8–9, 23–27.

67. Grierson, "Memorandum upon the Military Forces Required for Over-Sea Warfare," 4 January 1906, Robertson Papers, L.H.C.M.A., 1/2/6, page 7.

68. "The True Standard of Our Military Needs," c. 1906, Robertson Papers, L.H.C.M.A., 1/2/9.

69. Wilson diary, 30 December 1905 and 21 April 1905, Imperial War Museum, DS/MISC/80, reel 3.

70. Ibid., 12 September 1911, reel 4.

71. Tyler, *The British Army and the Continent*, 115, 119–122, 176–177.

72. Hew Strachan, "The Battle of the Somme and British Strategy," *Journal of Strategic Studies* 21 (1998): 79–95.

Belgium

Operational Plans and Tactics of a Neutral Country

Luc de Vos

On 28 June 1914, six young men armed with pistols, hand grenades, and cyanide capsules were ready to attempt to assassinate Archduke Franz Ferdinand, the nephew of and heir presumptive to Austria's Emperor Franz Joseph. They wanted the assassination to take place in Sarajevo, the capital of the province of Bosnia-Herzegovina, claimed by Serbia. The assassins, all about eighteen years of age, chose as a symbol not only the person and the place, but also a date that should fire imaginations: June 28 is the Serbian national day commemorating the defeat suffered at the hands of the Turks in Kosovo in 1389. That morning at about 1030 hours Gavrilo Princip shot the archduke and his wife with a Belgian FN pistol at close range.

At first, the upper classes were outraged by the villainous deed, but before long the tensions that had built up over the last decades poisoned the atmosphere between the existing alliances, the Triple Alliance (France, Great Britain, and Russia) and the Central Powers (Austria-Hungary and Germany). In Belgium the influential Catholic Church, becoming more nervous by the day, wanted to side with Vienna. But the Belgian government tried to maintain its policy of neutrality at all costs. Great outrage ensued when this internationally guaranteed neutrality was violated by Germany in August 1914.

Belgium's International Status and the 1814–1815 Congress of Vienna

When the French Napoleonic Empire was defeated the first time in 1814, the Great Powers, led by the Austrian chancellor Clemens von Metternich, met in Vienna to redraw the political map of Europe. The common goal of the statesmen was to isolate France and to prevent the spread of renewed revolutionary ideas in Europe by military means. Buffer states were to protect Europe from France and a system of international conferences would assist in suppressing nationalist and liberal tendencies.

But before the Vienna summit was able to complete its work, Napoleon returned from Elba and expelled King Louis XVIII from France. At the Battle of Waterloo in 1815, however, the "Corsican Dictator" was finally dealt a decisive blow. France was now pushed back to its 1792 borders and surrounded by buffer states from north to south: the Netherlands, the Grand Duchy of Luxembourg connected with the Netherlands by personal union, the historically ever-neutral Switzerland, and Piedmont-Sardinia. Belgium, having belonged to the French Republic since 1795, was forced to merge with the Netherlands into the United Kingdom of the Netherlands. This solution, contrary to Belgian national interests, was adopted under pressure from Great Britain.

For the United Kingdom of the Netherlands to be able to fulfill its intended function, it had to be protected from a French attack. Considering that the securing of "natural borders" was a high priority for France—in other words, the possession of the left complete bank of the Rhine River—such an attack was possible at any time. Therefore the Wellington Line was established along the French-Belgian border and along the Meuse River from Namur to Maastricht, with two fortified zones in Nieuport and Ostende. The fortifications established in the United Kingdom of the Netherlands were so numerous that there were not enough soldiers to man them. Thus, in the event of a French attack the United Kingdom of the Netherlands was to assume the defense of the coast and man the fortifications along the Scheldt River, while Prussia would defend the forts on the Meuse River.[1]

The 1830 revolution in France put the neutrality of the Netherlands to the test. Conservatives throughout Europe feared that the revolution would spread to the rest of the continent. The United Kingdom of the Netherlands had a special role in preventing such. It had to defend not only itself, but also the rest of Europe, against republican tendencies. For this reason, William I of the Netherlands and Prince of Orange questioned the British government whether it was necessary to reinforce the garrisons of the border fortifications in order to halt a possible French attack. It could well be expected that France would perceive such action as a provocation, since Britain was one of the five countries that had promised to defend "Dutch-Belgian" neutrality. In the end it was decided not to provoke France, although some forces were repositioned because the French had also deployed soldiers to the north and east.[2]

Ultimately, the threats from within proved to be stronger than those from without. Following the performance of the opera *La Muette de Portici* on 25 August 1830, a revolt broke out and grew into a revolution. On 18 November 1830, the Belgian National Congress proclaimed independence, which was guaranteed two days later by Great Britain, France, Prussia, Russia, and Austria. France and Great Britain were the primary supporters of this development. What were the reasons for that? The United Kingdom of the Netherlands was a fierce competitor of Great Britain in the field of trade. A breakup into a northern and a southern part would weaken the Netherlands' economic position and benefit British trade. France also supported the separation, because from a military perspective a small Belgium was easier prey than the United Kingdom of the Netherlands.

The Ten Days Campaign of 1831 and the Securing of Belgian Independence

Since the Congress of Vienna the artificially established United Kingdom of the Netherlands had within itself the seed of its own disintegration. The newly established independent Belgium was easy and attractive prey for both France and the Netherlands. As a compensation for insufficient means for self-defense, Belgium on 20 January 1831 was given the status of permanent neutrality, for which the five great European powers assumed the guarantee. In the XVIII Article Treaty of June 1831—the first practical result of the London conference of the Great Powers dealing with Belgium and the Netherlands after the 1830 Revolution—Belgian neutrality was declared as follows: "Belgium, within its borders such as they shall be traced in conformity with the principles laid down in the present preliminaries, shall form a perpetually neutral state. The five powers, without wishing to interfere in the internal administration of Belgium, guarantee to it that perpetual neutrality, as well as the integrity and the inviolability of its territory within the limits mentioned in the present Article [IX]."[3] Although the guarantors had reserved the right to intervene for the protection of their interests, Article X clearly stated that Belgium was allowed to defend itself from any foreign aggressor: "By a just reciprocity, Belgium shall be bound to observe the same neutrality toward all other states and not make any attempt against their internal or external tranquility, reserving itself, however, the right of defending itself against all foreign aggression."[4]

The five powers, however, did not intend to have their hands tied in the future and they decided to reject provisions that threatened to interfere with their interests. Article VII of the Protocol of 15 November 1831—revised in 1839 as the XXIV Article Treaty—states: "Belgium, within the boundaries specified in Articles I, II and IV, shall form an independent and perpetually neutral state. It shall be bound to observe such neutrality toward all other states."[5] In a series of protocols the Great Powers defined the future position of Belgium within the international community: "The five major powers have sole intention of assigning to Belgium a harmless position in the European system and offering it a role that simultaneously ensures its own happiness and the safety of others. Every nation has its respective rights, but Europe has its own rights too. It is the social system that has given Europe this right. The valid European agreements are already in force. Belgium must observe them and cannot break them. The events that led to the establishment of the new state in Europe do not give Belgium the right to change this general system of which it is a part. Likewise, any changes in the status of a long-existing state do not entitle [Belgium] to feel free of prior commitments."[6]

Countries committed to the maintenance of their neutrality could not enter into any alliances. The defense of their neutrality was, therefore, not easy. In addition, there was the problem that the Great Powers did not see an inseparable tie between the maintenance of peace in Europe and the support of the Belgian neutrality.

Despite the warnings of the Great Powers, King William I of the Netherlands did not want to accept the loss of the southern territories. During the Ten Days Campaign from 2 to 12 August 1831, Dutch troops invaded Belgium under the command of "Belgian" General Jozef Jacobus van Geen, who had decided upon the outbreak of the revolution to remain loyal to his king. It was only after the military intervention of France and the influence of British diplomacy that the independence of Belgium was restored. Similar conflicts had to be avoided in the future. Concerned about the balance of power on the Continent, Great Britain led the negotiations to normalize the relations between Belgium and the Netherlands.

The XXIV Article Treaty

The negotiations over Belgian neutrality stretched out over years. Only in 1839 did Belgium and the Netherlands sign a peace treaty, the so-called XXIV Article Treaty. Actually, it was an unfair agreement. Article XV, for example, stated that Antwerp harbor could not be used for military activities and thus remained a commercial port, as had already been established under the Treaty of Paris of 30 May 1814. The reason why Belgium was prepared to sign such an unfavorable agreement was its military weakness, which had been so pitifully exposed once more during the Ten Days Campaign. Only the article that guaranteed the young nation permanent neutrality was of any real advantage.

The Great Powers decided at the same time "to prevent by all means in their power a new conflict." They acted on the assumption that only an armed neutrality would be effective: "Without prejudice to Article III (imposing an unarmed neutrality on the Grand Duchy of Luxembourg), the other neutral states, of course, still have the right to improve their fortifications and other defenses."[7]

In addition to the Dutch threat, the politicians, in contrast to public opinion, primarily feared a French threat, especially during the first two decades after Belgian independence. This fear persisted until 1870, the year of the French defeat at the Battle of Sedan. The Belgian foreign minister, Sylvain Van de Weyer, described the French-Belgian relationship in the following terms: "Whoever the French foreign minister is, Talleyrand, Sebastiani, Molé, or Lamartine, it does not change France's attitude toward us. All these men—whose efforts we have experienced—had and will always have only one thought: they want to recapture Belgium totally or in part, and they always try to create opportunities to achieve that objective."[8]

In 1850 the French politician Adolphe Thiers wrote to King Leopold II: "Without a good means of defense you will be everyone's plaything."[9] In 1848 the construction of the large Antwerp fortifications started. In the event of the violation of Belgian neutrality, the Belgian Army could assemble there and wait for the forces of a guarantor power to arrive. This arrangement would only work, of course, in the case of a French or a Prussian attack. It was not designed to defend against a Dutch attack. Luckily, the king as well as the relevant government ministers were aware of the importance of maintaining good relations with their neighbor to the north. After 1848 the Netherlands no longer posed a threat to Belgium.

No external military threat was responsible for the so-called Crisis of 1848. Instead, the attitude of the Belgian and foreign press was the cause of the internal tensions. Some journalists encouraged the Belgian people to overthrow the monarchist regime and establish a republic. This also seemed possible because there were numerous French living in political exile in liberal Belgium, and they showed great affinity with the new regime in France. The ideological connection that would unite the new regime in Belgium with the French Republic could be an incentive to tie it to France. Such a development, of course, could be accepted neither by Belgium nor by any of the other Great Powers.[10]

The Risquons-Tout Incident made it clear that this danger was not just imaginary. Unemployed French and Belgian revolutionaries in France had combined to form a Belgian Legion. On 28 March 1848 an invasion disguised as "deportations" failed because of interference by Belgian railway workers. All the rebels were arrested. On the following day there was a clash between eighteen hundred insurgents and two hundred Belgian soldiers near Risquons-Tout. The latter reacted fast and forced the insurgents back. This incident, plus Napoleon III's accession to the French throne and hostile articles in the French press, led to increased military activity in Belgium.[11]

Seven forts in forward positions were built around Antwerp to protect the town's suburbs. The decision to build them had far-reaching consequences for the economic and demographic development of Antwerp, because no buildings could be erected within the firing zones of the forts' guns. It did not take long until political protests emerged, leading to the foundation of the Meeting Party. In addition, the king now had to deal with a Parliament that no longer accepted the principle that the monarch was solely responsible for foreign policy and defense. The protests of the Antwerp citizens and the increasingly important position of the Parliament delayed the completion of the already started extensions of the fortifications by several years. Not only were the fortifications strengthened, but the Belgian Army was increased as well. It now had one hundred thousand men under arms. At the same time, military service was extended to thirty months.[12]

Only during the Franco-Austro-Italian War of 1859 did Leopold II succeed in convincing his cabinet of the necessity of completing the Antwerp forts. Under the leadership of Henri-Alexis Brialmont, the next five years of construction produced enormous progress, and the works were completed in 1865. Apart from Paris, Antwerp was now the largest fortification system in Europe.

The Security Policy of Leopold II

Although France and Prussia were the guarantors of Belgian neutrality, it soon became apparent that they would sacrifice Belgium for the benefit of their own geopolitical interests. In the world of politics internationally guaranteed neutrality did not amount to much. In 1859 France advanced via the neutral Piedmont-Sardinia to support Italy against Austria in its fight for independence. Prussia also openly declared that it would infringe upon Belgian neutrality if it felt such an action to be necessary: "We also must not complicate our task by respecting Belgian neutrality."[13]

In consequence, neutrality only made sense when the guarantor states were prepared to respect it, and Belgian neutrality did not mean that Belgium could not be occupied by the guarantor states. The protocol of 20 January 1831 stated: "The Five Powers guarantee . . . in common the existence of the Belgian Kingdom and declare that none of them could under any circumstances invade or occupy it *without the consent of the four others.*" In fact, there was an international agreement that neutrality did not mean that a neutral area could no longer be traversed. Only The Hague Laws of Land Warfare described the status of a neutral country in a legally unambiguous way and declared a passage illegal. In the course of his policy to unite Germany under Prussian leadership, Otto von Bismarck tried to persuade Napoleon III to keep still by offering vague promises about possible territorial compensations at the Rhine and in Luxembourg.

After an unsuccessful effort to force Luxembourg to enter into a customs union, Napoleon III nevertheless attempted at the London Conference of 1867 to annex the Grand Duchy. That scheme failed because of the resistance of the other Great Powers. Luxembourg remained a member of the German *Zollverein* (customs union) and also enjoyed the neutrality guaranteed by the Great Powers; however, it had to raze the defensive fortifications around Luxembourg City. The town's Prussian garrison also had to be withdrawn. France, nevertheless, continued its efforts to control a part of the Luxembourg railroad network, which would have imposed a heavy economic burden on Belgium.

Despite evident foreign threat, the Belgian attitude was anti-militarist, since war was thought impossible. The fact that Belgium had luckily escaped the Franco-German War of 1870–1871 reinforced the blithe attitude of the population and its confidence in neutrality. It was partly thanks to the relative strength of the Belgian Army in relation to the French or Prussian armies that Belgium was not drawn into the Franco-German War. Since 1830 the Belgian forces had continually improved qualitatively and quantitatively, as the French military attaché in Belgium, Captain Louis-Lucien Demasur, reported in the 1860s: "Belgium is equipped with a significant army provided with excellent weapons, which under able command and forced by the circumstances to participate in a European war would bring its influence to bear."[14] With the knowledge of Belgium, Great Britain concluded a pact with France and Prussia in 1870 promising to respect the Belgian neutrality as long as the two Franco-German War opponents did the same.[15]

The naive confidence of the Belgian public in the passive neutrality initially frustrated Leopold II's efforts to further strengthen national defense. Only after 1878 was an additional outer line, the so-called Rupel–Nete Line, added to the Antwerp cordon of fortifications. The advanced positions had become necessary to protect the city center from enemy fire now possible from the greater ranges of artillery. Ten forts were added between 1878 and 1906—as far as the government's financial situation permitted. This outer line protected additional areas and nearly extended to the Dutch border in the north and the town of Mechelen in the south.

The courses of the Meuse and Sambre Rivers were also secured by forts. Both valleys had always been classical invasion routes. Once France and Germany had strengthened their own border defenses, Belgium had to follow, building barrier forts between 1887 and 1890. Namur and Liège were also secured by cordons of fortifications. Belgian defenses were now based on three major fortification systems: Antwerp, Namur, and Liège. The concept was a flexible one designed to contain a French attack (defense along the lines Antwerp–Namur and Namur–Liège), as well as a German invasion (defense along the lines Antwerp–Liège and Liège–Namur).

Pro-German Attitudes in the Catholic Regions

The Belgian monarchs were related to the royal families of France, Great Britain, Portugal, and Russia, but their origin was in Germany. It is, therefore, not surprising that the Belgian monarchs assumed a pro-German attitude, even in times of an imminent German invasion. The French military attaché, Captain Demasur, therefore, reported to Paris that this attitude would impede French diplomatic action. In particular, he perceived the good relationship between Leopold II and the German military attaché, Lieutenant Colonel Sommerfeld, as disadvantageous for France. Numerous members of the Belgian General Staff also appeared pro-German to Demasur. His successor shared his opinion: "The Belgian Army is provided with a good cadre and leadership. If required it is able to fight loyally and bravely. But its military leaders—the king and the General Staff—and the government, will they not endeavor to neutralize this force through making decisions which benefit too much the sole interests of Germany?"[16]

Furthermore, Belgium ordered German-made Krupp guns, and Germany recommended the defense of the Meuse valley. The Belgian leadership followed this recommendation because such a line of defense would not only delay a French advance to the Rhine River but also a German invasion. The plans already in place for the construction of a railway between Monschau and St. Vith—there already was a connection between Gladbach and Antwerp—stimulated German-Belgian trade and promoted pro-German attitudes. From the French perspective, the regular visits of Leopold II and his brother, the Count of Flanders, to Berlin were considered an affront. When the German kaiser paid a return visit to Brussels, Leopold and his brother wore the uniforms of their honorary Prussian regiment. Even the inhabitants of Brussels found such behavior odd, and their comments were accordingly critical.

In late 1880 the French military attachés revised their assessment of the effectiveness of the Belgian Army. They now considered that the Belgian soldiers lacked the necessary military fighting spirit. They also reported that the pro-German attitude continued at the higher levels of Belgian military command: "The impartiality of the Belgian people in its entirety . . . cannot really be doubted. They love their independence very much and do not feel collective sympathy for Germany, but quite on the contrary they admit openly that they feel ethnically and culturally connected to France. On the other hand, it is obvious that the court, the military leadership and a major part of the intellectual or financial elites admire the great and strong Reich to the east and enjoy describing in detail the numerous weaknesses that explain the decadence of their southern neighbor so well."

A discussion the French attaché Major Charles Haillot had with the Belgian deputy chief of the General Staff, Lieutenant Colonel Antonin de Selliers de Moranville, reinforced this impression: "For our Catholic and communal ideals, Belgium's accession to the Reich's federal system would involve fewer difficult circumstances than an unmistakable annexation by centralist and Jacobin France. Eat or be eaten, we still prefer the Bavarian recipe to the Provençal one. . . . Maybe we would gain Artois with the part of Flanders and Hainaut that you took away from us under Louis XIV. . . . If you are strong, you are our greatest danger. We will only be able to grow at their expense if you are weak." In short, Belgium between 1884 and 1914 was governed by a Catholic majority that preferred the Lutheran and therefore Christian Germany to an ecclesiophobic and republican France.

After the turn of the century the construction of a railway line was once again a cause for worry for the French government. The connection from Malmedy to Stavelot ran adjacent to Camp Elsenborn, which had been established in the border region a few years earlier. In the event of a war this base could be used as an assembly area for German forces that could use the Belgian railway to invade France. If the Belgian Army had a more martial posture, this would not have been a problem. But according to the report that Captain Louis Duruy, military attaché since 1909, sent to Paris, the fighting spirit of the Belgians did not live up to expectations. Additionally, there was no lack of German influence on the Belgian government: "The most typical behavior appears to be observing events from protected positions behind the Meuse. Also, the influence of the Germans on the Belgian government must not be underestimated. Some days ago a Belgian officer told me: 'From a practical perspective, the interest of the Belgian Army is to await the result of the first battles and then associate with the stronger party.'"

The death of Leopold II and Albert's accession to the throne did not bring about a change of the situation: "According to a French correspondent in Brussels, the new court in Brussels is said to be very pro-German. Its actual head is, by the way, the Countess of Flanders, who is of purely German descent. The new king has been educated in a German fashion and, in contrast to King Leopold and Prince Baudouin, has no affinity for France."

Even when it was commonly assumed that Germany rather than France would likely violate Belgian neutrality, there was no change in the attitude toward the neighbor to the east. Captain Eugène Génie, attaché since 1912, reported to Paris that "the Catholic government in Brussels would pass up no opportunity to express its partiality against France and for Germany."

Times of Change, 1904 to 1913

The 1907 Hague Laws of Land Warfare stipulated that the territory of a neutral state was inviolable and any passage required permission. Considering the arms race and the likeliness of an armed conflict in Europe, Belgium decided to modernize its existing fortifications, particularly those at Antwerp, Namur, and Liège, which were not capable of withstanding the new high explosive artillery shells. Brick forts were replaced by concrete—but only a few by reinforced concrete—and armored cupolas. The underlying assumption was that it would be impossible to transport the heaviest caliber guns over greater distances. In August 1914, Germany proved the contrary by using rail transport.

Eleven forts and twelve entrenchments were added to the outer line around Antwerp. Leopold II and his nephew and successor to the throne, Albert, were mainly responsible for the improvements. They successfully bypassed the government and Parliament, neither of which had much interest in military matters. Nor did the government understand the purpose of the far-reaching reforms, or even man key positions with people who had any idea of Belgium's military situation. Since Leopold and Albert had participated in German maneuvers, they knew that neither the existing fortifications nor the strength of the Belgian Army would suffice to stop the German military. "Sadly enough, we may only say that our strength and quality are currently insufficient from a military point of view, that we are completely powerless, and that even if the current situation continues, the poor morale of the army will become a threat to internal order."[17]

Thanks to the family ties to a member of the German General Staff, Karl von Hohenzollern, the brother-in-law of King Albert, the people in charge in Belgium were well informed about the intentions and military capabilities of their eastern neighbor. During Leopold's visit to Germany in 1904, Kaiser Wilhelm II tried to persuade the Belgian king to join an anti-French alliance in return for the restoration of the former Belgian territories in northern France previously ceded to Louis XIV. During the Agadir Crisis the German ambassador in London mentioned that in the event of a war against France an invasion into Belgium was planned. When King Albert visited Potsdam in 1913, Kaiser Wilhelm II unmistakably declared that the small neutral states not forming an alliance with Germany would be regarded as enemies.[18]

Belgian Plans for the Event of War: Personnel Strength

The mere development of military plans was not sufficient for defending Belgium. At first, the politicians had to be convinced that the existing number of forces was inadequate. The fact that Leopold II could only on his deathbed sign the law introducing general compulsory military service shows that this insight was not generally shared. With the support of Cardinal Désiré-Joseph Mercier, the previous conscription system was abolished in December 1909. From then on one son from every family was conscripted. Owing to the growing strength of the neighboring countries' military forces, further measures soon became necessary. On 28 May 1913 the Catholic prime minister Charles de Broqueville, who also held the minister of defense portfolio, succeeded in securing Parliament's consent to the introduction of general compulsory military service. On paper, the Belgian Army thus grew to 340,000 men, a number that was actually never achieved.

The *levée en masse* of 31 July 1914 mobilized 200,000 men. During the following weeks the force increased by 18,000 volunteers and another 18,000 conscripts who were drafted from parts of the country that were not yet occupied. The Belgian field army of 117,000 men was organized into six divisions. In contrast with the other European countries, the Belgian divisions had a strength on paper of 25,000 to 30,000 men each. Belgium also fielded a single cavalry division of 4,500 troopers. A division consisted of three or four brigades with two regiments each, a cavalry regiment, an artillery regiment equipped with thirty-six 75 mm and 150 mm guns, a separate artillery battalion equipped with twelve 75 mm field guns, and engineers and service support troops. The Belgian Army, however, had only about one hundred machine guns and it lacked heavy artillery. It only procured twelve howitzers from France in August 1914. The army had 37,600 horses, 2,600 trucks, and 1,500 passenger vehicles. Military aviation was still a very modest service equipped with only thirty aircraft.

The Belgian Buildup at the End of the Nineteenth Century

After expansion of the army, the Belgian General Staff had to prepare a plan for the defense of Belgium in the event of a German or a French attack. This was not an easy task, since the members of Parliament thought of it as their responsibility. Through a series of case studies the General Staff tried to plan the reactions of the Belgian Army to various scenarios. There was a "Hypothèse d'une invasion directe de notre pays par l'armée française" (a scenario of the French Army directly invading Belgium) for the case of a French invasion, and a "Hypothèse d'un passage de l'armée française par la Belgique" (a scenario of the French Army passing through Belgium) for the case of a German attack.[19]

In 1891 Lieutenant Joseph Begrand of the General Staff prepared a study that became the basis for the future Belgian deployment in 1914. This study was revised by Major Auguste Hamelrijck and forwarded to his superior, Lieutenant Colonel Félix Chapelié. In this analysis Begrand himself played the role of the Germans and planned an attack against France that violated Belgian neutrality. Following military logic, he described the potential German assembly areas and axes of advance. Begrand posited five different scenarios. Next, he war-gamed the Belgian Army's possible courses of action. He concluded by recommending a more effective distribution of the Belgian Army. What did this mean precisely?

Initially Begrand assumed a German advance along the left bank of the Meuse River, but he did not exclude a deployment along the right bank. The position of the Netherlands was also taken into consideration: "We believe that when the Germans have made the decision to violate the neutrality of Belgian territory and thus cross over to the left bank of the Meuse River and traverse the Haspengau plateau if their intent requires this, they will also march through Dutch Limburg—a narrow strip between Visé and Roermond. I have heard Dutch officers claiming that pertinent documents indicate the Dutch Army would be in no way concerned if foreign troops were to traverse this part of their country."[20] From this point Begrand examined the five scenarios, two of which assumed a deployment south of the Meuse, while the other three anticipated a breakthrough north of Liège.

Case No. 1: The first scenario was based on the assumption that the German forces would start out from the Belgian areas around Verviers–Eupen–Malmedy, which are German-speaking to this day, and advance along four axes from north to south to reach the French part of the Meuse between Mézières and Sedan. The first axis started in Malmedy and led along past Stavelot, Marche, and Wellin to end at Mézières. The second axis departed from Recht via Vielsalm, Laroche, Saint-Hubert, Rochehaut, and went on toward the French border. The third axis started at St. Vith and ran to Houffalize, Recogne, Bouillon, and terminated at Sedan. The last axis had its starting point in Reuland and stretched along Bastogne, Neufchâteau, Florenville or Cugnon, with Douzy as the final destination.

Case No. 2: After crossing the Meuse north of the Haute Fagnes (High Fens)—a high moor area—the Germans advanced toward the Val-d'Oise, thereby passing the valley between the Sambre and the Meuse. This scenario had two approach routes. The first started in Malmedy and ran by Stavelot, Hamoir, Emptienne, Ciney, Yvoir, and Chimay, and then continued toward the French border. The second route started at St. Vith and went through Vielsalm, Baraque Fraiture, Marche, Dinant, and Philippeville, to end in Maubert-Fontaine in France.

Case No. 3: The German First Army would assemble in the area of Aachen and cross the Meuse near Maastricht, advance via the plains of Hesbaye toward Charleroi, and either continue along the Meuse or advance in the valley between the Sambre and the Meuse. For the first axis the assumed crossing was near Maastricht. The route ran along Bilzen, Sint-Truiden, Tienen, Jodoigne, Charleroi, Beaumont, and farther toward the French border. The second axis began in Visé and went via Tongeren and Waremme to Philippeville.

Case No. 4: As in Case No. 3, the assembly area was Aachen. The German First Army would cross the Meuse near Maastricht and Visé and then march toward Antwerp. This would also violate the neutrality of the Netherlands. The routes of advance had to avoid the fortified town of Diest. Nonetheless, Begrand was not quite sure about which route the Germans would choose. He therefore posited an alternative for each axis. The first left Maastricht and went via Hasselt, Lummen, Tessenderloo, Veerle, and Herentals. The alternate route ran via Halen, Waanrode, Tielt, Aarschot, and Lier instead of Lummen. The second axis started in Visé and ran along Tongeren, Sint-Truiden, Tienen, Aarschot, and Lier. The alternative route started in Tienen and ran toward Leuven and Mechelen.

Case No. 5: In this scenario the assembly would take place in the Geilenkirchen–Gladbach area. The Meuse River would either be crossed at Maaseik only, or at both Maaseik and Roermond. The objective was Antwerp. Assuming the crossing of the border to take place in the north, the march toward Antwerp would be very short. The first axis went from Roermond to Herentals, along Meert, Lommel, and Mol. The second axis started in Maaseik and passed Leopoldsburg, Veerle, Markhoren, and Lier.

According to Begrand it was not unlikely that the Germans would attack the center of the Belgian defense and thus neutralize Antwerp right at the beginning of operations. The purpose of violating Belgium's neutrality was to reach France as quickly as possible, thus threatening Paris. If the Germans were to advance south of the Meuse River, then the larger part of the Belgian Army would remain intact and be available anytime to attack the flank of the German Army. This development would force Germany to deploy a significant number of troops to counter such a threat. From the German perspective, therefore, it was only logical to neutralize the Belgian Army in the north as a preemptive measure.

A later development confirmed Begrand's analysis. The difference was that the German force was large enough to march to Paris and at the same time keep the Belgian Army in check, while only having to modify slightly their original plan. Begrand also discussed the measures the Belgian Army could take to stop a German advance. Should the enemy thrust forward south of the Meuse via Belgian territory (Cases No. 1 and 2), and should the Belgian troops be concentrated relatively far away from the Meuse in the north, then the Germans still would be one day's march ahead of the Belgian Army, which would have to march south first before it could try to intercept the enemy. The Belgian troops would therefore only reach the Namur area when the German forces had already reached Nafraiture, near the French-Belgian border.

That situation was comparable to the German forces crossing the Meuse near Maastricht and attempting a southern breakthrough (Case No. 3), because the Belgians knew through their intelligence service that the Germans would assemble in Aachen, but not the direction toward which they would advance. Only when enemy forces reached the Meuse would it become clear whether they would go for Maastricht, Roermond, or Maaseik. Only that knowledge would clarify the German Army's deployment plan (No. 3, No. 4, or No. 5). In order to compensate for the strategic disadvantage of the Belgian Army, it was necessary to select the correct staging area and to deploy the forces in such a way that they would be able to catch up with the Germans and contain them, even when forced to react to the German movements.

One possible staging area was the triangle of Brussels–Mechelen–Leuven. Even better suited was the quadrangle of Leuven–Aarschot–Diest–Tienen. That position had several advantages. In the north it was protected by the Demer River, to the east by the Gete River, and it was relatively near the Meuse. Nonetheless, a deployment from that position would not reduce the difficulty of catching up with the Germans. Starting from that position, the Belgian forces would reach the German Army at Hoepertingen. Since they would arrive at approximately the same time as the Germans, Belgian forces would not have enough time to establish their positions. It therefore appeared more advantageous to occupy positions in the area of Sint-Truiden or along the Velpe River. If the German Army followed Case No. 4, the Belgian Army could deploy south of Diest and link its flank with the fort. Should the deployment follow Case No. 5, the Belgians could barricade behind the channel of Hasselt near Turnhout and conduct a delaying maneuver toward the direction of Herentout. A deployment farther east seemed unfeasible because of the nature of the terrain. Pine trees obstructed the fields of fire and bogs and dunes prevented a reasonable deployment.

Even with the deployment area of the Belgian Army well chosen, there was not much time and scope for action. Therefore, they had to play for time. That was the task of the cavalry division and the engineers. They had to ensure the timely arrival of the Belgian units at the locations where they could bring their influence to bear. South of the Meuse, felled trees could be used to block the enemy's advance on the main roads; north of the river, a series of bridges across rivers and channels could be demolished. However, these acts of sabotage could not be executed just anywhere. It was necessary to consult with the guarantor states to find out which routes they were going to use when supporting the Belgian Army in the enforcement of neutrality. The Belgians, therefore, hoped to avoid inadvertently slowing their advance by choosing the wrong places for barriers. Rather, the barriers should be established at positions the enemy had to pass (along roads and railway lines) and that could be defended by cavalry and, if possible, by infantry. The intent was to force the Germans to position themselves and to fight to fend off attacks while trying to repair the destructions and overcome the barriers.

All that should cause the Germans to lose crucial time for their advance. The barriers and destructions, however, should not be irreparable. Repairs had to be possible within a few hours or days at most. In order to correctly select positions where destructions should be carried out, Begrand recommended reconnoitering the courses of the rivers that ran parallel to the border.

At the end of his detailed analysis Begrand concluded that notwithstanding the deployment conducted by the Germans—an advance north or south of the Meuse—it would be vitally important for the Belgian Army to be ready to go to war in sufficient time and not to allow its lines of communication to Antwerp to be cut. That fortress was the most important base of the Belgian Army, because neither Namur nor Liège had depots large enough to supply the entire force. By maintaining communications with Antwerp, the Belgian Army would be able to operate freely in the triangle of Antwerp–Liège–Namur and would not be completely dependent on the Antwerp stocks. By abandoning the lines of communication with Antwerp, it would be forced to use the stocks from the two other fortified towns. Naturally that scenario would not apply in the case of a French invasion via Lille, or a German invasion via the northern parts of Belgium.

Major Hamelrijck, who commented on Begrand's operational study, suggested thinking about a central staging area for the army from where it could operate independently of the routes and objectives of the German invaders. According to Hamelrijck's calculations it was possible to deploy the army to the right bank of the Meuse in only twelve hours by using the railway network. Begrand noted that there were more than thirty train stations in the quadrangular staging area, in particular the large stations at Brussels, Schaarbeek, Mechelen, and Leuven.

The Eve of World War I

Deploying the Belgian Army for a war became the subject of heated discussions within the General Staff. As long as the enemy was unknown (France or Germany), the General Staff envisaged a central deployment of the infantry divisions near Ath, Namur, Liège, Asse, Brussels, and Leuven and of the cavalry division near Ottignies. Depending on the situation, these forces should be concentrated either around Namur, Ath, or Liège.[21]

When in May 1914 the avowed Catholic Antonin de Selliers de Moranville became chief of the General Staff, the deployment planning was modified. He prepared three plans. The first plan for the event of a German attack concentrated Belgian forces in the region Sint-Truiden, Houtaîn-l'Evêque, Hannuit,

Eghezée in the first line, and Tienen, Hamme-Mille, and Hoegaarden in the second line. The cavalry division should be positioned to the front. These units were not intended to defend the fortified positions of Liège and Namur. This plan had significant advantages. The Belgian forces could not be cut off from the Antwerp fortification, and the lines of communications allowed for a swift repositioning to Liège or toward the Meuse, should the opportunity arise to threaten the German flank. In addition, the plan took into account the arrival of the guarantor states' forces.[22] The second plan was designed to contain a French attack, and the third developed an option for the event that Belgium should find itself in an uncertain situation.

Selliers de Moranville later directed one of his adjutants, Major Henri Maglinse, to prepare yet another plan, which would immediately concentrate two divisions (the 3rd and 4th) west of the Meuse. The other divisions were to be positioned between Hannut, Sint-Truiden, and Hasselt and, if necessary, would march to the Meuse on foot. The deputy chief of the General Staff, Colonel Louis de Ryckel, preferred a defense at the Meuse.[23] There was no doubt that Germany would mobilize faster than Belgium, and he therefore expected the guarantor states to take the offensive. No matter how the situation evolved, the Germans would reach the Meuse relatively quickly.

The chief of the General Staff could count on the support of the war minister but not on the military adviser to the king, Captain Emile Galet. The latter also presented a plan for staging the Belgian Army based on deploying in the quadrangle between Liège-Visé-Engis-Odeur, with the intent of immediately defending Belgian territory at the borders. Many members of the General Staff regarded this plan as risky and venturesome.[24] But Galet assumed that Germany would commit only a limited number of its forces against Belgium and that he would know in advance who the enemy was. In this scenario the Belgian Army would indeed be capable of containing the German forces. Belgium's defense "cannot be restricted to defending the national flag in Antwerp, but has to start at the border."[25]

King Albert had to decide on the plan, taking into consideration the sensitivities in both Parliament and the army. By 31 July 1914 he still had not made a decision, but during the mobilization he decided in favor of the plan forwarded by de Ryckel: defending along the Meuse River. It was one thing, however, to choose a plan, and another to execute it. Unfortunately, there had been no preparations made for railway transport of the units.[26]

Circumstances compelled the Belgians to deploy the 3rd Division near Liège, the 4th Division near Namur, and the other divisions between the Gete and Dyle Rivers.

Leuven was to be the location of the headquarters. The cavalry division assumed a position between the Meuse and Gete with the mission of serving as an advance guard, and, in the event that Liège fell, conducting a rearward movement. The cavalry also would be available to contain a German breakthrough toward Maastricht.

The Violation of Belgium's Neutrality

After the assassination of the Austrian crown prince in Sarajevo, Belgium first hoped that it would be able to keep out of the emerging conflict, as it had in 1870. Only on 23 June 1914, when a war was clearly unavoidable, was a partial mobilization announced. After the German ultimatum to France and Russia, full mobilization was ordered. Nonetheless, Belgium declared again, in contrast to the ideas of its military leaders, that it wanted to remain neutral. King Albert sent a letter written in German, revised by his wife Queen Elisabeth, to his brother-in-law, Bavaria's King Ludwig III, asking not to begin a war. It remained unanswered.

On 2 August King Albert assumed direct command of the army. At 1900 hours the German ultimatum was submitted. It demanded free access to Belgian territory to preempt a French attack. The Belgian government had only twelve hours to reply. That night, the king presided over the Council of Ministers. After one hour, the Crown Council was summoned as well. With the exception of the Catholic Charles Woeste, all present rejected the German ultimatum: "The Belgian government was determined to avoid each and any assault on its rights with all means available." Although the Belgian people had great sympathy for orderly, stable, and Christian Germany, they were outraged.

In his speech before the House of Commons on 3 August, British foreign secretary Sir Edward Grey said that the violation of Belgium's neutrality was a reason for war. On 4 August 1914, Germany set in motion the Schlieffen-Moltke Plan. With German troops crossing the border, the Belgian military found itself facing the scenario it had always dreaded—fighting against the anticipated victor, Germany.

Notes

1. Luc de Vos, *Het effectief van de Belgische krijgsmacht en de militiewetgeving, 1830-1914* (Brussels, 1985), 107.

2. Arnold Smits, *1830, Scheuring in de Nederlanden, deel I: Holland stoot Vlaanderen af*, UGA (Kortrijk, 1983), 83-86.

3. Alfred de Ridder, *Histoire diplomatique du traité de 1839* (Brussels, Paris, 1920), 375; Alexander Fuehr, *The Neutrality of Belgium* (New York, 1915), appendix, http://net.lib.byu.edu/~rdh7/wwi/comment/belgneut/BelgTC.htm#TC.

4. E. Banning, *Les origines et les phases de la neutralité belge* (Brussels, 1927), 46; Fuehr, *The Neutrality of Belgium*, appendix, http://net.lib.byu.edu/~rdh7/wwi/comment/belgneut/BelgTC.htm#TC.

5. Banning, *Les origines et les phases de la neutralité belge*, 55; Fuehr, *The Neutrality of Belgium*, appendix, http://net.lib.byu.edu/~rdh7/wwi/comment/belgneut/BelgTC.htm#TC.

6. Banning, *Les origines et les phases de la neutralité belge*, 43.

7. Alfred de Ridder, *La crise de la neutralité belge de 1848* (Brussels, 1928), v.

8. Ibid., page vii.

9. E. Descamps, *La neutralité de la Belgique* (Brussels, Paris, 1902), 398.

10. De Ridder, *La crise de la neutralité belge de 1848*, viii.

11. De Vos, *Het effectief van de Belgische krijgsmacht en de militiewetgeving*, 98–100.

12. Ibid., 111–119.

13. De Ridder, *La crise de la neutralité belge de 1848*.

14. Albert Duchesne, "L'armée et la politique militaire belge de 1871 à 1920 jugés par les attachés militaires de France à Bruxelles," *Belgisch Tijdschrift voor Filosofie en Geschiedenis* 40, no. 2 (1961): 391–430, here page 397.

15. Descamps, *La neutralité de la Belgique*, 288f.

16. Cf. Duchesne, "L'armée et la politique militaire," *Belgisch Tijdschrift voor Filosofie en Geschiedenis* 40, nos. 2 and 4 (1961): 391–430 and 1092–1126, respectively; Albert Duchesne, "L'armée et la politique militaire," *Belgisch Tijdschrift voor Filosofie en Geschiedenis* 41, nos. 2 and 4 (1962): 371–384 and 1188–1219, respectively.

17. Marie-Rose Thielemans and Emile Vandewoude, *Le Roi Albert au travers de ses lettres inédites* (Brussels: Office international de librairie, 1982), 80–83.

18. Ibid., 85.

19. Brussels Army Museum, Russian Archives, Box 1106, Chart 185-14-2647.

20. Ibid.: Begrand, Etude stratégique op. cit., 14.

21. Henri Bernard, *Totale oorlog en revolutionaire oorlog*, vol. 1, *De 19de eeuw, de Eerste Werelddoorlog en de Russische Revolutie* (Brussels, 1993), 358.

22. Antonin de Selliers de Moranville, *Du haut de la tour de Babel* (Paris, 1925), 197–199.

23. Bernard, *Totale oorlog en revolutionaire oorlog*, 1:357f.

24. Ibid.

25. Emile Galet, *Sa Majesté le Roi Albert, commandant en chef devant l'invasion allemande* (Paris, 1931), 17.

26. Bernard, *Totale oorlog en revolutionaire oorlog*, 1:359.

Appendix

Deployment Plans, 1893–1914

Editorial Remarks

Theoretical map exercises, *Winterarbeiten* (literally "Winter Work," meaning assignments for officers as a substitute for maneuvers), or war games, provide only a limited explanation for the operational-strategic plans of a General Staff. The operational and strategic intentions of a General Staff in a specific situation can only be evaluated if lessons learned are translated into operational principles and *Aufmarschplanungen* (deployment plans). This also holds true for the plans of the *Grosser Generalstab* (Great General Staff) prior to the First World War.

After the end of the war in 1918, the German files on the plans of the General Staff were kept at the *Reichsarchiv*. That institution never made the *Aufmarschpläne* (deployment plans) of Schlieffen and Moltke the Younger available to the public. At best the *Reichsarchiv* issued paraphrased summaries or extracts. With the destruction of the *Heeresarchiv* (Army Archive) in Potsdam in April 1945, the *Aufmarschakten* (deployment files) of the *Grosser Generalstab* seemed to have been irretrievably lost. In discussions about the Schlieffen Plan and the issue of who was to blame for the war, many scholars have expressed their regret about this loss. Fortunately, a compilation of the *Aufmarschpläne* from 1893–1894 to 1914–1915, which had been prepared for the *Reichsarchiv* on the basis of available *Aufmarschakten,* survived the destruction of the *Heeresarchiv* and was deposited in the military archive of the German Democratic Republic under reference nunber Pr 3.2.12.1./2, in the subholdings *Chef des Generalstabs des Feldheeres* (Chief of the General Staff of the Field Army), in the holdings *Generalstab* (General Staff), and in the record group *Preussische Armee* (Prussian Army). In 1996 these holdings were taken over by the *Bundesarchiv/Militärarchiv* (Federal Archives, Military Division) in Freiburg, under the same reference number. In 2002 they were added to the holdings *Kriegsgeschichtliche Forschungsanstalt des Heeres* (War History Research Center of the Army) under reference number RH61/96.[1]

This file contains 171 handwritten or typed sheets of paper, some of them written on both sides, plus twenty cards with no dates indicated. In addition to the *Aufmarschpläne*, the file contains an eight-page typed study by an unknown author entitled "Die Verletzung der belgischen Neutralität" (The Violation of Belgian Neutrality); a four-page typed compilation of *Aufmarschanweisungen* for the Sixth and Seventh Armies for 1908 to 1914; a twelve-page typed study entitled "Stellungnahme zu den Bemerkungen zu den Aufgaben des Südflügels des deutschen Westheeres unter besonderer Berücksichtigung der Einstellung Moltkes zu ihnen" (Comment to the Remarks on the Tasks of the Southern Wing of the German West Army in due Consideration of Moltke's Opinion Regarding Such). Also included is a typed, undated statement by the president of the *Kriegsgeschichtliche Forschungsanstalt des Heeres,* Wolfgang Foerster titled "Stellungnahme zu den Bemerkungen des Generals Konrad Krafft von Dellmensingen zu Band I des Reichsarchiv-Werkes" (Comment on the Remarks by General Wolfgang Krafft von Dellmensingen on Volume I of the Reich Archive's Works). Since Krafft von Dellmensingen wrote the final version of his critical review of volume 1 of the World War I German official history in February 1931,[2] Foerster probably wrote his reply in that same year.

Nevertheless, it is impossible to determine the exact dates of the excerpts of the *Aufmarschakten*. There are two periods during which they might have been written. Since volume 1 of the official history contains several detailed hints about the *Aufmarschplanungen,*[3] it is possible that the excerpts from the *Aufmarschakten* were written in the early 1920s as preparatory notes for the official history. On the other hand, there are good reasons to assume that these excerpts were made only during the run-up to the publication of Friedrich von Boetticher's article entitled "Der Lehrmeister des neuzeitlichen Krieges"[4] (The Master of Modern War) in the early 1930s. With the exception of a few details, the map on the *Westaufmarsch* (Western Deployment) of 1899–1900 is identical to the *Aufmarschkarte* (Deployment Map) in Boetticher's article. The fact that an external member of the Reichsarchiv, retired Major Thilo von Bose, prepared compilations of Schlieffen's *Aufmarschplanungen* for Boetticher in 1931[5] supports the dating. While doing this work, Bose could have prepared a compilation of all of Schlieffen's and Moltke the Younger's *Aufmarschpläne* by using the *Aufmarschakten* available at the *Reichsarchiv.*

Except for the stenographic copies Foerster[6] made of the *Aufmarsch* II of 1912 and the *Aufmarschanweisungen* for 1914–1915, as well as some of his handwritten marginal notes, all the other handwritten copies and marginal notes cannot be associated with this file.

The *Aufmarschplanungen* of the *Grosse Generalstab* of the mobilization years from 1893–1894 to 1914–1915, which are published for the first time in this volume, do not feature the long-term operational plans of the German ground forces after the beginning of the war. They do highlight, however, both the establishment of the main point of the strategic effort on the right wing of the western front and the short-term operational objectives of the German field armies. They include exact time frames in mobilization days for the conduct of the operations, starting from the beginning of mobilization, for both the planned assault on Liège and a potential advance through the Netherlands. The initial objectives of the German wing armies for the deployment of 1907–1908 were Oudenarde, west of Brussels, for the First Army, the line from Ath northwest of Binche for the Second Army, and the line Thuin–Charleville for the Third Army.[7] This scheme of maneuver reveals the planned broad transit through Belgium and the intent to cross the Franco-Belgian border on a line north of Lille–Verdun.

Furthermore, it is possible with the help of these files to understand for the first time in an operational context the modifications that Moltke the Younger made to Schlieffen's *Aufmarschplanungen*—the decision to dispense with the transit through the Netherlands,[8] which resulted in the attack on Liège,[9] and the reinforcement of the left German wing. These modifications started with the mobilization year of 1908–1909. Simultaneously, it becomes clear that Moltke had planned the transit through Netherlands territory as a precautionary measure, in case the attack on Liège failed.[10]

In addition to new knowledge about the German *Aufmarschplanungen*, these files illustrate that the *Aufmarschplan* of 1906–1907—the last under Schlieffen's responsibility—provided for elements of the Third Army to quell potential labor unrest in Germany's Ruhr region, despite the fact that Schlieffen had often complained about a shortage of forces.[11] The files also show that there was an intent to wage war in coordination with the Austro-Hungarian Royal and Imperial Army in the east, but there was no joint operational plan, and since the mobilization year of 1913–1914 there were no preparations for the "*Grosse Ostaufmarsch*" (Great Eastward Deployment).[12] Moreover, the *Aufmarschplanungen* reveal that for a period of years nobody in the General Staff seriously considered the use of Italian forces against France, although arrangements existed for the transport of Italian forces into Alsace.[13] It is only in the *Aufmarschplan* of 1914–1915 that there is a certain conviction that the Italian General Staff would be obliged to send forces, and thus that Italy would enter the war on the side of the Reich.[14] The *Aufmarschanweisungen* for the mobilization year of 1914–1915, however, do not include instructions or specific plans for cooperation between German and Italian forces.

Thus, this volume not only illustrates the operational and strategic plans of Schlieffen and Moltke, but also shows the important domestic and foreign aspects of the work of the *Grosser Generalstab*. And for the first time we present a file-based analysis of Germany's *Aufmarschplanungen* prior to the First World War.

The original versions of the *Aufmarschpläne* printed in this volume are preserved as typed, handwritten, and stenographic versions. Compiled by a number of writers, the plans sometimes differ considerably from each other on punctuation, abbreviations, and the spelling of geographic names. Often the absence of the German letter "ß" on the old typewriters resulted in Straßburg being spelled as Strassburg. [English edition editor's note: For the purpose of this English edition the German letter "ß" has been replaced throughout with "ss," since most English readers who do not speak German will most likely be completely unfamiliar with the "ß" character.]

The editors of this volume have been very cautious in their treatment of these documents. We have harmonized or silently corrected the spellings of place and country names. Abbreviations and punctuations are taken from the original. [In the English translation most of the abbreviations are spelled out. Hence, infantry division for I.D., army corps for A.K., etc.] For layout reasons, the formats of some of the tables have been modified for the present edition. All in all, the editors have endeavored to achieve as much uniformity as possible.

Remarks by the "translators" from the old Sütterlin script and the stenographic parts of the text are marked in square [ ] brackets. A question mark indicates ambiguities. Three ellipsis points in square brackets [. . .] indicate illegibility in the handwriting. Corrections and other additions in the original, in several colors and handwritings, are included in the edition in brackets.

Notes

1. For the history of file RH61/96, see the chapter by Gerhard Gross in this volume.

2. For information on this, see Markus Pöhlmann, *Kriegsgeschichte und Geschichtspolitik: Der Erste Weltkrieg. Die amtliche deutsche Militärgeschichtsschreibung 1914–1956* (Paderborn, 2002), 307.

3. *Der Weltkrieg 1914–1918,* vol. 1, *Die Grenzschlachten im Westen,* ed. Reichsarchiv (Berlin, 1925), 49–65. (Volume 1 of the German official history of World War I.)

4. Cf. Friedrich von Boetticher, "Der Lehrmeister des neuzeitlichen Krieges," in *Von Scharnhorst zu Schlieffen 1806–1906: Hundert Jahre preussisch-deutscher Generalstab,* ed. Friedrich von Cochenhausen at the instigation of the Reichswehrministerium (Berlin, 1933), 249–319, here 266.

5. Boetticher to Marcks, 18 December 1931, BA-MA, Nachlass Boetticher, N 323/53.

6. Foerster used the Gabelsberger shorthand system in accordance with the so-called Vienna Decisions of 1895. The present stenograph, however, includes some more recent notations in accordance with the Berlin Decisions of 1902. The editors express their gratitude to Mr. Hans Gebhardt for the transcription of Foerster's shorthand texts.

7. Cf. Aufmarsch 1907–1908.

8. See Aufmarsch 1908–1909.

9. See Aufmarsch 1908–1909 and 1909–1910.

10. See Aufmarsch 1908–1909 and 1913–1914.

11. See Aufmarsch 1906–1907.

12. See Aufmarsch 1913–1914. Cf. Annika Mombauer, *Helmuth von Moltke and the Origins of the First World War* (Cambridge, 2001), 102–104.

13. "Preparations have been made for the deployment of an Italian army consisting of five army corps and two cavalry divisions to the Upper Rhine. In the current political situation, the Italian army is unlikely to arrive." Aufmarsch 1909–1910, 433. See also the chapter by Fuhrer and Olsansky in this volume.

14. See Aufmarsch 1914–1915.

Aufmarsch 1893–1894

(The only material available is the wartime Order of Battle and two *Aufmarsch* maps)

1. Western Army

First Army (4 army corps, 3 reserve divisions, 1 Landwehr brigade, 2 cavalry divisions.)
Command Post Merzig.
Deployment Line German border near Echternach–Sierck–Diedenhofen–Maizières and Metz–Niederbrücken southwest of Bolchen.
The area around Metz will be secured by XVI Army Corps, which is not under the operational control of any army.
Main Effort Left wing.

Second Army (3 army corps, 4 reserve divisions, 1 Landwehr brigade, 2 cavalry divisions.)
Command Post Saarbrücken.
Deployment Line Niederbrücken–Waibelskirchen–Bingen–Elwingen–Falkenberg–area east of Gesslingen.
Main Effort Right wing.

Third Army (3 army corps, 3 reserve divisions, 1 Landwehr brigade, 1 cavalry division.)
Command Post Saargemünd.
Deployment Line Area east of Gesslingen–Obrick–Laufingen–northern tip of Stock-Weiher (northwest of Saarburg).
Main Effort Exertion of pressure on both wings.

Fourth Army (4 army corps, 4 reserve divisions, 1 Landwehr brigade, 1 cavalry division.)
Command Post Zabern.
Deployment Line Northern tip of Stock–Weiher–Gondrexange–Lörchingen–Soldatenthal–leaving out the Vosges ridge –Ob. Haslach–Urmatt–Laubenheim–Innenheim.
Main Effort Right wing.

Army Detachment (1 army corps, 1 reserve division, 5½ Landwehr brigades.)
Command Post Colmar.
Deployment Line Dambach–Ingersheim–[Ensisheim]–Mühlhausen.
Main Effort Right wing.

Coastal Defense 5 Landwehr brigades.

Rear boundary of the lodgement area of the Western Armies
Pfalzel (northeast of Trier)–Neunkirchen–Zweibrücken–Hagenau–Rhine line from Strassburg to Basel.

Enemy stands opposite with 42 infantry divisions, 35 Landwehr brigades, 6½ cavalry divisions, massed in the area
Epinal–Toul–Bar le Duc.
Deployment completed on 17th mobilization day.

Main body of forces deployed on and behind the line
Belfort–Lure–Remiremont–Epinal–Vezelise–Toul–Verdun–Dun.

Outposts (strength: around 13 infantry divisions, 4 Landwehr brigades, 6½ cavalry divisions) along line
Belfort–St. Dié–Lunéville–Nancy–Pont-à-Mousson–Fresnes–Montmédy.

* * *

2. Eastern Army

Fifth Army	(3 army corps [one of them consisting of 3 infantry divisions], 4 reserve divisions, 6 Landwehr brigades, 3 cavalry divisions.)
Deployment Line	Along the German border, specifically: Southern Group: (2 army corps, 1 cavalry division) from Brezinka (on railway line Beuthen–Oswiecim)–Bodzanowitz (east of Rosenberg). Central Group: (2 infantry divisions) from Sternalice (east of Kreuzburg)–Wyschanow (northeast of Kempen). Northern Group: (2 cavalry divisions) from south of Kalisch–Robakowo (northeast of Sarotschin).
Main Effort	Right wing.
Army Detachment	(1 army corps, 2 reserve divisions, 7 Landwehr brigades, 1 cavalry division.)
Initial Deployment	In groups. Southern Group (1 reserve division) in and around Lautenburg Railway to be secured between Soldau and Lyck by 3 Landwehr brigades. Northern Group: (1 army corps, 1 reserve division) in the Gerdauen–Insterburg–Gumbinnen area. Outposts near Lyck
Main Effort	Left wing

Enemy is assembling in groups behind his border protection force made up of border guard troops and cavalry units, with:

Army of the Niemen	(15 infantry divisions) in the Wilna–Kowno–Grodno area. 12th through 32nd mobilization days (i.e., main body of forces completed deployment on 12th mobilization day, the remainder on 32nd mobilization day).

Army Detachment Bialystok

    (4 infantry divisions, 2 cavalry divisions) in and around Bialystok.
    14th through 16th mobilization days.

Army of the Vistula

    Center: (9½ infantry divisions, 4½ cavalry divisions) in the area south of Lomza.
    12th through 18th mobilization days.
    Main Reserve: (6 infantry divisions, 1½ cavalry divisions) around Bielsk.
    18th through 22nd mobilization days.

Fortress Garrisons

    (6½ reserve divisions) Nowo Georgiewsk, Warsaw, Iwangorod, Brest-Litowsk.
    11th through 14th mobilization days.

Army of the Bug

    (9 infantry divisions, 4 cavalry divisions, front facing south) in the Lublin–Brest-Litowsk–Cholm area.
    21st through 40th mobilization days.

Southwestern Army

    a. Right wing and reserve (12 infantry divisions, 7 cavalry divisions) in the Luck–Dubno–Kowno area.
    19th through 24th mobilization days.
    b. Left wing (6 infantry divisions, 4½ cavalry divisions) around Proskurow.
    14th through 22nd mobilization days.

Aufmarsch 1894–1895

(The only material available is a general railroad map of southwest Germany with entries titled: "Arrival of First Transports 1894/95")

Army	In the area Bischheim–Brumath
Command Post	Bischheim
Strength	$1^{1}/_{6}$ army corps (½ V, ½ VIII, $^{1}/_{6}$ IX Army Corps)
	26th mobilization day (i.e., initial deployment completed on 26th mobilization day).
Army	In the area Königshofen–Wasselnheim–Molsheim
Command Post	Königshofen
Strength	$1^{1}/_{6}$ army corps, 1 cavalry division (½ V, ½ VIII, $^{1}/_{6}$ IX Army Corps, and 2nd Cavalry Division)
	24th mobilization day.
Army	In the area Schlettstadt–Markirch–Rappoltsweiler
Command Post	Schlettstadt
Strength	$1^{1}/_{3}$ army corps, 1 cavalry division (½ VI, ½ X, $^{1}/_{3}$ IX Army Corps, and 3rd Cavalry Division)
	25th–26th mobilization day (i.e., initial deployment of main body of forces completed on 25th, the remainder on 26th mobilization day).
Army	In the area Colmar–Münster–Rufach
Command Post	Colmar
Strength	$1^{1}/_{3}$ army corps, 1 cavalry division (½ VI, ½ X, $^{1}/_{3}$ IX Army Corps, and 1st Cavalry Division)
	25th–26th mobilization day.

Aufmarsch 1895-1896

The following documents are available:
1. Wartime Order of Battle West.
2. Wartime Order of Battle East A.
3. Wartime Order of Battle East B.
4. Map Depicting Border Security by VIII, XVI, XV, XIV Army Corps.
5. Map Depicting Draft of *Aufmarsch* East A.

* * *

Re. 1-3

West

First Army	Second Army	Third Army	Fourth Army
4 army corps	4 army corps	4 army corps	4 army corps
1 reserve division		2 reserve divisions	
1 Landwehr brigade	1 Landwehr brigade	1 Landwehr brigade	1 Landwehr brigade
2 cavalry divisions	2 cavalry divisions	1 cavalry division	1 cavalry division
1st Army Detachment	2nd Army Detachment	OHL Reserve	
	1 army corps		
4 reserve divisions	4 reserve divisions	1 reserve division	
2 Landwehr brigades	4 Landwehr brigades	4 Landwehr brigades	

East

A		B	
Fifth Army	3rd Army Detachment	*Fifth Army*	3rd Army Detachment
5 army corps		4 army corps	
3 reserve divisions	4 reserve divisions	1 reserve division	5 reserve divisions
6 Landwehr brigades	1 Landwehr brigade	4 Landwehr brigades	3 Landwehr brigades
2⅔ cavalry divisions	1 cavalry division	1 cavalry division	2 cavalry divisions
Army Contingents in Silesia and Posen		4th Army Detachment	
		1 army corps	
1 reserve division		2 reserve divisions	
7 Landwehr brigades		7 Landwehr brigades	
1 cavalry brigade		1 cavalry division	

* * *

Re. 4 Stronger border guard detachments are marshaled near:

    Wasserbillig–Nennig
    hard east of Diedenhofen
    in and near Metz
    southwest of Mörchingen
    Colmar
    Mühlhausen

* * *

Re. 5

The draft appears to have been written before *Aufmarsch* East A and B were defined. The wartime Order of Battle of this draft deviates from the ones that were defined at a later time (A and B). The following, therefore, is only applicable to define the general operational idea for *Aufmarsch* East B.

3rd Army Detachment (4 reserve divisions, 1 Landwehr brigade, 1 cavalry division)
Command Post Briesen
Initial Deployment In the area Kulmsee–Schönsee–Briesen–Rheden
Planned Advance With 2 reserve divisions each via Gollub to Sierpc and via Strassburg to Biezun.

Fifth Army (4 army corps, 4 Landwehr brigades, 1⅔ Cavalry divisions)
Command Post Dt. Eylau
Initial Deployment In the area Jablonowo–Strassburg–Soldau–Neidenburg–Willenberg–Ortelsburg–Hohenstein–Neumark
Planned Advance 1 army corps via Mlawa–Ciechanow to Pultusk
1 army corps, 1 reserve division via Prasnysz–Makowo to Roshan.
1 army corps, 1 reserve division in two columns to Seljun (north of Roshan) to Nowowis (west of Ostrolenka)
1 army corps in two columns via Myschinez to Ostrolenka and to Nowogrod (west of Lomza)

4th Army Detachment (2 infantry divisions, 1 Landwehr brigade, 1 cavalry division)
Command Post Insterburg
Initial Deployment 1 infantry division each in and around Darkehmen and Insterburg
Outposts (1 infantry regiment, 1 cavalry brigade) south of Lyck.

Aufmarsch 1896–1897

The following documents are available:
  1. Wartime Order of Battle West
  2. Wartime Order of Battle East
  3. Map Depicting *Aufmarsch* East

* * *

Re. 1 and 2

West

First Army	Second Army	Third Army	Fourth Army
5 army corps	4 army corps	5 army corps	4 army corps
1 Landwehr brigade	1 Landwehr brigade	1 Landwehr brigade	1 Landwehr brigade
2 cavalry divisions	2 cavalry divisions	1 cavalry division	1 cavalry division
1st Army Detachment	2nd Army Detachment	Army Contingents in Ober-Elsass (Haut-Rhin)	Not assigned to an army
		1 army corps	
6 reserve divisions	5 reserve divisions	1 reserve division	
2 Landwehr brigades		4 Landwehr brigades	4 Landwehr brigades

East

Fifth Army	3rd Army Detachment	Army Contingents in Silesia and Posen
3 army corps		
4 reserve divisions	4 reserve divisions	
6 Landwehr brigades		7 Landwehr brigades
3 cavalry divisions	1 cavalry division	

Re. 3

3rd Army Detachment (4 reserve divisions, 1 cavalry division)

Initial Deployment   In the area Thorn–Gollub–Kulmsee
Planned advance   1 reserve division toward Lipno
     2 reserve divisions toward Rypin
     1 reserve division on stand-by

Fifth Army (3 army corps, 4 reserve divisions, 6 Landwehr brigades, 3 cavalry divisions)

Initial Deployment
     a. Right wing (2 army corps, 3 reserve divisions, 4 Landwehr brigades, 1⅔ cavalry divisions) in the area Graudenz–Strassburg–Soldau–Neidenburg–Hohenstein–Osterode–Dt. Eylau.
     Planned Advance
         1 army corps toward Suronim
         1 army corps with another 2 reserve divisions toward Mlawa, covered on the left flank by 1 reserve division on the road Hohenstein–Neidenburg.
     b. Left wing (1 army corps, 1 reserve division, 2 Landwehr brigades, 1 cavalry division) in and around Insternburg (1 army corps, 1 reserve division).
     Outpost
         (1 infantry regiment, 1 cavalry brigade) south of Lyck in and around Tilsit (1 Landwehr brigade)

Aufmarsch 1897–1898

The following documents are available:
1. Wartime Order of Battle West.
2. Wartime Order of Battle East.
3. Drafts of Deployment Tables for Each Army and the Cavalry Divisions of the East.

The annexes of the deployment tables are completely missing.

* * *

West

Cover of the initial deployment provided by 10 infantry divisions and 6 cavalry divisions, specifically:
- VIII Army Corps reinforced by 2 cavalry divisions.
- XVI Army Corps reinforced by 2 infantry brigades, 2 cavalry divisions, with main body of forces near Metz.
- XV Army Corps reinforced by 1 cavalry division, with the main body of forces near Saarburg.
- XIV Army Corps.

First Army	(3 army corps [incl. 1 reserve corps], 2 combined Landwehr brigades, 2 cavalry divisions.)
Command Post	Trier
Initial Deployment	Behind the line Petingen (northeast of Longich)–Hayingen (southwest of Diedenhofen) on the left bank of the Moselle.
	Left-wing army corps to the Friesingen–Gr. Hettingen–Algringen road.
Comments	1. The Belgian border must not be crossed.
	2. Notes for a defense of the Moselle between Sierck and Metz have been issued.

356

Second Army	(4 army corps [incl. 1 reserve corps], 1 combined Landwehr brigade, 1 cavalry division.)
Command Post	Metz
Initial Deployment	a. XVI Army Corps near Metz, otherwise...
	b. On the right bank of the Moselle, between the Moselle and Nied, north of the line Argannen–Gr. Tänchen.
	Right-wing army corps to the Diedenhofen–Argannen road.
	Left-wing army corps to the Beckingen–Busendorf–St. Barbara road.
Comments	Notes for a defense of the Moselle between Sierck and Metz have been issued.
Third Army	(4 army corps [incl. 2 reserve corps], 1 combined Landwehr brigade, 1 cavalry division.)
Command Post	Saarbrücken
Initial Deployment	Behind Deutsche Nied, between Nied and the Saarbrücken–Falkenberg railroad.
	Right-wing army corps to the Saarlouis–Bolchen–Waibelskirchen road.
	Left-wing army corps to Forbach–Ober-Homburg–Falkenberg road.
Fourth Army	(4 army corps, 1 combined Landwehr brigade, 1 cavalry division.)
Command Post	Saargemünd
Initial Deployment	Behind Mutterbach and the Saar.
	Right-wing army corps to the Brebach–Gr. Blittersdorf–Metzingen–Pfarrebersweiler road.
	Left-wing army corps to the Wolmünster–Rohrbach–Saar-Buckenheim (formerly Saarunion) road.
Fifth Army	(4 army corps [incl. 1 army corps of 3 infantry divisions], 2 combined Landwehr brigades, 1 cavalry division.)
Command Post	Hagenau

Initial Deployment	Behind the line Saar–Buckenheim–Pfalzburg. Right-wing army corps to the Lemberg–Glashütte–Adamsweiler–Eyweiler road. Left-wing army corps to the Monnenheim–Zabern–Pfalzburg road.
Sixth Army	(2 army corps, 2 reserve divisions, 1 combined Landwehr brigade.)

Army contingents in Ober-Elsass (1 army corps, 1 reserve division, 3 combined Landwehr brigades.)

Command Post	Strassburg
Initial Deployment	a. Right wing: North (2 reserve divisions) and west of Strassburg (2 army corps). Right-wing army corps to the Ittenheim–Wasselnheim road.
	b. Center: Holding the Voges passes, with the main body of the forces near Colmar (1 infantry division).
	c. Left wing: 2 infantry divisions near Mühlhausen provide cover against Belfort.
Comments	The Government of Strassburg shall make preparations to establish a position north of the Breusch River between Molsheim and Strassburg.
Unassigned to any Army	2 combined Landwehr brigades
Coastal Defense	4 combined Landwehr brigades at the disposal of the Deputy General Command.

* * *

East

Cover of the initial deployment and border protection provided by I Army Corps (reinforced by 1 cavalry division) and XVII Army Corps (reinforced by 4 cavalry divisions), to be replaced at a later time by combined Landwehr brigades and Landsturm.

Furthermore, border security only provided by Deputy General Commands II, V, and VI.

Total of active security forces: 5 infantry divisions, 5 cavalry divisions.

Seventh Army (5 army corps, 2 reserve divisions, 5 combined Landwehr brigades, 1 cavalry division.) Commander-in-Chief of the Seventh Army is also Commander-in-Chief of Field Army East.

Command Post Wehlau

Initial Deployment Assembly behind the Angerapp River in the area Rastenburg–Angerburg–Darkehmen–Insterburg–Nordenburg–Barten.

Eighth Army 3 army corps, 2 reserve divisions, 9 combined Landwehr brigades, 4 cavalry divisions, and one senior cavalry commander.

Command Post Graudenz

Initial Deployment Cavalry divisions united between Thorn–Jablonowo.

   a. Left wing (2 army corps) on the line Jablonowo–Dt. Eylau.

   b. Center (1 army corps, 1 reserve division) near Bromberg.

   c. Right wing (1 reserve division) near Breslau.

Aufmarsch 1898–1899

The following documents are available:
1. Wartime Order of Battle West.
2. Wartime Order of Battle East.
3. Directives for the Security of the *Aufmarsch* of the German Western Army *Westheer)*—1 Booklet.
4. Unloading Stations and Initial Billeting of the Armies in the Lodgment Area—1 Booklet.
5. Draft of Deployment Tables without Annexes for the Armies (Minus the Eighth Army) and the Western Cavalry Divisions.
6. Basic Principles for the *Aufmarsch* of the Western Army (Refers Mainly to the Arrival of Specific Formations).
7. Map Depicting *Aufmarsch* East.

* * *

1. West

Cover of the initial deployment and border security in Alsace provided by:
    VIII Army Corps reinforced by 2 cavalry divisions.
    XVI Army Corps reinforced by 2 infantry brigades, 3 cavalry divisions.
    XV Army Corps reinforced by 1 cavalry division.
    XIV Army Corps.

Marshaling — Beginning 6 hours after receipt of mobilization order:

VIII Army Corps:	2 infantry regiments, 1 cavalry regiment, 3 batteries vicinity Diedenhofen.
	½ infantry division in Trier (for invasion of Luxembourg).
	1 infantry brigade approaching Trier (for invasion of Luxembourg).

	2 cavalry divisions under Senior Cavalry Commander northwest of Diedenhofen.
XIV Army Corps:	With main body of forces in Metz. 1 infantry brigade near Herlingen. 1 infantry brigade, 2 squadrons, 3 batteries near Mörchingen. 1 infantry brigade, 2 squadrons near Bensdorf. 3 cavalry divisions under Senior Cavalry Commander south and southeast of Metz.
XV Army Corps:	1 infantry regiment, 1 cavalry regiment near Duss (Dieuze). Main body of forces of XV Army Corps near Saarburg. 1 cavalry division near Saarburg. Detachments south of the Saarburg–Zabern road. 1 special detachment in the Breusch valley.
XIV Army Corps:	1 infantry division near Colmar. 1 infantry division, 1 reserve division near Mühlhausen (for cover against Belfort).

Comments:
1. "According to not improbable intelligence, it is the intent of the enemy to march to Trier through Luxembourg with strong cavalry."
2. XVI and XV Army Corps and their cavalry divisions "must take into consideration that they might be brought forward without delay and deployed against the flank and rear of a break-in between Metz and Saarburg."

Enemy stands with his covering forces (some 8 infantry divisions, $6\frac{2}{3}$ cavalry divisions, light infantry battalions, customs and forest troops) in general line east of the Meuse from Stenay—along the eastern fringes of the

Côte Lorraine–Thiaucourt–Pont-à-Mousson–Nancy–Lunéville–Baccarat–alongside the ridge of the Vosges–Belfort.

In detail, the elements below are opposed as follows:

VIII Army Corps:	2 infantry divisions, 3 light infantry battalions, 3 cavalry divisions.
XVI Army Corps:	3 infantry divisions (two "near and in front of Nancy"), 6 light infantry battalions, 3⅔ cavalry divisions.
XV Army Corps:	About 2 infantry divisions.
XIV Army Corps:	Individual contingents of 2 different infantry divisions, 3 light infantry battalions.

First Army	4 army corps (incl. 1 reserve corps), 4 combined Landwehr brigades, 2 cavalry divisions under Senior Cavalry Commander.
Command Post	Remich
Initial Deployment	Behind the line Petingen (northeast of Longich)–Hayingen (southwest of Diedenhofen). Right-wing army corps to the Kruchten–Mersch–Mamer–Dippach road. Left-wing army corps to the Saarburg–Benrig [?]–Sierck–Diedenhofen road.
Comments:	1. The Belgian border must not be crossed. 2. Notes concerning defense of the Moselle line between Sierck and Metz have been issued.

Second Army	5 army corps (incl. 1 army corps of 3 infantry divisions), 1 combined Landwehr brigade, 2 cavalry divisions under Senior Cavalry Commander.
Command Post	Saarlouis
Initial Deployment	XVI Army Corps near Metz and the remainder east of the line Metzeresch–Füllingen. Right-wing army corps to road Merzig–Halsdorf–Kedingen–Metzeresch. Left-wing army corps to the Lisdorf–Überherrn–Kreuzwald–Buschborn–Lubeln–Füllingen road.

Comments:	Notes concerning the defense of the Moselle line between Sierck and Metz have been issued.
Third Army	(2 army corps, incl. 1 reserve corps)
Command Post	Saarbrücken
Initial Deployment	Behind the Deutsche Nied. Right-wing army corps to the Völklingen–Karlingen–St. Avold–Falkenberg Rail Station–Kriechingen road. Left-wing army corps to the Saarbrücken–Forbach–Kl. Ebersweiler–Falkenberg road.
Fourth Army	4 army corps, 1 combined Landwehr brigade, 1 cavalry division.
Command Post	Saargemünd
Initial Deployment	Behind Saar and Mutterbach Right-wing army corps to the Frauenberg–Bliegersweiler–Hanweiler–Wolferdingen–Metzingen–Pfarrebersweiler–Cappel road. Left-wing army corps to the Enchenberg–Lorenzen–Saar-Buckenheim (Saarunion)–Harskirchen road.
Fifth Army	4 army corps, 2 combined Landwehr brigades, 1 cavalry division.
Command Post	Buchsweiler
Initial Deployment	Behind the Saar-Buckenheim–Pfalzburg line. Right-wing army corps to the Ingweiler–Glashütte–Adamsweiler–Hirschland road. Left-wing army corps to the Hochfelden–Zabern–Pfalzburg/Lützelburg road.
Sixth Army	2 army corps (incl. 1 reserve corps), 3 reserve divisions, 5 combined Landwehr brigades.
Command Post	Strassburg
Initial Deployment	Near Strassburg and in Ober-Elsass. a. Right wing (4 reserved divisions) northwest and west of Strassburg in the area of

	Dunzenheim–Sulzbad– Oberschäffolsheim–Pfulgriesheim,
	b. Center (1 infantry division) near Colmar.
	c. Left wing (1 infantry division, 1 reserve division) near Mühlhausen (columns and trains remain on right bank of the Rhine and will only be committed if necessary).
Comments:	1. The Landwehr occupies the Rhine line of Strassburg–Hüningen.
	2. The government Strassburg issues orders for the preparation of a position north of the Breusch between Molsheim u. Strassburg. Notes about this position have been issued.
At the disposal of the Deputy General Command	3 combined Landwehr brigades.

* * *

2. East

Seventh Army	6 army corps (incl. 1 reserve corps), 2 reserve divisions, 5 combined Landwehr brigades, 1 cavalry division.
Command Post	Insterburg

Seventh Army commander is also Commander-in-Chief of the East

Initial Deployment	Behind the Angerapp River in the area Gr. Stürlack–Angerburg–Darkehmen–Gumbinnen–Insterburg–Saalau–Nordenburg–Barten–Rastenburg.

Planned advance as indicated in sketch,[1] with:

    1 army corps via Goldap toward Szittkehmen.
    1 army corps via Darkehmen toward Wyschtynjetz.
    1 army corps and 1 reserve division via Gumbinnen toward Pillupönen.
    1 army corps and 1 reserve division via Stallupönen toward Wirballen.

	1 army corps via Pillkallen toward Schirwindt. 1 infantry division remaining near Gr. Stürlack. 1 infantry division remaining near Ortelsburg.
Eighth Army	2 army corps, 4 reserve divisions, 9 combined Landwehr brigades, 4 cavalry divisions under Senior Cavalry Commander.
Initial Deployment	With the cavalry between Thorn and Jablonowo. Left group (1 army corps, 3 reserve divisions) in the area Strassburg–Gr. Koschlau–Löbau–Dt. Eylau–Riesenburg–Rheden. Central group 1 army corps, 1 reserve division near Bromberg. Right group 1 reserve division near Breslau. (This group is not indicated in the sketch; however, in accordance with *Aufmarsch* 1897–1898 its presence is to be assumed, as it is the only possibility of explaining the use of the reserve divisions that remain based on the wartime order of battle.)

At the disposal of the Deputy General Command of the II Army Corps
    1 combined Landwehr brigade.

Notes

1. The sketch is not available in the File RH61/96.

Aufmarsch 1899–1900[1]

The following documents are available:
1. Wartime Order of Battle I.[2]
2. Wartime Order of Battle II (West).
3. Wartime Order of Battle III (East).
4. Wartime Order of Battle West from 1 October 1899.
5. Wartime Order of Battle East from 1 October 1899.
6. Basic Principles for the Deployment of the West and East Armies in 1899–1900 with Attached
7.[3] Overviews of Unloading Stations and Initial Billeting of the Armies.
8. Deployment Tables (East) in Accordance with Wartime Order of Battle III.
9. Deployment Tables West in Accordance with Wartime Order of Battle West from 1 October 1899.
10. Deployment Tables East in Accordance with Wartime Order of Battle from 1 October 1899.
11. Deployment Tables for the Italian High Command, Including Map with Entries.

* * *

Re. 1   Wartime Order of Battle I

First Army	Second Army	Third Army	Fourth Army
5 army corps (incl. 1 reserve corps)	4 army corps	5 army corps (1 reserve corps)	4 army corps
3 combined Landwehr brigades	2 combined Landwehr brigades	1 combined Landwehr brigade	1 combined Landwehr brigade
4 cavalry divisions	2 cavalry divisions	2 cavalry divisions	1 cavalry division

Fifth Army	Sixth Army	Seventh Army	Eighth Army
4 army corps (1 reserve corps)	3 army corps	3 army corps (1 army corps of 3 infantry divisions/1 reserve corps)	2 army corps
	2 reserve divisions	1 reserve division	2 reserve divisions
2 combined Landwehr brigades	1 combined Landwehr brigade	4 combined Landwehr brigades	
2 cavalry divisions			

At the disposal of OHL	At the disposal of the Deputy General Command for Coastal Defense	In the area of XV Army Corps
13 combined Landwehr brigades	5 combined Landwehr brigades	6 Landwehr battalions

* * *

Re. 2   Wartime Order of Battle II (West)

First Army	Second Army	Third Army	Fourth Army
3 army corps (incl. 1 reserve corps)	3 army corps	4 army corps (1 reserve corps/1 army corps of 3 infantry divisions)	4 army corps
3 combined Landwehr brigades	2 combined Landwehr brigades	1 combined Landwehr brigade	1 combined Landwehr brigade
2 cavalry divisions		2 cavalry divisions	1 cavalry division

Fifth Army	Sixth Army	At the disposal of the Deputy General Command	In the area of XV Army Corps
4 army corps (1 reserve corps)	2 army corps (1 reserve corps/1 army corps of 3 infantry divisions)		
	3 reserve divisions		
2 combined Landwehr brigades	5 combined Landwehr brigades	3 combined Landwehr brigades	5 Landwehr battalions
1 cavalry division			

* * *

Re. 3 Wartime Order of Battle III (East)

Seventh Army	Eighth Army
4 army corps (incl. 2 reserve corps)	5 army corps (1 army corps of 3 infantry divisions)
2 reserve divisions	2 reserve divisions
8 combined Landwehr brigades	6 combined Landwehr brigades
3 cavalry divisions	2 cavalry divisions

* * *

Re. 4 Wartime Order of Battle West from 1 October 1899
Re. 5 Wartime Order of Battle East from 1 October 1899

West

First Army	Second Army	Third Army	Fourth Army
6 army corps (incl. 2 reserve corps, 1 reserve corps of 3 reserve divisions)	4 army corps (1 army corps of 3 infantry divisions)	4 army corps (1 reserve corps)	4 army corps

3 combined Landwehr brigades	2 combined Landwehr brigades	2 combined Landwehr brigades	1 combined Landwehr brigade
2 cavalry divisions	2 cavalry divisions	2 cavalry divisions	1 cavalry division
Fifth Army	*Sixth Army*	*Coastal defense at the disposal of the Deputy General Command*	*In the area of XV Army Corps*
4 army corps (1 reserve corps)	4 army corps (1 reserve corps/1 army corps of 3 infantry divisions)		
	2 reserve divisions		
2 combined Landwehr brigades	5 combined Landwehr brigades	3 combined Landwehr brigades	5 Landwehr battalions
1 cavalry division			

East

Seventh Army		Eighth Army	
1 reserve corps		2 army corps (1 army corps of 3 infantry divisions)	
1 reserve division		2 reserve divisions	
7 combined Landwehr brigades		7 combined Landwehr brigades	
		3 cavalry divisions	

* * *

Re. 3, 6, and 7 *Aufmarsch* East in accordance with wartime Order of Battle III

Seventh Army	4 army corps (incl. 2 reserve corps), 2 reserve divisions, 8 combined Landwehr brigades, 3 cavalry divisions under Senior Cavalry Commander.
Command Post	Graudenz
Initial Deployment	Cavalry before the Thorn–Jablonowo front. Right wing around Thorn and Bromberg/2

reserve corps, 1 reserve division.
(6 combined Landwehr brigades are deployed to the area of Deputy General Commands VI and V for border security.)
Left wing 1 army corps to the Briesen–Gollub road, 1 army corps to the Jablonowo–Strassburg road, 1 reserve division to the Bischofswerder–Strassburg road.

Eighth Army	5 army corps (incl. 1 army corps of 3 infantry divisions), 2 reserve divisions, 6 combined Landwehr brigades, 2 cavalry divisions
Command Post	Riesenburg
Eighth Army commander	is also Commander-in-Chief of the East.
Initial Deployment	In general behind the line Lautenburg–Neidenburg–Scheufelsdorf

Right wing 4 army corps, 1 reserve division in the area Bischofswerder–Lautenburg–Soldau–Ortelsburg–Allenstein, viz.

1 army corps to the Bischofswerder–Lautenburg road.

1 army corps to the Dt. Eylau–Löbau–Soldau road.

1 army corps to the Hohenstein–Neidenburg road.

1 army corps to the Allenstein–Jedwabno road. Center near Bischofsburg, Sensburg, Rastenburg, and Angerburg.

1 combined Landwehr brigade each, which is to replace an infantry division used for border security between Allenstein and Neidenburg, and Masurian Lakeland. This infantry division will than join the right wing.

Left wing 1 army corps, 1 reserve division, 1 combined Landwehr brigade, 1 cavalry division. In and around Gumbinnen near Tilsit 1 combined Landwehr brigade.

* * *

Re. 4, 6, and 7 *Aufmarsch* West from 1 October 1899

First Army	6 army corps (incl. 2 reserve corps, incl. 1 of 3 reserve divisions), 3 combined Landwehr brigades, 2 cavalry divisions under Senior Cavalry Commander.
Command Post	Gerolstein
Initial Deployment	Behind the German border from Malmedy to Dasburg in the area Aachen–Neuerburg–Wittlich–Cochem–Gerolstein–Düren. 4 army corps in 1st line, followed by 3 reserve divisions, 2 reserve divisions on the left echeloned rearwards. Right-wing army corps to the Montjoie-Elsenborn–Büttgenbach–Weismes–Malmedy road. Left-wing army corps to the Schönecken–Waxweiler–Krautscheid–south of Lichtenborn–Dasburg road. Cavalry initially subordinate to Second Army-stands in the line Bitburg–Wasserbillig.
Comment	"As soon as the French enter Luxembourg territory, the Germans will be required to cross the Luxembourg border in order to cover the deployment. Apart from that, command authority remains with the OHL"
Second Army	4 army corps (incl. 1 army corps of 3 infantry divisions), 2 combined Landwehr brigades, 2 cavalry divisions under Senior Cavalry Commander.
Command Post	Trier
Initial Deployment	Behind the Our, Sauer, and Moselle between Neuerburg and Remich Right: Speicher–Bitburg–Oberweis–Sinspelt–Geichlingen. Left: Mettlach–Remich. Cavalry in front of the line Rodemachern–Bus.

Comment	"VIII Army Corps (to the Trier–Wasserbillig–Grevenmacher road) is instructed to advance across the Luxembourg border as soon as the French enter Luxembourg territory in order to screen the German deployment. Apart from that, command authority remains with the OHL."
Third Army	4 army corps (incl. 1 reserve corps), 2 combined Landwehr brigades, 2 cavalry divisions under the Senior Cavalry Commander
Command Post	Saarlouis
Initial Deployment	Behind the line Launsdorf–Neunkirchen–Wölflingen–Merten–Kreuzwald. Right: Losheim–Merzig–Waldwiese–Launsdorf Left: Saarbrücken–Forbach–Emmersweiler–Gr. Rosseln–Ludweiler–Differten–Überherrn Merten. Cavalry in front of the line Bolchen–Falkenberg.
Comment	"As soon as the French enter Luxembourg territory, it will be necessary for the Germans to screen the deployment by having the First and Second armies cross the Luxembourg border. For the Third Army command authority in this case remains with the OHL."
Fourth Army	4 army corps, 1 combined Landwehr brigade, 1 cavalry division.
Command Post	Saargemünd
Initial Deployment	1 army corps (XVI) near Metz, the remainder behind the line Ober-Homburg–Cappel and the Mutterbach. Right: Wittersheim–Frauenberg–Bliesgeisweiler–Hanweiler–Wölferdingen–Metzingen–Merlenbach. Left: Wolmünster–Holbach–Rohrbach–Achen–Saaralben–Rech.
Comment	During initial deployment, the cavalry divisions of the Second and Third Armies (a total of 4 cavalry divisions) will be subordinate to the Fourth Army.

Fifth Army	4 army corps (incl. 1 reserve corps), 2 combined Landwehr brigades, 1 cavalry division.
Command Post	Buchsweiler
Initial Deployment	XV Army Corps, 1 cavalry division near Saarburg, the remainder behind the Saar between Saar-Buckenheim and Schalbach. Right: Bitsch–Lemberg–Enchenberg–Saar-Buckenheim–Harskirchen. Left: Obermodern–Lützelstein–Lahr–Sieweiler–Weyer.
Sixth Army	4 army corps (incl. 1 reserve corps and furthermore 1 army corps of 3 infantry divisions), reserve divisions, 5 combined Landwehr brigades.
Command Post	Zabern
Initial Deployment	Between Pfalzburg and Strassburg and in Ober-Elsass. Right group in the area Pfalzburg–Brumath–Herlisheim–Molsheim–Dagsburg. 2 army corps in 1st line. 1 reserve corps, echeloned on the left. 2 reserve divisions, echeloned on the left. Right: Zobersdorf–Prinzheim–Dettweiler–Zabern–Pfalzburg–Mittelborn. Left-wing reserve division to the Oberschäffolsheim–Ergersheim road. Left group: 2 infantry divisions, 1 reserve division near Colmar. 1 infantry division near Mühlhausen
Comments	1. Landwehr secures Rhine line Strassburg–Hüningen. 2. By order of Government of Strassburg, a position north of the Breusch is prepared between Molsheim and Strassburg. Notes for this defense position have been issued.

Royal Italian Army	5 army corps, 2 cavalry divisions.
Command Post	Altbreisach
Initial Deployment	On the right banks of the Rhine between Strassburg and Neubreisach.
	1st Transport Group:
	2 cavalry divisions, arriving on 7th to 11th mobilization day.
	3 cavalry divisions, arriving on 7th to 11th mobilization day.
	V and VI Army Corps arriving on 14th to 20th mobilization day.
	2nd Cavalry Division to advance on 20th mobilization day from Altbreisach via Colmar–Münster.
	3rd Cavalry Division marching from Kappel (southeast of Rheinau) via Molsheim is to have hooked up with the German 7th Cavalry Division south of Saarburg on 14th mobilization day.
	V and VI Army Corps leaving on 20th mobilization day are to arrive on 21st mobilization day.
	V Army Corps via Erstein–Niederehnheim–Barr–Thannweiler to Saales and via Rheinau–Behnfeld–Schlettstadt to Markich.
	VI Army Corps via Markolsheim–Colmar–Kaysersberg to Schmierlach and via Altbreisach–Winzenheim to Münster.
	2nd Transport Group:
	IX Army Corps will arrive by 26th, advance on 27th mobilization day.
	VIII Army Corps will arrive by 28th, advance on 29th mobilization day.
	X Army Corps will arrive by 26th, advance on 27th mobilization day.
	These corps will follow the V and VI Army Corps.

* * *

Re. 5, 6, and 7 *Aufmarsch* East from 1 October 1899

Seventh Army	1 reserve corps, 1 reserve division, 7 combined Landwehr brigades.
Command Post	Posen
Initial Deployment	1 reserve division each near Breslau, Posen, and Bromberg. Combined Landwehr brigades distributed along the German border.
Eighth Army	2 army corps, 2 reserve divisons, 7 combined Landwehr brigades, 3 cavalry divisions.
Command Post	Marienburg

Eighth Army commander is also Commander-in-Chief of the East.

Initial Deployment: 2 cavalry divisions in front of the line Thorn–Jablonowo.
Right Wing (1 army corps, 1 reserve division, 1 combined V Landwehr brigade) in the area Jablonowo–Strassburg–Bischofswerder.
Center (3 combined Landwehr brigades) near Sensburg, Rastenburg, Angerburg.
Left Wing (1 army corps, 1 reserve division, 1 combined Landwehr brigade, 1 cavalry division) near Gumbinnen, the combined Landwehr brigade near Tilsit.

Notes

1. The following memo in an unknown hand is attached to the collection of material on the *Aufmarsch* 1899–1900: "For the first time (from 1 Oct 99) strongly reduced deployment in the east. Seventh and Eighth Army in total 2 army corps, 1 reserve corps, 3 reserve divisions, 3 cavalry divisions, 14 Landwehr brigades, 9 divisions." [Altered from 9 to 10 divisions in unknown hand.] Furthermore, a map "*Westaufmarsch*: 1899–00" on a scale of 1:2,500,000 is attached to this *Aufmarsch*. The map is largely identical to sketch 19, "Westaufmarsch 1899–1900," in the article "Friedrich von Boetticher, Der Lehrmeister des neuzeitlichen Krieges," in *Von Scharnhorst zu Schlieffen 1806–1906: Hundert Jahre preussisch-deutscher Generalstab. Auf Veranlassung des Reichswehrministeriums bearbeitet von aktiven und ehemaligen Offizieren des Reichsheeres und zusammengestellt von Generalleutnant a.D. von Cochenhausen* (Berlin, 1933), 266.

2. The original wartime Orders of Battle I and II (West) include a remark in brackets that reads "There is nothing further available on this."

3. Before 6 and 7 there is a bracket and the remark "Only in accordance with wartime Order of Battle West from 1 Oct 99 and wartime Order of Battle III (East)."

Aufmarsch 1900–1901

The following documents are available:
1. Mobilization Schedule 01-02.
2. Basic Principles for *Aufmarsch* West including Overview of Unloading Stations and Initial Billeting of the Armies.
3. The Same for *Aufmarsch* East (Special Case).
4. Deployment Map West 1:100,000 in 6 Sections (1 is Missing).
5. Deployment Map East 1:100,000 in 4 Sections.

* * *

I. Excerpt from Mobilization Schedule 1900-01

1. In the event of mobilization the following positions will be consolidated:
    Moselstellung (Moselle Position) between Sierck and Metz
    Breuschstellung (Breusch Position) and the Vosges Barrier
    Neu-Breisach.
    On the Upper Rhine south of Strassburg (Gerstheim, Rheinau, Schönau, Markolsheim, Neuenburg, Hüningen).
    Marienburg.
    Graudenz.
    Glogau.
    Breslau.
    Masurian Lakes Line.
    Vistula Line from Kulm to the Nogat.

2. Coastal defense is established at:
    Borkum.
    Pellworm.
    Sylt.
    Brunsbüttel.
    Kiel Canal.

3. Objects to be destroyed.
>XIV Army Corps: viaduct of Dammerkirch, Lock 16 and 42 of the Rhone-Rhine Canal near Woltersdorf and Ile Napoleon.

4. Instructions for General Command VIII and 16th Infantry Division; report to Railroad Department regarding continuation of operations into Luxembourg, etc.

5. "W." maps are also intended for I and XVII Army Corps.

6. Preparation of Directives for the Commander-in-Chief of the East, First and Second Armies, and XX Army Corps.

7. Consider whether it will be necessary to establish a "commander-in-chief for a northern theater of war" and whether reinforcement of troops in the area of IX Army Corps is required. The Railroad Department has made preparations to transport immediately replacement forces to the Kiel–Altona line.

8. "If the Italian Army assembles in Baden and Alsace" wire to Italy that Prussian and Italian officers in Freiburg are to make initial preparations for "billeting and messing in the deployment area" on the 5th mobilization day.
>Consider that IX Italian Corps will unload in Alt-Breisach from the 16th mobilization day and have the most part of the deployment district of the XX Army Corps (formed of XIV Army Corps contingents) at its disposal.
>If at that time XX Army Corps has not yet crossed the Rhine, its deployment sector is to be moved south.

* * *

II. Aufmarsch West

First Army 4 army corps, 4 reserve divisons, 3 combined Landwehr brigades, 1 cavalry division.
Command Post Stadtkyll.
Initial Deployment Behind the border of Aachen–Maldingen
3 army corps in front line of Malmedy–Maldingen behind right-wing army corps, 1 army

corps following, another 2 reserve divisions echeloned on the right (near Aachen and Eupen). 1 each reserve division following behind the central and left army corps.[1]
Right-wing army corps to the Montjoie-Elsenborn-Büttgenbach-Weismes-Malmedy road.
Left: Reuth-Mehlen-Bleialf-Üttfeld-Burg Reuland-Ondler-Maldingen cavalry division south of St. Vith.

Second Army	4 army corps (incl. 1 reserve corps), 2 reserve divisions, 2 combined Landwehr brigades, 2 cavalry divisions under Senior Cavalry Commander.
Command Post	Trier.
Initial Deployment	Behind the border of Dasburg-Wasserbillig, 3 army corps in front line, 1 reserve division each following the right and central army corps, 1 reserve corps following the left-wing army corps. Right: Mürlenbach-Schönecken-Waxweiler-Krautscheid-south of Lichtenborn-Dasburg. Left wing-division to the Ehrang-Trier-Igel-Wasserbillig road. 1 each cavalry division east of Wellen and south of Sierck.
Third Army	4 army corps, 2 combined Landwehr brigades, 2 cavalry divisions under Senior Cavalry Commander.
Command Post	Saarlouis.
Initial Deployment	Behind the line Grevenmacher-Remich-Launsdorf-Niedaltdorf. 4 army corps in line. Right: Mandern-Saarburg-Grevenmacher. Left: Lebach-Saarwellingen-Saarlouis-Wallerfangen-Niedaltdorf. 1 each cavalry division near Metzeresch and Bolchen.

Fourth Army 3 army corps, 1 reserve divison, 1 combined Landwehr brigade, 1 cavalry division (together with cavalry division of Fifth Army under Senior Cavalry Commander).
Command Post Saargemünd.
Initial Deployment Behind the line Merten–Merlenbach–Cappel, 3 army corps in line, reserve division follows left-wing army corps.
Right: Sulzbach–St. Johann–Saarbrücken–Forbach–Ludweiler–Merten.
Left: Medelsheim–Bliesbrücken–Folpersweiler–Saargemünd–Püttlingen–Cappel, Cavalry division near St. Avold.

Fifth Army 4 army corps, 2 combined Landwehr brigades, cavalry division (together with cavalry division of Fourth Army under Senior Cavalry Commander).
Command Post Saar-Buckenheim.
Initial Deployment 1 army corps (XVI) near Metz, the remainder behind the line Ottweiler (west of Saaralben)–Altweiler–Weyer.
Right: Eppingen–Bettweiler–Weidesheim–Saaralben–Ottweiler.
Left: Ingweiler–Lützelstheim–Ottweiler–Weyer cavalry division south of Gr. Tänchen.

Sixth Army 4 army corps, 5 reserve divisions, 5 combined Landwehr brigades, 1 cavalry division.
Command Post Hochfelden.
Initial Deployment Vanguard of XV Army Corps and 1 cavalry division forward-based to Saarburg area, the remainder behind the line Pfalzburg–Zabern–Molsheim–Niederehnheim–Benfeld and west of Freiburg.
Right Wing: 3 army corps, 5 reserve divisions, 1 cavalry division behind the line Pfalzburg–Benfeld.
3 army corps (north of the Breusch) in line.
2 reserve divisions (south of the Breusch) in line.
3 reserve divisions behind the center (in the area

	Mittelschäffolsheim–Reichsstett–Sufflenheim). Right: Main body of XV Army Corps to marshal near Pfalzburg and Zabern. Left: Reserve division to the Strassburg–Benfeld road. Left Wing: 1 army corps to the Freiburg–Breisach road. Forward-based contingents near Colmar and Mühlhausen.

Coastal Defense	The 3 combined Landwehr brigades designated for this purpose in the area of the IX and X Army Corps are marshaled near:
	    Lübeck.
	    Lockstedter Lager.
	    Hannover–Hildesheim.

* * *

III. Aufmarsch East

Fifth Army	3 army corps (incl. 1 reserve corps), 6 reserve divisions, 2 combined Landwehr brigades, 3 cavalry divisions.
Command Post	Graudenz.

Initial Deployment	Behind the border from the Vistula to Strassburg, 3 army corp—followed by 1 reserve division each—in front line, behind the left wing 1 reserve division, behind the right wing 2 reserve divisions.
	Routes of advance:
	    Thorn–Leibitsch–Obrowo–Czernikowo
	    Schönsee–Gollub–Ostrowite
	    Jablonowo–Strassburg
	    1 cavalry division near Gnesen–Hohensalza
	    1 cavalry division near Schönsee
	    1 cavalry division near Strassburg

Sixth Army	4 army corps (incl. 1 reserve corps), 2 reserve divisions, 2 combined Landwehr brigades.

Command Post	Riesenburg.
Initial Deployment	Behind the line Lautenburg–Soldau–Neidenburg–Ortelsburg–Spirding-See.
	Right Group: 3 army corps between Lautenburg–Neidenburg.
	1 army corps to the Bischofswerder–Neumark–Lautenburg road.
	1 army corps to the Dt. Eylau–Löbau–Soldau road.
	1 army corps to the Reichenau–Hohenstein–Neidenburg road.
	Left Group: 1 reserve corps, 2 reserve divisions between Ortelsburg–Spirding-See.
	1 reserve corps to the Allenstein–Scheufelsdorf–Ortelsburg road.
	1 reserve division to the Bischofsburg–Rheinswein–Opukel-Mühle road.
	1 reserve division to the Peitschendorf–Alt-Ukka–Rudezanny road.
Seventh Army	5 army corps, 2 combined Landwehr brigades, 1 cavalry division.
Command Post	Korschen.
Initial Deployment	Behind the line Arys–Wronken (west of Marggrabowa)–Buddern (northeast of Angerburg)–Darkehmen.
	1 army corps to the Rastenburg–Rhein–Arys road.
	1 army corps to the Lötzen–Widminnen–Wronken road.
	1 army corps to the Barten–Drengfurth–Angerburg road.
	1 army corps to the Szallgirren–Trempen–Darkehmen road.
	1 army corps to the Gerdauen–Neidenburg–Angerburg–Buddern road.
	Cavalry division west of Marggrabowa.
Eighth Army	4 army corps, 5 reserve divisions, 1 combined Landwehr brigade, 2 cavalry divisions.

Command Post	Insterburg.
Initial Deployment	West of line Stallupönen–Gr. Schillehlen (south east of Ragnit).
	4 army corps in front line, with 3 reserve divisions following behind the right wing, and 2 reserve divisions following behind the left wing.
	1 army corps to the Judtschen–Gumbinnen–Grünweitschen road.
	1 army corps to the Insterburg–Nibudzschen–Kattenau road.
	1 army corps to the Georgenburg–Pellemingken–Kauschen–Spullen road.
	1 army corps to the Tilsit–Ragnit–Gr. Schillehlen and Szillen–Lengwethen–Gr. Schillehlen roads.
	1 cavalry division west of Wisztyniec.
	1 cavalry division east of Stallupönen.

At the disposal of Deputy General Command VI
    4 combined Landwehr brigades

At the disposal of Deputy General Command V
    2 combined Landwehr brigades

Notes

1. A sketch of the described deployment is provided on the left margin.

Aufmarsch 1901–1902

The following documents are available:
1. Mobilization Schedule Aufmarsch I and II.
2. Aufmarsch I.
   a. Basic Principles West and East (without Annexes).
   b. Border Security Map West.
   c. Deployment Map West.
   c. Deployment Tables East.
   d. Railroad Map Including Aufmarsch East.
3. Aufmarsch II.
   a. Basic Principles West and East (without Annexes).
   b. Map of Aufmarsch West 1:300,000.
   c. Railroad Map with Transport Routes for "Special Case" (=Aufmarsch II West).
   d. Map of Aufmarsch East.

* * *

I. Excerpt from Mobilization Schedule 1901–1902

a. Aufmarsch I:

1. In the event of mobilization the intent is to consolidate the following positions:
   Moselle Position.
   Breusch Position.
   Vosges barrier.
   Bridge fortifications of the Upper Rhine.
   Vistula line.
   Masurian Lakes line.
   Breslau.
   Glogau.

2. Preparation of directives for the initial operations of the First and Second Armies, the Senior Cavalry Commander West, and the Eighth Army.
3. The Railway Department has made preparations for the transport of replacement and reserve replacement forces from the districts of G, III, IV, X, XII, XIX Army Corps and the 3rd Division to the Kiel–Altona line upon special order.
4. Decide whether to appoint a "commander-in-chief for a northern theater of war" and whether a reinforcement of troops in the area of IX Army Corps is required.
5. a. Inform Italy that 1 general officer (plus staff) with deployment instructions and stipulations for food will arrive in Offenburg on 5th mobilization day, and that a simultaneous dispatch of Italian General Staff officers to Offenburg is requested.
    b. War maps for the Italian Army are kept at the stations of Kenzingen, Breisach, Strassburg.
    c. Should contingents of XIV Army Corps still be in the deployment area of the Italian Army upon the latter's arrival, XIV Army Corps is to vacate this area.
6. Railroad Department arranges for further measures in accordance with special regulations regarding the Oder barges provided for the Austrian Army with the V and VI Army Corps.

b. Aufmarsch II:

1. Preparation of directives for Seventh and Eighth Armies, the Senior Cavalry Commander East, the High Command West, VIII, XVI, II Bavarian, XV, and XIV Army Corps.
2. Preparations for Italian Army might be subject to modification, in particular a possible change of unloading stations.

* * *

II. Aufmarsch I

1. Aufmarsch I West

The available "basic principles" (without annexes) only contain instructions for the arrival of individual transports according to urgency, etc.
The number of armies and their approximate deployment areas can be

deduced from the overview of unloading stations of field train companies below.
First Army: Elsenborn, Stadtkyll, Jünkerath, Zülpich, Euskirchen.
Second Army: Gerolstein, Erdorf, Bitburg, Trier.
Third Army: Diedenhofen, Saarburg-Beurig, Merzig, Saarlouis, Saarbrücken.
Fourth Army: Diedenhofen, St. Ingbert, Bolchen, Saargemünd.
Fifth Army: Bitsch, Ingweiler, Hagenau, St. Avold.
Sixth Army: Brumath, Bischweiler, Ittenheim, Pfalzburg, Alt- and Neubreisach.

2. Aufmarsch I East:

Seventh Army	3 reserve divisions, 3 separate reserve brigades, 7 combined Landwehr brigades, 1 cavalry division.
Command Post	Posen.
Initial Deployment:	Behind the railroad line Myslowitz–Sarotschin–Gnesen–Hohensalza (where 7 combined Landwehr brigades are deployed).
	a) Right Wing: ½ reserve division each near Oppeln and Breslau.
	b) Center: 1 reserve division, 2 separate reserve brigades near Posen.
	c) Left Wing: 1 reserve division, 1 separate reserve brigade near Bromberg.
	Cavalry division south of Hohensalza.
Eighth Army	3 army corps, 2 separate reserve brigades, 7 combined Landwehr brigades, 2 cavalry divisions.
Command Post	Marienburg.

Eighth Army Commander is also Commander-in-Chief of the East.

Initial Deployment:	In the line Jablonowo–Montowo–Allenstein–Gumbinnen
	Right Wing: Near Jablonowo–Montowo (1 army corps, 1 separate reserve brigade) as well as near Allenstein (1 army corps) – 1 cavalry division near Strassburg.
	Center: Following the replacement of the border guard the fortifications of the Masurian Lakes will be occupied by 3 combined Landwehr

brigades.
Left Wing: (1 army corps, 1 separate reserve brigade, 1 cavalry division) around Gumbinnen, 1 combined Landwehr brigade near Tilsit.

* * *

Re. Aufmarsch I

Aufmarsch I West

First Army	5 army corps, 3 reserve divisions.
Command Post	Stadtkyll.
Initial Deployment:	Behind the border of Aachen–Sevenich in the area Aachen–Malmedy–Burg Reuland–Stadtkyll–Gemünd.
	4 army corps in line from Malmedy–Malscheid (southwest of Burg Reuland).
	1 army corps follows the right-wing army corps.
	2 reserve divisions follow the second army corps on the right.
	1 reserve division follows the third army corps on the right.
	Right-wing army corps to the Montjoie–Elsenborn–Malmedy road.
	Left: Roth–Bleialf–Burg Reuland–Malscheid.
	Cavalry division west of Burg Reuland.
Second Army	4 army corps (incl. 1 reserve corps).
Command Post	Trier.
Initial Deployment	Behind the border of Sevenich–Wasserbillig in the area Dasburg–Wasserbillig–Mertert–Hetzerath–Prüm.
	3 army corps in line, 1 army corps behind the left-wing army corps.
	Right: Prüm–Lichtenborn–Dasburg.
	Center: Bitburg–Oberweis–Sinspelt–Roth.
	Left-wing infantry division Trier–Wasserbillig.
Third Army	4 army corps, 3 cavalry divisions.
Command Post	Saarlouis.

Initial Deployment	Behind the line Moselle Wasserbillig–Remich–Ritzingen–Flasdorf–Filsdorf in the area Grevenmacher–Remich–Filsdorf–Schwalbach (east of Saarlouis)–Mettlach–Hentern (east of Saarburg/Rh). Right: Nieder Zerf–Saarburg–Beurig–Grevenmacher. Left: Schwalbach–Saarlouis–Niedaltdorf–Flasdorf. 1 cavalry division east of Grevenmacher. 1 cavalry division near Königsmachern. 1 cavalry division near Metzeresch.
Fourth Army Command Post Initial Deployment:	4 army corps, 2 cavalry divisions. Saargemünd. Behind the line of Busendorf–Marienthal in the area Busendorf–Püttlingen–Saargemünd–Saarbrücken. Right: Burbach–Malstatt–Waldgassen–Busendorf. Left: Folpersweiler–Püttlingen–Marienthal. 1 cavalry division near Bolchen. 1 cavalry division near St. Avold.
Fifth Army Command Post Initial Deployment:	4 army corps, 1 cavalry division. Saar-Buckenheim. XVI Army Corps near Metz (assumption since map does not indicate to which army XVI Army Corps is assigned). The remainder behind the line Johanns-Rohrbach–Wittersburg–Mittersheim in the area Johanns-Rohrbach–Wittersburg–Mittersheim–Finstingen–Weislingen–Schmittweiler (east of Saaralben). Right: Ormingen–Herbitzheim–Saaralben–Johanns-Rohrbach. Left: Weislingen–Wolfskirchen–Finstingen–Mittersheim. Cavalry division near Gr. Tänchen.

Sixth Army	4 army corps, 3 reserve divisions, 1 cavalry division.
Command Post	Zabern.
Initial Deployment:	Right Wing: 2 army corps, 2 reserve divisions, 1 cavalry division behind the line of the Saarkohlen Canal–Stockweiher–Gunderchingen (Gondrexange)–Alberschweiler–Pfalzburg. 2 army corps in line, each followed by 1 reserve division, cavalry division near Saarburg. Right: Saarburg–Gunderchingen. Left: Lützelburg–Harzweiler–Lörchingen. Left wing 2 army corps, 1 reserve division behind the line of Schirmeck–Kolrein (Colroy la Boche) in the area Schirmeck–Kolrein–Schlettstadt–Erstein–Molsheim. 2 army corps abreast, reserve division behind the center (in the area Benfeld–Erstein). Right: Molsheim–Schirmeck. Left: Schlettstadt–Steige–Kolrein.

* * *

III. Aufmarsch II

The First, Second, and Third Armies are employed in the west; the Fifth through Eighth Armies in the east. The documents available give no indication of the whereabouts of the Fourth Army.

1. Aufmarsch II West:

A French offensive is expected. Only after the direction of the offensive is identified will the transportation of the army corps begin. Until then, they will remain in garrison. The purpose is to launch a surprise attack on the enemy's wing or flank.

Precautionary measures are basically the same as with Aufmarsch I.
    VIII Army Corps assembles near Trier.
    XVI Army Corps assembles near Metz.
    (Garrisons [detachments] Mörchingen and Dieuze remain.)

Main body of XV Army Corps will not be transported to Saarburg.
The upper Rhine will be protected by Bavarian and Baden Landwehr.
Cavalry divisions will be transported as follows:
9th to Trier.
3rd to Diedenhofen.
Bavarian to Bolchen.
6th to Gr. Tänchen.
7th to Saarburg.

"Preparations made for the approach of the Italian army contingents will remain in force."

West Army High Command Hanover:

First Army	4 army corps (incl. 1 reserve corps), 1 reserve division, 3 combined Landwehr brigades, 2 cavalry divisions.
Command Post	Jünkerath.
Initial Deployment:	Right Group: 2 army corps in the area north of Kilburg–Schönecken–Prüm–Kronenberg–Gerolstein.
	Left Group: 1 army corps (VIII) around Trier.
	Reserve: 1 reserve division around Euskirchen, 1 reserve corps in the area Rheinbach–Ahrweiler.
Second Army	5 army corps, 3 combined Landwehr brigades, 1 cavalry division.
Command Post	Koblenz.
Initial Deployment:	Outpost 1 army corps (XVI) in Metz.
	Right Group: 3 army corps in the approximate area of Zell a/d Mosel–Kelberg–Mayen–Coblenz.
	Left Group: 1 army corps in the area northeast of Kreuznach.
Third Army	3 army corps (incl. 1 reserve corps), 1 reserve division, 4 combined Landwehr brigades, 2 cavalry divisions.
Command Post	Mainz

Initial Deployment   1. With 3 army corps (incl. 1 reserve corps) in the area Worms–Grünstadt–Kirchheimbolanden–Eckelsheim–Wörrstadt.
2. With 1 reserve division near Mannheim.
At the disposal of the Deputy General Command VI
4½ combined Landwehr brigades.

2. Aufmarsch II East (as far as indicated in map):

Fifth Army   3 army corps (incl. 1 reserve corps), 3 reserve divisions, 3 cavalry divisions.
Command Post   Graudenz.
Initial Deployment: 1 cavalry division each near Gnesen, Goolub, and Strassburg.
Right Wing: 2 army corps (incl. 1 reserve corps), 3 reserve divisions in the area Thorn–Gollub–Briesen–Kulmsee.
Left Wing: 1 army corps to road Jablonowo–Strassburg.

Sixth Army   4 army corps (incl. 1 reserve corps).
Command Post   Riesenburg.
Initial Deployment: Behind the line Lautenburg–Ortelsburg, viz. 1 army corps each to the following roads:
    Neumark–Lautenburg.
    Löbau–Gilgenburg–Usdau (north of Soldau).
    Hohenstein–(north of) Neidenburg
    Passenheim–Ortelsburg.

Seventh Army   4 army corps, 1 cavalry division.
Command Post   Rastenburg.
Initial Deployment: Behind the line Johannisburg–Lyck–Maggrabowa.
Cavalry division east of Maggrabowa.
1 army corps is deployed to each of the following roads:
    Peitschendorf (south of Sensburg)–Johannisburg.

          Gr. Konopken (southeast of Lötzen)–Arys–Drygallen.
          Widminnen–Lyck–Neuendorf (south of Lyck).
          Grabowen (south of Goldap)–Sokollen–Maggrabowa.

Eighth Army	5 army corps, 4 reserve divisions, 2 cavalry divisions.
Command Post	Insterburg.
Initial Deployment:	Along the German border from Mierunsken (west of Filipowo)–Schirwindt.

The units are deployed as follows:
    2 cavalry divisions east of Stallupönen.
    1 army corps to the Goldap–Filipowo road.
    1 army corps to the Walterkehmen–Duberningken road.
    1 army corps to the Trakehnen–Szittkehmen road.
    1 army corps, 1 reserve division to the Kattenau–Stallupönen–Kirbaty road.
    1 army corps, 1 reserve division to the Pillkallen–Schirwindt road.
    1 reserve division each near Szillen and Tilsit.

Aufmarsch 1902–1903

The following documents are available:
Only maps with entries...
1. Aufmarsch I.
   a) Map West.
   b) Railroad Map East.
2. Aufmarsch II.
   a) Map West.
   b) Map East.
3. Coastal Defense (Railroad Map).

* * *

1. Aufmarsch I

a. West:

First Army	4 army corps (incl. 1 reserve corps), 4 reserve divisions, 1 cavalry division.
Command Post	St. Vith.
Initial Deployment:	Behind the German border from Aachen to Roth (west of Bitburg).
	3 army corps on the line Malmedy–Roth.
	Right infantry division to the Sourbrodt–Malmedy road.
	Left infantry division to the Waxweiler–Neuenburg–Dasburg road.
	1 reserve corps, 1 reserve division to the Aachen–Montjoie road.
	1 reserve division near Düren–Nideggen.
	1 reserve division near Schleiden.
	1 reserve division near Kronenburg–Stadtkyll.
	Cavalry division west of Burg Reuland.

Second Army
Command Post
Initial Deployment:

3 army corps, 1 cavalry division.
Trier.
Behind the German border from Bollendorf (northwest of Echternach) to Besch (south of Remich).
Right-wing army corps to the Trier–[illegible]–Minden–Bollendorf road.
Left: Moselle crossing near Remich.
Cavalry division east of Grevenmacher.

Third Army
Command Post
Initial Deployment:

4 army corps (1 reserve corps), 1 cavalry division.
Diedenhofen.
Behind the line Püttlingen–Bust–Volkringen–Grossmövern (Gr. Mayeuvre).
Right: Waldwiese–Sierck–Ob. Kontz–Fixem–Rentgen.
Left: Busendorf–Endorf–Mondelingen–Grossmövern.
Cavalry division west of Diedenhofen.

Fourth Army

Command Post
Initial Deployment:

4 army corps, 2 reserve divisions, 2 cavalry divisions.
Metz.
Behind the German border from Grossmövern to Mardeningen (Mardigny).
4 army corps on the front line, 2 reserve divisions behind the left wing.
Right: Wigingen (Vigy)–Ennerchen (Ennery)–Machern (Maizières)–St. Privat–Wernheim (Verneville).
Left: pp. Schersingen (Cherisy)–Kuberneck (Coin Cuvry)–Corningen (Corny)–Arnaville.
1 cavalry division near Gravelotte.
1 cavalry division near Kurzel a/Nied.

Fifth Army

Command Post
Initial Deployment:

4 army corps (incl. 2 reserve corps), 2 reserve divisions, 2 cavalry divisions.
Mörchingen.
Behind the German border from Kemnat

(Chemanot) to Gerden (Lagarde).
Right: (XVI) marshals northwest of St. Jürgen (St. Iure).
Left: Duss (Dieuze)–Monhofen (Montcourt).
1 cavalry division each near Herlingen and Conthil (north of Duss).

Sixth Army
Command Post
Initial Deployment:

3 army corps, 1 cavalry division.
Saarburg.
Behind the line Mulsach (Moussey)–Bruschweiler.
Right group west of Saarburg.
1 army corps to the Finstingen–Langenberg–Mulsach road.
1 army corps to the Saarburg–St. Georg road.
1 cavalry division near Saarburg.
Left group in the area of Schirmeck.
1 army corps to the Mutzig–Schirmeck–Salzern (Saulxures)–Gutbrunn (Goutte) road.

Seventh Army
Command Post
Initial Deployment:

3 army corps, 2 reserve divisions.
Neubreisach.
In the area Colmar–Mühlhausen–Hüningen–Lörrach–Müllheim–Staufen–Breisach.
The units are deployed as follows:
    1 infantry division near Colmar.
    1 reserve division south of Neu-Breisach.
    1 army corps to the Heitersheim–Müllheim–Neuenburg–Banzenheim Road.
    1½ army corps, 1 reserve division to the Lörrach–Hüningen–Mühlhausen road.

b. Aufmarsch East:

The map does not indicate the designation of the armies; in general it should be the same as in 1901–1902.

Army

1 reserve division, 5 reserve brigades, 7 combined Landwehr brigades, 1 cavalry division.

Command Post

Posen (*not indicated*).

Initial Deployment:	Behind the railroad line Myslowitz–Sarotschin–Gnesen–Hohensalza (which is secured by 7 combined Landwehr brigades). 1 reserve division near Oppeln (½) and Breslau (½). 3 reserve brigades near Posen. 2 reserve brigades near Bromberg. 1 cavalry division south of Hohensalza.
Army	3 army corps, 2 separate reserve brigades, 6 combined Landwehr brigades, 2 cavalry divisions.
Command Post	Marienburg.
Army commander is also Commander-in-Chief of the East.	
Initial Deployment:	On the line Montowo–Allenstein–Gumbinnen. Right Wing: 1 army corps, 1 separate reserve brigade northwest of Montowo. 1 army corps near Allenstein. 1 cavalry division near Soldau. Center: 3 combined Landwehr brigades near Sensburg, Rastenburg, Angerburg. Left Wing: 1 army corps, 1 separate reserve brigade, 1 cavalry division near Gumbinnen. 1 combined Landwehr brigade near Tilsit.

* * *

2. Aufmarsch II

a. West:

First Army	5 army corps, 4 reserve divisions, 1 cavalry division.
Command Post	Trier.
Initial Deployment:	To the German border from Roth (west of Bitburg) to Wincheringen (south of Grevenmacher). 5 army corps in front line, behind the two wings 2 reserve divisions each. Right: Bitburg–Oberweis–Sinspelt–Roth. Left: Moselle crossing near Grevenmacher. Cavalry division east of Grevenmacher.

Second Army	4 army corps (incl. 1 reserve corps), 1 cavalry division.
Command Post	Ebersweiler.
Initial Deployment:	1 army corps (XVI) near Metz, the remainder behind the line Metzingen (west of Diedenhofen)–Bertringen (south of Diedenhofen)–Ennerchen (Ennery)– Contchen. Right: Metzerwiese–Diedenhofen–Metzingen. Left: Busendorf–Anzelingen–Gunderweiler (Gondreville). Cavalry division north of Ars a/d. Mosel.
Third Army	3 army corps (incl. 1 reserve corps), 1 reserve division.
Command Post	Saarbrücken.
Initial Deployment:	Behind the line Bolchen–Spittel (north of St. Avold)–Beningen (southwest of Forbach). Right: Teterchen–Bolchen. Left: Forbach–Rossbrücken.
Fourth Army	4 army corps (incl. 1 reserve corps), 2 cavalry divisions.
Command Post	Saarburg.
Initial Deployment:	Behind the line Saaralben–Finstingen–Gunderchingen (Gondrexange)–Salzern (Saulxures). Right Wing: 1 army corps each in the area of Saaralben and east of Finstingen and east of Saarburg and westward. Cavalry division south of Saarburg. Left Wing: 1 army corps to the Mutzig–Schirmeck–Salzern road.

Fifth Army
The initial deployment is identical to "Aufmarsch I West for the Seventh Army."

b. Aufmarsch II East:

Sixth Army	2 army corps, 4 reserve divisions, 1 cavalry division.

Command Post	Ortelsburg.
Initial Deployment:	Behind the German border from Gollub to northwest of Leman. Right Group: 1 army corps, 2 reserve divisions in the area Gollub–Strassburg–Jablonowo–Briesen. Planned advance: 1 army corps via pp. Sierpc–Racionz–Ciechanow. 1 reserve division via Rypin–Luronim–Kuczbork–Wierzbowo (northeast of Ciechanow) and Eastward. 1 reserve division via Zielun–Mlawa–Przasnysz. 1 cavalry division near Gr. Koschlau. Left Group: 1 army corps, 2 reserve divisions in the area Willenberg–Gr. Turoschheln–Aweyden–Ortelsburg. Planned advance: 1 reserve division via Zaremby–Berdowe–Lonki–Kadzidlo–Dombrowka and southward. 1 reserve division via Myszyniec–Lipniki–Kuzie–Dobrylas–Serwatki and southward. 1 army corps via Leman–Kolno–Staruski.
Seventh Army	5 army corps (incl. 1 reserve corps), 2 cavalry divisions.
Command Post	Lyck.
Initial Deployment:	Behind the German border from Sokollen am Berg (south of Bialla) to south of Szittkehmen. Right Group: 3 army corps, 1 cavalry division in the area Bialla–Lyck–Stradaunen Gingen. Cavalry division southeast of Lyck. Planned advance: 1 army corps via Gr. Prostken–Danowo–Orzechowka–Polkowo–Dolistowo and northeastward. 1 army corps via Borzymmen–Barglow–Netta–Kolnica–Sztabin (southwest of Lipsk). 1 army corps via Gingen–Augustow–Skieblewo (north of Lipsk). Left Group: 2 army corps in the area northeast of

	Marggrabowa–Goldap–Dubeningken. Planned advance: 1 army corps via Filipowo–Bakalarzewo–Dubowo (south of Suwalki)–Makarce–Rudawka (east of Sopokinie). 1 army corps via Przerosl–Suwalki–Krasnopol–Sejny–Kopciowo–Bzondowy (south of Kopciowo).
Eighth Army	2 army corps, 1 reserve division, 1 cavalry division.
Command Post	Gumbinnen.
Initial Deployment:	In the area Wisztyniec–Bilderweitschen–Gumbinnen. Cavalry division northwest of Kibaty.

* * *

3. Coastal Defense

Becomes effective on the 1st day of mobilization and will be conducted by Landsturm troops. From the 3rd day of mobilization these Landsturm troops will be reinforced by Landwehr troops.

a. Special "*Wartime garrisons*" (Landwehr troops) will be deployed to:
    Swinemünde.
    Kiel.
    Cuxhaven.
    Lehe (1906–1907 = Geestemünde).
    Wilhelmshaven.

b. *Reserves* (1 combined Landwehr brigade each) are deployed to:
    Stettin.
    Lübeck.
    Lockstedter Lager.
    Hannover.

c. Troops are deployed to the following islands:
Alsen:	1 company.
Sylt:	10 companies, 1 battery, ⅓ engineer company.
Amrum:	1 company.

Pellworm:	3 companies.
Nordstrand:	1 company.
Wangerooge:	1 company.
Norderney:	1 company.
Borkum:	16 companies, 2 batteries, ⅔ engineer company.

Aufmarsch 1903–1904

The following documents are available:
1. Mobilization Schedule 1903–1904.
2. Directives for Covering Aufmarsch West.
3. Directives for Covering Aufmarsch East.
4. Wartime Order of Battle West I.
5. Wartime Order of Battle East I.
6. Deployment Directives West (without Annexes).
7. Deployment Directives East (without Annexes).
8. Deployment Directives for Coastal Defense (for 1 Landwehr Brigade).

* * *

II. Excerpt from the "Directives for Covering the Deployment of the German Western Army in 1903–1904"

1. For the purpose of joint operations the seven cavalry divisions of the Western Army initially will be assigned to the Senior Cavalry Commander. The cavalry divisions are marshaled as follows:

9th Cav. Div.	near Sinspelt	Until Senior Cav. Commander assumes command assigned to…	VIII Army Corps
Guards Cav. Div.	near Sierck	Until Senior Cav. Commander assumes command assigned to…	XVI Army Corps
3rd Cav. Div.	west of Diedenhofen	Until Senior Cav. Commander assumes command assigned to…	XVI Army Corps
6th Cav. Div.	south of Metz	Until Senior Cav. Commander assumes command assigned to…	XVI Army Corps
8th Cav. Div.	near Rembach (Remilly)	Until Senior Cav. Commander assumes command assigned to…	XVI Army Corps
Bavarian Cav. Div.	Near Conthil	Until Senior Cav. Commander assumes command assigned to…	XVI Army Corps
7th Cav. Div.	Near Saarburg	Until Senior Cav. Commander assumes command assigned to…	XV Army Corps

2. *VIII Army Corps District*
   a. The district can be threatened particularly by French cavalry rallying at the Meuse between Verdun and Sedan.
   b. The main body of the 16th Infantry Division is at the disposal of the OHL in Trier.
   c. Bridges across the Moselle and Sauer from the mouth of the Our to Grevenmacher will be occupied immediately.
   d. Entering the Belgian and Luxembourg border areas is forbidden. If the French enter Luxembourg, however, an immediate advance across the Luxembourg border is authorized to cover the German deployment. In this case the issuance of the pertinent order is reserved for the General Command.
   e. There will be no disruption of the railroads leading to Belgium and Luxembourg, nor of the bridges across the Moselle and Sauer at the Luxembourg border.

3. *XVI Army Corps District*
The main body provides border security near Metz.
The Mörchingen garrison is stationed near Lemhofen (Lemoncourt) and Orhofen (Oricourt).
Furthermore, XVI Army Corps is reinforced by 3 infantry brigades (with 3 batteries, 1 squadron each) arriving at:
   Metzerwiese.
   Kadingen.
   Château-Salins.
12cm batteries will emplace near Illingen, Buss-Blettingen, and Rupeningen (Rugy).
"Do not put high priority on the destruction of railways on enemy territory."

4. *XV Army Corps District*
Main body deploys in the area of Zabern to the Hochfelden–Zabern–Pfalzburg–Saarburg road.
Detachment (former garrisons) near Dieuze.
Detachment (former garrisons) near Saarburg.
Detachment on the roads of the Vosges.
The following units will arrive:
   1 infantry brigade with 3 batteries near Geistkirch.
   1 infantry brigade with 3 batteries near Schirmeck.

5. *XIV Army Corps District*
Main body plus 1 reserve division deploy to Colmar.
Detachment (former garrison) near Schlettstadt.
Detachment (former garrison) near Colmar.
Detachment (former garrison) near Mühlhausen.
"In the event of a breakthrough of superior French forces, the troops stationed near Mühlhausen will withdraw to Colmar, and if necessary, across to the right bank of the Rhine."
"Upon receipt of the mobilization order or the opening of hostilities, the railroads leading into France are to be slightly disrupted at the border and in the outpost zone."

* * *

I. Excerpt from the Mobilization Schedule of 1903–1904

1. The following units are allocated for *Aufmarsch I*:
    Against France: 25 army corps, 7 cavalry divisions, 15 reserve divisions.
    Against Russia: 3 army corps, 4 cavalry divisions, 4 reserve divisions.
    For *Aufmarsch II*: "... The preparations for *Aufmarsch II* are written down only in the form of a study, since this *Aufmarsch* was considered the less probable case."
2. Positions to be consolidated as in the previous years: "Possible occupation of fortifications at the Isteiner Klotz, in accordance with its completion."
3. Consider whether memorandums and reconnaissance reports regarding Belgian routes of advance and water conditions should be attached to the deployment directives for First and Second Army headquarters.
4. Provision of VIII Army Corps forces in Trier 6 hours after mobilization is announced.
    Message to Railroad Department regarding the continued operation into Luxembourg.
5. Preparation of apparently necessary notifications to Austria and Italy. (Dispatch of senior officers.)
    "If an Italian army is transported to southern Germany, the procedure will be in accordance with plan."
    Files to be taken along include: "Copy of the agreement between the German Navy Admiralty Staff, the Italian Naval Ministry, and the Naval Section of the Austro-Hungarian Imperial Ministry."
    The boats to be provided to OHL by V and VI Army Corps will be transported to Austria.

6. Decision on the establishment of a "commander-in-chief of a northern theater of war" and preparation of transport on the line Kiel–Altona (as in previous years).

* * *

III. Aufmarsch I West

The most senior of the two Senior Cavalry Commanders assumes overall command of all seven cavalry divisions deploying to the area of the western border, and after receiving initial guidance from XVI Army Corps headquarters he conducts operations independently. At the beginning, the cavalry divisions will cover the deployment of the army, and without engaging in further activities will prevent the enemy from gaining intelligence.

    Later, the cavalry divisions will join their armies.

    For the assembly points of the cavalry divisions see II, 1.

Preliminary Remark:

The deployment directives indicate only: Location of command post, the field base of the communications zone (E.H.O.), and the headquarters.

The location of the headquarters is the only indication for tentative conclusions about grouping.

First Army	4 army corps, 4 reserve divisions, 3 combined Landwehr brigades.
Command Post	Montjoie.
E.H.O.[1]	Düren.
Corps Headquarters:	Euskirchen, Elsenborn training area, Zülpich and St. Vith.
Reserve Division Headquarters: Stolberg, Lammersdorf, Kelz, Stadtkyll.	
	2 army corps on the front line.
	1 reserve division, echeloned on the right.
	2 army corps, 1 reserve division in 2nd line.
	"Crossing the Belgian border is authorized only after explicit order issued by OHL." Luxembourg territory may be entered to cover the deployment *as soon as it is entered by the enemy.*"

Second Army 4 army corps, 1 reserve division, 2 combined Landwehr brigades, 3 cavalry divisions.
Command Post Bitburg.
E.H.O. Stadtkyll–Jünkerath.
Corps Headquarters: Prüm, Bitburg, Speicher, Trier.
Reserve Division Headquarters: Gindorf.
4 army corps in line, reserve division behind the center.

Third Army 3 army corps, 4 reserve divisions, 2 combined Landwehr brigades, 4 cavalry divisions.
Command Post Saarlouis.
E.H.O. Ottweiler.
Corps Headquarters: Saarburg, Merzig, Saarlouis.
Reserve Division Headquarters: Conz, Pellingen, Beckingen, Püttlingen.
3 army corps, 1 reserve division abreast, on the right wing 2, on the left wing 1 reserve division echeloned.

Fourth Army 4 army corps, 2 reserve divisions, 2 combined Landwehr brigades.
Command Post Forbach.
E.H.O. Neunkirchen.
Corps Headquarters: (XVI) Metz, Völklingen, Forbach, Saargemünd.
Reserve Division Headquarters: St. Ingbert, Blieskastel.
3 army corps abreast, 2 reserve divisions following behind the center.

Fifth Army 4 army corps, 2 combined Landwehr brigades.
Command Post Ingweiler.
E.H.O. Hagenau.
Corps Headquarters: Hornbach, Ingweiler, Neuweiler, Zabern.
4 army corps abreast.

Sixth Army 3 army corps, 2 reserve divisions, 2 combined Landwehr brigades.
Command Post Mutzig.
E.H.O. Strassburg.
Corps Headquarters: Wasselnheim, Mutzig, Behnfeld.

Reserve Division Headquarters: Vendenheim, Geispolsheim
    3 army corps abreast, 1 reserve division behind each wing.

Seventh Army	3 army corps, 2 reserve divisions, 1 combined Landwehr brigade.
Command Post	Colmar.
E.H.O.	Freiburg.
Corps Headquarters:	Schlettstadt, Colmar, Freiburg.

Reserve Division Headquarters: Gotenheim, Neuenburg.
    2 army corps in 1st line.
    1 army corps, 2 reserve divisions echeloned on the left.

Landwehr Troops on the Upper Rhine
    3½ Landwehr brigades.

Coastal Defense in the Sectors of IX and X Army Corps
    1⅓ combined Landwehr brigades. (Main body in Lockstedter Lager.)

IV. Aufmarsch I East

1. Excerpt from the "Directives for Covering the Deployment of the German Eastern Army in 1903–1904."

Specific instructions for VI, V, II Army Corps (which will be transported to the west and be replaced by Landwehr and Landsturm forces for the purposes of border security); and XVII and I Army Corps, which are generally instructed to refrain from blocking the expected breakthrough of the enemy cavalry (which might be followed by infantry battalions) with individual detachments. The intent instead is to leave the troops in garrison for the time being, and then to destroy the enemy only after he has paused to rest.

XVII Army Corps	reinforced by 1 reserve brigade, 1 combined Landwehr brigade, and 2 cavalry divisions (marshaled near Lautenburg and Thorn) will assemble in the area of Neumark, after having

	been replaced by Landwehr and Landsturm for border security.
I Army Corps	reinforced by 1 reserve brigade, 1 combined Landwehr brigade, and 2 cavalry divisions will marshal its main body and 1 cavalry division on the Angerapp and 1 cavalry division southwest of Tilsit.

Assumed Enemy Intent
VI and V Army Corps Districts: Breakthrough with cavalry for minor operations.
II Army Corps District: Threatened by I Cavalry Corps near Woclawek, which will advance against the Schneidemühl railroad junction and the Schneidemühl–Bromberg railroad.

XVII Army Corps District: Threatened by II Cavalry Corps, which will advance from Lomza–Ostrolenka–Mlawa–Rypin in the general direction of Allenstein–Elbing and against Dt. Eylau and from there against the Marienburg–Elbing railroad and Graudenz.
Furthermore, 1 cavalry division each can be expected from the directions of Grajewo and Ostrolenka.

I Army Corps District: Threat along the east front of the corps district from 2 cavalry divisions that will disrupt the mobilization of the I Army Corps and spread terror in the border districts.
1 cavalry division can be expected from the direction of Grajewo, and elements of II Cavalry Corps from the direction of Lomza–Ostrolenka (see above XVII Army Corps) are believed to have been instructed to destroy the railroad near Allenstein.

2.

Eighth Army (*Eastern Army*)	3 army corps, 4 reserve divisions, 6 combined Landwehr brigades, 4 cavalry divisions (incl. 2 cavalry divisions under the Senior Cavalry Commander). The following units are subordinate: In the V Army Corps sector, 2 combined Landwehr brigades. In the VI Army Corps sector, 3 combined

Command Post	Landwehr brigades. In the II Army Corps sector, 4 combined Landwehr brigades. Dt. Eylau
Initial Deployment:	
Right Wing:	1 army corps, 3 reserve divisions, 1 combined Landwehr brigade, 2 cavalry divisions behind the border from Thorn to Lauenburg, with 3 reserve divisions in the area of Thorn. 1 army corps in the area of Lautenburg. 1 cavalry division in the area of Lautenburg. 1 cavalry division in the area east of Thorn.
Center:	1 army corps near and south of Allenstein.
Left Wing:	1 army corps, 1 reserve division, 5 combined Landwehr brigades, 2 cavalry divisions behind the Angerapp to ensure that the Angerburg–Insterburg front is covered. 1 cavalry division marshals southwest of Tilsit. 1 cavalry division marshals near Gumbinnen (including Senior Cavalry Commander).

Notes

1. *Etappe Hauptort*, main base of the communications zone.

Aufmarsch 1904–1905

The following documents are available:
1. Mobilization Schedule 1904–1905.
2. Border Security Map West.
3. Border Security Map West including the Enemy Situation.
4. Two Border Security Maps East.
5. Wartime Order of Battle West-East Aufmarsch I.
6. Deployment Directives West (without Annexes).
7. Deployment Directives East I (without Annexes).
8. Deployment Directives East II (without Annexes).

* * *

I. Excerpt from Mobilization Schedule 1904–1905
(individual sheets are missing)

1. "Peacetime preparations provide for two types of deployment:
   Aufmarsch I assumes a state of war with France only. The following units are to be committed:

Against France:	26 army corps, 9 cavalry divisions, 15 reserve divisions.
In the East:	To prevent a complete removal of forces from the very beginning, the following units shall remain: 2 cavalry divisions, 4 reserve divisions.

   Aufmarsch II assumes a state of war with France and Russia. The following units are to be committed:

Against France:	23 army corps, 9 cavalry divisions, 15 reserve divisions.
Against Russia:	3 army corps, 2 cavalry divisions, 4 reserve divisions.

(Apparently, Aufmarsch West II would otherwise proceed exactly as West I without 3 army corps "since the First, Third, and Fourth Armies will be informed that XX, I, and XVII Army Corps will remain in the eastern theater.")

2. With regard to positions to be consolidated, the following is added to those of the previous years: Mainz.

II. Border Security West

The following units are committed to border security:

VIII Army Corps District from Reuland-Sierck Castle		
	1 combined infantry brigade	Waxweiler
	1 cavalry division	south of Neuerburg
	1 cavalry division, 1 infantry regiment	Area northeast of Echternach
	Main body of 16th Infantry Division	Trier
	1 infantry regiment	Wincheringen
XVI Army Corps District extending to Vic		
	1 combined infantry brigade	southwest of Sierck
	1 cavalry division	north of Diedenhofen
	1 cavalry division	west of Diedenhofen
	1 infantry regiment, 4 squadrons	near Diedenhofen
	1 combined infantry regiment	south of Blettingen
	1 infantry brigade, 4 squadrons	near Metz
	34th Infantry Division	Area south and southwest of Remlach (Remilly) where General Command XVI is located
	33rd Infantry Division	assembly south of Herlingen
	1 combined infantry brigade	near Mörchingen
	1 cavalry division each	Contchen
		Falkenberg
		Gr. Tänchen
		Leiningen
XV Army Corps District extending to Breuschtal near Salzern (Saulxures)		
	1 combined infantry brigade	near Duss (Dieuze)
	1 combined infantry brigade	Saarburg (HQ of 30th Infantry Division)
	1 cavalry division	Saarburg
	1 combined infantry brigade	Schirmeck
XIV Army Corps District extending to the Swiss border		
	1 combined infantry brigade	near Colmar (HQ of 39th Infantry Division)
	1 combined infantry brigade	Mühlhausen
	On the Rhine: security operations of Landwehr and Landsturm	

Enemy	Will secure the general line: Belfort–Vosges ridge (VII Army Corps)–Lunéville–east of Nancy (XX Army Corps)–Pont-à-Mousson–Thiaucourt–Westhang Côtes Lorraines–Verdun–west of the Meuse to Sedan (VI Army Corps). Apart from numerous individual infantry and light infantry battalions, forest and customs troops are committed:

    8 infantry divisions.
    8⅔ cavalry divisions.

Massed infantry divisions located at…
    Belfort   1.
    Bruyeres 1.
    Nancy   2.

Massed cavalry divisions are located at….
    Belfort.
    Bruyeres (⅓).
    Southwest of Lunéville.
    Lunéville.
    Nancy.
    North of Toul.
    Thiaucourt (⅓).
    East of Verdun.
    North of Verdun.
    Stenay.

* * *

III. Aufmarsch West

The nine cavalry divisions in the west are subordinate to the ranking Senior Cavalry Commander (as in 1903–1904), and to whom another two Senior Cavalry Commanders are subordinated.

Until the ranking Senior Cavalry Commander assumes command, the following units are committed to border security in the districts of the following army corps:

VIII Army Corps	2 cavalry divisions.
XVI Army Corps	6 cavalry divisions.
XV Army Corps	1 cavalry division.

The deployment directives indicate only the initial headquarters of the senior staffs.

First Army | 4 army corps [Guards, VII, XX, IX], 4 reserve divisions [5th, 13th, 17th, 29th], 5 combined Landwehr brigades.
Command Post | Bitburg.
E.H.O.[1] | Gerolstein.
Corps HQs | Zülpich, Schönecken, Bitburg, Welschbillig.
Reserve Division HQs | Ehran. The other 3 cannot be established.

Second Army | 4 army corps [II, X, IV, VIII], 2 reserve divisions [6th, 7th], 6 combined Landwehr brigades.
Command Post | Merzig.
E.H.O. | Trier.
Corps HQs | Trier, Saarburg, Merzig, Dillingen.
Reserve Division HQs | Wittlich, Hetzerath.

Third Army | 3 army corps [I, XVI, XVIII], 4 reserve divisions [15th, 19th, 21st, 22nd], 2½ combined Landwehr brigades.
Command Post | Saarbrücken.
E.H.O. | Neunkirchen.
Corps HQs | Saarlouis, Saarbrücken, Metz (XVI).
Reserve Division HQs | Diedenhofen, Aich (Ay), Metz–Sablon, Metz–Devant les Ponts.
Armored 12cm or 15cm batteries near Königsmachern, Illingen, Buss–Blettingen, and Rugy (south of Ennerchen [Ennery]).

Fourth Army | 4 army corps [II Bavarian, V, XI, XVII], 2 combined Landwehr brigades.
Command Post | Saargemünd.
E.H.O. | Homburg.
Corps HQs | Forbach, Gr. Blittersdorf, Saargemünd, Saaralben.

Fifth Army | 4 army corps [Guards Reserve, III, XV, XXI], 2 combined Landwehr brigades.
Command Post | Saar-Buckenheim (Saarunion).
E.H.O. | Ingweiler.
Corps HQs | Saar-Buckenheim, Diemeringen, Lützelstein, Saarburg.

Sixth Army	4 army corps [VI, XII, XIII, XIX], 2 combined Landwehr brigades.
Command Post	Wasselnheim.
E.H.O.	Brumath.
Corps HQs	Zabern, Mauersmünster, Mutzig, Barr.
Seventh Army	3 army corps [I Bavarian, III Bavarian, XIV], 5 reserve divisions [1st Bavarian, 26th, 28th, 23rd, 24th], 1 combined Landwehr brigade, in addition 3½ Landwehr brigades will secure the Rhine crossings, subordinated to XIV Army Corps.
Command Post	Neu-Breisach.
E.H.O.	Freiburg.
Corps HQs	Dambach, Schlettstadt, Colmar.
Reserve Division HQs	Neu-Breisach, Gottenheim, Neuenburg, Kandern, Hüningen.
For Coastal Defense	1⅓ combined Landwehr brigades.

* * *

IV. Border Security East

[...]²

* * *

V. Aufmarsch I East

Eastern Army

Eighth Army	4 reserve divisions, 2 cavalry divisions, 9 combined Landwehr brigades.
Command Post	Marienburg.

Commander is also Commander-in-Chief, East.

Operations in the eastern theater are not probable initially. Troops stationed there can be redeployed to other assignments. Should operations become necessary, the Commander-in-Chief, East will exercise independent command and control. Initially the forces will remain there for the sole purpose of preventing a complete lack of forces in the area.

Since this Aufmarsch does not assume a war with Russia, border violations must be strictly avoided.

Following the redeployment of the I, XVII, and newly formed XX Army Corps, the security of the country is ensured by the forces subordinated to Deputy General Command under the command of the Commander-in-Chief, East.

Subordination is as follows:

Deputy General Command I:	1 cavalry division, 2 reserve divisions, 1 combined Landwehr brigade.
Deputy General Command XVII:	1 cavalry division, 1 reserve division, 1 combined Landwehr brigade.
Deputy General Command II:	1 reserve division, 2 combined Landwehr brigades.
Deputy General Command V:	2 combined Landwehr brigades.
Deputy General Command VI:	3 combined Landwehr brigades.

In general, these forces are committed as provided in the ordinary "border security" (cf. item IV above)—with consideration for their reduced numbers.

* * *

VI. Aufmarsch II East

Eastern Army

Eighth Army	3 army corps, 4 reserve divisions, 2 cavalry divisions, 9 combined Landwehr brigades.
Command Post	Marienburg.

Commander is also Commander-in-Chief, East.

Initial deployment in 3 groups:
- 1 army corps, 1 reserve division, 1 cavalry division near and southeast of Dt. Eylau and Gosslershausen.
- 1 army corps, 1 reserve division near and southeast of Allenstein and Rotfliess–Bischofsburg.

1 army corps, 1 reserve division, 1 cavalry division across the Angerapp.
In addition, the following units are deployed to the area of...
Deputy General Command II Army Corps:
1 reserve division, 2 combined Landwehr brigades.
Deputy General Command V Army Corps:
2 combined Landwehr brigades.
Deputy General Command VI Army Corps:
2 combined Landwehr brigades.

Reconnaissance reports on combat positions on the left bank of the Vistula are kept with the governor of Thorn and the commander's office at Graudenz.

Notes

1. *Etappe Hauptort*, main base of the communications zone.
2. A detailed list of the individual border guard battalions is provided below.

Aufmarsch 1905–1906

The following documents are available:
1. Mobilization Schedule 1905–1906.
2. Wartime Order of Battle West I.
3. Border Security Map West.
4. Border Security Map East.
5. Deployment Directives West I (without Annexes).
6. Deployment Directives East (without Annexes).
7. Deployment Directives Coastal (without Annexes).

* * *

I. Excerpt from the Mobilization Schedule of 1905–1906

Item 1   Peacetime preparations plans are for two types of deployment: Aufmarsch West I against France only.
Aufmarsch West II and East, against France and Russia.
Upon activation of Aufmarsch West I, I, XVII, II, V, and III Army Corps will be given the mobilization order that contains the caveat "without security arrangements." If deployment "without security arrangements" is ordered, it must be determined which fortifications are to be activated.
Coastal defense will be effective in both deployments. Should its expansion or special defenses against Denmark be necessary, specific orders are required.

Item 2   In the event of Aufmarsch West I, the entire army without occupation forces will deploy to the west with eight armies of 26 army corps, 20 reserve divisions, 11 cavalry divisions, and 26½ Landwehr brigades.
In the event of Aufmarsch West II and East, seven armies will deploy to the west (First through Third, and Fifth through Eighth) consisting of 23 army corps, 16 reserve divisions, 9 cavalry divisions, and 19½ Landwehr brigades. One army (the Fourth)

of 3 army corps, 4 reserve divisions, 2 cavalry divisions, and 7 Landwehr brigades will deploy to the east.

In both instances, the 34th Landwehr Brigade is allocated for coastal defense, in addition to the occupying and Landsturm forces. It might become necessary to leave the 17th Reserve Division behind in Schleswig Holstein. Specific orders are required in this case.

Item 3 Preparations have been made for the deployment of an Italian army of 5 army corps and 2 cavalry divisions to the Upper Rhine. Its deployment depends on the political situation. In the event of activation, heavy field howitzer units of the siege regiments are to be assigned to the Italian army.

Item 19 Obtain His Majesty's order that the . . . reserve divisions are redesignated reserve corps.

Item 20 Issue the instruction for the . . . Oder River barges provided for V and VI Army Corps at the disposal of OHL to be transported to Austria.

Item 23 An order is required for the conscription of the railroad guard and the withdrawal of the border guard troops of XIV Army Corps from Alsace, which have not yet been dispatched by the railroad department.

Item 24 Decide whether to appoint a "commander-in-chief for a northern theater of war" or the siege army, and whether a reinforcement of troops in the area of IX Army Corps is required.

The Railroad Department will prepare redeployment of Ersatz[1] and reserve troops of III, IV, X, XII, and XIX Army Corps and 3rd Division to Holstein after the 10th day of mobilization.

* * *

II. Border Security Map West

Significant changes from the previous year. Some 8½ infantry and 8 cavalry divisions are tasked with border security, in particular:

VIII Army Corps District	From Aachen to Sierck along the border 1⅓ infantry regiments and cyclists, later Landsturm	
Main body	1 cavalry division	Düren
	1 combined infantry brigade	East of Malmedy
	1 cavalry division	St. Vieth

	1 cavalry division	Burg Reuland
	1 combined Landwehr brigade	East of Grevenmacher
Forward-based to Luxembourg:		
	16th Infantry Division	½ near Mersch
		½ in Luxembourg City
	1 combined infantry brigade	Weiler (south of Luxembourg City)
	1 cavalry division	Esch
XVI Army Corps District	Extending to Vic	
	1 combined infantry brigade	Kattenhofen
	1 cavalry division	North of Fentsch
	1 combined infantry brigade	Blettingen
	34th Infantry Division	Metz
	1 combined infantry brigade	Han a/d. Nied
	1 combined infantry brigade	Mörchingen
	1 cavalry division	Delme
	1 cavalry division	Chateau-Salins
XV Army Corps District	Extending to Breuschtal	
	1 combined infantry brigade	Duss (Dieuze)
	1 combined infantry brigade	Saarburg
	1 cavalry division	Southwest of Saarburg
	1 combined infantry brigade	Schirmeck
XIV Army Corps District	Extending to the Swiss border	
	Security operations forward to the Vosges ridge	
	39th Infantry Division	Colmar
	1 combined infantry brigade	Mühlhausen

* * *

III. Aufmarsch I West

The 11 cavalry divisions of the west are assigned as follows:

Senior Cavalry Commander 1	4th Cavalry Div. unloading station	Büderich
	1st Cavalry Div. unloading station	Crefeld
	Guards Cavalry Div. unloading station	Schezdt
Senior Cavalry Commander 2	9th Cavalry Div. unloading station	Düren
	2nd Cavalry Div. unloading station	St. Vith

	3rd Cavalry Div. unloading station	Burg Reuland
Senior Cavalry Commander 3	5th Cavalry Div. unloading station	Mellen (southeast of Grevenmacher)
	6th Cavalry Div. unloading station	Arsweiler
Temporarily assigned to XVI Army Corps	8th Cavalry Div. unloading station	Delme
	Bav. Cavalry Div. unloading station	Chateau-Salins
Temporarily assigned to XV Army Corps	7th Cavalry Div. unloading station	Saarburg

The 4th, 1st, Guards, and 9th Cavalry Divisions will deploy away from the border to prevent the early detection of OHL's intent. If the following units have not already advanced to or across the border earlier, they will do so upon arrival of the first infantry echelons of the armies:

4th Cavalry Division	To south of Straelen on the road to Venlo
1st Cavalry Division	West of Dülken on the road to Roermond
Guards Cavalry Division	Heinsberg on the road to Maaseyck
9th Cavalry Division	Aachen

Reconnaissance against the line Antwerpen–Wawre–Mezières–Dun–Verdun–Damvillers–Pont-à-Mousson–Nancy–Blamont–Baccarat.

"Do not enter Dutch or Belgian territory until OHL gives order to do so, or until the enemy enters, or until those states start hostilities. Gain prior intelligence about the conditions beyond the borders from agents and borderers."

"In the event of an advance into Holland and Belgium, the next task of the cavalry divisions (4th, 1st, and Guards) will be to seize the Meuse bridges in Venlo, Roermond, Maaseyck and the railroads, including rolling stock. Direction of the advance will be Brussels."

"The 9th Cavalry Division will advance to Liège, tasked with seizing the Aachen–Homburg–Herrn–Lüttich rail line and preventing the destruction of tunnels."

"Belgian and Dutch forces will be regarded as enemies if they put up resistance or if war is declared against those states."

First Army   3 army corps [IV, X, IX], 4 reserve corps [XVII; 19th, 22nd;[2] 7th, 3rd;[3] I], 3 combined Landwehr brigades.

Command Post   Viersen.

Initial Deployment   Behind the border at Goch–Heinsberg. In the area Goch–Heinsberg–Reydt–Grevenbroich–Neuss–Büderich.

         4 corps in line, strong left wing.
         2 corps behind the left wing.
         1 corps behind the right wing.

Second Army   4 army corps [I, II, VII, XX], 1 reserve corps [XIII], 4 combined Landwehr brigades.

Command Post   Aachen.

Initial Deployment   Behind the border at Heinsberg–Aachen, in the area of Odenkirchen–Erkelenz–Geilenkirchen–Aachen–Eschweiler–Jülich–Kerpen–Cöln.

         3 corps in line.
         2 corps behind the left wing.

Third Army   4 army corps [9th, 9th Reserve,[4] III, XVIII], 3 cavalry divisions, 2½ reserve corps [5th, 6th;[5] XXI; 2nd, 9th[6]], 4 combined Landwehr brigades.

Command Post   Gemünd.

Initial Deployment   Behind the border on the line Aachen–St. Vith in the area of Düren–north of Stolberg–north of Eupen–St. Vith–north of Prüm–east of Hillesheim–Gemünd–Meckenheim–Lechenich.

         4 corps in line.
         2 reserve corps behind the right wing.
         ½ reserve corps behind the left wing.

Fourth Army   3 army corps [V, XI, XVII], 3 combined Landwehr brigades.

Command Post   Bitburg.

Initial Deployment   Behind the border at Aldringen–Wallendorf in the area Aldringen–Wallendorf–Speicher–Prüm.

         3 army corps in line.

Fifth Army   3 army corps [VIII, XII, XIII, XIX], 3 combined Landwehr brigades.

Command Post   Trier.

Initial Deployment   VIII Army Corps will enter Luxembourg to seize the railroad, or deploy behind the line Wallendorf–north of Remich in the area Wallendorf–north of Remich–Wadern–Hermeskeil–Schweich.

Sixth Army   3 army corps [I Bavarian, II Bavarian, III Bavarian], 2 combined Landwehr brigades.

Command Post   Saarlouis.

Initial Deployment   Behind the border at Remich–Suftgen (north-northwest of Diedenhofen) in the area Remich–Suftgen–Busendorf–Saarlouis–east of Mettlach.
       3 army corps in line.

Seventh Army   3 army corps [VI, XIII, XVI], 3 reserve corps [IX, XV; 23, 24[7]], 3 combined Landwehr brigades.

Command Post   Metz.

Initial Deployment   Behind the line (north-northwest of Diedenhofen)–Gorz–Lorry (Lorringen)–Pagny near Coin (Paningen).
In the area Kaufen–Gorz–Lorringen–Paningen–Rollingen–Bolchen–south of Busendorf.
       5 corps in line.
       1 corps behind the left wing.

Eighth Army   3 army corps [XIV, XV, XXI], 3 reserve corps [XI; 1st Bavarian, 5th Bavarian;[8] 26; 28[9]], 1 combined Landwehr brigade.

Command Post   Saaralben.

Initial Deployment   Behind the border at Wingert (Vigny)–to the western fringes of the Vosges in the area Wingert–Château-Salins–south of Saarburg–Zabern–west of Saargemünd–St. Avold.
       3 army corps in 1st line, strong right wing.
       3 reserve corps in the 2nd line.
"XIV Army Corps does not leave troops in Alsace south of Strassburg."

"For the purpose of deceiving the enemy . . . XV and XIV Army Corps in Alsace south of Strassburg and in southern Baden . . . will have General Command XV announce billeting for 2 army corps in its corps district from Strassburg to Schlettstadt.
XIV Army Corps will announce billeting for 3 army corps and 1 cavalry division in southern Alsace, and for 6 army corps and 2 cavalry divisions in Baden between the Rhine near Neuerburg and Lake Constance...
The forces are expected to arrive from the 8th day of mobilization."

Deputy General Command XIV will secure the Rhine *on the Upper Rhine* with 3½ combined Landwehr brigades.
Coastal defense consisting of 1½ combined Landwehr brigades will be carried out along the *Baltic Sea* by Deputy General Commands I, XVII, II, and IX (without Imperial War Port of Kiel and security of the Kiel Canal); 1 combined Landwehr brigade will deploy in the Lockstedter Lager.
The Chief of the North Sea Naval Station will be responsible for the defense of the North Sea coast. He will be supported by Deputy General Command of the X Army Corps.

* * *

IV. Border Security East

Entries on the Border Security Map East generally indicate the same marshaling as in 1904–1905.

New formations:	11th Reserve Division	in Breslau
	9th Reserve Division	in Posen

* * *

V. Aufmarsch East

Fourth Army — 3 army corps, 4 reserve divisions, 2 cavalry divisions, 7 combined Landwehr brigades.
Command Post — Marienburg.
Fourth Army Commander is also Commander-in-Chief, East.
Initial deployment in 3 groups.

a.	1 army corps	Dt. Eylau
	1 cavalry division	Strassburg
	1 combined Landwehr brigade	Gosslershausen
b.	1 army corps	Allenstein
c.	1 army corps, 1 reserve division	Behind Angerapp
	1 cavalry division	East of Gumbinnen
	1 combined Landwehr brigade	Tilsit

The following units are deployed to the area of Deputy General Commands VI, V, II.

Border and railroad security	1 infantry brigade	Near Ostrowo
	5 combined Landwehr brigades	
Behind them	1 reserve division each	In Breslau, Posen, Znin

Notes

1. Replacement.

2. This indicates a corps, yet undesignated, composed of the 19th and 22nd Divisions.

3. This indicates a corps, yet undesignated, composed of the 7th and 3rd Divisions.

4. This indicates a corps, yet undesignated, composed of the 9th and 9th Reserve Divisions.

5. This indicates a corps, yet undesignated, composed of the 5th and 6th Divisions.

6. This indicates a half corps, yet undesignated, composed of the 2nd Division and elements of the 9th Division.

7. This indicates a corps, yet undesignated, composed of the 23rd and 24th Divisions.

8. This indicates a corps, yet undesignated, composed of the 1st Bavarian and 5th Bavarian Divisions.

9. This indicates a corps, yet undesignated, composed of the 26th and 28th Divisions.

Aufmarsch 1906–1907[1]

The following documents are available:
1. Mobilization Schedule 1906–1907.
2. Wartime Order of Battle West.
3. Wartime Order of Battle West II and East.
4. Wartime Order of Battle North.
5. Border Security Map West.
6. Border Security Map East (2 Items).
7. Deployment Map West 1:300,000 including Enemy Situation.
8. Deployment Map West 1:200,000.
9. Deployment Map East (Railroad Map).
10. Deployment Map North 1:300,000.
11. Coastal Defense Map.
12. Deployment Directives West (including Italian Army) (without Annexes).
13. Deployment Directives East (without Annexes)

* * *

I. Excerpt from the Mobilization Schedule of 1906–1907

Item 1 Peacetime preparations provide for two types of deployment:
Aufmarsch West I against France only.
Aufmarsch West II and East, against France and Russia.
Upon activation of Aufmarsch West I, the I, XVII, II, V, VI, and III Army Corps will be given the mobilization order that contains the caveat "without security arrangements," and a list of the fortifications to be activated.
Coastal defense will be effective in both deployments.
The Landsturm will be mobilized throughout the Reich.

Item 2 In the event of Aufmarsch West I, the entire army without occupation forces will deploy to the west with eight armies of 26 army corps, 12 reserve corps, 3 reserve divisions, 11 cavalry divisions and 26½ Landwehr brigades.

In the event of Aufmarsch West II and East, seven armies will deploy to the west (First, Third through Eighth) consisting of 23 army corps, 8 reserve corps, 4 reserve divisions, 9 cavalry divisions, and 19½ Landwehr brigades, and the Eastern Army consisting of 3 army corps, 3 reserve corps, 1 reserve division, 2 cavalry divisions, and 7 Landwehr brigades will deploy to the east.

Item 3 In both deployments, the IX Reserve Corps, 34th Landwehr Brigade, and Ersatz[2] and Landsturm troops of IX Army Corps are allocated for coastal defense in Schleswig Holstein and the security of the Kiel Canal. Preparations have been made for the marshaling of further contingents of the occupation army from the eastern fortifications and the area of the X, IV, III, Guards, XII, XIX Army Corps in Schleswig Holstein.

Item 4 Preparations have been made for the deployment of an Italian army consisting of 2 cavalry divisions and 5 army corps to the Upper Rhine. Its deployment depends on the political situation.

Item 5 Forces deployed to Southwest Africa are tasked with invading English territory in the event of a declaration of war against England.

The occupation force stationed in East Asia . . . (? No further entry)

Item 6 . . . In the event of Aufmarsch West II and East, preparations for the Second Army are suspended, instead preparations "East" are issued . . .

Item 10 For the purpose of deceiving the enemy, instructions for preparing billeting of army contingents in Upper Alsace and southern Baden have been included in the deployment directives for XIV and XV Army Corps.

Item 25 . . . possible order for the destruction of railroads in upper Alsace. Consider the commitment of Landwehr brigades on the Upper Rhine for the security of Alsace.

Item 34 Consider appointment of an army commander as commander-in-chief of that part of the western theater, which is outside the direct influence of the Supreme Headquarters.

* * *

II. Overview of the Wartime Orders of Battle

1 West

First Army		5 res.corps			
Second Army	4 army corps			5 g.³Ldw.brig.	
Third Army	4 army corps	1 res.corps		4 g.Ldw.brig.	
Fourth Army	4 army corps	1 res.div.	1 res.div.	4 g.Ldw.brig.	
Fifth Army	5 army corps			3 g.Ldw.brig.	
Sixth Army	5 army corps			6 g.Ldw.brig.	
Seventh Army	3 army corps	1 res.corps	2 res.div.	1 g.Ldw.brig.	
Eighth Army	1 army corps	4 res.corps			
Army cavalry					11 cav.div.
Upper Rhine				3½ g.Ldw.brig.	
Total:	26 army corps	12 res.corps	3 res.div.	26½ g.Ldw.brig.	11 cav.div.
Coastal defense				1½ g.Ldw.brig.	

2 West II and East

First Army		3 res.corps	1 res.div.		
Third Army	6 army corps	1 res.corps		6 g.Ldw.brig.	
Fourth Army	4 army corps	1 res.div.	1 res.div.	4 g.Ldw.brig.	
Fifth Army	4 army corps			1 g.Ldw.brig.	
Sixth Army	5 army corps			4 g.Ldw.brig.	
Seventh Army	3 army corps		2 res.div.	1 g.Ldw.brig.	
Eighth Army	1 army corps	3 res.corps			
Army cavalry					9 cav.div.
Upper Rhine				3½ g.Ldw.brig.	
Total:	23 army corps	8 res.corps	4 res.div.	19½ g.Ldw.brig.	9 cav.div.
Coastal defense				1½ g.Ldw.brig.	
Eastern Army	3 army corps	3 res.corps	1 res.div.	7 g.Ldw.brig.	2 cav.div.

3 North

IX Reserve Corps, Landwehr Corps, Guards Ersatz Corps, IX Ersatz Corps, 2 Landwehr brigades, 1 cavalry Ersatz brigade/Ersatz battery, 3 Ersatz light field howitzer batteries, 20 heavy batteries as well as assignments, columns pp.

* * *

III. Border Security West

Basically identical to 1905–1906 with minor variations.

* * *

IV. Aufmarsch West (I)

"The attitude of Holland is expected to be more friendly than hostile, whereas the attitude of Belgium is likely to be hostile. It cannot be ruled out that the English army will support Belgium. They can advance through Holland or land near Antwerp."
The 11 cavalry divisions of the west will be committed in a similar way as in 1905–1906.

Senior Cavalry Commander 1	(1st, 4th, Guards, 9th) advance in the direction of Antwerp–Brussels. To the front of the First, Second, Third Armies, north of the Belgian Meuse fortifications.
Senior Cavalry Commander 2	(2nd, 5th) advance in the direction of Montmédy–Hirson, to the front of the Fourth, Fifth Armies, south of the Belgian Meuse fortifications.
Senior Cavalry Commander 3	(3rd, 6th) will cover the initial deployment to the front of the Sixth Army, will have vastly superior cavalry with cyclists forward.

First Army
Command Post
Initial Deployment

5 reserve corps [I, IV, VII, IX, XI Reserve Corps].
Düsseldorf.
With 1 reserve corps (IX) behind the Dutch border on both sides of Goch in the area Goch–Xanten.
With 4 reserve corps in general east of the Rhine between Wesel and Cologne in the area Wesel–Uedingen–east of Neuss–northwest of Ehrenfeld–Cologne–Hohkeppel–Elberfeld–Dorsten.
"The army will cover the right flank of the force and be committed against Antwerp, whereas the Second Army will advance toward Brussels."

Second Army

Command Post

4 army corps [I, II, IX, X], 5 combined Landwehr brigades.
Krefeld.

Initial Deployment	Behind the Belgian-Dutch border from northwest of Geldern–northwest of Erkelenz, in the area Geldern–Kaldenkirchen–northwest of Erkelenz–Jakerath (southeast of Erkelenz)–Neuss–Crefeld–left banks of the Rhine from Uerdingen–Wesel.
	  2 army corps in the 1st line.
	  2 army corps in the 2nd line.
	"... Second Army will march toward Brussels... will coordinate with First Army in order to have continuous coverage of Antwerp without delaying its advance. Covering forces that had been left behind will be brought up quickly after having been relieved by First Army."

Third Army	4 army corps [III, IV, VII, XX], 1 reserve corps [III Reserve], 4 combined Landwehr brigades.
Command Post	Aachen.

Initial Deployment	Behind the border from northwest of Heinsberg–west of Montjoie in the area Heinsberg–Aachen–Montjoie–Lechenich–northeast of Wewelinghoven
	  3 army corps in the 1st line.
	   1 army corps and 1 reserve corps in the 2nd line.
	"... Third Army will advance between the Belgian Meuse fortifications and Brussels... will secure against Liège and Namur on the left banks of the Meuse and coordinate with the Fourth Army on the right banks of the Meuse. The advance must not be delayed in the process. Initially, reserve corps will be available for security, but will quickly be replaced by Landwehr brigades."

Comment	"VII Army Corps will be authorized to leave elements of the 14th Infantry Division behind to suppress unrest in the coal district; they will follow by train as soon as possible."

Fourth Army	4 army corps [Guards, Guards Reserve, XI, XVIII], 1 reserve corps [XIII Reserve], 1 reserve division [2nd], 4 combined Landwehr brigades.
Command Post	Stadtkyll.
Initial Deployment	Behind the border connecting to Third Army to north of Dasburg in the area Malmedy–St. Vith–Burg Reuland–Schoenecken–Gerolstein–Stadtkyll–Blankenheim–Münstereifel–Rheinbach–Rhine line from Königswinter–east of Brühl–Zülpich–southeast of Montjoie.

    4 army corps in line
        1 reserve corps and 1 reserve division behind the right wing.

"Fourth Army will send its right column XVIII and XVIII Reserve Corps via Huy to the left bank of the Meuse, where it will come under the command of the Third Army. They will take Huy with its old factories. The remainder of the army will establish contact with the Third Army between Namur and Givet and secure against the Meuse fortifications on the right bank of the Meuse."

Fifth Army	5 army corps [V, VIII, XVII, XII, XIV], 6 combined Landwehr brigades.
Command Post	Trier.
Initial Deployment	Contingents of VIII Army Corps have already advanced to Luxembourg; the remainder will join the Fourth Army behind the border to the north of Remich, in the border area to north of Remich–Losheim–Hermeskeil–Neumagen–Wittlich–Manderscheid–Waxweiler.

    5 army corps in line.

"Fifth Army will march against the line Givet–Sedan in such a way that when the force turns left the right wing will remain in concert with the advancing Fourth Army and the left wing with the Sixth Army."

Sixth Army	5 army corps [I Bavarian, II Bavarian, III Bavarian, VI, XIII], 6 combined Landwehr brigades.
Command Post	Diedenhofen.
Initial Deployment	Behind the Moselle from north of Remich–Sierck–Püttlingen–Kattenhofen–southeast of Fentsch–north of Fort Lorraine.
	In the area of the line as above St. Barbara (St. Barbe)–Waibelskirchen–Zimmingen–Saarlouis–Lebach–south of Wadern–Wahlen–Freudenburg.
	5 army corps in line
	"Sixth Army will move forward against the line Carignan–Longuyon . . . 6 Landwehr brigades are assigned to occupy the Nied position from Gr. Tänchen to the mouth. . . . Upon request, 4 Landwehr brigades of the Metz war establishment will be provided to Sixth Army Headquarters to reinforce the garrison in position."
Seventh Army	3 army corps [XIV, XV, XXI], 1 reserve corps [VI Reserve], 2 reserve divisions [26th, 28th], 1 combined Landwehr brigade.
Command Post	Mörchingen.
Initial Deployment	Behind the line Ars–Corningen (Corny)–Delm (Delme)–Wich (Vic)–Elfringen (Avricourt)–Alberschweiler–northeast of Lützelstein–south of Saar-Buckenheim (Saarunion)–east of Gr. Tennchen–Büdingen (southeast of St. Avold)–Falkenberg–Pangen (Pange).
	3 army corps, 2 reserve divisions in line.
	1 reserve corps behind the left wing.
	". . . The entire force with the exception of the Seventh Army will pivot to the left through Belgium. The left wing (Eighth Army) will push to Metz and cover the left flank of the force against Verdun from a reinforced position, if necessary.

"The Seventh Army will support these movements by fixing and holding the enemy at the Meurthe and Moselle. It should anticipate an attack of vastly superior forces and evade in time, in particular since the objective is a future deployment to reinforce the right wing. If necessary, it will retreat to south of Metz where a position at the Nied from Gr. Tänchen to the mouth of the Saar is prepared and occupied by Landwehr brigades. In this movement, 26th and 28th Reserve Divisions will retreat to the fortifications of Metz and be given appropriate instructions."

Eighth Army	1 army corps [XVI], 4 reserve corps [V, VIII, XII, I Bavarian Reserve].
Command Post	Saargemünd.
Initial Deployment	With XVI Army Corps north of the fortifications of Metz in the area Fort Lorraine–Kurzel. With 4 reserve corps behind the line Malstadt-Burbach–Saarbuckenheim, in the area Malstadt-Burbach–Saarbuckenheim–Bitsch–Homburg.

From the instruction issued by the headquarters: "Eighth Army moves forward closely behind and abreast of the Sixth Army, according to the latter's advance. It covers the left flank of the army against Verdun, while pushing to Metz. In coordination with the left wing of the Sixth Army, which advances against the line of Carignan–Longuyon, it will reinforce its position as required using all resources, including available guns from the fortress of Metz."

From the instruction of XVI Army Corps: "Eighth Army will insert its reserve corps between the Sixth and Seventh Armies and then cross the Moselle on the line Diedenhofen–Metz. ..."

From the instruction for the *Royal Italian Army*:
Command Post   Kenzingen
Projections

Command Post	13th mob. day	Kenzingen
2nd Cavalry Division	7th–11th mob. day	Breisach
3rd Cavalry Division	8th–12th mob. day	Kenzingen, Riegel
V Army Corps	11th–16th mob. day	Kenzingen, Riegel
VI Army Corps	14th–18th mob. day	Strassburg
VII Army Corps	15th–26th mob. day	Kenzingen, Riegel
VIII Army Corps	19th–26th mob. day	Strassburg
XI Army Corps	16th–24th mob. day	Breisach

"The German Seventh Army and the XV Army Corps in Saarburg form the left wing of the German Western Army. Their assembly will be completed approximately on the 19th mobilization day. By the time of arrival of the Italian army corps, the major part of XIV Army Corps will have been transported to the area Château-Salins–Mörchingen. In any event, the Italian army is responsible for its security and for covering its flank against southern Alsace and Belfort...."

"The Italian 3rd Cavalry Division is ordered to advance via Schlettstadt into the area west of Dambach along the Schlettstadt–Salles road on the 11th mobilization day. The Italian 2nd Cavalry Division is billeted near Neubreisbach."

* * *

Enemy Situation

French First Army   4 army corps, 4 reserve divisions, 1 cavalry division.
    Covering forces on the line Belfort–southwest of Schirmeck.
        3 infantry divisions = VII Army Corps.
        1 cavalry division.
        Light infantry battalions.
    Initial deployment on and behind the line Belfort–Charmes.
        1 army corps west of Belfort.
        2 army corps near Epinal.
        4 reserve divisions, dismounted behind the center of the front.

French Second Army   5 army corps, 4 reserve divisions, 4 cavalry divisions.
Covering forces on the line Cirey–Lunéville–Nancy–Pont-à-Mousson.
    1 army corps.
    3 cavalry divisions.
    Light infantry battalions.
Initial deployment on and behind the line Charmes–Toul.
    3 army corps in line.
    1 cavalry division in line.
    1 army corps echeloned on the left.
    1 reserve division, echeloned on the left.
    3 reserve divisions, dismounted behind the center of the front.

French Third Army   6 army corps, 3 reserve divisions.
Covering forces on the Côtes Lorraines, 2 infantry divisions of the VI Army Corps.
Initial deployment.
    With 1 army corps near Commercy west of the Meuse.
    3 army corps on line Ligny–Revigny–Domartin.
    1 army corps west of St. Dizier.
    3 reserve divisions on the line Vitry le François–Chalons.

French Fourth Army   4½ army corps, 4 reserve divisions, 3 cavalry divisions.
Covering forces behind the line Etain–Stenay–Sedan.
    1 infantry division, 3 cavalry divisions.
Initial deployment with 4 army corps on the line Ste. Menehould–Vouziers–southwest of Signy l'Abbaye.
    4 reserve divisions, echeloned on the left between Neufchâtel and Laon.

Approximate rear boundary of the lodgement area: west of Iussey (1.)–north of Chaumont (2.)–Vitry le François (3.)–Laon (4.).

* * *

V. Border Security East

Is in general the same as in 1904–1905.
The previous reserve divisions (in 1905–1906) are replaced by . . .
    VI Reserve Corps in Breslau.
    V Reserve Corps in Posen.

* * *

VI. Aufmarsch East

Eastern Army	3 army corps, 3 reserve divisions, 7 combined Landwehr brigades, 2 cavalry divisions.
Command Post	Marienburg.
Initial Deployment	In groups.

a.	The following units back up the Landwehr railway security (in addition to 1 infantry brigade near Ostrowo) on the line Kattowitz–Jarotschin–Gnesen–Thorn–Gosslershausen:		
	Near	Breslau	VI Reserve Corps
		Posen	V Reserve Corps
		Znin	3rd Reserve Division
b.	South and east of Dt. Eylau XVII Army Corps with subordinate 2nd Cavalry Division near Strassbourg		
c.	Northeast of Allenstein XX Army Corps		
d.	On the line Angerburg–Insterburg		I Army Corps
			I Reserve Corps
	East of Gumbinnen		1st Cavalry Division
	Near Tilsit		1 combined Landwehr Brigade

* * *

VII. Coastal Defense

Coastal defense on the North Sea Coast and in the area of the Kiel Imperial War Port, as well as in the Kiel Canal, is a responsibility of the Navy (cf. 1905–1906).

With regard to wartime garrisons and island garrisons, there is no basic change from 1902–1903. For the time being, the only reserves available are ½ combined Landwehr brigade each near Rendsburg and Heide. Anything else will be unnecessary due to Aufmarsch North.

* * *

VIII. Aufmarsch North

Based on the instruction for the Deputy General Command IX Army Corps and deployment map "North."

The initial deployment is carried out in two echelons from the 9th to the 10th mobilization day and from the 13th to the 17th mobilization day against the invasion of a hostile army landing in Jutland (presumed landing sites: Esberg, Kolding, Friedericia, and Röm, Sylt for smaller detachments). The second echelon will deploy only if necessary, the first in any event.

First echelon	IX Reserve Corps, IX Ersatz Corps, 34th Landwehr Brigade.
Second echelon	The remainder of the wartime order of battle listed on page 1.
Initial Deployment	IX Reserve Corps in Angeln, in the area Kappeln–Flensburg.
	Landwehr Corps in the area north of Schleswig.
	Guards Ersatz Corps in the area south of Schleswig.
	21st Landwehr Brigade near Eckernförde.
	18th Landwehr Brigade near Rendsburg.
	IX Ersatz Corps in the area Meldorf–Friedrichstadt.

"If the enemy approaches, it might become necessary to dam up the Treene. . . . Friedrichsstadt as well as the Eider and the Treene line are to be held." Numerous directives have been prepared for the destruction of bridges and railway lines. . . . Memos regarding the English and Danish armies have been issued.

Notes

1. Blue handwritten marginal note at the bottom left: "Aufmarsch I is identical to Schlieffen's Memorandum of December 1905."
2. Replacement.
3. *Gemischte*, combined.

Aufmarsch 1907–1908[1]

The following documents are available:
1. Mobilization Schedule 1907–1908.
2. Wartime Order of Battle West.
3. Wartime Order of Battle East.
4. Wartime Order of Battle North.
5. Border Security Map West.
6. Border Security Map East.
7. Border Security File West.
8. Border Security File East.
9. Deployment Map West 1:500,000 with Enemy Situation.
9a. Deployment Map West 1:300,000 with Enemy Situation.
10. Deployment Map West 1:200,000.
11. Deployment Directives West (including Italian Army) (without Annexes).
12. Deployment Directives East (without Annexes).

* * *

I. Excerpt from the Mobilization Schedule of 1907–1908

Item 1   Peacetime preparations provide for two types of deployment:
    Aufmarsch I (to the west only against France).
    Aufmarsch II (to the west and east against France and Russia).

Item 2   In the event of mobilization the following units will be established in addition to wartime manning and occupation forces:
    26 army corps (Guards, Guards Reserve, I–XXI, 3 Bavarian Army corps).
    13 reserve corps (I, III–X, XII, XIV, XVIII, I Bavarian).
    1 reserve division (2nd Guards Reserve Division).
    27½ combined Landwehr brigades.
    11 cavalry divisions.
    The III, IV, X, XII, XIV, I Bavarian Reserve Corps will consist

of two reserve divisions each; the I, V, VI, VII, VIII, IX, XVIII Reserve Corps will consist of one reserve division and two reserve infantry brigades each. (The intent is to augment the missing field artillery of these reserve corps with mobile Ersatz batteries.) By adding the 2nd Guards Reserve Division, a total of 20 reserve divisions will be established, plus the 1 Guards Reserve Division with the Guards Reserve Corps.

Item 3 In the event of Aufmarsch I (to the west only), all troops in the west listed under item 2 will be committed, with the exception of the IX Reserve Corps and . . . 4 combined Landwehr brigades.
In the event of Aufmarsch I (to the west only):
    26 army corps (including 12 reserve corps),
        1 reserve division (19th Reserve Division),
        20 combined Landwehr brigades,
        11 cavalry divisions,
organized in six armies. — 3½ combined Landwehr brigades are attached to Deputy General Command XIV and intended for the defense of the Upper Rhine.
Fortification workers will construct a field position on the Nied connecting to the fortifications of the Metz Fortress and farther to the mouth into the Saar.
Two army headquarters, "Stettin" (designated for the Northern Army) and "Posen" (designated for the Eastern Army), and the assigned rear area commands and units remain at the disposal of the Supreme Headquarters (Gr.H.Qu.).

Item 4 In the event of Aufmarsch II (to the west and east), the following forces in the west will be committed. They are also organized in 6 armies:
    23 army corps (including 9 reserve corps),
    1 reserve division (15th Reserve Division),
    13 combined Landwehr brigades,
    9 cavalry divisions.
In addition, 3½ combined Landwehr brigades will be committed on the Upper Rhine.
A special "Eastern Army" will be established to be committed in the east. It will consist of:
    3 army corps (I, XVII, XX),
    3 reserve corps (I, V, VI),
    7 combined Landwehr brigades,
    2 cavalry divisions.

Item 5 In Aufmarsch I (to the west only), the organization of the entire army into field armies and the allocation of individual units to those armies will be done in such a way that for the establishment of an eastern army (Aufmarsch II) contingents of each field army in the west will be detached and transferred to the eastern army. Another organizational structure of the armies in the west might therefore not become effective.

Item 6 In both deployments, the IX Reserve Corps, ... four combined Landwehr brigades, ... Ersatz and Landsturm forces of the IX Army Corps are designated for coastal defense in Schleswig Holstein, the security of the Kiel Canal, and the defense against enemy landings.

Item 7 Preparations have been made for the deployment of an Italian army consisting of five army corps and two cavalry divisions to the Upper Rhine. The deployment depends on the political situation, which cannot be anticipated.

Item 8 Orders will be issued for the occupation forces in Southwest Africa and East Asia. Those forces will be included, unless they have already received their orders in peacetime.

Item 22 Inform the Railroad Department whether it will transport the second echelon of the Northern Army.

Item 35 ... Consider whether XIV Army Corps, XXI and XV Army Corps or elements thereof should remain in Alsace.

Item 39 Consider moving forward elements of the First Army to occupy the bridges near Venlo, Roermond, and Maeseyck.

Item 40 Consider the subordination of the Senior Cavalry Commander to the army headquarters. ...

Item 41 Commander of the Sixth Army ... will be tasked to move ... to St. Avold unless the army remains in Alsace.

Item 44 If there is no intention of establishing the Northern Army, IX Reserve Corps and the Landwehr brigade will be brought forward.

Item 52 In the event of Aufmarsch I, consider the allocation of XIV Reserve Corps to the Fifth Army to be committed in the Nied position.

Item 53 Suggestion for an imperial cabinet order on the subordination of naval fortifications in Schleswig Holstein to the Supreme Army Command North.

* * *

II. Border Security West

No significant changes from the previous year.

* * *

III. Aufmarsch West

"The conduct of Belgium and the Netherlands will be questionable. Until a clarification of the mutual relations is achieved, security against military action of both states is necessary. The interference of an English army is probable; it may advance through Holland or land near Antwerp, or try to join France immediately near Calais."

The schedule for the army cavalry is similar to the previous year:

Senior Cavalry Commander 1:	(1st, Guards, 4th) Plans to advance First and Second Armies against the line Antwerp–Brussels–Mons. . . . It is important to establish the location of the Belgian army.
Senior Cavalry Commander 2:	(2nd, 5th, 9th) Advance south of the Belgian Meuse fortifications to the front of the Third Army, against the line Mons–Rozoy. . . . Establish the location of the Belgian army and detect the advance of the French forces through Belgium at an early stage.
Senior Cavalry Commander 3:	(3rd, 6th) Scout in front of the Fourth and the right wing of the Fifth Army against the Meuse on the line Sedan–Verdun. It is important to determine at an early stage whether the Meuse line is heavily occupied or whether there are any forward enemy movements via Verdun and across the Meuse north of Verdun.

With the Sixth Army:
    8th Cavalry Division reconnaissance via Pont-à-Mousson and toward Nancy.

Bavarian Cavalry Division reconnaissance toward Nancy and Lunéville.
7th Cavalry Division   reconnaissance of the same.

First Army   4 army corps, 4 reserve corps, 3 combined Landwehr brigades.
Command Post   Crefeld.
Initial Deployment   Behind the border from west of Kleve–west of Geilenkirchen, in the area Kleve–Geilenkirchen–Odenkirchen–Grevenbroich–Höhscheid (east of the Rhine)–Müllheim–Bottrop–south of Bacholt
West of the Rhine:
   3 army corps, 1 reserve corps in line, 1 army corps echeloned to the left east of the Rhine; 3 reserve corps in line.
Designated advance via Brussels in the direction of Audenarde, reserve corps against Antwerp.
"The First Army will advance to Brussels with its left wing, cover the right flank of the force and close off Antwerp with the reserve corps."

Second Army   5 army corps, 2 reserve corps, 6 combined Landwehr brigades.
Command Post   Eschweiler.
Initial Deployment   Connecting with the First Army behind the border to south of Malmedy, in the area Geilenkirchen–Malmedy–north of Münstereifel–Ahrweiler–Rhine line from Sinzig (at the mouth of the Ahr) – approx. 30 km north of Cologne.
   4 army corps in the 1st line;
   1 army corps, 2 reserve corps in the 2nd line.
Designated advance to the line Ath–northwest of Binche.
"The Second Army is to advance on both sides of Liege, and unite via Huy on the north bank of the Meuse and continue to march via Wawre–Gembloux to the west. It will have Liege encircled and the siege begun. . . . The old works of Huy

will be breached with the means available to the field army...."

Third Army

Command Post
Initial Deployment

6 army corps, 1 reserve division, 2 combined Landwehr brigades.
Gerolstein.
Contingents will move forward into Luxembourg, the remainder connecting with the Second Army behind the border at Wasserbillig, in the border area as above–Wittlich–Daun–Mayen–south of Ahrweiler.
    5 army corps in line.
    1 army corps, 1 reserve division echeloned on the right.
Designated advance to the line Thuin–Philippville–Couvin–Rocroi–area northeast of Charleville.
"Third Army will advance south of the Belgian Meuse fortifications against the line Charleroi-Charleville (Mezières) and encircle Namur on the south banks of the Meuse."

Fourth Army

Command Post
Initial Deployment

6 army corps, 1 reserve corps, 6 combined Landwehr brigades.
Merzig.
Connecting with Third Army behind the border at Fentsch, in the area of the border as above–Saarbrücken–Kusel–east of Oberstein–Neumagen a.d. Mosel.
    4 army corps in the 1st line.
    2 army corps, 1 reserve corps in the 2nd line.
Designated advance to a line east of Sedan–Carignan–Montmédy–Longuyon.
"The Fourth Army will advance with its right wing to Bouillon and turn to the line Sedan–Longuyon in order to advance against the Meuse north of Verdun. It will have the fortifications of Longwy and Montmédy encircled and attacked...."

Fifth Army	2 army corps, 3 reserve corps, 2 combined Landwehr brigades.
Command Post	St. Johann.
Initial Deployment	With XVI Army Corps north and northeast of Metz in the area Hayingen–Gr. Tänchen, with 1 army corps, 3 reserve corps (all 4 corps abreast) behind the line Hargarten–Püttlingen–Finstingen, in the area of this same line–east of Ingweiler–east of Homburg–Neunkirchen–Saarbrücken.

From the deployment directives of the army command, Government Metz, XVI Army Corps, and those for the commander of the "Field Position on the Nied":

"The Fifth Army will advance with its right wing to Pierrepont, southwest of Longuyon, linking up with the left wing of the Fourth Army and turn to the Longuyon–Briey–Metz road. Bring up the rear army corps behind XV Army Corps so that the connection to Metz is maintained. The Fifth Army will establish and retain permanent contact with the German army at Metz. In coordination with Metz and the field position on the Nied, it will secure the left wing of the army against enemy envelopment. Initially, it will assume a position on the Longuyon–Briey–Metz road or farther forward on the Upper Rhine via Conflans to Metz. The position will be reinforced with all means. The Fortress of Metz is assigned to the army. As there can be no threat to this fortress in this situation on the northern front, resources of the fortress are to be used to retain the position, if necessary. Follow the advance of the Fourth Army against the Meuse north of Verdun and assume a new position behind the Orne against enemy advance between Metz and Verdun, or from Verdun. The reinforcement of the position must not result in breaking the connection with the left wing of the Fourth Army...."

"The following units will be attached to the commander of the Field Position on the Nied:
      6 Landwehr brigades of the Fourth Army.
      2 Landwehr brigades of the Fifth Army.
      2 Landwehr brigades of Metz Fortress.
      8 heavy 12cm batteries of Metz Fortress."

"The Sixth Army is required to provide reinforcements for the Metz Fortress and the Field Position on the Nied at their own discretion in urgent situations."

"It is not expected that the Sixth Army will remain south of Metz."

Sixth Army	3 army corps, 2 reserve corps, 1 combined Landwehr brigade.
Command Post	St. Avold.
Initial Deployment	XIV Reserve Corps in and south of Metz. 3 army corps behind the border at St. Jürgen (St. Jure)–Falkringen (Foulerey), in the area of the border as above–Saarburg–Gr. Tänchen–southwest of St. Avold. 1 reserve corps, echeloned on the left around Zabern.

From the deployment directives of the army command, Government of Strassburg, XIV, XV, and Deputy XIV Army Corps:

"The Sixth Army will advance against Nancy in order to hold the enemy on the Meurthe and Moselle and to deceive him on the intent of the campaign. It may encounter vastly superior enemy forces and be attacked itself; but even if it is established that there are only insignificant enemy forces, a great service will have been rendered to the campaign. . . . The intent is to withdraw the Sixth Army after it has accomplished its mission and to transport it by rail to another theater of operations. The mission of the army imposes the highest requirements on the leadership, since a deception of the enemy can only be achieved by resolute action, while keeping open the possibility of retreating at any time. . . . In the event that the army does not retreat voluntarily, but is forced to do so by the enemy, coordination with the Fifth Army is a prerequisite for successful retreat as long as there are still strong elements of that army to the rear of the Sixth Army that restrict the latter's maneuvering space."

"The Government of Strassburg will probably be required to resort to its own forces and the cooperation with the Deputy General Command XIV Army Corps. It cannot be ruled out that the enemy will penetrate with strong forces into Alsace from Belfort and through the Vosges. This will not disrupt the the campaign plan as long as they do not cross the line Strassburg–Breusch position–Fort de Mutzig (Feste Kaiser Wilhelm II). The task of the Government, therefore, will be to hold this line. Any attempt by the enemy to advance west of Fort de Mutzig in the direction of Wasselnheim must be blocked with mobile forces of the fortress. . . ."

"Since the eastern front of Strassburg on the right bank of the Rhine is not strong, holding the Upper Rhine becomes more important for Strassburg as well. In the event that it becomes necessary to surrender the Upper Rhine, the railroads on the right bank leading to Strassburg will be severed in order to delay the supply of siege equipment against the eastern front."

"It cannot be ruled out that enemy forces will invade Upper Alsace before XIV and XV Corps are withdrawn. It is not in the interest of the operations plan that the corps allow themselves to be delayed.

Upper Rhine   3½ combined Landwehr brigades

Initial deployment of the Italian Army   5 army corps, 2 cavalry divisions
is identical to 1906–1907.

Enemy situation (Army boundaries are missing on the map.)
    The distribution of forces from Belfort up to Commercy is basically identical to 1906-1907. In contrast, the French northern wing is reinforced and somewhat extended to the north compared to the previous year.
    6 army corps are deployed to the line Revigny–Ste. Menehould–Vouziers–Signy l'Abba–southwest of Maubert-Fontaine.
    Another 3 army corps (on the line Vitry le François–Chalons–Champ de Chalons) are deployed behind the right wing of this line; they, in turn, have another three reserve divisions to their rear.
    4 reserve divisions are deployed behind the left wing of the line Revigny–Maubert–Fontaine:
        2 near Laon,
        1 near Soissons,
        1 near St. Quentin.

* * *

IV. Border Security East

No particular changes from the previous year. (Thus, the provisions for 1904–1905 are generally still in effect.)

* * *

V. Aufmarsch East

Eastern Army   a. 3 army corps, 1 reserve corps, 2 cavalry divisions, 2 combined Landwehr brigades.
b. In the sector of Deputy General Command II, 3 reserve divisions, 2 combined Landwehr brigades.
c. In the sector of Deputy General Command V, V Reserve Corps, 1 combined Landwehr brigade.
d. In the sector of Deputy General Command VI, VI Reserve Corps, 2 combined Landwehr brigades.

Command Post   Marienburg.
Upon arrival the commanding general "will probably find the troops in border security or assembling.... After assuming supreme command, he will order the commitment of the troops and use of war materiel, and conduct the operation at his own discretion."

Initial Deployment   (see 1906–1907) Will develop from the border security buildup as noted above. Initially the following units are attached:
I Army Corps: 1st Cavalry Division, I Reserve Corps, 1 combined Landwehr brigade.
XVII Army Corps: 2nd Cavalry Division, 1 combined Landwehr brigade.
XX Army Corps will insert between I and XVII Army Corps; both corps will assign troops to the XX Army Corps.

The following scheduled works are planned:
a. Consolidation of a reinforced position between

Königsberg and the Lagoon.

b. Reinforcement of the Vistula batteries on the left bank along the Pregel–Deime line may become more important for the operation. Preparations for its reinforcement are under way. . . .

Positions on the left bank for the defense of the Vistula line are reconnoitered. . . .

* * *

VI. Northern Army

IX Reserve Corps.
4 combined Landwehr brigades (with reinforced field artillery).
12 Ersatz (replacement) squadrons.
3 Landwehr battalions for coastal defense.
2 Landwehr battalions as island garrisons (Sylt, Pellworm).
2 foot artillery battalions.

The following units will be established only on specific order from O.H.L:

1 divisional headquarters.
3 combined Landwehr brigades.
12 Ersatz (replacement) squadrons.
19 field artillery batteries.
2 foot artillery battalions.

Notes

1. Blue handwritten note on the upper left: "Still completely in the spirit of Schlieffen."

Aufmarsch 1908–1909[1]

The following documents are available:
1. Instructions West.
2. Instructions East.
3. Border Security Files West.
4. Border Security Files East.
5. Border Security Map East.
6. Wartime Order of Battle West, East, North.
7. Wartime Order of Battle West.
8. Wartime Order of Battle East.
9. Deployment Map West 1:500,000 including the Enemy Situation.
10. Deployment Map West 1:300,000 (Two Copies).
11. Deployment Map West 1:200,000.
12. Deployment Directives West (without Annexes).
13. Deployment Directives East (without Annexes).

* * *

I. Border Security West

No significant changes from the previous year.

* * *

II. Aufmarsch West

"German interests require not entering Dutch territory. (Deploying forces should not enter the area directly bordering Holland for political and operational reasons.)" Compliance with this requirement depends on the conduct of Belgium and the resistance at Liege. Therefore, march routes are planned through Belgium alone, as well as through both Belgium and Holland. *The use of march routes through Holland is subject to the specific order of Supreme Army Command (OHL).*

A. *Advance through Belgium alone:*
The Second Army will open the blocked roads through Liege and Huy. For this purpose, it will line up before the initial deployment is completed (approximately on the 10th to 11th mobilization day). The First Army will follow via Aachen to the Belgian border. After taking Liege, the Second Army will clear the march routes between the Dutch border and Liege that are designated for the First Army, and wait for the arrival of that army.

B. *Advance through both Belgium and Holland* (only after a specific order is issued by the Supreme Army Command (OHL):
Should the Second Army fail to open the blocked roads through Liege, the scheduled attack against this fortress will be launched. No significant resistance is expected from Huy. The advance of the First Army will then proceed through Holland via the line Roermond–Maastricht. . . .
In this case, the Second Army also will march with the right column via Maastricht.

The advance will proceed as follows:

First Army	Toward Brussels, covering the right flank of the force.
Second Army	With the right wing to Wawre, with the left wing passing Namur on the north.
Third Army	Against the Meuse between Namur and Givet.
Fourth Army	With right wing to Fumay (south of Givet), then pivoting against the Meuse and the lower Semois to the line Fumay–Monthermé–Bouillon, in order to continue the march against the lower Sormonne and central Meuse. . . .
Fifth Army	With right wing toward Neufchateau, pivoting to the line Carignan–Longuyon, in order to continue toward the Meuse.
Sixth Army	Will advance with right wing in the direction of Longwy, pivoting to the Longuyon–Briey–Metz road. The right wing will move in the general direction of Pierrepont. It will maintain the connection of the German army with Metz and assume a position at its own discretion on the Longuyon–Briey–Metz road or farther forward across from Verdun. The fortifications of Metz will cover the left wing of the army in coordination with a subordinate fortified position on the Nied between Metz and Saarburg.[2]

Seventh Army	Will initially marshal in Lorraine between Metz and Saarburg in preparation for a French advance south of Metz. The intent is to deceive and detain the enemy with our own advance toward Namur.... The Army will organize its operations in such a way as to prevent an envelopment of the German army wing through capture or envelopment of the Nied position.... (It is not expected that the Seventh Army will remain in southern Lorraine).³
Senior Cavalry Commander 1:	(1st, 4th, 9th) Advance to the front of the First and Second Armies against the line Antwerp–Brussels–Charleroi. Establish location of the Belgian army and secure right wing of the force. The most important task in the follow-on course of events is to reconnoiter rapidly any French movements through Belgium in the direction of Namur and/or movement of the French left wing westward in the direction of Maubeuge and Lille.
Senior Cavalry Commander 2:	(Guards, 2nd, 8th) Advance to the front of the Third and Fourth Armies on the line Namur–Bouillon. Rapidly reconnoiter any French movements on both sides of the Meuse railroad from Namur to Mézières through Belgium or any movement of the French left wing in the direction of Maubeuge and south.
Senior Cavalry Commander 3:	(3rd, 6th) Reconnoiter to the front of the Fifth and Sixth Armies against the Meuse on line Sedan–Verdun, as well as between Verdun and Metz. It is important to determine as soon as possible whether the Meuse line is heavily occupied or whether enemy movements take place via Verdun and through the gaps between Verdun and Metz.

5th, 7th, Bavarian Cavalry Divisions—subordinated to the Seventh Army—will reconnoiter via Pont-à-Mousson, as well as toward Nancy and Toul.

(Some rear boundaries of the initial deployment are not indicated on the map.)

First Army[4]

    4 army corps [I, II, III, IV], 2 reserve corps [I, III], 6 combined Landwehr brigades. In the event of an eastern deployment (Ostaufmarsch), 1 army corps [I], 1 reserve corps [I], and 3 combined Landwehr brigades will be detached from the Army.

Command Post   Jülich

Initial Deployment   Some remote elements behind the Dutch border from Kaldenkirchen–northwest of Geilenkirchen; some elements to the rear of the Second Army from Geilenkirchen–Düren, in the approximate area Kaldenkirchen–northwest of Geilenkirchen–Düren–Rhine line from Cologne–approximately to the level of Crefeld.

    2 army corps, 1 reserve corps in the 1st line.
    2 army corps in the 2nd line.
    1 reserve corps in the 3rd line.
Designated advance across the line Vilvorde–Brussels–Hal.

Second Army[5]

    4 army corps [VII, IX, X, XI], 2 reserve corps [VII, X], 3 combined Landwehr brigades. In the event of an eastern deployment (Ostaufmarsch), ½ reserve corps [½ X Reserve Corps, 3 reserve divisions] will be detached from the Army.

Command Post   Stolberg

Initial Deployment   Connecting to the border sector of the First Army–north of St. Vith, in the border area as above –Schleiden–Euskirchen–Kerpen–Düren–Stolberg.

    4 army corps in the 1st line.

Comment	2 reserve corps in the 2nd line. Designated advance to the line Braine-Lalleud-Genappe-southwest of Gembloux. The following annexes were enclosed: Surprise raid against Liege and Huy. Draft of an attack against Liege and Huy.
Third Army[6]	4 army corps [Guards, Guards Reserve, XVIII, XX], 2 reserve corps [IV, XVIII], 1 reserve division, 2 combined Landwehr brigades. In the event of an eastern deployment (Ostaufmarsch), 1 army corps (XX) will be detached from the Army.
Command Post	Gerolstein
Initial Deployment	Contingents move forward to Luxembourg connecting with Second Army behind the border-south of Dasburg, in the area of the border as above-west of Wittlich-Daun-west of Montreal-Rheinbach. 3 army corps in the 1st line. 1 army corps, 2 reserve corps, 1 reserve division, in the 2nd line. Designated advance: to the line St. Gerard-Hossee (northwest and west of Dinant).
Fourth Army[7]	3 army corps [VIII, XII, XIX], 2 reserve corps [VIII, XII], 2 combined Landwehr brigades.
Command Post	Trier
Initial Deployment	VIII Army Corps and other elements move forward to Luxembourg, the remainder connect with the Third Army behind the border-south of Grevenmacher, in the approximate area of the border as above, Birkenfeld-Wittlich-Speicher. 2 army corps, 1 reserve corps in the 1st line. 1 army corps, 1 reserve corps in the 2nd line. Designated advance to the Maas-Semois line Fumay-Bouillon.

Fifth Army[8] 4 army corps [I Bavarian, II Bavarian, III Bavarian, V], 2 reserve corps [I, V], 3 combined Landwehr brigades. In the event of an eastern deployment (Ostaufmarsch), 1 combined Landwehr brigade and I Reserve Corps will be detached from the Army.

Command Post Losheim

Initial Deployment Elements move forward to Luxembourg; the remainder connect with the Fourth Army behind the border–south of Esch, in the area of the border as above, Busendorf–St. Ingbert–St. Wendel–Saarburg.
  3 army corps in the 1st line.
  1 army corps, 2 reserve corps in the 2nd line.
  Designated advance to the line St. Cecile (southeast of Bouillon)–Tellencourt (southeast of Virton).

"... since the Belgian and French borders will be crossed only upon completion of the overall deployment and when ordered by OHL, any army elements moved forward to Luxembourg might come under an early French attack. It will, therefore, be necessary to hold the Fifth Army on their left wing, for example at the Alzette...."

Sixth Army[9] 4 army corps [VI, XIII, XVI, XVII], 1 reserve corps [VI], 4 combined Landwehr brigades. In the event of an eastern deployment (Ostaufmarsch), 1 army corps [XVII], 1 reserve corps [VI], and 3 combined Landwehr brigades will be detached from the Army.

Command Post Saarbrücken

Initial Deployment Connecting with the Fifth Army behind the border to southwest of Metz, in the area of the border as above, corridor Bolchen–Saargemünd–Bitsch.
  3 army corps in the 1st line.
  1 army corps in the 2nd line.
  1 reserve corps in the 3rd line.
  Designated advance to a line southeast of Longuyon–Briey.

Comment	The fortress of Metz is attached to the Sixth Army. 9 combined Landwehr brigades, 8 gun batteries deploy to the Nied position.
Seventh Army[10]	3 army corps [XIV, XV, XXI], 1 reserve corps [XIV]
Command Post	St. Avold
Initial Deployment	With 2 army corps, 1 reserve corps connecting with the Sixth Army behind the border to south of Saarburg, in the area of the border as above, Finstingen–St. Avold with 1 army corps (XVI) to the Upper Rhine. As local guards of the Rhine bridges: 3½ combined Landwehr brigades.

"XIV Army Corps remains in Upper Alsace to cover the same and the Upper Rhine. But this must not result in the army corps being sacrificed to a superiority of the enemy and the enemy being given the opportunity to achieve a victory. Rather, it is important that the country will not be evacuated as soon as a state of war is effective and exposed to every action of the enemy. In the event that a serious enemy operation against Upper Alsace is identified, the army corps will withdraw across the Upper Rhine or to Strassburg…. It is important for German operations to retain both the Breusch line and the Upper Rhine, and to prevent the enemy from determining the conditions on the right bank of the Rhine."

The enemy situation has remained largely unchanged from 1907–08. Both army corps west of Dun have come closer to the Meuse.

* * *

III. Wartime Order of Battle of the Northern Army

IX Reserve Corps.
4 combined Landwehr brigades.

North Sea Islands:	Borkum	Reserve 79.
	Pellworm	1 Landwehr battalion.
	Sylt	2 Landwehr battalions.
	Coastal defense:	3 Landwehr battalions.

* * *

IV. Border Security East

No significant changes from the previous year.

* * *

V. Aufmarsch East

Wartime order of battle and directives are identical to that of 1907–1908[11]
    I, XVII, XX Army Corps.
    I, V, VI Reserve Corps.
    3rd Reserve Division.
    1st, 2nd Cavalry Division.
    7 combined Landwehr brigades.[12]

Notes

    1. Blue handwritten marginal note at the top: "Do not immediately enter Holland XIV Army Corps on the Upper Rhine." Handwritten in red: "For the first time, idea to quickly take Liege."

    2. Longer stenographic marginal note at the bottom left: "The Sixth Army will establish the permanent connection of the German army with the fortifications of Metz and secure the left wing of the army against envelopment in coordination with the fortified Nied position. It will assume position at its own discretion on the L. Br. Metz road or farther forward on Obain [illegible], or if the operations continue on the Orne, which is to be defended with all means. The involvement [illegible] must not result in breaking contact with the left wing of the Fifth Army."

    3. Longer stenographic marginal note at the top left: "The Seventh Army will marshal in southern Lorraine to prepare for an enemy advance between Metz and the Vosges, as well as for their own advance in the direction of Nancy. In the event that it is forced to retreat, the XIV Reserve of the fortifications of Metz are to be transferred to the defense of the fortifications and the northern position. The Army will organize its operations in such a way as to prevent an envelopment of the German army wing through capture or envelopment of the Nied position. . . . Coordinated action with the Sixth Army is required. For the time being, the XIV Army Corps of the Seventh Army will remain in Upper Alsace. A decision on its commitment will be made by the Supreme Army Headquarters."

    4. Handwritten note: the names of Hindenburg as designated commanding general and Matthiass as designated chief of staff of the First Army.

    5. Handwritten note: the names of Bülow as designated commanding general and Below as designated chief of staff of the Second Army.

6. Handwritten note: the names of Bock as designated commanding general and Roehl as designated chief of staff of the Third Army.

7. Handwritten note: the names of Treitschke as designated commanding general and Zwehl as designated chief of staff of the Fourth Army.

8. Handwritten note: the names of Leopold von Bayern as designated commanding general and Gündell as designated chief of staff of the Fifth Army.

9. Handwritten note: the names of Gilgenheimb as designated commanding general and Steuben as designated chief of staff of the Sixth Army.

10. Handwritten note: the names of Eichhorn as designated commanding general and Scholtz as designated chief of staff of the Seventh Army.

11. Handwritten note: the names of Goltz as designated commanding general and Unger as designated chief of staff of the Army in the East.

12. The following stenographic comment is written on the bottom of the page: "It is not expected that the Seventh Army will remain in southern Lorraine. Therefore, XIV Army Corps will have to fend for itself in Upper Alsace. It will conduct its operations independently until the Supreme Army Command orders its attachment to the Seventh Army. It is possible that strong enemy forces will advance from Belfort and through the Vosges into Upper Alsace, and simultaneously advance against the Fort de Mutzig. This will not disrupt the operational plan of the German army unless the enemy crosses the line Fort de Mutzig–Breusch position–Strassburg. Covering Upper Alsace must not result in the army corps being sacrificed to a superiority of the enemy and the enemy being given the opportunity to achieve a victory. Rather, it is important that the country will not be evacuated as soon as a state of war is in effect and exposed to every action of the enemy. If a serious enemy operation against Upper Alsace is identified, any resources of the country, the rolling stock, public coffers, material [word illegible] etc. are to be eliminated and the army corps is to withdraw. For future operations, consider retaining the Upper Rhine and the Bavarian line. Initially, the Bavarian line is protected by the fortifications of Strassburg and the Fort de Mutzig. Fortifications and forces assigned to provide local security do not completely cover the Upper Rhine. It is of great importance, however, to retain the right bank of the Rhine and to prevent the enemy from determining the conditions on that bank."

Aufmarsch 1909–1910[1]

The following documents are available:
1. Mobilization Schedule 1909–1910.
2. Border Security Map West.
3. Border Security Map East.
4. Directives for the Security of Aufmarsch I and II.
5. Wartime Order of Battle Aufmarsch I West.
6. Wartime Order of Battle Aufmarsch I East.
7. Wartime Order of Battle Aufmarsch II East and West.
8. Wartime Order of Battle Northern Army.
9. Deployment Directives Aufmarsch II West (without Annexes).
10. Deployment Directives Aufmarsch I East (without Annexes).
11. Deployment Directives Aufmarsch II West (without Annexes).
12. Deployment Directives Aufmarsch II East (without Annexes).

* * *

I. From Mobilization Schedule 1909–1910

Item 1   Germany must expect a war against France or Russia and a war against both states that England might join.
To what extent Germany can expect support from Austria or Italy will depend on the situation.
Arrangements have been made with the other states as well; Oberquartiermeister I[2] and the chief of the General Staff of the Army are aware of them.
Germany must mobilize the entire force in any case; partial mobilizations are impossible because the mobilization preparations of all corps are interconnected.
In the event of mobilization, Germany will establish the following force, apart from wartime garrisons and occupation forces:
   26 army corps.
   13 reserve corps, a total of 21 reserve divisions.

            1 reserve division.
            27½ combined Landwehr brigades.
            11 cavalry divisions.

Item 2   The following initial deployments have been prepared:
           Aufmarsch I: Large-scale western deployment against France only.
           Aufmarsch Ia: Large-scale western deployment against France,
           including a small-scale eastern deployment against Russia.
           In both cases for the large-scale western deployment, the
           deployment and organization of the Western Army, the number
           and distribution as well as the deployment of the individual armies
           are identical. Only in Aufmarsch Ia, the Eastern Army units (list
           included) are withdrawn from the individual field armies in the
           west and form the Eastern Army against Russia.
           Aufmarsch II: Large-scale eastern deployment against Russia, with
           ... corps remaining in their garrisons.
           Aufmarsch IIa: These elements are committed to the defensive
           western deployment against France.
           In all initial deployments, IX Reserve Corps will remain in
           Schleswig Holstein for coastal defense and the security of the Kiel
           Canal. Another option is to reinforce IX Reserve Corps with
           elements of the occupation army to form a Northern Army.

Item 3   The following scenarios will apply:
           Aufmarsch I if Russia is neutral.
           Aufmarsch Ia if France and Russia declare war.
           Aufmarsch II if France is neutral.
           Aufmarsch IIa if France sides with our enemies after the large-scale
           eastern deployment starts.

Item 4   Command and control of operations will be allocated as follows:
           For Aufmarsch I, by the Supreme Army Command.
           For Aufmarsch Ia, by the Supreme Army Command in the west,
           and in the east by Army Headquarters Posen, which is not
           deployed in the large-scale western deployment.
           For Aufmarsch II, by the Supreme Army Command in the east.
           For Aufmarsch IIa, in the west by Army Headquarters Hanover,
           which forms the Supreme Headquarters II.

458   Appendix

Item 5   Preparations have been made for the deployment of an Italian army consisting of 5 army corps and 2 cavalry divisions to the Upper Rhine. Considering the current political situation, it is impossible to count on the arrival of the Italian army.

Item 7   Distribution of forces for the various deployments:

West:

Aufmarsch I:	26 army corps, reserve formations: 12 army corps, 1 reserve division, 19 reserve divisions, 23½ Landwehr brigades, 11 cavalry divisions, 7 armies in total.
Comment:	Not allocated to Army Headquarters Posen.
Aufmarsch Ia:	23 army corps, reserve formations: 9 army corps, 1 reserve division, 15 reserve divisions, 16½ Landwehr brigades, 9 cavalry divisions, 7 armies in total.
Aufmarsch II:	Comment: The army elements listed in IIa in the garrisons.
Aufmarsch IIa:	11 army corps, reserve formations: 5 army corps, 7 reserve divisions, 10½ Landwehr brigades, 5 cavalry divisions, 3 armies in total.

North:

Aufmarsch I:	1 reserve corps, 4 Landwehr brigades.
Aufmarsch Ia:	1 reserve corps, 4 Landwehr brigades.
Aufmarsch II:	1 reserve corps, 4 Landwehr brigades.

East:

Aufmarsch I:	3 army corps, reserve formations: 3 army corps, 1 reserve division, 4 reserve divisions, 7 Landwehr brigades, 2 cavalry divisions, 1 army in total.

Aufmarsch II:	15 army corps, reserve formations: 7 army corps, 1 reserve division, 12 reserve divisions, 13 Landwehr brigades, 6 cavalry divisions, 4 armies in total.
Item 15d	A supreme cabinet order will order the Navy to assume either a small-scale or large-scale security posture.
Item 15i	In the event of England entering hostilities, consider the possibility of an enemy landing near Emden, in Schleswig Holstein or Jutland....
Item 59	Request permission from Belgium for a passage of forces. If the government rejects the request, issue an appeal directly to the population of Belgium.
Item 60	Inform Holland that even a victorious Germany will not violate Dutch independence. (see case file Z.A. Nr. 14065/08)
Item 61	General Staff officers will be assigned to the Second Army as commanders of the attack columns for the surprise raid on Liege. These officers have already reconnoitered the routes in peacetime.
Item 68	Consider whether and when reinforcements are to be sent to the Fifth Army for the accomplishment of its mission and from where (Seventh Army).
Item 69	Transfer of the I Bavarian Reserve Corps to Metz and the Nied position in the event of a withdrawal of the Sixth Army.
Item 89	If possible, assemble wartime order of battle in the respective corps districts. Furthermore, consider marshaling the cavalry divisions intended for the west in their training areas.
Item 92v	(Aufmarsch II) western corps will provide 13 foot artillery battalions in support of the attack forces to

Kowno ... consider the possibility of withdrawing siege artillery from the western fortifications. ...

Item 100   (Aufmarsch II) Consider possibility of reinforcing the eastern army with forces intended for the west.

* * *

II. Border Security West[3]

Border Security West remains basically unchanged. Since XIV Army Corps will remain in Alsace, the security measures for this area have been extended.

Strength of border security: 1 infantry division (Luxembourg),
8 combined infantry brigades,
11 cavalry divisions,
Individual units, battalions. ...

In the event of an enemy advance through the Vosges, the Mutzig–Schirmeck–Saales railroad will be destroyed. According to reliable intelligence, France will try to use agents to destroy the Rhine bridges. There will, however, be changes in the event of Aufmarsch II. Border security will be reduced to:

5 combined infantry brigades.
6 cavalry divisions,
Individual units, battalions, ...

VIII Army Corps	Will not enter Luxembourg. It will marshal near Saarburg i.Rh.—after the arrival of VIII Reserve Corps near Trier.
XVI Army Corps	Will marshal east of Metz; the Nied Position will not be consolidated.
XV Army Corps	Will marshal near Saarburg. Demolitions in enemy territory will be carried out.

* * *

III. Aufmarsch I: Large-Scale Western Deployment

This Aufmarsch closely follows the western deployment of the previous year. Again, routes of advance through Dutch territory are provided for the First Army if the conquest of Liege cannot be accomplished at an early stage. What is new is that Senior Cavalry Commander 3—in the year before on Luxembourg territory—will now take over the 3 southern cavalry divisions to the sector of the Sixth Army. Furthermore, the corps approaching the Luxembourg border will immediately move forward with its main force to the Alzette. There is a basic change in the grouping of the Seventh Army.

"Hostilities from Holland are not anticipated for the time being. The conduct of Belgium may be doubtful. . . . The interference of an English army is probable. . . . Benevolent neutrality can be expected from Switzerland.

(In some cases, the rear boundaries of the deployment areas are not indicated on the maps.)

First Army	4 army corps, 2 reserve corps, 6 combined Landwehr brigades. (In the event of a simultaneous small eastern deployment, 1 army corps, 1 reserve corps, 3 combined Landwehr brigades will not be included.)
Command Post	Grevenbroich.
Initial Deployment	Some remote elements behind the Dutch border from Kaldenkirchen–northwest of Geilenkirchen; some elements to the rear of the Second Army behind the line northwest of Geilenkirchen–Linnich–Eschweiler–Düren–Bergheim, in the approximate area of the line as above–northwest of Cologne (Rhine line)–at the level of Crefeld:

        3 army corps in the 1st line.
        1 army corps, 2 reserve corps in the 2nd line.

Plotted advance to the line west of Vilvorde–Brussels–Ruysbroeck.

Second Army	4 army corps, 2 reserve corps, 3 combined Landwehr brigades, 4 foot artillery battalions, 2 batteries of special guns. (1 army corps, ½ reserve corps, 1 combined Landwehr brigade.)
Command Post	Stolberg.
Initial Deployment	Connecting to the border sector of the First Army—southwest of Malmedy, in the approximate area of the border as above—north of

                Blankenheim–Adenau–Ahrweiler–Kerpen:
                    3 army corps in the 1st line.
                    1 army corps, 2 reserve corps in the 2nd line.
Plotted advance to the line Braine l'Alleud–Genappe–Sombreffe.
The following attachments were enclosed:
                1. Surprise raid against Liege and Huy.
                2. Draft of an attack against Liege.

Third Army	4 army corps, 2 reserve corps, 1 reserve division, 2 combined Landwehr brigades, 2 foot artillery battalions. (1 army corps.)
Command Post	Gerolstein.
Initial Deployment	Elements move forward to Luxembourg, the remainder connecting to Second Army behind the border to northeast of Diekirch in the area of the border as above–west of Wittlich–Gerolstein–east of Kaiseresch–east of Mayen:

                4 army corps in line.
                1 reserve corps, 1 reserve division to the rear of the right wing.

Plotted advance to the line Denée–Hastière (northwest and southwest of Dinant).
The following attachments were enclosed:
                1. Draft of an attack against Namur.
                2. Draft of an attack against Givet.

Fourth Army	4 army corps, 3 reserve corps, 3 combined Landwehr brigades, 1 cavalry division, 2 foot artillery battalions.
Command Post	Trier.
Initial Deployment	Elements move forward to Luxembourg, the remainder connecting to Third Army behind the border to southeast of Esch, in the area of the border as above–Lebach–Birkenfeld–Hetzerath:

                4 army corps in the 1st line.
                3 reserve corps in the 2nd line.

Plotted advance to the line Fumay–Virton: The army will attack Montmédy.

Fifth Army	4 army corps, 2 reserve corps, 5 combined Landwehr brigades, 1 cavalry division, 3 foot artillery battalions. (2 reserve corps, 3 combined Landwehr brigades.)
Command Post	Saarlouis.
Initial Deployment	Connecting to Fourth Army behind the border–west of Metz, in the area of the border as above–Buschborn–Saarbrücken–Zweibrücken–east of Homburg–east of St. Wendel–north of Saarlouis–north of Diedenhofen:

        2 army corps in the 1st line.
        2 army corps in the 2nd line.
        2 reserve corps in the 3rd line.

Plotted advance to a line south of Virton–Briey.
    Fortress of Metz and Nied position (containing 7 combined Landwehr brigades and 8 10cm batteries) are attached to this army.
    Initiate the seizure of Longwy.

Sixth Army	3 army corps, 1 reserve corps, 1 combined Landwehr brigade.
Command Post	St. Avold.
Initial Deployment	Behind the border from southwest of Metz–southwest of Saarburg, in the area of the border as above–west of Lützelburg–St. Avold–Gr. Tänchen.

"The Sixth Army will be tasked with deceiving the enemy by advancing against the Moselle and Meurthe and preventing him from redeploying his forces from this sector to his left wing. . . . In the event that an enemy offensive of strong enemy forces against southern Lorraine forces the Sixth Army to withdraw in order to avoid defeat, the latter's movements and those of the Seventh Army will be made in such a way as to prevent an encirclement of the German left wing through an envelopment of the Nied position. In the process, the Sixth Army will detach the I Bavarian Reserve Corps to the Fifth Army as reinforcement for Metz and the Nied position. Senior Cavalry Commander 3 is aware of the significance of identifying a French offensive across Moselle and Meurthe in sufficient time. The Sixth Army is not expected to remain south of Metz.

Seventh Army 3 army corps, 1 reserve corps. (On the Upper Rhine 3⅓ combined Landwehr brigades, 1 foot artillery battalion.)
Command Post Strassburg.
Initial Deployment With 2 army corps (XXI, XV) in the approximate area of Weissenburg–Zabern–Strassburg.
1 army corps (XIV) on the left banks of the Rhine—near Colmar, 39th Infantry Division, near Mühlhausen, 29th Infantry Division.
1 reserve corps (XIV Reserve Corps) on the right bank of the Rhine.
In the area northwest of Freiburg, 26th Reserve Division.
South of Mühlhausen, 28th Reserve Division.
The fortifications of Strassburg are attached to Seventh Army.

"Seventh Army initially will hold at the Rhine to cover Upper Alsace, to intervene on the left wing of the Sixth Army, or to move to another part of the theater of war by railway.

It is possible that strong enemy forces will invade Upper Alsace from Belfort and through the Vosges, and simultaneously advance against the Fort de Mutzig."

Enemy situation is identical to the previous year.

* * *

IV. Aufmarsch IIa Defensive Western Deployment against France

High Command of the Western Army Saarbrücken

"The High Command of the Western Army (*Grosses Hauptquartier* II) will direct the operations against France at its own discretion. Despite the superiority of the enemy and in the event that German forces have a headstart in mobilization, a rapid offensive into France must be included in the considerations. As long as France respects the sovereignty of the neutral states, Germany will not violate such neutrality without compelling military reasons. The neutrality of Switzerland must not be violated unless that country takes hostile action against us. It may be necessary to enter

Luxembourg territory, but in such an event sufficient legal grounds are desirable.... The construction of the Nied Position will be postponed under the prevailing circumstances. The High Command is free to have such construction carried out.... The deployment has been prepared according to plan and with the prerequisite that its implementation is definitely possible...."

Fifth Army	4 army corps, 3 reserve corps, 4 combined Landwehr brigades, 4 cavalry divisions under Senior Cavalry Commanders 1 and 3.
Command Post	Bolchen.
Initial Deployment	Between Burg Reuland–Metz. Senior Cavalry Commander 3 near Diedenhofen, XVI and XVIII Army Corps, Senior Cavalry Commander 1 between Metz–Dieuze. In detail: VII Army and VII Reserve Corps in the area of Bitburg and north. VIII Reserve Corps near Trier. VIII Army Corps near Saarburg i.Rh. XVIII Reserve near Diedenhofen. XVI Army Corps near Metz. XVIII Army Corps near Mörchingen. The fortifications of Diedenhofen and Metz are attached to Fifth Army.
Sixth Army	3 Bavarian army corps, 1 Bavarian reserve corps, 2 combined Landwehr brigades.
Command Post	Saarlouis.
Initial Deployment	Behind the Saar on the line Merzig–Saargemünd.
Seventh Army	4 army corps, 1 reserve corps, 1 cavalry division, 5 combined Landwehr brigades on the Upper Rhine.
Command Post	Strassburg.
Initial Deployment	XV Army Corps, 7th Cavalry Division near Saarburg in Lorraine. XIII Army Corps near Weissenburg. XXI Army Corps near Hagenau.

XIV Army Corps in Upper Alsace.
XIV Reserve Corps on the Upper Rhine and in Baden.

* * *

V. Border Security East

Basically unchanged.

* * *

VI. Aufmarsch Ia Small-Scale Eastern Deployment

Eastern Army	a.	I, XVII, XX Army Corps, I Reserve Corps.	2 combined Landwehr brigades, 1 and 2 Cavalry Reserve Divisions.
	b.	In the area of Deputy General Command II.	3 reserve divisions, 2 combined Landwehr brigades.
	c.	In the area of Deputy General Command V.	V Reserve Corps, 1 combined Landwehr brigade.
	d.	In the area of Deputy General Command VI.	VI Reserve Corps, 2 combined Landwehr brigades.

Command Post Marienburg.

Initial Deployment The troops of the army will at first be committed in border and railroad security operations in accordance with the directives issued to the General Commands for covering the deployment of the Eastern Army. (Displacement of the V and VI Reserve Corps by railroad can begin approximately on the 9th mobilization day.)

"A Russian offensive will probably be directed against East and West Prussia east of the Vistula. According to unconfirmed intelligence, the possibility cannot be ruled out that weaker forces will advance left of the Vistula—downstream to attack the Vistula fortifications from the West. For the time being, the other areas bordering Russia seem to be less threatened. The army headquarters will cover Prussian territory against a Russian offensive. It will command and control the operations at its own discretion. Delay of the Russian advance is desired. In a worst-case scenario, Prussia east of the Vistula must be given up until the Eastern Army is reinforced. The following special installations are for the defense of the country:

a. Defensive Installations	On the Masurian Lakes line.
b. Defensive Installations	On the Pregel–Deime line; to be completed by Headquarters I Army Corps by the 14th mobilization day....
c. Lagoon Connection Line	Will be built as a field position by the Government of Königsberg between Königsberg and the lagoon, connecting the fortification approximately from the 15th mobilization day. It will cover the movements of army elements via Pillau and the Spit....

* * *

VII. Aufmarsch II Large-Scale Eastern Deployment against Russia

"The German Eastern Army will deploy 4 armies between Gnesen and Tilsit for the offensive against Russia. The force must overcome the fortified line of the Narew, Bobr, and Niemen while being divided by the marshes of Bobr and Lenk (Lyck) east and south of Augustow. The northern group will advance north of the Lenk against the Niemen. The southern group will advance between Vistula and Lenk...."

First Army   2 army corps, 2 reserve corps, 5 combined Landwehr brigades.

Command Post   Bromberg.

Initial Deployment   After the initial assembly on the left bank of the Vistula in the area Gnesen–Hohensalze–Exin, the army will move to the right bank of the Vistula and marshal on the line Gollub–Soldau. "The army will advance against the Narew line Serock–Pultusk and cover the right flank against the Warsaw training area...."

Second Army   4 army corps, 2 reserve corps, 1 combined Landwehr brigade, 2 cavalry divisions.

Command Post   Dt. Eylau.

Initial Deployment   After the initial assembly between the Vistula and Lake Spirding, the army will concentrate in the area east of Dt. Eylau and deploy to the line Neidenburg–Johannisburg.

"The army will advance from the line Neidenburg–Johannisburg . . . in such a way that its right wing moves along the lower Orzyc and reaches the Narew between Pultusk and Rozan. . . . Attacking strongly fortified Lomsha with the forces available to the field army is pointless. The main attack must be launched against the Narew between the lower Orzyc and Lomsha; but the army also must secure its left wing against Lomsha and Ossowiec. . . . Keep in mind for the further operations that a fortified field position connects to south of Lomsha in the forest and the downs of Czerwony-Bor, which may extend to the Bug. . . ."

Third Army   5 army corps, 2 reserve corps, 3 combined Landwehr brigades, 2 cavalry divisions.
Command Post   Gerdauen.
Initial Deployment   Between Lyck and Pillkallen

"Third Army will advance against the fortified Niemen line of Grodno–Kowno, right wing north of the Lenk. . . . It must detain the enemy standing behind the Niemen in the front. The right wing should attack lightly fortified Grodno.—Any enemy advance from the direction of Grodno to Augustow and Raigrod, or against the flank of our columns marching north of Grodno, must be prevented. . . . A siege-like attack on Kowno is reserved. . . ."

Fourth Army   4 army corps, 2 reserve corps, 4 combined Landwehr brigades, 2 cavalry divisions under Senior Cavalry Commander 2.
Command Post   Wehlau.
Initial Deployment   North of the line Allenburg–Insterburg–Schirwindt.

"Fourth Army will envelop the fortified Niemen line in the direction of Wilna and attack the enemy right wing east of the Niemen. . . . Fourth Army must defend itself . . . against the enemy Schawly Group (1 army corps, 1 reserve corps). At least 4 active corps must be available to envelop the enemy wing. . . ."

Enemy

According to Austrian calculations (19 November 1909), the following forces are available against Germany and Austria. (Exactly the same as in 1902.):

First Army	15½ Divisions
Second Army	11½ Divisions
Third Army	9½ Divisions
Fourth Army	14½ Divisions
Fifth Army	5½ Divisions

* * *

VIII. Northern Army

IX Reserve Corps with 2 foot artillery battalions		
Headquarters of 35th Infantry Division with 4 combined Landwehr brigades and 12 Ersatz squadrons		
Island garrisons	Total of 8 brigades	1½ foot artillery battalions
Coastal defense		2 engineer companies

The following will be established only upon order from OHL: 2 combined Landwehr brigades, 16 field artillery batteries, 8 foot artillery batteries.

From the instructions of IX Army Corps for preparations to repel an enemy invasion in the corps sector, and the deployment directives of IX Army Corps and IX Reserve Corps:

"Enemy landings may take place in Jutland on the west coast near Esberg, and on the east coast at various positions from Aarhuus to Kolding. Following an enemy landing in Jutland, the enemy may advance on various routes via Ripen, Brorup and Kolding. . . . The east coast of Schleswig Holstein with its many bays from Hadersleben to Eckernförde is considered useless for enemy landings at any time. Opinions regarding the west coast have changed. Although there is little danger of landings of massive forces, minor undertakings are possible between Hoyersschleuse and Büsum. Fairly reliable intelligence states that the enemy will take the islands of Röm and Sylt in order to move advance forces forward to the Ripen–Tondern road. Refrain from mounting an offensive on Jutland. The units remaining in the corps district are intended as the base of a northern army, which will be established as required. The intent is to marshal reserve forces in Angeln and in the Schlei area, and Landwehr forces near and south of Friederichsstadt. In the event of an enemy invasion, prevent the enemy from advancing across the Schlei, Treene, and Eider. Such action, however, must in no way interfere with our own offensive. Enter Danish territory only in the event that an enemy state violates that country's neutrality, or if Denmark joins our enemies—which is not anticipated for the time being. . . ."

Notes

1. There is a blue marginal note at the top of the page: "New: Large-scale eastern deployment and changed setup of Seventh Army (Upper Alsace). In addition, there is a red marginal note: "Surprise raid on Liege."

2. Oberquartiermeister I, or O.G.I, was the directorate of the Great General Staff that included the 2nd Department (Operations and Deployments); the Railroad Department (Movements); and the 4th Department (Foreign Fortifications).

3. Blue marginal note at the right top in an unknown hand says: "New: Setup of Seventh Army."

Aufmarsch 1910–1911

The following documents are available:
1. Mobilization Schedule 1910–1911.
2. Wartime Order of Battle I West and East.
3. Wartime Order of Battle II West and East.
4. Wartime Order of Battle in the IX Army Corps District for Aufmarsch I and II.
5. Directives for the Security of Aufmarsch West.
6. Directives for the Security of Aufmarsch East.
7. Directives for the Security of Aufmarsch North.
8. Border Security Map West and East.
9. Deployment Map I West.
10. Deployment Map II West and II East.
11. Deployment directives I West and East (without Annexes).
12. Deployment directives II West and East (without Annexes).

* * *

I. Excerpts from the Mobilization Schedule 1910–1911

Item 1   Germany must expect a war against France or Russia and a war against both states, which England might join. To what extent Germany can expect support from Austria or Italy will depend on the situation. Arrangements have been made with the other states, of which *Oberquartiermeister* I and the chief of the General Staff of the Army are aware. In the event of mobilization Germany will establish the following forces—apart from wartime garrisons and occupation forces:

26 army corps	
13 reserve corps	A total of 27 reserve divisions
1 reserve division	
28½ combined Landwehr brigades	
11 cavalry divisions	

472 *Appendix*

Item 2   The following initial deployments are prepared:
Aufmarsch I West:
"Great Western Deployment" against France only.
Aufmarsch I West and East:
"Great Western Deployment" against France, including "Minor Eastern Deployment" against Russia.
For both the Great Western Deployment and the organization of the Western Army, the number, assignments, and deployments of the individual armies are unchanged. Only in "Aufmarsch I West and East" are units detached from the field armies in the west to form the "Eastern Army" against Russia.
Aufmarsch II East:
"Great Eastern Deployment" against Russia, including temporary positions of VII, VIII, IX, XVIII, XVI, XV, XIV, XIII, XXI, and I–III Bavarian Army Corps, plus reserve formations and Landwehr brigades and 3rd, 9th, 6th, 7th, and Bavarian Cavalry Divisions in their garrisons.
Aufmarsch II West:
Use of these elements for the "Western Deployment" against France. If this deployment is not executed, these elements will be committed in the east.
Aufmarsch North is prepared in conjunction with Aufmarsch I and II.

Item 5   Preparations have been made for the deployment of an Italian army consisting of 5 army corps and 2 cavalry divisions to the Upper Rhine. Considering the current political situation, it is impossible to count on the arrival of the Italian army.

Item 7   See below for the distribution of forces for the various deployments:

West

Aufmarsch I West:
26 army corps, reserve formations: 12 army corps, 1 reserve division, 25 reserve divisions, 24½ Landwehr brigades, 11 cavalry divisions, 7 armies in total.
Comment: Army Headquarters Posen is not allocated.

Aufmarsch I West and East:
> 23 army corps, reserve formations: 9 reserve corps, 18 reserve divisions, 17½ Landwehr brigades, 9 cavalry divisions, 7 armies in total.

Aufmarsch II East:
> Comment: The army elements listed in IIa in the garrisons.

Aufmarsch II West:
> 12 army corps, reserve formations: 5 army corps, 10 reserve divisions, 11½ Landwehr brigades, 5 cavalry divisions, 4 armies in total.
> Army Headquarters Berlin establishes . . . a special high command for the west "Gr.H.Qu. West."

North

Aufmarsch I West: 1 reserve corps, 4 Landwehr brigades.
Aufmarsch I West and East: 1 reserve corps, 4 Landwehr brigades.
Aufmarsch II East: 1 reserve corps, 4 Landwehr brigades.

East

Aufmarsch I West and East:
> 3 army corps, reserve formations: 1 reserve corps, 7 reserve divisions, 7 Landwehr brigades, 2 cavalry divisions, 1 army in total.
> Comment: Army Headquarters Posen assumes command authority in the east.

Aufmarsch I East:
> 14 army corps, reserve formations: 7 army corps, 1 reserve division, 15 reserve divisions, 13 Landwehr brigades, 6 cavalry divisions, 3 armies in total.

Item 39 Request the War Ministry to load all ammunition that is ready or to be completed at a later time onto trains and use all available means to make the . . . specified procurements.

Item 40 a. Issue order to the corps general commands Guards, II, III, IV, X, IX, XI, XII, and XIX to provide replacement troops for mobile deployment as quickly as possible (Ersatz Corps North).
b. Inform Railway Department of whether and when to transport Ersatz Corps North. . . .

　　　　c. Decide whether commander of Army Headquarters Posen shall assume command authority of the Northern Army.

Item 43　In the event of Aufmarsch II, units mobilized in the IX Army Corps District will remain in garrison. There will be no assembly of IX Reserve Corps nor of the Landwehr brigades of IX and X Army Corps. . . . Upon receipt of telegram "Aufmarsch II West ordered . . ." carry out the measures stipulated in "Preparations for Defense, etc." IX Army Corps will be committed in the west.

Item 45　Army Headquarters Posen with Rear Services Inspectorate reinforces Guards Headquarters Berlin. Guards will receive orders to remain in their garrisons on order to OHL. Consider committing them with the Northern Army or with siege armies (Aufmarsch I West).

Item 60　Depending on the results of the surprise attack on Liege . . . decide whether or not entering Holland during the advance is permitted. . . .

Item 88　Consider the supply of the following artillery force for the attack on Kowno: . . . 18 foot artillery battalions, 2 batteries of heavy coastal howitzers (Aufmarsch II East).

* * *

II. Border Security West

Instructions for Aufmarsch I and II are based on the same considerations as the previous year.

* * *

III. Aufmarsch I West

The deployment is identical as 1909–1910, except for a slightly different grouping of the Seventh Army. Violation of Dutch neutrality is a possibility only in the event that the conquest of Liège is delayed. Luxembourg will be occupied immediately, and if deployment takes place on Luxembourg territory, the main body will be deployed behind Alzette. For the purpose of coordinating the movements of Sixth and Seventh Armies and Senior

Cavalry Commander 3, one of the two army headquarters will be given command authority over the operations.

> Senior Cavalry Commander 1 advances against the line Antwerp–Brussels–Charleroi.
> Senior Cavalry Commander 2 advances against the Meuse south of Namur.
> Senior Cavalry Commander 3 reconnoiters against Nancy, Lunéville, Baccarat.

Advance will proceed as follows:
  First Army toward Brussels—will cover the right flank of the force.
  Second Army with right wing toward Wawre, left wing toward Namur.
  Third Army against the Meuse between Namur and Givet.
  Fourth Army with right wing to Fumay, then pivot toward the Meuse and lower Semois to the line Fumay–Monthermé–Bouillon–Virton, to continue the march against the lower Sormonne and central Meuse.
  Fifth Army moves with right wing via Rodemachern–Ewringen–Udange south of Arlon, pivots toward the line Virton–Briey–Metz to advance against the Meuse.
  Sixth Army and Seventh Armies[1] with Senior Cavalry Commander 3 will be tasked with deceiving the enemy by advancing against the Moselle and Meurthe and preventing him from redeploying his forces from that sector to his left wing.[2] This is a difficult task since the enemy might launch an offensive with strong forces himself in order to threaten the left wing of the German Army. It is essential to avoid defeat by enemy superiority and to withdraw in such a way as to counter an envelopment of the Nied Position. . . .[3]

(Some of the deployment sector rear boundaries are not indicated on the maps.)

First Army   4 army corps, 2 reserve corps, 1 reserve division, 6 combined Landwehr brigades.
                     (In the event of a simultaneous small eastern deployment, 1 army corps, 1 reserve corps, 1 reserve division, 3 combined Landwehr brigades will not be included.)

Command Post	Grevenbroich.

Initial Deployment	Some elements behind the Dutch border southwest of Geldern and northwest of Geilenkirchen; some elements to the rear of the Second Army behind the line north of Geilenkirchen–Eschweiler–Düren–Bergheim in the approximate area Geldern–north of Geilenkirchen–Düren–Bergheim–Rhine line approx. 20 km north of Cologne, at the level of Rheinberg.
	    3 army corps in the 1st line.
	    1 reserve division, echeloned on the right.
	    1 army corps, 2 reserve corps in the 2nd line.

Plotted advance to the line Wolwerthem–Dilbeck–Ruysbroeck.

Second Army	4 army corps, 2 reserve corps, 3 combined Landwehr brigades, 5 foot artillery battalions, 2 batteries of special guns. (1 army corps, 1 combined Landwehr brigade.)
Command Post	Stolberg.

Initial Deployment	Behind the Dutch-Belgian border from northwest of Geilenkirchen, southwest of Malmedy in the area of the border as above–north of Blankenheim–Adenau–south of Ahrweiler.
	    3 army corps in the 1st line.
	    1 army corps, 2 reserve corps in the 2nd line.

Plotted advance to the line Braine l'Alleud–Genappe–Sombre–Sombreffe.

Third Army	4 army corps, 1 reserve corps, 2 combined Landwehr brigades, 2 foot artillery battalions. (1 army corps.)
Command Post	Gerolstein.
Initial Deployment	Arriving elements immediately move forward to Luxembourg, the remainder connect to Second Army behind the border—10 km south of Dasburg in the area of the border as above, south of Bitburg–south of Wittlich– Kochem–Adenau–Blankenheim.

>3 army corps in the 1st line.
>
>1 army corps, 1 reserve corps in the 2nd line.

Plotted advance to the line Denée–Serville–Anthée (northwest and west of Dinant).

Fourth Army — 4 army corps, 3 reserve corps, 3 combined Landwehr brigades, 1 cavalry division, 2 foot artillery battalions.

Command Post — Trier.

Initial Deployment — Arriving elements immediately move forward to Luxembourg, the remainder connect to Third Army behind the border south of Esch, in the approximate area of the border as above–Sierck–Merzig–St. Wendel–Birkenfeld–north of Neumagen a.d. Mosel–south of Speicher.

>4 army corps in the 1st line.
>
>3 reserve corps in the 2nd line.

Plotted advance to the line Fumay–Bouillon–Limes (northwest of Virton).

Fifth Army — 4 army corps, 2 reserve corps, 5 combined Landwehr brigades, 3 foot artillery battalions. (2 reserve corps, 3 combined Landwehr brigades.)

Command Post — Saarlouis.

Initial Deployment — Connecting to Fourth Army behind the border southwest of Metz, in the area of the border as above–Flöringen (Fleury)–south of Bolchen–south of Forbach–Zweibrücken–Homburg–St. Wendel–Dillingen a.d. Saar–south of Merzig–north of Königsmachern.

>2 army corps in the 1st line.
>
>2 army corps in the 2nd line.
>
>2 reserve corps in the 2nd line.

Plotted advance to the line Bazailles (southeast of Longuyon)–Briey. Fortifications of Diedenhofen and Metz, including the Nied Position, are attached. A senior Landwehr commander with 7 combined Landwehr brigades and 8 10cm batteries are deployed to the Nied Position. Preparations have been made for the construction of a position in

	the intermediate terrain of the forward-deployed eastern batteries of the fortress of Metz.
Sixth Army	3 army corps, 1 reserve corps, 1 combined Landwehr brigade.
Command Post	St. Avold.
Initial Deployment	Connecting to Fifth Army behind the border from southwest of Metz–Saarburg, in the area of the border as above–Saaralben–west of Rohrbach–south of Zweibrücken–north of St. Avold–Kurzel–Flöringen (Fleury).
	3 army corps in line.
	1 reserve corps behind the left wing.
	"It cannot be expected that the Sixth Army will remain in south of Metz."
Seventh Army	3 army corps, 1 reserve corps, 1 combined Landwehr brigade. (Plus 3½ combined Landwehr brigades on the Upper Rhine.)
Command Post	Strassburg.
Initial Deployment	1 army corps (XXI) in the area Saar-Buckenheim–Saarburg.
	1 army corps (XV) in the area Zabern–Strassburg.
	1 army corps (XIV) in the area Colmar (39th Infantry Division), Mühlhausen (29th Infantry Division).
	1 reserve corps (XIV) behind the Rhine line from the Swiss border to the level of Schlettstadt. Fortresses of Bitsch, Strassburg, Upper Rhine fortifications are attached.
	Consider: . . . allocating XIV and XIV Reserve Corps for operations north of Strassburg.

* * *

IV. Aufmarsch II West

The High Command of the Western Army (*Grosses Hauptquartier* II, Saarbrücken) will command the operations of the four armies.

Despite the superiority of the enemy, a rapid offensive into France must be included in the considerations in the event of a head start in mobilization. "It is expected that strong enemy forces will advance from Belfort and through the Vosges into Upper Alsace at an early stage, and simultaneously advance against the Fort de Mutzig."

Fourth Army — 3 army corps, 2 reserve corps, 3 combined Landwehr brigades.
Command Post — Trier.
Initial Deployment — Behind the border of Burg Reuland–north of Sierck, in the approximate area of the border as above–Mettlach–Bernkastel–Lutzerath–Gerolstein–St. Vith.
    5 army corps in line.

Fifth Army — 3 army corps, 1 reserve corps, 2 combined Landwehr brigades, 4 cavalry divisions under 2 Senior Cavalry Commanders.
Command Post — Bolchen.
Initial Deployment — Connecting to Fourth Army behind the border–south of Duss (Dieuze) in the area of the border as above–Saaralben–Bolchen–Busendorf–corridor Wallerfangen–north of Lebach–north of Tholey–Wadern–north of Losheim–Sierck.
    3 army corps in line.
    1 reserve corps behind the right wing.
    Senior Cavalry Commander 3 west of Diedenhofen.
    Senior Cavalry Commander 1 to the front Solgen (Sologne)–Marsal.
Fortifications of Diedenhofen and Metz are attached.

Sixth Army — 3 army corps, 1 reserve corps, 2 combined Landwehr brigades.
Command Post — Saarbrücken.
Initial Deployment — Behind the line Saarlouis–Saargemünd–Saarbuckenheim–Lützelstein, in the area as above–Zweibrücken–St. Wendel–Saarlouis.
    4 army corps in line.

Seventh Army	3 army corps, 1 reserve corps, 4½ combined Landwehr brigades (including defense of the Upper Rhine).
Command Post	Strassburg.
Initial Deployment	Identical to the initial deployment of the Seventh Army in Aufmarsch I West, except for minor deviations in billeting. 1 army corps, 1 cavalry division in the area Finstingen–Saarburg–Pfalzburg–Lörchingen. 1 army corps in the area Brumath–Wasselnheim–Rosheim–Strassburg. 1 army corps in the area Colmar–Mühlhausen. 1 army corps behind the Rhine line from the Swiss border to the level of Schlettstadt.

* * *

V. Directives for the Security of Aufmarsch East

No significant changes from the previous year. Headquarters of 3rd Reserve Division is moved forward from Znin to Hohensalza. Information about suspected initial Russian actions includes:

> Objectives for a possible Russian cavalry incursion with some seven cavalry divisions.
> Objectives for Russian demolition patrols.
> Establishment of four border security detachments as reserve for the border guards.
> Measures for Russian railway security.

* * *

VI. Aufmarsch I East

Eastern Army	3 army corps, 3 reserve corps, 1 reserve division, 7 combined Landwehr brigades, 2 cavalry divisions.
Command Post	Marienburg.
Initial Deployment	Initially the forces will be attached to border security in accordance with existing directives.

Headquarters	I Army Corps	Insterburg
	I Reserve Corps	Angerburg
	1st Cavalry Division	Gumbinnen
	2nd Combined Landwehr Brigade	Tilsit
	XX Army Corps	Allenstein
	XVII Army Corps	Dt. Eylau
	2nd Cavalry Division	near Gosslershausen
	70th Combined Landwehr Brigade	near Gosslershausen
	3rd Reserve Division	Hohensalza
	5th Combined Landwehr Brigade	Gnesen
	6th Combined Landwehr Brigade	Mogilno
	V Reserve Corps	Posen
	17th Combined Landwehr Brigade	Wreschen
	VI Reserve Corps	Breslau
	22nd Combined Landwehr Brigade	Kreuzburg
	23rd Combined Landwehr Brigade	Königshütte

"A Russian offensive will probably be directed against East and West Prussia east of the Vistula. In the worst-case scenario, we will be forced to abandon Prussia east of the Vistula...."

* * *

VI. Aufmarsch II East

The German Eastern Army will deploy 3 field armies between Gnesen and Tilsit for an offensive against Russia. The force will cross the reinforced line of Narew, Bobr, and Niemen.
Securing its left wing, First Army will advance against Ossowiec between Vistula and Lenk (Lyck) against the Narew route Serock–Lomza–Wizna. Second Army will advance with its left wing to Grodno–Kowno south of Schirwindt–Sredniki. It will attack the Niemen line in order to hold the enemy to the front.
Third Army will circumvent the fortified Niemen line in the direction of Wilna and attack the enemy right wing east of the Niemen....

First Army	6 army corps, 1 reserve corps, 1 combined Landwehr brigade, 2 cavalry divisions, 2 foot artillery battalions.
Command Post	Dt. Eylau.

Initial Deployment	Initial assembly on both banks of the Vistula due to overstressing of railroad lines and then westward toward Gnesen. Afterward final deployment to the line Thorn–Johannisburg. 　　6 army corps in line. 　　1 reserve corps, 1 reserve division to the rear of the right wing. "Army left wing will prevent enemy attempts at breakthrough from Lomza–Ossowiec between First and Second Armies. . . ."
Second Army	4 army corps, 3 reserve corps, 3 combined Landwehr brigades, 2 cavalry divisions, 2 foot artillery battalions.
Command Post	Gerdauen.
Initial Deployment	On the line Lyck–Stallupönen, in the approximate area of Lyck–Stallupönen–Gerdauen–Rössel. 　　4 army corps, 1 reserve corps in line. 　　2 reserve corps behind the center. "The army right wing should attack weakly fortified Grodno. . . . A siege-like attack on Kowno is reserved. . . ."
Third Army	4 army corps, 3 reserve corps, 4 combined Landwehr brigades, 2 cavalry divisions under the Senior Cavalry Commander.
Command Post	Wehlau.
Initial Deployment	Behind the line Schirwindt–Heydekrug, in the area Schirwindt–Heydekrug–Labiau–Tabiau–Insterburg–Gumbinnen. 　　4 army corps in the 1st line. 　　3 reserve corps in the 2nd line.

The following units will remain in border security initially:

With Deputy General Cmd	VI:	2 combined Landwehr brigades.
	V:	1 combined Landwehr brigade.
	II:	2 combined Landwehr brigades.

* * *

North

The directives north for the general command of IX Army Corps are basically identical to those of the previous year.

"Fairly reliable intelligence indicates that the enemy will occupy the islands of Röm and Sylt in order to move advance troops forward to the Ripen-Tondern road, which will then secure a future landing. Should the landing of the advance forces fail, they will attempt to tie down the coastal defense forces in order to facilitate the landing of the main body in another place. Under enemy pressure, the advance forces will embark and follow the main body."

"In the event of an enemy landing in Jutland, an offensive into Jutland might be considered, depending on the actions of Denmark."

"The troops remaining in the (IX) corps district will serve as the base of a northern army, which will be established if required. . . ."

In the event of Aufmarsch I and II East, the following forces are available in the IX Army Corps District:
IX Reserve Corps.
4 combined Landwehr brigades under Senior Landwehr Commander.
Assignment of special forces.

Island garrisons	Borkum	1 reserve infantry regiment
	Pellworm	1 Landwehr battalion
	Sylt	2 Landwehr battalions
Coastal defense	3 Landwehr battalions	

Notes

1. Handwritten note in shorthand: "The Sixth and Seventh Armies, as well as Senior Cavalry Commander 3 will be tasked. . . ."

2. Note in shorthand on the left margin: Concerning the Seventh Army an earlier remark states: "The Seventh Army will only be temporarily deployed on the Rhine with XV, XIV Army Corps, and XIV Reserve Corps to defend Upper Alsace and the Upper Rhine against early enemy action. An advance of strong enemy forces in Alsace will not threaten the entire operation unless the enemy crosses the line Fort de Mutzig–Breusch Position–Strassburg."

3. Handwritten note in shorthand: "Withdrawing, the Sixth Army will detach an army corps, if possible the reserve corps, to the fortress of Metz as reinforcement of the Nied Position."

Aufmarsch 1911–1912

The following documents are available:
1. Mobilization Schedule 1911–1912.
2. Directives West and East including Information about Suspected Initial French and Russian Actions.
3. Border Security Map West and East.
4. Wartime Order of Battle I West, East.
5. Wartime Order of Battle II West and East.
6. Deployment Map West I.
7. Deployment Map East II.
8. Deployment Directives I West, East (without Annexes).
9. Deployment Directives II East, West (without Annexes).

* * *

I. Excerpt from the Mobilization Schedule 1911–1912

Item 1 . . . Germany will establish . . .

26 army corps	
13 reserve corps	total of 27 reserve divisions
1 reserve division	
28½ combined Landwehr brigades	
11 cavalry divisions	

Item 2 The following initial deployments are prepared:
Aufmarsch I West: Great Western Deployment.
Aufmarsch I West and East.
Aufmarsch II East: Great Eastern Deployment.
Aufmarsch II West.
Aufmarsch North.
Each Aufmarsch requires the establishment of new formations and an extreme strain on our military power.
A fortification of Berlin must be considered for an extreme emergency.

Item 3   The following will occur:
Aufmarsch I West and North—in the event that Russia is neutral.
Aufmarsch I West and East and North—in the event that France and Russia declare war.
Aufmarsch II East—in the event that France is neutral.
Aufmarsch II West and North—in the event that France sides with our enemies after Aufmarsch II East has started.

Item 7   Distribution of forces as indicated below:

West
Aufmarsch I West   26 army corps, reserve formations: 12 army corps, 1 reserve division, 25 reserve divisions, 24½ Landwehr brigades, 11 cavalry divisions, 7 armies in total.
Aufmarsch I West and East   23 army corps, reserve formations: 9 reserve corps, 18 reserve divisions, 17½ Landwehr brigades, 9 cavalry divisions, 7 armies in total.
Aufmarsch II East   Comment: Army elements listed in IIa in the garrisons.
Aufmarsch II West   12 army corps, reserve formations: 5 army corps, 10 reserve divisions, 11½ Landwehr brigades, 5 cavalry divisions, 3 armies in total.
                           Comment: Army Headquarters Berlin will establish a special high command of the western army (Supreme Headquarters II).

North
Aufmarsch I West   1 reserve corps, 4 Landwehr brigades.
Aufmarsch I West and East   1 reserve corps, 4 Landwehr brigades.
Aufmarsch II East   1 reserve corps, 4 Landwehr brigades.

East
Aufmarsch I West and East   3 army corps, reserve formations: 3 reserve corps, 1 reserve division, 15 reserve divisions, 7 Landwehr brigades, 2 cavalry divisions, 1 army in total.

Aufmarsch I East	14 army corps, reserve formations: 7 reserve corps, 1 reserve division, 15 reserve divisions, 13 Landwehr brigades, 6 cavalry divisions, 4 armies in total.
Item 16g:	Encourage military treaties and other agreements with other states (especially agreements with Belgium, Holland, and Luxembourg).
Item 52	Designate a joint commanding general for the Sixth and Seventh Armies and Senior Cavalry Commander 3. Furthermore, consider appointing one of the commanding generals as commander-in-chief of that part of the theater of war where the Supreme Headquarters (Gr.H.Qu.) cannot exercise direct influence.
Item 61	Depending on the outcome of the surprise raid on Liege by the Second Army, decide whether or not entering Holland during the advance will be authorized. . . .
Item 64	Consider whether and when reinforcements are to be sent to the Fifth Army for the accomplishment of its mission and from where (Seventh Army). In the further course of the advance, decide whether the Fourth Army or the Fifth Army will take Montmédy.
Item 65	Attach elements of Sixth Army to the Government of Metz and the Nied Position in the event of a withdrawal of the Sixth and Seventh Armies.
Item 74	(Aufmarsch I West and East) Decide on transmitting the order for the destruction of the railroads in Russia.

* * *

II. Border Security West

Aufmarsch I and II are basically identical to the previous year.
From the attached "Information about suspected initial French actions 1911–12":

1. ... According to not improbable older intelligence, the French intend to advance with strong cavalry to Trier through Luxembourg. The 4th Cavalry Division may enter the Grand Duchy of Luxembourg as early as the first mobilization day.
7. From the 1st mobilization day, XX Army Corps (24th, 12th, 30th Divisions) will be ready for action near and forward of Nancy. ...
8. In the event of a breakthrough of the 4 cavalry divisions in Lorraine, light infantry battalions and probably other troops are likely to follow the cavalry divisions in reserve.
12. It is possible that stronger French forces will invade Upper Alsace at an early stage ... on the 11th mobilization day the following forces may advance:
    From Belfort, XIX Army Corps, elements of VII Army Corps (14th Infantry Division), 8th Cavalry Division.
    Across the Vosges, the remainder of VII Army Corps (13th, 41st Infantry Divisions).
    Possibly elements of the XIII and XVI Army Corps from the direction of Epinal.

Intelligence on the English Army:
... It is possible that only elements of the regular field army (total strength: 119,000) will be deployed to the Continent, and that the English only intend to demonstrate but not engage in decisive combat. English forces may advance from the line Antwerp–Calais from the 14th mobilization day, or from the 16th mobilization day via the Danish border. ...

* * *

III. Aufmarsch I West

For the time being, hostilities from Holland are not expected. The conduct of Belgium can be doubtful. ... The intervention of an English army is probable. ...
The 11 cavalry divisions of the west are attached to Senior Cavalry Commanders 2, 1, 4, 3 (order from north to south).
The following forces will advance (similar to 1910–1911):

First Army	Toward Brussels, covering the right flank of the force.
Second Army	Across the line Wawre–Brussels.
Third Army	Against the Meuse between Namur and Givet.

Fourth Army
: With right wing to Fumay, pivoting toward the Meuse and lower Semois to the line Fumay–Monthermé–Bouillon–Virton, and to continue the march against the lower Sormonne and central Meuse. . . .

Fifth Army
: With left wing via Rodemachern–Ewringen–Udange (south of Arlon), pivoting toward the line Virton–Briey–Metz, to advance further against the Meuse.

Sixth and Seventh Army
: Will be tasked with detaining the enemy by advancing against Moselle and Meurthe and capturing the Manonviller Forts, and with preventing the enemy from withdrawing his forces from this area and shifting them to the left wing of his army. The task will be difficult because the enemy may launch an offensive with strong forces in this area.

First Army
: 4 army corps, 2 reserve corps, 1 reserve division, 6 combined Landwehr brigades.
(In the event of a simultaneous small eastern deployment, 1 army corps, 1 reserve corps, 1 reserve division, 3 combined Landwehr brigades will not be included.)

Command Post
: Grevenbroich.

Initial Deployment
: Behind the border from Kaldenkirchen to Herzogenrath, and behind the Second Army — south of Jülich–north of Düren–Bergheim, in the area of the line as above — Rhine line of 20 kilometers Cologne–Dinslaken.
  3 army corps in the 1st line.
  1 reserve division, echeloned on the right.
  1 army corps, 2 reserve corps in the 2nd line.

Plotted advance to the line Wolwerthem–Dilbeck–Ruysbroeck.

Second Army
: 4 army corps, 2 reserve corps, 3 combined Landwehr brigades, 3 foot artillery battalions, 2 batteries of heavy special projectiles. (1 army corps, 1 combined Landwehr brigade.)

Command Post
: Stolberg.

Initial Deployment	Behind the border connecting to the First Army from Herzogenrath–southwest of Malmedy, in the area of the Border as above– north of Blankenheim–Adenau–east of Ahrweiler– Rheinbach–Lechenich–Düren.

           3 army corps in the 1st line.
           1 army corps, 2 reserve corps in the 2nd line.

Plotted advance to the line Braine l'Alleud–Genappe–Sombreffe.
           Capturing Liege and Huy will be a responsibility of the army in the event that Belgium does not allow German forces to advance.

Third Army	4 army corps, 1 reserve corps, 2 combined Landwehr brigades, 2 foot artillery battalions. (1 army corps.)
Command Post	Gerolstein.
Initial Deployment	Arriving elements move forward with main body into Luxembourg to the Alzette, the remainder connecting to Second Army behind the border–south of Dasburg in the area of the border as above–south of Bitburg–south of Wittlich–Kochem–south of Adenau–Blankenheim–north of St. Vith.

Plotted advance to the line Denée–Serville–Anthée (northwest and west of Dinant).

           3 army corps in the 1st line.
           1 army corps, 1 reserve corps in the 2nd line.

Fourth Army	4 army corps, 3 reserve corps, 3 combined Landwehr brigades, 2 foot artillery battalions.
Command Post	Trier.
Initial Deployment	Arriving elements move forward to Luxembourg, the remainder connecting to Third Army behind the border–southeast of Esch–south of Sierck–south of Merzig–south of Lebach–north of St. Wendel–Birkenfeld–northeast of Neumagen a/d. Mosel.

           4 army corps in the 1st line.
           3 reserve corps in the 2nd line.

Plotted advance to the line Fumay–Bouillon–Limes (northwest of Virton).

Fifth Army — 4 army corps, 2 reserve corps, 5 combined Landwehr brigades, 2 foot artillery battalions. (2 reserve corps, 3 combined Landwehr brigades.)

Command Post — Saarlouis.

Initial Deployment — Connecting to Fourth Army behind the border–southwest of Metz, in the approximate area of the border as above–Flöringen (Fleury)–south of Bolchen–south of Forbach–west of Zweibrücken–Homburg–St. Wendel–south of Merzig–south of Sierck.

    2 army corps in the 1st line.
    2 army corps in the 2nd line.
    2 reserve corps in the 3rd line.

Plotted advance to the line Virton–Briey.

Fortifications of Diedenhofen and Metz including the Nied Position are attached.

Sixth Army — 3 army corps, 1 reserve corps, 1 combined Landwehr brigade.

Command Post — St. Avold.

Initial Deployment — Connecting to Fifth Army behind the border–north of Blamont, in the area of the border as above–west of Saar-Buckenheim–Walsheim (35 kilometers northeast of Saargemünd)–St. Avold.

    3 army corps in line.
    1 reserve corps behind the left wing.

Seventh Army — 3 army corps, 1 reserve corps, 2 foot artillery battalions, batteries of heavy coastal howitzers, on the Upper Rhine 3½ combined Landwehr brigades, 1 foot artillery battalion.

Command Post — Strassburg.

Initial Deployment — XXI Army Corps in the area north of Blamont–Saar-Buckenheim–Lützelburg.

XV Army Corps in the area southwest of Hagenau–Zabern–Molsheim.

XIV Army Corps with 39th Infantry Division

near Colmar, 29th Infantry Division near Mühlhausen.
XIV Reserve Corps behind the Rhine from the Swiss border — to the level of Schlettstadt.

* * *

IV. Aufmarsch II West

Three armies (1910–1911 = 4 armies) will deploy. Furthermore, "Troops in Upper Alsace" (commander-in-chief: commanding general of XIV Army Corps) will act independently.

The 5 cavalry divisions attached to:	Senior Cavalry Commander 4 (2 cavalry divisions) west of Diedenhofen.
	Senior Cavalry Commander 3 (3 cavalry divisions) between Metz and Saarburg.

Fifth Army — 3 army corps, 2 reserve corps, 3 combined Landwehr brigades, 2 cavalry divisions under the Senior Cavalry Commander 4.

Command Post — Trier.

Initial Deployment — Behind the border of Reuland–Perl, in the approximate area of the border as above–west of Hermeskeil–Bernkastel–Gerolstein.

    5 corps in line.

Sixth Army — 4 army corps, 1 reserve corps, 2 combined Landwehr brigades, 3 cavalry divisions under the Senior Cavalry Commander 3.

Command Post — St. Avold.

Initial Deployment — Connecting to the Fifth Army behind the border–across the ridge of the Vosges–Molsheim, approx. rear border of the deployment area Merzig–St. Avold–Zabern–Brumath.

    5 corps in line.
    XVIII Reserve Corps in the Diedenhofen area.
    XVI Army Corps in the Metz area.
    XVIII Army Corps in the Gr. Tänchen area.
    XXI Army Corps in the Saarburg area.

	XV Army Corps in the Strassburg area. Fortifications of Diedenhofen, Metz, Bitsch, and Strassburg are attached.
Seventh Army	4 army corps, 1 reserve corps, 4 combined Landwehr brigades.
Command Post	Saarbrücken.

Initial Deployment	In general behind the Saar line Saarlouis–Saargemünd–Saar-Buckenheim, in the area of the line as above–Buchsweiler–west of Bitsch–Pirmasens–Kaiserslautern–Homburg–St. Wendel.
	   4 army corps in line.
	   1 reserve corps to the rear of the center.

Troops in Upper Alsace	1 army corps (XIV), 1 reserve corps (XIV reserve Corps), 3½ combined Landwehr brigades.

Initial Deployment	XIV Army Corps
	   1 infantry division in the vicinity of Colmar.
	   1 infantry division in the vicinity of Mühlhausen.
	XIV Reserve Corps
	   On the eastern bank of the Rhine from the Swiss border to the level of Schlettstadt.

... The troops in Upper Alsace are left behind to cover Upper Alsace only for the purpose of not immediately surrendering the country to any enemy action as soon as a case of war is effective. A withdrawal of XIV Army Corps and, if possible, of XIV Reserve Corps ... must be considered. ... In the event that a serious enemy operation against Upper Alsace is detected ... withdraw troops. ... Consider retaining Upper Alsace for further operations.

* * *

V. Border Security East

Basically identical to the previous year.
From "Information about suspected initial Russian actions": Expect

invasion of East Prussia, and possibly West Prussia by the cavalry divisions that are already based at the border during peacetime. West of the Vistula such an invasion is less probable.

... In times of political tension, a secret partial mobilization of the Russians is expected, allowing them to cross the border before or no later than at the time of general mobilization or the declaration of war.

Intelligence on the possible invasion by the following forces is available:

a. Reinforced cavalry corps, 60 squadrons, 24 guns.
   Mission: Advance along the Lyck–Lötzen–Rastenburg railroad against the Insterburg–Rothfliess railroad; capture Lötzen (2 rifle regiments with 1 battery are specifically assigned for this task); railroad destruction; reconnaissance west of the Masurian Lakes.
b. 4th Cavalry Division: Advance against the Allenstein–Rothfliess–Korschen railroad. (Probably conduct a simultaneous advance with the above cavalry corps.)
c. Possibility of advancing with 2 cavalry divisions against Allenstein–Thorn railroad, continuing to Elbing.

Number of border security detachments increased to 8.

* * *

VI. Aufmarsch I East

Identical to the previous year. An army headquarters will be established to cover Prussian territory against Russian offensive..., delay of Russian advance is desirable. In worst case, Prussia east of the Vistula will be given up until the Eastern Army is reinforced with additional units.

* * *

VII. Aufmarsch II East

The German Eastern Army deploys four armies between Thorn and Tilsit to advance against the fortified line of the Narew, Bobr, and Niemen.

The intent is to move some of the off-loading forward at a later date, "unless the active corps of the [Russian] Warsaw and Wilna Armies and the cavalry divisions deploy early and disrupt the German deployment." The overstrain of the railroad will make necessary major shifts after off-loading.

| First Army | Has its right wing transported into Russian |

Second Army	territory even before the general advance; marches via Lipno–Willenberg against the Narew section Pultusk–Ostrolenka with the right wing heavily echeloned to the rear. Allocated for the advance against the Narew-Bobr section of Lomza–Ossowiec on the line Johannisburg–Lyck. The Second Army will be able to deploy only after the First and Third Armies because of the late arrival of the transportation. The army is responsible for covering the right and left flanks of the First and Third Armies against enemy action from the line Lomza–Ossowiec. Capture Lomza, and be ready to move from the 23rd mobilization day.
Third Army	Will advance from line north of Lyck–Wisztyniec toward the Niemen section of Grodno–Olita. Active corps will be ready to march on the 16th mobilization day.
Fourth Army	Will advance from line Wierzbolowo–Juborg between Jezioro–Zuwinty (lake) and the northern Niemen bend.
First Army	6 army corps, 1 reserve corps, 1 reserve division, 3 combined Landwehr brigades, 2 cavalry divisions under the Senior Cavalry Commander 1, 1 foot artillery battalion.
Command Post	Dt. Eylau.
Initial Deployment	Initial assembly on the line Hohensalza–Ortelsburg, then marshaling for the advance in line toward Lipno–Willenberg. 6 army corps in line. 1 army corps, 1 reserve division to the rear of the right wing.
Second Army	2 army corps, 1 reserve corps, 1 combined Landwehr brigade, 4 foot artillery battalions.
Command Post	Rhine.
Initial Deployment	Initial assembly in the approximate area of

Johannisburg–Lötzen, south of
Schippenbeil–Bischofsburg.
　　2 army corps in the 1st line.
　　1 reserve corps in the 2nd line.

Third Army

Command Post

Initial Deployment

3 army corps, 2 reserve corps, 2 combined Landwehr brigades, 2 cavalry divisions.
Darkehmen.
Initial assembly in the approximate area of Bialla, northwest of Wisztyniec, south of Gumbinnen–Gerdauen–Johannisburg, marshaling for the advance in line to Lyck–Wisztyniec.
　　3 army corps, 1 reserve corps in the 1st line.
　　1 reserve corps to the rear of the center.
"Since an enemy advance from Niemen is possible before the unloading is completed, the corps of the Third Army will initially marshal their forces within the designated deployment sector in defense-capable positions, and only gradually expand to the border."

Fourth Army

Command Post

Initial Deployment

3 army corps, 3 reserve corps, 2 combined Landwehr brigades, 2 cavalry divisions under the Senior Cavalry Commander 2.
Insterburg.
Initial assembly in the area Wierzbolowo–Heydekrug–Tapiau.
Marshaling for the advance in line Wierzbolowo–Jurborg.
　　3 army corps in the 1st line.
　　3 reserve corps in the 2nd line.

2 combined Landwehr brigades will remain in the VI Army Corps District.
1 combined Landwehr brigade will remain in the V Army Corps District.
2 combined Landwehr brigades will remain in the II Army Corps District.

* * *

VIII. North

Wartime orders of battle north in Aufmarsch I and II are identical.

IX Reserve Corps	
Senior Landwehr Commander with	4 combined Ldw. brigades
Island garrisons	3 reserve, 3 Landwehr battalions
Coastal defense	3 Landwehr battalions

From the deployment directives of IX Reserve Corps:
"Suitable unloading points for bringing in reinforcements: Meldorf, Heide, Lunden, Rendsburg, Schleswig, Eckernförde."
"Keep in mind that replacement (*Ersatz*) formations in the deployment area will be given time to develop internal cohesion before they are committed against the enemy."

Deployment Directives 1912
Aufmarsch II

The advance begins with the right wing, while the left wing (Third and Fourth Armies) will initially be held back.

East

First through Fourth Armies (except for XVII and XX Army Corps located in the border area) will deploy behind the fortified lake line northwest of Bischofstein–Rössel.

Second Army (XVII, XX, IV, XI Army Corps, IV Reserve Corps, 13th and 43rd combined Landwehr Brigades) will marshal for an advance against Lomza, Wizna, and Osowiec on the line Ortelsburg–Rhine. The Second Army will be responsible for covering the left and right flanks, respectively, of the First and Third Armies against enemy action from the line Lomza–Osowiec. Capture Lomza. Initiate capture of Osowiec on the left bank of the Bobr. After the fall of Lomza, launch an attack on Osowiec.

The army must determine to its front the accuracy of the intelligence on the suspected initial Russian actions, as provided in Annex 14. In the event that contrary to expectations the active units of the Russian Warsaw and Vilna Armies and the Russian cavalry divisions deploy early to disrupt the German deployment, the XVII and XX Army Corps at a minimum in coordination with the army's Cavalry Command 1 will be committed to the defense against the Warsaw Army.

The force will disembark on the right bank of the Vistula, approximately west to the line Strassburg–Dt. Eylau, and deploy by advancing to the line Mlawa–Willenberg.

First Army (II, V, X, III, VI Army Cprps, V, VI Reserve Corps, 3rd Reserve Division, 10th and 70th combined Landwehr Brigades, Senior Cavalry Commander 1, 2nd Cavalry Division, 5th Cavalry Division).

OHL plans to advance the active army corps of the First Army early in order to [illegible in the German original] . . . for the reserve corps that will arrive in the future.

The First Army will move forward against the Narew section of Pultusk–Ostrolenka with the front via the line Mlawa–Willenberg, while the right wing will be heavily echeloned to the rear.

Senior Cavalry Commander 1 will seize as early as possible the Mlawa railroad station and the gauge changing facility for the Russian gauge. He will detect to the front of the First Army any enemy advance from the line Novogeorgievsk–Ostrolenka, and he will clarify the situation on the southern bank of the Vistula. He will determine within this area the accuracy of the intelligence on the suspected initial Russian actions, as provided in Annex 14.

Last paragraph is identical to that of Second Army.

Third Army (XII, XIX, I Army Corps, I, XII Reserve Corps, Senior Cavalry Commander 2, 8th Cavalry Division, 1st Cavalry Division, 45th and 47th combined Landwehr Brigades).

Detrain on the line Lötzen–Angerburg–Darkehmen and to the west of it. Marshal Third Army for the advance—initially to the border—against the line Augustow–Wisztymiec from Lötzen, to the north to Darkehmen.

Senior Cavalry Commander 2 will detect to the front of Third Army any enemy advance from the line Grodno–Olika, and also within this area the correctness of the intelligence on suspected initial Russian actions, as provided in Annex 14.

The 4th Cavalry Division of the Fourth Army will reconnoiter in the same manner ahead of the front of the Fourth Army against the line Olita–Kowno.

Fourth Army (Guards, Guards Reserve Corps, X, III Reserve Corps, Guards Cavalry Division, 4th Cavalry Division, 2nd and 11th combined Brigades).

Owing to the strain on the railway, elements of the army will arrive late. If the situation permits, arrange with detraining commissioner to move forward the . . . from Reval on later days within the deployment district and report to OHL.

Since an enemy advance is possible before the detraining of the army is completed, marshal the arriving troops in defense-capable positions in the deployment area.

The Fourth Army will stand by from Insterburg to the north to Ragnit behind the Inster and lower Szcazuppe in order to follow at a later time the advance of the Third Army, echeloned to the rear south of the Niemen.

The Fourth Army will determine through the 4th Cavalry Division any enemy advance to its front from the line Olita-Kowno, and also the accuracy of the intelligence on suspected initial Russian actions, as provided in Annex 14.

The Fourth Army will determine through the Guards Cavalry Division the presense of the suspected enemy forces at Szawle, and if they are there, if they are in positions concealed from Wilna. To ensure the security of this reconnaissance, it will be necessary at an early stage to advance the Senior Cavalry Command into enemy territory by deceiving the enemy in the vicinity of Tauroggen.

The security of the left flank of the army and its deployment against enemy actions from the north and northeast are a responsibility of the army headquarters. The intent is to move the main body of the reserve forward from Königsberg to Tilsit.

West

Initially, France will be neutral. The possibility of a war against France remains. Avoid anything that France could consider a threat or [illegible in the German original] . . . reason for a breach of neutrality. The headquarters of the Border Corps must conduct careful and unobtrusive observation of activity beyond the border.

With a few, specifically ordered exceptions, all mobile units in the sector. . . . Army Corps will remain in their garrisons. Their commitment in either the east or the west is possible.

Perform coastal defense and the defense of the Kiel Canal according to plan. Initially refrain from marshaling IX Reserve Corps and the Landwehr brigade of IX Army Corps in Kappeln and near Freystadt.

In the event that the initial deployment is executed, the advanced party will arrive at the marshaling area only a few hours before the arrival of the lead units. It will be necessary, therefore, to plan security and billeting from the map while still in the garrisons.

3 armies (Fifth through Seventh)—High Command of the Western Army—Supreme Headquarters II.

The High Command of the Western Army will command the operations against France at its own discretion. In the event of a head start in mobilization, a rapid offensive into France must be considered despite the superiority of the enemy. Germany's situation does not permit the violation of the neutrality of other states without pressing military reasons, as long as France observes such neutrality. The neutrality of Switzerland must not be violated unless that country takes hostile action against us. Entering Luxembourg territory is allowed. VIII Army Corps is tasked with occupying the bridges leading across the Moselle, Sauer, and Our into Luxembourg.

OHL had planned for the XVI Army Corps to consolidate a position on the northern bank of the Nied—the Nied Position—from Metz to the confluence of the Nied with the Saar. Under the prevailing circumstances, the consolidation of the Nied position was postponed. The High Command of the Western Army is at liberty to have the construction completed and to issue the pertinent instructions to XVI Army Corps and the Fortress of Metz.

As soon as a state of war comes into effect, units will be left behind to cover Upper Alsace in order to avoid an immediate surrender of that territory to initial enemy action. The commanding general of XIV Army Corps is specifically advised in his deployment directive that the covering of Upper Alsace must not result in the troops there being sacrificed to a superior enemy force, which must be expected to appear early from the direction of Belfort and through the Vosges in a move coordinated with an offensive south of Metz. Such would provide the enemy with an opportunity to achieve success at little cost.

An enemy offensive will not necessarily disrupt the entire German operation unless the enemy crosses the line Fort de Mutzig–Breusch position–Strassburg.

Consider holding the Upper Rhine for follow-on operations by the forces in Upper Alsace. In the event that a surrender of the Upper Rhine cannot be avoided, the forces in Upper Alsace will effectively disrupt the Rhine bridges and the railroad leading north on the right bank of the Rhine, because the east fronts at Neu-Breisach and Strassburg do not have a line.

Fifth Army (5 army corps, 1 Senior Cavalry Commander, 2 cavalry divisions, 3 combined Landwehr brigades) will march between Burg-Reuland and Mettlach–Perl, with Senior Cavalry Commander west of Diedenhofen.

Sixth Army (5 army corps, 1 Senior Cavalry Commander, 3 cavalry divisions, 2 combined Landwehr brigades) will deploy between Sierck and Strassburg, with Senior Cavalry Commander between Metz and Strassburg.

Seventh Army (5 army corps, 3 combined Landwehr brigades) will marshal between Dillingen (northwest of Saarlouis) and Buchsweiler (west of Hagenau).

Troops in Upper Alsace (2 army corps, 3½ combined Landwehr brigades) will deploy on both sides of the Rhine north and south of Neu-Breisach.

In addition: *Italian Army* (5 army corps, 2 cavalry divisions).

Initially, XIV Army Corps and the attached XIV Reserve Corps will remain in the southern part of Baden and in Upper Alsace for the defense of Upper Alsace. Whether these two corps or the border security force of XIV and XV Army Corps (vicinity Mülhausen, vicinity Engelmar, vicinity Schirmena) will still be in this area when the Italian army arrives will depend on the situation.

In any case, the Italian army will be responsible for its own security, for covering its flank against Upper Alsace and Belfort, and for contacting adjacent forces.

Will deploy between Engelmar and Neu-Breisach (in the south) and Molsheim–Strassburg (in the north) a cavalry division near Rufach and Weiler from 7th to 30th mobilization day.

The main difference from previous drafts of Aufmarsch II West, e.g., 1901–1902, is that previously the offensive was to be left to the French.

If the major part of the German army is committed against Russia and the minor part against France, the French will not be able to avoid launching an offensive. In this case, it will be crucial to marshal the approach of the considerably weaker German Western Army as effectively as possible toward the direction of the enemy offensive.[1]

For this purpose, it will be necessary to await the direction of the French offensive. The forces assigned to the Western Army (excluding those committed to border security) will therefore remain in their garrisons, where the required rolling stock will be provided for transport.

As soon as the enemy intent is identified, the marshaling of the force will commence.

Notes

1. In another version: as favorably as possible, i.e., to achieve a surprise attack on a wing or flank of the enemy army.

Aufmarsch 1913–1914

The following documents are available:
1. Mobilization Schedule 1913–1914.
2. Wartime Order of Battle West and East.
3. Directives for the Security of Aufmarsch West, East, North.
4. Border Security Map West and East.
5. Deployment Map West.
   Deployment Map West II (Study).
   Deployment Map East.
   Deployment Map East II (Study).
6. Deployment Directives West and East.
7. Special Orders for the First and Second Surprise Raids on Liège.

* * *

I. Excerpt from the Mobilization Schedule 1913–1914

(The schedule is expanded and advanced, compared to previous years. In technical terms, it is completely different because it is organized in mobilization days.)

A. Preliminary remarks.

1. Germany's preparations for war must first and foremost be directed against France. It is probable that Russia and England will join the French Republic in a war against Germany. Considering the popular mood in France, a war waged by Germany against England or Russia alone is not expected. In the event that either England or Russia alone declares war, German diplomacy will have to force France to make a final statement. The extent to which Germany can expect support from Austria or Italy will depend on the circumstances. Austria is a natural enemy of Russia. Currently there is only hope for an Italian intervention at the French-Italian Alpine border. . . .

A mobilization of the Navy alone has not been prepared, but such a possibility must be taken into account.

In the event of mobilization, Germany will establish the following force—apart from wartime garrisons and occupation forces:

26 army corps	
13 reserve corps	a total of 27 reserve divisions
1 reserve division	
11 cavalry divisions.	
28½ combined Landwehr brigades	

Preparations have been made to combine "Ersatz units intended for possible mobile use" into an Ersatz army (Guards, IV, VIII, X, XIX, Bavarian Ersatz Division). Furthermore, the 55th combined Ersatz Brigade will be at the disposal of the Seventh Army.

2. Only one *Aufmarsch* has been prepared where German main forces will deploy to the western border against France.

The Eighth Army will remain in the east. It will either deploy against Russia (eastern deployment), or in the event of Russian neutrality it also will be committed against France.

The following forces will be marshaled for coastal defense and the security of the Kiel Canal in Schleswig-Holstein as northern deployment (*Nordaufmarsch*): IX Reserve Corps, Senior Landwehr Commander 1 with 4 combined Landwehr brigades.—If there is no threat to the German coasts, IX Reserve Corps and, if applicable, the Landwehr brigades attached to Senior Landwehr Commander 1 will be transferred to other theaters of war. Preparations for transport have been made.

The Ersatz Army can be committed to the western, eastern, or northern theaters of war, either in whole or in part.

As soon as mobilization is announced, all German fortifications—with the exception of Ingolstadt, Königstein, Spandau, and Neisse—will be armed. The following positions will be consolidated:

    Fortifications on the Upper Rhine.
    Breusch Position.
    Nied Position.
    Pregel–Deime Line.
    Position north of Bromberg.

Field position to connect the mouth of Obra and Posen.
Vistula Fortifications.
Masurian Lakes Line.

The fortification of Berlin has been considered in case of an extreme emergency.

The reinforcement of an army headquarters mobilized with ... guards corps can be deployed with the Eighth Army, the Ersatz Army, or in the western theater of war if several armies are concentrated under a combined senior command. ...

7. The initial distribution of German armed forces in various theaters of war will result in the following combination:

Theater of War	Army Corps	Reserve Formations			Cavalry Divisions	Number of Armies
		Reserve Corps/ Reserve Divisions	Composite Reserve Divisions	Combined Landwehr Brigades		
West	23	11/0	22	17½	10	7
East	3	1/1	3	7	1	1
North	–	1/0	2	4	–	–
Together in Western Theater of War, at Best	26	13/1	27	28½	11	8

Additionally, the Ersatz Army of 6 Ersatz divisions and 1 combined Ersatz brigade.

Main reserves of noteworthy strength will be available at the fortifications of Metz, Strassburg, Thorn, Königsberg, Posen.

B. Measures to be taken in the event of serious political tensions:

1. ... Make oral arrangements with Foreign Office that the following agreements must be reached immediately after mobilization is announced:
 a. With Belgium on the 1st mobilization day. Give the Belgian government a last-minute ultimatum on whether Belgium will be Germany's ally or enemy. Belgium must allow transit of German troops; open the fortifications of Liège, Huy, and Namur; secure the railroads and make them available; and prevent English landings.
 b. With Holland to prevent English landings. Negotiations must allow for

transit through the Dutch corridor around Maastricht as well as the use of the Dutch railroad line via Maastricht on a later mobilization day.

c. With Luxembourg transit must be allowed; railroads must be secured and made available.

Prepare proclamations for Belgium, Holland, and Luxembourg.

2. An officer shall deliver the order for the "Surprise Raid by Commanding General X Army Corps on Liège" to the Commanding General X Army Corps. The commanding general will not be allowed to leave Hanover.

3. Apply to the War Ministry for meeting the staffs of the senior cavalry commanders and cavalry divisions in their marshaling locations. Consider concentrating individual cavalry divisions in the marshaling area for training purposes.

4. . . . Drafting of reservists with border corps. . . . Reinforcement of garrison on the island of Borkum. . . . Reinforcement of peacetime garrison of high-risk fortifications. Leaving forces behind in Metz, Strassburg, Thorn after the fall exercises. . . . Obtain export bans. . . . Deployment of agents for destruction of railroads on enemy territory. . . . Preparations to stop Danish cattle exports from Esberg and Kopenhagen to England. Denmark will become dependent on German coal if England blocks the North Sea. . . . Cancellation of the Airship Agreement with France.

C. Measures to be initiated following the announcement of an "imminent threat of war."

1st Mobilization Day

7. Determine where to employ the Eighth Army in the west if its deployment against Russia is not necessary.

15. In the event of internal unrest following the departure of regular forces—especially in Berlin or the industrial districts—provide for the speedy introduction of reliable troops. The Landwehr brigades of IX and X Army Corps might be particularly suited for this purpose. If the worst case, we must fall back on the Ersatz units of the Guards, II, IX, and X Army Corps.

3rd Mobilization Day

7. In the event of a relocation of the deployment between Metz and the Vosges, unload as follows:

> II Bavarian Army Corps in Saargemünd, Folpersweiler, Blickweiler.

I Bavarian Army Corps in Kahlhausen, Oermingen, Domfessel.
III Bavarian Army Corps in Adamsweiler, Wingen, Ingweiler.
Bavarian Reserve Corps in Lemberg, Bitsch and Menschhofen, Obermodern.
Order foot march by XXI Army Corps.

7th Mobilization Day
2. Designate a joint commanding general for the Sixth and Seventh Armies and Senior Cavalry Commander 3. . . .

8th Mobilization Day
3. In the event of a failed first surprise raid on Liège, Second Army headquarters will report any intent to launch a new surprise raid.
4. As soon as it is understood that a siege-like attack against Liège is necessary, preparations will be made accordingly. . . .

10th Mobilization Day and Subsequent Days
3. . . . In the event that the line of the Meuse is occupied by the enemy, consider moving an infantry division of the Third Army forward to Dinant as an advance party to facilitate the crossing of the Meuse by the cavalry divisions under Senior Cavalry Commander 1.
6. Consider whether and when to send reinforcements to the Fifth Army for the accomplishment of its missions. The following forces might be considered as reinforcements:
   a. Elements of the Seventh Army, XIV Army Corps, or XIV Reserve Corps.
   b. Elements of the Eighth Army in the event that the eastern deployment does not take place. Withdrawal before the 15th mobilization day is not possible.
   c. IX Reserve Corps, if northern deployment is not necessary. Withdrawal is possible in the evening of 11th mobilization day.
   d. Elements of the Ersatz Army. Withdrawal is not possible before the 11th mobilization day.
In the event of an early attack by strong French forces between Metz and Strassburg, elements of the Fifth Army may be held east of Metz. In this case, take precautions to prevent the formation of a gap between the Fourth and Fifth Armies. If there is *no* French attack east of Metz, marshal the Fifth Army for an advance to the west, heavily echeloned on the left, approximately on the line Luxembourg–Diedenhofen.

7. Consider the capture of Namur by the Second or Third Army.

9. In the event of a withdrawal by the Sixth and Seventh Armies, provide elements of the Sixth Army to the government of Metz as reinforcements for the garrison of the Nied Position. The commitment of the Ersatz Army may be considered. The Nied Position, which is initally attached to the headquarters of the Fifth Army, may be detached to the joint commanding general of the Sixth and Seventh Armies, if applicable.

17. In the event of a Russian advance, consider damming the Nogat and the Netze and Obra marshes.

* * *

II. Border Security West

Identical to Border Security I West of the previous year. The following units are deployed:

2 cavalry divisions	near Aachen
1 cavalry division	near Malmedy
1 cavalry division	near Wiltz
1 cavalry division	west of Mersch
1 infantry division	Luxembourg (16th Infantry Division)
1 cavalry division	north of Esch
1 combined infantry brigade	Frisingen
1 combined infantry brigade	Gr. Hettingen
1 cavalry division	Fentsch
1 infantry regiment	Gr. Mayeuvre
1 combined infantry brigade	Nouilly ö. Metz
1 infantry regiment	Anserweiler
1 cavalry division	Delme
1 combined infantry brigade	Mörchingen
1 cavalry division	Château-Salins
1 combined infantry brigade	Dieuze
1 combined infantry brigade	Saarburg
1 cavalry division	southwest of Saarburg
⅔ reinforced infantry regiment	Schirmeck
1 battalion	east of Weiler
1 combined infantry brigade	Colmar
1 combined infantry brigade	Mühlhausen

The directives go into far greater detail than previous years.—
According to unconfirmed intelligence, the French are considering a surprise advance from their peacetime garrisons even before war is declared.

For the purpose of uniform implementation of border and railway security measures, XVI and XXI Army Corps will be attached to the inspector general of the Seventh Army Inspectorate Saarbrücken as soon as mobilization or an imminent threat of war are announced, or in the event of a surprise initiation of hostilities. The same applies to XV and XIV Army Corps with regard to Army Headquarters Brandenburg upon the arrival of the senior commander in Strassburg.

The intent is to marshal the following units after mobilization is completed:

XVI Army Corps	with main body near	Metz
XXI Army Corps	with main body near	Saarburg
XV Army Corps	with main body near	Strassburg

From "Intelligence in suspected initial French actions":

The assembly of French border security units against Germany (VI, XX, VII Corps; 4th, 2nd, 8th Cavalry Divisions; Army Headquarters Nancy) in their border security positions will take 1½ days. Pertinent orders will probably be issued prior to the general mobilization order. . . . By the evening of the 4th mobilization day, the 1st, 3rd, 5th, 6th, 7th Cavalry Divisions and the 9th and 10th, which might have to be established, also will have arrived. I Army Corps will take over border security at the Belgian-French border approximately at the same time, probably reinforced by II Army Corps and one . . . cavalry division.

The following actions will be possible before or immediately after the initial deployment is completed:

>An advance into Upper Alsace.
>
>Occupation of the Vosges passes.
>
>Conditions permitting, strong forces might enter Belgium and Luxembourg.
>
>Advance of the extreme left wing of I and II Army Corps to the Meuse on the line Givet–Namur.

* * *

III. Aufmarsch West

No significant changes from the previous year. The corps of the First Army, which had been deployed to south of Aachen in the previous year, have been incorporated into the Second Army for the time being.
The following actions have been planned for the capture of Liège: On the night of 4th to 5th mobilization day, a suprise raid with 5 advanced combined infantry brigades, including attachments. In the event of failure, a second surprise raid of 3 infantry divisions (including attachments) will be launched approximately on the 10th mobilization day. This surprise raid will be combined with a raid on Huy. If Liège has not fallen by the 12th mobilization day, the First Army will enter Dutch territory during the advance.
Another grouping takes place on the Upper Rhine, with the following forces committed:

Senior Cavalry Commander	1	Against the Meuse south of Namur, with main body in the direction of Dinant.
	2	Against the line Antwerp-Brussels.
	3	Reconnaissance against Nancy, Lunéville, Baccarat.
	4	Against Carigan–Dambillers.

The following units will advance:

First Army	Toward Brussels, covering the right flank of the army.
Second Army	Via the line Wawre–Brussels.
Third Army	Against the Meuse between Namur and Givet.
Fourth Army	Echeloned on the left, right wing via Bastogne toward Fumay; left wing via Luxembourg toward Neufchateau.
Fifth Army	Echeloned on the left; right wing via Arlon toward Etalle.

Fourth and Fifth Armies be prepared to pivot to the south.
Sixth Army and Seventh Army
    With Senior Cavalry Commander 3 under the combined senior command against the Moselle and Meurthe, capturing Fort Manonviller in order to hold the deployed French forces and prevent their redeployment to the French army left wing. Since an intervention by the Sixth Army and Senior Cavalry Commander 3 in a battle on the left bank of the Moselle via Metz or south may be desirable, the recommendation will be made to the

combined senior commander to concentrate the Sixth and Seventh Armies in the advance against the Moselle and Meurthe toward the right wing, and echelon this wing in depth.

First Army — 3 army corps, 2 reserve corps, 3 combined Landwehr brigades.
Command Post — Grevenbroich.
Initial Deployment — Behind the border at Heinsberg–Herzogenrath, in the area of the border as above–west of Puttern–Langewiehe, north of Düren–Rhine line, west of Hitdorf, north of Duisburg–Dülken.
    2 army corps in the 1st line.
    1 army corps echeloned on the left.
    2 reserve corps in the 2nd line.

Plotted advance to the line Wolwerthem–Dilbeck–Zuen.

Second Army — 5 army corps, 2 reserve corps, 2 combined Landwehr brigades.
Command Post — Montjoie.
Initial Deployment — Connecting to the First Army behind the border–St. Vith, in the area of the border as above–Hillesheim–Ahrweiler–south of Bergheim–Düren.
    4 army corps in the 1st line.
    1 army corps, 2 reserve corps in the 2nd line.

Plotted advance to the line Braine l'Alleud–Genappe–Sombreffe. Grant authority to VII Army Corps to leave 1 infantry brigade of VII Reserve Corps—and in the worst case 1 cavalry brigade and elements of 14th Infantry Division—behind to suppress unrest in the coal-mining district. . . .

Third Army — 3 army corps, 1 reserve corps, 1 combined Landwehr brigade.
Command Post — Prüm.
Initial Deployment — Connecting to Second Army behind the Belgian and Belgian-Luxembourg borders–northwest of Wiltz, in the area of the border as above–east of Vianden–Hetzerath–Pünderich.

3 army corps in the 1st line.
1 reserve corps to the rear of the right wing.
Plotted advance to the line Denée–Anthée (northwest and west of Dinant).

Fourth Army   3 army corps, 2 reserve corps, 1 combined Landwehr brigade.
Command Post   Trier.
Initial Deployment   Connecting to Third Army behind Belgian-Luxembourg and German-French borders–southwest of Esch, in the area of the border as above–Sierck–Merzig–east of Wadern–east of Hermeskeil–northeast of Schweich.
3 army corps in the 1st line.
2 reserve corps in the 2nd line.
Plotted advance to the line Fumay–Monthermé–Bouillon–Herbeumont.

Fifth Army   3 army corps, 2 reserve corps, 5 combined Landwehr brigades (under Senior Landwehr Commander 2).
Command Post   Saarbrücken.
Initial Deployment   Connecting to the Fourth Army behind the border–Mardeningen (Madigny), in the area of the border as above–Bolchen–Blittersdorf–Homburg–St. Wendel–south of Merzig–south of Sierck.
3 army corps in the 1st line.
2 reserve corps in the 2nd line.
Plotted advance to the line Florenville (south of Chiny)–Virton–Saulines (east of Longwy).
At any time, it may become necessary for the army to pivot into a position with the front to southwest or south in order to repel a French counterattack from the direction of Verdun.
In the course of the advance, the Fifth Army will probably have the mission of capturing Longwy and Montmédy.

Sixth Army   3 army corps, 1 reserve corps, 1 combined Landwehr brigade.
Command Post   St. Avold.
Initial Deployment   Connecting to the Fifth Army behind the

	border to north of Blamont, in the area of the border as above–Saaralben–southwest of Hornbach–St. Avold–Kurzel.
	   3 army corps in the 1st line.
	   1 army corps to the rear of the right wing.

Seventh Army	3 army corps, 1 reserve corps, 1 combined Landwehr brigade, in addition 3½ combined Landwehr brigades on the Upper Rhine.
Command Post	Strassburg.
Initial Deployment	XXI Army Corps in the area Saarburg–Saarbuckenheim–Lützelburg. XV Army Corps in the area Hagenau–Zabern–Molsheim. XIV Army Corps in Upper Alsace south of Baden, Cavalry Headquarters Müllheim. XIV Reserve Corps on the right bank of the Rhine in the approximate area Lahr–Burkheim–Freiburg.

"For the defense of Upper Alsace and south Baden, the following elements of the Seventh Army will be deployed as follows:
     39th Infantry Division of XIV Army Corps to the Vosges passes between Weiler and Münstertal.
     XIV Army Corps, XIV Reserve Corps to the Upper Rhine.

Their mission is only a temporary one. Do not forget the necessity of maintaining the strongest possible forces in direct coordination with the other elements of the Seventh Army. . . ."

* * *

IV. Border Security East

Apart from the loss of the active 77th Infantry Brigade near Ostrowo, there are no significant changes from the year before. The same applies to the enclosed "Intelligence about Suspected Initial Russian Actions."

V. Eastern Deployment

Excerpt from the "Specific Directives for the Commanding General of the Eighth Army":

"The Eighth Army will be tasked with the difficult mission:
1. To secure our eastern provinces against a Russian intervention.
2. To support the offensive planned by Austria. For this purpose, permanent liaison with the Austrian supreme command is required. Austria intends to attack from the line Lemberg–Krakow between the Bug and Vistula, with the left wing directed toward Ivangorod. The Austrian Army will provide timely information in the event that the execution of its operations is prevented by the enemy.

Re 1   The only decisive factor for the accomplishment of Task 1 is the overall situation after the Eighth Army has been alerted.

Re 2
      a. Austria has been promised immediate support for its attack by an advance of German troops from Silesia, which will link with the Austrian left wing. In particular . . .
      . . . to secure the left flank of the Austrian force;
      . . . to protect its railway transports from Bohemia;
      . . . in our own interest, in order to give the Austrians the continuous impetus for further advance.
      The following forces will be available for these offensive movements:
      22nd and 23rd combined Landwehr Brigades.
      Elements of the wartime garrison of Breslau (21st Landwehr Brigade)—only until the 10th mobilization day.
      Ersatz elements of VI Army Corps intended for mobile use from the 11th day of mobilization.
      The offensive will probably be directed toward Skarzlisko via Tschenstochau. This must be agreed with by the Austrian Supreme command.
      b. The intended Austrian offensive will be supported effectively if the Eighth Army succeeds in containing as many forces of the northern and western Russian army groups as possible in order to block them from the Austrian army, thus making combat easier for the latter. In the event of a Russian offensive against

East Prussia, it will probably be conducted with so many forces as to give relief to the Austrian army.

In the event that the Russians initially remain on the defensive toward Germany, an offensive move by the Eighth Army into Russia will be the only way to tie down strong Russian forces and prevent them from reinforcing those elements committed against Austria.

The general situation must dictate the direction of this offensive. If, in due consideration of the Russian forces situated farther north, an offensive toward the southeast past Warsaw becomes possible, then it must be understood that the Narev River and the fortifications of Pultusk, Ostrolenka, and Razan will offer no insurmountable obstacles.

Combined action with the Austrian Army must be considered for all such offensive movements of the Eighth Army.

The general situation will determine the extent to which an offensive move can be carried out.

If Russia commits particularly strong forces against the Eighth Army, it would not threaten the general situation. Ensure in adequate time a secure crossing of the Vistula River under all circumstances.

It is important to determine the direction of movement of the Russian central army at an early stage. The Szawle Group, which is initially situated in the north, also requires continuous observation."

Eighth Army   3 army corps, 1 reserve corps, 1 reserve division, 7 combined Landwehr brigades, 1 cavalry division.

Command Post   Marienburg.

Initial Deployment   Forces committed to border security:

23rd	combined Landwehr Brigade	Headquarters	Königshütte
22nd	combined Landwehr Brigade	Headquarters	Kreuzburg
18th	combined Landwehr Brigade	Headquarters	Wreschen
17th	combined Landwehr Brigade	Headquarters	Ostrowo
6th	combined Landwehr Brigade	Headquarters	Gnesen
3rd	Reserve Division	Headquarters	Hohensalza
70th	combined Landwehr Brigade	Headquarters	Gosslershausen
XVII	Army Corps	Headquarters	Dt. Eylau

XX	Army Corps	Headquarters	Allenstein
I	Reserve Corps	Headquarters	Nordenburg
I	Army Corps	Headquarters	Darkehmen
1	Cavalry Division	Headquarters	Gumbinnen
2nd	combined Landwehr Brigade	Headquarters	Tilsit

"Russia will remain neutral at first, although the possibility of a war remains." (From the directives for the army headquarters, which, for the time being, will remain in the east.)

* * *

V. North

The "Directives for the Security of the Deployment of an Army Marshaling in Schleswig Holstein" and the "Deployment Directives IX Reserve Corps" are almost identical to the year before.
The Senior Landwehr Commander, who is the commander of the four combined Landwehr brigades of the Landwehr Corps, is designated Senior Landwehr Commander 1.

* * *

VI. Studies

Aufmarsch II West and II East have been prepared as studies. Aufmarsch II West seems to be identical to the year before; however, for Aufmarsch II East advance arrows indicate that there will not be such a far-reaching movement for the First Army as in the year before, and the First Army will start from the line Thorn–Neidenburg.

Mobilization Schedule 1914–1915

General Information on the Deployment and the Political Situation

1. Germany's preparations for war are first and foremost directed against France. Russia will probably join France in a war against Germany. The English are expected to be hostile.
   Considering the popular mood in France, a war waged by Germany against Russia or England alone is not probable. In the event that either Russia or England nevertheless declares war alone, German diplomacy will have to force France to make a final decision. See Item 13 for specific points on Belgium, Holland, Luxembourg, Denmark, etc.
   In the event of a war against Russia, arrangements have been made with the Austro-Hungarian General Staff for a general offensive toward Russia.
   Italy is expected to join Germany in a war against France. The Italian General Staff will initiate the move of 2 cavalry divisions, and later an army consisting of 3 army corps, by railroad into southern Germany via Austria during the first days of mobilization. Furthermore, an intervention by Italian main forces at the French Alpine border is expected.
   Arrangements have been made with other states, of which the chief of the General Staff of the Army, *Oberquartiermeister* I, and the chief of 2nd ... are aware.
2. Germany can only mobilize its entire force. Since mobilization preparations for all army corps are interconnected, partial mobilizations are impossible.
   Upon mobilization the German army will establish:
   a) The Field Army, consisting of...

26 army corps.
13 reserve corps.
1 reserve division (3rd Reserve Division).
11 cavalry divisions (Guards, 1st through 9th Bavarian).
1 Landwehr corps.
24½ combined Landwehr brigades.

b) Wartime garrisons and occupation forces: Preparations are under way to combine "Ersatz formations for potential mobile use" into an Ersatz army (Guards, IV, VIII, X, XIX Bavarian Ersatz divisions, 55 combined Ersatz brigades, XIV). See Item 3.

Upon the mobilization order the Landsturm will be called up. Border security and coastal defense will be effective throughout the German Reich.

3. Only one *Aufmarsch* has been prepared for German main forces to deploy to the western border against France.

   If necessary, an army element will marshal southwest of Metz to provide a diversion from the main deployment. In the event of an early invasion by superior French forces into Lorraine, consideration should be given to withdrawing the deployment of the Sixth Army to the line St. Avold–Saaralben–Pfalzburg.

   In the east, the Eighth Army (4 corps, 1 reserve division, 1 cavalry division, Landwehr corps of 3 combined Landwehr brigades) will remain behind. The Eighth Army will either march immediately against Russia or will remain behind in the eastern corps districts while the mobilization and border security and coastal defense measures are executed according to plan, until decisions can be made on Eighth Army's further commitment.

   If Russia remains permanently neutral, the Eighth Army will probably be committed against France. Preparations for its redeployment have been made.

   After mobilization is completed, the following elements will be marshaled in Schleswig Holstein as the "Northern Deployment."

   IX Corps, with the two Landwehr Commands I and IX (33rd, 34th, 37th, 38th combined Landwehr Brigades).

   If there is no threat to the German coast, IX Corps and, conditions permitting, the Northern Brigade will be deployed to another theater of war.

   The Ersatz Army[1] can be committed to the western, eastern, or northern theaters of war, either in whole or by elements. The initial distribution of German field forces to the various theaters of war is as follows:

West	23 army corps	11 reserve corps		17½ combined Landwehr brigades	10 cavalry divisions
East	3 army corps	1 reserve corps	1 Landwehr Corps	3 combined Landwehr brigades	1 cavalry division
North		1 reserve division			
		1 reserve corps		4 combined Landwehr brigades	
Maximum total of forces in any one theater	26 army corps	13 reserve corps 1 reserve division	1 Landwehr Corps	24½ combined Landwehr brigades	11 cavalry divisions

The Ersatz Army will consist of 6 Ersatz divisions and 1 combined Ersatz brigade.

13. A general meeting of the Chief of the General Staff of the Army with the Imperial Chancellor, the Foreign Office, the War Ministry, the Military Cabinet, and the Chief of the Admiralty Staff will identify likely enemies and the attitudes of the allied and neutral powers in the event of war. If possible, a determination will be made on the likelihood of a redeployment of French forces from the ports on the African Mediterranean coast to France.
Oral arrangements will be made with the Imperial Chancellor and the Foreign Office for the following demands to be issued immediately after the announcement of mobilization:
a) To Belgium:
By 1800 hours on the 2nd mobilization day the Belgian government must decide whether Belgium will be Germany's friend or enemy; or if as a neutral state it will allow German forces to transit. That will require the Belgians to open immediately the fortifications of L. Huy and Namur to the German army; to make the railroads . . . available to us; and not to mobilize the Belgian army. If Belgium joins Germany's side, it must allow the transit of the German army by all means;

hold Namur against a possible surprise raid by the French army; and prevent English landings. A delay in the response of the Belgian government must not be allowed.

b) To Holland:

English landings must be prevented. The German army must be allowed to limit Dutch neutrality. (For the transit through the Dutch corridor around Maastricht see Item 71d). If the Second Army refrains from launching a surprise raid on Liege, immediately negotiate with Holland for unrestricted transit through the corridor.

c) To Luxembourg:

Transit must be allowed and railroads must be secured and be made available.

d) To Denmark:

Prevent English landings.

10th mobilization day and subsequent days:
Make the decision about the commitment of the Italian army.
The following courses of action are possible:
Advance immediately, connecting with Sixth and Seventh Armies.
Advance against the barrier fort line between Epinal and Belfort.
Ensure that the covering forces on the Upper Rhine screen the left flank of the Italian Army during its advance via the Vosges into France. The German deployment against France is based on the following intent:

1. The main body of the German force will advance through Belgium and Luxembourg into France. The advance—if the intelligence on the French deployment is correct—is intended as a turning movement anchored on the pivot point at Diedenhofen–Metz. The right wing of the force will determine the tempo of the turn. The movements of the inner armies will be directed in such a way as to maintain the cohesion of the force and the connection to Diedenhofen–Metz.
2. Army elements marshaling southeast of Metz will be responsible for the security of the left flank of the main body of the force—in addition to the fortifications of Diedenhofen and Metz.
3. The march routes through Liège must be open for the advance of the First and Second Armies. If Belgium allows the transit of the German force, the commanding general of X Army Corps will occupy Liège with forces that are ready to march early and have been positioned in

advance. If Belgium refuses right of passage, the following options are available for capturing Liège:

a. A surprise raid under the commanding general of X Army Corps with forces that are ready to march early and have been positioned in advance.

b. A surprise raid with strong forces under the direct command of the Second Army.

c. A siege-like attack,

For its actions against Liège, the Second Army will have all the roads south of the Dutch border at its disposal.... As soon as Liège is captured, the Second Army will clear the march routes designated for the First Army.... If the Second Army fails to open the blocked advance routes through Liège by the 12th mobilization day, it will initiate the scheduled attack by reserve and siege units against this fortification and bypass Liège in the south. In this case, the First Army will advance through Dutch territory—but only upon explicit order of the Supreme Army Command (OHL).

4. The order to start the general advance of the German main body will be issued as soon as the First and Second Armies are ready at the level of Liège.

Senior Cavalry Commander 2 with attached *Jäger*[2] battalions will be directly subordinate to OHL and will bypass Namur in the north and advance against the line Antwerp–Brussels–Charleroi in order to determine the location of the Belgian Army, the possible landing of English forces, and the possible presence of French forces in northern Belgium. Furthermore, he will be tasked with reconnoitering the area west of the Meuse along the route Namur–Givet, bypassing Namur in the north, and locating the left wing of the French Army. Senior Cavalry Commander 2 will provide intelligence to the command posts of the Second and First Armies. His reports to OHL will be submitted without delay.

The *First Army* will march toward Brussels and cover the right flank of the force. Its advance, in coordination with that of the Second Army, will be decisive in executing the turning movement.

The *Second Army* will advance with its right wing toward Wavre, with its left wing bypassing Namur in the north.

Senior Cavalry Commander 1 with attached *Jäger* battalion will be subordinate directly to OHL at the beginning of the general advance. He will advance to the front of the Third Army and the right wing of the Fourth Army against the Meuse, south of Namur, following the Meuse in the direction of Dinant. He will reconnoiter against the Meuse along the route Namur–Mezières and initially will ascertain whether the I and II French Army Corps have occupied the Meuse between Namur and Givet, or whether French forces are already east of the Meuse. Directives have been issued for him to provide intelligence to the command posts of the Third and Fourth Armies. His reports to the OHL will be submitted without delay.

The *Third Army*, despite the early deployment of the Second Army, will complete its deployment and begin the advance against the Meuse between Namur and Givet, only upon the order of OHL. Since the Third Army may be required to advance farther to encircle Namur on the southern front and capture Fort Charlemont near Givet, preparations will be made to facilitate the early replacement with rear formations of the forces intended for this purpose.

The *Fourth Army* will advance with its right wing echeloned on the left toward Fumay south of Givet, and with its left wing via Attert north of Arlon toward Neufchateau. The left wing of the Fourth Army and the right wing of the Fifth Army must coordinate with each other.

During the course of the advance, the Fourth Army must be prepared at any time to turn south against the Semois to relieve the Fifth Army, which will be the first to come under enemy attack. Later, while advancing across the Meuse, the Fourth Army might be required to intervene in support of the Third Army.

The forest terrain in the Belgian-French border area and the difficult terrain along the banks of the Meuse and lower Semois, which the Fourth Army must cross, requires decisive action by the individual columns in order to clear axes of advance for each other and to provide mutual support when exiting the forest zone.

Senior Cavalry Commander 4 with attached *Jäger* battalions will be directly subordinate to OHL and will advance toward Cargnau . . . and Damvillers, while continuing reconnaissance against the Meuse route Mezières–Mouzon–Stenay–Verdun–St. Mihiel. He will determine whether the Meuse north of Verdun is heavily occupied, or whether French forces are advancing from there against the Fourth and Fifth Armies via Verdun or between Verdun and Metz. Senior Cavalry Commander 4 is instructed to provide reports to the command post of the Fifth Army. His reports to OHL will be submitted without delay.

The Fifth Army during the general advance of the German main body will have the task of holding the pivot point of Diedenhofen–Metz connecting to the Fourth Army. For this purpose, the Fifth Army will be ready to advance starting from the line Bettenburg–Diedenhofen, initially maintaining echelonment in depth. The further advance of the Fifth Army will be executed heavily echeloned on the left, with the right wing from Bettenburg via Mamer–Arlon toward Florinville south of Cliny, while the left wing maintains the connection with Diedenhofen.

To repel with strong forces a French counterattack from the direction of Verdun, it may be necessary at any time for the Fifth Army to turn into a position with its front facing southwest or south. Therefore, it will be necessary to conduct early ground reconnaissance and arrange for precautionary provision of all resources available from Metz and Diedenhofen for the reinforcement and defense of a fortified forward position. The situation will determine the necessity for committing the main reserve at Metz.

During the further course of the advance, the Fifth Army will probably be tasked with capturing Longwy and Montmédy.

Sixth Army, *Seventh Army*, and *Senior Cavalry Commander 3*—those forces marshaling in the Imperial Territories[3] southeast of Metz— will be subordinate to the joint command of the senior of the two commanding generals. The joint senior commander is tasked with advancing toward the Moselle downriver of Frouard and the Meurthe, capturing Fort Manonviller, in order to block the assembled French forces and prevent their redeployment to the left wing of the French Army. This task may be overcome by events if the French launch an attack with superior forces between Metz and the Vosges. If the forces in the Imperial Territories are thus forced to withdraw, their movements will be such as to prevent a threat to the left wing of the German main body, which would come from a French envelopment of the Nied Position. If necessary, the Sixth Army will detach elements to reinforce the garrison of the Nied Position. In the event that the Sixth and Seventh Armies do not encounter superior French forces, elements of the Sixth Army and Senior Cavalry Commander 3 might be required to intervene in the battle on the left bank of the Moselle. The joint senior commander will decide the extent to which such action is necessary for the advance against the Moselle and the Meurthe. The Fifth Army command post will continuously receive intelligence.

If a French offensive is expanded into Upper Alsace, it will not necessarily disrupt our overall operation unless the enemy crosses the line Fort de Mutzig–Breusch Position–Strassburg. It is primarily the task of the governor of Strassburg to hold that line.

During the deployment movements the border area along Upper Alsace and southern Baden is the responsibility of the commanding general of the Seventh Army. Of those units attached to him, the main body of the 29th Infantry Division of the XV Army Corps will initially hold positions near the Vosges between Weileifel and Münstereifel; elements of the 29th Infantry Division of the XIV Army Corps will hold positions near Mühlhausen; the remainder of the XV Army Corps will marshal northwest of Strassburg; XIV Army Corps and XIV Reserve Corps will marshal on the Upper Rhine. For the security of Upper Alsace and south Baden, the covering forces on the Upper Rhine and those forces under the deputy commanding generals of the XV and XIV Army Corps will be attached to the commanding general of the Seventh Army.

The task of the commanding general of the Seventh Army in Upper Alsace and south Baden will only be temporary. The joint senior commander in the Imperial Territories will make every effort to commit the strongest elements of the Seventh Army to direct support of the Sixth Army. The 29th Infantry Division, which probably can be replaced in its border security mission by the 1st and 2nd combined Bavarian Landwehr Brigades, will be attached to the XV Army Corps in Strassburg *as soon as possible*. All requests for necessary rail transport will be submitted in a timely manner to the chief of the Field Railway Service....

The covering mission in Alsace must not result in the Seventh Army or elements thereof being sacrificed to a superior enemy force that might advance at an early stage from the direction of Belfort. Such a move probably would be in support of a French offensive between Metz and the Vosges. If the Seventh Army is tied down by such action, it would give the French an opportunity to achieve a success at little cost. Rather, it is much more important to repel an early advance of weak French forces in order to prevent Alsace from being surrendered without resistance to enemy action. The command post of the Seventh Army will, therefore, identify specifically in its directives whether it is facing a hasty advance by inferior French forces, or a deliberate advance by strong French forces from the direction of Belfort and north.

If an advance by superior enemy forces into Upper Alsace is identified, the territory will be stripped of all resources useful to the enemy—rolling stock, public funds, etc. The units of the Seventh Army will be withdrawn to Strassburg (XV Army Corps) and to the right bank of the Rhine (XIV Army Corps). The Rhine bridges and the railroads on the left bank of the Rhine will be permanently destroyed. . . .

At that moment at the latest, the Seventh Army with the strongest possible forces will be freed to provide direct support to the Sixth Army. The situation of the Sixth Army will determine the direction of the support and the mode of transport—foot march or rail.
After the evacuation of Upper Alsace, south Baden must be defended. Whether the Landwehr units primarily intended for that task will be sufficient, or whether they will require reinforcement by occupation forces from the XV Army Corps or from elements of the XIV Reserve Corps, will be determined by the situation. If necessary, the Seventh Army command post may commit all occupation forces of the XIV Army Corps. Identify the command relationships on the Upper Rhine. The deputy commanding general of the XIV Army Corps is a potential senior commander for the Upper Rhine. He will, therefore, be constantly informed about the overall situation.

Notes

1. Replacement Army.
2. Elite light infantry.
3. Alsace and Lorraine.

Glossary of German Military Terms and Acronyms

This glossary includes some German military terms and abbreviations used in the German edition of the book that do not appear in this edition because they have been rendered in English. They are included here as an aid to anyone who wants to reference the German edition, or who wants to undertake additional reading about the Schlieffen Plan.

Absicht	intent, commander's intent
Abteilung	department, also battalion
AK	abbreviation for *Armeekorps*
Alpenjäger	mountain light infantry
Angriffskrieg	offensive war
Anweisung	instruction, directive
AOK	abbreviation for *Armee Oberkommando*
Armeekorps	army corps, a standard German infantry corps
Armee Oberkommando	army senior command, the headquarters for a German numbered field army
Artillerieschutzstellung	artillery security zone
Aufklärung	reconnaissance
Aufmarsch	deployment
Aufmarschabteilung	Deployment Department
Aufmarschakten	deployment files
Aufmarschanweisungen	deployment directives
Aufmarschkarten	deployment maps
Aufmarschmappe	deployment folder
Aufmarschpläne	deployment plans
Aufmarschplanung	deployment planning
Auftragstaktik	mission-oriented command and control

527

Bahnfahrt	rail movement
Bayerisches Kriegsarchiv	Bavarian War Archives, located in Munich
Bayer. KA	abbreviation for *Bayerisches Kriegsarchiv*
BA/MA	abbreviation for *Bundesarchiv/Militärarchiv*
Bewegungskrieg	mobile warfare
Bundesarchiv/Militärarchiv	Military Archives Branch of the German Federal Archives, presently located in Freiburg, Germany
Bundeswehr	Armed Forces of the Federal Republic of Germany
CSG	abbreviation for *Conseil Supérieur de la Guerre*, French Supreme War Counsel
Denkschrift	memorandum
Der Weltkrieg 1914–1918	title of the fourteen-volume German official history of World War I
Durchbruch	breakthrough
D.V.E.	abbreviation for *Druckvorschriftenetat*, the pre-1918 designation and numbering system for military manuals
EHO	abbreviation for *Etappe Hauptort*
Einbruch	break-in
Eisenbahnbüro	Railway Division (Austrian)
EK	abbreviation for *Ersatzkorps*
Ersatz	replacement, reserve
Ersatzkorps	replacement corps
Erstes Generalquartiermeister	first quartermaster general, the seniormost deputy to the chief of the Great General Staff
Etappe Hauptort	main base of the communications zone
Etappenbüro	Supply Division (Austrian)
Evidenzbüro	Intelligence Division (Austrian)
Fall	case
Feldeisenbahnwesen	Field Railway Service
Feldmunitionswesen	Field Ordnance Service
Fussartillerie	foot artillery, the German heavy artillery
Gegenangriff	deliberate counterattack
Gegenstoss	hasty counterattack

Glossary of German Military Terms and Acronyms 529

geheim	secret
Geheimrat	privy councillor, a German government official
gemischte	combined
Generalkommando	general command, a corps headquarters
Generalquartiermeister	quartermaster general, the chief of a directorate of the Great General Staff
Generalstab	General Staff
Generalstabsreisen	General Staff rides, a training exercise for General Staff officers
Grenzschutz	border security
Gr.H.Qu.	abbreviation for *Grosses Hauptquartier*
Grosser Generalstab	Great General Staff, in Berlin, as opposed to the General Staff with troops
Grosses Hauptquartier	general headquarters
Hauptwiderstandslinie	main line of resistance
Heeresarchiv	Army Archives
Ia	German General Staff officer in charge of operations
Ic	German General Staff officer in charge of intelligence
Immediatrecht	the right of direct access to the kaiser
Jäger	literally "hunter," elite light infantry units
Kaiserheer	Imperial Army, the German Army of World War I
Kaiserliche Armee	Imperial Armed Forces, the German military of World War I
Kaiserlich und Königliche Armee	Imperial and Royal Armed Forces, the Austrian military of World War I
Kriegsakademie	War Academy, the principal training institution of the German General Staff
Kriegsgeschichtliche Abteilung	War History Department
Kriegshandwerk	military tradecraft
Kriegsrüstung	war armaments
Kriegsspiele	war games, analytical procedures to test war plans
Kriegstagebuch	war diary
Kriegswirtschaft	war economy
Kriegszustand	state of war

KTB	abbreviation for *Kriegstagebuch*
K.u.K.	abbreviation for *Kaiserlich und Königliche* (Austrian)
Lage	situation
Lageskizzen	situation sketches
Landesbeschreibungsbüro	Area Studies Division (Austrian)
Landsturm	territorial assault force, Germany's second tier reserve
Landwehr	territorial defense force, Germany's first tier reserve
Materialschlacht	battle of attrition
Militärgeschichte	military history
Mobilmachung	mobilization
Mörser	literally "mortar," but actually the German designation for a very heavy howitzer, such as the Krupp 420 mm *Dicke*
Nachlass	posthumous personal papers
Nachrichtendienst	Intelligence Service
NL	abbreviation for *Nachlass*
Nordaufmarsch	northern deployment
Nordstoss	northern thrust
Oberost	German general headquarters on the eastern front
Oberste Heeresleitung	Supreme Army Command, the operational headquarters of the German Army in the field
l'offensive à outrance	attack in the extreme (French)
OHL	abbreviation for *Oberste Heeresleitung*
Operationsabteilung	Operations Division
Operationsbüro	Operations Division (Austrian)
Operationsplan	operations plan, war plan
operatives Ziel	operational objective
Ostaufmarsch	eastern deployment
Ostheer	German Army on the World War I eastern front
Reichsarchiv	Reich Archives
Reichskanzler	Reich chancellor, the head of the German government

Reichslande	Imperial territories. Areas that were not part of the semi-autonomous German states, and therefore came under the direct administration of the Reich. In the case of World War I on the western front, the former French territories of *Elsass* (Alsace) and *Lothringen* (Lorraine)
Reservekorps	reserve corps
RK	abbreviation for *Reservekorps*
Rückmarsch	retrograde march
Schlussaufgaben	key taskings
Schlussbesprechung	final, or wrap-up discussion
Schwerpunkt	center of gravity, main effort
SHA	abbreviation for *Service Historique de l'Armée de Terre,* the Historical Service of the French Army, located in Vincennes, France
Staatskunst	statecraft
Stabschef	chief of staff
Stellung	position, line, trench
Stellungskrieg	trench warfare
streng geheim	top secret
Totalsieg	total victory
Umfassung	envelopment, a military encircling maneuver
Vernichtungsschlacht	battle of annihilation
Vollmacht	full power, authority delegated to a General Staff officer to issue orders in the name of the commander
Wehrmacht	German armed forces of World War II
Weisung	directive
Weisungsführung	command by directive
Weltkrieg	world war
Westaufmarsch	western deployment
Westheer	German Army on the World War I western front

Contributors

Dr. Hans Ehlert, Colonel (Ret.) was from 2004 to 2010 Director of the Military History Research Institute (MGFA) in Potsdam and President of the German Commission for Military History. Focus of work: Security policy and military history of the Federal Republic of Germany and the German Democratic Republic. Hans Ehlert is the author of many publications on the history of the *Bundeswehr* and the National People's Army. For example: *Genosse General! Biographische Skizzen zur Militärelite der DDR* (edited with Armin Wagner) (Berlin, 2003); *Militär, Staat und Gesellschaft in der DDR: Forschungsfelder Ergebnisse, Perspektiven* (edited with Matthias Rogg) (Berlin, 2004); *Die Militär- und Sicherheitspolitik in der SBZ/DDR: Eine Bibliographie (1945–1995)* (München, 1996) (editor); "Innenpolitische Auseinandersetzungen um die Pariser Verträge und die Wehrverfassung 1954 bis 1956," in Hans Ehlert, Christian Greiner, and Georg Meyer Bruno Thoss, *Die NATO-Option,* Anfänge westdeutscher Sicherheitspolitik 1945–1956, 3 (München, 1993), 235–560.

Prof. Dr. Michael Epkenhans is Director of Research at the Center for Military History and Social Sciences of the German Armed Forces in Potsdam. He also teaches modern history as well as military history at both Potsdam University and Hamburg University. His main research interests are naval history and the history of the German Armed Forces on foreign missions. Currently he is working on an edition of the private papers of the chief of German military intelligence during World War I, Colonel Nicolai, as well as an edition of important documents on the "Anglo-German Naval Race 1900–1914" in conjunction with the British Navy Records Society. His most important publications include: *Preussen, Aufstieg und Fall einer Grossmacht* (Stuttgart, 2011); *Geschichte Deutschlands (1648–2008)* (Stuttgart, 2008); *Grand Admiral Alfred von Tirpitz: A Biography* (New York, 2008); *Albert Hopman: Das ereignisreiche Leben eines "Wilhelminers": Tagebücher, Briefe und Aufzeichnungen 1901–1920* (München, 2004); *Die wilhelminische Flot-*

tenrüstung 1908–1914: Weltmachtstreben, industrieller Fortschritt, soziale Integration (München, 1991).

Dr. Robert T. Foley is Reader in Defence Studies at King's College London and teaches at the Joint Services Command and Staff College. His books include *Alfred von Schlieffen's Military Writings* (London: Frank Cass, 2004); *German Strategy and the Path to Verdun: Erich von Falkenhayn and the Development of Attrition, 1870–1916* (Cambridge: Cambridge Univ. Press, 2005), which was awarded the Royal Historical Society's Gladstone Prize in 2005; and, with H. B. McCartney, *The Somme: An Eyewitness History* (London: Folio Society, 2006). Dr. Foley is the Co-Director of the First World War Research Group at King's College London and is leading the First World War centenary commemorations at the Defence Academy of the United Kingdom.

Dr. Hans Rudolf Fuhrer is a former head of the Department of Military History at the Military Academy at the Swiss Federal Institute of Technology in Zurich and was Associate Professor (Privatdozent) for Swiss military history at the University of Zurich. His publications include: *Die Schweizer Armee im Ersten Weltkrieg: Bedrohung, Landesverteidigung und Landesbefestigung,* Habilitation (Zurich, 2003); *General Ulrich Wille: Vorbild den einen— Feindbild den andern* (Zurich, 2003); *Der schweizerische Generalstab,* vol. 11, *Alle roten Pfeile kamen aus Osten—zu Recht? Das Bild und die Bedrohung der Schweiz 1945–1966 im Licht östlicher Archive* (Baden, 2010).

Colonel Dr. Gerhard P. Gross is head of the department German Military History before 1945 at the Center for Military History and Social Science. He is the author of a number of books and articles dealing with the Imperial German Army and Navy. For example: *Mythos und Wirklichkeit: Geschichte des operativen Denkens im deutschen Heer von Moltke d.Ä. bis Heusinger* (Paderborn, 2012); *Preussen, Aufstieg und Fall einer Grossmacht* (Stuttgart, 2011); *Die vergessene Front—der Osten 1914/15: Ereignis, Wirkung, Nachwirkung* (Paderborn, 2006); "Das Dogma der Beweglichkeit: Überlegungen zur Genese der deutschen Heerestaktik im Zeitalter der Weltkriege," in *Erster Weltkrieg Zweiter Weltkrieg: Ein Vergleich.* Edited for the Militärgeschichtliches Forschungsamtes by Bruno Thoss and Hans-Erich Volkmann (Paderborn, 2002).

Prof. Emeritus Dr. Klaus Hildebrand was Professor of modern history at Bonn University. He has published extensively on German history and international relations in the nineteenth and twentieth centuries. His most important publications include *Das vergangene Reich: Deutsche Aussenpolitik 1871–1945* (Stuttgart, 1995).

Prof. Dr. Günther Kronenbitter currently teaches modern history and cultural anthropology at the University of Augsburg. He specializes in the history of international relations and military history in the long nineteenth century with a special focus on the Habsburg Monarchy. His dissertation on the conservative Friedrich Gentz was published in 1994, and his second book on the politics of the Austro-Hungarian army in 2003: *"Krieg im Frieden": Die Führung der k.u.k. Armee und die Grossmachtpolitik Österreich-Ungarns 1906–1914*.

Dr. Jan Kusber is Professor and Chair for Eastern European History at the Johannes Gutenberg-University in Mainz, Germany. He is the author of *Krieg und Revolution in Russland, 1904–1906: Das Militär im Verhältnis zu Wirtschaft, Autokratie und Gesellschaft* (Stuttgart, 1997), *Eliten- und Volksbildung im Zarenreich während des 18. und in der ersten Hälfte des 19. Jahrhunderts: Studien zu Diskurs, Gesetzgebung und Umsetzung* (Stuttgart, 2004), and *Kleine Geschichte St. Petersburgs* (Regensburg, 2009), and with Ilya Gerasimov and Alexander Semyonov he is coeditor of *Empire Speaks Out? Languages of Rationalization and Self-Description in the Russian Empire* (Leiden, 2009).

Dr. Annika Mombauer is Senior Lecturer in History at the Open University in Milton Keynes, England. Her research specialism is the origins of the First World War. Recent publications include *Die Julikrise* (Munich: C. H. Beck, 2014), *The Origins of the First World War: Diplomatic and Military Documents* (Manchester: Manchester Univ. Press, 2013), and "The Fischer Controversy after 50 Years" special issue of the *Journal of Contemporary History* 48, no. 2 (April 2013). She is currently working on a comparative history of the Battle of the Marne of 1914 to be published by Cambridge University Press.

Dr. Michael Olsansky is the current head of the Department of Military History at the Military Academy at the Swiss Federal Institute of Technology in Zurich and he periodically lectures at the University of Zurich. His main research topics are Swiss military history in the twentieth century and the evolution of warfare in the interwar period. He received his Ph.D. in 2012 from the University of Zurich for his thesis "Von Landkriegstaktik und Taktikdebatten: Militärisches Denken der schweizerischen und österreichischen Offizierseliten nach dem Ersten Weltkrieg im historischen Vergleich." His publications include "The Development of the Swiss Army's Combat Methods after the First World War," in *Small Powers in the Age of Total War*, ed. H. Amersfoort and W. Klinkert (Leiden, 2011).

Dr. Stefan Schmidt is the author of *Frankreichs Aussenpolitik in der Julikrise 1914* (Munich, 2009). In 2008 he joined the Research Services of the German Bundestag. From 2010 to 2012 he worked in the Policy Planning Staff of the CDU/CSU Parliamentary Group. In 2012 he became head of the office of the chairman of the CDU Baden-Wuerttemberg.

Dr. Dieter Storz is curator at the Bavarian Army Museum in Ingolstadt. His previous publications were *Rifle and Carbine 98* (Vienna, 2006), *German Military Rifles*, vol. 1, *From the Werder Rifle to the M/71.84. Rifle* (Vienna, 2011), and *German Military Rifles*, vol. 2, *88 and 91 Firearms* (Vienna, 2012).

Dr. Hew Strachan has been Chichele Professor of the History of War at the University of Oxford and a Fellow of All Souls College since 2002, and was Director of the Oxford Programme on the Changing Character of War between 2003 and 2012. He also serves on the Strategic Advisory Panel of the Chief of the Defence Staff and on the UK Defence Academy Advisory Board, as well as being a Trustee of the Imperial War Museum, a Commonwealth War Graves Commissioner, and a member of both the National Committee for the Centenary of the First World War and the Council of the International Institute for Strategic Studies. He is also a Fellow of Corpus Christi College, Cambridge, and Visiting Professor at the University of Glasgow. He was elected a Fellow of the Royal Society of Edinburgh in 2003 and was awarded an Hon. D. Univ. by the University of Paisley in 2005. In 2010 he chaired a task force on the implementation of the Armed Forces Covenant for the prime minister. In 2011 he was the inaugural Humanitas Visiting Professor in War Studies at the University of Cambridge and became a specialist adviser to the Joint Committee on the National Security Strategy. He is a Deputy Lieutenant for Tweeddale, and a Brigadier in the Queen's Bodyguard for Scotland (Royal Company of Archers). In December 2012, *Foreign Policy* magazine included him in its list of top global thinkers for the year. He was knighted in the 2013 New Year's Honours.

Dr. Luc de Vos is a former colonel of the Belgian Army and Emeritus Professor from the Catholic University Leuven and from the Royal Military Academy in Brussels. He has published forty-one books in Dutch and French about military history. He was president of the International Commission for Military History for ten years and is currently president of the National Library of Belgium.

Major General David T. Zabecki, USA (Ret.) holds a Ph.D. in military history from Britain's Royal Military College of Science, Cranfield University. He is an honorary senior research fellow in the War Studies Programme at the University of Birmingham. In 2012 he held the Dr. Leo A. Shrifren Distinguished Chair in Military History at the U.S. Naval Academy, Annapolis. He is also the chief military historian of the Weider History Group, the world's largest publisher of history magazines. He is the author of *Steel Wind: Colonel Georg Bruchmüller and the Birth of Modern Artillery* (Westport, Conn.: Preager, 1994), and *The German 1918 Offensives: A Case Study in the Operational Level of War* (London: Routledge, 2006.) He is the editor-in-chief of the four-volume encyclopedia *Germany at War: 400 Years of Military History* (Santa Barbara: ABC-CLIO, 2014).

Index

The names of military units appear in alphabetical rather than numerical order; for example, "5th Cavalry Division" appears before "1st Cavalry Division."

Aachen (Germany), 331
Aarschot (Belgium), 333
Adriatic Crisis (1912), 25
Aehrenthal, Alois von, 28, 29, 190, 196, 201
aerial reconnaissance, 145, 159, 184n148
Afflerbach, Holger, 26
Afghanistan, 22
Africa, 213, 279, 438, 519
Agadir Crisis. *See* Morocco Crisis (1911)
Airship Agreement, 506
Albert I (King of Belgium), 49, 328–29, 335, 336
Albrecht (Archduke of Austria), 195
Aldershot Garrison (England), 309, 310
Algeciras Conference (1906), 27
Allenstein–Rothfliess–Korschen railroad, 493
Allenstein–Thorn railroad, 493
All-German Union, 292n82
Alsace (France), 102, 140–41, 220, 275, 343, 453, 454n3, 479, 483n2, 487, 492, 501–2, 509, 524–25
Andrássy, Julius, 19
Andrian-Werburg, Leopold von, 20

Anglo-Japanese Agreement (1902), 303
Anglo-Russian Agreement (1907), 303
Ante Portas telegram, 274–76, 290n51
Antwerp (Belgium), 111, 132–33n154, 265, 322–23, 324, 326, 327, 328, 332, 334, 335, 439, 440, 510
Army Archive (*Heeresarchiv*; Potsdam), 69, 263; access to records in, 87–88, 95; establishment of, 87; General Staff records stored in, 87, 92, 95–96, 341; holdings catalog of, 95; inventory lists of, in Moscow Archive, 128n85; WWII destruction of, 2, 7, 68, 88, 341. *See also* Reich Archive (*Reichsarchiv*; Potsdam)
Army Bill, 131n132
artillery, 131n128, 158–60, 184n134
artillery projectiles, 3
Asia, 438
Asia Convention (1907), 22
Asquith, Herbert, 23, 295
Asse (Belgium), 334
Ath (Belgium), 334
Audéoud, Alfred, 273
Aufmarsch I (State of War with France Only): combat strength involved in, 107; deployment plans 1901–1902, 384–89; deployment plans

540 Index

Aufmarsch I *(cont.)*
  1902–1903, 393–96; deployment plans 1903–1904, 403, 404–8; deployment plans 1904–1905, 409, 411–14; deployment plans 1905–1906, 73, 416, 418–23; deployment plans 1906–1907, 132–33n154, 424–25, 427–33; deployment plans 1907–1908, 436, 437–38; deployment plans 1909–1910, 457–58; deployment plans 1910–1911, 472–78; deployment plans 1911–1912, 484–86, 487–91; East, 386–89, 395–96, 406–8, 413–15, 422–23, 472, 473–74, 480–81, 484–86, 493; North, 435; Paris envelopment in, 116–17; West, 385–86, 393–95, 404–6, 411–13, 418–22, 427–33, 439–44, 472–73, 474–78, 484–85, 487–91
Aufmarsch Ia (Small-Scale Eastern Deployment), 457–58, 466–67
Aufmarsch II (State of War with Russia and France): deployment directives 1912, 497–502; deployment plans 1901–1902, 389–92; deployment plans 1902–1903, 395–98; deployment plans 1903–1904, 403; deployment plans 1904–1905, 409–10; deployment plans 1905–1906, 73, 416–17; deployment plans 1906–1907, 424–25, 434; deployment plans 1907–1908, 436, 437–38; deployment plans 1909–1910, 457–60, 467–68; deployment plans 1910–1911, 472, 473, 474, 478–80, 481–83; deployment plans 1911–1912, 342, 484–85, 491–95; East, 397–98, 434, 445–46, 472, 473, 481–83, 493–95, 497–99; handwritten copies of, 342; West, 389–92, 396–97, 472, 473, 478–80, 491–92, 499–502
Aufmarsch IIa (Defensive Western Deployment Against France), 457–58, 464–66
Aufmarschanweisungen. See deployment directives (*Aufmarschanweisungen*)
Aufmarschpläne, 73, 87, 95–96, 107, 341. *See also* deployment plans (*Aufmarschpläne*; *Aufmarschplanungen*)
Aufmarschplanungen, 10, 341. *See also* deployment plans (*Aufmarschpläne*; *Aufmarschplanungen*)
Auftragstaktik, 101
Austria, 321, 324–25
Austria-Hungary: alliance-/bloc-building by, 21, 192, 268 (*see also* Triple Alliance); Balkans policy of, 201; constitutional situation of, 189; declining power of, 230; deployment plans of, 12; détente/rapprochement efforts of, 26, 27–30; in French war plans, 216, 225–26, 230; German agreements/cooperation with, 196, 198–200; German Double Alliance with, 21, 265; German intelligence on, 265; German war plan and, 98, 114, 503, 514; operational planning of, 9, 191–96; in Russian war plans, 249, 251, 253, 254–55, 256; Sprecher's relationship with, 273; statecraft/military tradecraft relationship in, 17, 20; strategic position of, 190; in Swiss operational planning, 268–69, 270, 271; war planning by, 189
Austrian Army Archives, 69, 81n10
Austro-German War (1866), 78, 142, 193, 283, 292n89, 298, 299
Austro-Hungarian Dual Monarchy, 4, 28, 196
Austro-Hungarian Foreign Ministry, 190
Austro-Hungarian General Staff: Area

Studies Division, 191; Conrad von Hötzendorf as chief of, 190; German agreements/cooperation with, 196, 201–6; German war plan and, 517; Intelligence Division, 191, 197, 271–72; operational planning by, 191–98; Operations Division, 190, 191–92, 194–95, 200, 201; organization of, 190–92, 197; political control over lacking, 196; Railway Division, 190, 191, 192, 193, 194; responsibilities of, 189; Schlieffen Plan and, 202; Sprecher Affair and, 271–72, 289n40; Supply Divisions, 190–91; Switzerland and, 272–73; tensions with Foreign Ministry, 190, 196; tensions within, 197

Austro-Hungarian Imperial and Royal Army (*K.u.K.* Army): combat power of, 251; deployment plans 1901–1902, 385; echelon deployment scheme of, 193–94; German coordination with, 204–6; German war plan and, 343, 514–15; mobilization of, 199, 248; reorganization of, 193; Russian military intelligence on, 251–52; Schlieffen's view of, 75; spy network of, 197; territorial augmentation scheme of, 193–94. *See also* Austro-Hungarian General Staff

Austro-Hungarian Imperial and Royal Army—armies: First Army, 200; Second Army, 200; Third Army, 200

Austro-Hungarian Imperial Ministry, 403

Austro-Hungarian Military Chancellery, 195–96

Austro-Hungarian War Ministry, 189, 190, 194–95

Baccarat (France), 475, 510
Baghdad Railway, 29

bag maneuver (*Sackmanöver*), 148, 150, 151, 175, 179n39, 181n66
balance-of-power system, 30–32, 217–18, 230, 322
Balfour, Arthur, 22
Balkan states, 191, 201, 202, 230
Balkan Wars (1912–1913), 25, 27, 158, 213, 249, 250, 252–53, 279
Baltic Sea, 422
Baltischport *entrevue* (1912), 29
Basel (Switzerland), 267, 282, 288n29
Battle of Sedan (1870), 323
Battle of Waterloo (1815), 320
Baudouin (Prince of Belgium), 328
Bauer, Max, 161–62, 170, 173, 182n95
Bavarian Army Supreme Command, 142. *See also* Sixth Army
Bavarian Cavalry Division (Germany), 401, 419
Bavarian Ersatz Division (Germany), 504, 518
Bavarian General Staff, 142
Bavarian Reserve Corps (Germany), 507
Bayern, Leopold von, 455n8
Bayon (France), 162, 164–65
Beck, Ludwig, 6
Beck-Rzikowsky, Friedrich von, 81n10, 190, 195, 199, 201
Before the War (Haldane), 293
Begrand, Joseph, 330–34
Belgian Army, 323, 324; deployment of, 334–36; effectiveness of, 327–28; in German war plans, 419, 521; increases in strength of, 265, 266, 329–30; modernization of, 328–29; operational planning involving, 330–34
Belgian Army—divisions: 3rd Infantry Division, 335; 4th Infantry Division, 335
Belgian Council of Ministers, 336

Belgian General Staff, 13, 330–36
Belgian Legion, 324
Belgian National Congress, 321
Belgian Parliament, 324, 328, 329, 330, 335
Belgium, 7, 13; BEF deployment in, 296; border fortifications of, 106, 326, 328; in British war plans, 312; Catholicism and pro-German attitudes in, 326–28; conscription in, 329–30; in French war plans, 98–99, 220–23, 224, 231, 232–33n12; German intelligence on, 265–66; German invasion of, 58–59, 73, 139–40, 144, 210–11, 262–63, 336; German ultimatum to, 336; German war plan and, 44–45, 57, 58, 73, 106, 111, 116, 131n124, 134n178, 144, 427, 447–48, 459, 460–61, 486, 487, 505–6, 519–21; independence of (1830–1831), 321–22; Moltke Plan vs. Schlieffen Plan, 48–50, 58–59, 61n5; Netherlands merged with, 320–21; operational planning of, 9, 330–36; railroads in, 73, 155, 263, 327, 505; in Russian war plans, 254; self-defense rights of, 321; Ten Days Campaign (1831), 322, 323
Belgium—neutral status of, 313; Congress of Vienna and, 320–21; early threats to, 324–25; French respect of, 221–22, 265–66, 288n28; German violation of, 25, 79–80, 95, 108, 112–13, 221–22, 319, 336; German war plan and, 108, 112–13, 419, 439; Moltke Plan vs. Schlieffen Plan, 50, 52–53; moral aspects of violating, 45; treaties guaranteeing, 321–24, 325
Below, Otto von, 454n5
Berchtold, Leopold, 27, 28, 29

Berlepsch, Otto von, 289n43
Berlin (Germany), 484, 505, 506
Berlin Decisions (1902), 345n6
Berner Tagwacht (Swiss newspaper), 271
Bernhardi, Friedrich von, 266
Bern Officers' Association, 261
Berstein, Eduard, 26
Bertie, Francis, 217
Bethmann Hollweg, Theobald von, 4, 17, 29, 136n196, 281, 284–85, 519
Bircher, Eugen, 152
Bismarck, Herbert von, 278
Bismarck, Otto von, 2–3, 21, 30–31, 325
Bit War, 31
Björkoe meeting (1905), 29, 76
Bloch, Ernest, 27
Bock und Polach, Max von, 455n6
Boer uprisings, 306
Boer War, 22, 62n9, 113, 298, 301, 304
Boetticher, Friedrich von, 133n161; access to Schlieffen's papers, 91–92, 123n35, 123–24n37; career background of, 122–23n30; *Denkschrift* copy of, 125n61; General Staff rides as researched by, 130n116; Groener and, 123n30, 123n35; papers of (*Nachlass*), 11, 15n13, 89–90, 123n30, 124n37; research on Schlieffen, 89, 94, 95, 101–2; writings of, 342; Zuber thesis and, 97
Bonjour, Edgar, 286n2
Border Corps (Germany), 500
border security: East, 413, 422, 434, 445, 466, 492–93, 513; maps, 409; West, 410–11, 417–18, 427, 439, 460, 474, 486–87, 508–9
Bornand (French-Swiss officer), 273
Bose, Thilo von, 92, 342
Bosnia-Herzegovina, 193–94, 319

Bosnian Annexation Crisis (1908–1909), 25, 27, 33, 48, 201, 249
Bosworth, Richard, 234n25
Brackenbury, Henry, 299, 301
Brain of the Army, The (Wilkinson), 299
Brialmont, Henri-Alexis, 324
British Army: command structure of, 309–10, 313; continentalism and, 297–304, 312, 313–14; deficiencies of, 298; Egyptian Campaign (1882), 298, 301, 310; German intelligence on, 487; German war plan and, 439; Intelligence Division, 301–2; mobilization of, 293; principles vs. doctrine in, 311, 313–14; reorganization of, 301; training/instruction in, 310–11
British Army, The (Grierson), 301
British Army and the Continent, The (Tyler), 295
British Army Council, 309, 310
British Army in India Committee, 304
British Committee of Imperial Defence (CID), 295, 296, 297, 304, 306–7, 312–13
British Expeditionary Force (BEF), 23, 48; anticipated size of, 309; combat strength of, 215; command structure of, 309; creation of, 294–95, 310; in French war plans, 211–12, 218–20, 221; Indian Army and, 304; WWI defeats of, 313
British General Staff: colonial contingencies of, 306; continentalism of, 297, 299–304, 308, 309, 310–14; creation of, 296–97, 298–300, 306, 309–10; French consultations with, 223, 293, 294, 303; German model for, 299, 304–5, 307; operational planning of, 305–6; organizational structure of, 306–10; training/instruction and, 310–11; writ of, 304
British National Service League, 300
British Parliament, 293, 296
British Royal Navy, 223–24, 293–94, 295, 296, 299, 506
British War Office, 299, 304
Brockhaus Encyclopedia, 1
Bronsart von Schellendorff, Paul, 299
Broqueville, Charles de, 329
Brosch von Aarenau, Alexander, 196
Brussels (Belgium), 111, 132–33n154, 327, 333, 334, 440, 475, 487, 510, 520
Buchlau meeting (1908), 28
Bug River, 200, 514
Bukovina, 257
Bülow, Bernhard von, 60n1, 62n9, 74–75, 77, 113, 134n178
Bülow, Karl von, 454n5
Bundesarchiv/Militärarchiv (BA/MA; Freiburg), 88, 89, 90, 92, 94, 96, 120n4, 122n29, 128n91, 341–42
Burgundy Gate, 263, 264, 267

Calais (France), 439
Calwell, Charles, 295
Camberley (England), 310
Cambon, Jules, 24, 25
Cambon, Paul, 216, 217, 219
Campbell-Bannerman, Henry, 298–99
Camp Elsenborn (French military facility), 327
Cannae model, 4, 6, 8–9, 98, 138, 175, 210
Caprivi, Leo von, 19
Cardwell system, 310
Castelnau, Édouard de, 147, 153–54, 170, 211–12, 223–24, 233n17
Catholic Church, 319, 326–28, 329, 334, 336
Central Powers, 319. *See also* Austria-Hungary; German Reich

Chamberlain, Joseph, 22
Chapelié, Félix, 330
Charmes Gap, 157, 162
Chavannes (French-Swiss officer), 273
Churchill, Winston S., 18, 296
CID. *See* British Committee of Imperial Defence (CID)
Citadel of Bitche, 140
Claparède, Alfred de, 275
coastal defense, 377, 399–400, 422, 434, 500
Cold War, 30, 31, 32
Compulsory Service (Hamilton), 308
Congress of Vienna (1814–1815), 319–21
Congress Poland, 198
Conrad von Hötzendorf, Franz, 17, 47, 279; Aehrenthal and, 190, 196; as Austro-Hungarian General Staff chief, 190; as brigade/divisional commander, 199–200; correspondence of, 61n7, 201–2; criticism directed at, 197; deployment planning by, 192–93, 194–95, 199–201; German General Staff coordination with, 12, 201–6; motivation of, 201–2; replaced by Schemua, 203–4; Sprecher Affair and, 272
conscription, 103, 105, 312
Conseil supérieur de la défense nationale (CSDN; France), 212, 213, 214, 221, 222, 235n31
Conte, Arthur, 233n14
continentalism, 297–304, 308, 309, 310–14
Convention of 1888, 277–78, 279
Convention of 1898, 278
counterattack doctrine, 98–100, 129n103
Cowans, John, 307
Crewe, Lord, 296

Crisis of 1848, 323–24
Crispi, Francesco, 277
Crowe, Eyre, 300
cult of the offensive, 19, 211
Curragh Mutiny (1914), 297, 300
customs unions, 325
Czernin, Otto, 20

Daniels, Emil, 26
Danilov, Yuri N., 225, 249, 251, 253
Defense Bill (1899), 104
Delcassé, Théophile, 24, 222, 229–30
Delian League, 27
Demasur, Louis-Lucien, 325, 326
Demer River, 333
Denkschrift für einen Krieg gegen Frankreich (Schlieffen memorandum; 1905), 1, 5–6, 7, 10, 11, 70; campaign plan in, 86; facsimiles of, 90–91, 125n61; first post-WWI citation of, 90; German Army expansion as main objective of, 85–86, 103–5; as infeasible, 105–8; Moltke's marginal notes, 91, 117–18; as operational plan, 95, 108–11; original version, 90–92; post-WWI controversy over, 88; Ritter edition, 85, 88, 90, 125n61; storage of, 85, 87, 90–92, 96, 97–98, 120n4, 124n46; Switzerland as non-objective in, 264–65, 284. *See also* Schlieffen Plan
Denmark, 416, 469–70, 487, 506, 520
"Deployment and Operational Intentions of the French in a Future German-French War" (General Staff study), 63n22
deployment directives (*Aufmarschanweisungen*), 11, 87, 139–41, 142–45, 497–502
deployment files (*Aufmarschakten*), 87, 341, 342

deployment folder (*Aufmarschmappe*), 96
deployment maps (*Aufmarschkarten*), 88, 342
deployment plans (*Aufmarschpläne*; *Aufmarschplanungen*): 1896–1897, 107, 354–55; 1897–1898, 356–59; 1898–1899, 360–65; 1899–1900, 99, 366–76; 1900–1901, 377–83; 1901–1902, 100, 384–92; 1902–1903, 109, 113, 393–400; 1903–1904, 113, 401–8; 1904–1905, 409–15; 1905–1906, 73, 109, 174–75, 416–23; 1906–1907, 97, 106, 107–8, 111, 116–17, 132–33n154, 343, 424–35; 1907–1908, 343, 436–46; 1908–1909, 56, 118, 343, 447–55; 1909–1910, 63n26, 118, 141, 204, 345n13, 456–70; 1910–1911, 471–83; 1911–1912, 342, 484–96; 1913–1914, 63n30, 118, 343, 503–16; 1914–1915, 57–59, 342, 343; destruction of, at end of mobilization year, 87, 95, 96; existence of confirmed, 95–96, 341–42; original versions of, 344; storage of, 96, 341–42. *See also* Aufmarsch I (State of War with France Only); Aufmarsch II (State of War with Russia and France)
deployment table drafts, 356, 360
deployment tables, 366
Deputy General Command (Germany), 358
Deputy General Command I (Germany), 414, 422
Deputy General Command II (Germany), 359, 414, 415, 422, 423, 445, 466, 482
Deputy General Command V (Germany), 359, 383, 414, 415, 423, 445, 466, 482
Deputy General Command VI (Germany), 359, 383, 414, 415, 423, 445, 466, 482
Deputy General Command IX (Germany), 422, 435
Deputy General Command XIV (Germany), 422, 437, 443
Deputy General Command XVII (Germany), 414, 422
Deuringer, Karl, 141–42, 153
Deutsche Revue, 3–4
De Vos, Luc, 13
Dieckmann, Wilhelm: access to Schlieffen's papers, 88; career background of, 126n70; Foerster and, 107; on German defense expenditures, 134n173; on Schlieffen and political considerations, 111–13, 135n181; on Schlieffen and preventitive war, 60 n1; Schlieffen criticized by, 131n132; writings of, 86, 103–4, 127n79; Zuber thesis and, 68–71, 86, 92–95, 96, 98, 99, 103–4, 107, 108, 109, 111
Diedenhofen (Lorraine), 109, 132n154, 465, 479, 520, 523
Diest (Belgium), 333
Dieuze (France), 163, 164
Dilke, Charles, 299
"Directives for Covering the Deployment of the German Eastern Army in 1903–1904," 406–7
"Directives for Covering the Deployment of the German Western Army in 1903–1904," 401–3
Directives for the Security of the *Aufmarsch* of the German Western Army *Westheer* (booklet), 360
"Directives for the Security of the Deployment of an Army Marshaling in Schleswig Holstein," 516

D'Ombrain, Nicholas, 294, 295
Dommes zu Handen, Wilhelm von, 151, 152, 181n84, 265–66, 267
Double Alliance, 21, 265
Doumergue, Gaston, 217–18, 228
Douzy (France), 331
Dual Alliance, 79, 268. *See also* France; Russia
Dubail, Auguste, 147, 158, 214
Du Cane, John P., 307
Dupont, Charles, 233n13
Durnovo, Petr G., 251
Duruy, Louis, 328
Düsseldorf (Germany), 132n154
Dutch Army, 331, 419
Duties of the General Staff, The (Bronsart von Schellendorff), 299
Dyle River, 335

Eastern Army: deployment plans 1906–1907, 425, 434; deployment plans 1907–1908, 437, 445–46; deployment plans 1909–1910, 466–69; deployment plans 1910–1911, 480–83; deployment plans 1911–1912, 493–95; leadership of, 455n11
Eastern Deployment Plan, 64n39, 69
East German Army, military archives of, 88, 96
East Prussia, 156, 198, 199, 205, 214, 220, 224–27, 252, 255–57, 466, 481, 493, 514–15
École supérieur de la guerre, 224
Eghezée (Belgium), 335
Egli, Karl, 273
Egypt, 22
Egyptian Army, 306
Egyptian Campaign (1882), 298, 301, 310
Eichhorn, Hermann von, 455n10
XVIII Article Treaty (1831), 321–22
XVIII Army Corps (Germany):
deployment plans 1904–1905, 412; deployment plans 1905–1906, 420; deployment plans 1906–1907, 429; deployment plans 1907–1908, 436; deployment plans 1908–1909, 451; deployment plans 1909–1910, 465; deployment plans 1911–1912, 491
18th combined Landwehr Brigade (Germany), 515
18th Landwehr Brigade (Germany), 435
XVIII Reserve Corps (Germany), 429, 436, 437, 451, 465, 491
Eighth Army (Germany): deployment plans 1897–1898, 359; deployment plans 1898–1899, 365; deployment plans 1899–1900, 367, 368, 369, 370, 375, 375n1; deployment plans 1900–1901, 382–83; deployment plans 1901–1902, 385, 386–87, 392; deployment plans 1902–1903, 399; deployment plans 1903–1904, 407–8; deployment plans 1904–1905, 413–15; deployment plans 1905–1906, 416, 421; deployment plans 1906–1907, 111, 425, 426, 431; deployment plans 1913–1914, 504–5, 506, 507, 514–16; mobilization schedules 1914–1915, 518
VIII Army Corps (Germany): deployment directives 1912, 500; deployment plans 1897–1898, 356; deployment plans 1898–1899, 360–62; deployment plans 1901–1902, 385, 389; deployment plans 1903–1904, 401, 402, 403; deployment plans 1904–1905, 410, 411–12; deployment plans 1905–1906, 417–18, 421; deployment plans 1906–1907, 429; deployment plans 1907–1908, 436; deployment plans 1908–1909, 451; deployment plans

1909–1910, 460, 465; deployment plans 1913–1914, 504
VIII Army Corps (Italy), 374
8th Cavalry Division (Germany):
deployment directives 1912, 498;
deployment plans 1903–1904, 401;
deployment plans 1905–1906, 419;
deployment plans 1907–1908, 439;
deployment plans 1908–1909, 449;
deployment plans 1911–1912, 487;
deployment plans 1913–1914, 509;
mobilization schedules 1914–1915, 518
VIII Ersatz Corps (Germany), 518
VIII Reserve Corps (Germany), 431, 436, 437, 451, 465
Einem, Karl von, 104, 105, 132n139
"Einige Bemerkungen über die Entstehungsgeschichte des Schlieffenplans" (Dieckmann), 94, 127n79
Elbe River, 99
XI Army Corps (Germany):
deployment directives 1912, 497;
deployment plans 1904–1905, 412;
deployment plans 1905–1906, 420;
deployment plans 1906–1907, 429;
deployment plans 1907–1908, 436;
deployment plans 1908–1909, 450;
deployment plans 1910–1911, 473
11th combined Landwehr Brigade (Germany), 499
11th Reserve Division (Germany), 422
XI Reserve Corps (Germany), 421, 427
Elisabeth (Queen of Belgium), 336
Elze, Walter, 103
Encyclopedia Britannica, 298
Engis (Belgium), 335
Entente, 13
Entente Cordiale (1904), 22, 24, 216, 302
entrevues, 29

Epinal (France), 159, 175–76
Ersatz Army, 78–79, 149–50, 417, 425, 473, 496, 504–5, 507, 508, 518–19
Ersatzkorps, 105
Esher, Lord, 306–7
European System, 21, 25, 29–30, 231
Ewart, J. Spencer, 303

Falkenhausen, Ludwig von, 266
Falkenhayn, Erich von, 8, 9, 59, 161, 162
Feldeisenbahnwesen (Field Railway Service), 139
Ferguson, Niall, 18
Feste Kaiser Wilhelm II, 140
Field Army, 517–18
Field Railway Service, 524
Field Service Regulations, 308, 309, 311
XV Army Corps (Germany):
deployment directives 1912, 502;
deployment plans 1897–1898, 356; deployment plans 1898–1899, 360–62; deployment plans 1899–1900, 368, 369; deployment plans 1900–1901, 380–81; deployment plans 1901–1902, 385, 390; deployment plans 1903–1904, 401, 402; deployment plans 1904–1905, 410, 411–12; deployment plans 1905–1906, 418, 421–22; deployment plans 1906–1907, 425, 430, 432; deployment plans 1907–1908, 436, 438, 442, 444; deployment plans 1908–1909, 453; deployment plans 1909–1910, 460, 464, 465; deployment plans 1910–1911, 483n2; deployment plans 1911–1912, 490, 492; deployment plans 1913–1914, 509, 513; during Lorraine campaign, 140, 146, 159, 166; mobilization schedules 1914–1915, 524–25

Fifth Army (Germany): deployment directives 1912, 501; deployment plans 1896–1897, 355; deployment plans 1897–1898, 357–58; deployment plans 1898–1899, 363; deployment plans 1899–1900, 367, 368, 369, 373; deployment plans 1900–1901, 380–81; deployment plans 1901–1902, 386, 388, 391; deployment plans 1902–1903, 109, 394–95, 397; deployment plans 1903–1904, 405; deployment plans 1904–1905, 412; deployment plans 1905–1906, 99, 109, 416, 421, 452; deployment plans 1906–1907, 425, 426, 427; deployment plans 1907–1908, 438, 442; deployment plans 1908–1909, 448, 449; deployment plans 1909–1910, 463, 465; deployment plans 1910–1911, 475, 477–78, 479; deployment plans 1911–1912, 488, 490, 491; deployment plans 1913–1914, 507, 510, 512; leadership of, 455n8; Lorraine/Vosges operational objective, 140; mobilization schedules 1914–1915, 522, 523

Fifth Army (Russia), 469

V Army Corps (Germany): deployment directives 1912, 498; deployment plans 1901–1902, 385; deployment plans 1903–1904, 406, 407; deployment plans 1904–1905, 412; deployment plans 1905–1906, 416, 417, 420; deployment plans 1906–1907, 424, 429; deployment plans 1907–1908, 436; deployment plans 1908–1909, 452; deployment plans 1911–1912, 495

V Army Corps (Italy), 374

5th Bavarian Cavalry Division (Germany), 450

5th Bavarian Reserve Division (Germany), 421, 423n8

5th Cavalry Division (Germany): deployment directives 1912, 498; deployment plans 1905–1906, 419; deployment plans 1906–1907, 427; deployment plans 1907–1908, 439; deployment plans 1913–1914, 509; mobilization schedules 1914–1915, 518

5th combined Landwehr Brigade (Germany), 481

V Reserve Corps (Germany), 431, 436, 452, 466, 481, 498

5th Reserve Division (Germany), 412, 423n5

55th combined Landwehr Brigade (Germany), 504

First Army (Austria-Hungary), 200

First Army (France), 147, 153, 158–60, 170–71, 288n29, 432

First Army (Germany), 135n189; in Belgian war plans, 331–32; deployment directives 1912, 497, 498; deployment plans 1896–1897, 354; deployment plans 1897–1898, 356; deployment plans 1898–1899, 362; deployment plans 1899–1900, 366, 367, 368–69, 371; deployment plans 1900–1901, 378–79; deployment plans 1901–1902, 385, 386, 387, 390; deployment plans 1902–1903, 109, 393, 396; deployment plans 1903–1904, 403, 404; deployment plans 1904–1905, 409–10, 412; deployment plans 1905–1906, 109, 416, 420; deployment plans 1906–1907, 111, 132–33n154, 425, 426, 427; deployment plans 1907–1908, 343, 440; deployment plans 1908–1909, 448, 449, 450; deployment plans 1909–1910, 460–61, 467; deployment plans 1910–1911, 475–76, 481–82; deployment plans 1911–1912, 487, 488, 493–94; deployment plans 1913–1914, 510, 511; leadership of, 454n4; during Liège *coup de main*, 53, 63n30; mobilization schedules 1914–1915, 520–21

First Army (Russia), 257, 469

I Army Corps (France), 522

I Army Corps (Germany): deployment directives 1912, 498; deployment plans 1897–1898, 358; deployment plans 1900–1901, 378; deployment plans 1903–1904, 406–7; deployment plans 1904–1905, 412, 414; deployment plans 1905–1906, 416, 420; deployment plans 1906–1907, 424, 427; deployment plans 1907–1908, 436, 437, 445; deployment plans 1908–1909, 450; deployment plans 1909–1910, 466–67; deployment plans 1910–1911, 481; deployment plans 1913–1914, 509, 516

1st Army Detachment (Germany), 354

I Bavarian Army Corps (Germany): deployment plans 1904–1905, 413; deployment plans 1905–1906, 421; deployment plans 1906–1907, 430; deployment plans 1907–1908, 436; deployment plans 1908–1909, 452; deployment plans 1913–1914, 507; during Lorraine campaign, 140, 163, 168

I Bavarian Reserve Corps (Germany), 140, 421, 431, 436–37, 463

1st Bavarian Reserve Division (Germany), 413, 423n8

1st Cavalry Division (Germany): deployment directives 1912, 498; deployment plans 1905–1906, 418, 419; deployment plans 1906–1907, 427; deployment plans 1907–1908, 439, 445; deployment plans 1908–1909, 449; deployment plans 1910–1911, 481; deployment plans 1913–1914, 509, 516; mobilization schedules 1914–1915, 518

1st combined Bavarian Landwehr Brigade (Germany), 524

1st Guards Reserve Division (Germany), 437

I Reserve Corps (Germany), 420, 427; deployment directives 1912, 498; deployment plans 1907–1908, 436, 437, 445; deployment plans 1908–1909, 450, 452; deployment plans 1909–1910, 466; deployment plans 1910–1911, 481; deployment plans 1913–1914, 516

Fischer, Fritz, 2, 14n3, 76

Fisher, John A., 18, 295, 296

Foch, Ferdinand, 223, 224

Foerster, Wolfgang: access to Schlieffen's papers, 87; career background of, 5; critical reviews written by, 342; *Denkschrift* copy of, 90–91, 92, 125n52; *Denkschrift* marginal notes made by, 93, 107, 345n6; on *Denkschrift* purpose, 58; deployment records confirmed by, 95–96; Krafft and, 144; as Reich Archive director, 5–6; Ritter Schlieffen Plan publication and, 92; Schlieffen Plan feasibility and, 105–6; Schlieffen's papers and, 5–6; shorthand system used by, 345n6

Foley, Robert T., 10, 11, 86, 111, 113

Forgách, János, 20

Forrer, Ludwig, 270, 273–74, 289n40

Förster, Stig, 93, 103, 105

Fort de Manonviller, 148, 157, 158, 488, 510, 523

Fort de Mutzig, 479
45th combined Landwehr Brigade (Germany), 498
41st Infantry Division (Germany), 487
47th combined Landwehr Brigade (Germany), 498
43rd combined Landwehr Brigade (Germany), 497
Foster, Hubert, 308
477th Infantry Replacement Battalion (Germany), 126n70
XIV Army Corps (Germany): deployment directives 1912, 501–2; deployment plans 1897–1898, 356; deployment plans 1898–1899, 360–62; deployment plans 1900–1901, 378; deployment plans 1901–1902, 385; deployment plans 1903–1904, 403; deployment plans 1904–1905, 410, 413; deployment plans 1905–1906, 417, 418, 421–22; deployment plans 1906–1907, 425, 429, 430, 432; deployment plans 1907–1908, 436, 438, 444; deployment plans 1908–1909, 453, 454n1; deployment plans 1909–1910, 464, 466; deployment plans 1910–1911, 483n2; deployment plans 1911–1912, 490–91, 492; deployment plans 1913–1914, 507, 509, 513; during Lorraine campaign, 140, 146, 168; mobilization schedules 1914–1915, 524–25
14th Infantry Division (Germany), 487, 511
XIV Reserve Corps (Germany): deployment plans 1907–1908, 436–37; deployment plans 1908–1909, 453; deployment plans 1909–1910, 464, 466; deployment plans 1910–1911, 483n2; deployment plans 1911–1912, 491, 492; deployment plans 1913–1914, 507, 513; during Lorraine campaign, 140; mobilization schedules 1914–1915, 525

Fourth Army (France), 433
Fourth Army (Germany): deployment directives 1912, 497, 499; deployment plans 1896–1897, 354; deployment plans 1897–1898, 357; deployment plans 1898–1899, 363; deployment plans 1899–1900, 99, 366, 367, 368–69, 372; deployment plans 1900–1901, 380; deployment plans 1901–1902, 386, 388; deployment plans 1902–1903, 109, 394, 397; deployment plans 1903–1904, 405; deployment plans 1904–1905, 409–10, 412; deployment plans 1905–1906, 109, 416–17, 420, 425; deployment plans 1906–1907, 426, 427, 429; deployment plans 1907–1908, 441, 442; deployment plans 1908–1909, 448, 449, 451; deployment plans 1909–1910, 462, 468; deployment plans 1910–1911, 475, 477; deployment plans 1911–1912, 488, 489, 494, 495; deployment plans 1913–1914, 507, 510, 512; leadership of, 455n7; mobilization schedules 1914–1915, 522
Fourth Army (Russia), 469
IV Army Corps (Germany): deployment directives 1912, 497; deployment plans 1901–1902, 385; deployment plans 1904–1905, 412; deployment plans 1905–1906, 417, 420; deployment plans 1906–1907, 425, 428; deployment plans 1907–1908, 436; deployment plans 1908–1909, 450; deployment plans 1910–1911, 473; deployment plans 1913–1914, 504

4th Cavalry Division (Germany): deployment directives 1912, 498, 499; deployment plans 1905–1906, 418, 419; deployment plans 1906–1907, 427; deployment plans 1907–1908, 439; deployment plans 1908–1909, 449; deployment plans 1911–1912, 487, 493; deployment plans 1913–1914, 509; mobilization schedules 1914–1915, 518

IV Ersatz Corps (Germany), 518

4th Infantry Division (Belgium), 335

IV Reserve Corps (Germany), 427, 436–37, 451, 497

France: alliance-/bloc-building by, 21, 22–23, 24–26, 38n48, 77, 213, 216; BEF deployment in, 296; Belgian independence guaranteed by, 321, 324, 325; as Belgian threat, 323; in Belgian war plans, 330; border fortifications of, 48, 70, 78, 85, 97, 116, 138, 159; in British war plans, 306, 312–13; détente/rapprochement efforts of, 26–27, 39n62; German ultimatum to, 336; German war plan and, 44–45, 58, 98, 108–9, 252–53, 409, 416, 424, 436, 456–57, 471–72, 485, 499–500, 502, 503, 517 (*see also* Aufmarsch I [State of War with France Only]; Aufmarsch II [State of War with Russia and France]; Schlieffen Plan); Great Britain as Entente partner of, 13; Moltke Plan vs. Schlieffen Plan operations against, 46–51, 55–57, 62n9; Napoleonic-era, 319–20; operational planning of, 9, 58, 63n22, 252 (*see also* Plan XVII [France]); railroads in, 155; Revolution of 1830, 320–20; in Russian war plans, 252–53; in Schlieffen Plan, 210; statecraft/military tradecraft relationship in, 18, 19–21; Swiss neutrality and, 264–65, 275–76; in Swiss operational planning, 268–70, 271; two-front war scenario and, 114–20

Franckenstein, Georg von, 20

Franco-Austro-Italian War (1859), 324–25

Franco-German War (1870–1871), 78, 193, 298, 299, 323, 325

Franco-Russian Alliance (1892–1917), 3, 4, 12–13, 21, 24, 55, 249

Franz, Gunther, 256

Franz Ferdinand (Archduke of Austria): assassination of, 4, 20, 319, 336; Austro-Hungarian operational planning and, 195–96; official function of, 195; as successor to the throne, 195

Franz Joseph I (Emperor of Austria), 190, 195, 196

Frauendienst, Werner, 92

French, John, 297

French Army, 56, 288n29; artillery as used by, 184n134; Chasseurs Alpines units, 165; combat power of, 236n37; German war plan and, 133n161, 432–33, 487, 519–20, 522; Lorraine/Vosges offensive of, 149–50, 184n133, 220–24; materiel deficiencies, 233–34n17; mobilization speed of, 115, 129n98; numerical superiority of, 99–100, 146–47, 149, 214, 234n22; Plan XVII, 12; Russian consultations with, 252; Schlieffen Plan operational objective against, 1, 11, 97, 108, 116, 264

French Army—armies: First Army, 147, 153, 158–60, 170–71, 288n29, 432; Second Army, 146, 147, 153–54, 170–71, 233n17, 433; Third Army, 433; Fourth Army, 433

French Army—corps: I Army Corps, 522; II Army Corps, 522; VI Army Corps, 433; VII Army Corps, 432
French Foreign Ministry, 213, 221, 222
French General Staff: British consultations with, 223, 293, 294, 303; foreknowledge of German intentions, 210–11; Joffre as chief of, 211; *offensive à outrance* planned by, 212, 214, 220–24, 231, 233–34n17; operational planning of (*see* Plan XVII [France]); Russian consultations with, 234n22, 252, 256–57
French Navy Ministry, 222
French-Swiss, 273
French War Ministry, 222
Freytag-Loringhoven, Hugo von, 2
Frieser, Karl-Heinz, 6
From Private to Field Marshal (Robertson), 302
Fuhrer, Hans Rudolf, 13
Fuller, William, 232n7, 251, 252

Galet, Emile, 335
Galicia, 202–3, 205–6, 252, 253, 254, 255, 257
Gatrell, Peter, 257
Gebhardt, Hans, 345n6
Gebsattel, Ludwig von, 160
General Command VIII (Germany), 378
General Command XV (Germany), 422
General Command XVI (Germany), 410
Generals (TV documentary), 137
General Staff rides (*Generalstabsreisen*), 11; after-action analysis sessions, 130n116; archival storage of, 123n36; details of, in enemy hands, 82n30; disagreements during, 128n92; in the East (*Generalstabreisen im Osten*; 1901), 88, 115; envelopment idea and, 108–9, 110–11; France as objective in, 101–3; German force strength assumptions during, 106–7; officer training during, 129–30n112; political foundations of, 134n177; records of, 87, 89–90; Schlieffen's use of, 71–73, 81n27, 101–3, 129–30n112; in the West (*Generalstabreisen im Westen*; 1904), 117, 128n92; in the West (*Generalstabreisen im Westen*; 1905), 89–90, 101–3, 124n39, 130n120; in Zuber thesis, 71–73, 101, 106–7
Geneva (Switzerland), 269, 270
Génie, Eugène, 328
George, Lloyd, 312
German Army: archives of (*see* Army Archive [*Heeresarchiv*; Potsdam]); artillery types in, 131n128; Belgian defense planning against, 330–36; combat power of, 99, 114, 117, 236n37, 251; deficiencies of, 121n7; development of, 94, 131n132; HQ Brandenburg, 509; HQ Nancy, 509; as insufficient for Schlieffen Plan, 105–8; leadership crisis in, 171–74; mobilization speed of, 129n98; operational/strategic planning for, 87; organizational structure of, 173–74; peacetime strength of, 132n149; Russian military intelligence on, 252; Schlieffen Plan and expansion of, 85–86, 103–5; strength of, 62n8, 214. *See also specific military unit*
German Army—armies: First Army (*see* First Army [Germany]); Second Army (*see* Second Army [Germany]); Third Army (*see* Third

Army [Germany]); Fourth Army (*see* Fourth Army [Germany]); Fifth Army (*see* Fifth Army [Germany]); Sixth Army (*see* Sixth Army [Germany]); Seventh Army (*see* Seventh Army [Germany]); Eighth Army (*see* Eighth Army [Germany])

German Army—battalions: 477th Infantry Replacement Battalion, 126n70

German Army—brigades: 1st combined Bavarian Landwehr Brigade, 524; 2nd combined Bavarian Landwehr Brigade, 524; 2nd combined Landwehr Brigade, 481, 499, 516; 5th combined Landwehr Brigade, 481; 6th combined Landwehr Brigade, 481, 515; 10th combined Landwehr Brigade, 498; 11th combined Landwehr Brigade, 499; 13th combined Landwehr Brigade, 497; 18th combined Landwehr Brigade, 515; 18th Landwehr Brigade, 435; 21st Landwehr Brigade, 435, 514; 22nd combined Landwehr Brigade, 481, 514, 515; 23rd combined Landwehr Brigade, 481, 514, 515; 33rd combined Landwehr Brigade, 518; 34th combined Landwehr Brigade, 417, 425, 435, 518; 37th combined Landwehr Brigade, 518; 38th combined Landwehr Brigade, 518; 43rd combined Landwehr Brigade, 497; 45th combined Landwehr Brigade, 498; 47th combined Landwehr Brigade, 498; 55th combined Landwehr Brigade, 504; 70th combined Landwehr Brigade, 481, 498, 515; 77th Infantry Brigade, 513

German Army—commanding units: Bavarian Army Supreme Command, 142; Deputy General Command, 358; Deputy General Command I, 414, 422; Deputy General Command II, 359, 414, 415, 422, 423, 445, 466, 482; Deputy General Command IX, 422; Deputy General Command V, 359, 383, 414, 415, 423, 445, 466, 482; Deputy General Command VI, 359, 383, 414, 415, 423, 445, 466, 482; Deputy General Command IX, 435; Deputy General Command XIV, 422, 437, 443; Deputy General Command XVII, 414, 422; General Command VIII, 378; General Command XV, 422; General Command XVI, 410; Senior Cavalry Commander 1 (*see* Senior Cavalry Commander 1 [Germany]); Senior Cavalry Commander 2, 418, 427, 439, 449, 475, 498, 510, 521; Senior Cavalry Commander 3 (*see* Senior Cavalry Commander 3 [Germany]); Senior Cavalry Commander 4, 491, 510, 522–23; Senior Cavalry Commander East, 385; Senior Cavalry Commanders, 404, 411; Senior Cavalry Commander West, 385; Senior Landwehr Commander 1, 504, 516, 518; Senior Landwehr Commander 2, 512; Senior Landwehr Commander 9, 518

German Army—corps: I Army Corps (*see* I Army Corps [Germany]); I Bavarian Army Corps, 140, 163, 168, 413, 421, 430, 436, 452, 507; I Bavarian Reserve Corps, 140, 421, 431, 436–37, 463; I Reserve Corps (*see* I Reserve Corps [Germany]); II Army Corps (*see* II Army Corps

German Army—corps *(cont.)* [Germany]); II Bavarian Corps, 140, 157, 385, 412, 421, 430, 436, 452, 506; II Cavalry Corps, 407; III Army Corps (*see* III Army Corps [Germany]); III Bavarian Corps, 140, 413, 421, 430, 436, 452, 507; IV Army Corps (*see* IV Army Corps [Germany]); IV Ersatz Corps, 518; IV Reserve Corps, 427, 436–37, 451, 497; V Army Corps (*see* V Army Corps [Germany]); V Reserve Corps, 431, 436, 452, 466, 481, 498; VI Army Corps (*see* VI Army Corps [Germany]); VI Reserve Corps, 430, 436, 437, 445, 452, 466, 481, 498; VII Army Corps (*see* VII Army Corps [Germany]); VII Reserve Corps, 427, 436, 437, 450, 465, 511; VIII Army Corps (*see* VIII Army Corps [Germany]); VIII Ersatz Corps, 518; VIII Reserve Corps, 431, 436, 437, 451, 465; IX Army Corps (*see* IX Army Corps [Germany]); IX Ersatz Corps, 426, 435; IX Reserve Corps (*see* IX Reserve Corps [Germany]); X Army Corps (*see* X Army Corps [Germany]); X Ersatz Corps, 518; X Reserve Corps, 436–37, 450, 499; XI Army Corps, 412, 420, 429, 436, 450, 473, 497; XI Reserve Corps, 421, 427; XII Army Corps, 385, 417, 421, 425, 429, 436, 451, 473, 498; XII Reserve Corps, 431, 436–37, 451, 498; XIII Army Corps, 421, 430, 436, 452, 465; XIII Reserve Corps, 420, 429; XIV Army Corps (*see* XIV Army Corps [Germany]); XIV Reserve Corps (*see* XIV Reserve Corps [Germany]); XV Army Corps (*see* XV Army Corps [Germany]); XVI Army Corps (*see* XVI Army Corps [Germany]); XVII Army Corps (*see* XVII Army Corps [Germany]); XVII Reserve Corps, 420; XVIII Army Corps, 412, 420, 429, 436, 451, 465, 491; XVIII Reserve Corps, 429, 436, 437, 451, 465, 491; XIX Army Corps, 385, 417, 421, 425, 436, 451, 473, 487, 498, 504; XIX Ersatz Corps, 518; XX Army Corps (*see* XX Army Corps [Germany]); XXI Army Corps (*see* XXI Army Corps [Germany]); Bavarian Reserve Corps, 507; Guards Army Corps, 412, 425, 429, 436, 451, 473, 499, 504, 506; Guards Ersatz Corps, 426, 518; Guards Reserve Army Corps, 412, 429, 436, 437, 451, 499

German Army—divisions: 1st Bavarian Reserve Division, 413, 423n8; 1st Cavalry Division, 418, 419, 427, 439, 445, 449, 481, 498, 509, 516, 518; 1st Guards Reserve Division, 437; 2nd Cavalry Division, 418, 427, 439, 445, 449, 481, 498, 509, 518; 2nd Guards Reserve Division, 436, 437; 2nd Reserve Division, 422, 423n6; 3rd Cavalry Division, 401, 419, 427, 432, 439, 449, 509; 3rd Infantry Division, 417; 3rd Reserve Division, 420, 423n3, 480, 481, 498, 515, 518; 4th Cavalry Division (*see* 4th Cavalry Division [Germany]); 5th Bavarian Cavalry Division, 450; 5th Bavarian Reserve Division, 421, 423n8; 5th Cavalry Division, 419, 427, 439, 498, 509, 518; 5th Reserve Division, 412, 423n5; 6th Cavalry Division, 401, 419, 427, 439, 449, 509, 518; 6th Reserve Division, 412, 422, 423n5; 7th Bavarian Cavalry

Index 555

Division, 450; 7th Cavalry Division, 374, 401, 419, 440, 465, 509, 518; 7th Reserve Division, 412, 420, 423n3; 8th Cavalry Division, 401, 419, 439, 449, 487, 498, 509, 518; 9th Cavalry Division, 401, 418, 419, 423n4, 427, 439, 449, 518; 9th Reserve Division, 422, 423n4, 423n6; 11th Reserve Division, 422; 12th Infantry Division, 487; 13th Infantry Division, 487; 13th Reserve Division, 412; 14th Infantry Division, 487, 511; 16th Infantry Division, 378, 402, 410, 418; 17th combined Landwehr Division, 481, 515; 17th Reserve Division, 412; 22nd Reserve Division, 420, 423n2; 23rd Reserve Division, 413, 421, 423n7; 24th Infantry Division, 413, 421, 423n7, 487; 26th Reserve Division, 413, 421, 423n9, 430–31, 464; 28th Reserve Division, 413, 421, 423n9, 430–31, 464; 29th Infantry Division, 412, 464, 491, 524; 30th Infantry Division, 487; 33rd Infantry Division, 410; 34th Infantry Division, 410, 418; 35th Infantry Division, 469; 39th Infantry Division, 418, 464, 490–91, 513; 41st Infantry Division, 487; Bavarian Cavalry Division, 401, 419; Bavarian Ersatz Division, 504, 518; Guards Cavalry Division, 401, 418, 419, 427, 439, 449, 499, 518

German Army—regiments: 9th Infantry Regiment, 126n70

German Council of State, 113

German Foreign Office, 2, 28, 44, 134n177, 505, 519

German High Seas Fleet, 7, 22

Germanism, 281–83, 292n82

German Navy, 434, 459, 504

German Navy Admiralty Staff, 403

German Railway Administration, 290n58

German Reich, 17; alliance-/bloc-building by, 21–26, 192, 268 (*see also* Triple Alliance); Austro-Hungarian agreements/cooperation with, 196, 198–200, 265; in Belgian war plans, 330–36; in British war plans, 223–24, 305–6; declaration of war, 257; détente/rapprochement efforts of, 26–30, 76, 112–13, 134n172; "encirclement" of, 54–55, 77; foundation myth of, 78; in French war plans, 224–31; geographic position of, 3, 4, 45–46, 54–55, 114, 115; Italian troop passage to, 272, 276–80; railroads in, 266, 327; relations with Switzerland, 13; in Russian war plans, 249–50, 251, 252–53, 254–57; Sprecher's relationship with, 273; statecraft/military tradecraft relationship in, 17; in Swiss operational planning, 268–70; Switzerland/Swiss as viewed in, 281–83; unification of (1871), 114; as world power, 14n3; WWI defeat of, 51; *Zollverein* (customs union), 325

German Reichbahn, 267

German reunification, 88

German-Swiss, 273, 281, 285

German War Ministry, 46, 77, 79, 103–5, 117, 519

German War Planning 1891–1914 (Dieckmann), 92–93

Germany, Federal Republic of, 6

Germany, Weimar Republic: Russian spies in, 251

Gertsch (German-Swiss officer), 273

Gete River, 333, 335, 336
Gilgenheimb, Leopold von, 455n9
Givet (Belgium), 462, 475
Gladbach (Germany), 327
Gneisenau, August Neidhardt von, 183n119
Goltz, Colmar von der, 455n11
Gooch, John, 294, 295
Görlitz, Walter, 92
Graf Schlieffen und der Weltkrieg (Foerster), 5
Grand Couronné, 157, 170–71
Graudenz (East Prussia), 359
Great Britain: alliance-/bloc-building by, 22–26, 38n48, 54, 77, 216, 303; Belgian independence guaranteed by, 321, 322, 325; Continental commitment of, 13; détente/rapprochement efforts of, 28–30, 39nn62, 79, 112–13; entrance into WWI, 19, 53, 135n188, 262, 336; France as Entente partner of, 13; in French war plans, 211–12, 215–21, 223–24, 231, 312–13; German war plan and, 45, 57, 65n56, 76–77, 98, 427, 439, 456, 457, 459, 471, 503, 505, 517, 520; operational planning of, 9; public opinion in, 217–18; statecraft/military tradecraft relationship in, 17, 18–19; in Swiss operational planning, 268; trade competitors, 321. *See also* British entries
Greiner, Helmut, 86, 110
Grey, Edward, 23, 24–25, 28, 216–18, 293, 296, 336
Grierson, James M., 298, 300–301, 302, 305–6, 310
Griff nach der Weltmacht (Fischer), 14n3
Grigorovič, Ivan K., 248
Groener, Wilhelm, 136n195; access to Schlieffen's papers, 88; Boetticher and, 92, 123n30, 123n35; career background of, 5; *Denkschrift* copy of, 90, 125n52; Krafft criticized by, 138–39; Lorraine/Vosges campaign criticized by, 150, 155; on Marne failure, 59; on Moltke, 46; on Schlieffen Plan alterations, 61n6; as Schlieffen supporter, 5, 45
Gross, Gerhard P., 10, 11, 15n13, 60n1
Grosser Ostaufmarsch, 55, 63n26, 204
Guards Army Corps (Germany): deployment directives 1912, 499; deployment plans 1904–1905, 412; deployment plans 1906–1907, 425, 429; deployment plans 1907–1908, 436; deployment plans 1908–1909, 451; deployment plans 1910–1911, 473; deployment plans 1913–1914, 504, 506
Guards Cavalry Division (Germany): deployment directives 1912, 499; deployment plans 1903–1904, 401; deployment plans 1905–1906, 418, 419; deployment plans 1906–1907, 427; deployment plans 1907–1908, 439; deployment plans 1908–1909, 449; mobilization schedules 1914–1915, 518
Guards Ersatz Corps (Germany), 426, 518
Guards Reserve Army Corps (Germany), 412, 429, 436, 437, 451, 499
Gündell, Erich von, 455n8

Habsburg Empire, 195, 196, 251
Habsburg Monarchy, 189, 190, 192–93, 198, 214. *See also* Austria-Hungary
Haeften, Hans von, 92, 135n188, 152
Haffner, Sebastian, 137
Hagenau (Alsace), 357

Hague Laws of Land Warfare, The, 325, 328
Hahnke, Anna Josefa von, 91, 125n57
Hahnke, Elizabeth von, 70, 91, 92, 120n4, 124n46
Hahnke, Wilhelm von, 62n9, 70, 90, 91, 97–98, 102, 113, 123–24n37, 124n39, 125n61, 136n195
Haig, Douglas, 303–4, 309, 311
Haillot, Charles, 327
Haldane, Richard Burdon, 293–94, 295, 304
Haldane Mission (1912), 29, 61n5
Halder, Franz, 92, 286
Hamelrijck, Auguste, 330
Hamilton, Ian, 308
Hamme-Mille (Belgium), 335
Hankey, Maurice, 295
Hannuit (Belgium), 334, 335
Hanover (Germany), 506
Harcourt, Lewis, 296
Hardinge, Charles, 24–25, 304
Hartington Commission, 301
Hasse, Ernst, 282–83
Hasselt (Belgium), 335
Hausen, Max von, 59–60
Haussman, Conrad, 4
Heeringen, Josias von, 145, 147–48, 166, 168
Henderson, G. F. R., 302, 311
Herentals (Belgium), 332
Herr, Georges Frédéric, 160, 184n133
Hertling, Georg von, 49
Herwig, Holger, 65n67
Heusinger, Adolf, 8
High Command West (Germany), 385, 464, 478–79, 500
Higher Cavalry Command 3, 140, 158
Hildebrand, Klaus, 9–10
Hindenburg, Paul von, 5, 89, 454n4
Hintze, Paul von, 23
Hitler, Adolf, 6

Hitler-Stalin Pact (1939), 93
Hoegaarden (Belgium), 335
Hohenzollern, Karl von, 329
Holland. *See* Netherlands
Holmes, Terence, 68, 71, 86, 106
Holstein, Friedrich von, 2, 76, 112, 134n177
Hordlicka, Eugen, 271–72
Houtaîn-l'Evêque (Belgium), 334
Hoyos, Alexander, 20
Huy (Belgium), 462, 489, 505, 519

Ideology of the Offensive, The (Snyder), 232n7
Imperial Defence (Wilkinson), 299
Imperialist System, 30–34
Imperial Royal *Landwehr* (Austria), 189. *See also* Austro-Hungarian Imperial and Royal Army (*K.u.K.* Army)
Imperial Territories (*Reichslande*), 138; Deployment Directives in, 139–41, 142–45; German leadership in, 141–42. *See also* Lorraine/Vosges campaign (1914)
India, 299, 300, 302, 306
Indian Army, 303, 304, 309
Indian General Staff, 304
Insterburg–Rothfliess railroad, 493
Interwar Era, 79
Inventing the Schlieffen Plan (Zuber), 14
Irvine, Dallas D., 296
Italian Army, 140, 272; deployment directives 1912, 501–2; deployment plans 1899–1900, 374; deployment plans 1900–1901, 378; deployment plans 1901–1902, 385; deployment plans 1903–1904, 403; deployment plans 1905–1906, 417; deployment plans 1906–1907, 425, 432; deployment plans 1907–1908, 438; deployment plans 1909–1910,

Italian Army *(cont.)*
  345n13, 458; deployment plans 1910–1911, 472; deployment plans 1914–1915, 343; mobilization schedules 1914–1915, 517, 520; Switzerland and, 272, 276–80, 290nn59–60
Italian Army—corps: V Army Corps, 374; VI Army Corps, 374; VIII Army Corps, 374; IX Army Corps, 374, 378; X Army Corps, 374
Italian Army—divisions: 2nd Cavalry Division, 374, 432; 3rd Cavalry Division, 374, 518
Italian General Staff, 276, 277, 278, 343, 385, 517
Italian High Command, 366
Italian Naval Ministry, 403
Italy: Africa expeditionary force of, 213; alliance-/bloc-building by, 204, 213, 216, 268 *(see also* Triple Alliance); annexationist policy of, 272; in Austro-Hungarian war plans, 190, 191–92, 199–201; border forces of, 213–14, 235n31; Franco-Austro-Italian War (1859), 324–25; in French war plans, 213–15, 224, 235n31; German intelligence on, 265; German war plan and, 503, 517; independence war of, 324–25; naval blockade of, 277; Schlieffen's view of, 279; in Swiss operational planning, 268–69, 270, 271
Italy: The Least of the Great Powers (Bosworth), 234n25
Izvol'skiy, Aleksandr P., 28, 213, 214, 217, 218, 256

Jäger battalions (Germany), 521, 522–23
Jagow, Gottlieb von, 136n196
Japan, 21, 22, 77, 158, 185n171, 303.

  See also Russo-Japanese War (1904–1905)
Jäschke, Gotthard, 92
Jews, 254
Joffre (Conte), 233n14
Joffre, Joseph, 18, 19; Belgian neutrality respected by, 288n28; biographers of, 233n14; on British intervention timing, 219; Castelnau appointed deputy chief of staff by, 211; as French General Staff chief, 211, 212; German railroad system studied by, 266; Lorraine/Vosges campaign (1914), 147, 150, 153, 157, 160–61, 170–71; memoirs of, 212, 234n22, 266; operational planning by, 220–21, 222–23, 227, 228, 234n22; restraining orders given by, 58; Russian consultations with, 252
Jomini, 311
Journal for Military History, 60n2
journalism, 191
July (1914) Crisis, 9–10, 12–13, 17–18, 20, 24–25, 29, 33, 196, 209, 227, 231, 248, 312
Jura Mountains, 262–63, 264
Jutland (Germany), 459, 469

Kaiser maneuvers, 130n112, 272, 284–85
Kant, Immanuel, 32
Keller, Arnold, 269–70
Kennan, George F., 6
Kenworthy, J. M., 18
Kessel, Eberhard, 92
key taskings (*Schlussaufgaben*), 87, 89, 100–101
KGFA files, 80n8
Kiderlen-Wächter, Alfred von, 28
Kiel Canal, 422, 425, 434, 500, 504
Kiel Imperial War Port, 434
Kiessling, Friedrich, 26, 27, 30

Kiev Military District, 250–51, 252
Kitchener, Horatio, 297, 303
Kluck, von (General), 130n120
Knötel, Richard, 301
Kokovtsov, Vladimir N., 252–53
Kolster, Walter, 134n178
Königsberg (East Prussia), 467, 505
Köpke, Martin, 78
Korfes, Otto, 93, 126n70
Krafft von Dellmensingen, Konrad von: on "bag maneuver," 181n66; biographers of, 139; correspondence of, 144–45; critical reviews written by, 342; criticism directed at, 138–39, 143–44, 152–53, 154–55; as Imperial Territories force commander, 141–42; Lorraine/Vosges deployment orders and, 142–45; Lorraine/Vosges Moselle/Nancy attack, 161, 163–64, 166, 167–70, 171, 172; Lorraine/Vosges offensive and, 151–54; Lorraine/Vosges uncertainties and, 148–49; Moltke the Younger and, 178–79n27; as Sixth Army chief of staff, 138, 178n27; troop morale and, 148; war diary of, 167, 184n138
Krauss, Alfred, 197
Kreppel, Otto, 162
"Krieg gegen das mit England verbündete Frankreich" (Groener Denkschrift version), 125n52
"Krieg gegen Frankreich" (Foerster Denkschrift version), 125n52
Kriegsrüstung und Kriegswirtschaft (Dieckmann et al.), 104, 126n70
Kriegsspiele. See war games (*Kriegsspiele*)
Kronenbitter, Günther, 12
Krumreich, Gerd, 220
Kuhl, Hermann von, 5, 72, 105, 130n120

K.u.K. Army. *See* Austro-Hungarian Imperial and Royal Army (*K.u.K.* Army)
Kusber, Jan, 12–13

labor unrest, 343
Lagoon Connection Line, 467
Lambi, Ivo N., 14n6
Landwehr Corps (Germany), 426
Lauenstein, Otto von, 75–76, 82n37
"Lehrmeister des neuzeitlichen Krieges, Der" (Boetticher), 342
Leopold II (King of Belgium), 323, 324, 326, 327, 328–29
Lerchenfeld, Hugo von und zu, 49–50
Leuven (Belgium), 333, 334, 336
Lichnowsky, Karl Max von, 163
Liddell Hart, Basil H., 299, 305, 313
Liège (Belgium): Belgian Army deployed at, 334–35; in Belgian war plans, 331, 334; fortifications at, 263, 326, 328, 335; German *coup de main* on, 45, 50, 52–53, 61n5, 118, 136n191; in German war plans, 343, 440–41, 447–48, 459, 460–61, 462, 470n1, 474, 486, 489, 505–6, 507, 510, 520–21; Moltke the Younger and, 136n191
Lithuania, 201
London (England), 310
London Conference (1867), 325
Longwy (France), 441, 463, 512, 523
Lorraine (France), 56, 118, 131n124, 487, 518
Lorraine, Battle of (1914), 11–12
Lorraine/Vosges campaign (1914): artillery used in, 158–60; "bag" trap (*Sackmanöver*) in, 148, 150, 151, 175, 179n39, 181n66; Battle of Mulhouse, 147, 149; casualties in, 176–77; controversy over, 138–39, 154–55; failure of, 167–

Lorraine/Vosges campaign *(cont.)* 68, 170–71; French offensive in, 143–44, 149–50, 156–57, 220–24, 264; German fortifications during, 159, 220; German leadership in, 141–42; German offensive in, 150–54; military significance of, 174–76; Moselle crossing, 161, 165–66; operational impact of, 137–38; operational objective of, 139–45; "Position de Nancy" attack, 161, 163–74; pursuit mission in, 154–58; in Russian war plans, 254; scholarship on, 139, 141–42; separation from western front, 137; trench warfare during, 160, 168; troop morale in, 148; uncertainties in, 145–50
Louis XVIII (King of France), 320
Ludendorff, Erich, 52, 61n6, 90, 96, 104–5, 144, 182n95
Ludwig III (King of Bavaria), 336
Lunéville (France), 475, 510
Luxembourg: Bismarck and, 325; as French buffer state, 320; French fortifications in, 99; French offensive in, 98–99; in French war plans, 220–21; German occupation of, 53, 57, 163; German war plan and, 44, 50, 98–99, 116, 264, 452, 465, 474, 486, 487, 506, 520; Lorraine/Vosges campaign (1914) and, 139–40; neutrality of, 50, 108, 323; OHL HQs in, 164; railroads in, 506; in Russian war plans, 254; Zuber thesis and, 98–99
Luzzati, Luigi, 289n40
Lwow (Galicia), 257
Lyttelton, Nelville, 306

Maaseik (Belgium), 332, 333
Maastricht (Netherlands), 331, 333, 520

machine guns, 3
Maglinse, Henri, 335
Malmedy (Belgium), 331
Manchuria, Japanese invasion of (1894), 158
Mantey, Friedrich von, 62n12
map exercises (*Winterarbeit*), 341
Marksmanship School (Walenstadt, Switzerland), 273
Marne, Battle of the (1914), 9; aftermath of, 171; German defeat at, 171, 173; German force strength during, 257; Lorraine/Vosges battles and, 137; Moltke as scapegoat for, 45, 51, 59; TV documentary on, 137; Zuber thesis concerning, 86
Marne River, 102
Marx, Wilhelm, 5
mass armies, 3–4
Masurian Lakes, 226
Matin (magazine), 230
Matthiass, Paul, 102, 454n4
Maubert-Fontaine (France), 331
Maurice, J. F., 297–98
McDermott, J., 294
McKenna, Reginald, 295–96
Mecheln (Belgium), 326, 333
media coverage, 191
Meinecke, Friedrich, 6
Mercier, Désiré-Joseph, 329
Mertz von Quirnheim, Hermann, 151; access to Schlieffen's papers, 87–88; Dieckmann as son-in-law of, 126n70; Krafft criticized by, 139, 141, 143–44, 154–55, 169; during Lorraine campaign, 150, 163, 167; Sixth Army leadership criticized by, 152–53
Mesopotamia Commission, 304
Messimy, Adolphe, 227
Metternich, Clemens von, 319–20
Metz (France), 56, 102, 111, 112, 117,

140, 149, 151, 159, 175–76, 220, 357, 437, 453, 463, 465, 479, 505, 520
Metzger, Joseph, 200
Meurthe River, 141, 143, 443, 463, 475, 488, 510–11
Meuse railroad, 449
Meuse River, 144, 210–11, 233n13, 302, 320, 326, 330–34, 335, 336, 419, 441, 448, 475, 487–88, 507, 509, 522–23
Mézières (France), 331
Michel, Victor Constant, 266
militarism, 18–19
Military History Research Institute (Potsdam), 9–14, 261–62
military professionalization, 196
military tradecraft (*Kriegshandwerk*), 7. *See also* statecraft/military tradecraft relationship
Millerand, Alexandre, 222
Mittler, Max, 282
mobile warfare, 158
mobilization schedules: 1900–1901, 377–78; 1901–1902, 384–85; 1903–1904, 403–4; 1904–1905, 409–10; 1905–1906, 416–17; 1906–1907, 424–25; 1907–1908, 436–38; 1909–1910, 456–60; 1910–1911, 471–74; 1911–1912, 484–86; 1913–1914, 503–8; 1914–1915, 517–25. *See also* deployment plans (*Aufmarschpläne*; *Aufmarschplanungen*)
Moltke, Adam von, 64n37
Moltke, Helmut von, the Elder, 297, 300, 301; memorandum of 1888, 264; military significance of, 1, 2; Schlieffen as follower of, 6, 7; war plans of, 114–15; WWI as predicted by, 26
Moltke, Helmut von, the Younger: Austro-Hungarian General Staff coordination with, 12, 201–6; blamed for Marne defeat, 45, 51, 59; correspondence of, 61n7, 201–2; *Denkschrift* copy in possession of, 92, 97; *Denkschrift* marginal notes made by, 91; deployment instructions of, 265; deployment plans of, 95, 341–42; dismissal of, 144; as Great General Staff chief, 17, 43, 67, 85, 143, 144, 201; Italy as viewed by, 279; key taskings of, 87; Krafft and, 143, 178–79n27; papers of (*Nachlass*), 123n36; political decisions and, 134n177; pre-WWI planning by, 17, 44; Schlieffen and, 97–98, 105, 117–19; Schlieffen Plan modified by, 8, 61n6, 97–98, 144, 209, 343; Sprecher Affair and, 272, 273; Sprecher and, 274–76, 286, 290n51; staff rides led by, 71–72; two-front war as viewed by, 119; von Einem and, 132n139; WWI duration predicted by, 135n188. *See also* Moltke Plan
Moltke Plan, 64n37; Dutch/Belgian neutrality in, 52–53, 61n5; eastern front strategy in, 53–54; French intentions and, 55–57; Germany's "encirclement" and, 54–55; mobilization of, 336; moral aspects of, 45; Schlieffen Plan differences, 50–51, 53–57; Schlieffen Plan parallels, 45–50, 61n7, 62n12, 435n1; Switzerland as non-objective of, 262–63, 280; WWI use of, 43; Zuber thesis and, 57–60
Mombauer, Annika, 10–11, 69, 86, 111, 113, 262
Monschau (Germany), 327
Montenegro, 192
Montmédy (France), 441, 462, 512, 523
Moritz, Albrecht, 76

Morley, John, 296
Morocco, 22
Morocco Crisis (1905), 3, 62n9, 76–77, 79, 113, 293
Morocco Crisis (1911), 13, 19, 27, 46, 312, 329
Moselle River, 102, 140, 141, 143, 148, 154, 157–58, 161, 165–66, 264, 443, 463, 475, 488, 500, 510–11, 524
Mountain Brigade 15 (Switzerland), 271
Mountain Brigade 18 (Switzerland), 271
Mudra, Bruno von, 47
Mulhouse (France), 146
Mulhouse (France), Battle of (1914), 147, 149
Müller, Eduard, 270
Müller, Thomas, 139, 174
Mürzsteg Program, 28
Musulin, Alexander von, 20

Namur (Belgium), 326, 328, 334, 335, 441, 462, 475, 505, 508, 519–20
Nancy (France), 56, 99, 107, 109, 153–54, 175–76, 443, 450, 454n3, 475, 487, 509, 510; Position de, 157, 161, 163–74
Napoleon, 297, 300, 319–20
Napoleonic era, 22, 32
Napoleon III (Emperor of France), 324, 325
Narev Army, 202–3, 205
Narev River, 199, 205, 468, 515
nationalism, 284
National People's Army Military Archive (Potsdam, East Germany), 88, 96, 128n91, 341
Navy and German Power Politics 1862–1914, The (Lambi), 14n6
Neman Army, 199
Neman River, 201, 253, 257

Netherlands, 7, 331; in Belgian war plans, 330–32; Belgium merged with, 320–21; as economic lifeline, 118; as French buffer state, 320; German march through, 63n30, 73, 79–80, 136n191; German war plan and, 73, 111, 116, 118, 343, 427, 439, 447, 454n1, 459, 461, 474, 486, 487, 506, 520, 521; neutrality of, 50, 52, 320–21, 419, 474; railroads in, 73; Ten Days Campaign (1831), 322, 323
Nicholas II (Tsar of Russia), 76, 248, 250, 253, 255
Nicholas Nickolaevich (Grand Duke of Russia), 249–50, 257
Nicholson, William, 303, 309
Nied position, 151, 437, 442, 448–49, 454nn2–3, 463, 465, 475, 500, 508
Nieuport (Belgium), 320
XIX Army Corps (Germany): deployment directives 1912, 498; deployment plans 1901–1902, 385; deployment plans 1905–1906, 417, 421; deployment plans 1906–1907, 425; deployment plans 1907–1908, 436; deployment plans 1908–1909, 451; deployment plans 1910–1911, 473; deployment plans 1911–1912, 487; deployment plans 1913–1914, 504
XIX Ersatz Corps (Germany), 518
19th Reserve Division (Germany), 420, 423n2, 437
IX Army Corps (Germany): deployment directives 1912, 500; deployment plans 1900–1901, 381; deployment plans 1901–1902, 385; deployment plans 1904–1905, 412; deployment plans 1905–1906, 417, 420; deployment plans 1906–1907, 425, 427; deployment plans

1907–1908, 436; deployment plans 1908–1909, 450; deployment plans 1909–1910, 469–70; deployment plans 1910–1911, 473, 474, 483; deployment plans 1913–1914, 506; mobilization schedules 1914–1915, 518
IX Army Corps (Italy), 374, 378
9th Cavalry Division (Germany): deployment plans 1903–1904, 401; deployment plans 1905–1906, 418, 419; deployment plans 1906–1907, 427; deployment plans 1907–1908, 439; deployment plans 1908–1909, 449; mobilization schedules 1914–1915, 518
IX Ersatz Corps (Germany), 426, 435
9th Infantry Division (Germany), 423n4
9th Infantry Regiment (Germany), 126n70
9th Reserve Division (Germany), 422, 423n4, 423n6
IX Reserve Corps (Germany): deployment directives 1912, 500, 516; deployment plans 1905–1906, 421; deployment plans 1906–1907, 425, 426, 427, 435; deployment plans 1907–1908, 436, 437, 438, 446; deployment plans 1908–1909, 453; deployment plans 1909–1910, 457, 469–70; deployment plans 1910–1911, 474, 483; deployment plans 1911–1912, 496; deployment plans 1913–1914, 504, 507
North Atlantic Treaty Organization (NATO), 8, 27
Northern Army (Germany): deployment plans 1907–1908, 438, 446; deployment plans 1908–1909, 453; deployment plans 1909–1910, 469–70; deployment plans 1910–1911, 472, 474, 483; deployment plans 1911–1912, 496
North Sea, 434, 506
North Sea Naval Station, 422
"Notizen und Material für eine Untersuchung über Graf Schlieffen und die Entwicklung des deutschen Heeres" (Dieckmann), 94, 104, 127n79

Oder River, 99
Odeur (Belgium), 335
offensive, cult of the, 19, 211
Olsansky, Michael, 13
Oncken, Hermann, 113
Option Freytag, 102–3, 130n116, 130n120
Option Kuhl, 102–3, 130n116
Option Steuben, 102, 130n116
Organisation des Nachrichtendienstes von 1906, 265
Ostende (Belgium), 320
Ostheer, 198, 200
Ottignies (Belgium), 334
Ottoman Empire, 230, 253
Our River, 500

Pageot, Gaston Léonce Edouard, 266–67
Paléologue, Maurice, 19, 26–27, 30, 95, 227–28
Pan-German League, 282, 283
Paris (France), 85, 101, 102–3, 108–9, 120–21n6, 130n115, 130n120, 133n157, 332
Paris, Treaty of (1814), 323
Paul, Apostle, 34
Pedroncini, Guy, 223
Peloponnesian League, 27
Persia, 22
Philippe (Prince of Belgium; Count of Flanders), 327

564 Index

Pichon, Stéphan, 229
Piedmont-Sardinia, 320, 324
Plan XVI (France), 210
Plan XVII (France), 12, 19; Austria-Hungary in, 225–26; Belgian neutrality in, 221–22, 224, 232–33n12; British intervention in, 211–12, 215–21, 223–24; deployment options in, 223; failure of, 231; foreknowledge of German intentions, 210–11; French offensive in, 147, 220–23, 224, 233–34n17; German intelligence on, 55–56; introductory section (*Bases du Plan*), 219; Italy in, 213–15, 224; Moltke Plan vs. Schlieffen Plan, 55–57; Russian intervention in, 215, 216, 220, 224–31; Switzerland in, 266–67
Plan 18 (Russia), 253
Plan 19 (Russia), 20, 225, 253–57
Plans of War, The (Gooch), 294
Pöhlmann, Markus, 4–5, 15n13
Poincaré, Raymond, 18, 213, 214, 216–17, 218, 219–20, 223–24, 228, 229, 230, 272
Poland, 198, 201, 254
Polish–White Russian territory, 250–51
Pollio, Alberto, 279
Porch, Douglas, 233–34n17
Port Arthur, Battle of (1904), 185n171
Portuguese colonialism, 29
Posen (Eastern Army HQs), 225, 355, 437, 472, 474, 505
Potsdam *entrevue* (1910), 29, 30
preemptive war, 46, 113–14
Prete, Roy A., 220
Preussischen Jahrbücher, 26
pre-WWI European System, 1–2, 9; alliances/ententes in, 21–26, 38n48; bloc system in, 27–30; détente/rapprochement efforts in, 26–30, 39nn62, 79; Imperialist System in, 30–34; statecraft/military tradecraft relationship in, 17–21, 33–34
Princip, Gavrilo, 319
Prospect of War, The (Gooch), 294
Prussia, 19, 178–79n27, 321, 325, 466, 481, 493. *See also* East Prussia; Franco-German War (1870–1871)
Prussian-Austrian War. *See* Austro-German War (1866)
Prussian-German Great General Staff (*Grosse Generalstab*), 87; Austro-Hungarian agreements/cooperation with, 196, 201–6; as Austro-Hungarian General Staff model, 197; as British General Staff model, 299, 304–5, 307; deployment plans of, 342–44; history of, 2, 86; military intelligence collection capabilities of, 265; officer's handbook, 72–73; officer training in, 101, 129–30n112; operational planning of, 105; organizational structure of, 307, 470n2; political control over lacking, 196; Railway Division, 87, 122n30, 378, 385, 417, 438, 473; records of, 87–88, 122n29, 123–24n37; responsibilities of, 86–87; Sprecher and, 289n43; status of, 304–5; Switzerland and, 272–73, 280–85; tensions within, 117, 128n92; two-front war and, 119–20; war plan secrecy maintained by, 69, 72–73, 87. *See also* General Staff rides (*Generalstabsreisen*)

railroads, 3, 73, 115, 120n5, 190, 201
Rambervillers (France), 165, 171
Raulff, Heiner, 14n6, 76
Rawlinson, Henry, 308
Recht (Belgium), 331
Recipe for Victory ("Siegesrezept Schlieffens"), 88

Redern, Erich von, 169
Redl, Alfred, 197, 251–52
Regenauer, Kurt von, 81n10
Reich Archive (*Reichsarchiv*; Potsdam): access to records in, 88, 92, 123n35; Dieckmann as researcher at, 68; document searches at, 69–70; establishment of, 87; Foerster as director of, 5–6; General Staff records stored in, 87, 88, 90, 91, 95–96, 97, 341; Historical Division, 87, 91; historical objectivity of doubted, 264; inventory lists of, in Moscow Archive, 128n85; Lorraine/Vosges campaign analysis of, 143–44, 154, 155; Mertz as director of, 126n70, 139; official historiography of, 103, 154, 155, 342; Schlieffen papers stored in, 123–24nn36–37, 124n39; southern front source materials in, 264–65, 287n11; WWI series of, 138; WWII destruction of, 86. *See also* Army Archive (*Heeresarchiv*; Potsdam)
Reichstag, 46
Rennenkampf, Paul von, 257
Renouvin, Pierre, 227–28
Repington, Charles à Court, 311
Reuland (Belgium), 331
Revolution of 1830 (France), 320–21
Rhine River, 264, 267, 320, 326, 422, 425, 437, 454n1, 483n2, 513, 524
rifles, 3
Risquons-Tout Incident (1848), 324
Ritter, Gerhard: *Denkschrift* edition of, 85, 88, 90, 125n61; on Schlieffen as apolitical, 114, 133–34n170; Schlieffen Plan as critiqued by, 6–8, 67, 110, 210; on Schlieffen's strategic planning, 127n83; statecraft/military tradecraft relationship as viewed by, 17–18; Zuber thesis and, 105, 110, 111, 114

Roberts, Frederick, 300, 301, 312
Robertson, William, 301–3, 305, 307–8, 311, 312, 313
Rödiger, Aleksandr F., 249
Roehl, Maximilian von, 455n6
Roermond (Netherlands), 332, 333
Romania, 192, 204
Rovno (Ukraine), 200–201
Royal Hungarian *Honvéség*, 189. *See also* Austro-Hungarian Imperial and Royal Army (*K.u.K.* Army)
Ruhr region (Germany), labor unrest in, 343
Rupel–Nete Line, 326
Rupprecht (Prince of Bavaria), 156; correspondence of, 144–45; criticism directed at, 143–44, 171, 181n85; diary of, 154, 157; Lorraine/Vosges campaign (1914), 157–58, 163–64, 168–70, 171, 174–75; military abilities of, 142; as Sixth Army commander, 139, 141–42, 147; on trench warfare, 160; troop morale and, 148
Russia: alliance-/bloc-building by, 21, 22–23, 24–26, 38n48, 54–55, 303; alliance with France, 3, 4, 12–13, 55; in Austro-Hungarian war plans, 191–92, 197–98, 199–201, 204–6; Belgian independence guaranteed by, 321, 324; in British war plans, 299, 306; communications technology in, 255–56; détente/rapprochement efforts of, 28–30, 76, 112, 134n172; in French war plans, 215, 216, 220, 224–31; German ultimatum to, 336; German war plan and, 98, 110, 204–6, 277, 409, 414, 416, 424, 436, 456–57, 466–67, 471–72, 481, 485, 493, 502, 503, 514–15, 517 (*see also* Aufmarsch II

Russia *(cont.)*
[State of War with Russia and France]; Schlieffen Plan); historiography on, 247–48; as Indian threat, 299, 300, 302; Moltke Plan vs. Schlieffen Plan operations against, 46–47, 53–54; operational planning of, 9, 232n7; railroads in, 197, 228–29, 493; Schlieffen Plan operational objective against, 1; statecraft/military tradecraft relationship in, 20; structural weakness of, 248, 257; in Swiss operational planning, 268–69; two-front war scenario and, 114–20. *See also* Russo-Japanese War (1904–1905)

"Russia Is Ready" (newspaper article; Sukhomlinov), 248

Russian Army: in Austro-Hungarian war plans, 198, 199, 202–3; combat power of, 251; deficiencies of, 110, 248–51, 255–56; German war plan and, 468–69, 493; increases in strength of, 55, 118, 230; military intelligence collection capabilities of, 251–53; mobilization of, 115–16, 199, 248, 493; multiethnic makeup of, 254; Narev Army, 202–3, 205; Neman Army, 199; Plan 19 mobilization scenarios, 20, 225, 253–57; as police force, 250; redeployment of, 198; Schlieffen's dismissive view of, 74–76, 79, 82n37

Russian Army—armies: First Army, 257, 469; Second Army, 255–56, 257, 469; Third Army, 469; Fifth Army, 469

Russian Council of State Defense, 249

Russian General Staff, 225, 226, 234n22, 249–50, 252, 256–57

Russian-German Reinsurance Treaty (1887), 3, 21

Russian Navy, 249, 250, 255

Russian Revolution (1905), 12, 76, 78, 79, 248, 250

Russian Revolution (1917), 247

Russian State Council, 255

Russian War Ministry, 248, 249–50, 252–53

"Russia Wishes for Peace, but Is Ready for War" (newspaper article; Sukhomlinov), 248

Russo-Japanese War (1904–1905): artillery use in, 158, 185n171; Battle of Port Arthur (1904), 185n171; British-German relations and, 76–77; German war plan and, 110, 116, 118, 200; Russian Army deficiencies exposed in, 74–75, 79, 248–51; Russian Army regeneration following, 118; Russian defeat in, 12, 200

Ryckel, Louis de, 335

sabotage, 333–34
Saletta, Tancredi, 278
Salisbury, Robert A., 22
Sambre River, 233n13, 326
Samsonov, Aleksandr V., 257
Sandžak railway project, 201
Sarajevo (Bosnia-Herzegovina), 319, 336
Sauer River, 500
Sazonov, Sergey D., 24, 213, 218, 253, 256
Scheldt River, 320
Schemua, Blasius, 203–4, 205–6
Scheurer, Karl, 272–73
Schleswig-Holstein (Germany), 459, 469, 504, 516, 518
Schlieffen, Alfred von: army/armaments policy of, 94–95; counterattack doctrine of, 98–100, 129n103; criticism directed at, 117, 131n132, 209; death of,

136n195; deployment plans of, 95, 341–42; as Great General Staff chief, 2, 3, 6, 7, 67, 69, 85, 113, 199; Italy as viewed by, 279; key taskings of, 87; memorandum of 1891, 123n36; memorandum of 1894, 70; memorandum of 1898, 98–99, 264; memorandum of 1905 (see *Denkschrift für einen Krieg gegen Frankreich*; Schlieffen Plan); memorandum of 1912, 55, 88; military significance of, 1; Moltke the Younger and, 97–98, 105, 117–19; papers of (*Nachlass*), 87, 88, 90–92, 123–24nn36–37; political decisions and, 60n1, 111–14, 116, 133–34n170, 134n177, 135n181; Recipe for Victory ("Siegesrezept Schlieffens"), 88; retirement of, 60n1, 61n5, 77, 104, 117, 136n195, 201; scholarship on, 2, 15n13; staff rides led by, 71–73, 129–30n112; two-front war as viewed by, 3–4, 114–20; war games commanded by, 98, 100–101, 129–30n112; writings of, 1, 3–4

Schlieffen, Elizabeth von. *See* Hahnke, Elizabeth von

Schlieffen, Maria von, 120n4, 124n46

Schlieffen Plan: Austro-Hungarian General Staff knowledge of, 202; Cannae model in, 210; defined, 202; Dutch/Belgian neutrality in, 52–53, 61n5; eastern front strategy in, 53–54, 255; as existent, 65n67; French intentions and, 55–57; Germany's "encirclement" and, 54–55; historiographical debate over, 2, 8–14, 57–60, 85–86, 209–10 (*see also* Zuber thesis); implementation of, 131n130, 136n195; as infeasible, 105–8; mobilization of, 336; Moltke Plan differences, 50–51, 53–57; Moltke Plan influenced by, 43; Moltke Plan parallels, 45–50, 61n7, 62n12, 435n1; Moltke's modifications of, 8, 61n6, 97–98, 117–19, 144, 174, 209, 343; political considerations and, 111–14, 116; post-WWI controversy over, 88; post-WWI historiographical criticism of, 4–6; post-WWII historiographical criticism of, 6–8; post-WWI version, 44; pre-WWI European System and, 19; Schlieffen's operational alterations to, 108–11; Switzerland as non-objective of, 261–63, 264–65, 280–85; traditional interpretation of, 1–2, 7–8, 67, 85; two-front war in, 114–20; wide envelopment principle (*Umfassung*), 8, 12, 70–71, 93, 97–98, 108–9; Zuber questioning of (*see* Zuber thesis)

"Schlieffenplan, Der" (Dieckmann), 86, 92–95, 96, 103–4, 108, 127n79

Schlieffenplan, Der (Military History Research Institute), 14

"Schlieffen Plan" symposium (German Military History Research Institute), 9–14, 261–62

Schlieffen School, 5, 45, 71, 117

Schlussaufgaben. *See* key taskings (*Schlussaufgaben*)

Schmidt, Stefan, 12

Schmidt von Knobelsdorff, Konstantin, 142

Scholtz, Friedrich von, 455n10

Schroeder, Paul W., 230

Scott, H. M., 26

Second Army (Austria-Hungary), 200

Second Army (France), 146, 147, 153–54, 170–71, 233n17, 433

Second Army (Germany), 135n189; deployment directives 1912, 497; deployment plans 1896–1897, 354; deployment plans 1897–1898, 357; deployment plans 1898–1899, 362–63; deployment plans 1899–1900, 366, 367, 368–69, 371–72; deployment plans 1900–1901, 379; deployment plans 1901–1902, 385, 386, 387–88, 390; deployment plans 1902–1903, 109, 394, 397; deployment plans 1903–1904, 403, 405; deployment plans 1904–1905, 412; deployment plans 1905–1906, 109, 416, 420; deployment plans 1906–1907, 111, 132–33n154, 425, 426, 427–28; deployment plans 1907–1908, 343, 440–41; deployment plans 1908–1909, 448, 449, 450–51; deployment plans 1909–1910, 461–62, 467–68; deployment plans 1910–1911, 475, 476, 482; deployment plans 1911–1912, 486, 487, 488–89, 494–95; deployment plans 1913–1914, 507, 508, 510, 511; leadership of, 454n5; during Liège *coup de main*, 53; mobilization schedules 1914–1915, 520–21

Second Army (Russia), 255–56, 257, 469

II Army Corps (France), 522

II Army Corps (Germany): deployment directives 1912, 498; deployment plans 1903–1904, 406, 407, 408; deployment plans 1904–1905, 412; deployment plans 1905–1906, 416, 420; deployment plans 1906–1907, 424, 427; deployment plans 1907–1908, 436; deployment plans 1908–1909, 450; deployment plans 1910–1911, 473; deployment plans 1911–1912, 495; deployment plans 1913–1914, 506, 509

2nd Army Detachment (Germany), 354

II Bavarian Corps, 385; deployment plans 1904–1905, 412; deployment plans 1905–1906, 421; deployment plans 1906–1907, 430; deployment plans 1907–1908, 436; deployment plans 1908–1909, 452; deployment plans 1913–1914, 506; during Lorraine campaign, 140, 157

II Cavalry Corps (Germany), 407

2nd Cavalry Division (Germany): deployment directives 1912, 498; deployment plans 1905–1906, 418; deployment plans 1906–1907, 427; deployment plans 1907–1908, 439, 445; deployment plans 1908–1909, 449; deployment plans 1910–1911, 481; deployment plans 1913–1914, 509; mobilization schedules 1914–1915, 518

2nd Cavalry Division (Italy), 374, 432

2nd combined Bavarian Landwehr Brigade (Germany), 524

2nd combined Landwehr Brigade (Germany), 481, 499, 516

2nd Guards Reserve Division (Germany), 436, 437

2nd Reserve Division (Germany), 422, 423n6

Secrétan, Edouard, 273

Sedan (France), 331

Sedan, Battle of (1870), 323

Seine River, 101

Selliers de Moranville, Antonin de, 327, 334–35

Selves, Justin de, 221, 222

Senior Cavalry Commander 1 (Germany): deployment directives 1912, 498; deployment plans

1905–1906, 418; deployment plans 1906–1907, 427; deployment plans 1907–1908, 439; deployment plans 1908–1909, 449; deployment plans 1909–1910, 465; deployment plans 1910–1911, 475; deployment plans 1913–1914, 507, 510; mobilization schedules 1914–1915, 522

Senior Cavalry Commander 2 (Germany): deployment directives 1912, 498; deployment plans 1905–1906, 418; deployment plans 1906–1907, 427; deployment plans 1907–1908, 439; deployment plans 1908–1909, 449; deployment plans 1910–1911, 475; deployment plans 1913–1914, 510; mobilization schedules 1914–1915, 521

Senior Cavalry Commander 3 (Germany): deployment plans 1905–1906, 419; deployment plans 1906–1907, 427; deployment plans 1907–1908, 439; deployment plans 1908–1909, 449–50; deployment plans 1909–1910, 461, 463, 465; deployment plans 1910–1911, 474–75, 479; deployment plans 1911–1912, 486, 491; deployment plans 1913–1914, 507, 510–11; mobilization schedules 1914–1915, 523–25

Senior Cavalry Commander 4 (Germany), 491, 510, 522–23

Senior Cavalry Commander East (Germany), 385

Senior Cavalry Commanders (Germany), 404, 411

Senior Cavalry Commander West (Germany), 385

Senior Landwehr Commander 1 (Germany), 504, 516, 518

Senior Landwehr Commander 2 (Germany), 512

Senior Landwehr Commander 9 (Germany), 518

Serbia, 4, 17, 190, 192, 200, 216, 319

XVII Army Corps (Germany): deployment directives 1912, 497; deployment plans 1897–1898, 358; deployment plans 1900–1901, 378; deployment plans 1903–1904, 406; deployment plans 1904–1905, 410, 412, 414; deployment plans 1905–1906, 416, 420; deployment plans 1906–1907, 424, 429; deployment plans 1907–1908, 436, 437, 445; deployment plans 1908–1909, 452; deployment plans 1909–1910, 466; deployment plans 1910–1911, 481; deployment plans 1913–1914, 515

17th combined Landwehr Division (Germany), 481, 515

XVII Reserve Corps (Germany), 420

17th Reserve Division (Germany), 412

7th Reserve Division (Germany), 412, 420, 423n3

Seventh Army (Germany), 11, 56; deployment directives 1912, 501; deployment plans 1897–1898, 359; deployment plans 1898–1899, 364–65; deployment plans 1899–1900, 367, 368, 369–70, 375, 375n1; deployment plans 1900–1901, 382; deployment plans 1901–1902, 385, 386, 391–92; deployment plans 1902–1903, 395, 398–99; deployment plans 1903–1904, 406; deployment plans 1904–1905, 413; deployment plans 1905–1906, 416, 421; deployment plans 1906–1907, 111, 425, 426, 430–31, 432; deployment plans 1908–1909, 342, 449, 450, 453, 454n3; deployment plans 1909–1910, 342, 461, 463, 464, 465–66, 470n1, 470n3;

Seventh Army (Germany) *(cont.)*
deployment plans 1910–1911, 342, 474–75, 478, 483n2; deployment plans 1911–1912, 342, 486, 488, 490–91, 492; deployment plans 1913–1914, 342, 504, 507, 508, 509, 510–11, 513; fortifications of, 159; French superior numbers and, 146–47, 149; leadership of, 455n10; Lorraine/Vosges combat, 146, 147, 150–54; Lorraine/Vosges Moselle/Nancy attack, 164–66, 168, 171; Lorraine/Vosges operational objective, 140–41, 142–45; Lorraine/Vosges pursuit mission, 155–57; mobilization schedules 1914–1915, 520, 523–25; war diary of, 184n148

VII Army Corps (France), 432

VII Army Corps (Germany): deployment plans 1904–1905, 411, 412; deployment plans 1905–1906, 420; deployment plans 1906–1907, 428; deployment plans 1907–1908, 436; deployment plans 1908–1909, 450; deployment plans 1909–1910, 465; deployment plans 1911–1912, 487; deployment plans 1913–1914, 509, 511

7th Bavarian Cavalry Division (Germany), 450

7th Cavalry Division (Germany), 374; deployment plans 1903–1904, 401; deployment plans 1905–1906, 419; deployment plans 1907–1908, 440; deployment plans 1909–1910, 465; deployment plans 1913–1914, 509; mobilization schedules 1914–1915, 518

VII Reserve Corps (Germany), 427, 436, 437, 450, 465, 511

70th combined Landwehr Brigade (Germany), 481, 498, 515

77th Infantry Brigade (Germany), 513

Seven Year Military Bill (1894), 131n132

Siedlce Thrust, 205

Sieger, Ludwig von, 166–67

Silesia, 355, 514

Sint-Truiden (Belgium), 333, 334, 335

XVI Army Corps (Germany): deployment directives 1912, 500; deployment plans 1897–1898, 356–57; deployment plans 1898–1899, 360–62; deployment plans 1900–1901, 380; deployment plans 1901–1902, 385, 389; deployment plans 1903–1904, 401, 402, 404; deployment plans 1904–1905, 410, 411–12; deployment plans 1905–1906, 418, 421; deployment plans 1906–1907, 431; deployment plans 1907–1908, 436, 442; deployment plans 1908–1909, 452; deployment plans 1909–1910, 460, 465; deployment plans 1911–1912, 491; deployment plans 1913–1914, 509

16th Infantry Division (Germany), 378, 402, 410, 418

Sixth Army (Germany), 11, 56; artillery of, 159–60, 184n138; as "Bavarian" army, 138; deployment directives 1912, 501; deployment plans 1897–1898, 358; deployment plans 1898–1899, 363–64; deployment plans 1899–1900, 367, 368, 369, 373; deployment plans 1900–1901, 380–82; deployment plans 1901–1902, 386, 389, 391; deployment plans 1902–1903, 109, 395, 397–98; deployment plans 1903–1904, 405–6; deployment plans 1904–1905, 413; deployment plans 1905–1906, 416, 421; deployment plans 1906–1907, 425, 426, 430;

deployment plans 1907–1908, 438, 439, 443–44; deployment plans 1908–1909, 342, 448, 449, 452–53, 454n2; deployment plans 1909–1910, 342, 461, 463, 465; deployment plans 1910–1911, 342, 474–75, 478, 479–80, 483n3; deployment plans 1911–1912, 342, 486, 488, 490, 491–92; deployment plans 1913–1914, 342, 508, 510–11, 512–13; dynastic concerns in, 152–53; French superior numbers and, 146–47, 149; leadership of, 138, 139, 171–74, 455n9; Lorraine/Vosges combat, 146, 150–54, 159–60, 184n138; Lorraine/Vosges Moselle/Nancy attack, 161–71; Lorraine/Vosges operational objective, 139–41, 142–45; Lorraine/Vosges pursuit mission, 154–58; mobilization schedules 1914–1915, 518, 520, 523–25; OHL and, 142, 152, 171–74; war diary of, 149, 150
VI Army Corps (France), 433
VI Army Corps (Germany): deployment directives 1912, 498; deployment plans 1901–1902, 385; deployment plans 1903–1904, 406, 407; deployment plans 1904–1905, 411, 413; deployment plans 1905–1906, 417, 421; deployment plans 1906–1907, 424, 430; deployment plans 1907–1908, 436; deployment plans 1908–1909, 452; deployment plans 1911–1912, 495; deployment plans 1913–1914, 509, 514
VI Army Corps (Italy), 374
6th Cavalry Division (Germany): deployment plans 1903–1904, 401; deployment plans 1905–1906, 419; deployment plans 1906–1907, 427; deployment plans 1907–1908, 439;

deployment plans 1908–1909, 449; deployment plans 1913–1914, 509; mobilization schedules 1914–1915, 518
6th combined Landwehr Brigade (Germany), 481, 515
VI Reserve Corps (Germany): deployment directives 1912, 498; deployment plans 1906–1907, 430; deployment plans 1907–1908, 436, 437, 445; deployment plans 1908–1909, 452; deployment plans 1909–1910, 466; deployment plans 1910–1911, 481
6th Reserve Division (Germany), 412, 422, 423n5
Snyder, Jack, 232n7, 234n17
Sommerfeld (German military attaché), 326
Special Archive (Moscow, Russia), 122n22, 128n85
"Specific Directives from the Commanding General of the Eighth Army," 514–16
Spiers, Edward, 294–95
Sprecher Affair, 271–73, 289n40
Sprecher von Bernegg, Theophil: as German-Swiss citizen, 273; intelligence service contacts of, 271–73; memorandum of 1906, 268–70, 288–89n32; memorandum of 1912, 270–71; Moltke *Ante Portas* assurance and, 274–76, 290n51; Moltke correspondence with, 286; as Swiss General Staff chief, 261; as Swiss intelligence service, 268
Staff College, 296, 302, 308–9
staff rides (British), 308
staff rides (German). *See* General Staff rides (*Generalstabsreisen*)
Staff Work (Foster), 308
Stalin, Joseph, 93

Stanhope Memorandum (1888), 298, 310
statecraft (*Staatskunst*), 7
statecraft/military tradecraft relationship, 8, 9–10, 17–21
St. Avold (France), 145
Stein, Hermann von, 61n6, 90, 136n195, 152, 162
"Stellungnahme zu den Bemerkungen des Generals Konrad Krafft von Dellmensingen zu Band I des Reichsarchiv-Werkes" (Foerster), 342
"Stellungnahme zu den Bemerkungen zu den Aufgaben des Südflügels des deutschen Westheeres unter besonderer Berücksichtigung der Einstellung Moltkes zu ihnen" (anon. study), 342
Stetten, Otto von, 146
"Stettin" (Northern Army HQs), 437
Steuben, Kuno von, 455n9
Stone, Norman, 248
Storz, Dieter, 11–12
St. Petersburg Military District, 252
Strachan, Hew, 13
Strasbourg (France), 102, 175–76, 220, 358, 443–44, 505, 524; fortress of, 140, 464
St. Vith (Belgium), 327, 331
Sudan, 306
Sukhomlinov, Vladimir A., 248, 249, 250, 253–54
Supreme Army Command (*Oberste Heeresleitung*; OHL): criticism directed at, 138, 142; in German war plans, 454n3, 457; HQs, 457, 486; Lorraine/Vosges pursuit mission and, 154–58; low-country neutrality and, 447–48, 521; Operations Division, 138; Political Division, 151; Sixth Army and, 142, 152, 171–74

Swiss Army, 264, 266, 273–74, 288–89n32
Swiss Army—corps: III Army Corps, 273
Swiss Federal Council, 266–68, 273, 274
Swiss Federal Institute of Technology (Zurich), 273
Swiss General Staff: Austro-Hungarian consultations with, 272; German/Austrian influence on, 266; operational deliberations of, 267–76; Sprecher von Bernegg as chief of, 261
Switzerland: border fortifications of, 276; as French buffer state, 320; in French war plans, 266–67, 288n29; German intelligence on, 265; as German non-objective, 261–63, 264–65, 280–85; Germanophilia in, 281–83, 292n82; German population of, 282; German sources involving, 263–66; German view of, 281–83; German war plan and, 461, 464; Italian troop passage through, 272, 276–80, 290nn59–60; military intelligence collection capabilities of, 268, 270; neutrality of, 261–63, 264–65, 271–73, 274, 275–76, 278, 289n43, 461, 464; operational planning of, 9, 13, 267–76; political power structure in, 276; railroads in, 267; self-defense capability of, 283–85; strategic defensive planning by, 270–71; strategic location of, 286n2; topography of, 262–63
Szábo, István, 252
Szápáry, Friedrich, 20

Tannenburg, Battle of (1914), 257
Tappen, Gerhard, 52, 90, 144–45, 152, 154, 156, 161, 162, 166

Taschenbuch des Generalstabsoffiziers (*General Staff Officer's Handbook*), 72–73
Taylor, A. J. P., 293
Ten Days Campaign (1831), 322, 323
X Army Corps (Germany): deployment directives 1912, 498; deployment plans 1900–1901, 381; deployment plans 1901–1902, 385; deployment plans 1904–1905, 412; deployment plans 1905–1906, 417, 420, 422; deployment plans 1906–1907, 425, 427; deployment plans 1907–1908, 436; deployment plans 1908–1909, 450; deployment plans 1910–1911, 473; deployment plans 1913–1914, 504, 506
X Army Corps (Italy), 374
10th combined Landwehr Brigade (Germany), 498
X Ersatz Corps (Germany), 518
X Reserve Corps (Germany), 436–37, 450, 499
Thiers, Adolphe, 323
3rd Reserve Division (Germany): deployment directives 1912, 498; deployment plans 1905–1906, 420, 423n3; deployment plans 1910–1911, 480, 481; deployment plans 1913–1914, 515; mobilization schedules 1914–1915, 518
Third Army (Austria-Hungary), 200
Third Army (France), 433
Third Army (Germany): deployment directives 1912, 497, 498, 499; deployment plans 1896–1897, 354; deployment plans 1897–1898, 357; deployment plans 1898–1899, 363; deployment plans 1899–1900, 366, 367, 368–69, 372; deployment plans 1900–1901, 379; deployment plans 1901–1902, 386, 390–91; deployment plans 1902–1903, 109, 394, 397; deployment plans 1903–1904, 405; deployment plans 1904–1905, 409–10, 412; deployment plans 1905–1906, 109, 416, 420; deployment plans 1906–1907, 343, 425, 426, 427, 428; deployment plans 1907–1908, 343, 441; deployment plans 1908–1909, 448, 449, 451; deployment plans 1909–1910, 462, 468; deployment plans 1910–1911, 475, 476–77, 482; deployment plans 1911–1912, 487, 489, 494, 495; deployment plans 1913–1914, 507, 508, 510, 511–12; leadership of, 455n6; mobilization schedules 1914–1915, 522
Third Army (Russia), 469
III Army Corps (Germany): deployment directives 1912, 498; deployment plans 1901–1902, 385; deployment plans 1904–1905, 412; deployment plans 1905–1906, 416, 420; deployment plans 1906–1907, 424, 425, 428; deployment plans 1907–1908, 436; deployment plans 1908–1909, 450; deployment plans 1910–1911, 473
III Army Corps (Switzerland), 273
3rd Army Detachment (Germany), 355
III Bavarian Corps (Germany): deployment plans 1904–1905, 413; deployment plans 1905–1906, 421; deployment plans 1906–1907, 430; deployment plans 1907–1908, 436; deployment plans 1908–1909, 452; deployment plans 1913–1914, 507; during Lorraine campaign, 140
3rd Infantry Division (Belgium), 335
3rd Cavalry Division (Germany): deployment plans 1903–1904, 401; deployment plans 1905–1906, 419;

3rd Cavalry Division (Germany) *(cont.)*
deployment plans 1906–1907, 427;
deployment plans 1907–1908, 439;
deployment plans 1908–1909, 449;
deployment plans 1913–1914, 509;
mobilization schedules 1914–1915, 518
3rd Cavalry Division (Italy), 374, 432
3rd Infantry Division (Germany), 417
III Reserve Corps (Germany), 436–37, 450, 499
XIII Army Corps (Germany), 421, 430, 436, 452, 465
13th combined Landwehr Brigade (Germany), 497
13th Infantry Division (Germany), 487
XIII Reserve Corps (Germany), 420, 429
13th Reserve Division (Germany), 412
30th Infantry Division (Germany), 487
38th combined Landwehr Brigade (Germany), 518
35th Infantry Division (Germany), 469
34th combined Landwehr Brigade (Germany), 417, 425, 435, 518
34th Infantry Division (Germany), 410, 418
39th Infantry Division (Germany), 418, 464, 490–91, 513
37th combined Landwehr Brigade (Germany), 518
33rd combined Landwehr Brigade (Germany), 518
33rd Infantry Division (Germany), 410
Thirty Years War, 33
Tibet, 22
Tienen (Belgium), 333, 335
Times (London), 311
Tirpitz, Alfred von, 7, 62n9
Tirpitz Plan, 22
Tisza, István, 196
Toul (France), 109, 159, 175–76, 450

trade, German-Belgian, 327
Treaty of Paris (1814), 323
Treaty of Versailles (1919), 79
Treitschke, Heinrich von, 455n7
trench warfare, 160, 168
Trier (Germany), 356, 487
Triple Alliance, 26, 192, 198, 204, 213, 214, 268, 276, 277–78, 319. *See also* Austria-Hungary; German Reich; Italy
Triple Entente, 213
Turkey, 60
XII Army Corps (Germany):
deployment directives 1912, 498;
deployment plans 1901–1902, 385;
deployment plans 1905–1906, 417, 421; deployment plans 1906–1907, 425, 429; deployment plans 1907–1908, 436; deployment plans 1908–1909, 451; deployment plans 1910–1911, 473
12th Infantry Division (Germany), 487
XII Reserve Corps (Germany), 431, 436–37, 451, 498
XX Army Corps (Germany):
deployment directives 1912, 497;
deployment plans 1900–1901, 378; deployment plans 1904–1905, 410, 411, 412, 414; deployment plans 1905–1906, 420; deployment plans 1906–1907, 428; deployment plans 1907–1908, 436, 437, 445; deployment plans 1908–1909, 451; deployment plans 1909–1910, 466; deployment plans 1910–1911, 481; deployment plans 1911–1912, 487; deployment plans 1913–1914, 509, 516
28th Reserve Division (Germany), 413, 421, 423n9, 430–31, 464
XXI Army Corps (Germany):
deployment plans 1904–1905, 412;

deployment plans 1905–1906, 420, 421; deployment plans 1906–1907, 430; deployment plans 1907–1908, 436, 438; deployment plans 1908–1909, 453; deployment plans 1909–1910, 464, 465; deployment plans 1911–1912, 490, 491; deployment plans 1913–1914, 507, 509, 513; during Lorraine campaign, 140, 146
21st Landwehr Brigade (Germany), 435, 514
XXIV Article Treaty (1839), 322–24
24th Infantry Division (Germany), 487
24th Reserve Division (Germany), 413, 421, 423n7
29th Infantry Division (Germany), 464, 491, 524
29th Reserve Division (Germany), 412
22nd combined Landwehr Brigade (Germany), 481, 514, 515
22nd Reserve Division (Germany), 420, 423n2
26th Reserve Division (Germany), 413, 421, 423n9, 430–31, 464
23rd combined Landwehr Brigade (Germany), 481, 514, 515
23rd Reserve Division (Germany), 413, 421, 423n7
two-front war, 2–4, 114–20
Tyler, J. E., 295, 313

Ukraine, 254
Ungarschitz, Leopold Berchtold von und zu, 17
Unger, Kurt von, 455n11
United Kingdom of the Netherlands, 320–21
United States, 21, 22, 306
Urbas, Emanuel von, 20
Urner, Klaus, 283
U.S. National Archives (Washington, DC), 88

Van de Weyer, Sylvain, 323
Van Geen, Jozef Jacobus, 322
Vannovskiy, Petr S., 249
Velpe River, 333
Verdun (Lorraine), 108, 109, 110, 111, 133n157, 512, 523
"Verletzung der belgischen Neutralität, Die" (anon. study), 342
Versailles, Treaty of (1919), 79
Vienna, Congress of (1814–1815), 319–21
Vienna Decisions (1895), 345n6
Virchow, Rudolph, 32
Visé (Belgium), 331–32, 335
Vistula River, 99, 200, 225, 226, 253, 254, 466, 481, 493, 497, 514
Viviani, René, 30
Vosges Mountains, 146, 161, 165, 487, 513. *See also* Lorraine/Vosges campaign (1914)

Waldersee, Alfred von, 2, 53–54, 55, 64n39, 90, 114, 134n177, 205
Wallach, Jehuda, 114, 262
Wallis (Switzerland), 269
"War" (Maurice), 298
warfare: changing character of, 3–4; political dimension of, 111–14; two-front war, 2–4, 114–20
war games (*Kriegsspiele*), 11, 71, 72; archival storage of, 123n36; envelopment idea and, 108–9; German force strength assumptions during, 107; officer training during, 129–30n112; records of, 87, 89; Schlieffen's use of, 107, 129–30n112; Zuber thesis and, 98, 100–101, 107, 108
War Historical Research Institute, 87, 88, 126n70, 341
War in History, 60n2, 67
Warsaw Military District, 250–51, 252

Warsaw Pact, 27
wartime orders of battle, 408; I, 366–67, 376n2, 409; II (West), 367–68, 376n2; III (East), 368, 369–70, 376n3; East, 354, 356, 360; East (from 1 October 1899), 369, 375; Northern Army, 453; West, 354, 356, 360; West (from 1 October 1899), 368–69, 371–74, 376n3
Waterloo, Battle of (1815), 183n119, 320
Wawre (Belgium), 475, 487, 510, 521
Wehlau (East Prussia), 359
"Welche Nachrichten besass der deutsche Generalstab über Mobilmachung und Aufmarsch des französischen Heeres in den Jahren 1885-1914" (Greiner), 110
Wellington Line, 320
Weltkrieg 1914-1918, Der, 88, 126n70
Wenninger, Karl von, 8–9, 125n57, 145, 152, 161, 168
Western Army, 432
western front, 137
Wetzell, Georg, 138
Wilhelm (Crown Prince of Prussia), 142
Wilhelm II (Kaiser), 46; Anglophobic tirades of, 301; Belgian neutrality and, 329; Belgian visits of, 327; Bismarck dismissed by, 21; détente/rapprochement efforts of, 112, 134n172; General Staff access to, 86–87; German defense expenditures approved by, 134n173; on German war intentions, 59–60; "Kaiser maneuvers" attended by, 272, 273–74; Luxembourg occupation and, 163; Russo-German treaty signed by (1905), 76; Schlieffen replaced by, 60n1; Swiss visits of, 281, 284–85; Switzerland/Swiss as viewed by, 281, 283, 284

Wilkinson, Spenser, 299–300
Wille, Gerhard Ulrich, 271, 273
William I (King of the Netherlands and Prince of Orange), 320, 322
Williamson, Samuel, 216
Wilsberg, Klaus, 26, 29
Wilson, Arthur, 295
Wilson, Henry, 19, 294–95, 297, 300, 302–3, 304, 306, 307, 308, 310–11, 312–13
Wilson, Keith M., 38n48
Woeste, Charles, 336
Wolff, Theodor, 20
Wolseley, Garnet, 297, 298, 299, 300
World War I: British entrance into, 19, 53, 135n188, 262, 336; cultural historical interpretation of, 247–48; German apologism following, 79; German official history of, 88, 126n70; Germany defeated in, 51, 79; as inevitable, 26, 28; Moltke Plan used during, 43; outbreak of, 1, 14n3, 44, 336; *Reichsarchiv* series on, 138; Swiss popular view of, 261; WWII scholarly research on halted, 93. *See also* Lorraine/Vosges campaign (1914); Marne, Battle of the (1914); pre-WWI era
World War II, 2, 6, 7, 68, 86, 88, 93, 263, 280

Xylander, Oskar von, 163
Xylander, Rudolf von, 147–48, 156, 162, 163, 172, 173–74

Yates, C. L., 311

Zatschek, Heinz, 145, 179n42
Zayontchkovskiy, A. M., 232n7
ZDF (television network), 137
Zeebrugge (Belgium), 265
Zhilinskiy, Yakov Grigor'evich, 227

Zoellner, Eugen, 90, 168
Zollverein (customs union), 325
Zuber, Terence, 50; historiographical debate initiated by, 2, 8–14, 43–45, 57–60, 85–86, 114; writings of, 14
Zuber thesis, 92; as apologist, 79; context lacking in, 74–79; critiques of, 79–80, 209; German deployment (1914) as defensive, 57, 67, 79, 85, 98–103, 120–21n6, 129n103, 131n124; historiographical debate over, 60n2; Moltke Plan and, 57–60; operational planning vs. larger context in, 74–79; Paris envelopment in, 101–3, 108–9, 130n115; Schlieffen as apolitical technocrat, 111–14, 133–34n170, 135n181; Schlieffen Plan and German Army expansion in, 85–86, 103–5; Schlieffen Plan as aberration, 108–11; Schlieffen Plan as "doctrine," 57–58, 59; Schlieffen Plan as infeasible, 105–8, 121n8; Schlieffen Plan as myth, 10, 57, 59, 60n2, 67, 85, 114; Schlieffen Plan storage and, 97–98, 120n4, 124n46; source problems in, 68–74, 80n8; sources used to support, 68–74, 85–86, 92–95, 114
Zurich (Switzerland), 282
Zwehl, Johann von, 455n7